U0107624

中英文对照版（第2版）

英语说文解字

〔美〕诺曼·刘易斯／著

王威 刘博／译

谭新木／审订

庖丁解牛般的单词艺术

WORD POWER MADE EASY

北京大学出版社

PEKING UNIVERSITY PRESS

著作权合同登记号　图字：01-2013-4044

图书在版编目（CIP）数据

英语说文解字：中英文对照版：第二版／（美）诺曼·刘易斯著；王威，刘博译. -- 北京：北京大学出版社，2022.5

ISBN 978-7-301-31305-3

Ⅰ. ①英… Ⅱ. ①诺… ②王… ③刘… Ⅲ. ①英语—词汇—自学参考资料 Ⅳ. ①H313

中国版本图书馆 CIP 数据核字（2020）第 048696 号

Word Power Made Easy, by Norman Lewis, ISBN 978-0-671-74190-7.

Copyright ⓒ The Knopf Doubleday Publishing Group, New York, U. S. A

本书简体中文版ⓒ北京大学出版社，经由博达著作权代理有限公司，2013

书　　　名：英语说文解字（中英文对照版）（第二版）
　　　　　　YINGYU SHUO WEN JIE ZI(ZHONG YING WEN DUIZHAO BAN)(DI ER BAN)
著作责任者：［美］诺曼·刘易斯　著　　王威　刘博　译
责 任 编 辑：刘文静
标 准 书 号：ISBN 978-7-301-31305-3
出 版 发 行：北京大学出版社
地　　　址：北京市海淀区成府路 205 号 100871
网　　　址：http://www.pup.cn　　　新浪微博:@北京大学出版社
电 子 信 箱：编辑部 pupwaiwen@put.cn　总编室 zpup@pup.cn
电　　　话：邮购部 010-62752015　　　发行部 010-62750672
　　　　　　编辑部 010-62754382　　　出版部 010-62754962
印　刷　者：北京盛通印刷股份有限公司
经　销　者：新华书店
　　　　　　710 毫米×1000 毫米　　16 开本　　34 印张　　800 千字
　　　　　　2014 年 6 月第 1 版　　2022 年 5 月第 2 版　　2024 年 7 月第 3 次印刷
定　　　价：118.00 元

译 者 序

《英语说文解字》是一本关于如何在短时间内迅速建立超级词汇量的学习手册,在英语国家畅销不衰,而对于母语不是英语的读者来说,它可能更具有非凡的意义。

与市面上大多数词汇学习手册不同,《英语说文解字》强调的并非单纯的单词学习技巧,而是从语言的本质特征出发来考察词汇的意义,探究高效的学习方法。本书的出发点是,语言是思维的载体,是知识、概念和思想的符号;丰富的词汇量有助于掌握新知识、新概念和新思想,而学习词汇也要从知识、概念和思想入手。为此不能单纯地为学词汇而学词汇,将词汇积累变成枯燥、乏味、干瘪的机械过程。

本书从概念入手,分门别类将表达相同或相似概念的核心词汇组合在一起,考察这些词汇意义上的联系和区别。在形式上,通过对单词词源、词根和词缀的研究,帮助读者掌握构词法,做到触类旁通,举一反三,在掌握核心词汇的基础上迅速扩充词汇量。每一个英语单词不再是孤立的个体,而是与其他词汇有机联系在一起的要素,是各种概念的活泼的表现形式。本书被誉为"最有效的英语词汇积累工具",绝不是浪得虚名。

全书编排严谨,内容丰富,每一章既有对概念和构词法的详细讲解,又配备了大量的练习和测试,帮助读者复习和巩固所学内容。此外,书中还插入了大量的典故、故事,各种学习方法的介绍和比较,各种奇特的语言现象的分析与评论。全书语言幽默生动,使读者能够轻轻松松地学到新词汇、新概念,真正体会英文书名 Word Power Made Easy 的涵义。此次改版在原有基础上,对文字、排版进行了优化和调整,使其在细节上更方便读者阅读。高聪颖先生对全书文字进行了细致的校对,在此也表示感谢。

本书适合具有一定英文水平但面临词汇瓶颈的读者阅读。尤其对备考 SAT、TOEFL、GRE 和 GMAT 等国际考试需要在短期内掌握大量词汇的读者来说,更是必不可少的案头书。

HOW TO USE THIS BOOK FOR MAXIMUM BENEFIT
如何从本书获得最大收益(原序)

1. This is not a reading book...
这不是一本阅读书……

Don't read this book!

Instead，*work* with it. *Write* in it，*talk aloud* to it，*talk back* to it—use your pen or pencil，your voice，not just your eyes and mind.

Learning，*real learning*，goes on only through *active participation*.

When a new word occurs in a chapter，*say it aloud*！（The phonetic respelling will help you pronounce it correctly.）

不要阅读这本书！

而是动手用它。在里面书写,大声和它交流,与它顶嘴——不仅仅运用你的眼睛和思维,还要拿起你的钢笔或铅笔,张开你的嘴巴。

学习,真正的学习,只能通过积极的参与。

当一个新词出现在某一章节中时,大声将它朗读出来!(语音重拼会帮助你正确发音。)

When you do the matching exercises，use a pen or pencil. *Write your responses*！（Check the key that immediately follows each exercise after you have filled in all the answers.）

When you do the "Yes-No"，"True-False"，or "Same-Opposite" exercises，use your *pen or pencil to indicate the appropriate response*，then check with the key when you have completed the whole exercise.

进行配对练习时,使用钢笔或铅笔。写出你的回答!(填写完所有答案之后,与练习后紧跟的答案核对。)

进行"是—否""真—假"或"同义词—反义词"练习时,用钢笔或铅笔标出恰当的答案,完成全部练习之后,核对答案。

When you are asked to fill in words that fit definitions，*write your answers*；then check the key both to see if you have responded with the right word and also to make sure your spelling is correct.

要求你填写符合定义的词汇时,写出你的答案;然后核对答案,检验你写出的是否是正确的词汇,同时也能够检验拼写。

When you do the *Review of Etymology* exercises，make sure to fill in the English word containing the prefix，root，or suffix required—use a chapter word，or any other word that comes to mind.（Coin words if you like！）

Pay special attention to the *Chapter Reviews*. Are the words still fresh in your mind? Do you remember the meaning of each root studied in the previous sessions? In these *Reviews*，you are not only testing your learning but also tightening up any areas in which you discover lacks, weaknesses, or lapses of memory.

进行词源复习练习时,确保填写的英语词汇包含要求的前缀、词根或后缀——使用章节中刚学到的词汇或者任何其他你能够想到的词汇。(如果你喜欢,也可以创造词汇!)

尤其要重视章节复习。在你的脑海中,这些词汇是否新鲜依旧?你是否记得之前学习的每个词根的含义?通过这些复习,你不仅可以检验自己的学习效果,同时可以强化学得不够、掌握不牢、记得不清的部分。

2. Master the pronunciation system!

掌握音标系统!

Saying words *aloud*, and saying them *right*, is half the battle in feeling comfortable and assured with all the new words you are going to learn. Every word taught is respelled to show its pronunciation, so pay close attention to how the phonetic symbols work.

在学习新单词的过程中,"大声"说,说"正确",能使学习变得轻松并建立信心。每个学过的单词被标出了读音,所以请注意音标是如何使用的。

(a) First, master the "schwa"!

首先,掌握"非重读音节的元音"!

Almost every English word of two or more syllables contains one or several syllables in which the vowel sound is said *very* quickly. For example:

"*Linda* spoke to her *mother about a different idea* she had." →Read the *previous sentence aloud* at *normal conversational* speed.

Read it again. Listen to how the -*a* of *Linda*; the -*er* of *mother*; the *a*- of *about*; the -*er* and -*ent* of *different*; and the -*a* of *idea* sound.

Very quick—very short! Right?

几乎每个由两个或者多个音节组成的英文单词都包含一个或几个元音读得非常快的音节,例如:

"琳达对她妈妈说她有个不同的想法。"→用正常的语速读这个句子。

再读一次,听一下-a 在 Linda,-er 在 mother,-a 在 about,-er 和-ent 在 different,-a 在 idea 中的发音。

非常快——非常短! 对吗?

Phonetically respelled, these words are represented as:

从发音上把这些词重新拼写出来:

1. *Linda*   LIN′-də
2. *mother*   MUTH-ər
3. *about*   ə-BOWT′
4. *different*   DIF′-ər-ənt
5. *idea*   Ī-DEE′-ə

The symbol "ə", called a *schwa*, represents the quick, short vowel sound in the five words above.

Now look back at the sentence preceded by an arrow.

The italicized words are rewritten as:

字符"ə",叫做"schwa"(非重读音节的元音),指以上 5 个单词中发音短而快的元音。

请看前一页（即第 ii 页中间——译者注）箭头之后的英文原句。

这个句子里的斜体字是：

1. *previous*   PREE′-vee-əs
2. *sentence*   SEN′-təns
3. *aloud*   ə-LOWD′
4. *normal*   NAWR′-məl
5. *conversational*   kon′-vər-SAY′-shən-əl

You will find ə in almost all words that are phonetically respelled throughout this book. Say the five italicized words aloud and make sure you understand how the *schwa* (ə) sounds.

你会发现在本书中几乎所有标有音标的单词中，都有"ə"出现。大声读上面的 5 个斜体单词，确定你理解了非重读元音"ə"的发音。

(b) *Next*，*understand accent*.

下一步，了解重音。

Look at word (5) above：*conversational*：kon′-vər-SAY′-shən-əl. Note that there are *two* accent marks，one on *kon′*，another on *SAY′*. Note also that *kon′* is in lower-case letters，*SAY′* in capitals. Both syllables are stressed，but the one in capitals (*SAY′*) sounds stronger (or louder) than the one in lower case (*kon′*). Say *conversational* aloud，noting the difference.

Say these three words，taken from Chapter 3，*aloud*，noticing the variation in stress between the lower-case and the capitalized syllables：

看一下上面第 5 个单词：conversational：kon′-vər-SAY′-shən-əl。

注意有两个重音标志，一个在 kon′上，另外一个在 SAY′上。同时注意 kon′是由小写字母组成的，而 SAY′是由大写字母组成的。两个音节都要发重音，但大写的(SAY′)听起来比小写的(kon′)更强(或更大声)。大声读"conversational"，体验一下这种差别。

大声读以下来自第 3 章的 3 个词，注意大写音节和小写音节之间的差别。

1. *egomaniacal*   ee′-gō-mə-NĪ′-ə-kəl
2. *altercation*   awl′-tər-KAY′-shən
3. *anthropological*   an′-thrə-pə-LOJ′-ə-kəl

(c) *Be careful of the letter* "*S*" (*or* "*s*") *in phonetic respellings*. S (*or s*) is always *hissed*，as in *see*，*some*，*such*. After an *-n*，you will be tempted to *buzz* (or "voice") the *-s*，because final *-ns* is usually pronounced *-nz*，as in *wins*，*tons*，*owns*，etc. (Say these three words aloud—hear the *z* at the end?) *Resist the temptation*! S (*or s*) is *always hissed* in phonetic respellings!

注意音标中的"s"的发音。S(或 s)总是发不出声的"嘶"音，如在 see，some，such 中。在-n 后，往往会被引诱发出低沉(或出声)的-s 音，因为以 ns 结尾的单词-ns 往往发-nz 音，如在 wins，tons，owns 等词中。(大声读这 3 个词——听到结尾的 z 音了吗?)抵制住这个诱惑! S(或 s)在音标中永远都发不出声的"嘶"音!

Say these words aloud：

大声读出下面的单词：

1. *ambivalence*   am-BIV′-ə-ləns
2. *affluence*   AF′-lσσ-əns
3. *opulence*   OP′-yə-ləns
4. *sentence*   SEN′-təns

(d) The symbol ī or Ī is pronounced *eye*, to rhyme with *high*, *sigh*, *my*, etc.,
no matter where you find it. For example：

不管在哪里见到符号 ī 或 Ī，发音都为 eye，与 high，sigh，my 等词同韵。例如：

1. *fights*   FĪTS
2. *spy*   SPĪ
3. *malign*   mə-LĪN′
4. *civilize*   SIV′-ə-Iīz′

[*I* or *i*（without the top bar）is pronounced as in *it*, *sit*, *pitch*.]

[I 或 i(上面不带横杠)发音如同在 it,sit,pitch 里。]

(e) *All consonants have their normal sounds.*

Except for *G*（or *g*），which is *always pronounced as in give*，*girl*，*get*，*go*.

所有的辅音都有正常的发音。

G(或 g)除外，它们发音总是像在 give,girl,get 和 go 里一样。

1. *agree*   ə-GREE′
2. *pagan*   PAY′-gən
3. *again*   ə-GEN′

(f) *The vowel sounds are as follows*：

元音发音如下：

SYMBOL   EXAMPLE
1. A, a   *cat*（KAT）
2. E, e   *wet*（WET）
3. I, i   *sit*（SIT）
4. O, o   *knot*（NOT）
5. U, u   *nut*（NUT）
6. AH, ah   *martinet*（mahr′-tə-NET′）；
7. AW, aw   *for*（FAWR）；*incorrigible*（in-KAWR′-ə-jə-bəl）

8. AY，ay   *ate*（AYT）; *magnate*（MAG'-nayt）

9. EE，ee   *equal*（EE'-kwəl）; *clandestinely*（klan-DES'-tən-lee）

10. Ō，ō   *toe*（TŌ）; *concerto*（kən-CHUR'-tō）

11. OŎ，oŏ   *book*（BOŎK）; *prurient*（PROŎR'-ee-ənt）

12. OO̅，oō   *doom*（DOōM）; *blue*（BLOō)）

13. OW，ow   *about*（ə-BOWT'）

14. OY，oy   *soil*（SOYL）

15. ING，ing   *taking*（TAYK'-ing）

（g）*TH* or *th* is pronounced as in *thing*; *TH* or *th* is pronounced as in *this*.

TH 或 th 如同在 thing 里的发音; T̅H̅或t̅h̅如同在 this 里的发音。

3. a word（or words）on western and eastern pronunciation
单词在西部和东部的读音

In the New York City area，and in parts of New Jersey and other eastern states，the syllables -*ar*，-*er*，-*or*，-*off*，and -*aw* are pronounced somewhat differently from the way they are said in the Midwest and in the West.

In New York City，for example，the words below are generally pronounced as follows：

在纽约市区和在新泽西的部分地区以及其他东部的一些州,音节-ar、-er、-or、-off 和-aw 在发音上与中西部和西部的一些地区有所差别。

例如,在纽约市区下面这些单词的发音为:

orange	AHR'-ənj
talk	TAWK̈
coffee	KAW'-fee
sorority	sə-RAHR'-ə-tee
incorrigible	in-KAHR'-ə-jə-bəl
disparage	dis-PAR'-əj（A as in HAT）
merry	MER'-ee（E as in WET）
marry	MAR'-ee（A as in HAT）
astronaut	AS'-trə-nawt'
Harry	HAR'-ee（A as in HAT）

In the Midwest and West，on the other hand，the same words are usually said approximately as follows：

另一方面,在中西部和西部地区,同样的单词发音大概是这样的:

orange	AWR'-ənj
talk	TOK
coffee	KOF'-ee

sorority	sə-RAWR'-ə-tee
incorrigible	in-KAWR'-ə-jə-bəl
disparage	dis-PAIR'-əj
merry	MAIR'-ee
marry	MAIR'-ee
astronaut	AS'-trə-not'
Harry	HAIR'-ee

Nothing so radical here that a person brought up in Brooklyn or the Bronx cannot understand a native of Los Angeles or San Francisco—it's just that each one thinks *the other* has an accent!

In California, for example, *Mary*, *merry*, and *marry* sound almost exactly a-like—in New York, they are usually heard as quite different words.

不过还不至于严重到一个在布鲁克林或者布朗克斯长大的人,听不懂地道的洛杉矶或圣弗朗西斯科人的程度,他们不过觉得彼此有口音罢了。

例如,在加利福尼亚,Mary, merry 和 marry 听起来差不多,而在纽约,这些词听起来则有明显的区别。

(So, to be sexist for a moment, if the men at a party in Manhattan say, "Let's all make merry!", Mary doesn't feel that she is about to be seduced by the males!)

(因此,暂时"性别主义者"一下,如果男人们在曼哈顿的一个聚会上说"大家高兴起来",Mary 不会误认为是男的在挑逗她!)

In the phonetic respellings throughout the book, the western pronunciations of words with the syllables remarked on above are used. This is done largely because I myself have lived in the Los Angeles area for some fourteen years, and have had to retrain my pronunciation (having come from New York City, where I was born, and lived all my life until 1964) so that my friends and students would stop making fun of the way I speak.

在本书的音标注释里,凡包含以上音节的单词,都以西部发音为准。之所以这样做,很大程度上是因为我在洛杉矶地区生活了 14 年,为了使我的朋友和学生们不再打趣我的音调,我不得不改变我的口音(我来自纽约,在那里出生,并且一直生活到 1964 年)。

Neither form of pronunciation is any better nor any more euphonious than the other. Throughout the country, pronunciation varies not only from region to region or state to state, but often from city to city! The changes are slight and subtle, but they do exist, and an expert can easily pinpoint the geographical source of a person's language patterns almost down to a few square miles in area.

没有哪种口音比其他口音更好,或者更动听。在全国范围内,口音不仅因地区或州而变化,并且经常是连城市之间的口音都有所变化。这种变化虽然轻微和微妙,但确实存在,从一个人的口音上,专家能很容易地判定出他的生活地域,有时甚至能精确到几英里的范围。

If you are an Easterner，you will have no difficulty translating the pronunciations of words like *sorority*，*incorrigible*，*disparage*，and *astronaut*（all words discussed in later chapters）into your own comfortable language patterns.

假如你是个生活在东部的人，你就能够根据你舒服的发音方式轻松发出诸如 sorority, incorrigible, disparage 和 astronaut 之类的词（这些词将要在后面几章里讨论）。

4. Why etymology?
为什么要了解词源学？

Etymology（et′-ə-MOL′-ə-jee）deals with the origin or derivation of words.

When you know the meaning of a root（for example，Latin *ego*，I or self），you can better understand，and more easily remember，*all* the words built on this root.

词源学是探究单词的起源和演变的。

当你知道一个词根的意思时（例如，拉丁字根 ego 的意思是"我""自我"），你就能更好地理解、更容易地记住所有包含这个词根的单词。

Learn one root and you have the key that will unlock the meanings of up to ten or twenty words in which the root appears.

Learn *ego* and you can immediately get a handle on *egocentric*，*egomaniac*，*egoist*，*egotist*，and *alter ego*.

Learn *anthropos*（Greek，mankind），and you will quickly understand，and never forget，*anthropology*，*misanthropy*，*anthropoid*，*anthropocentric*，*anthropomorphic*，*philanthropy*，and *anthropophobia*. Meet any word with *anthropo-* in it，and you will have at least some idea of its meaning.

掌握一个词根，你就有了一把钥匙，能够解开 10 个或 20 个包含此字根的单词的涵义。

学习了 ego 之后，你就能立即领会 egocentric，egomaniac，egoist，egotist 和 alter ego 这些单词的意思。

学习了 anthropos（希腊语，意为"人类"），你就能很快了解，并且永远不会忘记 anthropology，misanthropy，anthropoid，anthropocentric，anthropomorphic，philanthropy 和 anthropophobia。遇到任何包含 anthropo-的单词，你至少大概能猜到它是什么意思。

In the *etymological*（et′-ə-mə-LOJ′-ə-kəl）approach to vocabulary building：
- You will learn about *prefixes*，*roots*，and *suffixes*—
- You will be able to figure out unfamiliar words by recognizing their structure，the building blocks from which they are constructed—
- You will be able to construct words correctly by learning to put these building blocks together in the proper way—and
- You will be able to derive verbs from nouns，nouns and verbs from adjectives，adjectives from nouns，etc. —and do all this correctly.

从词源学的角度积累词汇，你将：
- 学习单词的前缀、词根和后缀；
- 能根据单词的结构、构成元素，推出陌生单词的意思；
- 通过学习将这些构词元素以适当的方式放在一起，能正确地构建单词；
- 能从名词猜测出动词，从形容词推测出名词和动词，从名词推测出形容词，等等——并且能正确地完成这些。

Learn how to deal with etymology and you will feel comfortable with words—you will use new words with self-assurance—you will be able to figure out thousands of words you hear or read even if you have never heard or seen these words before.

That's why the best approach to new words is through etymology[1]—as you will discover for yourself as soon as you start to work on chapter 3!

掌握如何利用词源学后,你就会觉得得心应手地学习单词——你会很有把握地使用新单词——你也能猜出这数以千计单词的意思,即使是从没见过、听过的新词。

这就是为什么通过词源学学习单词是最好的方法——就如你很快会在第 3 章里发现的那样。

5. But what are nouns, verbs, and adjectives?

但是,名词、动词和形容词又是什么呢?

You probably know.

But if you don't, you can master these parts of speech (and reference will be made to *noun forms*, *verb forms*, and *adjective forms* throughout the book) within the next five minutes.

你可能明白。

但是,如果你不明白,接下来 5 分钟的讲解能够使你掌握这些词性(本书会经常提及所讲解词汇的名词形式、动词形式和形容词形式)。

(a) A *noun* is a word that can be preceded by *a*, *an*, *the*, *some*, *such*, or *my*.

名词前面会出现 a、an、the、some、such 或 my 等词汇。

An *egoist* (noun)

Such *asceticism* (noun)

The *misogynist* (noun)

(Nouns, you will discover, often end in conventional suffixes: *-ness*, *-ity*, *-ism*, *-y*, *-ion*, etc.)

(你会发现,名词通常以-ness,-ity,-ism,-y,-ion 等为后缀结尾。)

(b) A *verb* is a word that fits into the pattern, "Let us _____." A verb has a past tense.

动词是能够嵌入"Let us _____."模式的词汇。动词有过去式形式。

---

1. Incidentally, Latin scholars will notice that I present a Latin verb in the first person singular, present tense (*verto*, I turn), but call it an infinitive (*verto*, to turn). I do this for two reasons: ① *verto* is easier for a non-Latin scholar to pronounce (the actual infinitive, *vertere*, is pronounced WAIR′-tə-ray); and ② when I studied Latin fifty years ago, the convention was to refer to a verb by using the first person singular, present tense.

If you are not a Latin scholar, you need not bother to read this footnote—if you've already done so, forget it!

顺便提一下,拉丁语学者会注意到,我将一个第一人称单数、现在时的拉丁语动词(verto,我转向)称为不定式(verto,转向)。这样做出于两个原因:① verto 的发音对于非拉丁语学者来说更容易(不定式的准确形式是 vertere,读音为 WAIR′-tə-ray);② 50 年前我学习拉丁语时,规定是使用第一人称单数现在时来表示动词。

如果你不是拉丁语学者,你不用费心阅读此脚注——如果你已经读完,请将它忘记!

Let us *equivocate*（verb）—past tense：*equivocated*.

Let us *alternate*（verb）—past tense：*alternated*.

Let us *philander*（verb）—past tense：*philandered*.

（Verbs，you will discover，often end in conventional suffixes：*-ate*，*-ize*，*-fy*，etc.）

（你会发现,动词通常以-ate,-ize,-fy 等为后缀结尾。）

（c）An *adjective* is a word that fits into the pattern，"You are very _____."

形容词是能够嵌入"You are very _____."模式的词汇。

You are very *egoistic*（adjective）.

You are very *introverted*（adjective）.

You are very *misogynous*（adjective）.

（Adjectives，you will discover，often end in conventional suffixes：*-ic*，*-ed*，*-ous*，*-al*，*-ive*，etc.）

（你会发现,形容词通常以-ic,-ed,-ous,-al,-ive 等为后缀结尾。）

And *adverbs*，of course，are generally formed by adding *-ly* to an adjective：*misogynous*→*misogynously*；*educational*→*educationally*；etc.

当然,副词的形式通常是在形容词后加-ly,如:misogynous→misogynously,educational→educationally,等等。

That's all there is to it!（Did it take more than five minutes? Maybe ten at the most?）

这就是词性的所有内容!（是否超过了 5 分钟? 也许最多花费 10 分钟?）

6. How to work for best results?

如何达到最佳效果?

If you intend to work with this book seriously（that is，if your clear intention is to add a thousand or more new words to your present vocabulary—add them permanently，unforgettably—add them so successfully that you will soon find yourself using them in speech and writing），I suggest that you give yourself every advantage by carefully following the laws of learning：

如果你打算认真学习这本书的内容(也就是说,如果你的目标明确,要使目前的词汇量增加 1,000 个或更多——而且是永久性的记忆——非常成功地增加词汇,以至于你很快能发现自己在言语和书写中开始使用这些词汇),那么我建议你仔细遵循以下学习法则:

（a）*Space your learning*.

确定学习步骤。

Beginning with Chapter 3，every chapter will be divided into "sessions". Each session may take one half hour to an hour and a half，depending on the amount of material and on your own speed of learning.

Do one or two sessions at a time—three if you're going strong and are all involved—and always decide when you stop *exactly when* you will return. （I remind you to do this later in the book，since such a procedure is of crucial importance.）

从第 3 章开始,每一章被分成了"节"。每节花费的时间不等,从半个小时到一个半小时,这取决于材料的数量和你自己的学习速度。

一次完成 1 到 2 节——如果你水平提高并完全沉浸在其中,一次可以完成 3 节——但是,当你停下来的时候,一定要确定好下一次学习的时间。(我提醒你在之后的内容一定要这样做,因为这个程序十分关键。)

(b) *Do not rush—go at your own comfortable speed.*

不可心急——以最适合自己的速度进行。

Everyone learns at a different pace. Fast learners are no better than slow learners—it's the end result that counts, not the time it takes you to finish.

每个人学习的步调不尽相同。学习速度快的人不一定比速度慢的人学得好——最终效果才算数,而非花费时间的长短。

(c) *Review.*

复习。

When you start a new session, go back to the last exercise of the previous session (usually *Can you recall the words*? or *Chapter Review*), cover your answers, and test your retention—do you have quick recall after a day or so has elapsed?

开始新章节学习时,回顾之前部分最后的练习(通常是"你能够写出这些词汇吗"或"章节复习"),不要看答案,检验你的记忆——一天或几天之后,你是否还能快速回忆起这些词汇?

(d) *Test yourself.*

自我测验。

You are not aiming for a grade, or putting your worth on the line, when you take the three Comprehensive Tests (Chapters 8, 13, and 17)—rather you are discovering your weaknesses, if any; deciding where repairs have to be made; and, especially, experiencing a feeling of success at work well done. (In learning, too, nothing succeeds like success!)

Use these three tests, as well as the abundant drill exercises, as aids to learning. No one is perfect, no one learns in the exact same way or at the same rate as anyone else. Find the optimum technique and speed for *your* unique learning patterns—and then give yourself every opportunity to exploit your actual, latent, and potential abilities.

But most important (as I will remind you several times throughout the book)— develop a routine and stick to it!

进行三次综合测验时(第 8 章、第 13 章和第 17 章),你的目标并不是分数,也不是考察自己的价值——你的目标是发现自己可能存在的弱点;确定需要弥补之处;尤其要感受一种完美地完成任务之后成功的喜悦。(没有什么比成功更让人欣慰的,在学习中也是如此!)

利用这三个综合测验和丰富的练习作为学习的辅助材料。没有人是完美的,每个人学习的方式不同,学习的速度也不同。为你自己独特的学习模式寻找最佳技巧和速度——然后抓住每次机会,开发自己真实的、隐伏的和潜在的能力。

但是最重要的是(在本书中我会不断地提醒你)——制定一套日程表,并持之以恒。

Disclaimer:

Occasionally in these pages, owing to the deficiency of the English language, I have used *he*/*him*/*his* meaning *he or she*/*him or her*/*his or her* in order to avoid awkwardness of style.

He，*him*，and *his* are *not* intended as exclusively masculine pronouns—they may refer to either sex or to both sexes.

免责声明：

因为英语语言的缺陷，在本书中，我偶尔使用 he，him，his 来表示 he(she)，him(her)，his(her)，以避免文体怪异。

He，him 和 his 并非专门用来指阳性代词——它们可以指阳性或阴性，或两性皆指。

CONTENTS
正文目录

HOW TO USE THIS BOOK FOR MAXIMUM BENEFIT

Why this is not a book to be *read*; how to learn to pronounce the new words *correctly*; how the *etymological* approach works better than any other method for learning words quickly and permanently; how to master nouns, verbs, adjectives, and adverbs in five to ten minutes; how to use the psychological principles of learning to sharpen your verbal skills.

为什么本书不是用于阅读；如何掌握新单词的正确读音；为何利用词源快速学习词汇、长效记忆词汇的方法优于其他方法；如何用 5 到 10 分钟掌握名词、动词、形容词和副词；如何运用关于学习的心理学原理来提升语言技巧。

PART ONE　　GETTING OFF TO A GOOD START
第一部分　　建立一个良好的开端

1. HOW TO TEST YOUR PRESENT VOCABULARY

How vocabulary growth of the average adult compares with that of children; a simple test to show you whether your vocabulary is below average, average, above average, excellent, or superior in range, verbal speed, and responsiveness; important evidence of the close relationship between vocabulary and success.

一般成年人学习词汇的速度和孩子相比怎么样；一个简单的测试，检验你的词汇范围、说话速度和反应能力，来确定你的词汇量是低于平均水平、高于平均水平、优秀还是非常优秀；词汇量和成功密切相关的重要证据。

2. HOW TO START BUILDING YOUR VOCABULARY

How building your vocabulary will enrich your thinking, increase your self-assurance in speaking and writing, and give you a better understanding of the world and of yourself; why it is necessary to recapture the "powerful urge to learn"; why your age makes little difference; how this book is designed to build a college-size vocabulary in two to three months.

扩大词汇量如何能丰富你的思维,增强你说话和写作的自信,使你更好地理解这个世界和你自己;为什么重新获得"强烈的学习欲望"尤为重要;为什么扩展词汇量与年龄无关;本书如何能够使你在两到三个月之内达到大学水平的词汇量。

3. HOW TO TALK ABOUT PERSONALITY TYPES (*Sessions 1—3*)

Words that describe all kinds and sorts of people, including terms for self-interest, reactions to the world, attitudes to others, skill and awkwardness, marital states, hatred of man, of woman, and of marriage. How one session of pleasant work can add more words to your vocabulary than the average adult learns in an entire year; why it is necessary to develop a comfortable time schedule and then *stick to it*.

描述各种各样个性类型的人物,包括与自我利益、世界观、对他人的态度、通达与笨拙、婚姻状况、厌恶男人、厌恶女人和厌恶婚姻生活等概念相关的术语。愉快地学习一段时间所掌握的词汇量,如何能比一般成年人一整年学到的词汇量还多;为什么制订一个合适的学习时间表并坚持执行是必不可少的。

4. HOW TO TALK ABOUT DOCTORS (*Sessions 4—6*)

Words that relate to medical specialists and specialties. Terms for experts in disorders of the female organs; childhood diseases; skin ailments; skeletal deformities; heart ailments; disorders of the nerves, mind, and personality. How self-discipline and persistence will ultimately lead to complete mastery over words.

与医学专家和专业相关的词汇;治疗女性组织紊乱、儿童疾病、皮肤疾病、骨骼畸形、心脏疾病,以及神经、心智、人格紊乱等疾病的专家术语;自律和恒心如何引导你完全掌握词汇。

5. HOW TO TALK ABOUT VARIOUS PRACTITIONERS (*Sessions 7—10*)

Words that describe a variety of professions, including those dealing with the human mind, teeth, vision, feet, handwriting, aging, etc. How you are becoming more and more conscious of the new words you meet in your reading.

描述各种各样职业的词汇,包括那些与人的心理、牙齿、视力、脚、书写、衰老等相关的职业。阅读时,你对新词如何变得越来越警觉。

6. HOW TO TALK ABOUT SCIENCE AND SCIENTISTS
(*Sessions 11－13*)

Words that describe students of human development，of the heavens，of the earth，of plant and animal life，of insect forms，of words and language，of social organization. Books on psychology that will add immeasurably both to your store of new words and ideas，and also to your understanding of yourself and of other people.

　　描述人类进化、天体、地球、植物与动物、昆虫、词汇与语言、社会组织等科目的学生的词汇。关于心理学的书籍不但可以极大地丰富你的新词，储备新概念，还使你更好地了解自己和其他人。

7. HOW TO TALK ABOUT LIARS AND LYING（*Sessions 14－17*）

Words that accurately label different types of liars and lying. Terms that relate to fame，artistry，reform，heredity，time，place，suffering，etc. Four lasting benefits you have begun to acquire from your work in vocabulary building.

　　准确描述不同种类骗子与谎言的词汇；与名誉、艺术才能、改造、遗传、时间、地点、苦难等相关的词汇。你从词汇扩建的学习中获得的四个长远利益。

8. HOW TO CHECK YOUR PROGRESS（*Session 18*）

Comprehensive Test Ⅰ：A 120-item test of your learning in *Part Ⅰ*.

　　综合测验Ⅰ：测试包含 120 道题，测验第一部分的学习成果。

PART TWO　GAINING INCREASED MOMENTUM
第二部分　加大马力

9. HOW TO TALK ABOUT ACTIONS（*Sessions 19－23*）

Verbs that accurately describe important human activities. Excursions into expressive terms for good and evil，doing，saying，wishing，and pleasing. Further proof that you can learn，in a few weeks or less，more new words than the average adult learns in an entire year.

　　描述人类重要行为的动词，了解一些表达好坏、行为、语言、愿望和取悦他人的相关术语。更多的证明证明，你能通过几个星期或更短的时间掌握普通成年人一整年才能掌握的新词。

10. HOW TO TALK ABOUT VARIOUS SPEECH HABITS
（*Sessions 24－27*）

Words that explore in depth all degrees and kinds of talk and silence. More books that will increase your alertness to new ideas and new words.

准确描述不同程度和不同种类的健谈和寡言。更多能够增加你对新概念和新词汇敏感程度的书目。

11. HOW TO INSULT YOUR ENEMIES（*Sessions 28－31*）

Terms for describing a disciplinarian, toady, dabbler, provocative woman, flag waver, possessor of a one-track mind, freethinker, sufferer from imaginary ailments, etc. Excursions into words relating to father and mother, murder of all sorts, sexual desires, and various manias and phobias. Magazines that will help you build your vocabulary.

描述严格的纪律奉行者、谄媚之人、浅涉文艺之人、蛮横的女人、狂热的爱国者、独行其是之人、自由的思想者、饱受虚构的疾病折磨的人等概念的术语。了解一些与父母、各种谋杀、性欲、各种疯狂和恐惧相关的词汇。对词汇的扩建有帮助的推荐书目。

12. HOW TO FLATTER YOUR FRIENDS（*Sessions 32－37*）

Terms for describing friendliness, energy, honesty, mental keenness, bravery, charm, sophistication, etc. Excursions into expressive words that refer to ways of eating and drinking, believing and disbelieving, looking and seeing, facing the present, past, and future, and living in the city and country. How the new words you are learning have begun to influence your thinking.

描述友善、精力、诚实、敏锐的思维、勇敢、魅力、老练等概念的术语。了解描述吃喝方式、信与不信，看与看见，面对现在、过去和将来，居住于城市和乡村的方式的表意词汇。你学到的新词给自己的思维带来了怎样的影响？

13. HOW TO CHECK YOUR PROGRESS（*Session 38*）

Comprehensive Test II：A 120-item test of your achievement in *Part II*.

综合测验Ⅱ：测试包含120道题，测验第二部分的学习成果。

PART THREE FINISHING WITH A FEELING OF COMPLETE SUCCESS
第三部分 以圆满成功的感觉收尾

Comprehensive Test III：A 120-item test of your achievement in *Part III*

综合测验Ⅲ：测试包含 120 道题，测验第三部分的学习成果。

Answers to Teaser Questions in Chapters 3－7，9－12，and 14－16.

第 3－7 章、第 9－12 章和第 14－16 章的难题答案。

The five simple，but vital，steps to take so that you can keep your vocabulary ever developing，ever increasing. How your vocabulary will continue to grow only if you remain on the search for new ideas. The best means for making this search successful.

保证词汇继续增长、继续扩展的五个简单但重要的步骤。只有不断探索新概念，你的词汇量才会继续增加；使这种探索取得成功的最佳手段。

BRIEF INTERMISSIONS
简短插叙目录

PART ONE
GETTING OFF TO A GOOD START

第一部分
建立一个良好的开端

1

HOW TO TEST YOUR PRESENT VOCABULARY
如何测试现有词汇量

Once—as a child—you were an expert, an accomplished virtuoso, at learning new words.

Today, by comparison, you are a rank and bumbling amateur.

在儿童时期,你曾经是一位专家,在学习新词汇方面,你是一位杰出的学者。

在今天,相比之下,你仅仅是一位笨口拙舌的业余选手。

Does this statement sound insulting?

It may be—but if you are the average adult, it is a statement that is, unfortunately, only too true.

Educational testing indicates that children of ten who have grown up in families in which English is the native language have recognition vocabularies of over twenty thousand words—

这些话听起来是否刺耳?

这些话也许有些无礼。但是,不幸的是,如果你是普通成年人,这些话再真实不过。

教育测试显示,在以英语为母语的家庭中成长的 10 岁儿童拥有两万多个认知词汇——

And that these same ten-year-olds have been learning new words at a rate of many hundreds a year since the age of four.

In astonishing contrast, studies show that adults who are no longer attending school increase their vocabularies at a pace *slower than twenty-five to fifty words annually.*

此外,同样是这些 10 岁儿童从 4 岁起便开始以每年几百个词汇的速度学习新词。

与之形成惊人对比的是,研究显示,不再上学的成年人每年词汇的增加数量少于 25 至 50 个。

How do you assess your own vocabulary?

Is it quantitatively healthy?

Rich in over-all range?

Responsive to any situation in which you may find yourself?

Truly indicative of your intellectual potential?

More important, is it still growing at the same rapid clip as when you were a child?

你如何评估自己的词汇?

你的词汇量是否符合标准?

你的词汇是否在各个领域都十分丰富?

你是否认为自己能够应付任何场合?

是否真正显示出你的智力潜能?

更重要的是,你的词汇增长速度是否与童年时期相同?

Or，as with most adults，has your rate of increase dropped drastically since you left school? And if so，do you now feel that your vocabulary is somewhat limited，your verbal skills not as sharp as you would like them to be?

Let us check it out.

I challenge you to a series of tests that will measure your vocabulary range，as well as your verbal speed and responsiveness.

或者,你的情况是否与大多数成年人相似? 你的词汇增长速度是否在你离开学校后骤减? 如果的确如此,你现在是否感觉自己的词汇量在某种程度上十分有限? 你的口语技巧是不是并没有自己希望的那么敏捷?

让我们加以测验。

以下一系列测试对你的词汇范围、语言速度和反应速度做出衡量。

A TEST OF VOCABULARY RANGE
词汇范围测试

Here are sixty brief phrases，each containing one italicized word；it is up to you to check the closest definition of each such word. To keep your score valid，refrain，as far as possible，from wild guessing. The key will be found at the end of the test.

这里有 60 个短语,每个都包含一个斜体单词,找出每个单词最确切的解释,为了使你的分数有效,尽量避免毫无根据地猜测答案。答案参见测验后面。

1. *disheveled* appearance：（a）untidy，（b）fierce，（c）foolish，（d）peculiar，（e）unhappy

2. a *baffling* problem：（a）difficult，（b）simple，（c）puzzling，（d）long，（e）new

3. *lenient* parent：(a) tall，(b) not strict，(c) wise，(d) foolish，(e) severe

4. *repulsive* personality：(a) disgusting，(b) attractive，(c) normal，(d) confused，(e) conceited

5. *audacious* attempt：(a) useless，(b) bold，(c) foolish，(d) crazy，(e) necessary

6. *parry* a blow：(a) ward off，(b) fear，(c) expect，(d) invite，(e) ignore

7. *prevalent* disease：(a) dangerous，(b) catching，(c) childhood，(d) fatal，(e) widespread

8. *ominous* report：（a）loud，（b）threatening，（c）untrue，（d）serious，

(e) unpleasant

9. an *incredible* story：(a) true，(b) interesting，(c) well-known，(d) unbelievable，(e) unknown

10. an *ophthalmologist*：(a) eye doctor，(b) skin doctor，(c) foot doctor，(d) heart doctor，(e) cancer specialist

11. will *supersede* the old law：(a) enforce，(b) specify penalties for，(c) take the place of，(d) repeal，(e) continue

12. an *anonymous* donor：(a) generous，(b) stingy，(c) well-known，(d) one whose name is not known，(e) reluctant

13. performed an *autopsy*：(a) examination of living tissue，(b) examination of a corpse to determine the cause of death，(c) process in the manufacture of optical lenses，(d) operation to cure an organic disease，(e) series of questions to determine the causes of delinquent behavior

14. an *indefatigable* worker：(a) well-paid，(b) tired，(c) skillful，(d) tireless，(e) pleasant

15. a confirmed *atheist*：(a) bachelor，(b) disbeliever in God，(c) believer in religion，(d) believer in science，(e) priest

16. endless *loquacity*：(a) misery，(b) fantasy，(c) repetitiousness，(d) ill health，(e) talkativeness

17. a *glib* talker：(a) smooth，(b) awkward，(c) loud，(d) friendly，(e) boring

18. an *incorrigible* optimist：(a) happy，(b) beyond correction or reform，(c) foolish，(d) hopeful，(e) unreasonable

19. an *ocular* problem：(a) unexpected，(b) insoluble，(c) visual，(d) continual，(e) imaginary

20. a notorious *demagogue*：(a) rabble-rouser，(b) gambler，(c) perpetrator of financial frauds，(d) liar，(e) spendthrift

21. a *naive* attitude：(a) unwise，(b) hostile，(c) unsophisticated，(d) friendly，(e) contemptuous

22. living in *affluence*：(a) difficult circumstances，(b) countrified surroundings，(c) fear，(d)wealth，(e) poverty

23. in *retrospect*：(a) view of the past，(b) artistic balance，(c) anticipation，(d) admiration，(e) second thoughts

24. a *gourmet*：(a) seasoned traveler，(b) greedy eater，(c) vegetarian，(d) connoisseur of good food，(e) skillful chef

25. to *simulate* interest：(a) pretend，(b) feel，(c) lose，(d) stir up，(e) ask for

26. a *magnanimous* action：(a) puzzling，(b) generous，(c) foolish，(d) unnecessary，(e) wise

27. a *clandestine* meeting：(a) prearranged，(b) hurried，(c) important，

(d) secret, (e) public

28. the *apathetic* citizens: (a) made up of separate ethnic groups, (b) keenly vigilant of their rights, (c) politically conservative, (d) indifferent, uninterested, uninvolved, (e) terrified

29. to *placate* his son: (a) please, (b) help, (c) find a job for, (d) make arrangements for, (e) change a feeling of hostility to one of friendliness

30. to *vacillate* continually: (a) avoid, (b) swing back and forth in indecision, (c) inject, (d) treat, (e) scold

31. a *nostalgic* feeling: (a) nauseated, (b) homesick, (c) sharp, (d) painful, (e) delighted

32. feel *antipathy*: (a) bashfulness, (b) stage fright, (c) friendliness, (d) hostility, (e) suspense

33. be more *circumspect*: (a) restrained, (b) confident, (c) cautious, (d) honest, (e) intelligent

34. an *intrepid* fighter for human rights: (a) fearless, (b) eloquent, (c) popular, (d) experienced, (e) famous

35. *diaphanous* material: (a) strong, (b) sheer and gauzy, (c) colorful, (d) expensive, (e) synthetic

36. a *taciturn* host: (a) stingy, (b) generous, (c) disinclined to conversation, (d) charming, (e) gloomy

37. to *malign* his friend: (a) accuse, (b) help, (c) disbelieve, (d) slander, (e) introduce

38. a *congenital* deformity: (a) hereditary, (b) crippling; (c) slight, (d) incurable, (e) occurring at or during birth

39. a definite *neurosis*: (a) plan, (b) emotional disturbance, (c) physical disease, (d) feeling of fear, (e) allergic reaction

40. made an *unequivocal* statement: (a) hard to understand, (b) lengthy, (c) politically motivated, (d) clear and forthright, (e) supporting

41. *vicarious* enjoyment: (a) complete, (b) unspoiled, (c) occurring from a feeling of identification with another, (d) long-continuing, (e) temporary

42. *psychogenic* ailment: (a) incurable, (b) contagious, (c) originating in the mind, (d) intestinal, (e) imaginary

43. an *anachronous* attitude: (a) unexplainable, (b) unreasonable, (c) belonging to a different time, (d) out of place, (e) unusual

44. her *iconoclastic* phase: (a) artistic, (b) sneering at tradition, (c) troubled, (d) difficult, (e) religious

45. a *tyro*: (a) dominating personality, (b) beginner, (c) accomplished musician, (d) dabbler, (e) serious student

46. a *laconic* reply: (a) immediate, (b) assured, (c) terse and meaningful,

(d) unintelligible, (e) angry

47. *semantic* confusion: (a) relating to the meaning of words, (b) pertaining to money, (c) having to do with the emotions, (d) relating to mathematics, (e) caused by inner turmoil

48. *cavalier* treatment: (a) courteous, (b) haughty and highhanded, (c) negligent, (d) affectionate, (e) expensive

49. an *anomalous* situation: (a) dangerous, (b) intriguing, (c) unusual, (d) pleasant, (e) unhappy

50. *posthumous* child: (a) cranky, (b) brilliant, (c) physically weak, (d) illegitimate, (e) born after the death of the father

51. feels *enervated*: (a) full of ambition, (b) full of strength, (c) completely exhausted, (d) troubled, (e) full of renewed energy

52. shows *perspicacity*: (a) sincerity, (b) mental keenness, (c) love, (d) faithfulness, (e) longing

53. an unpopular *martinet*: (a) candidate, (b) supervisor, (c) strict disciplinarian, (d) military leader, (e) discourteous snob

54. *gregarious* person: (a) outwardly calm, (b) very sociable, (c) completely untrustworthy, (d) vicious, (e) self-effacing and timid

55. generally *phlegmatic*: (a) smug, self-satisfied, (b) easily pleased, (c) nervous, high-strung, (d) emotionally unresponsive, (e) lacking in social graces

56. an *inveterate* gambler: (a) impoverished, (b) successful, (c) habitual, (d) occasional, (e) superstitious

57. an *egregious* error: (a) outstandingly bad, (b) slight, (c) irreparable, (d) unnecessary, (e) deliberate

58. *cacophony* of a large city: (a) political administration, (b) crowded living conditions, (c) cultural advantages, (d) unpleasant noises, harsh sounds, (e) busy traffic

59. a *prurient* adolescent: (a) tall and gangling, (b) sexually longing, (c) clumsy, awkward, (d) sexually attractive, (e) soft-spoken

60. *uxorious* husband: (a) henpecked, (b) suspicious, (c) guilty of infidelity, (d) fondly and foolishly doting on his wife, (e) tightfisted, penny-pinching

KEY: 1-a, 2-c, 3-b, 4-a, 5-b, 6-a, 7-e, 8-b, 9-d, 10-a, 11-c, 12-d, 13-b, 14-d, 15-b, 16-e, 17-a, 18-b, 19-c, 20-a, 21-c, 22-d, 23-a, 24-d, 25-a, 26-b, 27-d, 28-d, 29-e, 30-b, 31-b, 32-d, 33-c, 34-a, 35-b, 36-c, 37-d, 38-e, 39-b, 40-d, 41-c, 42-c, 43-c, 44-b, 45-b, 46-c, 47-a, 48-b, 49-c, 50-e, 51-c, 52-b, 53-c, 54-b, 55-d, 56-c, 57-a, 58-d, 59-b, 60-d

Your score (one point for each correct choice):

你的分数是(每答对一题得一分):_____。

The Meaning of Your Score:

0—11: below average

12—35: average

36—48: above average

49—54: excellent

55—60: superior

你的分数意味着:

0—11 分:低于平均水平

12—35 分:平均水平

36—48 分:高于平均水平

49—54 分:优秀

55—60 分:非常优秀

A TEST OF VERBAL SPEED
语言速度测验

PART 1
第一部分

This is a timed test.

In no more than three minutes (time yourself, or have someone time you), decide whether the word in column B is the *same* (or *approximately the same*) in meaning as the word in column A; *opposite* (or *approximately opposite*) in meaning; or whether the two words are merely *different*.

Circle S for *same*, O for *opposite*, and D for *different*.

You will not have time to dawdle or think too long, so go as fast as you can.

这是一个限时测验。

在不超过 3 分钟的时间内(你自己或请别人给你计时),确定 A 栏的单词和 B 栏的单词在意思上是相同(或大致相同)、相反(或大致相反),或者这两个单词不相关。

S 代表相同,O 代表相反,D 代表不同。

你没有太多的时间犹豫和停留,要尽可能快地做出判断。

COLUMN A	COLUMN B			
1. sweet	sour	S	O	D
2. crazy	insane	S	O	D
3. stout	fat	S	O	D
4. big	angry	S	O	D
5. danger	peril	S	O	D
6. help	hinder	S	O	D
7. splendid	magnificent	S	O	D

8.	love	hate	S	O	D
9.	stand	rise	S	O	D
10.	furious	violent	S	O	D
11.	tree	apple	S	O	D
12.	doubtful	certain	S	O	D
13.	handsome	ugly	S	O	D
14.	begin	start	S	O	D
15.	strange	familiar	S	O	D
16.	male	female	S	O	D
17.	powerful	weak	S	O	D
18.	beyond	under	S	O	D
19.	live	die	S	O	D
20.	go	get	S	O	D
21.	return	replace	S	O	D
22.	growl	weep	S	O	D
23.	open	close	S	O	D
24.	nest	home	S	O	D
25.	chair	table	S	O	D
26.	want	desire	S	O	D
27.	can	container	S	O	D
28.	idle	working	S	O	D
29.	rich	luxurious	S	O	D
30.	building	structure	S	O	D

PART 2
第二部分

This is also a timed test.

In no more than three minutes (again, time yourself or have someone time you), write down as many *different* words as you can think of that start with the letter *D*.

Do *not* use various forms of a word, such as *do*, *doing*, *does*, *done*, *doer*, etc.

Space is provided for 125 words. You are not expected to reach that number, but write as fast as you can and see how many blanks you can fill in before your time is up.

这也是一个限时测验。

在不超过 3 分钟的时间内(也是你自己或请别人给你计时),写出尽可能多的以 D 开头的不同的单词。

不要用同一个单词的不同形态,例如 do, doing, does, done, doer 等。

下面有 125 个空格,你不必都填满,但在规定的时间内,要尽可能快地写出来。

1. _____
2. _____
3. _____
4. _____
5. _____
6. _____
7. _____
8. _____
9. _____
10. _____
11. _____
12. _____
13. _____
14. _____
15. _____
16. _____
17. _____
18. _____
19. _____
20. _____
21. _____
22. _____
23. _____
24. _____
25. _____
26. _____
27. _____
28. _____
29. _____
30. _____
31. _____
32. _____
33. _____
34. _____
35. _____
36. _____
37. _____
38. _____
39. _____

40. _____
41. _____
42. _____
43. _____
44. _____
45. _____
46. _____
47. _____
48. _____
49. _____
50. _____
51. _____
52. _____
53. _____
54. _____
55. _____
56. _____
57. _____
58. _____
59. _____
60. _____
61. _____
62. _____
63. _____
64. _____
65. _____
66. _____
67. _____
68. _____
69. _____
70. _____
71. _____
72. _____
73. _____
74. _____
75. _____
76. _____
77. _____
78. _____

79. _____	103. _____
80. _____	104. _____
81. _____	105. _____
82. _____	106. _____
83. _____	107. _____
84. _____	108. _____
85. _____	109. _____
86. _____	110. _____
87. _____	111. _____
88. _____	112. _____
89. _____	113. _____
90. _____	114. _____
91. _____	115. _____
92. _____	116. _____
93. _____	117. _____
94. _____	118. _____
95. _____	119. _____
96. _____	120. _____
97. _____	121. _____
98. _____	122. _____
99. _____	123. _____
100. _____	124. _____
101. _____	125. _____
102. _____	

KEY：

Part 1：1-O，2-S，3-S，4-D，5-S，6-O，7-S，8-O，9-S，10-S，11-D，12-O，13-O，14-S，15-O，16-O，17-O，18-D，19-O，20-D，21-S，22-D，23-O，24-S，25-D，26-S，27-S，28-O，29-S，30-S

Part 2：Any English word starting with D is correct unless it is merely another form of a previous word on the list.

任何一个以 D 开头的单词都是正确答案，但要排除同一单词的不同形式。

Scoring：

PART 1
第一部分

If you have up to 10 correct answers，credit your score with 25 points.

If you have 11—20 correct answers，credit your score with 50 points.

21—25 correct answers—75 points.

26—30 correct answers—100 points.

答对 10 个或以下,得 25 分。

答对 11—20 个,得 50 分。

答对 21—25 个,得 75 分。

答对 26—30 个,得 100 分。

Your Score on Part 1：

你第一部分的得分：＿＿＿＿＿

PART 2
第二部分

Up to 30 words：25 points

31—50 words：50 points

51—70 words：75 points

71—125 words：100 points

写出 30 个或以下:25 分

31—50 个单词:50 分

51—70 个单词:75 分

71—125 个单词:100 分

Your Score on Part 2：

你第二部分的得分：＿＿＿＿＿

TOTAL SCORE(总分)

On Verbal Speed：

语言速度：＿＿＿＿＿

The meaning of your verbal speed score：

0—50 below average

51—75 average

76—100 above average

125—150：excellent

175—200：superior

你的分数意味着:

0—50 分:低于平均水平

51—75 分:平均水平

76—100 分:高于平均水平

125—150 分:优秀水平

175—200 分:非常优秀

A TEST OF VERBAL RESPONSIVENESS
反应速度测验

PART 1
第一部分

Write in the blank in column B a word starting with the letter P that is the *same*, or *approximately the same*, in meaning as the word given in column A.

Example: look _____ peer

Warning: Every answer *must* start with the letter P.

在 B 栏的空格中写出以字母 P 开头的单词,其意思要与 A 栏中对应的单词相同或大致相同。

举例:look   peer

注意:所填的每个单词必须以 p 开头。

A	B	A	B
1. bucket	_____	14. location	_____
2. trousers	_____	15. stone	_____
3. maybe	_____	16. inactive	_____
4. forgive	_____	17. fussy	_____
5. separate	_____	18. suffering	_____
6. likely	_____	19. castle	_____
7. annoy	_____	20. gasp	_____
8. good-looking	_____	21. fear	_____
9. picture	_____	22. twosome	_____
10. choose	_____	23. artist	_____
11. ugly	_____	24. sheet	_____
12. go	_____	25. collection	_____
13. dish	_____		

PART 2
第二部分

Write in the blank in column B a word starting with the letter G that is *opposite*, *approximately opposite*, or *in contrast to* the word given in column A.

Example: stop   *go*

Warning: Every answer *must* start with the letter G.

在 B 栏的空格中写出以 G 开头的单词,其意思要与 A 栏对应的单词相反或大致相反,或者意思相对。

举例:stop   go

注意:所填的每个单词必须以 G 开头。

A	B		A	B
1. lose	_____		14. ugly	_____
2. midget	_____		15. stingy	_____
3. special	_____		16. awkward	_____
4. lady	_____		17. little	_____
5. take	_____		18. rough	_____
6. moron	_____		19. bride	_____
7. sad	_____		20. ripe	_____
8. boy	_____		21. unwanting	_____
9. happy	_____		22. unprotected	_____
10. plain	_____		23. experienced	_____
11. hello	_____		24. scarcity	_____
12. here	_____		25. unappreciative	_____
13. bad	_____			

KEY：

Part 1：If more than one answer is given, count as correct any word you have written that is the same as any *one* of the answers.

如果答案不止一个,你写出与任何一个正确答案相同的单词,都算作正确。

1-pail, pan, 2-pants, 3-perhaps, possibly, probably, 4-pardon, 5-part, 6-probable, possible, perhaps, 7-pester, 8-pretty, 9-photograph, painting, 10-pick, 11-plain, 12-proceed, 13-plate, platter, 14-place, 15-pebble, 16-passive, 17-particular, picky, 18-pain, 19-palace, 20-pant, puff, 21-panic, 22-pair, 23-painter, 24-page, 25-pack

Part 2：If more than one answer is given, count as correct any word you have written that is the same as any *one* of the answers.

如果答案不止一个,你写出与任何一个正确答案相同的单词,都算作正确。

1-gain, get, garner, grab, glean, grasp, grip, 2-giant, gigantic, great, gross, 3-general, 4-gentleman, 5-give, 6-genius, 7-glad, gleeful, gleesome, 8-girl, 9-gloomy, glum, grieving, grumpy, 10-gaudy, grand, grandiose, 11-goodbye, 12-gone, 13-good, 14-good-looking, 15-generous, giving, 16-graceful, 17-great, giant, gigantic, 18-gentle, 19-groom, 20-green, 21-greedy, grasping, 22-guarded, 23-green, 24-glut, gobs, 25-grateful

Scoring：

Score Parts 1 and 2 together. Write in the blank the *total* number of correct responses you made：_____

第一部分和第二部分的得分加在一起。在空格中填上你正确答案的总数：_____

The meaning of your verbal responsiveness score：

$$0—10：below\ average$$
$$11—20：average$$
$$21—30：above\ average$$
$$31—40：excellent$$
$$41—50：superior$$

你的得分意味着：

0—10 分：低于平均水平

11—20 分：平均水平

21—30 分：高于平均水平

31—40 分：优秀

41—50 分：非常优秀

VOCABULARY AND SUCCESS
词汇量与成功的关系

Now you know where you stand. If you are in the below average or average group, you must consider, seriously, whether an inadequate vocabulary may be holding you back. (If you tested out on the above average, excellent, or superior level, you have doubtless already discovered the unique and far-reaching value of a rich vocabulary, and you are eager to add still further to your knowledge of words.)

Let us examine, briefly, some of the evidence that points to the close relationship between vocabulary and personal, professional, and intellectual growth.

The Human Engineering Laboratory found that the *only* common characteristic of successful people in this country is an unusual grasp of the meanings of words. The Laboratory tested the vocabularies of thousands of people in all age groups and in all walks of life—and discovered that those people drawing down the highest salaries made the highest scores. Consider very thoughtfully the explanation that the director of the Laboratory offered for the relationship between vocabulary and success：

现在你已经了解自己的词汇水平。如果你的词汇量低于平均水平或相当于平均水平，你必须严肃地思考一下，如此低水平的词汇量是否给你带来了负面影响。（如果你的词汇量到达了"高于平均水平""优秀"或"非常优秀"的级别，你一定已经发现了丰富的词汇量给你带来的独特而且影响长远的好处。同时，你也越发地追求更加丰富的词汇知识。）

让我们来简短地介绍一些科学证据，说明词汇量与个人、专业以及知识领域成功的紧密关系。

人类工程实验室发现本国成功人士唯一的共同点是对词汇的意义具有超乎寻常的理解。实验室对不同年龄段、不同职业的几千个人的词汇量进行测试——结果发现，拿最高薪酬的人所得分数最高。仔细思考实验室主任的以下论述，他的论述说明了词汇量和成功的紧密关系：

"Why do large vocabularies characterize executives and possibly outstanding men and women in other fields? The final answer seems to be that words are the instruments by means of which men and women grasp the thoughts of others and with which they do much of their own thinking. They are the tools of thought. "

There is other evidence.

At many universities, groups of freshmen were put into experimental classes for the sole purpose of increasing their knowledge of English words. *These groups did better in their sophomore, junior, and senior years than control groups of similarly endowed students who did not receive such training.*

And still more evidence:

At the University of Illinois, entering students were given a simple twenty-nine-word vocabulary test. The results of this test could be used, according to Professor William D. Templeman, to make an accurate prediction of future academic success—or lack of success—over the entire four year college course. "If a student has a superior vocabulary," states Professor Templeman, "it will probably follow that he will do better work academically. "

And finally:

Educational research has discovered that your I. Q. is intimately related to your vocabulary. Take a standard vocabulary test and then an intelligence test—the results in both will be substantially the same.

"高层管理人士和其他领域的杰出人物都具备一个共同点：词汇量尤为丰富。原因何在？最终的答案似乎是这样：男人和女人通过词汇来掌握他人的想法，也使用词汇来进行思考。词汇是思维的工具。"

再来看另外一个证据。

现在，很多大学会将几组新生分为实验班，其目的是增加英语词汇知识。这些学生在大二、大三以及大四的表现都要比没有接受训练的控制组中的学生出色。

还有更多的证据：

在伊利诺伊大学，入学新生要进行 29 个词汇的简单测试。根据威廉姆·D.坦普尔曼教授的观点，这个测试的结果可以用来准确推断学生在未来四年课程中学术方面的成就或者欠缺。坦普尔曼教授说："如果学生词汇量较大，他在学术上也会取得更好的成绩。"

最后：

近年来的教育研究发现，人的智商高低和词汇量有紧密的联系。词汇量测试和智商测试两者的结果基本一致。

YOU CAN INCREASE YOUR VOCABULARY

增加词汇，你能做到

The more extensive your vocabulary, the better your chances for success, other things being equal—success in attaining your educational goals, success in moving ahead in your business or professional career, success in achieving your intellectual potential.

假设其他条件相同，你拥有的词汇量越广泛，成功的机会就越多——例如成功地达到自己的教育目标，在商业或职业生涯更上一层楼，以及在需要发挥个人智力潜能方面取得成功。

And you *can* increase your vocabulary—faster and easier than you may realize.

You can, in fact, accomplish a tremendous gain in less than two to three months of concentrated effort, even if you do only one session a day—in less time if you do two or more sessions a day.

Furthermore—

You can start improving your vocabulary immediately—and within a few days you can be cruising along at such a rapid rate that there will be an actual change in your thinking, in your ability to express your thoughts, and in your powers of understanding.

Does this sound as if I am promising you the whole world in a neat package with a pretty pink ribbon tied around it? I am. And I am willing to make such an unqualified promise because I have seen what happens to those of my students at New York University and at Rio Hondo College in Whittier, California, who make sincere, methodical efforts to learn more, many more, words.

而且，你可以增加你的词汇量——比你想象的更快、更容易。

事实上，仅仅通过两三个月时间的集中努力，你就会取得巨大的进步，即使你一天仅仅完成一小节——如果每天完成两节或更多，你取得巨大进步所需的时间会更少。

此外——

你可以立即开始扩充自己的词汇——用不了几天，你的进步速度飞快，而你的思维、表达思想的能力以及理解力也会随之发生质的变化。

这听起来似乎是我在许诺，用漂亮的粉色丝带捆绑的礼物盒装下全世界送给你？事实的确如此。我愿意做出这样毫无保留的承诺，因为在我的纽约大学和加利福尼亚州惠蒂尔深河学院的学生身上，我的确看到了突飞猛进的进步。他们就是这样通过真切系统的努力，学到了越来越多的词汇。

2

HOW TO START BUILDING YOUR VOCABULARY
如何开始构建词汇

When you have finished working with this book，you will no longer be the same person.

You can't be.

If you honestly read every page，if you do every exercise，if you take every test，if you follow every principle，you will go through an intellectual experience that will effect a radical change in you.

阅读这本书,你会被彻底地改变。

你一定会经历很大的改变。

如果你认真地阅读每一页,做每一个练习,完成每一个测试,依照每一个原则做事,你会经历思想上的变革,得到一个全新的自我。

For if you systematically increase your vocabulary，you will also sharpen and enrich your thinking；push back your intellectual horizons；build your self-assurance；improve your facility in handling the English language and thereby your ability to express your thoughts effectively；and acquire a deeper understanding of the world in general and of yourself in particular.

原因在于,在你系统地增加词汇量的同时,你也是在塑造、丰富你的思维,扩大知识面,增加自信心,改善语言习得机制和提高有效表达思想的能力;也是在整体上更透彻地理解世界,尤其是对你自己的理解。

Increasing your vocabulary does not mean merely learning the definitions of large numbers of obscure words；it does not mean memorizing scores of unrelated terms. What it means—what it can only mean—is becoming acquainted with the multitudinous and fascinating phenomena of human existence for which words are，obviously，only the verbal descriptions.

增加词汇量并不仅仅意味着记忆许多晦涩难懂的词汇的定义;也不是指记忆许多不相关的术语。增加词汇量的意义,也是其唯一的意义,就是熟知存在于人类当中大量的令人着迷的现象,显然只有语言能对其做出描述。

Increasing your vocabulary—properly，intelligently，and systematically—means treating yourself to an all-round，liberal education.

And surely you cannot deny that such an experience will change you intellectually—ly—

Will have a discernible effect on your methods of thinking—on your store of information—on your ability to express your ideas—on your understanding of human problems.

恰当地、明智地、系统地增加你的词汇量意味着给自己进行一次全方位变革性的教育。

并且,你绝不会否认,这样的经历会从思想上为你带来变化——

这会对你的思维方式、信息储存、表达观点的能力,以及你对人类问题的认识等起到有效的作用。

HOW CHILDREN INCREASE THEIR VOCABULARIES
儿童如何增加词汇量

The typical ten-year-old, you will recall, has a recognition vocabulary of over twenty thousand words—and has been learning many hundreds of new words every year since the age of four.

You were once that typical child.

You were once an accomplished virtuoso at vocabulary building.

你会记得,正常的 10 岁儿童认知词汇量超过两万,从 4 岁起,他们的词汇量是以每年几百个新词的速度扩充的。

你曾经就是那个有代表性的儿童。

你在词汇扩建方面曾经是杰出的学者。

What was your secret?

Did you spend hours every day poring over a dictionary?

Did you lull yourself to sleep at night with *Webster's Unabridged*?

Did you keep notebooks full of all the new words you ever heard or read?

Did you immediately look up the meaning of any new word that your parents or older members of your family used?

Such procedures would have struck you as absurd then, as absurd as they would be for you today.

你的秘诀是什么?

你是否每天花费几个小时钻研词典?

你是否每晚熬夜仔细查阅韦氏词典?

你的笔记本是否塞满了你听到或者读到的每个生词?

你是否孜孜不倦地查阅父母或者家里年老成员使用的所有生词的定义?

这些程序在当时可能使你感到荒谬,即使在今天你也会感觉到它们十分荒唐。

You had a much better, much more effective, and considerably less self-conscious method.

Your method was the essence of simplicity: day in and day out you kept learning; you kept squeezing every possible ounce of learning out of every waking moment; you were an eternal question box, for you had a constant and insatiable desire to know and understand.

其实你使用了更好、更高效、更自然的方法。

你的方法再简单不过:你每天都在不停地学习;只要你醒着,你就在学习;你有问不完的问题,因为你想要知道、想去理解,这个欲望是无止境的、无法被满足的。

HOW ADULTS STOP BUILDING THEIR VOCABULARIES
成年人是如何停止构建词汇的

Then, eventually, at some point in your adult life (unless you are the rare exception), you gradually lost your compulsive drive to discover, to figure out, to understand, to know.

Eventually, therefore, you gradually lost your need to increase your vocabulary—your need to learn the words that could verbalize your new discoveries, your new understanding, your new knowledge.

最终,当你达到成年后的某个时期,你逐渐失去了去发现、领会、理解和了解事物的难以抑制的动力(除非你是少数例外)。

因此,你最终也会逐渐失去扩充词汇的需求——学习能够表达你的新发现、新理解和新知识的词汇的需求。

Roland Gelatt, in a review of Caroline Pratt's book *I Learn from Children*, describes this phenomenon as follows:

All normal human beings are born with a powerful urge to learn. Almost all of them lose this urge, even before they have reached maturity. It is only the few... who are so constituted that lack of learning becomes a nuisance. This is perhaps the most insidious of human tragedies.

在对凯若琳·普拉特的新书《我向儿童学习》的评论中,罗兰德·格莱特用以下的文字描述了这种现象:

所有正常人类出生时都具有巨大的学习欲望。后来,几乎所有人又都失去了这个欲望,甚至在他们尚未成熟时就失去了。只有少数人……他们如此塑造自己,以至于不学习成为了一种烦心事。这恐怕是人类最隐含不露的悲剧。

Children are wonders at increasing their vocabularies because of their "powerful urge to learn." They do not learn solely by means of words, but as their knowledge increases, so does their vocabulary—for words are the symbols of ideas and understanding.

(If you are a parent, you perhaps remember that crucial and trying period in which your child constantly asked "Why?" The "Why?" is the child's method of finding out. How many adults that you know go about asking and thinking "Why?" How often do you yourself do it?)

因为儿童有"巨大的学习欲望",所以从词汇增加的角度来讲,他们是奇迹。他们不仅通过词汇这一渠道本身来学习,还通过知识的增加来扩大词汇量——因为词汇是思想和理解的符号。

(如果你为人父母,你一定记得那个令你厌烦却又关键的阶段。在这个阶段中,你的孩子不断地问"为什么"。通过问"为什么",孩子们去发现世界。又有几个你认识的成年人会问"为什么"或者思考"为什么"呢? 你自己是否经常这样做?)

The adults who "lose this urge," who no longer feel that "lack of learning becomes a nuisance," stop building their vocabularies. They stop learning, they stop growing intellectually, they stop changing. When and if such a time comes, then, as Mr. Gelatt so truly says, "This is perhaps the most insidious of human tragedies." But fortunately the process is far from irreversible.

If you have lost the "powerful urge to learn," you can regain it—you can regain your need to discover, to figure out, to understand, to know.

"失去了这个欲望"的成年人再也感觉不到"不学习是一种烦心事"，也就停止了构建词汇。他们停止了学习，停止了心智上的发展，也停止了变化。人生的这个阶段就好比格莱特先生说的那样："这恐怕是人类最隐含不露的悲剧。"但是幸运的是，这个过程并不是不可逆转的。

即使你曾经失去"学习的欲望"，你也能够重新获得它——你能够重新获得去发现、领会、理解和了解事物的需求。

And thus you can start increasing your vocabulary at the same rate as when you were a child.

I am not spouting airy theory. For over thirty-five years I have worked with thousands of adults in my college courses in vocabulary improvement, and I can state as a fact, and without qualification, that：

If you can recapture the "powerful urge to learn" with which you were born, you can go on increasing your vocabulary at a prodigious rate—

No matter what your present age.

这样，你就能够以童年时的速度开始扩充自己的词汇。

我并不是纸上谈兵。在过去的 35 年中，我已接触成千上万个成年人，他们修习我开设的如何扩充词汇量的大学课程，我可以实事求是、毫无保留地说：

只要你能重新获得这种与生俱来的"巨大的学习欲望"，你就能够以非凡的速度继续增加词汇量——

无论你现在多大年龄。

WHY AGE MAKES LITTLE DIFFERENCE IN VOCABULARY BUILDING
为什么扩展词汇量与年龄无关

I repeat, *no matter what your present age.*

You may be laboring under a delusion common to many older people.

You may think that after you pass your twenties you rapidly and inevitably lose your ability to learn.

That is simply not true.

我再重复一遍，无论你现在多大年龄，你都可以扩展词汇。

你可能和许多其他老年人一样，饱受错觉之苦。

你可能会认为，过了 20 岁，你很快并且无法避免地失去了学习的能力。

这种想法并不是事实。

There is no doubt that the years up to eighteen or twenty are the best period for learning. Your own experience no doubt bears that out. And of course *for most people* more learning goes on faster up to the age of eighteen or twenty than ever after, even if they live to be older than Methuselah. (That is why vocabulary increases so rapidly for the first twenty years of life and comparatively at a snail's pace thereafter.)

毫无疑问，18 岁或者 20 岁之前是学习的最好阶段。你自己的经历也说明了这一点。而且，对于大多数人来说，哪怕他们比玛土撒拉[1] 活的时间更长，他们吸收新知识更多、更快的阶段也主要是在 18 岁或 20 岁之前，而不是以后。（这一点也可以解释为什么人的词汇量在 20 岁之前可以突飞猛进，而在 20 岁之后增长速度却如蜗牛一般。）

But (and follow me closely)—

The fact that most learning is accomplished before the age of twenty does not

---

1. 玛土撒拉是《圣经》记载的寿命最长的人，他活了 969 岁。——译者注

mean that very little learning can be achieved beyond that age.

What *is* done by most people and what *can* be done under proper guidance and motivation are two very, very different things—as scientific experiments have conclusively shown.

但是（请注意听我的）——

20 岁之前完成大部分学习这一事实并不意味着 20 岁之后就没有什么可学的。

大多数人做的是一回事，而这些人在恰当的引导和激发之下能够做的完全是另一回事。这一点，科学实验已经给出了肯定的答案。

Furthermore—

The fact that your learning ability may be best up to age twenty does not mean that it is absolutely useless as soon as your twentieth birthday is passed.

Quite the contrary.

Edward Thorndike，the famous educational psychologist，found in experiments with people of all ages that although the learning curve rises spectacularly up to twenty，it remains steady for at least another five years. After that，ability to learn (according to Professor Thorndike) drops very, very slowly up to the age of thirty-five，and drops a bit more but *still slowly* beyond that age.

再者——

20 岁之前人们的学习能力最佳并不意味着 20 岁之后学习能力的完全丧失。

事实并非如此。

通过对不同年龄段的人进行实验研究，著名教育心理学家爱德华·桑戴克发现，20 岁之前，学习曲线增加速度非常明显；之后的至少 5 年，曲线仍然维持稳定；直到 35 岁之前，学习曲线以非常非常慢的速度下降（根据桑戴克教授的研究）；35 岁之后，学习速度相对下降稍快，但总体下降速度仍然很慢。

And—

Right up to senility the *total* decrease in learning ability after age twenty is never more than 15 percent!

That does not sound，I submit，as if no one can ever learn anything new after the age of twenty.

Believe me，the old saw that claims you cannot teach an old dog new tricks is a baseless，if popular，superstition.

而且——

从 20 岁直到完全衰老之前，学习能力的总下降幅度不大于 15％！

我认为这个事实表明，并不是没有人能够在 20 岁之后学习新的知识。

相信我，认为"老狗学不会新花招"一类的观点虽然普遍，但却是毫无根据的盲目臆测。

So I repeat：no matter what your age，you can go on learning efficiently，or start learning once again if perhaps you have stopped.

You can be thirty，or forty，or fifty，or sixty，or seventy—or older.

No matter what your age，you can once again increase your vocabulary at a prodigious rate—providing you recapture the "powerful urge to learn" that is the key to vocabulary improvement.

所以我要重申，无论你年龄有多大，你都可以继续有效地学习；或者如果你已经停止学习，你绝对可以重新开始。

无论你是 30 岁、40 岁、50 岁，还是 60 岁或 70 岁——甚至更加年长，你都可以重新开始学习。

无论你多大年龄,都可以重新以惊人的速度增加词汇,前提是,你必须重新获得增加词汇的关键——"强烈的学习欲望"。

Not the urge to learn "words"—words are only symbols of ideas.

But the urge to learn facts, theories, concepts, information, knowledge, understanding—call it what you will.

Words are the symbols of knowledge, the keys to accurate thinking. Is it any wonder then that the most successful and intelligent people in this country have the biggest vocabularies?

It was not their large vocabularies that made these people successful and intelligent, but their *knowledge*.

不是学习"词汇"的欲望——词汇仅仅是思想的符号。

而是学习事实、理论、概念、信息、知识和提高理解力的欲望——随你怎么称呼它。

词汇是知识的符号,是准确思维的关键。那么,一个国家最成功、最智慧的人士正是那些拥有最多词汇量的人,这一点也不足为奇。

其实,不是巨大的词汇量本身使这些人成功、聪慧,而是他们的知识。

Knowledge, however, is gained largely through words,

In the process of increasing their knowledge, these successful people increased their vocabularies.

Just as children increase *their* vocabulary at a tremendous, phenomenal rate during those years when their knowledge is increasing most rapidly.

然而,知识很大程度上是通过词汇获得的。

在增加知识的过程中,这些成功人士也在增加词汇。

当儿童如饥似渴地以最快的速度吸收新知识的同时,他的词汇量也以惊人、显著的速度增长着。

Knowledge is chiefly in the form of words, and from now on, in this book, you will be thinking *about*, and thinking *with*, new words and new ideas.

知识主要是以词汇的形式呈现的。从现在开始,在阅读本书的过程中,你将会思考新词汇、新概念,并用新词汇、新概念进行思考。

WHAT THIS BOOK CAN DO FOR YOU

这本书对你有何用

This book is designed to get you started building your vocabulary—effectively and at jet-propelled speed—by helping you regain the intellectual atmosphere, the keen, insatiable curiosity, the "powerful urge to learn" of your childhood.

The organization of the book is based on two simple principles: ① words are the verbal symbols of ideas, and ② the more ideas you are familiar with, the more words you know.

本书的设计意在帮助你重新获得思考氛围,重拾儿童时代热忱的、永不满足的好奇心和"强烈的学习欲望",以此使你开始增加词汇量。

本书的结构基于两条简明的准则:第一,词汇是概念的语言符号;第二,人们熟知的概念越多,词汇量也就越大。

So, chapter by chapter, we will start with some central idea—personality types, doctors，science，unusual occupations，liars，actions，speech habits，insults，compliments，etc.—and examine ten basic words that express various aspects of the idea. Then，using each word as a springboard，we will explore any others which are related to it in meaning or derivation，so that it is not unlikely that a single chapter may discuss，teach，and test close to one hundred important words.

所以，我们会逐章从最核心的概念出发——个性类型、医生、科学、不同寻常的职业、谎言制造者、行动、言语习惯、羞辱、赞扬等——然后对表达某一概念各个方面的 10 个基本词汇做出详尽解释。然后，以每个词汇为出发点，我们会挖掘意义上或者起源上与其相关的其他词汇。这样，每一章探讨、讲解、测验的词汇很可能达到 100 个。

Always，however，the approach will be from the idea. First there will be a "teaser preview" in which the ideas are briefly hinted at；then a "headline"，in which each idea is examined somewhat more closely；next a clear，detailed paragraph or more will analyze the idea in all its ramifications；finally the word itself，which you will meet only after you are completely familiar with the idea.

但是，本书的视角总是从概念出发。首先是"引读"，简要暗示概念；然后是"提要"，对每个概念进一步解释说明；接下来是更加清晰、详尽的段落（一个或者多个），对概念的方方面面进行分析；最后才是词汇，只有在你完全理解概念之后，词汇才会出现。

In the *etymology* (derivation of words) section，you will learn what Greek or Latin root gives the word its unique meaning and what other words contain the same，or related，roots. You will thus be continually working in related fields，and there will never be any possibility of confusion from "too muchness," despite the great number of words taken up and tested in each chapter.

在词源（词汇衍生）部分，你将学习赋予词汇独特含义的希腊语和拉丁语词根；同时，也会了解其他哪些词语也包含同样或者相关的词根。这样，你会在相关的领域不断获取词汇，即使每个章节出现或者测试的单词再多，也不会因为"内容太多"而有混淆的可能。

Successful people have superior vocabularies. People who are intellectually alive and successful in the professional or business worlds are accustomed to dealing with ideas，are constantly on the search for new ideas，build their lives and their careers on the ideas they have learned. And it is to readers whose goal is *successful* living (in the broadest meaning of the word successful) that this book is addressed.

成功人士具有非常丰富的词汇量。那些头脑活跃，在专业领域或商界取得成功的成功人士，他们都善于思考概念，并不断寻求新的概念，在学到的概念之上改善生活、发展事业。这本书正是写给那些以"成功"（指最广泛意义上的成功）为目标的读者。

A NOTE ON TIME SCHEDULES
关于学习计划

From my experience over many years in teaching，I have become a firm believer in setting a goal for all learning and a schedule for reaching that goal.

You will discover that each chapter is divided into approximately equal sessions，and that each session will take from thirty to forty-five minutes of your time，depending on how rapidly or slowly you enjoy working—and bear in mind that everyone has an optimum rate of learning.

通过多年教学经验,我坚定地相信任何学习都要有确定的目标,为了达到目标,也必须制定学习计划。

你会发现,每一章被分为大致相等的几个小节,每个小节需要花费 30 到 45 分钟的时间。时间长短取决于你自己喜欢的速度——谨记,每个人都有自己的最佳学习速度。

For best results, do one or two sessions at a time—spaced studying, with time between sessions so that you can assimilate what you have learned, is far more efficient, far more productive, than gobbling up great amounts in indigestible chunks.

Come back to the book every day, or as close to every day as the circumstances of your life permit.

Find a schedule that is comfortable for you, and then stick to it.

为了达到最好效果,一次完成一或两个小节,合理分配小节与小节之间的间隔时间,这样你才能够吸收学到的内容。与囫囵吞枣一口气学大量内容相比,这种方法更高效,效果更佳。

每天学习一点点,或者根据你生活允许的情况安排时间,尽量做到每天学习。

找到适合自己的节奏,然后持之以恒。

Avoid interrupting your work until you have completed a full session, and always decide, before you stop, *exactly when* you will plan to pick up the book again.

Working at your own comfortable rate, you will likely finish the material in two to three months, give or take a few weeks either way.

However long you take, you will end with a solid feeling of accomplishment, a new understanding of how English words work, and—most important—how to make words work for you.

在完成整个小节的内容之前,避免中断学习。在停歇之前确定下次学习的准确时间。

按照适合自己的节奏学习,你可能在两到三个月之内完成材料,时间上允许有几周的出入。

无论花费多长时间,你都会在最后获得踏实的成就感,重新理解英语词汇的功能,最重要的是,如何使用词汇为自己服务。

3

HOW TO TALK ABOUT PERSONALITY TYPES
如何描述个性类型

（Sessions 1－3 ）

What word best describes your personality if you:

* *are interested solely in your own welfare?*
* *constantly talk about yourself?*
* *dedicate your life to helping others?*
* *turn your mind inward?*
* *turn your mind outward?*
* *hate humanity?*
* *hate women?*
* *hate marriage?*
* *lead a lonely，austere existence?*

如何分别描述下列各项体现的人物个性：
* 他只关心自己的安乐
* 他不停地谈论关于自己的一切
* 他将自己的生命致力于帮助他人
* 他思想内敛
* 他思想外张
* 他愤世嫉俗
* 他讨厌女性
* 他畏惧婚姻
* 他喜欢独处,对自己的道德要求严格

SESSION 1
第 1 节

Every human being is, in one way or another, unique.

Everyone's personality is determined by a combination of genetic and environmental factors.

Let us examine ten personality types (one of which might by chance be your very own) that result from the way culture, growth, family background, and environment interact with heredity.

And, of course, we begin not with the words, but with the ideas.

每个人都是独一无二的,或以这样的方式,或以那样的方式。

每个人的个性都由基因和环境因素组合决定。

下面让我们剖析 10 种个性类型(其中一种可能碰巧就是你的个性类型),这 10 种个性类型是文化、成长、家庭背景和环境与遗传相互作用的结果。

当然,我们从概念入手,而非词汇。

IDEAS
概念

1. me first
以我为先

Your attitude to life is simple, direct, and aboveboard—every decision you make is based on the answer to one question: "What's in it for me?" If your selfishness, greed, and ruthless desire for self-advancement hurt other people, that's too bad. "This is a tough world, pal, dog eat dog and all that, and I, for one, am not going to be left behind!"

An *egoist*

这样的人对生活的态度简单、直接、明了——他所做的每个决定都基于对一个问题的回答:"这件事会给我带来什么?"如果他为了得到自我利益而表现出的自私、贪婪和无情的欲望伤害到他人,那只能怪别人太倒霉了。"朋友,这是一个无情的世界,狗咬狗,人人都为自己,而我呢? 我在这方面也绝不会落后于他人。"

他是一个 egoist(利己主义者)。

2. the height of conceit
自负至极

"Now, let's see. Have you heard about all the money I'm making? Did I tell you about my latest amorous conquest? Let me give you my opinion—I know, because I'm an expert at practically everything!" You are boastful to the point of being obnoxious—you have only one string to your conversational violin, namely, *yourself*; and on it you play a number of monotonous variations: what *you* think, what *you* have done, how good *you* are, how *you* would solve the problems of the world, etc. ad nauseam. [1]

---

1. etc. ad nauseam:etc. 拉丁语 et cetera 的简写形式,意为"及其他等等""诸如此类";ad nauseam,拉丁语,意为"令人作呕的"。这两个词放在一起 etc. adnauseam 即意为"还有很多其他令人作呕的言语"。——译者注

An egotist

"现在大家听好了。你们听说过我赚到了多少大钱吗？我是否告诉过你们我最近的一次成功艳遇？让我来告诉你我的观点——我非常了解，因为我几乎在任何事情上都是专家!"这个家伙的自夸程度已经达到了令人相当厌恶的程度——他用来演奏的小提琴上只有一根琴弦，这根琴弦就是他自己；而在这唯一的一根琴弦上，他却演奏出了太多单调乏味的曲调：他的观点是什么，他做过什么，他有多么优秀，他会如何处理身边的问题，还有很多其他令人作呕的言语。

他是一个 egotist(自大者)。

3. let me help you

让我来帮助你

You have discovered the secret of true happiness—concerning yourself with the welfare of others. Never mind your own interests, how's the next fellow getting along?

An altruist

他已经发现了幸福的真正秘密——将自己和他人的安乐联系起来。他从不考虑自己的利益，从不考虑下一个伙计是否好相处？

他是一个 altruist(利他主义者)。

4. leave me alone

离我远点儿

Like a biochemist studying a colony of bacteria under the microscope, you minutely examine your every thought, feeling, and action. Probing, futile questions like "What do other people think of me?", "How do I look?", and "Maybe I shouldn't have said that?" are your constant nagging companions, for you are unable to realize that other people do not spend as much time and energy analyzing you as you think.

You may seem unsocial, yet your greatest desire is to be liked and accepted. You may be shy and quiet, you are often moody and unhappy, and you prefer solitude or at most the company of one person to a crowd. You have an aptitude for creative work and are uncomfortable engaging in activities that require co-operation with other people. You may even be a genius, or eventually turn into one.

An introvert

像一位生物化学家正研究着显微镜下的一团细菌，他每时每刻都在审视自己的观点、体会和行为。他无休无止地在心里唠叨，刨根问底地追问自己一些没有答案的问题："其他人对我有怎样的看法？""我看起来怎么样？""我可能不应该那样说？"因为他意识不到别人根本不会花费那么多时间和精力去像他一样分析他自己。

他看起来可能并不擅长交际，但是他最大的愿望却是被别人喜欢、接受。他可能很害羞，喜欢安静；他经常会情绪化，不开心；他更喜欢独处，或者他宁愿身边只有一个人陪伴，也不要一群人的喧闹。他对于需要创造力的工作颇有天资；而当需要和他人配合时，他就会很不自在。他甚至有可能是个天才，或者最终总会成为天才。

他是一个 introvert(内向的人)。

5. let's do it together

让我们合作吧

You would be great as a teacher, counselor, administrator, insurance agent. You can always become interested—sincerely, vitally interested—in other people's problems. You're the life of the party, because you never worry about the effect of your actions, never inhibit yourself with doubts about dignity or propriety. You are usually happy, generally full of high spirits; you love to be with people—lots of people. Your thoughts, your interests, your whole personality are turned outward.

An *extrovert*

他会是出色的教师、顾问、行政官员、保险代理人。因为他总能全心全意地、热情地被他人的问题所吸引。他从不担心自己的行为会造成怎样的后果,也从来不因担心自己的行为会有损尊严、不合时宜而约束自己,所以他是掌控全局的人。他总是处于兴奋的状态,情绪亢奋,他喜欢和人相处——人越多越好。他的思想,他的兴趣,他的整个人格都是外张的。

他是一个 extrovert(外向的人)。

6. neither extreme

与大多数人相同

You have both introverted and extroverted tendencies—at different times and on different occasions. Your interests are turned, in about equal proportions, both inward and outward. Indeed, you're quite normal—in the sense that your personality is like that of most people.

An *ambivert*

他既有内向、又有外向的性格倾向——不同的时间和不同的场合表现不同。他的兴趣既内敛,又外张,两者比例大致相同。他的性格符合大多数人的特点,从这个意义上来说,他非常正常。

他是一个 ambivert(中向性格者)。

7. people are no damn good

没有人是好东西

Cynical, embittered, suspicious, you hate everyone. (Especially, but never to be admitted, *yourself*?) The perfectibility of the human race? "Nonsense! No way!" The stupidity, the meanness, and the crookedness of most mortals ("Most? Probably all!")—that is your favorite theme.

A *misanthrope*

他愤世嫉俗,他充满怨恨,他疑心重重,他讨厌任何人(尤其是他自己,不过从不承认?)。如果你问:"人类物种真的可以近乎完美吗?"他会说:"胡说! 不可能!"大多数人都愚蠢、卑鄙、狡诈("大多数? 可能所有人都是这个死样!")——这才是他最喜欢讨论的主题。

他是一个 misanthrope(厌世者)。

8. women are no damn good

没有一个女人是好东西

Sometime in your dim past, you were crossed, scorned, or deeply wounded by a woman (a mother, or mother figure, perhaps?). So now you have a carefully constructed defense against further hurt—you hate *all* women.

A *misogynist*

在他阴暗不幸的过去的某个时刻,他曾被某个女人阻挠、讥笑或者深深地伤害(这个女人或许是一位母亲或者是母亲一样的人?)所以现在,他仔细地构筑了防卫心理,以预防遭到更深的伤害——他憎恨、惧怕所有的女性。

他是一个 misogynist(厌恶女人的人)。

9. "marriage is an institution—and who wants to live in an institution?"

"婚姻就是约束——谁又愿意在约束中活着呢?"

You will not make the ultimate *legal* commitment. Members of the opposite sex are great as lovers, roommates, apartment-or house-sharers, but *not* as lawfully wedded spouses. The ties that bind are too binding for you. You may possibly believe, and possibly, for yourself, be right, that a commitment is deeper and more meaningful if freedom is available without judicial proceedings.

A misogamist

他永远不会给出最终的法律承诺。异性作为情人、室友、公寓或房屋合租人都是不错的选择,但是他们成为合法婚姻伴侣就不行了。使夫妻紧紧相连的纽带对他来说是过度的束缚。他可能持有这样的信条,而且对他本人来说可能也是正确的,就是无须司法程序的约束、保留自由空间的承诺更为深刻、更有意义。

他是一个 misogamist(厌恶结婚的人)。

10. "... that the flesh is heir to..."

"……身心的疼痛无法逃避,这才叫圆满……"

Self-denial, austerity, lonely contemplation—these are the characteristics of the good life, so you claim. The simplest food and the least amount of it that will keep body and soul together, combined with abstinence from fleshly, earthly pleasures, will eventually lead to spiritual perfection—that is your philosophy.

An ascetic

自我否定、禁欲、独自冥想——他宣称这些才是幸福生活的特征。只食用维持人类不会死去的、最简单、最少量的食物,禁止享受任何肉体的、人间的乐趣,才能够最终达到精神上的圆满——这就是他的哲学。

他是一个 ascetic(禁欲主义者)。

USING THE WORDS
单词应用

You have been introduced to ten valuable words—but in each case, as you have noticed, you have first considered the ideas that these words represent. Now *say* the words—each one is respelled phonetically so that you will be sure to pronounce it correctly. [1]

Say each word aloud. This is the first important step to complete mastery. As you hear a word in your own voice, think of its meaning. Are you quite clear about it? If not, reinforce your learning by rereading the explanatory paragraph or paragraphs.

你已经阅读对于以上 10 个有价值的单词的介绍——正如你所注意到的一样,每种个性类型之下,你都是最先获得词汇所代表的概念。现在我们读这些词汇——每个单词都按照发音重新拼写,保证你的发音完全正确。

大声读出每个单词。这是完全掌握词汇的关键步骤之一。当你听到单词从自己口中读出时,思考单词的意义。你是否对单词的含义有了彻底的了解? 如果没有完全掌握,你可以再看相关的解释,巩固之前的学习。

Can you pronounce the words?
你能读出这些单词吗?

1. *egoist*   EE'-gō-ist

---

1. See Introduction, Section 2, *Master the pronunciation system*.
参见第二节介绍,掌握发音系统

2. *egotist*　　　　　　　EE′-gō-tist

3. *altruist*　　　　　　　AL′-trōō-ist

4. *introvert*　　　　　　IN′-trə-vurt′

5. *extrovert*　　　　　　EKS′-trə-vurt′

6. *ambivert*　　　　　　AM′-bə-vurt′

7. *misanthrope*　　　　　MIS′-ən-thrōp′

8. *misogynist*　　　　　mə-SOJ′-ə-nist

9. *misogamist*　　　　　mə-SOG′-ə-mist

10. *ascetic*　　　　　　　ə-SET′-ik

Can you work with the words?
你能灵活使用这些词汇了吗?

You have taken two long steps toward mastery of the expressive words in this chapter—you have thought about the ideas behind them, and you have said them aloud.

For your third step, match each personality with the appropriate characteristic, action, or attitude.

在掌握本章表示个性类型词汇的道路上,你已经向前迈进了两大步——你不仅已经思考了词汇背后隐藏的概念,也大声地朗读了这些词汇。

第三步是做以下练习,在右栏中挑选出与左栏词汇相对应的个性类型。

1. egoist　　　　　　　　a. turns thoughts inward

2. egotist　　　　　　　　b. hates marriage

3. altruist　　　　　　　　c. talks about accomplishments

4. introvert　　　　　　　d. hates people

5. extrovert　　　　　　　e. does not pursue pleasures of the flesh

6. ambivert　　　　　　　f. is interested in the welfare of others

7. misanthrope　　　　　　g. believes in self-advancement

8. misogynist　　　　　　　h. turns thoughts both inward and outward

9. misogamist　　　　　　i. hates women

10. ascetic　　　　　　　　j. turns thoughts outward

KEY:1-g, 2-c, 3-f, 4-a, 5-j, 6-h, 7-d, 8-i, 9-b, 10-e

Do you understand the words?
你对这些词汇是否已经透彻地理解?

Now that you are becoming more and more involved in these ten words, find out if they can make an immediate appeal to your understanding. Here are ten questions—can you indicate, quickly, and without reference to any previous definitions, whether the correct answer to each of these questions is *yes* or *no*?

现在,既然你已经越来越熟悉这些词汇,我们来测试你是否能在看到词汇之后立即做出联想。以下是 10 个问题——你是否能以最快的速度判断出每个问题的对错(注意不能参考之前的定义)?

1.	Is an *egoist* selfish?	YES	NO
2.	Is modesty one of the characteristics of the *egotist*?	YES	NO
3.	Is an *altruist* selfish?	YES	NO
4.	Does an *introvert* pay much attention to himself?	YES	NO
5.	Does an *extrovert* prefer solitude to companionship?	YES	NO
6.	Are most normal people *ambivert*?	YES	NO
7.	Does a *misanthrope* like people?	YES	NO
8.	Does a *misogynist* enjoy the company of women?	YES	NO
9.	Does an *ascetic* lead a life of luxury?	YES	NO
10.	Does a *misogamist* try to avoid marriage?	YES	NO

KEY：1-yes，2-no，3-no，4-yes，5-no，6-yes，7-no，8-no，9-no，10-yes

Can you recall the words?

你能够写出这些词汇吗?

You have thus far reinforced your learning by saying the words aloud, by matching them to their definitions, and by responding to meaning when they were used in context.

Can you recall each word, now, without further reference to previous material? And can you spell it correctly?

你已经完成了新词的发音练习,并将词汇和定义配对,回答了有关词汇含义的问题。

在不参考前面资料的情况下,你还记得每一个词吗? 你能根据简短的定义在右侧拼写出正确的单词吗?

1.	Who lives a lonely, austere life?	1.	A _____
2.	Whose interests are turned outward?	2.	E _____
3.	Who is supremely selfish?	3.	E _____
4.	Who hates people?	4.	M _____
5.	Whose interests are turned both inward and outward?	5.	A _____
6.	Who is incredibly conceited?	6.	E _____
7.	Who is more interested in the welfare of others than in his own?	7.	A _____
8.	Who hates women?	8.	M _____
9.	Whose interests are turned inward?	9.	I _____
10.	Who hates marriage?	10.	M _____

KEY：1-ascetic，2-extrovert，3-egoist，4-misanthrope，5-ambivert，6-egotist，7-altruist，8-misogynist，9-introvert,10-misogamist

(End of Session 1)

SESSION 2
第 2 节

ORIGINS AND RELATED WORDS
词源及相关词汇

Every word in the English language has a history—and these ten are no exception. In this section you will learn a good deal more about the words you have been working with; in addition, you will make excursions into many other words allied either in meaning, form, or history to our basic ten.

英语的每个单词都有一段历史——这里的 10 个单词也不例外。在这个部分,你将更深入地了解这 10 个单词。此外,你也会认识和这 10 个基本词汇在词义、词形或者词源上相关的其他一些词汇。

1. the ego
词根:ego(我)

Egoist and *egotist* are built on the same Latin root—the pronoun *ego*, meaning *I*. *I* is the greatest concern in the *egoist's* mind, the most overused word in the *egotist's* vocabulary. (Keep the words differentiated in your own mind by thinking of the *t* in *talk*, and the additional *t* in *egotist*.) *Ego* itself has been taken over from Latin as an important English word and is commonly used to denote one's concept of oneself, as in, "What do you think your constant criticisms do to my *ego*?" *Ego* has also a special meaning in psychology—but for the moment you have enough problems without going into that.

If you are an *egocentric* (ee'-gō-SEN'-trik), you consider yourself the *center* of the universe—you are an extreme form of the *egoist*. And if you are an *egomaniac* (ee'-gō-MAY'-nee-ak), you carry *egoism* to such an extreme that your needs, desires, and interests have become a morbid obsession, a *mania*. The *egoist* or *egotist* is obnoxious, the *egocentric is* intolerable, and the *egomaniac* is dangerous and slightly mad.

Egocentric is both a noun ("What an *egocentric* her new roommate is!") and an adjective ("He is the most *egocentric* person I have ever met!").

To derive the adjective form of *egomaniac*, add *-al*, a common adjective suffix. Say the adjective aloud:

egomaniacal　　　ee'-gō-mə-NĪ'-ə-kəl

Egoist 和 Egotist 两个词具有相同的拉丁语词根——代词 ego,意为"我"。"我"是 egoist(利己主义者)最关心的问题,也是 egotist(自大者)的词汇里出现最频繁的词。(egotist 比 egoist 多了字母 t,把 t 想做 talk 中的 t,这样便于区分 egoist 和 egotist。)英语将 ego 从拉丁语中借入,ego 成为了一个非常重要的英语单词,通常被用来指人们对自我的意识,例如:"你认为你不断地批评会对我有怎样的影响?"Ego 在心理学中具有特殊含义——在这里我们不做过多介绍,因为你已经有足够多的问题了。

一个 egocentric(以自我为中心的人)会把自己视为全宇宙的中心——他是 egoist 的极端。而一个 egomaniac(自大狂)会将 egoism 发挥到极致,他病态地着迷于自己的需要、欲望和兴趣,变成了 mania(狂热)。egoist 或者 egotist 令人讨厌,egocentric 让人无法忍受,而 egomaniac 就有些危险,并且轻度疯癫。

egocentric 既是名词("她的新室友真是个以自我为中心的人!"),又是形容词("他是我见过的最以自我为中心的人!")。

在 egomaniac 的词尾添加常见形容词后缀-al,便得到形容词形式。大声朗读形容词:egomaniacal,ee′-gō-mə-NĪ′-ə-kəl。

2. others

词根:others(他者)

In Latin, the word for *other* is *alter*, and a number of valuable English words are built on this root.

拉丁语中表示"他者"的词是 alter,许许多多宝贵的英语词汇都建立在这个词根之上。

Altruism (AL′-tr$\overline{oo}$-iz-əm), the philosophy practiced by *altruists*, comes from one of the variant spellings of Latin *alter*, other. *Altruistic* (al-tr$\overline{oo}$-lS′-tik) actions look toward the benefit of *others*. If you *alternate* (AWL′-tər-nayt′), you skip one and take the *other*, so to speak, as when you play golf on *alternate* (AWL′-tər-nət) Saturdays.

Altruism 是 altruist 的处世哲学,两个词来源于拉丁词 alter 拼写变体之一,意思是"他者"。altruistic 行为顾及他人的利益。如果你 alternate,你会跳过一个而选择另外一个。例如,you play golf on alternate Saturdays 是指"你这个周六不打高尔夫,下个周六打"。

An *alternate* (AWL′-tər-nət) in a debate, contest, or convention is the *other* person who will take over if the original choice is unable to attend. And if you have no *alternative* (awl-TUR′-nə-tiv), you have no *other* choice.

辩论、竞赛或者会议中的 alternate,是指当原选手无法参加时,需要有其他人来取代他。而当说你没有别的 alternative 时,是指你没有其他选择。

You see how easy it is to understand the meanings of these words once you realize that they all come from the same source. And keeping in mind that *alter* means *other*, you can quickly understand words like *alter ego*, *altercation*, *and alteration*.

你瞧,只要你意识到他们来自于同样的词根,理解这些词汇就变得非常容易。知道了 alter 就是 other(其他)的意思,你就能够很快理解 alter ego,altercation 和 alteration 的词义。

An *alteration* (awl′-tə-RAY′-shən) is of course a change—a making into something *other*. When you *alter* (AWL′-tər) your plans, you make *other* plans.

Alteration 当然表示一种变化——变成其他的东西。当你 alter(改变)你的计划时,你也就是做了其他的计划。

An *altercation* (awl′-tər-KAY′-shən) is a verbal dispute. When you have an *altercation* with someone, you have a violent disagreement, a "fight" with words. And why? Because you have *other* ideas, plans, or opinions than those of the person on the *other* side of the argument. *Altercation*, by the way, is stronger than *quarrel* or *dispute*—the sentiment is more heated, the disagreement is likely to be angry or even hot-tempered, there may be recourse, if the disputants are human, to profanity or obscenity. You have *altercations*, in short, over pretty important issues, and the word implies that you get quite excited.

altercation 是指言语上的争执——当你和别人有 altercation 时,你们会有激烈的争吵,一场文字"战斗"。为什么?

因为你和对方有不同的(其他的)观点、计划或主张。顺便说一句,altercation 在某种程度上要比 quarrel(争吵)或者 dispute(争执)强烈——情绪更加火爆,双方都很生气,甚至大发雷霆;如果争执者是人类,甚至可能会使用不敬或者淫秽的言语。简而言之,你会在重大问题上发生争吵,althrcations 一词也意味着你会变得非常激愤。

Alter ego (AWL′-tər EE′-gō), which combines *alter*, other, with *ego*, I, self, generally refers to someone with whom you are so close that you both do the same things, think alike, react similarly, and are, in temperament, almost mirror images of each other. Any such friend is your *other I*, your *other self*, your *alter ego*.

Alter ego(知己、密友)将 alter(另一个)和我们刚刚学习的 ego(我)结合起来,是指和你关系非常亲密的人,他和你做同样的事情,有相像的思维方式,会做出类似的反应,而在性格上,你们几乎是彼此的镜中影像。任何这样的朋友都是你的另一个我,你的另一个自己,你的 alter ego。

USING THE WORDS
单词应用

Can you pronounce the words?
你能读出这些单词吗?

Digging a little into the derivation of three of our basic words, *egoist*, *egotist*, and *altruist*, has put us in touch with two important Latin roots, *ego*, I, self, and *alter*, other, and has made it possible for us to explore, with little difficulty, many other words derived from these roots. Pause now, for a moment, to digest these new acquisitions, and to say them *aloud*.

深入地剖析 3 个基本词汇 egoist,egotist 和 altruist 的派生词,使我们接触到了两个重要的拉丁词根 ego(我)和 alter(另外的,其他),也使我们能够毫不费力地探究由这些词根派生的其他词汇。现在让我们停下来消化这些新内容,大声读出这些单词。

1.	*ego*	EE′-gō
2.	*egocentric*	ee-gō-SEN′-trik
3.	*egomaniac*	ee-gō-MAY′-nee-ak
4.	*egomaniacal*	ee′-gō-mə-NĪ′-ə-kəl
5.	*altruism*	AL′-trōō-iz-əm
6.	*altruistic*	al-trōō-IS′-tik
7.	to *alternate*(*v.*)	AWL′-tər-nayt′
8.	*alternate* (*adj. or noun*)	AWL′-tər-nət
9.	*alternative*	awl-TUR′-nə-tiv
10.	*alteration*	awl′-tər-AY′-shən
11.	to *alter*	AWL′-tər
12.	*altercation*	awl′-tər-KAY′-shən
13.	*alter ego*	AWL′-tər EE′-gō

Can you work with the words?（Ⅰ）
你能灵活使用这些词汇了吗？（Ⅰ）

You have seen how these thirteen words derive from the two Latin roots *ego*, I, self, and *alter*, other, and you have pronounced them aloud and thereby begun to make them part of your active vocabulary.

Are you ready to match definitions to words?

你已经看到这13个词汇是如何从两个拉丁语词根派生而来：ego(我)和 alter(其他)。你已经大声朗读了它们，因此，你已经开始使它们成为你主动词汇的一部分。

准备好为这些词选择正确的解释了吗？

1. ego	a. one who is excessively fixated on his own desires, needs, etc.
2. egocentric	b. to change
3. altruism	c. argument
4. to alternate	d. one's concept of oneself
5. to alter	e. take one, skip one, etc.
6. altercation	f. philosophy of putting another's welfare above one's own

KEY：1-d，2-a，3-f，4-e，5-b，6-c

Can you work with the words?（II）
你能灵活使用这些词汇了吗？（II）

1. egomaniacal	a. a change
2. altruistic	b. other possible
3. alternative	c. interested in the welfare of others
4. alteration	d. one's other self
5. alter ego	e. a choice
6. alternate (*adj.*)	f. morbidly, obsessively wrapped up in oneself

KEY：1-f，2-c，3-e，4-a，5-d，6-b

Do you understand the words?
你对这些词汇是否已经透彻地理解？

If you have begun to understand these thirteen words, you will be able to respond to the following questions.

如果你已经开始理解这13个词汇，你就能够快速并正确地对以下问题做出回答。

1. Is rejection usually a blow to one's *ego*? YES NO
2. Are *egocentric* people easy to get along with? YES NO
3. Does an *egomaniac* have a normal personality? YES NO
4. Are *egomaniacal* tendencies a sign of maturity? YES NO
5. Is *altruism* a characteristic of selfish people? YES NO
6. Are *altruistic* tendencies common to egoists? YES NO
7. Is an *alternate* plan necessarily inferior? YES NO
8. Does an *alternative* allow you some freedom of choice? YES NO
9. Does *alteration* imply keeping things the same? YES NO
10. Do excitable people often engage in *altercations*? YES NO
11. Is your *alter ego* usually quite similar to yourself? YES NO

KEY: 1-yes，2-no，3-no，4-no，5-no，6-no，7-no，8-yes，9-no，10-yes，11-yes

Can you recall the words?
你能够写出这些词汇吗?

Have you learned these words so well that you can summon each one from your mind when a brief definition is offered? Review first if necessary; then, without further reference to previous pages, write the correct word in each blank. Make sure to check your spelling when you refer to the Key.

你对这些单词的学习是否已经达到了根据简短的定义想起相应词汇的程度？如果有必要，首先复习之前学习的内容，然后在不参考前面内容的前提下，在空格中写出恰当的词。对照答案的时候记住也检查你的拼写是否正确。

1. one's other self   1. A _____
2. to change   2. A _____
3. a heated dispute   3. A _____
4. excessively, morbidly obsessed with one's own   4. E _____
   needs, desires, or ambitions
5. unselfish; more interested in the welfare of   5. A _____
   others than in one's own
6. utterly involved with oneself; self-centered   6. E _____
7. a choice   7. A _____
8. one who substitutes for another   8. A _____

KFY: 1-alter ego, 2-alter, 3-altercation, 4-egomaniacal, 5-altruistic, 6-egocentric, 7-alternative, 8-alternate

(End of Session 2)

SESSION 3
第 3 节

ORIGINS AND RELATED WORDS
词源及相关词汇

1. depends on how you turn
   词义取决于你如何"转向"

Introvert, *extrovert*, and *ambivert* are built on the Latin verb *verto*, to turn. If your thoughts are constantly turned inward (*intro-*), you are an *introvert*; outward (*extro-*), an *extrovert*; and in both directions (*ambi-*), an *ambivert*. The prefix *ambi-*, both, is also found in *ambidextrous* (am′-bə-DEKS′-trəs), *able to use both hands with equal skill*. The noun is *ambidexterity* (am′-bə-deks-TAIR′-ə-tee).

introvert,extrovert 和 ambivert 3 个词的构词基于拉丁语动词 verto,意为 turn(转向)。如果你的思想总是转向内部 (intro),你就是个 introvert;思想转向外部(extro),你就是个 extrovert;如果两种(ambi)情况都有发生,你就是个 ambivert。前缀 ambi-也出现在单词 ambidextrous 中,ambi 意为 both(两者),整个词表示"能够同样熟练地使用双手的"。其名词形式为 ambidexterity。

Dexterous (DEKS′-tə-rəs) means *skillful*, the noun *dexterity* (deks-TAIR′-ə-tee) is *skill*. The ending *-ous* is a common adjective suffix (*famous*, *dangerous*, *perilous*, etc.); *-ity* is a common noun suffix (*vanity*, *quality*, *simplicity*, etc.).

(Spelling caution: Note that the letter following the *t-* in *ambidextrous* is *-r*, but that in *dexterous* the next letter is *-e*.)

Dexter is actually the Latin word for *right hand*—in the *ambidextrous* person, both hands are *right hands*, so to speak.

dexterous 表示"有技巧的",名词 dexterity 表示"技巧"。结尾的-ous 是常见的形容词后缀,(例如 famous, dangerous, perilous 等);-ity 是常见的名词后缀(例如 vanity, quality, simplicity 等)。

(拼写要点:注意在 ambidextrous 中 t 后面是 r,而在 dexterous 中,t 后面的字母则是 e。)

dexter 在拉丁语中表示"右手"——可以说,一个 ambidextrous 的人的两只手都是右手。

The right hand is traditionally the more skillful one; it is only within recent decades that we have come to accept that "lefties" or "southpaws" are just as normal as anyone else—and the term *left-handed* is still used as a synonym of *awkward*.

通常右手是更有技巧的手;只是在近代我们才逐渐接受"善用左手的人"或者"左撇子"也和其他人一样正常——而人们仍然将 left-handed 视为"笨拙"的同义词。

The Latin word for the *left hand* is *sinister*. This same word, in English, means *threatening*, *evil*, or *dangerous*, a further commentary on our early suspiciousness of left-handed persons. There may still be some parents who insist on forcing left-handed children to change (though left-handedness is inherited, and as much an integral part of its possessor as eye color or nose shape), with various unfortunate results to the child—sometimes stuttering or an inability to read with normal skill.

"左手"对应的拉丁语是 sinister。在英语里,sinister 表示"险恶的""邪恶的"或者"危险的",人们习惯上对善用左手的人持猜疑的态度,所以,这个词汇的含义又是对这一点的进一步诠释。现在,仍然有一些家长坚持让天性左撇子的孩子做出改变(尽管左手习惯是从父母继承而来的,与眼睛的颜色和鼻子的形状一样,都是我们不可或缺的一部分),这可能会带来各种各样不幸的结果——通常是结巴或者丧失正常的阅读技巧。

The French word for the *left hand* is *gauche*, and, as you would suspect, when we took this word over into English we invested it with an uncomplimentary meaning. Call someone *gauche* (GŌSH) and you imply clumsiness, generally social rather than physical. (We're fight back to our age-old misconception that left-handed people are less skillful than right-handed ones.) A *gauche* remark is tactless; a *gauche* offer of sympathy is so bumbling as to be embarrassing; *gaucherie* (GŌ'-shə-ree) is an awkward, clumsy, tactless, embarrassing way of saying things or of handling situations. The *gauche* person is totally without finesse.

左手的法语词是 gauche。正如你猜到的一样,当这个词被借入到英语中时,人们会赋予它贬义。称人为 gauche,就是在暗示他笨拙,通常都是指社交方面而非身体方面。(现在你会发现,我们又回到了对善用左手的人的传统错误观点,认为他们没有其他人灵巧。)a gauche remark 意为"不机智的言语";a gauche offer of sympathy 指笨拙地表达同情心,反而令人难堪;gaucherie 是指说话或者处理问题的方式奇怪、笨拙、缺乏策略、令人难堪。the gauche person 指"完全不机智的这类人"。

And the French word for the *right hand* is *droit*, which we have used in building our English word *adroit* (ə-DROYT'). Needless to say, *adroit*, like *dexterous*, means *skillful*, but especially in the exercise of the mental facilities. Like *gauche*, *adroit*, or its noun *adroitness*, usually is used figuratively. The *adroit* person is quick-witted, can get out of difficult spots cleverly, can handle situations ingeniously. *Adroitness* is, then, quite the opposite of *gaucherie*.

法语中表示右手的词是 droit,在构建英语词 adroit 时使用了这个词。毋庸置疑,adroit 和 dexterous 一样,指"有技巧的",但通常用来指脑力劳动方面。和 gauche 一样,adroit 及其名词形式 adroitness 通常都用来表示象征性的含义。adroit person 反应灵敏,能够机智地摆脱困境,能够有才能地掌控局势。名词 adroitness 和 gaucherie 是一对反义词。

2. love, hate, and marriage
爱,恨和婚姻

Misanthrope, *misogynist*, and *misogamist* are built on the Greek root *misein*, to hate. The *misanthrope* hates mankind (Greek *anthropos*, mankind); the *misogynist* hates women (Greek *gyne*, woman); the *misogamist* hates marriage (Greek *gamos*, marriage).

Anthropos, mankind, is also found in *anthropology* (an-thrə-POL'-ə-jee), the study of the development of the human race; and in *philanthropist* (fə-LAN'-thrə-pist), one who loves mankind and shows such love by making substantial financial contributions to charitable organizations or by donating time and energy to helping those in need.

misanthrope, misogynist 和 misogamist 三个词的构词基于希腊语词根 misein,意为"憎恨"。misanthrope 憎恨人类(anthropos,希腊语,人);misogynist 憎恨女人(gyne,希腊语,女人);misogamist 憎恨婚姻(gamos,希腊语,婚姻)。

anthropos 指人类,出现在另外两个词中:anthropology 指对人类的研究,人类学;philanthropist(慈善家)——指热爱人类、通过向慈善机构做出大量财富贡献或奉献时间和精力帮助那些有需要的人们来表现爱的人。

The root *gyne*，woman，is also found in *gynecologist*（jinə-KOL'-ə-jist）. the medical specialist who treats female disorders. And the root *gamos*，marriage，occurs also in *monogamy*（mə-NOG'-ə-mee），*bigamy*（BIG'-ə-mee），and *polygamy*（pə-LIG'-ə-mee）.

（As we will discover later，*monos* means *one*，*bi-* means *two*，*polys* means *many*.）

So *monogamy* is the custom of only *one* marriage（at a time）.

Bigamy，by etymology，is *two* marriages—in actuality，the unlawful act of contracting another marriage without divorcing one's current legal spouse.

词根 gyne 指女人，也出现在 gynecologist 中，gynecologist 指专门医治女性疾病的医生。gamos 指婚姻，出现在 monogamy，bigamy，和 polygamy 等词中。

（我们在之后的内容会发现 monos 表示一个，bi-表示两个，polys 表示多个。）

所以，monogamy 是指一夫一妻制的习俗。

从词源角度讲，bigamy 是同时存在的两次婚姻，这是在未与目前合法配偶离婚的基础上与另外一个配偶结婚的不合法行为。

And *polygamy*，by derivation *many* marriages，and therefore etymologically denoting plural marriage for either males *or* females，in current usage generally refers to the custom practiced in earlier times by the Mormons，and before them by King Solomon，in which the man has as many wives as he can afford financially and/or emotionally. The correct，but rarely used，term for this custom is *polygyny*（pə-LIJ'-ə-nee）—*polys*，many，plus *gyne*，woman.

What if a woman has two or more husbands，That custom is called *polyandry*（pol-ee-AN'-dree），from *polys* plus Greek *andros*，male.

polygamy 从派生角度表示多次婚姻，因此，从词源角度讲表示男性或女性多次婚姻。目前，这个用法通常用来表示早期摩门教以及比摩门教更早的所罗门国王施行的习俗，在这些时代，男性可以迎娶许多妻子，只要他在经济上和（或）情感上能够承担得起。这种习俗的正确形式是 polygyny，由 polys（许多）和 gyne（女人）组成，但是人们较少使用这个形式。

一个女人拥有两个或更多个丈夫，我们应该如何称呼这种婚姻呢？这种习俗被称为 polyandry，由 polys 和希腊语表示男性的词汇 andros 组成。

3. making friends with suffixes
与后缀组成新单词

English words have various forms，using certain suffixes for nouns referring to persons，other suffixes for practices，attitudes，philosophies，etc，and still others for adjectives.

通过使用某些表示人的名词后缀，表示行为、态度、哲学等的后缀，以及其他表示形容词的后缀，英语词汇能够衍变出许多不同形式。

Consider：

Person	*Practice，etc.*	*Adjective*
1. misanthrope or misanthropist	misanthropy	misanthropic

2. misogynist	misogyny	misogynous *or* misogynistic
3. gynecologist	gynecology	gynecological
4. monogamist	monogamy	monogamous
5. bigamist	bigamy	bigamous
6. polygamist	polygamy	polygamous
7. polygynist	polygyny	polygynous
8. polyandrist	polyandry	polyandrous
9. philanthropist	philanthropy	philanthropic
10. anthropologist	anthropology	anthropological

You will note, then, that *-ist* is a common suffix for a person; *-y* for a practice, attitude, etc. ; and *-ic* or *-ous* for an adjective.

你会注意到,-ist 常常用作表示人的后缀,后缀-y 表示行为、态度等,-ic 或-ous 表示形容词。

4. living alone and liking it
独自居住并乐此不疲

Ascetic is from the Greek word *asketes*, monk or hermit.

A monk lives a lonely life—not for him the pleasures of the fleshpots, the laughter and merriment of convivial gatherings, the dissipation of high living. Rather, days of contemplation, study, and rough toil, nights on a hard bed in a simple cell, and the kind of self-denial that leads to a purification of the soul.

That person is an *ascetic* who leads an existence, voluntarily of course, that compares in austerity, simplicity, and rigorous hardship with the life of a monk.

The practice is *asceticism* (ə-SET′-ə-siz-əm), the adjective *ascetic*.

ascetic 来源于拉丁语 asketes,指和尚或者隐士。

和尚独自生活——寻欢作乐的愉悦、酒宴聚会中的欢笑和喜悦、放荡的上流生活,都不是他的追求。相反,不分昼夜地冥想、学习,身体的辛劳,在简陋的棚屋里硬板床上度过无数个夜晚,以及能够达到心灵净化的自我克制,这些才是他的目标。

那个能够自发地过和尚一样禁欲、简单、艰苦生活的人,就可以被称为 ascetic。

其行为叫做 asceticism,形容词形式是 ascetic。

REVIEW OF ETYMOLOGY
复习词源

Notice how efficiently you can master words by understanding their etymological structure. Stop for a moment to review the roots, prefixes, and suffixes you have studied. Can you recall a word we have discussed in this chapter that is built on the indicated prefix, root, or suffix?

注意从词源结构入手掌握新单词是多么有效。重新复习一下你已经学到的词根、前缀和后缀。你能想起来在本章中学习过的一个新单词吗? 这个单词包含我们已经介绍过的前缀、词根或后缀。

PREFIX，ROOT，SUFFIX	MEANING	EXAMPLE
1. *ego*	self，I	_____
2. *alter*	other	_____
3. *intro-*	inside	_____
4. *extro-*	outside	_____
5. *verto*	turn	_____
6. *ambi-*	both	_____
7. *misein*	hate	_____
8. *anthropos*	mankind	_____
9. *gyne*	woman	_____
10. *gamos*	marriage	_____
11. *asketes*	monk	_____
12. *centrum*	center	_____
13. *mania*	madness	_____
14. *dexter*	right hand	_____
15. *sinister*	left hand	_____
16. *gauche*	left hand	_____
17. *droit*	right hand	_____
18. *monos*	one	_____
19. *bi-*	two	_____
20. *polys*	many	_____
21. *andros*	male	_____
22. *-ist*	person who (*noun suffix*)	_____
23. *-y*	Practice，custom，etc. (*noun suffix*)	_____
24. *-ous*	adjective suffix	_____
25. *-ity*	quality，condition，etc. (*noun suffix*)	_____

USING THE WORDS
单词应用

Can you pronounce the words？（Ⅰ）
你能读出这些单词吗？（Ⅰ）

Say each word aloud! Hear it in your own voice! *Say it often enough so that you feel comfortable with* it，*noting carefully from the phonetic respelling exactly how it should sound*.

Remember that the first crucial step in mastering a word is to be able to say it with ease and assurance.

大声读出每个单词！听自己读音！尽可能多地说出这个单词来，直到你感到非常熟练为止。仔细阅读音标以明确这些单词的正确发音。

记住，掌握新单词的最关键的一步就是能正确和轻松地把它读出来。

1. *ambidextrous*	am-bə-DEKS'-trəs
2. *ambidexterity*	am'-bə-deks-TAIR'-ə-tee
3. *dexterous*	DEKS'-trəs
4. *dexterity*	deks-TAIR'-ə-tee
5. *sinister*	SIN'-ə-stər
6. *gauche*	GŌ-SH (Say the English word *go*, then quickly add -*sh*.)
7. *gaucherie*	GŌ'-shə-ree
8. *adroit*	ə-DROYT'
9. *adroitness*	ə-DROYT'-nəss
10. *anthropology*	an-thrə-POL'-ə-jee
11. *anthropologist*	an-thrə-POL'-ə-jist
12. *anthropological*	an'-thrə-pə-LOJ'-ə-kəl
13. *philanthropist*	fə-LAN'-thrə-pist
14. *philanthropy*	fə-LAN'-thrə-pee
15. *philanthropic*	fil-ən-THROP'-ik
16. *gynecologist*	gīn (*or* jin *or* jīn)-ə-KOL'-ə-jist
17. *gynecology*	gīn(*or* jin *or* jīn)-ə-KOL'-ə-jee
18. *gynecological*	gīn(*or* jin *or* jīn)-ə-kə-LOJ'-ə-kəl
19. *monogamist*	mə-NOG'-ə-mist
20. *monogamy*	mə-NOG'-ə-mee
21. *monogamous*	mə-NOG'-ə-məs

Can you pronounce the words？（Ⅱ）

你能读出这些单词吗？（Ⅱ）

1. *bigamist*	BIG'-ə-mist
2. *bigamy*	BIG'-ə-mee
3. *bigamous*	BIG'-ə-məs
4. *polygamist*	pə-LIG'-ə-mist
5. *polygamy*	pə-LIG'-ə-mee
6. *polygamous*	pə-LIG'-ə-məs
7. *polygynist*	pə-LIJ'-ə-nist
8. *polygyny*	pə-LIJ'-ə-nee
9. *polygynous*	pə-LIJ'-ə-nəs
10. *polyandrist*	pol-ee-AN'-drist

11. *polyandry*	pol-ee-AN'-dree
12. *polyandrous*	pol-ee-AN'-drəs
13. *misanthropist*	mis-AN'-thrə-pist
14. *misanthropy*	mis-AN'-thrə-pee
15. *misanthropic*	mis-ən-THROP'-ik
16. *misogyny*	mə-SOJ'-ə-nee
17. *misogynous*	mə-SOJ'-ə-nəs
18. *misogynistic*	mə-soj'-ə-NIS'-tik
19. *misogamy*	mə-SOG'-ə-mee
20. *misogamous*	mə-SOG-ə-məs
21. *asceticism*	ə-SET-ə-siz-əm

Can you work with the words? (Ⅰ)
你能灵活使用这些词汇了吗？（Ⅰ）

Check on your comprehension! See how successfully you can match words and meanings!

检查一下你的理解。看看能否顺利地将单词与词意匹配在一起！

1. ambidextrous	a. evil, threatening
2. dexterous	b. hating mankind
3. sinister	c. skillful
4. gauche	d. awkward
5. misanthropic	e. capable of using both hands with equal skill

KEY：l-e，2-c，3-a，4-d，5-b

Can you work with the words? (Ⅱ)
你能灵活使用这些词汇了吗？（Ⅱ）

1. anthropology	a. system of only one marriage
2. gynecology	b. hatred of women
3. monogamy	c. illegal plurality of marriages
4. bigamy	d. study of human development
5. misogyny	e. study of female ailments

KEY：l-d，2-e，3-a，4-c，5-b

Can you work with the words? (Ⅲ)

你能灵活使用这些词汇了吗?(Ⅲ)

1. polygamy   a. devotion to a lonely and austere life
2. misogamy   b. skill, cleverness
3. asceticism   c. custom in which one man has many wives
4. philanthropy   d. love of mankind
5. adroitness   e. hatred of marriage

KEY: 1-c, 2-e, 3-a, 4-d, 5-b

Can you work with the words? (Ⅳ)

你能灵活使用这些词汇了吗?(Ⅳ)

1. polygynist   a. student of the development of mankind
2. polyandrist   b. one who engages in charitable works
3. anthropologist   c. male with a plurality of wives
4. gynecologist   d. women's doctor
5. philanthropist   e. female with a plurality of husbands

KEY: 1-c, 2-e, 3-a, 4-d, 5-b

Do you understand the words?

你对这些词汇是否已经透彻地理解?

1. Can *ambidextrous* people use either the left or right hand equally well?   YES   NO
2. Should a surgeon be manually *dexterous*?   YES   NO
3. Is a *sinister*-looking person frightening?   YES   NO
4. Is *gaucherie* a social asset?   YES   NO
5. Is an *adroit* speaker likely to be a successful lawyer?   YES   NO
6. Is a student of *anthropology* interested in primitive tribes?   YES   NO
7. Does a *gynecologist* have more male than female patients?   YES   NO
8. Is *monogamy* the custom in Western countries?   YES   NO
9. Is a *misogamist* likely to show tendencies toward *polygamy*?   YES   NO
10. Is a *bigamist* breaking the law?   YES   NO
11. Is a *philanthropist* generally altruistic?   YES   NO
12. Does a *misanthropist* enjoy human relationships?   YES   NO
13. Does a *misogynist* enjoy female companionship?   YES   NO

14. Are unmarried people necessarily *misogamous*?　　　YES　　NO

15. Are bachelors necessarily *misogynous*?　·　　　YES　　NO

16. Is *asceticism* compatible with luxurious living
and the pursuit of pleasure?　　　　　　　　　YES　　NO

17. Does a *polyandrist* have more than one husband?　　YES　　NO

KEY：1-yes，2-yes，3-yes，4-no，5-yes，6-yes，7-no，8-yes，9-no，10-yes，11-yes，12-no，13-no，14-no，15-no，16-no，17-yes

---

Can you recall the words?
你能够写出这些词汇吗？

1. philosophy of living austerely　　　　　　1. A _____
2. hatred of women　　　　　　　　　　　　2. M _____
3. hatred of marriage　　　　　　　　　　　3. M _____
4. hatred of mankind　　　　　　　　　　　4. M _____
5. skillful　　　　　　　　　　　　　　　　5. D _____
6. awkward　　　　　　　　　　　　　　　6. G _____
7. evil, threatening　　　　　　　　　　　　7. S _____
8. describing hatred of women (*adj.*)　　　　8. M _____
　　　　　　　　　　　　　　　　　　　　or M _____
9. skill　　　　　　　　　　　　　　　　　9. A _____
10. pertaining to hatred of marriage (*adj.*)　10. M _____
11. pertaining to hatred of mankind (*adj.*)　11. M _____
12. social custom of plural marriage　　　　　12. P _____
　　　　　　　　　　　　　　　　　　　　or P _____
　　　　　　　　　　　　　　　　　　　　or P _____
13. unlawful state of having more than one spouse　13. B _____
14. doctor specializing in female disorders　14. G _____
15. custom of one marriage at a time　　　　15. M _____
16. one who hates the human race　　　　　16. M _____
　　　　　　　　　　　　　　　　　　　　or M _____
17. able to use both hands with equal skill　17. A _____
18. study of mankind　　　　　　　　　　　18. A _____
19. one who loves mankind　　　　　　　　19. P _____
20. skill in the use of both hands　　　　　20. A _____

KEY：1-asceticism，2-misogyny，3-misogamy，4-misanthropy，5-dexterous，6-gauche，7-sinister，8-misogynous or misogynistic，9-adroitness，10-misogamous，

11-misanthropic, 12-polygamy, polyandry, *or* polygyny, 13-bigamy, 14-gynecologist, 15-monogamy, 16-misanthropist *or* misanthrope, 17-ambidextrous, 18-anthropology, 19-philanthropist, 20-ambidexterity

CHAPTER REVIEW
章节复习

A. Do you recognize the words?

你认识这些单词吗?

1. Puts selfish desires first: (a) egoist, (b) egotist, (c) altruist
2. Is self-analytical: (a) extrovert, (b) introvert, (c) ambivert
3. Hates women: (a) misogamist, (b) misanthrope, (c) misogynist
4. One's other self: (a) altercation, (b) alter ego, (c) alteration
5. Awkward, clumsy: (a) adroit, (b) dexterous, (c) gauche
6. Plural marriage as a custom: (a) bigamy, (b) polygamy, (c) monogamy
7. Study of human development: (a) asceticism, (b) philanthropy, (c) anthropology
8. Plurality of husbands as a custom: (a) misogyny, (b) polygyny, (c) polyandry

KEY: l-a, 2-b, 3-c, 4-b, 5-c, 6-b, 7-c, 8-c

B. Can you recognize roots?

你能认出这些词根吗?

ROOT	MEANING	EXAMPLE
1. *ego*	_____	egoist
2. *alter*	_____	alternative
3. *verto*	_____	introvert
4. *misein*	_____	misogynist
5. *anthropos*	_____	anthropologist
6. *gyne*	_____	gynecologist
7. *gamos*	_____	bigamy
8. *centrum*	_____	egocentric
9. *dexter*	_____	dexterous
10. *droit*	_____	adroit
11. *monos*	_____	monogamy
12. *andros*	_____	polyandry

KEY: 1-self, 2-other, 3-to turn, 4-to hate, 5-mankind, 6-woman, 7-marriage, 8-center, 9-right hand, 10-right hand, 11-one, 12-male

TEASER QUESTIONS FOR THE AMATEUR ETYMOLOGIST
词源小测验

Suppose you met the following words in your reading. Recognizing the roots on which they are constructed, could you figure out the meanings? Write your answers on the blank lines.

假如在阅读当中你遇到了下面的单词。通过识别构成该单词的词根,你能明白它的意思吗? 在空白横线上写出你的答案。

1. *anthropocentric* : _____

   _____

2. *andromania* : _____

   _____

3. *gynandrous* : _____

   _____

4. *monomania* : _____

   _____

5. *misandrist* : _____

   _____

(Answers in Chapter 18.)

(答案见第 18 章)

STICK TO YOUR TIME SCHEDULE!
坚持你的学习计划

In three sessions, you have become acquainted with scores of new, vital, exciting words. You understand the ideas behind these words, their various forms and spellings, their pronunciation, their derivation, how they can be used, and exactly what they mean. I do not wish to press a point unduly, but it is possible that you have learned more new words in the short time it took you to cover this chapter than the average adult learns in an entire year. This realization should make you feel both gratified and excited.

Funny thing about time. Aside from the fact that we all, rich or poor, sick or well, have the same amount of time, exactly twenty-four hours every day (that is looking at time from a static point of view), it is also true that we can always find time for the things we enjoy doing, almost never for the things we find

通过这三个小节的学习,你已经熟悉了几个新词汇,这些词既关键又令人兴奋。你了解到这些词汇背后的概念,知道了词汇的不同形式、拼写、发音、派生,还有它们的用法及准确含义。我不愿过分强调这一点,但你可能通过短短的时间学完本章,学到了比普通成年人用一整年时间所学到的还要多的词汇。意识到这一点,你应该感到既荣幸又兴奋。

时间是个有趣的东西。无论富裕还是贫穷,无论生病还是健康,我们所有人每天拥有相同的时间——24小时(当然是从静态的角度观察)。除了这个事实,另外一个事实也是毋庸置疑的——只要是我们感兴趣的事情,我们总会抽出时间去做;而对于我

unpleasant (and that is looking at time from the dynamic point of view). I am not merely being philosophical— I am sure you will agree with this concept if you give it a little thought.

If you have enjoyed learning new words, accepting new challenges, gaining new understanding, and discovering the thrill of successful accomplishment, then make sure to stay with the time schedule you have set up for yourself.

A crucial factor in successful, ongoing learning is routine.

Develop a comfortable time routine, persevere against all distractions, and you will learn anything you sincerely want to learn.

So, to give yourself an edge, write here the day and hour you plan to return to your work:

DAY(星期)：_____

DATE(日期)：_____

TIME(时间)：_____

(End of Session 3)

们觉得无趣的事情，我们却总是没有时间(这一次是从动态的角度分析)。我不是在讲哲学，只要你仔细思考片刻，你一定也会同意这个观点。

如果你一直享受于学习新词汇、接受新挑战、获得新理解和发现成功达到目标时的兴奋，那么你要确保坚持你为自己设定的时间规划。

成功、不间断地学习的关键因素是有规律地学习。

为自己设定一个适合自己的时间规划，坚持不懈，抛开纷扰，你将学到任何你真正想要学习的知识。

所以，在这里写下你计划下次阅读本书的日期和时间，以帮助自己建立优势。

Brief Intermission One
简短插叙一

TEST YOUR GRAMMAR
语法小测验

How good is your English? Have you ever said *me* and then wondered if it shouldn't have been *I*—or vice versa? Do you sometimes get a little confused about *lay* and *lie* or *who* and *whom*? Perhaps you are often a little less than certain about the distinction between *effect* and *affect*, *principal* and *principle*, *childish* and *childlike*?

Here is a series of quick tests that will show you how skillful you are in using the right word in the right place, that will give you a reliable indication of how your language ability compares with the average.

你的英语水平如何？使用了宾格形式的 me 之后，你是否疑惑也许使用主格形式 I 才是正确的？反之亦然？对于 lay 和 lie, who 和 whom 的用法你是否有些混淆？对于 effect 和 affect, principal 和 principle, childish 和 childlike 等词汇，你能否正确区分它们？

以下是一系列测验，通过测验会发现你是否善于在恰当的地方使用合适的词语；也能够清楚地表明和普通人相比，你的语言能力到底如何。

TEST Ⅰ—EASY
测验Ⅰ——简单

If your English is every bit as good as average, you will have no difficulty making a proper choice in at least eight of the following ten sentences.

如果你的英语水平中等，在以下 10 个句子当中至少可以轻松地为 8 个句子选出恰当的词语。

1. There is a beautiful moon out tonight and Estelle and I are going for a stroll—would you like to come along with (she and I, her and me?)

2. Your husband doesn't believe that you are older than (I, me).

3. Maybe we're not as rich as (they, them), but I bet we're a lot happier.

4. Does your child still (lay, lie) down for a nap after lunch?

5. When we saw Mary openly flirting with Nellie's husband, we (could, couldn't) hardly believe our eyes.

6. You should (of, have) put more vermouth into the martini.

7. Does your company (leave, let) you have as long a lunch break as you would like?

8. Harriet feels that her (brothers-in-law, brother-in-laws) are impossible to get

along with.

9. "What (kind of, kind of a) car are you looking for?" asked the salesman.

10. Mrs. White was delighted that the Fennells had invited John and (she, her) to their party.

Is your English up to par? HERE ARE THE CORRECT ANSWERS
你的英语水平还算像样? 以下是正确答案。

1-her and me, 2-I, 3-they, 4-lie, 5-could, 6-have, 7-let, 8-brothers-in-law, 9-kind of, 10-her

TEST Ⅱ—HARDER
测验 Ⅱ —— 稍难

Choose correctly in at least seven of the following problems to consider that your skill is distinctly above average—get all ten right to conclude that you rarely, if ever, make an error in grammar.

以下问题如果能答对 7 道或者 7 道以上,你的英语水平则明显高于普通水平;如果全部答对,说明你很少犯语法错误。

1. What (effect, affect) has the new administration's policies had on investor confidence?

2. A feeling of one's worth is one of the (principle, principal) goals of psychological therapy.

3. There's no sense (in, of) carrying on that way.

4. I can't remember (who, whom) it was.

5. The infant (lay, laid) quietly sucking its thumb.

6. No one but (she, her) ever made a perfect score on the test.

7. In the early days of frontier history, horse thieves were(hanged, hung).

8. Neither of your responses(are, is)satisfactory.

9. Either of these two small cars, if properly maintained,(is, are)sure to give over thirty miles pergallon in highway driving.

10. Tell(whoever, whomever)is waiting to come in.

Is your English above average? HERE ARE THE CORRECT ANSWERS
你的英语是否高于普通水平? 以下是正确答案。

KEY: 1-effect, 2-principal, 3-in, 4-who, 5-lay, 6-her, 7-hanged, 8-is, 9-is, 10-whoever

TEST Ⅲ—HARDEST

测验 Ⅲ——最难

Now you can discover how close you are to being an expert in English. The next ten sentences are no cinch—you will be acquitting yourself creditably if you check the correct word five times out of ten. And you have every right to consider yourself an expert if you get nine or ten right.

现在你会发现，你距离成为英语专家只有一步之遥。以下的 10 个句子难度很大——如果能答对半数，你应该用钦佩的眼光重新审视自己。如果答对 9 个以上，你有绝对的权利认为自己已经是专家。

1. We have just interviewed an applicant(who，whom)the committee believes is best qualified for the position.

2. She is one of those gifted writers who(turns，turn)out one best seller after another.

3. Don't sound so (incredulous，incredible)；what I am saying is absolutely true.

4. We were totally (disinterested，uninterested)in the offer.

5. This recipe calls for two (cupsful，cupfuls) of sugar.

6. Are you trying to (infer，imply) by those words that he is not to be trusted？

7. We thought the actress to be (she，her)，but we weren't sure.

8. Was it (she，her) you were talking about？

9. Your criteria (is，are) not valid.

10. "It is I who (is，am) the only friend you've got，" she told him pointedly.

Are you an expert？ **HERE ARE THE CORRECT ANSWERS**

你是专家吗？以下是正确答案。

KEY：1-who，2-turn，3-incredulous，4-uninterested，5-cupfuls，6-imply，7-her，8-she，9-are，10-am

---

4

HOW TO TALK ABOUT DOCTORS
如何描述各科医生

(Sessions 4 — 6)

TEASER PREVIEW
引读

What is the title of the doctor who specializes in:

* *internal medicine?*
* *female ailments?*
* *pregnancy and childbirth?*
* *the treatment and care of infants and young children?*
* *skin disorders?*
* *diseases of the eye?*
* *heart problems?*
* *the brain and nervous system?*
* *mental and emotional disturbances?*

如何称呼专门从事以下方面工作的医生：
* 内科医学
* 治疗女性疾病
* 接生
* 专门医治儿童疾病
* 治疗皮肤病
* 治疗眼科疾病
* 专门医治心脏疾病
* 专门医治脑部和神经系统疾病
* 治疗心理和情绪障碍

SESSION 4
第 4 节

In this chapter we discuss ten medical specialists—what they do, how they do it, what they are called.

在这一章里我们会讨论 10 类医学专家的工作内容、工作方式，以及他们的职业名称。

IDEAS
概念

1. What's wrong with you?
你的问题出在哪里？

To find out what ails you and why, this specialist gives you a thorough physical examination, using an impressive array of tests: X-ray, blood chemistry, urinalysis, cardiogram, and so on.

An internist

他的专长是找出你的具体疾病以及原因。为了得到诊断结果，他会通过一系列仪器对你进行详尽、周密的检查：X光、血化学指标、尿检、心电图等。

这位医生是 internist(内科医生)。

2. Female troubles?
女性疾病？

This specialist treats the female reproductive and sexual organs.

A gynecologist

这位专科医生专门医治女性生育问题和女性专有的疾病。

这位医生是 gynecologist(妇科医生)。

3. Having a baby?
接生？

This specialist delivers babies and takes care of the mother during and immediately after the period of her pregnancy.

An obstetrician

他为怀孕女性接生，并在生产过程中和产后照顾生育母亲。

这位医生是 obstetrician(妇产科医生)。

4. Is your baby ill?
你的宝贝生病了？

You know the common childhood maladies—mumps, whooping cough, chicken pox, measles. This specialist limits his practice to youngsters, taking care of babies directly after birth, supervising their diet and watching over their growth and development, giving them the series of inoculations that has done so much to decrease infant mortality, and soothing their anxious parents.

A *pediatrician*

你一定听说过这些儿童常见疾病——流行性腮腺炎、百日咳、水痘和麻疹等。他的工作针对儿童,照顾新生儿,观察他们的饮食和成长,为新生儿接种疫苗,减少新生儿死亡率,安慰担忧的父母。

这位医生是 pediatrician(儿科医生)。

5. Skin clear?

皮肤是否健康?

You have heard the classic riddle："What is the best use for pigskin?" Answer："To keep the pig together." Human skin has a similar purpose：it is, if we get down to fundamentals, what keeps us all in one piece. And our outer covering, like so many of our internal organs, is subject to diseases and infections of various kinds, running the gamut from simple acne and eczemas through impetigo, psoriasis, and cancer. There is a specialist who treats all such skin diseases.

A *dermatologist*

你一定听说过这个经典谜语:"猪皮的最佳用途是什么?"答:"使猪的身体完整。"人类的皮肤有相同的功能:追根溯底,皮肤使我们成为一个整体。而我们最外层的皮肤和内脏一样,会生病,会被各种疾病感染,轻者痤疮、湿疹,重者小脓疱疹、梅毒,甚至皮肤癌。有一位医治所有这方面病患的专家。

这位医生是 dermatologist(皮肤科医生)。

6. Eyes okay?

你的视力可好?

The physician whose specialty is disorders of vision (myopia, astigmatism, cataracts, glaucoma, etc.) may prescribe glasses, administer drugs, or perform surgery.

An *ophthalmologist*

他的专业领域是眼疾(近视、散光、白内障、青光眼等)。他可能为你验光配镜、开药或者手术。

这位医生是 ophthalmologist(眼科医生)。

7. How are your bones?

你的骨头还好吗?

This specialist deals with the skeletal structure of the body, treating bone fractures, slipped discs, clubfoot, curvature of the spine, dislocations of the hip, etc., and may correct a condition either by surgery or by the use of braces or other appliances.

An *orthopedist*

他的专业领域是身体骨骼构造,医治骨折、腰间盘突出、畸形足、脊柱弯曲、髋关节错位等。他可能会通过手术或使用支架和其他器材来纠正骨骼畸形。

这位医生是 orthopedist(骨科医生)。

8. Does your heart go pitter-patter?

你的心脏跳动正常吗?

This specialist treats diseases of the heart and circulatory system.

A *cardiologist*

他专门医治心脏和循环系统疾病。

这位医生是 cardiologist(心脏病专家)。

9．Is your brain working?

你大脑运转正常吗?

This physician specializes in the treatment of disorders of the brain，spinal cord，and the rest of the nervous system.

A neurologist

他专门医治大脑功能紊乱、脊髓疾病和其他神经系统的疾病。

这位医生是 neurologist(神经科医生)。

10．Are you neurotic?

你的心智正常吗?

This specialist attempts to alleviate mental and emotional disturbances by means of various techniques，occasionally drugs or electroshock，more often private or group psychotherapy.

A psychiatrist

这个领域的专家致力于用不同的方法来缓解精神和情绪方面的紊乱,有时会使用药物和电击治疗,大多数时候是进行个体或群体的心理治疗。

这位医生是 psychiatrist(精神病医生)。

USING THE WORDS
单词应用

Can you pronounce the words?
你能读出这些单词吗?

Words take on a new color if you hear them in your own voice; they begin to belong to you more personally，more intimately，than if you merely hear or read them. As always，therefore，*say the words aloud* to take the first，crucial step toward complete mastery.

让自己听到自己的读音,词汇会呈现出不一样的色彩;与仅仅听和阅读相比,它们开始属于你个人,和你关系更加亲密。因此,坚持把大声朗读放在第一位,始终是彻底掌握单词的关键一步。

1. *internist* — in-TURN′-ist
2. *gynecologist* — gīn (*or* jin *or* jīn)-ə-KOL′-ə-jist
3. *obstetrician* — ob-stə-TRISH′-ən
4. *pediatrician* — pee′-dee-ə-TRISH′-ən
5. *dermatologist* — dur-mə-TOL′-ə-jist
6. *ophthalmologist* — off-thal-MOL′-ə-jist
7. *orthopedist* — awr-thə-PEE′-dist
8. *cardiologist* — kahr-dee-OL′-ə-jist
9. *neurologist* — noor-OL′-ə-jist
10. *psychiatrist* — sī (*or* sə)-KĪ′-ə-trist

Can you work with the words?
你能灵活使用这些词汇了吗?

Match each doctor to the field.
将医生名称与相关专科配对。

FIELDS	DOCTORS
1. mental or emotional disturbances	a. internist
2. nervous system	b. gynecologist
3. skin	c. obstetrician
4. diagnosis; internal organs	d. pediatrician
5. infants	e. dermatologist
6. female reproductive organs	f. ophthalmologist
7. eyes	g. orthopedist
8. heart	h. cardiologist
9. pregnancy, childbirth	i. neurologist
10. skeletal system	j. psychiatrist

KEY: 1-j, 2-i, 3-e, 4-a, 5-d, 6-b, 7-f, 8-h, 9-c, 10-g

Do you understand the words?
你对这些词汇是否已经透彻地理解?

1. Is an *internist* an expert in diagnosis?   YES   NO

2. Is a *gynecologist* familiar with the female reproductive organs?   YES   NO

3. Does an *obstetrician* specialize in diseases of childhood?   YES   NO

4. Does a *pediatrician* deliver babies?   YES   NO

5. If you had a skin disease, would you visit a *dermatologist*?   YES   NO

6. If you had trouble with your vision would you visit an *orthopedist*?   YES   NO

7. Is an *ophthalmologist* an eye specialist?   YES   NO

8. Does a *cardiologist* treat bone fractures?   YES   NO

9. Is a *neurologist* a nerve specialist?   YES   NO

10. If you were nervous, tense, overly anxious, constantly fearful for no apparent reasons, would a *psychiatrist* be the specialist to see?   YES   NO

KEY：1-yes，2-yes，3-no，4-no，5-yes，6-no，7-yes，8-no，9-yes，10-yes

Can you recall the words?
你能够写出这些词汇吗？

Write the name of the specialist you might visit or be referred to:
写出下面这些你可能会拜访或被引荐的专科医生名称：

1. for a suspected brain disorder	1. N _____
2. for a thorough internal checkup	2. I _____
3. if you have a skin disease	3. D _____
4. if you have a heart problem	4. C _____
5. if you are tense, fearful, insecure	5. P _____
6. if you are pregnant	6. O _____
7. for some disorder of the female reproductive organs	7. G _____
8. for a checkup for your two-month-old child	8. P _____
9. for faulty vision	9. O _____
10. for curvature of the spine	10. O _____

KEY：1-neurologist，2-internist，3-dermatologist，4-cardiologist，5-psychiatrist，6-obstetrician，7-gynecologist，8-pediatrician，9-ophthalmologist，10-orthopedist

(End of Session 4)

SESSION 5
第 5 节

ORIGINS AND RELATED WORDS
词源及相关词汇

1．inside you
身体内部

Internist and *internal* derive from the same Latin root，*internus*，inside．The *internist* is a specialist in *internal medicine*，in the exploration of your *insides*．This physician determines the state of your internal organs in order to discover what's happening *within* your body to cause the troubles you're complaining of．

Do not confuse the *internist* with the *intern* (also spelled *interne*)，who is a medical graduate serving an apprenticeship *inside* a hospital．

internist 和 internal 词源相同，都源于拉丁语词根 internus，意为"在……内部"。internist 是开 internal medicine（内科药物）的专家，是为身体内部做检查的专家。他能够确定各个器官的状态，能够发现引起不适的内部器官到底有何异样。

不要把 internist 和 intern（也可以写成 interne）混淆，后者是指在医院里实习的医学专业毕业生。

2．doctors for women
为女性诊疗的医生

The word *gynecologist* is built on Greek *gyne*，woman，plus *logos*，science；etymologically，*gynecology* is the science (in actual use，the medical science) of women．Adjective：*gynecological* (gīn [*or* jin *or* jīn]-ə-kə-LOJ'-ə-kəl)．

Obstetrician derives from Latin *obstetrix*，midwife，which in turn has its source in a Latin verb meaning *to stand*—midwives stand in front of the woman in labor to aid in the delivery of the infant．

The suffix *-ician*，as in *obstetrician*，*physician*，*musician*，*magician*，*electrician*，*etc*．，means *expert*．

Obstetrics (ob-STET'-riks) has only within the last 150 years become a respectable specialty．No further back than 1834，Professor William P．Dewees assumed the first chair of *obstetrics* at the University of Pennsylvania and had to brave considerable medical contempt and ridicule as a result—the delivery of children was then considered beneath the dignity of the medical profession．

Adjective：*obstetric* (ob-STET'-rik) or *obstetrical* (ob-STET'-rə-kəl)．

妇科疾病的专家 gynecologist 由希腊语 gyne（意为"女性"）和 logos（意为"科学"）组成；从词源上看，gynecology 是关于女人的科学（在实际应用中，一般特指医药科学方面），形容词是 gynecological。

obstetrician 来源于拉丁语 obstetrix（意为"接生婆"），obstetrix 又来源于表示"站"的一个拉丁语的词——接生婆在接生之前需要站在女人面前，准备好迎接即将出世的婴儿。

后缀-ician 意为"专家"，如 obstetrician，physician，musician，magician，electrician 等词。

obstetrics(产科学)在最近的 150 年才成为一个受尊敬的学科。最早在 1834 年,威廉姆·P.迪威斯成为宾夕法尼亚大学首席产科医生,不得不去勇敢面对众多的鄙视和嘲笑,因为当时接生工作被医学界所不齿。

形容词:obstetric 或 obstetrical。

3.children
儿童

Pediatrician is a combination of Greek *paidos*, child; *iatreia*, medical healing; and *-ician*, expert.

Pediatrics (pee-dee-AT'-riks), then, is by etymology the medical healing of a child. Adjective:*pediatric* (pee-dee-AT'-rik).

(The *ped-* you see in words like *pedestal*, *pedal*, and *pedestrian* is from the Latin *pedis*, foot, and despite the identical spelling in English has no relationship to Greek *paidos*.)

pediatrician 由三个希腊语词汇组成:paidos,表示儿童;iatreia,表示医疗康复;-ician,表示专家。

那么,从词源角度讲,pediatrics 表示儿童的医疗康复。形容词形式为:pediatric。

(pedestal,pedal 和 pedestrian 中包含的 ped-来自拉丁语 pedis,表示脚,与希腊语词汇 paidos 无关,虽然它们在英语中拼写形式相同。)

Pedagogy (PED-ə-gō'-jee),which combines *paidos* with *agogos*, leading, is, etymologically, *the leading of children*. And to what do you lead them? To learning, to development, to growth, to maturity. From the moment of birth, infants are led by adults—they are taught, first by parents and then by teachers, to be self-sufficient, to fit into the culture in which they are born. Hence, *pedagogy*, which by derivation means *the leading of a child*, refers actually to the principles and methods of teaching. College students majoring in education take certain standard *pedagogy* courses—the history of education; educational psychology; the psychology of adolescents; principles of teaching; etc. Adjective:*pedagogical* (ped-ə-GOJ'-ə-kəl).

pedagogy 结合了 paidos 和 agogos(引导),从词源理解,这个词表示"对儿童的引导"。而你又引导儿童去做什么呢?你引导他去学习、发展、成长,从而走向成熟。从出生那一刻开始,儿童便接受成人的引导——最初由家长教育,然后是老师,最后达到能够自立,以适应他所生存的社会。这样,pedagogy 从最初严格意义上所指的"对儿童的引导"引申到现在的"教育的原则和方法"。教育专业的学生要选修标准 pedagogy courses(教育学课程),包括教育史、教育心理学、青少年心理、教学原理等。形容词形式是:pedagogical。

A *pedagogue* (PED'-ə-gog) is versed in *pedagogy*. But *pedagogue* has an unhappy history. From its original, neutral meaning of *teacher*, it has deteriorated to the point where it refers, today, to a narrow-minded, strait-laced, old-fashioned, dogmatic teacher. It is a word of contempt and should be used with caution.

一位 pedagogue 精通教育的原则和方法。但是 pedagogue 这个词有一段不愉快的历史。pedagogue 最初的含义是中性的,指"教师"。而现在,它的含义已经变质,指心胸狭隘、顽固拘谨、思想陈旧、陈腐教条的老师。它是贬义词,使用时要小心谨慎。

Like *pedagogue*, *demagogue* (DEM'-ə-gog) has also deteriorated in meaning. By derivation a leader (*agogos*) of the people (*demos*), a *demagogue* today is actually one who attempts, in essence, to *mislead* the people, a politician who foments discontent among the masses, rousing them to fever pitch by wild oratory, in an attempt to be voted into office.

Once elected, *demagogues* use political power to further their own personal ambitions or fortunes.

Many "leaders" of the past and present, in countries around the world, have been accused of *demagoguery* (dem-ə-GOG′-ə-ree). Adjective: *demagogic* (dem-ə-GOJ′-ik).

和 pedagogue 相似，demagogue 的词义也发生了质变。从派生角度来讲，agogos 指"领袖"，demos 指"人民"，demagogue 应该指"人民的领袖"。而现在，demagogue 的基本含义指"企图误导人民的人"。他是一位政客，他挑拨事端，通过狂热的演讲煽动选民，以得到票选从政。

一旦当选，demagogues 利用政治权力去追求自己的野心或增加自己的财富。

无论是过去或是现在，许多这样的"领袖"出现在世界各国，人们指责他们的 demagoguery（煽动行为）。形容词形式是：demagogic。

4. skin-deep
皮肤深处

The *dermatologist*, whose specialty is *dermatology* (dur-mə-TOL′-ə-jee), is so named from Greek *derma*, skin. Adjective: *dermatological* (dur′-mə-tə-LOJ′-ə-kəl).

See the syllables *derma* in any English word and you will know there is some reference to *skin*—for example, a *hypodermic* (hī-pə-DUR′-mik) needle penetrates *under* (Greek, *hypos*) the *skin*; the *epidermis* (ep-ə-DUR′-mis) is the outermost layer of *skin*; a *taxidermist* (TAKS′-ə-dur-mist), whose business is *taxidermy*. (TAKS′-ə-dur-mee), prepares, stuffs, and mounts the *skins* of animals; a *pachyderm* (PAK′-ə-durm) is an animal with an unusually thick *skin*, like an elephant, hippopotamus, or rhinoceros; and *dermatitis* (dur-mə-TĪ′-tis) is the general name for any *skin* inflammation, irritation, or infection.

dermatologist, 皮肤科医生，专业为 dermatology, 皮肤医学，词根为希腊语 derma, 意为"皮肤"。形容词形式是 dermatological。

在英语单词中看到 derma 这个音节，你就会知道这个词或多或少与皮肤有关——例如，hypodermic needle（皮下注射器针头）穿透皮肤，到达皮肤下层（希腊语 hypo）；epidermis 指最外层的皮肤；taxidermist, 动物标本剥制师，是指准备、剥制和裱贴动物皮肤的人；pachyderm, 指厚皮类动物，例如大象、河马和犀牛；dermatitis 是任何皮肤炎症、过敏或者感染的统称。

5. the eyes have it
与眼睛相关

Ophthalmologist—note the *ph* preceding *th*—is from Greek *ophthalmos*, eye, plus *logos*, science or study. The specialty is *ophthalmology* (off′-thal-MOL′-ə-jee), the adjective *ophthalmological* (off′-thal-mə-LOJ′-ə-kəl).

An earlier title for this physician, still occasionally used, is *oculist* (OK′-yə-list), from Latin *oculus*, eye, a root on which the following English words are also built:

ophthalmologist——注意 ph 后面紧跟 th——源于希腊语中的 ophthalmos 一词，意为"眼睛"，加上 logos 意为"科学"或"研究"。此专业领域叫做 ophthalmology，形容词为 ophthalmological.

早期这个领域的医师被称为 oculist，现在偶尔也会使用这个称谓。oculist 来源于拉丁语 oculus 一词，意为"眼睛"，以下几个英语单词都有这个词根：

1. *ocular* （OK′-yə-lər）—an adjective that refers to the eye

2. *monocle* （MON′-ə-kəl）—a lens for one （*monos*）eye，sported by characters in old movies as a symbol of the British so-called upper class

3. *binoculars* （bə-NOK′-yə-lərz）—field glasses that increase the range of two （*bi*-）eyes

4. And，strangely enough，*inoculate* （in-OK′-yə-layt′），a word commonly misspelled with two *n's*. When you are *inoculated* against a disease，an "eye"，puncture，or hole is made in your skin，through which serum is injected.

1. ocular——形容词 ocular，与眼睛相关；

2. monocle——单片（monos）眼镜，在一些老电影中，往往作为英国上层社会的一种象征；

3. binoculars——双筒望远镜，增加双（*bi*-）眼的视野；

4. inoculate——奇怪，inoculate（预防接种）这个词经常被错拼为 innoculate，出现两个 n。当你为预防疾病而接种时，你的皮肤上会留下一个"眼"，小孔，或小洞，血清从这里注射进去。

Do not confuse the *ophthalmologist* or *oculist*，a medical specialist，with two other practitioners who deal with the eye—the *optometrist* （op-TOM′-ə-trist） and *optician* （op-TISH′-ən）.

Optometrists are not physicians，and do not perform surgery or administer drugs；they measure vision，test for glaucoma，and prescribe and fit glasses.

Opticians fill an *optometrist's* or *ophthalmologist's* prescription，grinding lenses according to specifications；they do not examine patients.

Optometrist combines Greek *opsis*，*optikos*，sight or vision，with *metron*，measurement—the *optometrist*，by etymology，is one who measures vision. The specialty is *optometry* （op-TOM′-ə-tree）.

Optician is built on *opsis*，*optikos*，plus -*ician*，expert. The specialty is *optics* （OP′-tiks ）.

Adjectives：*optometric* （op-tə-MET′-rik） or *optometrical* （op-tə-MET′-rə-kəl），*optical*（OP′-tə-kəl）.

注意不要将 ophthalmologist 或 oculist（专科医生）的称谓与另外两个眼科从业者混淆——optometrist（验光技师）和 optician（配镜师）。

optometrist 不是医师，不允许进行手术或药物治疗——他们测视力、检查青光眼、开处方和配眼镜。

而 optician 只能按照验光技师或者眼科医生的处方，根据规格制备镜片；他并不为患者做检查。

optometrist 由希腊语的 opsis，optikos（意为"视力"）和 metron（意为"测量"）构成——optometrist，从词源上看是一个测量视力的人，其专业领域为 optometry（验光）。

optician 由 opsis，optikos 加上 -ician（专家）构成，其专业领域为 optics（光学）。

形容词：optometric 或 optometrical，optical.

REVIEW OF ETYMOLOGY
复习词源

PREFIX, ROOT, SUFFIX	MEANING	ENGLISH WORD
1. *internus*	inside	_____
2. *gyne*	woman	_____
3. *obstetrix*	midwife	_____
4. *paidos*	child	_____
5. *pedis*	foot	_____
6. *agogos*	leading, leader	_____
7. *demos*	people	_____
8. *derma*	skin	_____
9. *hypos*	under	_____
10. *ophthalmos*	eye	_____
11. *oculus*	eye	_____
12. *monos*	one	_____
13. *bi-*	two	_____
14. *-ician*	expert	_____
15. *opsis, optikos*	vision, sight	_____
16. *metron*	measurement	_____

USING THE WORDS
单词应用

Can you pronounce the words? (Ⅰ)
你能读出这些单词吗？(Ⅰ)

1. *intern（e）* — IN′-turn
2. *gynecology* — gīn-ə-KOL′-ə-jee, jin-ə-KOL′-ə-jee, *or* jīn-ə-KOL′-ə-jee
3. *gynecological* — gīn-ə-kə-LOJ′-ə-kəl, jin-ə-kə-LOJ′-ə-kəl *or* jīn-ə-kə-LOJ′-ə-kəl
4. *obstetrics* — ob-STET′-riks
5. *obstetric* — ob-STET′-rik
6. *obstetrical* — ob-STET′-rə-kəl
7. *pediatrics* — pee-dee-AT′-riks
8. *pediatric* — pee-dee-AT′-rik

9. *pedagogy*   PED$'$-ə-gō-jee
10. *pedagogical*   ped-ə-GOJ$'$-ə-kəl
11. *pedagogue*   PED$'$-ə-gog
12. *demagogue*   DEM$'$-ə-gog
13. *demagoguery*   dem-ə-GOG$'$-ə-ree
14. *demagogic*   dem-ə-GOJ$'$-ik

Can you pronounce the words? (Ⅱ)
你能读出这些单词吗? (Ⅱ)

1. *dermatology*   dur-mə-TOL$'$-ə-jee
2. *dermatological*   dur$'$-mə-tə-LOJ$'$-ə-kəl
3. *hypodermic*   hī-pə-DURM$'$-ik
4. *epidermis*   ep-ə-DUR$'$-mis
5. *taxidermist*   TAKS$'$-ə-dur-mist
6. *taxidermy*   TAKS$'$-ə-dur-mee
7. *pachyderm*   PAK$'$-ə-durm
8. *dermatitis*   dur-mə-TĪ$'$-tis
9. *ophthalmology*   off-thal-MOL$'$-ə-jee
10. *ophthalmological*   off$'$-thal-mə-LOJ$'$-ə-kəl
11. *oculist*   OK$'$-yə-list
12. *ocular*   OK$'$-yə-lər
13. *monocle*   MON$'$-ə-kəl
14. *binoculars*   bə-NOK$'$-yə-lərz
15. *inoculate*   in-OK$'$-yə-layt$'$
16. *optometrist*   op-TOM$'$-ə-trist
17. *optometry*   op-TOM$'$-ə-tree
18. *optometric*   op-tə-MET$'$-rik
19. *optometrical*   op-tə-MET$'$-rə-kəl
20. *optician*   op-TISH$'$-ən
21. *optics*   OP$'$-tiks
22. *optical*   OP-tə-kəl

Can you work with the words? (Ⅰ)
你能灵活使用这些词汇了吗? (Ⅰ)

1. gynecology   a. principles of teaching
2. obstetrics   b. stuffing of skins of animals
3. pediatrics   c. specialty dealing with the delivery of newborn infants
4. pedagogy   d. stirring up discontent among the masses

5. demagoguery   e. treatment of skin diseases

6. dermatology   f. specialty dealing with women's diseases

7. taxidermy   g. specialty dealing with the treatment of children

KEY：1-f，2-c，3-g，4-a，5-d，6-e，7-b

Can you work with the words? (Ⅱ)
你能灵活使用这些词汇了吗？（Ⅱ）

1. hypodermic   a. elephant
2. epidermis   b. eye doctor
3. pachyderm   c. under the skin
4. dermatitis   d. one who measures vision
5. ophthalmologist   e. lens grinder
6. optometrist   f. outer layer of skin
7. optician   g. inflammation of the skin

KEY：1-c，2-f，3-a，4-g，5-b，6-d，7-e

Do you understand these words?
你对这些词汇是否已经透彻地理解？

1. Does a treatise on *obstetrics* deal with childbirth? YES NO
2. Does *gynecology* deal with the female reproductive organs? YES NO
3. Is *pediatrics* concerned with the diseases of old age? YES NO
4. Does *pedagogy* refer to teaching? YES NO
5. Is a *pedagogue* an expert teacher? YES NO
6. Is a *demagogue* interested in the welfare of the people? YES NO
7. Is a lion a *pachyderm*? YES NO
8. Is the *epidermis* one of the layers of the skin? YES NO
9. Is *dermatitis* an inflammation of one of the limbs? YES NO
10. Is a *taxidermist* a medical practitioner? YES NO
11. Is an *ophthalmologist* a medical doctor? YES NO
12. Is an *optometrist* a medical doctor? YES NO
13. Does an *optician* prescribe glasses? YES NO

KEY: 1-yes，2-yes，3-no，4-yes，5-no，6-no，7-no，8-yes，9-no，10-no，11-yes，12-no，13-no

Can you recall the words?

你能够写出这些词汇吗？

1.	specialty of child delivery	1. O _____
2.	outer layer of skin	2. E _____
3.	principles of teaching	3. P _____
4.	thick-skinned animal	4. P _____
5.	skin inflammation	5. D _____
6.	one who foments political discontent	6. D _____
7.	one who sells optical equipment	7. O _____
8.	medical graduate serving his apprenticeship	8. I _____
9.	treatment of childhood diseases	9. P _____
10.	practice of stirring up political dissatisfaction for purely personal gain	10. D _____
11.	one who stuffs the skins of animals	11. T _____
12.	another title for *ophthalmologist*	12. O _____
13.	treatment of female ailments	13. G _____
14.	medical specialty relating to diseases of the eye	14. O _____
15.	one-lens eyeglass	15. M _____
16.	pertaining to the eye	16. O _____
17.	one who measures vision	17. O _____

KEY: 1-obstetrics，2-epidermis，3-pedagogy，4-pachyderm，5-dermatitis，6-demagogue，7-optician，8-intern *or* interne，9-pediatrics，10-demagoguery，11-taxidermist，12-oculist，13-gynecology，14-ophthalmology，15-monocle，16-ocular，17-optometrist

(End of Session 5)

SESSION 6
第 6 节

ORIGINS AND RELATED WORDS
词源及相关词汇

1. the straighteners
使骨骼长直

The *orthopedist* is so called from the Greek roots *orthos*, straight or correct, and *paidos*, child. The *orthopedist*, by etymology, straightens children. The term was coined in 1741 by the author of a textbook on the prevention of childhood diseases— at that time the correction of spinal curvature in children was a main concern of practitioners of *orthopedics* (awr-thə-PEE′-diks).

orthopedist,骨科医师,来源于希腊语词根 orthos(使……挺直)和 paidos(儿童)。从词源上看,orthopedist 就是“使儿童挺直”的意思。这个单词是在 1741 年,由一个儿童疾病预防教科书的作者发明——在那时,矫正儿童的脊柱畸形是骨骼医师们遇到的最多的状况。

Today the specialty treats deformities, injuries, and diseases of the bones and joints (of adults as well as children, of course), often by surgical procedures.
Adjective：*orthopedic* (awr-thə-PEE′-dik).

而现在这一领域主要是治疗骨头和关节的畸形、损伤和疾病(当然是儿童和成人均包括在内),经常会通过手术矫治。形容词形式为 orthopedic。

Orthodontia (awr-thə-DON′-shə), the straightening of teeth, is built on *orthos* plus *odontos*, tooth. The *orthodontist* (awr-thə-DON′-tist) specializes in improving your “bite”, retracting “buck teeth”, and by means of braces and other techniques seeing to it that every molar, incisor, bicuspid, etc. is exactly where it belongs in your mouth.
Adjective：*orthodontic* (awr-thə-DON′-tik).

orthodontia,意为“牙齿矫正术”,由 orthos 和 odontos(牙齿)构成。orthodontist(正齿牙医)专门改善你牙齿的“啮合”状况,矫正“龅牙”,以及通过牙齿矫正器和其他技术手段确保你的臼齿、切齿、犬齿等都长在你的嘴里合适的地方。形容词形式为 orthodontic。

2. the heart
心脏

Cardiologist combines Greek *kardia*, heart, and *logos*, science.
The specialty is *cardiology* (kahr-dee-OL′-ə-jee), the adjective *cardiological* (kahr′-dee-ə-LOJ′-ə-kəl).
So a *cardiac* (KAHR′-dee-ak) condition refers to some malfunctioning of the heart; a *cardiogram* (KAHR′-dee-ə-gram′) is an electrically produced record of the heartbeat. The instrument that produces this record is called a *cardiograph* (KAHR′-dee-ə-graf′).

cardiologist 融合了希腊词语 kardia(心脏),logos(科学)。

其专业领域为 cardiology,其形容词形式是 cardiological。

cardiac condition 是指心脏的机能不健全;cardiogram 意为"心电图";而为心电图做记录的器械是 cardiograph,心电图仪。

3. the nervous system
神经系统

Neurologist derives from Greek *neuron*, nerve, plus *logos*, science.

Specialty：*neurology* (noor-OL′-ə-jee); adjective：*neurological* (noor-ə-LOJ′-ə-kəl).

Neuralgia (noor-AL′-ja) is acute pain along the nerves and their branches; the word comes from *neuron* plus *algos*, pain.

neurologist 源于希腊语词根 neuron(指神经)和 logos(意为"科学")。

其专业领域称为 neurology (神经病学);形容词为 neurological.

neuralgia (神经痛)是沿着神经及其分支的尖锐的疼痛,此单词是由 neuron 加 algos(意为"疼痛")构成

Neuritis (noor-Ī′-tis), is inflammation of the nerves.

Neurosis (noor-Ō′-sis), combining *neuron* with *-osis*, a suffix meaning *abnormal* or *diseased condition*, is not, despite its etymology, a disorder of the nerves, but rather, as described by the late Eric Berne, a psychiatrist, "... an illness characterized by excessive use of energy for unproductive purposes so that personality development is hindered or stopped. A man who spends most of his time worrying about his health, counting his money, plotting revenge, or washing his hands, can hope for little emotional growth."

Neurotic (noor-OT′-ik) is both the adjective form and the term for a person suffering from *neurosis*.

neuritis,是指神经的炎症。

neurosis,是由 neuron 和后缀-osis 组合在一起的,后缀的意思为"不正常"或"病态"。并不是指神经系统紊乱(虽然从词源构成上看起来是这个意思),而是正如已故的精神病学家艾瑞克·伯恩所描述的那样:"……因过度把能量消耗在没有结果的目的上面,而导致的一种人格发展阻滞和停止的病症。一个人如果大部分时间都在担忧自己的健康、数钱、设计报复,或者不停地洗手,是不可能指望心智有多大的发展空间的。"

neurotic 既是形容词,也用来指患有此种病症的人。

4. the mind
意识

A *neurosis* is not a form of mental unbalance. A full-blown mental disorder is called a *psychosis* (sī-KŌ′-sis), a word built on Greek *psyche*, spirit, soul, or mind, plus *-osis*.

A true *psychotic* (sī-KOT′-ik) has lost contact with reality—at least with reality as most of us perceive it, though no doubt *psychotic* (note that this word, like *neurotic*, is both a noun and an adjective) people have their own form of reality.

neurosis 不是某种精神上的失衡。彻底的精神紊乱称作 psychosis,由希腊语中的 psyche(意为"灵魂"或者"意识")加-osis 构成。

一个彻底的 psychotic 完全和现实脱离——至少是我们大多数人认为的"现实",虽然毫无疑问的是 psychotic(请注意这个词,和 neurotic 一样,既可做形容词,也可做名词)也有他们自己的"现实"。

Built on *psyche* plus *iatreia*, medical healing, a *psychiatrist* by etymology is a mind-healer. The specialty is *psychiatry* (sī- *or* sə-KĪ-ə-tree); the adjective is *psy-chiatric* (sī-*kee*-AT′-rik).

Pediatrics, as you know, is also built on *iatreia*, as is *podiatry* (pə-DĪ′-ə-tree), discussed in the next chapter, and *geriatrics* (jair′-ee-AT′-riks), the specialty deal-ing with the particular medical needs of the elderly. (This word combines *iatreia* with Greek *geras*, old age.)

The specialist is a *geriatrician* (jair′-ee-ə-TRISH′-ən), the adjective is *geriatric* (jair′-ee-AT′-rik).

词根 psyche 加 iatreia(意为"医疗"),从词源看,psychiatrist 就是"精神治疗者",这个领域叫做 psychiatry,其形容词是 psychiatric。

pediatrics,如你所知,也是建立在词根 iatreia 上,如在 podiatry(将要在下一章讨论)和 geriatrics 中一样。geriatrics 是关于老年特殊医疗的领域,这个单词由词根 iatreia 和希腊语中的 geras 构成,geras 意为年老的)。

这方面的专家称为 geriatrician,形容词为 geriatric。

REVIEW OF ETYMOLOGY
复习词源

ROOT, SUFFIX	MEANING	ENGLISH WORD
1. *orthos*	straight, correct	_____
2. *paidos* (*ped-*)	child	_____
3. *odontos*	tooth	_____
4. *kardia*	heart	_____
5. *logos*	science; study	_____
6. *neuron*	nerve	_____
7. *algos*	pain	_____
8. *-osis*	abnormal or diseased condition	_____
9. *-itis*	inflammation	_____
10. *psyche*	spirit, soul, mind	_____
11. *iatreia*	medical healing	_____
12. *geras*	old age	_____

USING THE WORDS
单词应用

Can you pronounce the words? (Ⅰ)
你能读出这些单词吗?(Ⅰ)

1. *orthopedics* awr-thə-PEE′-diks
2. *orthopedic* awr-thə-PEE′-dik
3. *orthodontia* awr-thə-DON′-shə
4. *orthodontist* awr-thə-DON′-tist

  5. *orthodontic*　　　　　　　awr-thə-DON$'$-tik
  6. *cardiology*　　　　　　　kahr-dee-OL$'$-ə-jee
  7. *cardiological*　　　　　　kahr$'$-dee-ə-LOJ$'$-ə-kəl
  8. *cardiac*　　　　　　　　KAHR$'$-dee-ak
  9. *cardiogram*　　　　　　　KAHR$'$-dee-ə-gram$'$
  10. *cardiograph*　　　　　　KAHR$'$-dee-ə-graf$'$

Can you pronounce the words?（Ⅱ）
你能读出这些单词吗？（Ⅱ）

  1. *neurology*　　　　　　　noor-OL$'$-ə-jee
  2. *neurological*　　　　　　noor-ə-LOJ$'$-ə-kəl
  3. *neuralgia*　　　　　　　noor-AL$'$-jə
  4. *neuritis*　　　　　　　noor-Ī$'$-tis
  5. *neurosis*　　　　　　　noor-Ō$'$-sis
  6. *neurotic*　　　　　　　noor-OT$'$-ik
  7. *psychosis*　　　　　　　sī-KŌ$'$-sis
  8. *psychotic*　　　　　　　sī-KOT$'$-ik
  9. *psychiatry*　　　　　　　sī- *or* sə-KĪ$'$-ə-tree
  10. *psychiatric*　　　　　　sī-kee-AT$'$-rik
  11. *geriatrics*　　　　　　　jair$'$-ee-AT$'$-riks
  12. *geriatrician*　　　　　　jair$'$-ee-ə-TRISH$'$-ən
  13. *geriatric*　　　　　　　jair$'$-ee-AT$'$-rik

Can you work with the words?（Ⅰ）
你能灵活使用这些词汇了吗？（Ⅰ）

  1. orthopedics　　　　　　a. nerve pain
  2. orthodontia　　　　　　b. specialty dealing with medical problems of
　　　　　　　　　　　　　　　the elderly
  3. neuralgia　　　　　　　c. straightening of teeth
  4. neuritis　　　　　　　　d. inflammation of the nerves
  5. geriatrics　　　　　　　e. treatment of skeletal deformities

KEY：1-e，2-c，3-a，4-d，5-b

Can you work with the words?（Ⅱ）
你能灵活使用这些词汇了吗？（Ⅱ）

  1. cardiogram　　　　　　a. record of heart beats
  2. cardiograph　　　　　　b. mental unbalance

3. neurosis   c. emotional disturbance

4. psychosis   d. treatment of personality disorders

5. psychiatry   e. instrument for recording heartbeats

KEY：1-a, 2-e, 3-c, 4-b, 5-d

Do you understand the words?

你对这些词汇是否已经透彻地理解？

1. A *gynecologist's* patients are mostly men.   TRUE   FALSE
2. *Ophthalmology* is the study of eye diseases.   TRUE   FALSE
3. *Orthopedics* is the specialty dealing with the bones and joints.   TRUE   FALSE
4. A *cardiac* patient has a heart ailment.   TRUE   FALSE
5. A person with a bad "bite" may profit from *orthodontia*.   TRUE   FALSS
6. *Neuralgia* is a disease of the bones.   TRUE   FALSE
7. A *neurosis* is the same as a *psychosis*.   TRUE   FALSE
8. *Neuritis* is inflammation of the nerves.   TRUE   FALSE
9. *Psychiatry* is a medical specialty that deals with mental, emotional, and personality disturbances.   TRUE   FALSE
10. A *cardiograph* is a device for recording heartbeats.   TRUE   FALSE
11. *Psychiatric* treatment is designed to relieve tensions, fears, and insecurities.   TRUE   FALSE
12. A doctor who specializes in *pediatrics* has very old patients.   TRUE   FALSE
13. A *geriatrician* has very young patients.   TRUE   FALSE

KEY：1-F, 2-T, 3-T, 4-T, 5-T, 6-F, 7-F, 8-T, 9-T, 10-T, 11-T, 12-F, 13-F

Can you recall the words?

你能够写出这些词汇吗？

1. specialist who straightens teeth   1. O _____
2. nerve pain   2. N _____
3. medical specialty dealing with bones and joints   3. O _____
4. medical specialty dealing with emotional   4. P _____

disturbances and mental illness

5. inflammation of the nerves 　　　　　　5. N _____

6. emotional or personality disorder 　　　6. N _____

7. mentally unbalanced 　　　　　　　　　7. P _____

8. pertaining to the heart 　　　　　　　　8. C _____

9. specialty dealing with medical problems 　9. G _____

　　of the elderly

10. instrument that records heart action 　　10. C _____

11. record produced by such an instrument 　11. C _____

KEY：1-orthodontist，2-neuralgia，3-orthopedics，4-psychiatry，5-neuritis，6-neurosis，7-psychotic，8-cardiac，9-geriatrics，10-cardiograph，11-cardiogram

CHAPTER REVIEW
章节复习

A. Do you recognize the words?

你认识这些单词吗?

1. Specialist in female ailments：

　　(a) obstetrician，(b) gynecologist，(c) dermatologist

2. Specialist in children's diseases：

　　(a) orthopedist，(b) pediatrician，(c) internist

3. Specialist in eye diseases：

　　(a) cardiologist，(b) opthalmologist，(c) optician

4. Specialist in emotional disorders：

　　(a) neurologist，(b) demagogue，(c) psychiatrist

5. Pertaining to medical treatment of the elderly：

　　(a) neurological，(b) obstetric，(c) geriatric

6. Straightening of teeth：

　　(a) orthodontia，(b) orthopedic，(c) optometry

7. Personality disorder：

　　(a) neuritis，(b) neuralgia，(c) neurosis

8. Mentally unbalanced：

　　(a) neurotic，(b) psychotic，(c) cardiac

9. Principles of teaching：

　　(a) demagoguery，(b) pedagogy，(c) psychosis

KEY：1-b，2-b，3-b，4-c，5-c，6-a，7-c，8-b，9-b

B. Can you recognize roots?

你能认出这些词根吗?

ROOT	MEANING	EXAMPLE
1. *internus*		internist
2. *paidos* (*ped-*)		pediatrician
3. *pedis*		pedestrian
4. *agogos*		pedagogue
5. *demos*		demagogue
6. *derma*		dermatologist
7. *hypos*		hypodermic
8. *ophthalmos*		ophthalmologist
9. *oculus*		monocle
10. *opsis*, *optikos*		optician
11. *metron*		optometrist
12. *orthos*		orthopedist
13. *odontos*		orthodontist
14. *kardia*		cardiologist
15. *logos*		anthropologist
16. *neuron*		neurologist
17. *algos*		neuralgia
18. *psyche*		psychiatrist
19. *iatreia*		psychiatry
20. *geras*		geriatrics

KEY：1-inside，2-child，3-foot，4-leading，5-people，6-skin，7-under，8-eye，9-eye，10-view，vision，sight，11-measurement，12-straight，correct，13-tooth，14-heart，15-science，study，16-nerve，17-pain，18-mind，19-medical healing，20-old age

TEASER QUESTIONS FOR THE AMATEUR ETYMOLOGIST

词源小测验

1. Thinking of the roots *odontos* and *paidos* (spelled *ped-* in English)，figure out the meaning of *pedodontia*：_____

2. Recall the roots *kardia* and *algos*. What is the meaning of *cardialgia*?_____

3. Of *odontalgia*?_____

4. *Nostos* is the Greek word for a *return* (home). Can you combine this root with *algos*, pain, to construct the English word meaning *homesickness*? _____

(*Answers in Chapter 18*)
(答案见第 18 章)

TWO KEYS TO SUCCESS：SELF-DISCIPLINE AND PERSISTENCE
两个成功的关键：自律和坚持

You can achieve a superior vocabulary in a phenomenally short time—given self-discipline and persistence.

你能在很短的时间内掌握大量词汇——只要自律和坚持。

The greatest aid in building self-discipline is，as I have said，a matter of devising a practical and comfortable schedule for yourself and then *keeping to that schedule*.

要建立自律最重要的是,正如我前面说的那样,要为自己制订切实可行且快慢适中的学习计划,并且坚持执行。

Make sure to complete *at least* one session each time you pick up the book，and always decide exactly when you will continue with your work before you put the book down.

当你拿起本书时,要确保至少完成一个小节——在确定下次的阅读时间之前,千万不要放下这本书。

There may be periods of difficulty—then is the time to exert the greatest self-discipline，the most determined persistence.

学习过程中一定会遇到艰难的时刻——届时也将是最需要原则和耐心的时刻。

For every page that you study will help you attain a mastery over words；every day that you work will add to your skill in understanding and using words.

本书每一页的学习都有助于你掌握单词;每天的学习将增加你理解和运用单词的能力。

(*End of Session 6*)

Brief Intermission Two
简短插叙二

RANDOM NOTES ON MODERN USAGE
现代用法随笔

English grammar is confusing enough as it is—what makes it doubly confounding is that it is slowly but continually changing.

This means that some of the strict rules you memorized so painfully in your high school or college English courses may no longer be completely valid.

Following such outmoded principles, you may think you are speaking "perfect" English, and instead you may sound stuffy and pedantic.

英语语法本身已经够令人困惑的了——而更让人备感困惑的是,英语语法正在缓慢而持续地演变。

这也意味着你在高中或者大学的英语课上绞尽脑汁背诵的严谨的语法规则可能已经不再完全可靠了。

遵循那些过时的原则,你可能认为自己说着一口"完美"的英语,而实际上你说的是陈旧、古板的英语。

The problem boils down to this: If grammatical usage is gradually becoming more liberal, where does educated, unaffected, informal speech end? And where does illiterate, ungrammatical speech begin?

The following notes on current trends in modern usage are intended to help you come to a decision about certain controversial expressions. As you read each sentence, pay particular attention to the italicized word or words. Does the usage square with your own language patterns? Would you be willing to phrase your thought in just terms? Decide whether the sentence is right or wrong, then compare your conclusion with the opinion given in the explanatory paragraphs that follow the test.

问题可以归结于此:如果语法一代比一代自由,受过良好教育的人们所使用的、自然的、非正式的语言又会发展至何处? 错误的、不符合语法的言语又是从何时开始的呢?

以下对于当代语言趋势的说明旨在帮助你判断一些有争议的表达。阅读每个句子时,要对斜体字尤其注意。这些用法与你的语言模式相符吗? 你会愿意改用这些表达吗? 判断以下句子对错,并做出总结。将你的总结与测试之后给出的解释做比较。

TEST YOURSELF
自我测试

1. If she drinks too many dry martinis,   RIGHT   WRONG
   she'll surely *get sick*.
2. Have you *got* a dollar?   RIGHT   WRONG
3. No one loves you except *I*.   RIGHT   WRONG
4. Please *lay* down.   RIGHT   WRONG

5. *Who* do you love?	RIGHT	WRONG
6. Neither of these cars *are* worth the money	RIGHT	WRONG
7. The judge sentenled the murderer to be *hung*.	RIGHT	WRONG
8. Mother, *can* I go out to play?	RIGHT	WRONG
9. Take two *spoonsful* of this medicine every three hours.	RIGHT	WRONG
10. Your words seem to *infer* that Jack is a liar	RIGHT	WRONG
11. I *will* be happy to go to the concert with you.	RIGHT	WRONG
12. It is *me*.	RIGHT	WRONG
13. Go *slow*.	RIGHT	WRONG
14. Peggy and Karen are *alumni* of the same high school.	RIGHT	WRONG
15. I *would* like to ask you a question.	RIGHT	WRONG

1. If she drinks too many dry martinis, she'll surely *get sick*.

　　如果她喝太多的干苦艾酒,她一定会病的。

RIGHT. The puristic objection is that *get* has only one meaning—namely, *obtain*. However, as any modern dictionary will attest, *get* has scores of different meanings, one of the most respectable of which is *become*. You can *get* tired, *get* dizzy, *get* drunk, or *get* sick—and your choice of words will offend no one but a pedant.

　　正确。语言纯正癖者认为 get 只有一个含义——获得。然而,无论查阅任何一本词典,我们都能够发现 get 有许多种不同的含义,其中最重要的含义之一就是"become"(变得)。你可能会 get tired, get dizzy, get drunk, 或者 get sick——使用 get 不会使你惹恼任何人,除非他是书呆子。

2. Have you *got* a dollar?

　　你有一美元吗?

RIGHT. If purists get a little pale at the sound of "*get* sick", they turn chalk white when they hear *have got* as a substitute for *have*. But the fact is that *have got* is an established American form of expression. Jacques Barzun, noted author and literary critic, says: "*Have you got* is good idiomatic English—I use it in speech without thinking about it and would write it if colloquialism seemed appropriate to the passage."

　　正确。如果语言纯正癖者听到人们使用 get sick 会脸色难看,那么,当他们听到 have got 被用来作为 have 的同义词使用时,脸色会变得像粉笔一样苍白。而事实是,have got 是既定了的美式表达。哥伦比亚大学著名学者和文学评论家雅克·巴尔赞说过:"Have you got 很符合语言习惯——在演讲中我会不假思索地使用,如果篇章是口语体风格,写作中我也会使用。"

3. No ones loves you except *I*.

　　除了我,没有人爱你。

WRONG. In educated speech, *me* follows the preposition *except*. This problem is troublesome because, to the unsophisticated, the sentence sounds as if it can be completed to "No one loves you, except *I* do," but current educated usage adheres to the technical rule that a preposition requires an objective pronoun (*me*).

错误。在规范的表达中，except 之后要使用 me。这个用法有点令人困惑，因为对于普通人来讲，这个句子看起来好像能够补全为"No one loves you，except I do."但是目前的规范用法忠实于语法规则，认为介词后需接代词宾格(me)。

4. Please *lay* down.

　　请躺下。

WRONG. Liberal as grammar has become，there is still no sanction for using *lay* with the meaning of *recline*. *Lay* means to place，as in "*Lay* your hand on mine." *Lie* is the correct choice.

错误。尽管语法已经变得自由，但是 lay 仍然没有被赋予 recline(躺下)的意思。lay，意为"放"，如"把你的手放在我的手上"，lie 为正确答案。

5. *Who* do you love?

　　你爱谁?

RIGHT. "The English language shows some disposition to get rid of *whom* altogether，and unquestionably it would be a better language with *whom* gone." So wrote Janet Rankin Aiken，of Columbia University，way back in 1936. Today，many decades later，the "disposition" has become a full-fledged force.

The rules for *who* and *whom* are complicated，and few educated speakers have the time，patience，or expertise to bother with them. Use the democratic *who* in your everyday speech whenever it sounds right.

正确。早在 1936 年，哥伦比亚大学珍妮特·兰金·艾肯写道："英语语言显示出抛弃 whom 的态势，毫无疑问，没有了 whom，英语将变得更好。"许多年过去了，今天，这个态势已经成为了正式的趋势。

who 和 whom 的使用规则相当复杂。如今，受到正规教育的说话者很少有人会有充裕的时间、耐心或者专门知识去纠缠这些规则。在日常表达中只要听起来合适，你尽管用更为通俗的 who。

6. Neither of these cars *are* worth the money.

　　两辆车都不值这个价钱。

WRONG. The temptation to use *are* in this sentence is，I admit，practically irresistible. However，"neither of" means "neither *one* of" and *is*，therefore，is the preferable verb.

错误。我承认，在这个句子中使用 are 的诱惑是难以抗拒的。但是，"neither of"相当于"neither one of"，第三人称单数形式 is 是最佳形式。

7. The judge sentenced the murderer to be *hung*.

　　杀人犯被处以绞刑。

WRONG. A distinction is made，in educated speech，between *hung* and *hanged*. A picture is *hung*，but a person is *hanged*—that is，if such action is intended to bring about an untimely demise.

错误。在规范的言语中，hung 和 hanged 是有区别的。照片被挂起来是 hung，而人被处以绞刑则是 hanged——如果行为的目的是为了带来过早的死亡，则要使用 hanged。

8. Mother，*can* I go out to play?

　　妈妈，我可以去外面玩吗?

RIGHT. If you insist that your child say *may*，and nothing but *may*，when asking for permission，you may be considered puristic. *Can* is not discourteous，incorrect，or vulgar—and the newest editions of the authoritative dictionaries fully sanction the use of *can* in requesting rights, privileges, or permission.

正确。如果在孩子请求允许时，你坚持他们使用 may，只使用 may，你可能被看成语言纯正癖者。can 并不失礼，并不是错误或粗鲁的用法——权威词典最新版完全赋予 can 具有要求权力、特权或允许的用法。

9. Take two *spoonsful* of this medicine every three hours.

每三个小时喝两勺药。

WRONG. There is a strange affection, on the part of some people, for *spoonsful* and *cupsful*, even though *spoonsful* and *cupsful* do not exist as acceptable words. The plurals are *spoonfuls* and *cupfuls*.

I am taking for granted, of course, that you are using one spoon and filling it twice. If, for secret reasons of your own, you prefer to take your medicine in two separate spoons, you may then properly speak of "*two spoons full* (not *spoonsful*) of medicine."

错误。尽管 spoonsful 和 cupsful 这样的词汇并不存在，一些人却对这样的用法莫名地喜欢。复数形式是 spoonfuls 和 cupfuls。

当然，我是理所当然地认为你用一个勺子或者杯子盛了两次。如果由于某些只有你自己知道的原因，你更喜欢用两个分开的勺子吃药，那么你就可以说"two spoonsfull（not spoonsful）of medicine"。

10. Your words seem to *infer* that Jack is a liar.

从你的话中似乎能推测杰克是个撒谎者。

WRONG. *Infer* does not mean *hint* or *suggest*. *Imply* is the proper word; to *infer* is to draw a conclusion from another's words.

错误。infer 并没有 hint 或者 suggest 等暗示的意思。符合本句的词汇是 imply；infer 意为"从别人的言词中做出推论"。

11. I *will* be happy to go to the concert with you.

我很愿意和你去音乐会听音乐。

RIGHT. In informal speech, you need no longer worry about the technical and unrealistic distinctions between *shall* and *will*. The theory of modern grammarians is that *shall-will* differences were simply invented out of whole cloth by the textbook writers of the 1800s. As the editor of the scholarly *Modern Language Forum* at the University of California has stated, "The artificial distinction between *shall* and *will* to designate futurity is a superstition that has neither a basis in historical grammar nor the sound sanction of universal usage."

正确。在非正式言中，你无需担心 shall 和 will 之间严格的、不切实际的区别。当代语法家认为 shall 和 will 的区别仅仅是 19 世纪教科书编撰者的臆造。正如加利福尼亚大学《当代语言论坛》的学术类编辑所说："对 shall 和 will 在表示将来意义上的刻意区分既没有历史语法基础，也没有普遍用法上有力的证据。"

12. It is *me*.

是我。

RIGHT. This "violation" of grammatical "law" has been completely sanctioned by current usage. When the late Winston Churchill made a nationwide radio address from New Haven, Connecticut, many, many years ago, his opening sentence was: "This is *me*, Winston Churchill." I imagine that the purists who were listening fell into a deep state of shock at these words, but of course Churchill was simply using the kind of down-to-earth English that had long since become standard in informal educated speech.

正确。这个用法曾经被归类为违反语法规则,现在已经被惯用法批准了。当温斯顿·丘吉尔在康涅狄格州的纽黑文进行全国性的广播演说时,他的开场白是:"This is me. Winston Churchill." 我相信,听到这样的话语,语言纯正癖者一定被震惊了,但是丘吉尔不过使用了已经在规范的非正式表达中成为标准表达方式的常规英语。

13. Go *slow*.

慢点走。

RIGHT. "Go *slow*" is not, and never has been, incorrect English—every authority concedes that *slow* is an adverb as well as an adjective. Rex Stout, well-known writer of mystery novels and creator of *Detective Nero Wolfe*, remarked:"Not only do I use and approve of the idiom *Go slow*, but if I find myself with people who do not, I leave quick."

正确。"Go slow"现在不是错误的表达,过去也从来不是——每本词典都承认 slow 既是副词,又是形容词。著名的推理小说作家、《侦探尼禄·沃尔夫》的创作者雷克斯·斯托特说过:"我使用并赞同使用 go slow 这个习语;如果我身边的人不赞同这个习语,我会马上离开。"

14. Peggy and Karen are *alumni* of the same high school.

Peggy 和 Karen 是同一个高中的女毕业生。

WRONG. As Peggy and Karen are obviously women, we call them *alumnae* (ə-LUM′-nee); only male graduates are *alumni* (ə-LUM′-nī).

错误。很明显,Peggy 和 Karen 是女学生,我们称她们为 alumnae;男毕业生才能被称为 alumni。

15. I *would* like to ask you a question.

我想问你一个问题。

RIGHT. In current American usage, *would* may be used with *I*, though old-fashioned roles demand I *should*.

Indeed, in modern speech, *should* is almost entirely restricted to expressing probability, duty, or responsibility.

As in the case of the charitable-looking dowager who was approached by a seedy character seeking a handout.

"Madam," he whined, "I haven't eaten in five days."

"My good man," the matron answered with great concern, "you should force yourself!"

正确。在当代美式英语用法中,would 可以与 I 连用。只有严格的、过时的语法规则要求使用 I should。

事实上,在当代话语中,should 几乎完全局限于表示职责或可能性。我们来看下面的对话。

例如,一个邋遢的人接近一位看起来乐善好施的贵妇人,求她给点施舍。

"夫人,"他哭啼着说,"我已经五天没有吃饭了。"

"可怜的人呐,"夫人关心地说道,"你应该强迫自己吃!"

5

HOW TO TALK ABOUT VARIOUS PRACTITONERS
如何描述各种从业者

$(Sessions\ 7-10\ )$

TEASER PREVIEW
引读

What practitioner:

* *is a student of human behavior?*

* *follows the techniques devised by Sigmund Freud?*

* *straightens teeth?*

* *measures vision?*

* *grinds lenses?*

* *treats minor ailments of the feet?*

* *analyzes handwriting?*

* *deals with the problems of aging?*

* *uses manipulation and massage as curative techniques?*

什么从业者从事以下工作：
* 研究人类行为
* 依照西格蒙德·弗洛伊德设计的治疗手段
* 矫正牙齿
* 测量视力
* 制备镜片
* 治疗轻微脚疾
* 分析笔迹
* 处理老年化问题
* 用推拿和按摩作为医疗技术

SESSION 7
第 7 节

An ancient Greek mused about the meaning of life, and *philosophy* was born. The first Roman decided to build a road instead of cutting a path through the jungle, and *engineering* came into existence. One day in primitive times, a human being lent to another whatever then passed for money and got back his original investment plus a little more—and *banking* had started.

Most people spend part of every workday at some gainful employment, honest or otherwise, and in so doing often contribute their little mite to the progress of the world.

We explore in this chapter the ideas behind people's occupations—and the words that translate these ideas into verbal symbols.

古希腊人思考生命的意义,于是哲学产生了。古罗马人最先想到修路,而不再在丛林中开辟小路,于是工程学产生了。原始社会里的某一天,一个人将当时被视为货币的东西借出,后来不但拿回原有投资,还得到了部分盈余——于是银行业产生了。

大多数人都在每个工作日用部分的时间从事某种职业以获取报酬,无论诚实与否。也正是这样,他们用微小的力量为世界的进步做出了贡献。

本章,我们将探索职业背后的概念——以及象征这些概念的词汇。

IDEAS
概念

1. behavior
行为

By education and training, this practitioner is an expert in the dark mysteries of human behavior—what makes people act as they do, why they have certain feelings, how their personalities were formed—in short, what makes them tick. Such a professional is often employed by industries, schools, and institutions to devise means for keeping workers productive and happy, students well-adjusted, and inmates contented. With a state license, this person may also do private or group therapy.

A *psychologist*

通过教育和训练,这个从业者是研究人类行为黑暗谜团的专家,研究诸如人们行为的动机、某些情感的原因、人格形成的途径——简而言之,是什么激发人类行为。他们经常受雇于工厂,保持工人的高产和幸福感;也常受雇于学校,使学生更好地适应环境;或受雇于社会机构,使人们心安。获得州执照后,他可以进行私人或团体治疗。

他是一位 psychologist(心理学家)。

2. worries, fears, conflicts
焦虑,恐惧、矛盾

This practitioner is a physician, psychiatrist, or psychologist who has been specially trained in the techniques devised by Sigmund Freud, encouraging you to delve into that part of your mind called "the unconscious." By reviewing the experiences, traumas, feelings, and thoughts of your earlier years, you come to a better understanding of your present worries, fears, conflicts, repressions, insecurities, and nervous tensions—thus taking the first step in coping with them. Treatment, consisting largely in listening to, and helping you to interpret the meaning of, your free-flowing ideas, is usually given in frequent sessions that may well go on for a year or more.

A psychoanalyst

他是内科医生、精神病医生或心理医生,专门接受过西格蒙德·弗洛伊德设计的治疗手段的培训;他能够帮助你挖掘他称之为"无意识"的那部分思维。这样,通过回顾你早年的经历、创伤、感觉和想法,使你更好地理解目前的焦虑、恐惧、矛盾、压抑、不安和精神紧张——这是消除以上症状的第一步。他利用大部分时间聆听你意识的自由涌动,并帮你进行解析,他频繁与你全面进行治疗,疗程可能需要一年或者更长时间。

他是一位 psychoanalyst(心理分析学家)。

3. teeth
牙齿

This practitioner is a dentist who has taken postgraduate work in the straightening of teeth.

An orthodontist

他是一位牙科医生,大学毕业后从事矫正牙齿的工作。
他是一位 orthodontist(牙齿矫正医师)。

4. eyes
眼睛

This practitioner measures your vision and prescribes the type of glasses that will give you a new and more accurate view of the world.

An optometrist

他为你测量视力,确定眼镜类型和度数,让你清晰地看到世界。
他是一位 optometrist(验光技师)。

5. glasses
眼镜

This practitioner grinds lenses according to the specifications prescribed by your optometrist or ophthalmologist, and may also deal in other kinds of optical goods.

An optician

他根据验光技师或者眼科专家的处方制备镜片,或其他光学设备。
他是一位 optician(配置眼镜技师)。

6. bones and blood vessels
骨头和血管

This practitioner is a member of the profession that originated in 1874, when Andrew T. Still devised a drugless technique of curing diseases by massage and other manipulative procedures, a technique based on the theory that illness may be caused by the undue pressure of displaced bones on nerves and blood vessels.

Training is equal to that of physicians, and in most states these practitioners may also use the same methods as, and have the full fights and privileges of, medical doctors.

An osteopath

这类从业者从事的专业源于 1874 年——安德鲁·T. 斯蒂尔发明了通过按摩和推拿的非药物性治疗骨病的技术。这种治疗手段的理论依据是:错位的骨头对神经和血管的压迫可能导致病痛。

他们的训练方法和内科医生一样,在很多州,他们采用的治疗方法和经历的甘苦与一般医生也没什么区别。

他是一位 osteopath(正骨医生)。

7. joints and articulations
关节

The basic principle of this practitioner's work is the maintenance of the structural and functional integrity of the nervous system. Treatment consists of manipulating most of the articulations of the body, especially those connected to the spinal column. Licensed and legally recognized in forty-five states, this professional has pursued academic studies and training that parallel those of the major healing professions.

A chiropractor

这类从业者的基本工作就是维护神经系统的结构和功能完整。治疗方法包括对全身的关节,尤其是对连接脊柱的关节,进行推拿。美国已有 45 个州为这类专业颁发了许可证,从法律上予以承认,这类专业的学术研究和培训与主要的治疗专业的研究和培训类似。

他是一位 chiropractor(按摩技师)。

8. feet
脚

This practitioner treats minor foot ailments—corns, calluses, bunions, fallen arches, etc., and may perform minor surgery.

A podiatrist

这类从业者治疗轻微脚疾——鸡眼、老茧、拇囊炎、足弓下陷等。通常也做些小手术。

他是一位 podiatrist(足科医生)。

9. writing
书写

This practitioner analyzes handwriting to determine character, personality, or aptitudes, and is often called upon to verify authenticity of signatures, written documents, etc.

A graphologist

这类从业者通过分析笔迹,来推断书写人的性格、个性以及某些倾向,并且还经常被要求鉴别文件或其他物体上面签名的真伪。

他是一位 graphologist(笔迹学家)。

10. getting older
变老

This social scientist deals with the financial, economic, sexual, social, retirement, and other non-medical problems of elderly.

A gerontologist

这类社会科学家研究包括与老年人有关的金融、经济、性、社交、退休以及其他的非医学类问题。

他是一位 gerontologist(老年问题专家)。

USING THE WORDS
单词应用

Can you pronounce the words?
你能读出这些单词吗?

1.	*psychologist*	sī-KOL′-ə-jist
2.	*psychoanalyst*	sī-kō-AN′-ə-list
3.	*orthodontist*	awr-thə-DON′-tist
4.	*optometrist*	op-TOM′-ə-trist
5.	*optician*	op-TISH′-ən
6.	*osteopath*	OS′-tee-ə-path
7.	*chiropractor*	KĪ-rə-prək′-tər
8.	*podiatrist*	pə-DĪ′-ə-trist
9.	*graphologist*	graf-OL′-ə-jist
10.	*gerontologist*	jair′-ən-TOL′-ə-jist

Can you work with the words?
你能灵活使用这些词汇了吗?

PRACTITIONERS	INTERESTS
1. psychologist	a. vision
2. psychoanalyst	b. "the unconscious"
3. orthodontist	c. bones and blood vessels
4. optometrist	d. lenses and optical instruments
5. optician	e. feet
6. osteopath	f. teeth
7. chiropractor	g. problems of aging
8. podiatrist	h. joints of the spine
9. graphologist	i. handwriting
10. gerontologist	j. behavior

KEY： 1-j，2-b，3-f，4-a，5-d，6-c，7-h，8-e，9-i，10-g

Do you understand the words?
你对这些词汇是否己经透彻地理解?

1. A *psychologist* must also be a physician.   TRUE   FALSE

2. A *psychoanalyst* follows Freudian techniques.   TRUE   FALSE

3. An *orthodontist* specializes in straightening teeth.　　　　TRUE　　FALSE

4. An *optometrist* prescribes and fits glasses.　　　　TRUE　　FALSE

5. An *optician* may prescribe glasses.　　　　TRUE　　FALSE

6. An *osteopath* may use massage and other manipulative techniques.　　　　TRUE　　FALSE

7. A *chiropractor* has a medical degree.　　　　TRUE　　FALSE

8. A *podiatrist* may perform major surgery.　　　　TRUE　　FALSE

9. A *graphologist* analyzes character from handwriting.　　　　TRUE　　FALSE

10. A *gerontologist* is interested in the non-medical problems of adolescence.　　　　TRUE　　FALSE

KEY：l-F，2-T，3-T，4-T，5-F，6-T，7-F，8-F，9-T，10-F

Can you recall the words?
你能够写出这些词汇吗?

1. delves into the unconscious
2. uses either massage and manipulation or other standard medical procedures to treat illness
3. takes care of minor ailments of the feet
4. straightens teeth
5. analyzes handwriting
6. grinds lenses and sells optical goods
7. deals with the non-medical problems of aging
8. manipulates articulations connected to the spinal column
9. studies and explains human behavior
10. measures vision and prescribes glasses

1. P _____
2. O _____
3. P _____
4. O _____
5. G _____
6. O _____
7. G _____
8. C _____
9. P _____
10. O _____

KEY：1-psychoanalyst，2-osteopath，3-podiatrist，4-orthodontist，5-graphologist，6-optician，7-gerontologist，8-chiropractor，9-psychologist，10-optometrist

(End of Session 7)

SESSION 8
第 8 节

ORIGINS AND RELATED WORDS
词源及相关词汇

1. the mental life
   心理

Psychologist is built upon the same Greek root as *psychiatrist*—*psyche*，spirit，soul，or mind. In *psychiatrist*，the combining form is *iatreia*，medical healing. In *psychologist*，the combining form is *logos*，science or study；a *psychologist*，by etymology，is one who studies the mind.

The field is *psychology* （sī-KOL′-ə-jee），the adjective *psychological* （sī-kə-LOJ′-ə-kəl）.

psychologist 与 psychiatrist 基于同样希腊语词根——psyche，意为"精神""灵魂"或"意识"。psychiatrist 是 psyche 与 iatreia(治愈)的结合；psychologist 是 psyche 与希腊语 logos 的结合。logos 意为"科学或研究"，所以 psychologist 是对人类心理进行研究的人，"心理学家"。

其专业领域是 psychology，心理学；形容词形式是 psychological。

Psyche （SĪ′-kee）is also an English word in its own right—it designates the mental life，the spiritual or non-physical aspect of one's existence. The adjective *psychic* （SĪ′-kik）refers to phenomena or qualities that cannot be explained in purely physical terms. People may be called *psychic* if they seem to possess a sixth sense，a special gift of mind reading，or any mysterious aptitudes that cannot be accounted for logically. A person's disturbance is *psychic* if it is emotional or mental，rather than physical.

Psyche combines with the Greek *pathos*，suffering or disease，to form *psychopathic* （sī-kə-PATH′-ik），an adjective that describes someone suffering from a severe mental or emotional disorder. The noun is *psychopathy* （sī′-KOP′-ə-thee）.

希腊语 psyche 单独使用也是英语单词——意为"心理生活，人类存在的精神或者非实体方面"。形容词形式 psychic 指"无法从实体方面解释的现象或者特质"。例如，如果说某个人是 psychic，这个人可能拥有第六感，一种具有心灵感应的特异功能，或者无法用逻辑解释的神奇能力。如果说一个人的毛病是 psychic，则是指这个人的问题在于情绪或心理，而非身体。

psyche 与希腊语 pathos(苦难或疾病)相结合，形成 psychopathic，形容词，用来描述遭受严重精神和情绪紊乱的状态。名词形式为 psychopathy。

The root *psyche* combines with Greek *soma*，body，to form *psychosomatic* （sī′-kō-sə-MAT′-ik），an adjective that delineates the powerful influence that the mind，especially the unconscious，has on bodily diseases. Thus，a person who fears the consequence of being present at a certain meeting will suddenly develop a bad cold or backache，or even be injured in a traffic accident，so that his appearance at this meeting is made impossible. It's a real cold，it's far from ad imaginary backache，and of course one cannot in any sense doubt the reality of the automobile that injured him. Yet，according to the *psychosomatic* theory of medicine，his unconscious made him susceptible to the cold germs，caused the backache，or forced him into the path of the car.

psyche 与希腊语 soma(身体)相结合，形成 psychosomatic，形容词，指"心理，尤其是无意识心理对身体疾病有重大影响的"。这样，如果一个人惧怕参加某个会议，他就会突然患重感冒、背痛，甚至在交通事故中受伤，这样他就可以避免在会议中出现。感冒并非假装，背痛也不是幻觉，当然任何人也不能否认被汽车碾过的事实。但是，根据身心病医学理论，他的无意识心理使他容易受到细菌的感染，使他背痛，甚至强迫他靠近加速的汽车。

A *psychosomatic* disorder actually exists insofar as symptoms are concerned (headache，excessive urination，pains，paralysis，heart palpitations)，yet there is no organic cause within the body. The cause is within the *psyche*, the mind. Dr. Flanders Dunbar，in *Mind and Body*，gives a clear and exciting account of the interrelationship between emotions and diseases.

身心紊乱会产生各种症状——头疼、尿频、疼痛、瘫痪、心悸——却找不到身体内部组织原因。原因就在于 psyche，心理。弗兰德斯·邓巴博士在《心理与身体》中清晰、生动地叙述了情感和疾病的关系。

Psychoanalysis (sī'-ko-ə-NAL'-ə-sis) relies on the technique of deeply，exhaustively probing into the unconscious，a technique developed by Sigmund Freud. In oversimplified terms，the general principle of *psychoanalysis* is to guide the patient to an awareness of the deep-seated，unconscious causes of anxieties，fears，conflicts，and tension. Once found，exposed to the light of day，and thoroughly understood，claim the *psychoanalysts*，these causes may vanish like a light snow that is exposed to strong sunlight.

psychoanalysis(精神分析学)依靠对西格蒙德·弗洛伊德开创的潜意识深度地、全方位地挖掘，简而言之，psychoanalysis 的普遍原理是引导患者意识到其焦虑、矛盾和紧张根深蒂固的无意识原因。psychoanalyst 认为，原因一旦找到并充分理解，病因就像暴露在强光下的雪花，马上消失不见。

Consider an example：You have asthma，let us say，and your doctor can find no physical basis for your ailment. So you are referred to a *psychoanalyst* (or *psychiatrist* or clinical *psychologist* who practices *psychoanalytically* oriented therapy).

With your therapist you explore your past life，dig into your unconscious，and discover，let us say for the sake of argument，that your mother or father always used to set for you impossibly high goals. No matter what you accomplished in school，it was not good enough—in your mother's or father's opinion (and such opinions were always made painfully clear to you)，you could do better if you were not so lazy. As a child you built up certain resentments and anxieties because you seemed unable to please your parent—and (this will sound farfetched，but it is perfectly possible) as a result you became asthmatic. How else were you going to get the parental love，the approbation，the attention you needed and that you felt you were not receiving?

例如，你患有哮喘，而且医生找不到疾病的身体根源。于是，他将你交给 psychoanalyst(或从事精神分析疗法的精神科医生或心理医生)。

你和精神分析医生一起探究你过去的生活，挖掘你的无意识。为了论证，假定你发现你的父母亲习惯为你指定过高的、难于实现的目标。无论你在学校的表现多么出色，你都做得不够好——按照他们的观点(而他们又常常过于直接地告诉你他们的观点)，如果不过于懒惰，你可以做得更好。孩子无法取悦父母，你开始愤恨、焦虑——(这听起来可能牵强，但是很可能发生），结果，你患上了哮喘。还有什么办法能使你得到你认为无法得到的父母的爱、认可和关注呢？

In your sessions with your therapist, you discover that your asthma is emotionally, rather than organically, based—your ailment is *psychogenic* (sī'-kō-JEN'-ik), of *psychic* origin, or (the terms are used more or less interchangeably although they differ somewhat in definition) *psychosomatic*, resulting from the interaction of mind and body. (*Psychogenic* is built on *psyche* plus Greek *genesis*, birth or origin.)

And your treatment? No drugs, no surgery—these may help the body, not the e-motions. Instead, you "work out" (this is the term used in *psychoanalytic* [sī-kō-an'-ə-LIT'-ik] parlance) early trauma in talk, in remembering, in exploring, in interpreting, in reliving childhood experiences. And if your asthma is indeed *psychogenic* (or *psychosomatic*), therapy will very likely help you; your attacks may cease, either gradually or suddenly.

Freudian therapy is less popular today than formerly; many newer therapies—Gestalt, bioenergetics, transactional analysis, to name only a few—claim to produce quicker results.

通过几个疗程的治疗，你了解到哮喘基于情感原因，而非身体器官失灵。于是，你的哮喘是 psychogenic——心理性的，或者 psychosomatic，由身心的交替作用造成的。（虽然这些术语的意思有些差异，但它们基本上可以互相替代使用；psychogenic 是 psyche 加希腊语 genesis 演变而成的，genesis 意为"出生"或"源于"。）

如何治疗呢？无需服药或手术——这些只能改变身体组织，无法改变心理。你通过与 psychoanalyst 的谈话、回忆、探索、解释和重视你儿时的经历，逐步"work out"（心理分析师使用的话语，指"恢复"）。而且，如果哮喘的确是 psychogenic，psychoanalysis 对你会很有帮助；哮喘可能不再发作，或逐渐减少，或突然停止。

现在弗洛伊德疗法已没过去盛行；很多更新的治疗方法——格式塔理论、生物能量学、交流分析理论等，都宣称能迅速找到病因，并且见效快。

In any case, *psychotherapy* (sī-kō-THAIR'-ə-pee) of one sort or another is the indicated treatment for *psychogenic* (or *psychosomatic*) disorders, or for any personality disturbances. The practitioner is a *psychotherapist* (sī-kō-THAIR'-ə-pist) or *therapist*, for short; the adjective is *psychotherapeutic* (sī-kō-thair'-ə-prōō'-tik).

总之，psychotherapy（精神疗法）是一种对于心理紊乱和人格障碍的常规疗法，其从业者是一个 psychotherapist（心理治疗师）或者缩写为 therapist。形容词形式是 psychotherapeutic。

REVIEW OF ETYMOLOGY
复习词源

ROOT, SUFFIX	MEANING	ENGLISH WORD
1. *psyche*	spirit, soul, mind	_____
2. *iatreia*	medical healing	_____
3. *-ic*	adjective suffix	_____
4. *soma*	body	_____
5. *genesis*	birth, origin	_____
6. *pathos*	suffering, disease	_____

USING THE WORDS
单词应用

Can you pronounce the words?
你能读出这些单词吗?

1.	*psychology*	sī-KOL′-ə-jee
2.	*psychological*	sī′-kə-LOJ′-ə-kəl
3.	*psyche*	SĪ′-kee
4.	*psychic*	SĪ′-kik
5.	*psychopathic*	sī-kə-PATH′-ik
6.	*psychopathy*	sī′-KOP′-ə-thee
7.	*psychopath*	SĪ′-kə-path
8.	*psychosomatic*	sī′-kō-sə-MAT′-ik
9.	*psychoanalysis*	sī′-kō-ə-NAL′-ə-sis
10.	*psychoanalytic*	sī-kō-an′-ə-LIT′-ik
11.	*psychogenic*	sī-ko-JEN′-ik
12.	*psychotherapy*	sī-kō-THAIR′-ə-pee
13.	*psychotherapist*	sī-kō-THAIR′-ə-pist
14.	*psychotherapeutic*	sī-kō-thair′-ə-PY OO′-tik

Can you work with the words?
你能灵活使用这些词汇了吗?

1.	psychology	a.	mental or emotional disturbance
2.	psyche	b.	psychological treatment based on Freudian techniques
3.	psychic	c.	general term for psychological treatment
4.	psychopathy	d.	originating in the mind or emotions
5.	psychosomatic	e.	one's inner or mental life, or self-image
6.	psychoanalysis	f.	study of the human mind and behavior
7.	psychogenic	g.	describing the interaction of mind and body
8.	psychotherapy	h.	pertaining to the mind; extrasensory
9.	psychopath	i.	person lacking in social conscience or inner censor

KEY：1-f，2-e，3-h，4-a，5-g，6-b，7-d，8-c，9-i

Do you understand the words?

你对这些词汇是否已经透彻地理解?

1. *Psychological* treatment aims at sharpening the intellect.	TRUE	FALSE
2. *Psychic* phenomena can be explained on rational or physical grounds	TRUE	FALSE
3. *Psychopathic* personalities are normal and healthy.	TRUE	FALSE
4. A *psychosomatic* symptom is caused by organic disease.	TRUE	FALSE
5. Every therapist uses *psychoanalysis*.	TRUE	FALSE
6. A *psychogenic* illness originates in the mind or emotions.	TRUE	FALSE
7. A *psychotherapist* must have a medical degree.	TRUE	FALSE
8. *Psychoanalytically* oriented therapy uses Freudian techniques.	TRUE	FALSE
9. A *psychopath* is often a criminal.	TRUE	FALSE

KRY: 1-F, 2-F, 3-F, 4-F, 5-F, 6-T, 7-F, 8-T, 9-T

Can you recall the words?

你能够写出这些词汇吗?

1. one's inner or mental life, or self-image	1. P _____
2. the adjective that denotes the interactions, especially in illness, between mind and body	2. P _____
3. mentally or emotionally disturbed	3. P _____
4. study of behavior	4. P _____
5. extrasensory	5. P _____
6. treatment by Freudian techniques	6. P _____
7. pertaining to the study of behavior (*adj.*)	7. P _____
8. of mental or emotional origin	8. P _____
9. general term for treatment of emotional disorders	9. P _____
10. antisocial person	10. P _____

KRY: 1-psyche, 2-psychosomatic, 3-psychopathic, 4-psychology, 5-psychic, 6-psychoanalysis, 7-psychological, 8-psychogenic, 9-psychotherapy, 10-psychopath

(End of Session 8)

SESSION 9
第 9 节

ORIGINS AND RELATED WORDS
词源及相关词汇

1. the whole tooth
整牙

Orthodontist, as we discovered in Chapter 4，is built on *orthos*，straight，correct，plus *odontos*，tooth.

A *pedodontist*（pee′-dō-DON′-tist）specializes in the care of children's teeth—the title is constructed from *paidos*，child，plus *odontos*. The specialty：*pedodontia*（pee′-dō-DON′-sha）; the adjective：*pedodontic*（pee′-dō-DON′-tik）.

A *periodontist*（pair′-ee-ō-DON′-tist）is a gum specialist—the term combines *odontos* with the prefix *peri-*，around，surrounding.（As a quick glance in the mirror will tell you，the gums surround the teeth，more or less.）

Can you figure out the word for the specialty? _____.

For the adjective? _____.

An *endodontist*（en′-dō-DON′-tist）specializes in work on the pulp of the tooth and in root-canal therapy—the prefix in this term is *endo-*，from Greek *endon*，inner，within.

Try your hand again at constructing words. What is the specialty? _____. And the adjective? _____.

The prefix *ex-*，out，combines with *odontos* to form *exodontist*（eks′-ō-DON′-tist）. What do you suppose，therefore，is the work in which this practitioner specializes? _____.

And the term for the specialty? _____.

For the adjective? _____.

正如我们在第 4 章发现的，orthodontist 是由 orthos(意为"使……变直")和 odontos(意为"牙齿")构成的。

一个 pedodontist(儿科牙医)的专业领域就是儿童的牙齿护理——这个称谓由 paidos(意为"儿童")加上 odontos 组成。这个专业领域称为 pedodontia(儿童牙科学)，形容词为 pedodontic。

periodontist 是牙床专家——这一术语由 odontos 和前缀 peri-(意为"周围""包围")组成。(瞄一眼镜子，你就会发现牙齿或多或少被牙床包围着。)

你是否能写出此领域的名称?

它的形容词是什么?

一个 endodontist(牙髓学专家)的专业领域是牙髓和牙根管的治疗，这一术语中的前缀 endo-，源自希腊语 endon，意为"内部""在……里面"。

再做一下关于组词的训练，这一领域是什么? 形容词是什么?

前缀 ex-，意为"外面"，和 odontos 一起构成 exodontist，根据这些你能猜出这种从业者具体是从事什么领域的吗?

这一术语的研究领域叫什么?

它的形容词是什么？

2. measurement
度量

The *optometrist*, by etymology, measures vision——the term is built on *opsis*, *optikos*, view, vision, plus *metron*, measurement.

Metron is the root in many other words：

（1）*thermometer*（thər-MOM'-ə-tər）—an instrument to measure heat（Greek *therme*, heat）.

（2）*barometer*（bə-ROM'-ə-ter）—an instrument to measure atmospheric pressure（Greek *baros*, weight）; the adjective is *barometric*（bair'-ə-MET'-rik）.

（3）*sphygmomanometer*（sfig'-mō-mə-NOM'-ə-tər）—a device for measuring blood pressure（Greek *sphygmos*, pulse）.

（4）*metric* system—a decimal system of weights and measures, long used in other countries and now gradually being adopted in the United States.

optometrist,从词源上来看,是测量视力的——这一术语源于 opsis, optikos,意为"视野""视力",加上 metron(意为"度量")。

metron 是很多单词的词根：

（1）thermometer——测量温度的仪器(希腊语词根 therme,意为"热")。

（2）barometer——测量气压的仪器(希腊语词根 baros,意为"重量")形容词形式是 barometric.

（3）sphygmomanometer——测量血压的仪器(希腊语词根 sphygmos,意为"脉搏")。

（4）metric system——一种十进位的重量测量系统,已在其他国家使用很久,现在在美国也逐渐被采用。

3. bones, feet, and hands
骨头,脚,手

Osteopath combines Greek *osteon*, bone, with *pathos*, suffering, disease. *Osteopathy*（os'-tee-OP'-ə-thee）, you will recall, was originally based on the theory that disease is caused by pressure of the bones on blood vessels and nerves. An *osteopathic*（os'-tee-ə- PATH'-ik）physician is not a bone specialist, despite the misleading etymology—and should not be confused with the *orthopedist*, who is.

osteopath 由两个希腊语词汇组成:osteon(骨头)和 pathos(苦难或疾病)。你能够记起,osteopathy 最初基于疾病由血管和神经对骨头的压力引起。an osteopathic physician 并不是骨骼专家,虽然词源具有误导性——不应该与骨骼专家 orthopedist(骨科医生)混淆。

The *podiatrist*（Greek *pous*, *podos*, foot, plus *iatreia*, medical healing）practices *podiatry*（pə-DĪ'-ə-tree）. The adjective is *podiatric*（pō'-dee-AT'-rik）.

podiatrist 是足病医生(希腊语 pous,podos 表示"脚",iatreia 表示"医疗康复"),参与 podiatry(足病治疗),形容词形式为 podiatric。

The root *pous*, *podos* is found also in：

（1）*octopus*（OK'-tə-pəs）, the eight-armed（or, as the etymology has it, eight-footed）sea creature（Greek *okto*, eight）.

（2）*platypus*（PLAT'-ə-pəs）, the strange water mammal with a duck's bill, webbed feet, and a beaver-like tail that reproduces by laying eggs.（Greek *platys*, broads, flat—hence, by etymology, a flatfoot!)

(3) *podium* (PŌ′-dee-əm), a speaker's platform, etymologically a place for the feet. (The suffix -*ium* often signifies "place where", as in *gymnasium*, *stadium*, *auditorium*, etc.)

(4) *tripod* (TRĪ′-pod), a three-legged (or "footed") stand for a camera or other device (*tri-*, three).

(5) *chiropodist* (kə-ROP′-ə-dist), earlier title for a podiatrist, and still often used. The specialty is *chiropody* (kə-ROP′-ə-dee).

Chiropody combines *podos* with Greek *cheir*, hand, spelled *chiro-* in English words. The term was coined in the days before labor-saving machinery and push-button devices, when people worked with their hands and developed calluses on their upper extremities as well as on their feet. Today most of us earn a livelihood in more sedentary occupations, and so we may develop calluses on less visible portions of our anatomy.

词根 pous, podos 也出现在其他词汇中：

(1) octopus, 章鱼, 长有八条（词源表示八只脚的）触须的海洋生物（希腊语 okto 表示八）。

(2) platypus, 鸭嘴兽, 是一种奇怪的水生哺乳动物, 长有鸭喙、脚蹼和像海狸一样的尾巴, 通过产卵繁殖。（希腊语 platys 表示宽的、平的——因此, 从词源理解, 本词汇表示扁平足!）

(3) podium, 讲台, 从词源讲表示脚部站立的地方。（后缀-ium 表示"……的地方", 例如 gymnasium 健身房、stadium 体育场、auditorium 礼堂等。）

(4) tripod, 三脚架, 三条腿（或三只脚）的架子, 可以支撑照相机或其他器材（tri-表示三）。

(5) chiropodist, podiatris 的早期用法, 意为足疗师, 仍然被频繁使用。其专业为 chiropody（足疗）。

chiropody 将 podos 与希腊语 cheir(手)结合, cheir 在英语词汇中的拼写变成 chiro。这个词汇在节省劳动力的机械时代和按钮装置被发明之前形成, 那时的人们用双手劳动, 因此手和脚长满老茧。今天, 我们中的大多数通过需要长期伏案的工作谋生, 因此, 我们身体一些不太可见的部位可能长满"老茧"。

Chiropractors heal with their hands—the specialty is *chiropractic* (kī′-rō-PRAK′-tik).

Cheir (*chiro-*), hand, is the root in *chirography* (kī-ROG′-rə-fee). Recalling the *graph-* in *graphologist*, can you figure out by etymology what *chirography* is? ___

_____.

An expert in writing by hand, or in penmanship (a lost art in these days of electronic word-processing)[1], would be a *chirographer* (kī-ROG′-rə-fər); the adjective is *chirographic* (kī′-rō- GRAF′-ik).

If the suffix -*mancy* comes from a Greek word meaning *foretelling* or *prediction*, can you decide what *chiromancy* (Kī′-rō-man′-see) must be? _____.

The person who practices *chiromancy* is a *chiromancer* (Kī′-rō-man′-sər); the adjective is *chiromantic* (kī′-rō-MAN′-tik).

chiropractors 是按摩师, 他们用手为患者治疗, 其专业为 chiropractic, 按摩疗法。

---

1. But see calligrapher in the next session.

calligrapher（书法家）见下一小节。

cheir(chiro-)表示手,是 chirography 的词根。回忆 graphologist 中的 graph-,你能够从词源想出 chirography 的含义吗?

书法或书法艺术专家(自动文字处理时代成为遗失的艺术)可以被称为 chirographer;形容词形式是 chirographic。

如果与来自希腊语表示预测或推测的后缀-mancy 组合,你能够确定 chiromancy 的含义吗?

研究 chiromancy 的人被称为 chiromancer,手相家;形容词形式是 chiromantic。

REVIEW OF ETYMOLOGY
复习词源

PREFIX, ROOT, SUFFIX	MEANING	ENGLISH WORD
1. *orthos*	straight, correct	_____
2. *odontos*	tooth	_____
3. *paidos*(ped-)	child	_____
4. *-ic*	adjective suffix	_____
5. *peri-*	around, surrounding	_____
6. *endo-*	inner, within	_____
7. *ex-*	out	_____
8. *opsis optikos*	vision	_____
9. *metron*	measurement	_____
10. *therme*	heat	_____
11. *bares*	weight	_____
12. *sphygmos*	pulse	_____
13. *osteon*	bone	_____
14. *pathos*	suffering, disease	_____
15. *pous, podos*	foot	_____
16. *okto*	eight	_____
17. *platys*	broad, fiat	_____
18. *-ium*	place where	_____
19. *tri-*	three	_____
20. *cheir*(chiro-)	hand	_____
21. *mancy*	prediction	_____
22. *iatreia*	medical healing	_____

USING THE WORDS
单词应用

Can you pronounce the words?(Ⅰ)
你能读出这些单词吗?(Ⅰ)

1. *pedodontist*   pee'-dō-DON'-tist

2. *pedodontia*   pee'-dō-DON'-shə

3. *pedodontic*   pee′-dō-DON′-tik

4. *periodontist*   pair′-ee-ō-DON′-tist

5. *periodontia*   pair′-ee-ō-DON′-shə

6. *periodontic*   pair′-ee-ō-DON′-tik

7. *endodontist*   en′-dō-DON′-tist

8. *endodontia*   en′-dō-DON′-shə

9. *endodontic*   en′-dō-DON′-tik

10. *exodontist*   eks′-ō-DON′-tist

11. *exodontia*   eks′-ō-DON′-shə

12. *exodontic*   eks′-ō-DON′-tik

13. *thermometer*   thər-MOM′-ə-tər

14. *barometer*   bə-ROM′-ə-tər

15. *barometric*   bair′-ə-MET-′rik

16. *sphygmomanometer*   sfig′-mō-mə-NOM′-ə-tər

Can you pronounce the words? (Ⅱ)

你能读出这些单词吗?(Ⅱ)

1. *osteopathy*   os′-tee-OP′-ə-thee

2. *osteopathic*   os′-tee-ə-PATH′-ik

3. *podiatry*   pə-DĪ′-ə-tree

4. *podiatric*   pō′-dee-AT′-rik

5. *octopus*   OK′-tə-pəs

6. *platypus*   PLAT′-ə-pəs

7. *podium*   PŌ′-dee-əm

8. *tripod*   TRĪ′-pod

9. *chiropodist*   kə-ROP′-ə-dist

10. *chiropody*   kə-ROP′-ə-dee

11. *chiropractic*   kī′-rō-PRAK′-tik

12. *chirography*   kī-ROG′-rə-fee

13. *chirographer*   kī-ROG′-ro-fər

14. *chirographic*   kī′-rə-GRAF′-ik

15. *chiromancy*   KĪ′-rə-man′-see

16. *chiromancer*   KĪ′-rə-man′-sər

17. *chiromantic*   kī′-rə-MAN′-tik

Can you work with the words? (Ⅰ)

你能灵活使用这些词汇了吗?(Ⅰ)

1. orthodontia   a. dental specialty involving the pulp and root canal

2. pedodontia   b. instrument that measures atmospheric pressure

3. periodontia   c. specialty arising from the theory that pressure of the bones on nerves and blood vessels may cause disease

4. endodontia   d. specialty of child dentistry

5. exodontia   e. blood—pressure apparatus

6. barometer   f. treatment of minor ailments of the foot

7. sphygmomanometer   g. instrument to measure heat

8. osteopathy   h. specialty of tooth extraction

9. podiatry   i. specialty of tooth straightening

10. thermometer   j. specialty of the gums

KEY：1-i, 2-d, 3-j, 4-a, 5-h, 6-b, 7-e, 8-c, 9-f, 10-g

Can you work with the words? (Ⅱ)
你能灵活使用这些词汇了吗？（Ⅱ）

1. octopus   a. speaker's platform

2. platypus   b. maintenance of integrity of the nervous system by manipulation and massage

3. podium   c. palm reading

4. chiropody   d. eight-armed sea creature

5. chiropractic   e. handwriting

6. chirography   f. treatment of minor ailments of the foot

7. chiromancy   g. egg-laying mammal with webbed feet

KEY：1-d, 2-g, 3-a, 4-f, 5-b, 6-e, 7-c

Do you understand the words?
你对这些词汇是否已经透彻地理解？

1. *Orthodontia* is a branch of dentistry.   TRUE   FALSE

2. Doctors use *sphygmomanometers* to check blood pressure.   TRUE   FALSE

3. *Osteopathic* physicians may use standard medical procedures.   TRUE   FALSE

4. *Chiropractic* deals with handwriting.   TRUE   FALSE

5. *Chiropody* and *podiatry* are synonymous terms.   TRUE   FALSE

6. A *podium* is a place from which a lecture might be delivered.   TRUE   FALSE

7. A *pedodontist* is a foot doctor.   TRUE   FALSE

8.	A *periodontist* is a gum specialist.	TRUE	FALSE
9.	A *endodontist* does root-canal therapy.	TRUE	FALSE
10.	An *exodontist* extracts teeth.	TRUE	FALSE
11.	A *barometer* measures heat.	TRUE	FALSE
12.	An *octopus* has eight arms.	TRUE	FALSE
13.	A *platypus* is a land mammal.	TRUE	FALSE
14.	A *tripod* has four legs.	TRUE	FALSE
15.	A *chirographer* is an expert at penmanship.	TRUE	FALSE
16.	A *chiromancer* reads palms.	TRUE	FALSE

KEY：1-T，2-T，3-T，4-F，5-T，6-T，7-F，8-T，9-T，10-T，11-F，12-T，13-F，14-F，15-T，16-T

Can you recall the words? (Ⅰ)
你能够写出这些词汇吗？(Ⅰ)

1. pertaining to child dentistry (*adj.*)   1. P＿＿＿＿
2. pertaining to treatment of the foot (*adj.*)   2. P＿＿＿＿
3. blood-pressure apparatus   3. S＿＿＿＿
4. three-legged stand   4. T＿＿＿＿
5. pertaining to the treatment of diseases by manipulation to relieve pressure of the bones on nerves and blood vessels (*adj.*)   5. O＿＿＿＿
6. pertaining to handwriting (*adj.*)   6. C＿＿＿＿
7. gum specialist   7. P＿＿＿＿
8. treatment of ailments of the foot   8. P＿＿＿＿ *or* C＿＿＿＿
9. stand for a speaker   9. P＿＿＿＿
10. dentist specializing in treating the pulp of the tooth or in doing root-canal therapy   10. E＿＿＿＿

KEY：1-pedodontic，2-podiatric，3-sphygmomanometer，4-tripod，5-osteopathic，6-chirographic，7-periodontist，8-podiatry or chiropody，9-podium，10-endodontist

Can you recall the words? (Ⅱ)
你能够写出这些词汇吗？(Ⅱ)

1. pertaining to the specialty of tooth extraction (*adj.*)   1. E＿＿＿＿
2. pertaining to the measurement of atmospheric pressure (*adj.*)   2. B＿＿＿＿

3. palm reading (*noun*)   3. C_____

4. handwriting   4. C_____

5. the practice of manipulating bodily articulations to relieve ailments   5. C_____

6. egg-laying mammal   6. P_____

7. eight-armed sea creature   7. O_____

8. instrument to measure heat   8. T_____

KEY：1-exodontic，2-barometric，3-chiromancy，4-chirography，5-chiropractic，6-platypus，7-octopus，8-thermometer

---

(End of Session 9)

SESSION 10
第 10 节

ORIGINS AND RELATED WORDS
词源及相关词汇

1. writing and writers
书写和作家

The Greek verb *graphein*, to write, is the source of a great many English words. We know that the *graphologist* analyzes handwriting, the term combining *graphein* with *logos*, science, study, The specialty is *graphology* (grə-FOL′-ə-jee), the adjective *graphological* (graf′-ə-LOJ′-ə-kəl).

希腊语动词 graphein 表示写,是许多英语词汇的根源。

我们知道 graphologist(笔相家)对书写进行分析,这个词汇是 graph(书写)和 logos(科学,研究)的组合。其专业为 graphology,笔迹学;形容词形式是 graphological。

Chirographer is built on *graphein* plus *cheir*(*chiro-*), hand. Though *chirography* may be a lost art, *calligraphy* (kə-LIG′-rə-fee) is enjoying a revival. For centuries before the advent of printing, *calligraphy*, or penmanship as an artistic expression, was practiced by monks.

A *calligrapher* (kə-LIG′-rə-fər) is called upon to design and write announcements, place cards, etc. , as a touch of elegance. The adjective is *calligraphic* (kal′-ə-GRAF′-ik).

Calligraphy combines *graphein* with Greek *kallos*[1], beauty, and so, by etymology, means *beautiful writing*.

chirograher 建立在 graphein 和 cheir(chiro-,表示手)的基础上。虽然 chirography 可能是一种遗失的艺术,但是 calligraphy,书法,却正经历复兴。在印刷出现之前的几个世纪,和尚练习书法或书法艺术,使其成为一种艺术表达。

calligrapher 是书法家,人们请求书法家设计、书写布告和座位卡片等,这会创造一种高雅的感觉。形容词形式是 calligraphic。

calligraphy 将 graphein 与表示美丽的希腊语 kallos 组合在一起,从词源理解,表示美丽的书写。

If a word exists for artistic handwriting, there must be one for the opposite—bad, scrawly, or illegible handwriting. And indeed there is—*cacography* (kə-KOG′-rə-fee), combining *graphein* with Greek *kakos*, bad, harsh.

By analogy with the forms of *calligraphy*, can you write the word for:

有优美的书写,必定也有与之相对的书写——糟糕的、潦草的、不容易辨认的书写。确实有相应的单词 cacography,它是由 graphein 和希腊词 kakos("坏的""粗糙的")组成的。

参照 calligraphy 的各种形式,你能写出下面的单词吗?

---

1. An entrancing word that also derives from *kallos* is *callipygian* (kal′-ə-PIJ′-ee-ən), an adjective describing a shapely or attractive rear end, or a person so endowed—the combining root is *pyge*, buttocks.

另外一个由 kallos 衍变而来的、令人着迷的单词是 callipygian,它是一个形容词,用来形容匀称或迷人的臀部,或有着健美臀部的人,它的词根是 pyge(意为"臀部")。

One who uses bad or illegible handwriting? _____.

Pertaining to, or marked by, bad handwriting (*adjective*)? _____.

Graphein is found in other English words：

(1) *cardiograph* （discussed in Chapter 4）—etymologically a "heart writer" (*kardia*, heart).

(2) *photograph*—etymologically, "written by light" (Greek *photos*, light).

(3) *phonograph*—etymologically, a "sound writer" (Greek *phone*, sound).

(4) *telegraph*—etymologically a "distance writer" (Greek *tele-*, distance).

(5) *biography*—etymologically "life writing" (Greek, *bios*, life).

(Many of these new roots will be discussed in greater detail in later chapters.)

Graphein 也出现在其他的英语单词中：

(1) cardiograph(已在第 4 章中讨论过)——从词源上看其本义是一个"心脏的书写者"(kardia,心脏)。

(2) photograph——从词源上看其本义是一个"用光写的"(希腊语 photos,光)。

(3) phonograph——从词源上看其本义是一个"声音的书写者"(希腊语 phone,声音)。

(4) telegraph——从词源上看其本义是一个"距离的书写者"(希腊语前缀 tele,距离)。

(5) biography——从词源上看其本义是一个"生命的书写"(希腊语 bios,生命)。

(许多这样的新词根,我们会在以后的章节里详细加以讨论。)

2. aging and the old
老化和老人

We know that a *geriatrician* specializes in the medical care of the elderly. The Greek word *geras*, old age, has a derived form, *geron*, old man, the root in *gerontologist*. The specialty is *gerontology*(jair′-ən-TOL′-ə-jee), the adjective is *gerontological*(jair′-ən-tə-LOJ′-ə-kəl).

我们知道,专门从事老年人医疗的人称为 geriatrician。希腊语 geras,意为"老年",有一个派生形式 geron(意为"老男人"),在 gerontologist 中有这个词根。其专业领域是 gerontology,形容词形式是 gerontological。

The Latin word for *old* is *senex*, the base on which *senile*, *senescent*, *senior*, and *senate* are built.

(1) *senile* (SEE′-nīl)—showing signs of the physical and/or mental deterioration that generally marks very old age. The noun is *senility* (sə-NIL′-ə-tee).

(2) *senescent* (sə-NES′-ənt)—aging, growing old. (Note the same suffix in this word as in *adolescent*, growing into an adult, *convalescent*, growing healthy again, and *obsolescent*, growing or becoming obsolete.) The noun is *senescence* (sə-NES′-əns).

(3) *senior* (SEEN′-yər)—older. Noun：*seniority* (seen-YAWR′-ə-tee).

(4) *senate* (SEN′-ət)—originally a council of older, and presumably wiser, citizens.

在拉丁语中,senex 表示老,由此衍生出来的单词有 senile,senescent,senior 和 senate。

(1) senile——因为非常老,所以在体力和精神方面出现衰退迹象。名词形式是 senility。

(2) senescent——老化,变老。(注意相同后缀的词,adolescent,正在变成一个成年人;convalescent,正在恢复健康;obsolescent,正在被抛弃。)其名词形式为 senescence。

(3) senior——年长。名词形式为 seniority。

(4) senate——原本的意思是年长者委员会,成员被认为更睿智。

REVIEW OF ETYMOLOGY
复习词源

PREFIX, ROOT, SUFFIX	MEANING	ENGLISH WORD
1. *graphein*	to write	_____
2. *cheir* (*chiro-*)	hand	_____
3. *kallos*	beauty	_____
4. *-er*	one who	_____
5. *-ic*	adjective suffix	_____
6. *pyge*	buttocks	_____
7. *kakos*	bad, harsh	_____
8. *kardia*	heart	_____
9. *photos*	light	_____
10. *tele-*	distance	_____
11. *bios*	life	_____
12. *geras*	old age	_____
13. *geron*	old man	_____
14. *senex*	old	_____
15. *-escent*	growing, becoming	_____

USING THE WORDS
单词应用

Can you pronounce the words?
你能读出这些单词吗?

1. *graphology*   grə-FOL′-ə-jee

2. *graphological*   graf′-ə-LOJ′-ə-kəl

3. *calligraphy*   kə-LIG′-rə-fee

4. *calligrapher*   kə-LIG′-rə-fər

5. *calligraphic*   kal′-ə-GRAF′-ik

6. *callipygian*   kal′-ə-PIJ′-ee-ən

7. *cacography*   kə-KOG′-rə-fee

8. *cacographer*   kə-KOG′-rə-fər

9. *cacographic*   kak′-ə-GRAF′-ik

10. *gerontology*   jair′-ən-TOL′-ə-jee

11. *gerontological*   jair′-ən-tə-LOJ′-ə-kəl

12. *senile*   SEE'-nīl
13. *senility*   sə-NIL'-ə-tee
14. *senescent*   sə-NES'-ənt
15. *senescence*   sə-NES'-əns

Can you work with the words?
你能灵活使用这些词汇了吗?

1. graphology
2. calligraphy

3. callipygian
4. cacography
5. gerontology
6. senility
7. senescence

a. possessed of beautiful buttocks
b. science of the social, economic, etc. problems of the aged
c. condition of aging or growing old
d. deteriorated old age
e. analysis of handwriting
f. ugly, bad, illegible handwriting
g. beautiful handwriting; handwriting as an artistic expression

KEY: 1-e, 2-g, 3-a, 4-f, 5-b, 6-d, 7-c

Do you understand the words?
你对这些词汇是否已经透彻地理解?

1. *Graphology* analyzes the grammar, spelling, and sentence structure of written material.   TRUE   FALSE
2. A *calligrapher* creates artistic forms out of alphabetical symbols.   TRUE   FALSE
3. Tight slacks are best worn by those of *callipygian* anatomy.   TRUE   FALSE
4. *Cacographic* writing is easy to read.   TRUE   FALSE
5. *Gerontology* aims to help old people live more comfortably.   TRUE   FALSE
6. *Senile* people are old but still vigorous and mentally alert.   TRUE   FALSE
7. In a society dedicated to the worship of youth, *senescence* is not an attractive prospect.   TRUE   FALSE

KEY: 1-F, 2-T, 3-T, 4-F, 5-T, 6-F, 7-T

Can you recall the words?

你能够写出这些词汇吗？

1. pertaining to the study of the non-medical problems of the aged (*adj.*)	1. G _____
2. growing old (*adj.*)	2. S _____
3. pertaining to handwriting as an artistic expression (*adj.*)	3. C _____
4. one who uses ugly, illegible handwriting	4. C _____
5. mentally and physically deteriorated from old age	5. S _____
6. pertaining to the analysis of handwriting (*adj.*)	6. G _____
7. possessed of beautiful or shapely buttocks	7. C _____

KEY：1-gerontological，2-senescent，3-calligraphic，4-cacographer，5-senile，6-graphological，7-callipygian

CHAPTER REVIEW

章节复习

A. Do you recognize the words?

你认识这些单词吗？

1. Practitioner trained in Freudian techniques：(a) psychologist，(b) psychoanalyst，(c) psychotherapist

2. Foot doctor：(a) podiatrist，(b) osteopath，(c) chiropractor

3. Handwriting analyst：(a) graphologist，(b) chirographer，(c)cacographer

4. Mentally or emotionally disturbed：(a) psychological，(b) psychopathic，(c) psychic

5. Originating in the emotions：(a) psychic，(b) psychogenic，(c) psychoanalytic

6. Describing bodily ailments tied up with the emotions：(a)psychosomatic，(b) psychopathic，(c) psychiatric

7. Gum specialist：(a)periodontist，(b) pedodontist，(c) endodontist

8. Specialist in tooth extraction：(a) orthodontist，(b) exodontist，(c) endodontist

9. Blood-pressure apparatus：(a) barometer，(b) thermometer，(c) sphygmomanometer

10. Prediction by palm reading：(a) chirography，(b) chiropody，(c) chiromancy

11. Possessed of a shapely posterior：(a) calligraphic，(b) callipygian，(c) adolescent

12. Artistic handwriting：(a) calligraphy，(b) chirography，(c)graphology

13. Growing old：(a) senile，(b) geriatric，(c) senescent

14. Medical specialty dealing with the aged：(a) gerontology，(b) geriatrics，(c) chiropractic

15. Antisocial person who may commit criminal acts：(a) psychopath，(b) sociopath，(c) osteopath

---

KEY：1-b，2-a，3-a，4-b，5-b，6-a，7-a，8-b，9-c，10-c，11-b，12-a，13-c，14-b，15-a and b

---

B. Can you recognize roots?

你能认出这些词根吗？

ROOT	MEANING	EXAMPLE
1. *psyche*	_____	psychiatry
2. *iatreia*	_____	podiatry
3. *soma*	_____	psychosomatic
4. *pathos*	_____	osteopath
5. *orthos*	_____	orthodontia
6. *paidos* (*ped-*)	_____	pedodontist
7. *odontos*	_____	exodontist
8. *pous*, *podos*	_____	platypus
9. *cheir* (*chiro-*)	_____	chiropodist
10. *okto*	_____	octopus
11. *graphein*	_____	graphology
12. *kallos*	_____	calligraphy
13. *pyge*	_____	callipygian
14. *kakos*	_____	cacography
15. *photos*	_____	photography
16. *tele-*	_____	telegraph
17. *bios*	_____	biography
18. *geras*	_____	geriatrics
19. *geron*	_____	gerontology
20. *senex*	_____	senate

KEY：1-mind，2-medical healing，3-body，4 disease，5-straight，correct，6-child，7-tooth，8-foot，9-hand，10-eight，11-to write，12-beauty，13-buttocks，14-bad，ugly，15-light，16-distance，17-life，18-old age，19-old man，20-old

TEASER QUESTIONS FOR THE AMATEUR ETYMOLOGIST
词源小测验

1. Latin *octoginta* is a root related to Greek *okto*, eight. How old is an *octogenarian* (ok′-tə-jə-NAIR′-ee-ən)? _____.

2. You are familiar with *kakos*, bad, harsh, as in *cacography*, and with *phone*, sound, as in *phonograph*. Can you construct a word ending in the letter *y* that means *harsh*, *unpleasant sound*?

_____. (Can you pronounce it?)

3. Using *callipygian* as a model, can you construct a word to describe an ugly, unshapely rear end? _____

_____. (Can you pronounce it?)

4. Using the prefix *tele-*, distance, can you think of the word for a field glass that permits the viewer to see great distances? _____. How about a word for the instrument that transmits sound over a distance? _____. Finally, what is it that makes it possible for you to view happenings that occur a great distance away? _____.

(Answers in Chapter 18)

（答案见第18章）

BECOMING WORD-CONSCIOUS
你对词汇的敏感度加强了

Perhaps, if you have been working as assiduously with this book as I have repeatedly counseled, you have noticed an interesting phenomenon.

This phenomenon is as follows: You read a magazine article and suddenly you see one or more of the words you have recently learned. Or you open a book and there again are some of the words you have been working with. In short, all your reading seems to call to your attention the very words you've been studying.

Why? Have I, with uncanny foresight, picked words which have suddenly and inexplicably become popular among writers? Obviously, that's nonsense.

如果你依照我的建议孜孜不倦地阅读这本书,你一定已经注意到一个有趣的现象。

当你阅读期刊文章时,你突然发现文章里面竟然出现了刚刚学过的词汇;而当你打开一本书,你再次发现了本书中学习的词汇。简而言之,无论你阅读哪些材料,你总会注意到刚刚学过的词汇。

原因何在? 是因为我深谋远虑,挑选的词汇都突然间成为了作家笔下最常用的词汇? 很明显,这个解释没有道理。

The change is in you. You have now begun to be alert to words, you have developed what is known in psychology as a "mind-set" toward certain words. Therefore, whenever these words occur in your reading you take special notice of them.

The same words occurred before—and just as plentifully—but since they presented little communication to you, you reacted to them with an unseeing eye, with an ungrasping mind. You were figuratively, and almost literally, blind to them.

Do you remember when you bought, or contemplated buying, a new car? Let's say it was a Toyota. Suddenly you began to see Toyotas all around you—you had a Toyota "mind-set."

It is thus with anything new in your life. Development of a "mind-set" means that the new experience has become very real, very important, almost vital.

If you have become suddenly alert to the new words you have been learning, you're well along toward your goal of building a superior vocabulary. *You are beginning to live in a new and different intellectual atmosphere—nothing less*!

On the other hand, if the phenomenon I have been describing has not yet occurred, do not despair. It will. I am alerting you to its possibilities—recognize it and welcome it when it happens.

(End of Session 10)

变化在于你！现在,你对词汇的敏感度加强了,这种变化在心理学领域被称为"思维定式"。这样,无论学过的词汇出现在哪里,你总会特别关注它们。

这些单词在你过去的阅读当中也出现过——数量也同样多——但是因为过去你并未对它们有充分的理解,所以,你对它们视而不见,想而不思。委婉说来,你并未刻意考虑这些词的含义。从比喻的意义甚至实际的意义上来说,你没有看见这些词汇。

你是否记得曾在某时你购买或者计划购买一辆新轿车？例如你想购买一台丰田车。你会突然发现生活中增添了许多丰田车——因为你具有了丰田"思维定式"。

这种"思维定式"针对你生活中的新鲜事物。发展出一种"思维定式",便意味着这种新鲜事物对于你已经变得非常真实、重要,它已经成为你的部分。

如果你突然开始对学过的单词更加警觉,你正在朝着掌握超级词汇量的目标大步迈进。你已经开始拥有一种新的、不同的思维方式——对,就是如此！

如果以上描述的情况尚未发生,不要气馁。这个时刻总会到来。我提醒你关注这个可能性——当这个时刻到来的时候,你要认清并欢迎它的到来。

Brief Intermission Three
简短插叙三

HOW GRAMMAR CHANGES
语法如何变化

If you think that grammar is an exact science, get ready for a shock. Grammar is a science, all right—but it is most inexact. There are no inflexible laws, no absolutely hard and fast rules, no unchanging principles. Correctness varies with the times and depends much more on geography, on social class, and on collective human caprice than on the restrictions found in textbooks.

In mathematics, which is an exact science, five and five make ten the country over—in the North, in the South, in the West; in Los Angeles and Coral Gables and New York. There are no two opinions on the matter—we are dealing, so far as we know, with a universal and indisputable fact.

如果你坚信语法是一门精确的科学,接下来的话一定会使你震惊。语法的确是一门科学,但是它并非精确——没有不变的法则,没有绝对、彻底的规定,没有恒定的原则。语法的正确性随时代而变,更多取决于地理、社会等级和大众用法等因素,而非教科书上常见的限定。

数学则是一门精确的科学。无论在美国北部、南部还是西部,无论在洛杉矶、珊瑚墙还是纽约,5 加 5 都等于 10。这个问题没有第二个答案——据我们所知,这是一个普遍的、不容置辩的事实。

In grammar, however, since the facts are highly susceptible to change, we have to keep an eye peeled for trends. What are educated people saying these days? Which expressions are generally used and accepted on educated levels, which others are more or less restricted to the less educated levels of speech? The answers to these questions indicate the trend of usage in the United States, and if such trends come in conflict with academic rules, then the rules are no longer of any great importance.

Grammar follows the speech habits of the majority of educated people—not the other way around. That is the important point to keep in mind.

The following notes on current trends in modern usage are intended to help you come to a decision about certain controversial expressions. As you read each sentence, pay particular attention to the italicized word or words. Does the usage square with your own language patterns? Would you be willing to phrase your thoughts in just such terms? Decide whether the sentence is right or wrong, then compare your conclusion with the opinions given following the test.

然而,语法时刻在变化,我们必须时刻关注新的趋势。受教育人们的言语有哪些特点? 哪些表达方式在受过教育的群体中是被普遍使用并接受的? 哪些更局限于教育程度较低的群体中使用? 这些问题的答案表明了美国语言用法的趋势。如果这些趋势与学术规则相矛盾,那么规则就不再重要。

语法以大多数受教育人士的语言习惯为依据——而非相反。这是我们必须谨记的一点。

以下对当代用语目前趋势的说明旨在帮助你判断某些有争议的表达。阅读句子时,尤其注意斜体单词。这些用法是否与你自己的语言模式相同? 你是否愿意用这些说法来表达你的思想? 判断以下句子对错,将你的观点与测验之后的总结相比较。

TEST YOURSELF
自我测试

1. Let's keep this between you and *I*.	RIGHT	WRONG
2. I'm your best friend, *ain't* I?	RIGHT	WRONG
3. Five and five *is* ten.	RIGHT	WRONG
4. I never saw a man get so *mad*.	RIGHT	WRONG
5. Every one of his sisters *are* unmarried.	RIGHT	WRONG
6. He visited an *optometrist* for an eye operation.	RIGHT	WRONG
7. Do you *prophecy* another world war?	RIGHT	WRONG
8. *Leave* us not mention it.	RIGHT	WRONG
9. If you expect to *eventually succeed*, you must keep trying.	RIGHT	WRONG

1. Let's keep this between you and *I*.
   让它成为你和我之间的秘密。

WRONG. Children are so frequently corrected by parents and teachers when they say *me* that they cannot be blamed if they begin to think that this simple syllable is probably a naughty word. Dialogues such as the following are certainly typical of many households.

错误。当儿童使用 me 时,他们总是被父母或者老师纠正。事实上,他们不应该被如此责备,因为过度责备会使孩子们认为 me 这个简单的音节非常淘气。以下对话是许多家庭的家常便饭。

"Mother, can me and Johnnie go out and play?"

"No, dear, not until you say it correctly. You mean 'May Johnnie and I go out to play?'"

"Who wants a jelly apple?"

"Me!"

"Then use the proper word."

(The child becomes a little confused at this point—there seem to be so many "proper" and "improper" words.)

(这时孩子很困惑——他们听到太多"恰当"和"不恰当"的字眼。)

"Me, *please*!"

"No, dear, not *me*."

"Oh. *I*, please?"

(This sounds terrible to a child's ear. It completely violates his sense of language, but he does want the jelly apple, so he grudgingly conforms.)

(对于孩子来说,这样的话糟糕极了。这完全破坏了他的语言感,但是孩子太想吃果冻苹果,所以他还是很不情愿地改正。)

"Who broke my best vase?"

"It wasn't me!"

"Is that good English, Johnnie?"

"Okay, it wasn't I. But honest, Mom, it wasn't me—I didn't even touch it!"

And so, if the child is strong enough to survive such constant corrections, he decides that whenever there is room for doubt, it is safer to say *I*.

Some adults, conditioned in childhood by the kind of misguided censorship detailed here, are likely to believe that "between you and *I*" is the more elegant form of expression, but most educated speakers, obeying the rule that a preposition governs the objective pronoun, say "between you and *me*."

所以,即使孩子足够坚强,能够面对无休止的纠正,在日后的使用中,一旦有不确定情况,他就会认为使用 I 更安全。

儿时被错误引导的成年人会认为 between you and I 是更高雅的表达形式,但是大多数受教育的人士遵从介词后要接代词宾格,使用 between you and me。

2. I'm your best friend, *ain't* I?

　　我是你最好的朋友,不是吗?

WRONG. As linguistic scholars have frequently pointed out, it is unfortunate that *ain't I*? is unpopular in educated speech, for the phrase fills a long-felt need. *Am I not*? is too prissy for down-to-earth people; *amn't I*? is ridiculous; and *aren't I*, though popular in England, has never really caught on in America. With a sentence like the one under discussion you are practically in a linguistic trap—there is no way out unless you are willing to choose between appearing illiterate, sounding prissy, or feeling ridiculous.

错误。语言学者已经多次指出,很不幸,ain't I 不是受教育人士的常用语。Am I not? 对于务实的人来说太过讲究;amn't I 的形式又太荒谬;aren't I 在英国虽然是惯用法,但是在美国从未流行。使用这个句子实际上是掉入了语言的陷阱——你无路可逃,只能在文盲的用法、刻板的用法或荒谬的用法中做一选择。

"What is the matter with *ain't I*? for *am I not*?" language scholar Wallace Rice once wrote. "Nothing whatever, save that a number of minor grammarians object to it. *Ain't I*? has a pleasant sound once the ears are unstopped of prejudice." Mr. Rice has a valid point there, yet educated people avoid *ain't I*? as if it were catching. In all honesty, therefore, I must say to you: don't use *ain't I*? except humorously. What is a safe substitute? Apparently none exists, so I suggest that you manage, by some linguistic calisthenics, to avoid having to make a choice. Otherwise you may find yourself in the position of being damned if you do and damned if you don't.

语言学者华莱士·赖斯曾经写道:"用 ain't I 代替 am I not 有何不可? 事实上并没有任何理由,只是一些不知名的文法家反对这个用法。如果你的耳朵经受得住偏见的言语,ain't I 也是很悦耳的声音。"赖斯先生的观点很有道理,但是受教育人士避免使用 ain't I,视其为传染病。所以,我不得不告诉你:不要使用 ain't I,除非刻意的幽默。你一定想问,是否有安全的替代品？很明显,没有。所以我建议你设法用一些语言技巧,尽可能避免使用 ain't I。否则,你会处于进退两难的境遇。

3. Five and five *is* ten.

5 加 5 等于 10。

RIGHT. But don't jump to the conclusion that "five and five *are* ten" is wrong—both verbs are equally acceptable in this or any similar construction. If you prefer to think of "five-and-five" as a single mathematical concept, say *is*. If you find it more reasonable to consider "five and five" a plural idea, say *are*. The teachers I've polled on this point are about evenly divided in preference, and so, I imagine, are the rest of us. Use whichever verb has the greater appeal to your sense of logic.

正确。但是不要得出结论,认为"Five and five are ten"错误。在这个以及其他相似的结构中,两个动词都正确。如果你认为"5 加 5"是一个独立的数学概念,使用 is。如果你发现更有理由认为"5 加 5"是复数概念,使用 are。我所调查的老师在这两个使用偏好上人数持平。我相信,我们也是如此。所以,你可以随意用任何一个,只要它对你的逻辑感更有吸引力。

4. I never saw a man get so *mad*.

我从没见过一个人变得如此生气。

RIGHT. When I questioned a number of authors and editors about their opinion of the acceptability of *mad* as a synonym for *angry*, the typical reaction was:"Yes, I say *mad*, but I always feel a little guilty when I do."

Most people do say *mad* when they are sure there is no English teacher listening; it's a good sharp word, everybody understands exactly what it means, and it's a lot stronger than *angry*, though not quite as violent as *furious* or *enraged*. In short, *mad* has a special implication offered by no other word in the English language; as a consequence, educated people use it as the occasion demands and it is perfectly correct. So correct, in fact, that every authoritative dictionary lists it as a completely acceptable usage. If you feel guilty when you say *mad*, even though you don't mean *insane*, it's time you stopped plaguing your conscience with trivialities.

正确。我曾经询问过一些作家和编辑,是否能够接受 mad 作为 angry 的同义词。大多数人的回答是:"是的,我会使用 mad,但是每次使用之后,我都会有种内疚感。"

如果确定没有英语老师在身边,大多数人会使用 mad。这是一个敏锐的词语,每个人都明白其中的含义:尽管 mad 没有 furious 或 enraged 激烈,其表达的情感也要比 angry 强烈。简而言之,与英语语言中其他单词相比,mad 具有一种特殊的含义。这样,如果情景需要,受教育的人士就会使用 mad,这个用法也是完全正确的。事实上,这个用法从未被质疑,以至于每本权威词典中都能找到这个词条。所以,如果你仍然为使用 mad 而感到内疚,虽然你明白 mad 并非指 insane,你也应该不再用这样琐碎的想法折磨自己的精神了。

5. Every one of his sisters *are* unmarried.

他的姐妹都未婚。

WRONG. *Are* is perhaps the more logical word, since the sentence implies that he has more than one sister and they are all unmarried. In educated speech, however, the tendency is to make the verb agree with the subject, even if logic is violated in the process—and the better choice here would be *is*, agreeing with the singular subject, *every one*.

错误。are 看起来更符合逻辑,因为句子暗示出他不止一个姐妹,而且姐妹都未婚。但是,受教育人士倾向于使动词与主语保持一致,即使违反了逻辑——所以,这里最佳选择是 is,与单数主语 every one 保持一致。

6. He visited an *optometrist* for an eye operation.

他去找验光师做眼部手术。

WRONG. If the gentleman in question did indeed need an operation, he went to the wrong doctor. In most states, optometrists are forbidden by law to perform surgery or administer drugs—they may only prescribe and fit glasses. And they are not medical doctors. The M. D. who specializes in the treatment of eye diseases, and who may operate when necessary, is an *ophthalmologist*. (See Chapter 4.)

错误。如果这个患有眼疾的绅士的确需要手术治疗,他找错了人。大多数州禁止验光师进行手术或者开处方药——他们只能为病人测量视力、配置眼镜。验光师不是医生。专业治疗眼疾、在有必要的情况下为患者手术的医学硕士被称为 ophthalmologist(参考第 4 章)。

7. Do you *prophecy* another world war?

你会预言另一次世界大战吗?

WRONG. Use *prophecy* only when you mean *prediction*, a noun. When you mean *predict*, a verb, as in this sentence, use *prophesy*. This distinction is simple and foolproof. Therefore we properly say:"His *prophecy* (*prediction*) turned out to be true," but "He really seems able to *prophesy* (*predict*) political trends." There is a distinction also in the pronunciation of these two words. *Prophecy* is pronounced PROF′-ə-see; *prophesy* is pronunced PROF′-ə-sī′.

错误。如果指 prediction(名词),你才能使用 prophecy——本句中指 predict(动词),只能使用 prophesy。区别简单、万无一失。因此,正确的说法是:"His prophecy (prediction) turned out to be true." "He really seems able to prophesy (predict) political trends."两个单词的读音也有所不同。prophecy 读音为 PROF′-ə-see;prophesy 读音为 PROF′-ə-si′。

8. *Leave* us not mention it.

我们不要再提它了。

WRONG. On the less sophisticated levels of American speech, *leave* is a popular substitute for *let*. On educated levels, the following distinction is carefully observed: *let* means *allow*; *leave* means *depart*. (There are a few idiomatic exceptions to this rule, but they present no problem.) "*Let* me go" is preferable to "*Leave* me go" even on the most informal of occasions, and a sentence like "*Leave* us not mention it" is not considered standard English.

错误。从非学术角度讲,leave 在美国口语中常用来替代 let。对于受教育人士来说,以下区别被严格遵守:Let 指 allow(允许);leave 指 depart(离开)。(少数习语除外,但这些例外并不影响规则。)即使是在最不正式的场合,"Let me go"比"Leave me go"更适用;而"Leave us not mention it"这样的表达被视为不规范。

9. If you expect to *eventually succeed*, you must keep trying.

如果你希望最后能成功,你必须不断努力。

RIGHT. We have here, in case you're puzzled, an example of that notorious bugbear of academic grammar, the "split infinitive."(An infinitive is a verb preceded by *to*: *to succeed*, *to fail*, *to remember*.)

Splitting an infinitive is not at all difficult—you need only insert a word between the *to* and the verb：to *eventually succeed*，to *completely fail*，to *quickly remember*.

　　正确。为了避免困惑,我们在这里简单介绍学术语法中臭名昭著的怪胎——不定式分裂。(不定式是由 to 和动词组成的形式,如：to succeed，to fail，to remember。)

　　将不定式分裂也绝非难事——只需要在 to 和动词之间插入另外一个词：to eventually succeed，to completely fail，to quickly remember。

Now that you know how to split an infinitive, the important question is, is it legal to do so? I am happy to be able to report to you that it is not only legal, it is also ethical, moral, and sometimes more effective than to not split it. Benjamin Franklin, Washington Irving, Nathaniel Hawthorne, Theodore Roosevelt, and Woodrow Wilson, among many others, were unconscionable infinitive splitters. And modern writers are equally partial to the construction.

　　现在你已经了解如何分裂不定式。但是问题是,这样做是否正确? 我要很开心地向你汇报,分裂不定式不仅正确,而且符合"伦理"和"道德",有时甚至比不分裂更耐用。本杰明·富兰克林,华盛顿·欧文,纳撒尼尔·霍桑,西奥多·罗斯福,伍德罗·威尔逊,及其他许多人都"肆无忌惮"地使用分裂不定式。此外,当代作家也同样钟情于此结构。

To bring this report up to the minute, I asked a number of editors about their attitude toward the split infinitive. Here are two typical reactions.

An editor at Doubleday and Company："The restriction against the split infinitive is, to my mind, the most artificial of all grammatical rules. I find that most educated people split infinitives regularly in their speech, and only eliminate them from their writing when they rewrite and polish their material."

　　为了得到入时的答案,我询问了许多编辑,以求他们对于分裂不定式的看法。以下是两种典型回答。

　　道布尔戴出版公司的编辑说道:"我认为,对分裂不定式的限制是所有语法规则中最做作的。大多数受教育人士在言语中经常使用分裂不定式,而只有在修改作品、润色语言时,才会删除它们。"

An editor at *Reader's Digest*："I want to defend the split infinitive. The construction adds to the strength of the sentence—it's compact and clear. This is to loudly say that I split an infinitive whenever I can catch one."

And here, finally, is the opinion of humorist James Thurber, as quoted by Rudolf Flesch in *The Art of Plain Talk*："Word has somehow got around that the split infinitive is always wrong. This is of a piece with the outworn notion that it is always wrong to strike a lady."

I think the evidence is conclusive enough—it is perfectly correct to consciously split an infinitive whenever such an act increases the strength or clarity of your sentence.

　　《读者文摘》的编辑说道:"我想为分裂不定式做辩护。这个结构为句子增添了力量——它简洁、明了。只要有机会,我就会将不定式分裂。"

　　最后是幽默作家詹姆斯·瑟伯的观点:"总有人认为分裂不定式是错误的。这就好像一种过时的观点,认为打女人是不对的。鲁道夫·弗莱奇在《说话艺术》中引用了这段话。"

　　我认为证据已经足够令人信服——无论何时,如果分裂不定式能够增强句子的力量和清晰度,它就是完全正确的。

6

HOW TO TALK ABOUT SCIENCE AND SCIENTISTS
如何描述各门科学及科学家

(*Sessions 11—13*)

TEASER PREVIEW
引读

What scientist：

* *is interested in the development of the human race?*
* *is a student of the heavens?*
* *explores the physical qualities of the earth?*
* *studies all living matter?*
* *is a student of plant life?*
* *is a student of animal life?*
* *is professionally involved in insects?*
* *is a student of language?*
* *is a student of the psychological effects of words?*
* *studies the culture, structure, and customs of different societies?*

哪些科学家：
* 对人类发展感兴趣
* 研究天体
* 探索地球的物理特性
* 研究生物
* 研究植物
* 研究动物
* 专业研究昆虫
* 研究语言
* 研究语言的心理作用
* 研究不同社会的文化、结构和风俗

SESSION 11
第 11 节

A true scientist lives up to the etymological meaning of his title "one who knows." Anything scientific is based on facts—observable facts that can be recorded, tested, checked, and verified.

Science, then, deals with human knowledge—as far as it has gone. It has gone very far indeed since the last century or two, when we stopped basing our thinking on guesses, wishes, theories that had no foundation in reality, and concepts of how the world *ought* to be; and instead began to explore the world as it *was*, and not only the world but the whole universe. From Galileo, who looked through the first telescope atop a tower in Pisa, Italy, through Pasteur, who watched microbes through a microscope, to Einstein, who deciphered riddles of the universe by means of mathematics, we have at last begun to fill in a few areas of ignorance.

Who are some of the more important explorers of knowledge—and by what terms are they known?

一位真正的科学家无愧于其头衔的词源含义——"知道的人"。任何科学都基于事实——基于可观察的、能够记录、测试、检验和证明的事实。

那么,科学则是涉及人类知识——人类迄今掌握的知识。在过去的一二百年,科学的确已经取得了巨大的进步:我们不再将将思考建立在猜测、愿望或一些在现实世界没有基础的理论之上,也不将其建立在认为世界应该怎样的观念之上;取而代之的是对现实世界的探索,而且延伸到对整个宇宙的探索。从伽利略在意大利比萨斜塔顶用望远镜观察月球,到巴斯德用显微镜观察微生物,再到爱因斯坦用数学解开宇宙谜团,人类终于开始填补认知的空白。

哪些人是更重要的知识探索者? 他们又是被如何称呼的?

IDEAS
概念

1. Whither mankind?
   人类何处去?

The field is all mankind—how we developed in mind and body from primitive cultures and early forms.

An *anthropologist*

他的研究全部与人类相关——在精神和身体两个方面,人类是如何从原始文化和早期形式发展至今的?
这是一位 anthropologist(人类学家)。

2. What's above?
   上面的世界是怎样的?

The field is the heavens and all that's in them—planets, galaxies, stars, and other universes.

An *astronomer*

他的领域是天体以及与天体有关的一切——星球、银河系、恒星和其他星系。
他是一位 astronomer(天文学家)。

3. And what's below?

下面的世界又是怎样的?

The field is the comparatively little and insignificant whirling ball on which we live—the earth. How did our planet come into being, what is it made of, how were its mountains, oceans, rivers, plains, and valleys formed, and what's down deep if you start digging?

A geologist

他的专业领域研究我们所生活的这个相对来说体积和重要性都较小的转动着的星球——地球。他研究地球的形成过程、组成部分,研究高山、海洋、河流、平原和峡谷的形成原因,研究地下最深处。

他是一位 geologist(地质学家)。

4. What is life?

什么是生命?

The field is all living organisms—from the simplest one-celled amoeba to the a-mazingly complex and mystifying structure we call a human being. Plant or animal, flesh or vegetable, denizen of water, earth, or air—if it lives and grows, this scien-tist wants to know more about it.

A biologist

他研究所有有机体——从最简单的单细胞变形虫到最复杂、最神秘的结构——人类。植物或动物、肉类或蔬菜,水里、地上或空气中的生物——只要有机体存在、生长,他就想对其有更多的了解。

他是一位 biologist(生物学家)。

5. flora

植物

Biology classifies life into two great divisions—plant and animal. This scientist's prov-ince is the former category—flowers, trees, shrubs, mosses, marine vegetation, blossoms, fruits, seeds, grasses, and all the rest that make up the plant kingdom.

A botanist

生物学将生命一分为二——植物和动物。这位科学家的职责是研究前者——花、树、灌木、苔藓、水生植物、花朵、水果、种子、草以及所有组成植物王国的其他生物。

他是一位 botanist(植物学家)。

6. and fauna

动物

Animals of every description, kind, and condition, from birds to bees, fish to fowl, reptiles to humans, are the special area of exploration of this scientist.

A zoologist

各种类型、种类和条件下的动物,无论是鸟或蜜蜂,鱼或家禽,爬行类或人类,都是这位科学家独特的探索领域。

他是一位 zoologist(动物学家)。

7. and all the little bugs

所有小昆虫

There are over 650,000 different species of insects, and millions of individuals of every species—and this scientist is interested in every one of them.

An entomologist

地球上有 65 万种昆虫之多,而每种昆虫有成千上万的个体——他对其中任何一只都兴趣十足。

他是一位 entomologist(昆虫学家)。

8. tower of Babel
巴别塔

This linguistic scientist explores the subtle, intangible, elusive uses of that unique tool that distinguishes human beings from all other forms of life—to wit: language. This person is, in short, a student of linguistics, ancient and modern, primitive and cultured, Chinese, Hebrew, Icelandic, Slavic, Teutonic, and every other kind spoken now or in the past by human beings, not excluding that delightful hodgepodge known as "pidgin English," in which a piano is described as "big box, you hit 'um in teeth, he cry," and in which Hamlet's famous quandary, "To be or not to be, that is the question...," is translated into "Can do, no can do—how fashion?"

A philologist

这位语言科学家探索一种独一无二的工具的微妙、空灵和难以捉摸的用法,这种工具将人类和其他所有生命形式区分开来——语言。简而言之,这个人研究语言:古代语言或现代语言、原始语言或文明语言;他研究汉语、希伯来语、冰岛语、斯拉夫语、日耳曼语或者任何其他在现代或者过去人类使用或者曾经使用过的语言,包括令人愉悦的大杂烩——洋泾浜。在洋泾浜英语中,钢琴被描述为一个"大盒子,你打击他的牙,他会叫喊",而哈姆雷特最为人知的困惑:"生存还是毁灭,这是个问题……"被翻译成:"能做,不能做——该怎么做?"

他是一位 philologist(语文学家)。

9. What do you really mean?
你到底是什么意思?

This linguistic scientist explored the subtle, intangible, elusive relationship between language and thinking, between meaning and words; and is interested in determining the psychological causes and effects of what people say and write.

A semanticist

这位语言科学家研究语言与思维、意义与词汇之间微妙、空灵和捉摸不定的关系。他的兴趣是找到我们所使用的语言心理层面的因果关系。

他是一位 semanticist(语义学家)。

10. Who are your friends and neighbors?
谁是你的朋友和邻居?

This scientist is a student of the ways in which people live together, their family and community structures and customs, their housing, their social relationships, their forms of government, and their layers of caste and class.

A sociologist

他研究人们相处的方式、家庭和社区的结构与习俗、住房、社会关系、政府形式和不同的阶层和等级。

他是一位 sociologist(社会学家)。

USING THE WORDS
单词应用

Can you pronounce the words?
你能读出这些单词吗？

1.	*anthropologist*	an'-thrə-POL'-ə-jist
2.	*astronomer*	ə-STRON'-ə-mər
3.	*geologist*	jee-OL'-ə-jist
4.	*biologist*	bī-OL'-ə-jist
5.	*botanist*	BOT'-ə-nist
6.	*zoologist*	zō-OL'-ə-jist
7.	*entomologist*	en'-tə-MOL'-ə-jist
8.	*philologist*	fə-LOL'-ə-jist
9.	*semanticist*	sə-MAN'-tə-sist
10.	*sociologist*	sō-shee-OL'-ə-jist *or* sō'-see-OL'-ə-jist

Can you work with the words?
你能灵活使用这些词汇了吗？

SCIENTIST	PROFESSIONAL FIELD
1. anthropologist	a. community and family life
2. astronomer	b. meanings and psychological effects of words
3. geologist	c. development of the human race
4. biologist	d. celestial phenomena
5. botanist	e. language
6. zoologist	f. insect forms
7. entomologist	g. the earth
8. philologist	h. all forms of living matter
9. semanticist	i. animal life
10. sociologist	j. plant life

KEY: 1-c, 2-d, 3-g, 4-h, 5-j, 6-i, 7-f, 8-e, 9-b, 10-a

Can you recall the words?
你能够写出这些词汇吗？

1.	insects	1.	E _____
2.	language	2.	P _____
3.	social conditions	3.	S _____

4. history of development of mankind
5. meanings of words
6. plants
7. the earth
8. the heavenly bodies
9. all living things
10. animals

4. A _____
5. S _____
6. B _____
7. G _____
8. A _____
9. B _____
10. Z _____

KEY：1-entomologist，2-philologist，3-sociologist，4-anthropologist，5-semanticist，6-botanist，7-geologist，8-astronomer，9-biologist，10-zoologist

(End of Session 11)

SESSION 12
第 12 节

ORIGINS AND RELATED WORDS
词源及相关词汇

1. people and the stars
   人与星体

Anthropologist is constructed from roots we are familiar with—*anthropos*, mankind, and *logos*, science, study.

The science is *anthropology* (an′-thrə-POL′-ə-jee). Can you write the adjective form of this word? _____. (Can you pronounce it?)

> anthropologist 包括我们之前学到的词根：希腊语 anthropos(人)，和 logos(科学、学习)。
> 这门科学被称为 anthropology，你能写出它的形容词形式吗？(你会发音吗？)

Astronomer is built on Greek *astron*, star, and *nomos*, arrangement, law, or order. The *astronomer* is interested in the arrangement of stars and other celestial bodies. The science is *astronomy* (ə-STRON′-ə-mee), the adjective is *astronomical* (as′-trə-NOM′-ə-kəl), a word often used in a non-heavenly sense, as in "the *astronomical* size of the national debt." *Astronomy* deals in such enormous distances (the sun, for example, is 93,000,000 miles from the earth, and light from stars travels toward the earth at 186,000 miles per *second*) that the adjective *astronomical* is applied to any tremendously large figure.

> astronomer，天文学家，由希腊语 astron 和 nomos 组成：astron 意为"星体"；nomos 意为"排列、法则或规则"。天文学家对天体的排列和其他天体感兴趣。他的专业是 astronomy，天文学，形容词形式是 astronomical。astronomical 也经常出现在与天体意义不相关的表达中，例如 the astronomical size of the national debt，天文数字的国债。astronomy 研究遥远的距离(例如，太阳距离地球 9,300 万英里；星体发出的光以每秒 186,000 英里的速度靠近地球)；形容词 astronomical 则被用来表示巨大的数字。

Astron, star, combines with *logos* to form *astrology* (ə-STROL′-ə-jee), which assesses the influence of planets and stars on human events. The practitioner is an *astrologer* (ə-STROL′-ə-jər). Can you form the adjective? _____. (Can you pronounce it?)

By etymology, an *astronaut* (AS′-tro-not′) is a sailor among the stars (Greek *nautes*, sailor). This person is termed with some what less exaggeration a *cosmonaut* (KOZ′-mə-not′) by the Russians (Greek, *kosmos*, universe). *Nautical* (NOT′-ə-kəl), relating to sailors, sailing, ships, or navigation, derives also from *nautes*, and *nautes* in turn is from Greek *naus*, ship—a root used in *nausea* (etymologically, ship-sickness or seasickness!).

Aster (AS′-tər) is a star shaped flower. *Asterisk* (AS′-tə-risk), a star-shaped symbol (＊), is generally used in writing or printing to direct the reader to look for a footnote. *Astrophysics* (as′-trə- FIZ′-iks) is that branch of physics dealing with heavenly bodies.

词根 astron 与 logos 相结合,形成 astrology,"占星术"。占星术考查行星和恒星对人类事件的影响。这个理论的从业者叫作 astrologer,"占星家"。你能写出形容词形式吗?(你会发音吗?)

从词源学角度看,一个"astronaut"就是星际间的水手(希腊语 nautes,意即"水手"),这种人在俄语中被称为 cosmonaut,较少有夸张意味(希腊语 kosmos,意为"宇宙")。nautical 和水手、航行、船、航海有关,也是由 nautes 演变而来,而 nautes 则源于希腊语中的 naus,意为"船"——nausea 就有这个词根(意为"晕船")。

aster 指一种星状花朵;asterisk 是一种星状标记(＊),常见于写作和印刷品中,旨在告诉读者阅读脚注;astrophysics,天体物理学,是物理学分支,研究天体的物理组成。

Disaster (də-ZAS′-tər) and *disastrous* (də-ZAS′-trəs) also come from *astron*, star. In ancient times it was believed that the stars ruled human destiny; any misfortune or calamity, therefore, happened to someone because the stars were in opposition. (*Dis-*, a prefix of many meanings, in this word signifies *against*.)

disaster 和 disastrous 也源于 astron,星体。在古代,人类相信星体统治人们的命运;因此,任何不幸或灾难的发生都预示着有与其相悖的星体。(Dis-有多种意义的前缀,在此单词中意为"反对"。)

Nomos, arrangement, law, or order, is found in two other interesting English words. For example, if you can make your own laws for yourself, if you needn't answer to anyone else for what you do, in short, if you are independent, then you enjoy *autonomy* (aw-TON′-ə-mee), a word that combines *nomos*, law, with *autos*, self. *Autonomy*, then, is self-law, self-government. The fifty states in our nation are fairly *autonomous* (aw-TON′-ə-məs), but not completely so. On the other hand, in most colleges each separate department is pretty much *autonomous*. And of course, one of the big reasons for the revolution of 1776 was that America wanted *autonomy*, rather than control by England.

Nomos 指"排列、法则或规则",出现在另外两个有趣的英语单词中。

例如,如果你能够为自己制定法则,如果你无需按照别人的指示行事,简言之,如果你很独立,那么就可以说你享有 autonomy。autonomy 结合了 nomos(法则)和 auto(自己)。那么,autonomy 就是"自治、自主"。美国的 50 个州是相对自治但不是完全自治的。另外,大多数学院的每一个院系也相当 autonomous。当然,1776 年革命的主要原因之一是美国要求 autonomy,想摆脱英国的控制。

You know the instrument that beginners at the piano use to guide their timing? A pendulum swings back and forth, making an audible click at each swing, and in that way governs or orders the measure (or timing) of the player. Hence it is called a *metronome* (MET′-rə-nōm′), a word that combines *nomos* with *metron*, measurement.

你知道钢琴初学者用什么工具来确定每个小节的开头结尾吗?钟摆前后摆动,每次摆动会发出咔嗒声,以此来指导和控制演奏者的节奏。这样,这个工具被称为 metronome(节拍器)。metronome 结合了 nomos 和 metron(测量)。

2. the earth and its life

地球和生命

Geologist derives from Greek *ge* (*geo-*), earth. The science is *geology* (jee-OL′-ə-jee). Can you write the adjective? _____. (Can you pronounce it?)

Geometry (jee-OM′-ə-tree)—*ge* plus *metron*—by etymology "measurement of the earth," is that branch of mathematics treating of the measurement and properties of solid and plane figures, such as angles, triangles, squares, spheres, prisms, etc. (The etymology of the word shows that this ancient science was originally concerned with the measurement of land and spaces on the earth.)

The mathematician is a *geometrician* (jee′-ə-mə-TRISH′-ən), the adjective is *geometric* (jee′-ə-MET′-rik).

Geography (jee-OG′-rə-fee) is writing about (*graphein*, to write), or mapping, the earth. A practitioner of the science is a *geographer* (jee-OG′-rə-fər), the adjective is *geographic* (jee-ə-GRAF′-ik).

(The name *George* is also derived from *ge* [*geo-*], earth, plus *ergon*, work—the first George was an earth-worker or farmer.)

geologist,地质学家,专业为 geology(地质学),你能写出它的形容词形式吗?(你会发音吗?)

geometry——ge 加 metron——从词源看其本义为"对地球的度量",是一门研究立体和平面的度量及特性的数学分支。比如角、三角形、正方形、球体、棱柱体等。(从词源上可以看出,这门历史悠久的科学源于对地球上土地和空间的测量。)

专门研究这门学科的数学家称为 geometrician,形容词是 geometric.

geography 是写关于地球的文字或是地图(graphein,意为"书写"),从事这门科学的人被称为 geographer,其形容词是 geographic。

(人名 George 也是由 ge[geo-,土地],加上 ergon[工作]而来的——第一个 George 是一个与土地相关的工作者,即农民。)

Biologist combines *bios*, life, with *logos*, science, study. The science is *biology* (bī-OL′-ə-jee). The adjective? _____.

Bios, life, is also found in *biography* (bī-OG′-rə-fee), writing about someone's *life*; *autobiography* (aw′-tə-bī-OG′-rə-fee), the story of one's *life* written by *oneself*; and *biopsy* (BĪ′-op-see), a medical examination, or view (*opsis*, *optikos*, view, vision), generally through a microscope, of living tissue, frequently performed when cancer is suspected. A small part of the tissue is cut from the affected area and under the microscope its cells can be investigated for evidence of malignancy. A *biopsy* is contrasted with an *autopsy* (AW′-top-see), which is a medical examination of a corpse in order to discover the cause of death. Th *autos* in *autopsy* means, as you know, *self*—in an *autopsy*, etymologically speaking, the surgeon or pathologist determines, by actual view or sight rather than by theorizing (i. e. , "by viewing or seeing for oneself"), what brought the corpse to its present grievous state.

biologist 由 bios(生命)和 logos(科学,研究)结合而成。biologist 从事研究生物的科学。你能写出它的形容词形式吗?

bios(生命,生活)也出现在其他词汇中:biography(传记),是对某人生活的记录;autobiography(自传),是由某人自己撰写的生活记录;biopsy(活检),是指为了确定疾病而用显微镜对从"活着的"身体取下的组织进行检查。医生通常使用 biopsy 来确定患者是否患有癌症。医生从患者受感染部分切下一小块组织,然后在显微镜下观察细胞,寻找癌细胞繁殖的证据。biopsy 与 autopsy 不同,autopsy 指尸体解剖,是为了找到死因而进行的医疗检查。当然,词根 autos 在 autopsy 中指"自己"——从词源学上看,在尸检中,外科医生或病理学家通过实际观察——而不是通过理论——确定致死原因。

Botanist is from Greek *botane*, plant. The field is *botany* (BOT′-ə-nee); the adjective is *botanical* (bə-TAN′-ə-kəl).

Zoologist is from Greek *zoion*, animal. The science is *zoology*. The adjective? _____. The combination of the two *o*'s tempts many people to pronounce the first three letters of these words in one syllable, thus: *zoo*. However, the two *o*'s should be separated, as in *co-operate*, even though no hyphen is used in the spelling to indicate such separation. Say zō-OL'-ə-jist, zō-OL'-ə-jee, zō'-ə-LOJ'-ə-kəl. *Zoo*, a park for animals, is a shortened form of *zoological gardens*, and is, of course, pronounced in one syllable.

The *zodiac* (ZŌ-dee-ak) is a diagram, used in astrology, of the paths of the sum, moon, and planets; it contains, in part, Lain names for various animals—*scorpio*, scorpion; *leo*, lion; *cancer*, crab; *taurus*, bull; *aries*, ram; and *pisces*, fish. Hence its derivation from *zoion*, animal.

The adjective is *zodiacal* (zō-DĪ-ə-kəl).

botanist 基于希腊语 botane,"植物"。专业为 botany,"植物学";形容词形式为 botanical。

zoologist(动物学家),学科为 zoology(动物学),形容词形式是什么? 两个 o 的组合会引导许多人将前三个字母读为一个音节:zoo。尽管 oo 没有用连字符分开,oo 也应分开发音,与 co-operate 中的 oo 相似。所以,zoologist 的音标为 zō-OL'-jist,zoology 的音标为 zō-OL'-o-jee。zoo,"动物园",是 zoological gardens 的缩写,它的发音才是一个音节。

Zodiac(黄道带),astrology(占星学)术语,指描绘太阳、月亮和其他行星运行轨迹的图表;它部分地包含了以拉丁文的动物名称命名的星座——scorpio(天蝎座),scorpion(蝎子);leo(狮子座),lion(狮子);cancer(巨蟹座),crab(螃蟹);taurus(金牛座),bull(公牛);aries(白羊座),ram(公羊)以及 pisces(双鱼座),fish(鱼)。所以它也是从希腊语 zoion (动物)派生而来的。

形容词是 zodiacal(黄道带的)。

REVIEW OF ETYMOLOGY
复习词源

PREFIX, ROOT	MEANING	ENGLISH WORD
1. *anthropos*	mankind	_____
2. *logos*	science, study	_____
3. *astron*	star	_____
4. *nautes*	sailor	_____
5. *naus*	ship	_____
6. *dis-*	against	_____
7. *nomos*	arrangement, law, order	_____
8. *autos*	self	_____
9. *metron*	measurement	_____
10. *ge* (*geo-*)	earth	_____
11. *graphein*	to write	_____
12. *bios*	life	_____
13. *opsis*, *optikos*	view, vision, sight	_____
14. *botane*	plant	_____
15. *zoion*	animal	_____

USING THE WORDS
单词应用

Can you pronounce the words?（Ⅰ）
你能读出这些单词吗？（Ⅰ）

1. *anthropology*   an′-thrə-POL′-ə-jee
2. *anthropological*   an′-thrə-pə-LOJ′-ə-kəl
3. *astronomy*   ə-STRON′-ə-mee
4. *astronomical*   as′-trə-NOM′-ə-kəl
5. *astrology*   ə-STROL′-ə-jee
6. *astrological*   as′-trə-LOJ′-ə-kəl
7. *astronaut*   AS′-trə-not′
8. *cosmonaut*   KOZ′-mə-not′
9. *nautical*   NOT′-ə-kəl
10. *aster*   AS′-tər
11. *asterisk*   AS′-tə-risk
12. *disaster*   də-ZAS′-tər
13. *disastrous*   də-ZAS′-trəs

Can you pronounce the words?（Ⅱ）
你能读出这些单词吗？（Ⅱ）

1. *geology*   jee-OL′-ə-jee
2. *geological*   jee′-ə-LOJ′-ə-kəl
3. *geometry*   jee-OM′-ə-tree
4. *geometrician*   jee′-ə-mə-TRISH′-ən
5. *geometric*   jee-ə-MET′-rik
6. *geography*   jee-OG′-rə-fee
7. *geographer*   jee-OG′-rə-fər
8. *geographical*   jee′-ə-GRAF′-ə-kəl
9. *biology*   bī-OL′-ə-jee
10. *biological*   bī′-ə-LOJ′-ə-kəl
11. *biography*   bī-OG′-rə-fee
12. *biographer*   bī-OG′-rə-fər
13. *biographical*   bī′-ə-GRAF′-ə-kəl

Can you pronounce the words?（Ⅲ）
你能读出这些单词吗？（Ⅲ）

1.	*autonomy*	aw-TON′-ə-mee
2.	*autonomous*	aw-TON′-ə-məs
3.	*metronome*	MET′-rə-nōm′
4.	*autobiography*	aw′-tə-bī-OG′-rə-fee
5.	*autobiographer*	aw′-tə-bī-OG′-rə-fər
6.	*autobiographical*	aw-tə-bī′-ə-GRAF′-ə-kəl
7.	*biopsy*	BĪ′-op-see
8.	*autopsy*	AW′-top-see
9.	*botany*	BOT′-ə-nee
10.	*botanical*	bə-TAN′-ə-kəl
11.	*zoology*	zō-OL′-ə-jee
12.	*zoological*	zō-ə-LOJ′-ə-kəl
13.	*zodiac*	ZŌ′-dee-ak
14.	*zodiacal*	zō-DĪ′-ə-kəl

Can you work with the words?（Ⅰ）
你能灵活使用这些词汇吗？（Ⅰ）

1. anthropology	a.	theory of the influence of planets and stars on human events
2. astronomy	b.	science of earth-mapping
3. astrology	c.	science of all living matter
4. geology	d.	science of human development
5. biology	e.	science of plants
6. geometry	f.	science of the composition of the earth
7. botany	g.	science of animal life
8. zoology	h.	science of the heavens
9. geography	i.	mathematical science of figures, shapes, etc.

KEY: 1-d, 2-h, 3-a, 4-f, 5-c, 6-i, 7-e, 8-g, 9-b

Can you work with the words?（Ⅱ）
你能灵活使用这些词汇吗？（Ⅱ）

1. autopsy	a.	"sailor among the stars"
2. biopsy	b.	star-shaped flower
3. biography	c.	story of one's own life

4. autobiography   d. dissection and examination of a corpse to determine the cause of death

5. zodiac   e. great misfortune

6. astronaut   f. "sailor of the universe"

7. cosmonaut   g. story of someone's life

8. aster   h. diagram of paths of sun, moon, and planets

9. disaster   i. instrument to measure musical time

10. autonomy   j. self-rule

11. metronome   k. examination of living tissue

KEY: 1-d, 2-k, 3-g, 4-c, 5-h, 6-a, 7-f, 8-b, 9-e, 10-j, 11-i

Do you understand the words?

你对这些词汇是否已经透彻地理解？

1. Are *anthropological* studies concerned with plant life?   YES   NO
2. Are *astronomical* numbers extremely small?   YES   NO
3. Is an *astrologer* interested in the time and date of your birth?   YES   NO
4. Are *nautical* maneuvers carried on at sea?   YES   NO
5. Does a *disastrous* earthquake take a huge toll of life and property?   YES   NO
6. Do *geological* investigations sometimes determine where oil is to be found?   YES   NO
7. Does a *geometrician* work with mathematics?   YES   NO
8. Do *geographical* shifts in population sometimes affect the economy of an area?   YES   NO
9. Does a *biographical* novel deal with the life of a real person?   YES   NO
10. Is *botany* a biological science?   YES   NO
11. Is the United States politically *autonomous*?   YES   NO
12. Is a *biopsy* performed on a dead body?   YES   NO
13. Is a *metronome* used in the study of mathematics?   YES   NO
14. Is an *autopsy* performed to correct a surgical problem?   YES   NO
15. Does an author write an *autobiography* about someone else's life?   YES   NO

Can you recall the words?（Ⅰ）
你能够写出这些词汇吗？（Ⅰ）

1. pertaining to the science of animals (*adj.*)　　1. Z＿＿＿＿＿
2. pertaining to the science of plants (*adj.*)　　2. B＿＿＿＿＿
3. dissection of a corpse to determine the cause of death　3. A＿＿＿＿＿
4. story of one's life, self-written　　4. A＿＿＿＿＿
5. pertaining to the science of all living matter (*adj.*)　5. B＿＿＿＿＿
6. science of the measurement of figures　　6. G＿＿＿＿＿
7. pertaining to the science of the earth's composition (*adj.*)　7. G＿＿＿＿＿
8. branch of physics dealing with the composition of celestial bodies　8. A＿＿＿＿＿
9. star-shaped flower　　9. A＿＿＿＿＿
10. very high in number; pertaining to the science of the heavens (*adj.*)　10. A＿＿＿＿＿
11. science of heavenly bodies　　11. A＿＿＿＿＿
12. science of the development of mankind　　12. A＿＿＿＿＿
13. person who believes human events are influenced by the paths of the sun, moon, and planets　13. A＿＿＿＿＿

Can you recall the words?（Ⅱ）
你能够写出这些词汇吗？（Ⅱ）

1. microscopic examination of living tissue　　1. B＿＿＿＿＿
2. self-government　　2. A＿＿＿＿＿
3. time measurer for music　　3. M＿＿＿＿＿
4. voyager among the stars　　4. A＿＿＿＿＿
5. traveler through the universe　　5. C＿＿＿＿＿
6. great misfortune　　6. D＿＿＿＿＿

7. mapping of the earth (*noun*)   7. G _____

8. self-governing (*adj.*)   8. A _____

9. diagram used in astrology   9. Z _____

10. pertaining to such a diagram (*adj.*)   10. Z _____

11. pertaining to ships, sailing, etc.   11. N _____

12. star-shaped symbol   12. A _____

13. story of a person's life   13. B _____

KEY: 1-biopsy, 2-autonomy, 3-metronome, 4-astronaut, 5-cosmonaut, 6-disaster, 7-geography, 8-autonomous, 9-zodiac, 10-zodiacal, 11-nautical, 12-asterisk, 13-biography

(End of Session 12)

SESSION 13
第 13 节

ORIGINS AND RELATED WORDS
词源及相关词汇

1. cutting in and out
切割

Flies, bees, beetles, wasps, and other insects are segmented creatures—head, thorax, and abdomen. Where these parts join, there appears to the imaginative eye a "cutting in" of the body.

Hence the branch of zoology dealing with insects is aptly named *entomology*, from Greek *en-*, in, plus *tome*, a cutting. The adjective is *entomological* (en'-tə-mə-LOJ'-ə-kəl).

(The word *insect* makes the same point—it is built on Latin *in-* in, plus *sectus*, a form of the verb meaning to *cut*.)

苍蝇、蜜蜂、甲壳虫、黄蜂,以及其他的昆虫都是身体分节的生物——头,胸和腹部。这些部位的连接处,对一个富有想象力的人来说,就像是身体的一种"切入"。

因此,关于昆虫的动物学学分支有一个很贴切的名字,叫作 entomology(昆虫学),来自希腊语的 en-,意为"在里面,里面",加上 tome"切割"。形容词是 entomological。

(insect 这个词也有同样构成——拉丁字母 in 意为"在里面,里面",加上 sectus,动词,意为"切"。)

The prefix *ec-*, from Greek *ek-*, means *out*. (The Latin prefix, you will recall, is *ex-*.) Combine *ec-* with *tome* to derive the words for surgical procedures in which parts are "cut out," or removed: *tonsillectomy* (the tonsils), *appendectomy* (the appendix), *mastectomy* (the breast), *hysterectomy* (the uterus), *prostatectomy* (the prostate), etc.

前缀 ec-,来自于希腊字母 ek-,意为"外面"(你可能会想起拉丁语的前缀 ex)。由 ec-和 tome 衍变出专指手术中"切开"或"去除"的部分:tonsillectomy (the tonsils),appendectomy (the appendix), mastectomy (the breast), hysterectomy (the uterus), prostatectomy (the prostate)等。

Combine *ec-* with Greek *kentron*, center (the Latin root, as we have discovered, is *centrum*), to derive *eccentric* (ək-SEN'-trik)—out of the *center*, hence deviating from the normal in behavior, attitudes, etc., or unconventional, odd, strange. The noun is *eccentricity* (ek'-sən-TRIS'-ə-tee).

由 ec-和希腊语的 kentron"中心"(我们会发现,其拉丁词根为 centrum)演变出 eccentric——"中心之外",由此引申为偏离正常行为、态度等,或不寻常的、古怪的、陌生的。名词形式为 eccentricity。

2. more cuts
更多关于切割的词根

The Greek prefix *a-* makes a root negative; the *atom* (AT'-əm) was so named at a time when it was considered the smallest possible particle of an element, that is, one that could *not* be cut any further. (we have long since spilt the atom, of course, with results, as in most technological advances, both good and evil.) The adjective is *a-tomic* (ə-TOM′-ik).

The Greek prefix *ana-* has a number of meanings, one of which is *up*, as in *anat-omy* (ə-NAT′-ə-mee), originally the *cutting up* of a plant or animal to determine its structure ,later the bodily structure itself. The adjective is *anatomical* (an′-ə-TOM′-ə-kəl).

希腊语前缀 a-是一个表示否定的词根;atom 曾经被认为是构成物质不可分割的最小颗粒。(当然,随着科技的发展,很久以前我们就能分开"atom"了——无论这种科技是好还是坏。)其形容词是 atomic。

希腊语前缀 ana-有多重意思,其中一个意思就是"向上",如 anatomy,原意为切开动物或植物确定其结构,后来指其结构本身。其形容词形式为 anatomical。

Originally any book that was part of a large work of many volumes was called a *tome* TŌM—etymologically, a part *cut* from the whole. Today, a *tome* designates, often dispar-agingly, an exceptionally large book, or one that is heavy and dull in content.

The Greek prefix *dicha-*, in two, combines with *tome* to construct *dichotomy* (dī-KOT′-ə-mee), a splitting in two,a technical word used in astronomy, biology, botany, and the science of logic. It is also employed as a non-technical term, as when we refer to the *dichotomy* in the life of a man who is a government clerk all day and a night-school teacher after working hours, so that his life is, in a sense, spilt into two parts. The verb is *dichotomize* (dī-KOT′-ə-mīz′); the adjective is *dichoto-mous* (dī-KOT′-ə-məs). *Dichotomous* thinking is the sort that divides everything into two parts—good and bad; white and black; Democrats and Republicans; etc. An unknown wit has made this classic statement about *dichotomous* thinking:"there are two kinds of people:those who divide everything into two parts,and those who do not. "

起初,一部包含很多分册的书中任何分册都可以称为 tome——从词源上看,其本义是从整体中切出来的一部分,现在,tome 通常有贬义的意味,指非常大或者内容很沉闷无味的书。

希腊语前缀 dicha-,意为"分为两部分",和 tome 一起组成 dichotomy,意思是"一分为二",是一个用在天文学、生物学、植物学和逻辑科学上的术语。它也被用作非技术术语,因此我们可以用来指白天做公务员,晚上下班后做教师的人,其生活是 dichotomy,从某种意义上说,其生活是分成两半的。其动词形式是 dichotomize;形容词是 dichotomous。dichotomous thinking 意思是任何事物要一分为二地看待——好的和坏的、白的和黑的、民主党和共和党等。一个不知名的智者曾经这样评论 dichotomous thinking:"有两种人:一些人把任何事都分为两部分,另一些人则不。"

Imagine a book ,a complicated or massive report, or some other elaborate docu-ment—now figuratively cut on or through it so that you can get to its essence, the very heart of the idea contained in it. What you have is an *epitome* (ə-PIT′-ə-mee), a condensation of the whole. (From *epi-* , on, upon, plus *tome*)

An *epitome* may refer to a summary, condensation, or abridgment of language , as in "Let me have an *epitome* of the book," or"Give me the *epitome* of his speech. "

设想一本书、一个复杂浩繁的报告,或是其他一些详尽的文件——形象地说,现在你在上面切割,或者将其切开,你就可以到达其核心,也就是其中包含的中心思想。你已经得到了一个 epitome,整体的浓缩。(epitome 由前缀 epi 意为"在……上",加上 tome 构成。)

epitome 可以用来指一个对语言的总结、摘要或是节录,如 let me have an epitome of the book(给我这本书的摘要),

give me the epitome of his speech(给我他演讲的摘要)。

More commonly, *epitome* and the verb *epitomize* (ə-PIT′-ə-miz′) are used in sentences like "She is the *epitome* of kindness," or "That one act *epitomizes* her philosophy of life." If you cut everything else away to get to the *essential* part, that part is a representative cross-section of the whole. So a woman who is the *epitome* of kindness stands for all people who are kind; and an act that *epitomizes* a philosophy of life represents, by itself, the complete philosophy.

更为普遍的是,epitome 和动词 epitomize 用在如 She is the epitome of kindness(她是善良的化身),或 That one act epitomizes her philosophy of life(那种行为体现了她的人生哲学。假如你从表及里,探寻本质部分,那么这部分就是整体事物中具有代表性的横切面。所以一个是善良"化身"的女人,是所有善良的人的代表。体现一种人生哲学的行为本身就是这种哲学的全部。

3. love and words
爱和单词

Logos, we know, means *science* or *study*; it may also mean *word* or *speech*, as it does in *philology* (fə-LOL′-ə-jee), etymologically *the love of words* (from Greek *philein*, to love, plus logos), or what is more commonly called *linguistics* (ling-GWIS′-tiks), the science of language, a term derived from Latin *lingua*, tongue.

Can you write, and pronounce, the adjective form of *philology*? _____.

正如我们所了解的,logos 意为"科学"或"研究";还有"词语"或者"演讲"的意思,如它在 philology 中,本义为"语句之爱"(来自于希腊语 philein,"去爱",加 logos),或者可以更普遍地称为 linguistics,语言学,由拉丁语的 lingua,意为"舌头",演变而来。

你能读出、写出 philology 的形容词形式吗?

4. more love
更多的爱

Philanthropy (fə-LAN′-thrə-pee) is by etymology the love of mankind—one who devotes oneself to *philanthropy* is a *philanthropist* (fə-LAN′-thrə-pist), as we learned in Chapter 3; the adjective is *philanthropic* (fil-ən-THROP′-ik).

philanthropy(慈善业)本义为"对人类的爱"——一个投身于 philanthropy 的人被称为 philanthropist(慈善家),正如我们在第 3 章所学的那样;形容词是 philanthropic。

The verb *philander* (fə-LAN′-dər), to "play around" sexually, be promiscuous, or have extramarital relations, combines *philein* with *andros*, male. (*Philandering*, despite its derivation, is not of course exclusively the male province. The word is, in fact, derived from the proper name conventionally given to male lovers in plays and romances of the 1500s and 1600s.) One who engages in the interesting activities catalogued above is a *philanderer* (fə-LAN′-dər-ər).

动词 philander,意为"在性上很放荡""淫乱""有婚外情的",由 philein 和 andros(意为"男性")构成,(philandering 尽管其词根中有"男性",但并不只指男性。这个词实际上源于公元 1500—1600 年期间,对戏剧和爱情小说中男性情人的普遍性称谓,符合其本义。)有以上所列兴趣的行为的人就是一个"philanderer"。

By etymology, *philosophy* is the love of wisdom (Greek *sophos*, wise); *Philadelphia* is the City of Brotherly Love (Greek *adelphos*, brother); *philharmonic* is the love of music or harmony (Greek *harmonia*，harmony)；and a *philter*，a rarely used word，is a love potion. Today we call whatever arouses sexual desire an *aphro-disiac* (af′-rə-DIZ′-ee-ak′)，from *Aphrodite*，the Greek goddess of love and beauty.

Aphrodisiac is an adjective as well as a noun，but a longer adjective form，*aph-rodisiacal* (af′-rə-də-ZĪ′-ə-kəl)，is also used.

从词源上看，philosophy(哲学)是"爱智慧"的意思(希腊语 sophos，"智慧")；Philadelphia(费城)是"兄弟之爱之城"(希腊语 adelphos，"兄弟")；philharmonic(交响乐团)是"爱音乐与和声"(希腊语中 harmonia，"和谐")；philter(春药)是一剂"爱药"，现在这个词已很少使用。现在我们称所有能催发人性欲的东西为 aphrodisiac，来自希腊语的 Aphrodite，是希腊爱与美丽的女神。

aphrodisiac 既是形容词，也是名词，但另外一个更为长一点的形容词形式是 aphrodisiacal，也同时在使用。

A *bibliophile* (BIB′-lee-ə-fīl′) is one who loves books as collectibles，admiring their binding，typography，illustrations，rarity，etc. —in short，a book collector. The combining root is Greek *biblion*，book.

An *Anglophile* (ANG′-glə-fīl′) admires and is fond of the British people，customs，culture，etc. The combining root is Latin *Anglus*，English.

bibliophile 是一个喜欢收集书的人，他喜欢欣赏书籍的装订、排版、插图，以及它的珍稀等。总之，就是一个书籍收集者。其中有一个希腊语词根 biblion，意为"书"。

Anglophile 是仰慕和喜欢英格兰人民以及其风俗、文化等，其中的拉丁词根 Anglus，意为"英国的"。

5. words and how they affect people
单词以及他们如何影响人们

The *semanticist* is professionally involved in *semantics* (sə-MAN′-tiks). The adjective is *semantic* (sə-MAN′-tik) or *semantical* (sə-MAN′-tə-kəl).

Semantics，like *orthopedics*，*pediatrics*，and *obstetrics*，is a singular noun despite the *-s* ending. Semantics *is*，not *are*，an exciting study. However，this rule applies only when we refer to the word as a science or area of study. In the following sentence，*semantics* is used as a plural："The *semantics* of your thinking *are* all wrong."

Two stimulating and highly readable books on the subject，well worth a visit to the library to pick up，are *Language in Thought and Action*，by S. I. Hayakawa，and *People in Quandaries*，by Dr. Wendell Johnson.

语义学者就是专门致力于语义研究的人，其形容词是 semantic 或 semantical。

semantics(语义学)和 orthopedics(整形手术)，pediatrics(儿科学)和 obstetrics(产科学)一样，虽然都是以-s 结尾，但却都是单数形式。语义学 is(而不是 are)一个令人兴奋的学科。然而，这项规则仅适用于当单词指某门科学或某个研究领域时。在下面的句子里 semantics 用作复数：The semantics of your thinking are all wrong.(你认为的这些语义全都是错的)。

关于这方面，有两本具有启发性和高度可读性的书，非常值得借来一读。一本是 Language in Thought and Action，作者是 S. I. Hayakawa；另一本是 People in Quandaries，作者是 Dr. Wendell Johnson。

6. how people live
人们如何生活

The profession of the *sociologist* is *sociology* (sō′-shee-OL′-ə-jee *or* sō-see-OL′-ə-jee). Can you write and pronounce the adjective？ _____.

社会学家的专业是社会学，你能写出、读出其形容词形式吗？

Sociology is built on Latin *socius*, companion,[1] plus *logos*, science, study. *Socius* is the source of such common words as *associate*, *social*, *socialize*, *society*, *sociable*, and *antisocial*; as well as *asocial* (ay-SŌ′-shəl), which combines the negative prefix *a-* with socius.

sociology 其中有拉丁词根 socius,意为"陪伴",并且再加上 logos,意为"科学"。常用词如 associate, social, social-ize, society, sociable 和 antisocial 均由 socius 衍生而来;asocial 由表示否定的前缀 a-, 和 social 组成。

The *antisocial* person actively dislikes people, and often behaves in ways that are detrimental or destructive to society or the social order (*anti-*, against).

On the other hand, someone who is *asocial* is withdrawn and self-centered, avoids contact with others, and feels completely indifferent to the interests or welfare of society. The *asocial* person doesn't want to "get involved."

antisocial 的人,非常不喜欢人,其行为常常对社会和社会秩序造成破坏。

另一方面,"asocial"的人往往是退缩和以自我为中心,避免和其他人接触,对社会事务非常冷淡,这类人缺乏"参与感"。

REVIEW OF ETYMOLOGY
复习词源

PREFIX，ROOT	MEANING	ENGLISH WORD
1. *en-*	in	_____
2. *tome*	a cutting	_____
3. *in-*	in	_____
4. *sectus*	cut	_____
5. *kentron* (*centrum*)	center	_____
6. *a-*	not，negative	_____
7. *ana-*	up	_____
8. *dicha-*	in two	_____
9. *epi-*	on, upon	_____
10. *logos*	word, speech	_____
11. *lingua*	tongue	_____
12. *philein*	to love	_____
13. *sophos*	wise	_____

---

1. *Companion* itself has an interesting etymology—Latin *com-*, with, plus *panis*, bread. If you are social, you enjoy breaking bread with companions. *Pantry* also comes from *panis*, though far more than bread is stored there.

companion 本身有一个很有意思的起源——拉丁语中的 com-,意为"和",加上 panis(面包),如果你是个"social"的人,即你乐意和同伴分享面包。pantry(食品储存室)由 panis(面包)演变而来,虽然它并不单指面包贮存在那里。

14. *adelphos*   brother   _____

15. *biblion*   book   _____

16. *Anglus*   English   _____

17. *socius*   companion   _____

18. *anti-*   against   _____

USING THE WORDS
单词应用

Can you pronounce the words? (Ⅰ)
你能读出这些单词吗?(Ⅰ)

1. *entomology*   en′-tə-MOL′-ə-jee
2. *entomological*   en′-tə-mə-LOJ′-ə-kəl
3. *eccentric*   ək-SEN′-trik
4. *eccentricity*   ək′-sən-TRIS′-ə-tee
5. *atom*   AT′-əm
6. *atomic*   ə-TOM′-ik
7. *anatomy*   ə-NAT′-ə-mee
8. *anatomical*   an′-ə-TOM′-ə-kəl
9. *tome*   TŌM
10. *dichotomy*   dī-KOT′-ə-mee
11. *dichotomous*   dī-KOT′-ə-məs
12. *dichotomize*   dī-KOT′-ə-mīz′

Can you pronounce the words? (Ⅱ)
你能读出这些单词吗?(Ⅱ)

1. *epitome*   ə-PIT′-ə-mee
2. *epitomize*   ə-PIT′-ə-mīz′
3. *philology*   fə-LOL′-ə-jee
4. *philological*   fil′-ə-LOJ′-ə-kəl
5. *linguistics*   ling-GWIS′-tiks
6. *philanthropy*   fə-LAN′-thrə-pee
7. *philanthropist*   fə-LAN′-thrə-pist
8. *philanthropic*   fil′-ən-THROP′-ik
9. *philander*   fə-LAN′-dər
10. *philanderer*   fə-LAN′-dər-ər

Can you pronounce the words? (Ⅲ)
你能读出这些单词吗？（Ⅲ）

1.	*philter*	FIL′-tər
2.	*aphrodisiac*	af′-rə-DIZ′-ee-ak′
3.	*aphrodisiacal*	af′-rə-də-ZĪ′-ə-kəl
4.	*bibliophile*	BIB′-lee-ə-fil′
5.	*Anglophile*	ANG′-glə-fil′
6.	*semantics*	sə-MAN′-tiks
7.	*semantic*	sə-MAN′-tik
8.	*semantical*	sə-MAN′-tə-kəl
9.	*sociology*	sō′-shee-OL′-ə-jee *or*
		sō′-see-OL′-ə-jee
10.	*sociological*	sō′-shee-ə-LOJ′-ə-kəl *or*
		sō′-see-ə-LOJ′-ə-kəl
11.	*asocial*	ay-SŌ′-shəl

Can you work with the words? (Ⅰ)
你能灵活使用这些词汇了吗？（Ⅰ）

1.	entomology	a.	physical structure
2.	eccentricity	b.	summary; representation of the whole
3.	anatomy	c.	science of the meanings and effects of words
4.	dichotomy	d.	linguistics
5.	epitome	e.	science dealing with insects
6.	philology	f.	science of social structures and customs
7.	semantics	g.	charitable works
8.	sociology	h.	that which causes sexual arousal
9.	aphrodisiac	i.	strangeness; oddness; unconventionality
10.	philanthropy	j.	condition or state of being split into two parts

KEY：1-e，2-i，3-a，4-j，5-b，6-d，7-c，8-f，9-h，10-g

Can you work with the words? (Ⅱ)
你能灵活使用这些词汇了吗? (Ⅱ)

1. dichotomize		a.	dull, heavy book
2. epitomize		b.	love potion; aphrodisiac
3. philander		c.	pertaining to the study of language
4. philter		d.	one fond of British people, customs, etc.
5. bibliophile		e.	pertaining to the science of group cultures, conventions, etc.
6. Anglophile		f.	to split in two
7. asocial		g.	withdrawn from contact with people
8. tome		h.	book collector
9. philological		i.	to summarize
10. sociological		j.	to engage in extramarital sex

KEY: 1-f, 2-i, 3-j, 4-b, 5-h, 6-d, 7-g, 8-a, 9-c, 10-e

Do you understand the words?
你对这些词汇是否已经透彻地理解?

1. Is a *philanderer* likely to be faithful to a spouse?	YES	NO
2. Did Dr. Jekyll-Mr. Hyde lead a *dichotomous* existence?	YES	NO
3. Is an egoist the *epitome* of selfishness?	YES	NO
4. Is a *philanthropist* antisocial?	YES	NO
5. Is an *aphrodisiac* intended to reduce sexual interest?	YES	NO
6. Is a *bibliophile's* chief aim the enjoyment of literature?	YES	NO
7. Does a *philologist* understand etymology?	YES	NO
8. Is a *semanticist* interested in more than the dictionary meanings of words?	YES	NO
9. Is an *asocial* person interested in improving social conditions?	YES	NO
10. Is a light novel considered a *tome*?	YES	NO

KEY: 1-no, 2-yes, 3-yes, 4-no, 5-no, 6-no, 7-yes, 8-yes, 9-no, 10-no

Can you recall the words?
你能够写出这些词汇吗？

1. pertaining to the study of social customs (*adj.*)	1. S _____
2. pertaining to the psychological effects of words (*adj.*)	2. S _____ *or* S _____
3. lover and collector of books	3. B _____
4. make love promiscuously	4. P _____
5. pertaining to the science of linguistics (*adj.*)	5. P _____
6. pertaining to the study of insects (*adj.*)	6. E _____
7. one who admires British customs	7. A _____
8. smallest particle, so-called	8. A _____
9. pertaining to the structure of a body (*adj.*)	9. A _____
10. a dull, heavy book	10. T _____
11. split in two (*adj.*)	11. D _____
12. to split in two	12. D _____
13. a condensation, summary, or representation of the whole	13. E _____
14. to stand for the whole; to summarize	14. E _____
15. pertaining to charitable activities (*adj.*)	15. P _____
16. out of the norm; odd	16. E _____
17. one who "plays around"	17. P _____
18. arousing sexual desire (*adj.*)	18. A _____ *or* A _____
19. science of the manner in which groups function	19. S _____
20. self-isolated from contact with people	20. A _____

KEY：1-sociological，2-semantic *or* semantical，3-bibliophile,4-philander，5-philological，6-entomological，7-Anglophile，8-atom，9-anatomical，10-tome，11-dichotomous，12-dichotomize，13-epitome，14-epitomize，15-philanthropic，16-eccentric，17-philanderer，18-aphrodisiac *or* aphrodisiacal，19-sociology，20-asocial

CHAPTER REVIEW
章节复习

A. Do you recognize the words?
你能认出这些单词吗？

1. Student of the stars and other heavenly phenomena：(a) geologist，(b) astronomer，(c) anthropologist
2. Student of plant life：(a) botanist，(b) zoologist，(c) biologist
3. Student of insect life：(a) sociologist，(b) entomologist，(c) etymologist
4. Student of the meaning and psychology of words：(a) philologist，(b) semanticist，(c) etymologist
5. Analysis of living tissue：(a) autopsy，(b) biopsy，(c) autonomy
6. That which arouses sexual desire：(a) zodiac，(b) bibliophile，(c) aphrodisiac
7. Self-governing：(a) autobiographical，(b) autonomous，(c) dichotomous
8. Part that represents the whole：(a) epitome，(b) dichotomy，(c) metronome
9. One who physically travels in space：(a) astronomer，(b) astrologer，(c) astronaut
10. One who has extramarital affairs：(a) cosmonaut，(b) philanderer，(c) philanthropist

---

KEY：1-b，2-a，3-b，4-b，5-b，6-c，7-b，8-a，9-c，10-b

B. Can you recognize the roots?
你能认出这些词根吗？

ROOT	MEANING	EXAMPLE
1. *anthropos*	_____	anthropology
2. *logos*	_____	philology
3. *astron*	_____	astronomy
4. *nautes*	_____	astronaut
5. *nomos*	_____	metronome
6. *autos*	_____	autonomy
7. *ge (geo-)*	_____	geology
8. *graphein*	_____	biography
9. *opsis, optikos*	_____	autopsy
10. *zoion*	_____	zodiac
11. *tome*	_____	entomology
12. *sectus*	_____	insect
13. *lingua*	_____	linguistics
14. *philein*	_____	philanthropy

15. *sophos*　　_____　philosophy
16. *biblion*　　_____　bibliophile
17. *Anglus*　　_____　Anglophile
18. *socius*　　_____　sociology
19. *logos*　　_____　biology
20. *bios*　　_____　biopsy

KEY：1-mankind，2-word，speech，3-star，4-sailor，5-law，order，arrangement，6-self，7-earth，8-to write，9-view，vision，sight，10-animal，11-a cutting，12-cut，13-tongue，14-to love，15-wise，16-book，17-English，18-companion，19-science，study，20-life

TEASER QUESTION FOR THE AMATEUR ETYMOLOGIST
词源小测验

1. Recalling the root *sophos*, wise, and thinking of the English word *moron*, write the name given to a second-year student in high school or college: _____.
Etymologically, what does this word mean? _____

2. Based on the root *sophos*, what word means *worldly-wise*? _____.

3. Thinking of *bibliophile*, define *bibliomaniac*: _____
_____.

4. These three words, based on *lingua*, tongue, use prefixes we have discussed.
Can you define each one?
(a) monolingual　_____
(b) bilingual　_____
(c) trilingual　_____
Can you, now, guess at the meaning of *multilingual*? _____

_____

How about *linguist*? _____
_____.

What do you suppose the Latin root *multus* means? _____.
(Think of *multitude*.)

5. With *Anglophile* as your model, can you figure out what country and its people, customs, etc. each of the following admires?
(a) Francophile　_____
(b) Russophile　_____
(c) Hispanophile　_____
(d) Germanophilo　_____
(e) Nipponophile　_____

(f) Sinophile _____

6. Using roots you have learned, and with *bibliophile* as your model, can you construct a word for:

(a) one who loves males: _____

(b) one who loves women: _____

(c) one who loves children: _____

(d) one who loves animals: _____

(e) one who loves plants: _____

(Answers in Chapter 18)

(答案见第 18 章)

WHERE TO GET NEW IDEAS
从哪里吸取新概念?

People with superior vocabularies, I have submitted, are the people with ideas. The words they know are verbal symbols of the ideas they are familiar with—reduce one and you must reduce the other, for ideas cannot exist without verbalization. Freud once had an idea and had to coin a whole new vocabulary to make his idea clear to the world. Those who are familiar with Freud's theories know all the words that explain them—the *unconscious*, the *ego*, the *id*, the *superego*, *rationalization*, *Oedipus complex*, and so on. Splitting the atom was once a new idea—anyone familiar with it knew something about *fission*, *isotope*, *radioactive*, *cyclotron*, etc.

正如之前所讲,具有超大词汇量的人一定熟知许多概念。他所掌握的词汇正是他所熟知的概念的语言符号——去其一必然去其二,没有词汇则没有概念。弗洛伊德表达前所未有的概念时,不得不创造出一系列新词,让人们去准确理解他的观点。熟知弗洛伊德理论的人一定知道解释这些理论的词汇——无意识、自我、本我、超我、理性化、俄狄浦斯情结等。原子分裂是新概念——了解这一概念的人一定熟知这些词汇——裂变、同位素、放射性的、回旋加速器等等。

Remember this: your vocabulary indicates the alertness and range of your mind. The words you know show the extent of your understanding of what's going on in the world. The size of your vocabulary varies directly with the degree to which you are growing intellectually.

谨记:词汇量是思维敏捷程度的体现。你所熟知的词汇能够体现你对现有世界的理解程度。你拥有的词汇量大小与你智力增长的程度直接相关。

You have covered so far in this book several hundred words. Having learned these words, you have begun to think of an equal number of new ideas. A new word is not just another pattern of syllables with which to clutter up your mind—a new word is a new idea to help you think, to help you understand the thoughts of others, to help you express your own thoughts, to help

至此,我们已经学习了几百个词汇。通过学习新词,你也开始思考同样数目的概念。每个新词并不是使你头脑混乱的几个音节的叠加——相反,每个新词是一个新概念帮助你思考,帮助你理解他人的思维,帮助你清楚表达自己的思维,帮助你拥有更智慧的人生。

you live a richer intellectual life.

Realizing these facts, you may become impatient. You will begin to doubt that a book like this can cover all the ideas that an alert and intellectually mature adult wishes to be acquainted with. Your doubt is well-founded.

One of the chief purposes of this book is to get you started, to give you enough of a push so that you will begin to gather momentum, to stimulate you enough so that you will want to start gathering your own ideas.

Where can you gather them? From good books on new topics.

How can you gather them? By reading on a wide range of new subjects.

Reference has repeatedly been made to psychology, psychiatry, and psychoanalysis in these pages. If your curiosity has been piqued by these references, here is a good place to start. In these fields there is a tremendous and exciting literature—and you can read as widely and as deeply as you wish.

What I would like to do is offer a few suggestions as to where you might profitably begin—how far you go will depend on your own interest.

I suggest, first, half a dozen older books (older, but still immensely valuable and completely valid) available at any large public library.

The Human Mind, by Karl A. Menninger

Mind and Body, by Flanders Dunbar

The Mind in Action, by Eric Berne

Understandable Psychiatry, by Leland E. Hinsie

A General Introduction to Psychoanalysis, by Sigmund Freud

Emotional Problems of Living, by O. Spurgeon English and Gerald H. J. Pearson

Next, I suggest books on some of the newer approaches in psychology. These are available in inexpensive paperback editions as well as at your local library.

听到这些事实,你一定开始心急。你开始怀疑,这样一本书是否能够覆盖所有概念,而这些正是一位思维敏捷的智慧人士所应当熟知的概念? 你的怀疑是合理的。

本书的主要目的之一是使你开始学习,给予你足够的动力,这样,你才能以强劲的势头扩充自己的概念。

在哪里能获取到新概念呢? 从大量关于新话题的书中获取。

怎样才能获取新概念? 通过在广阔的领域阅读关于新话题的读物获取新概念。

在以上章节中,我们已经反复涉及心理学、精神治疗法和心理分析。如果你已经被这些新的概念激发出极大的好奇心,这里就是你开始的好地方。这些领域拥有极大数目并令人振奋的著作——你可以尽情地广泛阅读、深入研究。

为了让你有个好的开端,我所能做的就是提些建议——你进步的多少取决于你自己的兴趣。

我首先建议 6 本比较"老一点"的书(老一点,但仍旧很有价值和现实影响),这些书在大一点的公共图书馆里都有。

其次,我再推荐一些更新一点的关于心理学方面的书籍,都是些并不贵的平装本,在你当地的图书馆里也能找到。

I Ain't Well—But I Sure Am Better, by Jess Lair, Ph. D.

The Disowned Self, by Nathaniel Brandon

A Primer of Behavioral Psychology, by Adelaide Bry

I'm OK—You're OK, by Thomas A. Harris, M. D.

Freedom to Be and Man the Manipulator, by Everett L. Shostrum

Games People Play, by Eric Berne, M. D.

Love and Orgasm, *Pleasure and The Language of the Body*, by Alexander Lowen, M. D.

The Transparent Self, by Sydney M. Jourard

Don't Say Yes When You Want to Say No, by Herbert Fen sterheim and Jean Baer

Gestalt Therapy Verbatim, by Frederick S. Perls

Born to Win, by Muriel James and Dorothy Jongeward

Joy and Here Comes Everybody, by William C. Schutz

The Fifty-Minute Hour, by Robert Lindner

(End of Session 13)

Brief Intermission Four
简短插叙四

HOW TO AVOID BEING A PURIST
如何避免成为语言纯正癖者

Life, as you no doubt realize, is complicated enough these days. Yet puristic textbooks and English teachers with puristic ideas are striving to make it still more complicated. Their contribution to the complexity of modern living is the repeated claim that many of the natural, carefree, and popular expressions that most of us use every day are "bad English", "incorrect grammar", "vulgar", or "illiterate".

In truth, many of the former restrictions and "thou shalt nots" of academic grammar are now outmoded—most educated speakers quite simply ignore them.

你一定已经发现,现代生活足够复杂。然而,持有语言纯正癖观点的教科书或英语教师仍然力求使生活更加复杂。虽然大多数人在日常生活中所使用的表达是自然的、顺畅的、普遍的,但语言纯正癖者仍然不断声称这样的语言是"糟糕的英语""错误的语法""粗俗的"或者"文盲的"语言,他们对现代生活复杂程度的贡献之大正体现于此。

其实,许多学术语法对形式的限制和用法的规定早已过气——大多数受教育人士对这样的语法完全不予理会。

Students in my grammar classes at Rio Hondo College are somewhat nonplused when they discover that correctness is not determined by textbook rules and cannot be enforced by school teacher edict. They invariably ask: "Aren't you going to draw the line somewhere?"

It is neither necessary nor possible for any one person to "draw the line." That is done—and quite effectively—by the people themselves, by the millions of educated people throughout the nation.

Of course certain expressions may be considered "incorrect" or "illiterate" or "bad grammar"—not because they violate puristic rules, but only because they are rarely if ever used by educated speakers.

得知教科书上的规则和政府法令无法规定语言正确与否时,在深河学院上我的语法课的学生感到十分困惑。他们总是问:"难道对与错不需要任何界限吗?"

不管由何人来"划清界限"都是不必要,也是不可能的。使用语言的人们和英语国家成千上万受教育人士已经划出了界线,而且非常有效。

当然,某些表达可以被视为"错误的""文盲的"或者"糟糕的",但这并非因为它们违反了纯正癖者的语法规则,而是因为即使曾经有受教育人士如此使用,这个使用频率也是相当之低。

Correctness, in short, is detemined by current educated usage.

The following notes on current trends in modern usage are in tended to help you come to a decision about certain controversial expressions. As you read each sentence, pay particular attention to the italicized word or words. Does the usage square with your own language patterns? Would you be willing to phrase your thoughts in just such terms? Decide whether the sentence is "right" or "wrong," then compare your conclusions with the opinions given after the test.

简而言之，正确与否取决于当今时代受教育人士的主流用法。

以下对当代用法趋势的解释旨在帮助你确定某些颇有争议的表达。阅读每个句子时，尤其注意斜体词。这些用法是否与你的语言习惯相符？你是否愿意按照以下用法表达？判断句子正误，然后将你的观点与测验后的解释相比较。

TEST YOURSELF
自我测试

1. Let's not walk any *further* right now.   RIGHT   WRONG
2. Some people admit that their *principle* goal in life is to become wealthy.   RIGHT   WRONG
3. What a *nice* thing to say!   RIGHT   WRONG
4. He's *pretty* sick today.   RIGHT   WRONG
5. I feel *awfully* sick.   RIGHT   WRONG
6. Are you going to invite Doris and *I* to your party?   RIGHT   WRONG

1. Let's not walk any *further* right now.
我们现在不要再走更远了。

RIGHT. In the nineteenth century, when professional grammarians attempted to Latinize English grammar, an artificial distinction was drawn between *farther* and *further*, to wit: *farther* refers to space, *further* means to a *greater extent* or *additional*. Today, as a result, many teachers who are still under the forbidding influence of nineteenth-century restrictions insist that it is incorrect to use one word for the other.

正确。19 世纪，专业文法家试图将英语语法拉丁化，在 farther 和 further 之间也做出了"人为的"划分：farther 形容"空间"，further 形容"程度"。所以，今天的一些教师仍然饱受 19 世纪这一顽固划分的影响，坚持认为这两个词互换是错误的用法。

To check on current attitudes toward this distinction, I sent the test sentence above to a number of dictionary editors, authors, and professors of English, requesting their opinion of the acceptability of *further* in reference to actual distance. Sixty out of eighty-seven professors, over two thirds of those responding, accepted the usage without qualification. Of twelve dictionary editors, eleven accepted *further*, and in the case of the authors, thirteen out of twenty-three accepted the word as used. A professor of English at Cornell University remarked: "I know of no justification for any present-day distinction between *further* and *farther*"; and a consulting editor of the Funk and Wagnalls dictionary said, "There is nothing controversial here. As applied to spatial distance, *further* and *farther* have long been interchangeable."

为了了解当今人们对 farther 与 further 的区分，我把上面这个句子发给许多词典编撰者、作家和英语教授，询问 further 是否可以用来修饰距离。87 位教授中,60 位无条件认可此用法,超过回复者总数的 2/3。12 位词典编撰者中,11 位认可此用法;23 位作家中,13 位接受此用法。一位康奈尔大学英语教授说道:"现在,我找不到任何理由将两者强制区别开来";芬克和瓦格纳词典的顾问编辑说道:"毫无争议。修饰空间距离时,further 和 father 早已可以相互替换。"

Perhaps the comment of a noted author and columnist is most to the point: "I like both *further* and *farther*, as I have never been able to tell which is which or why one is any farther or further than the other."

也许一位著名作家和专栏作家的答复最为中肯:"farther 与 further,两者我都喜欢使用;我无法分辨两者有何不同,也不明白什么情况下一个比另一个更恰当。"

2. Some people admit that their *principle* goal in life is to become wealthy.

一些人承认他们生活的主要目标是变得富有。

WRONG. In speech, you can get *principal* and *principle* confused as often as you like, and no one will ever know the difference—both words are pronounced identically. In writing, however, your spelling will give you away.

There is a simple memory trick that will help you if you get into trouble with these two words. *Rule* and *principle* both end in *-le*—and a princip*le* is a *rule*. On the other hand, *principal* contains an *a*, and so does *main*—and princip*al* means m*a*in. Get these points straight and your confusion is over.

错误。在对话中,你可以尽情混淆 principle 与 principal,没有人会知道你用的是哪个词——因为它们具有相同的发音。但在写作时,你的拼写会出卖你。

如果记忆这两个词的拼写有困难,这里提供一个简单的记忆窍门。rule 与 principle 都以 le 结尾——而 principle(原则)就是一种 rule(规则)。而 principal 和 main 都包含字母 a——principal 就是 main 的意思。记住这个窍门,你不会再有任何疑团。

Heads of schools are called *principals*, because they are the main person in that institution of learning. The money you have in the bank is your *principal*, your *main* financial assets. And the stars of a play are *principals*—the *main* actors.

Thus, "Some people admit that their *principal* (main) goal in life is to become wealthy," but "Such a *principle* (rule) is not guaranteed to lead to happiness."

一校之长被称为 principal,因为他是学校的主要人物;你在银行的存款是 principal,因为这是你的主要财务资产;戏剧中的主演也被称为 principals,因为他们是主要演员。

因此,例句应该修改为 Some people admit that their principal goal in life is to become wealthy(一些人承认他们生活的主要目标是变得富有),而 Such a principle(rule)is not guaranteed to lead to happiness。(而这个原则无法保证幸福。)

3. What a *nice* thing to say!

多么动听的说法!

RIGHT. Purists object to the popular use of *nice* as a synonym for *pleasant*, *agreeable*, or *delightful*. They wish to restrict the word to its older and more erudite meaning of *exact* or *subtle*. You will be happy to hear that they aren't getting anywhere.

When I polled a group of well-known authors on the acceptability in everyday speech of the popular meaning of *nice*, their opinions were unanimous; not a single dissenting voice, out of the twenty-three authors who answered, was raised against the usage. One writer responded: "It has been right for about 150 years..."

正确。语言纯正癖者反对将 nice 视为 pleasant，agreeable 或 delightful 的同义词，他们希望将其含义限制为 exact 或 subtle。他们未能如愿，你一定为此欢喜。

对于 nice 日常用法的可接受性，我请教许多著名作家，他们的观点是一致赞同的；23 位作家无一例外。一位作家说道："150 年来，人们一直是这样使用 nice 的……"

Editors of magazines and newspapers questioned on the same point were just a shade more conservative. Sixty out of sixty-nine accepted the usage. One editor commented："I think we do not have to be nice about *nice* any longer. No one can eradicate it from popular speech as a synonym for *pleasant*, or *enjoyable*, or *kind*, or *courteous*. It is a workhorse of the vocabulary, and properly so."

The only valid objection to the word is that it is *overworked* by some people，but this shows a weakness in vocabulary rather than in grammar.

As in the famous story of the editor who said to her secretary："There are two words I wish you would stop using so much. One is 'nice' and the other is 'lousy.'"

"Okay，" said the secretary, who was eager to please. "What are they?"

我所询问的期刊和报纸编辑稍微保守一些；69 位编辑中，60 人赞同此用法。一位主编说到："我认为我们无须将 nice 限定在古老的定义上。没有人能够阻止 nice 在日常口语中用作 pleasant，enjoyable，kind 或 courteous 的同义词。这个词'吃苦耐劳'，这样用也没有什么不妥。"

唯一一站得住脚的反对理由是，许多人过多地使用 nice，但这并非是语法问题，而是词汇量贫乏的问题。

下面这个有名的对话说明了 nice 的常用性。一位编辑对他的秘书说：

"There are two words I wish you would stop using so much. One is 'nice'，and the other is 'lousy'."

"好的，"秘书渴望取悦上司，"它们是什么?"（What are they?）[1]

4. He's *pretty* sick today.
他今天非常不舒服。

RIGHT. One of the purist's pet targets of attack is the word *pretty* as used in the sentence under discussion. Yet all modern dictionaries accept such use of *pretty*, and a survey made by a professor at the University of Wisconsin showed that the usage is established English.

对。pretty 的这种用法被语言纯正癖者所诟病，但所有现代的字典，都接受 pretty 的此种用法，威斯康辛大学一名教授所做的一项调查发现，pretty 的这种用法已经是被广为接受了的。

5. I feel *awfully* sick.
我感到难受极了!

RIGHT. Dictionaries accept this usage in informal speech and the University of Wisconsin survey showed that it is established English.

The great popularity of *awfully* in educated speech is no doubt due to the strong and unique emphasis that the word gives to an adjective—substitute *very*，*quite*，*extremely*，or *severely* and you considerably weaken the force.

On the other hand，it is somewhat less than cultivated to say "I feel *awful sick*，" and the wisdom of using *awfully* to intensify a *pleasant* concept（"What an *awfully* pretty child"; "That book is *awfully* interesting"）is perhaps still debatable，

---

1. 秘书将上司的话理解为：我希望你不要过多使用两个词。一个词很亲切，另一个污秽。——译者注

though getting less and less so as the years go on.

正确。字典已经承认这是在非正式演讲中的正确用法,并且威斯康辛大学的上述调查表明,这也是被广为接受的用法。

awfully 受到受教育人士的极大欢迎,这无疑要归功于它给所修饰的形容词带来的强烈的、特别的强调效果——将 awfully 替换为 very,quite,extremely 或 severely 中的任何一个,都会极大地削弱这种效果。

需要注意的是,“I feel awful sick”的说法不是很文雅;虽然对使用 awfully 来强化“喜悦”之意的用法的争议越来越少,但这个争议仍然没有完全消除。(例如,What an awfully pretty girl;That book is awfully interesting.)

6. Are you going to invite Doris and *I* to your party?

你会邀请我和多丽丝去参加你的晚会吗?

WRONG. Some people are almost irresistibly drawn to the pronoun *I* in constructions like this one. However, not only does such use of *I* violate a valid and useful grammatical principle, but, more important, it is rarely heard in educated speech. The meaning of the sentence is equally clear no matter which form of the pronoun is employed, of course, but the use of *I*, the less popular choice, may stigmatize the speaker as uneducated.

Consider it this way: You would normally say, "Are you going to invite *me* to your party?" It would be wiser, therefore, to say, "Are you going to invite Doris and *me* to your party?

错误。这样的句子中,许多人都会情不自禁地使用 I。但是,这个用法不仅违反合理和实用的语法规则,也不存在于受教育人士的言语中——这点更为重要。无论使用主格或是宾格形式,都不影响句子意思的表达;但是使用 I 这个不太常用的用法会给你打上“文盲”的烙印。

这样理解或许更加容易:你通常会说:“Are you going to invite me to your party?”因此,“Are you going to invite Doris and me to your party”的表达更为明智。

7

HOW TO TALK ABOUT LIARS AND LYING
如何描述各类骗子与谎言

（*Sessions 14—17*）

TEASER PREVIEW
引读

What kind of liar are you if you：

* *have developed a reputation for falsehood?*
* *are particularly skillful?*
* *cannot be reformed?*
* *have become habituated to your vice?*
* *started to lie from the moment of your birth?*
* *always lie?*
* *cannot distinguish fact from fancy?*
* *suffer no pangs of conscience?*
* *are suspiciously smooth and fluent in your lying?*
* *tell vicious lies?*

哪些词能够用来描述这样的骗子：

* 他谎话连篇，因此而臭名昭著
* 他的谎言天衣无缝
* 他屡教不改，无药可救
* 他说谎成瘾，恶习难改
* 说谎是他的天性
* 他永远在撒谎
* 他无法分辨事实与幻想
* 他肆无忌惮、良心泯灭
* 他油嘴滑舌、不假思索
* 他撒的谎非常恶毒

SESSION 14
第 14 节

It was the famous Greek philosopher and cynic Diogenes who went around the streets of Athens, lantern in hand, looking for an honest person.

This was over two thousand years ago, but I presume that Diogenes would have as little success in his search today. Lying seems to be an integral weakness of mortal character—I doubt that few human beings would be so brash as to claim that they have never in their lives told at least a partial untruth. Indeed, one philologist goes so far as to theorize that language must have been invented for the sole purpose of deception. Perhaps so. It is certainly true that animals seem somewhat more honest than humans, maybe because they are less gifted mentally.

古希腊著名哲学家、犬儒学派代表人物狄奥根尼手里打着灯笼,在雅典的街道上寻找诚实的人。

这发生在两千多年前。换作今天,我猜想狄奥根尼不会有任何收获。说谎似乎成了人类无法摆脱的弱点——我猜没有任何人敢于轻言他从不说谎。甚至有语言学家得出理论,认为发明语言的主要目的就是去欺骗。这也许是对的。所以,动物在某种程度上比人类更可信,因为它们在智力上没有人类发达。

Why do people lie? To increase their sense of importance, to escape punishment, to gain an end that would otherwise be denied them, out of long-standing habit, or sometimes because they actually do not know the difference between fact and fancy. These are the common reasons for falsification. No doubt there are other, fairly unique, motives that impel people to distort the truth. And, to come right down to it, can we always be certain what is true and what is false?

If lying is a prevalent and all-too-human phenomenon, there would of course be a number of interesting words to describe different types of liars.

Let us pretend (not to get personal, but only to help you become personally involved in the ideas and words) that you are a liar.

The question is, what kind of liar *are* you?

人类为什么说谎? 增加重要感;躲避惩罚;达到不撒谎无法达到的目的;已经撒谎成性;或仅仅因为无法分辨事实与幻想。这些都是常见的原因。当然,还有许多其他特别的动机,驱使人们扭曲事实。而且说到底,人们总是能够确定孰是孰非吗?

如果说谎是普遍存在的、是人性不可避免的,那么自然会有许多有趣的词汇来描述不同类型的骗子。

让我们假设你是个说谎者(不是人身攻击,而仅仅是帮你设身处地地理解这些概念和单词)。

问题是,你是哪种说谎者?

IDEAS
概念

1. you don't fool even some of the people
　　你谁都糊弄不了

Everybody knows your propensity for avoiding facts. You have built so solid and unsavory a reputation that only a stranger is likely to be misled—and then, not for long.

A notorious liar

所有人都了解你回避事实的倾向。你已经牢牢建立了令人极度厌恶的名声,恐怕只有陌生人才会听信你的话——但即使这样也持续不了多久。

你是一个 notorious liar(臭名昭著的骗子)。

2. to the highest summits of artistry
达到了说谎艺术的最高境界

Your ability is top-drawer—rarely does anyone lie as convincingly or as artistically as you do. Your skill has, in short, reached the zenith of perfection. Indeed, your mastery of the art is so great that your lying is almost always crowned with success—and you have no trouble seducing an unwary listener into believing that you are telling gospel truth.

A consummate liar

你能力超群——没有人能够像你一样编造出如此具有说服力和如此圆熟的谎言。简而言之,你的技巧已经达到了完美的极致。事实上,你的撒谎技巧如此娴熟,所以你的把戏总是成功——你轻轻松松就能让毫无戒心的听者将你的谎言视为福音书般的真理。

你是一个 consummate liar(精湛的骗子)。

3. beyond redemption or salvation
无可救药的骗子

You are impervious to correction. Often as you may be caught in your fabrications, there is no reforming you—you go right on lying despite the punishment, embarrassment, or unhappiness that your distortions of truth may bring upon you.

An incorrigible liar

虽然你的把戏经常被人戳穿,但是你却不知悔改——即使要面对惩罚、难堪或者随其谎言而来的不幸,你仍然继续说谎。

你是一个 incorrigible liar(无可救药的骗子)。

4. too old to learn new tricks
习惯根深蒂固而无法学习新的把戏

You are the victim of firmly fixed and deep-rooted habits. Telling untruths is as frequent and customary an activity as brushing your teeth in the morning, or having toast and coffee for breakfast, or lighting up a cigarette after dinner (if you are a smoker). And almost as reflexive.

An inveterate liar

你是根深蒂固习惯的受害者。对你来说,说谎已成为频繁而寻常之事,就像清晨刷牙,或像为早餐预订面包或咖啡,或像饭后点起一根香烟(如果你抽烟的话)。说谎几乎已经成了条件反射。

你是一个 inveterate liar(成瘾的骗子)。

5. an early start
从出生便开始说谎

You have such a long history of persistent falsification that one can only suspect that your vice started when you were reposing in your mother's womb. In other words，and allowing for a great deal of exaggeration for effect，you have been lying from the moment of your birth.

A congenital liar

你坚定不移的说谎习惯历史悠久，人们只能怀疑你从娘胎里便开始了这个恶习。换句话说，你从出生那一刻起便开始说谎——请允许我夸张一点点。

你是一个 congenital liar(天生的骗子)。

6. no letup
无休止的谎言

You never stop lying. While normal people lie on occasion，and often for special reasons，you lie continually—not occasionally or even frequently，but over and over.

A chronic liar

你的谎言从不停止。正常人偶尔会说谎，而且往往出于特殊原因，但你是持续地说谎——不是偶尔，甚至也不是经常，而是无休无止！

你是一个 chronic liar(习惯性的骗子)。

7. a strange disease
奇怪的毛病

You are not concerned with the difference between truth and falsehood；you do not bother to distinguish fact from fantasy. In fact，your lying is a disease that no antibiotic can cure.

A pathological liar

你不知道对与错之间的区别，你根本懒得去区分事实与幻想。实际上，你撒谎的习性是一种无药可医的病。

你是一个 pathological liar(精神错乱的骗子)。

8. no regrets
毫无悔意

You are completely without a conscience. No matter what misery your fabrications may cause your innocent victims，you never feel the slightest twinge of guilt. Totally unscrupulous，you are a dangerous person to get mixed up with.

An unconscionable liar

你良心泯灭。无论你的谎言会给无辜的受害者带来怎样的悲剧，你从来不觉得有一丁点的愧疚。你毫无道德原则，跟你打交道是危险之事。

你是一个 unconscionable liar(没有良心的骗子)。

9. smooth
油腔滑调

Possessed of a lively imagination and a ready tongue，you can distort facts as smoothly and as effortlessly as you can say your name. But you do not always get away with your lies.

Ironically enough，it is your very smoothness that makes you suspect：your answers are too quick to be true. Even if we can't immediately catch you in your lies，we have learned from unhappy past experience not to suspend our critical faculties when you are talking. We admire your nimble wit，but we listen with a skeptical ear.

A glib liar

你具有丰富的想象力和一副伶牙俐齿，能够像说自己的名字一样流利、毫不费力地扭曲事实。但是你的谎言并非时刻奏效。

讽刺的是，正是你高超的技巧出卖了你——你的回答太敏捷了，显得不可信。即使我们无法立刻戳穿你的谎言，我们也能够从过往不愉快的经历中吸取教训——听到你讲话时，我们会时刻保持挑剔的态度。我们赞美你敏捷的头脑，但是别忘了，我们也有一对多疑的耳朵。

你是一个 glib liar(口齿伶俐的骗子)

10. outstanding
技术超群

Lies，after all，are bad—they are frequently injurious to other people，and may have a particularly dangerous effect on you as a liar. At best，if you are caught you suffer some embarrassment. At worst，if you succeed in your deception your character becomes warped and your sense of values suffers. Almost all lies are harmful；some are no less than vicious.

If you are one type of liar，*all* your lies are vicious—calculatedly，predeterminedly，coldly，and advisedly vicious. In short，your lies are so outstandingly hurtful that people gasp in amazement and disgust at hearing them.

An egregious liar

谎言毕竟是坏事——它们经常会给他人带来伤害；而对说谎者来说，往往也会带来尤为危险的后果。如果被戳穿，哪怕是最好的结果，你也要忍受难堪——而最坏的结果是，如果你的谎言奏效，你的灵魂会扭曲，价值观也会变得低下。几乎所有的谎言都是有害的；有些谎言就是恶毒。

如果你是这样的一类骗子，你所有的谎言都是恶毒的——你的谎言都是深思熟虑、精心设计、故意恶毒的言语。简而言之，你的谎言可怕至极，普通人在听到你的谎言时，只能在恐惧和惊讶中屏住呼吸。

你是一个 egregious liar(过分的、异乎寻常的骗子)。

In this chapter the ten basic words revolve rather closely around a central core. Each one，however，has a distinct，a unique meaning，a special implication. Note the differences.

在这章中，这 10 个基本单词都紧密围绕同一个核心。但每个词都有鲜明的、独特的含义，都有特殊的隐含之意。请注意它们之间的区别。

TYPE OF LIAR	SPECIAL IMPLICATION
1. *notorious*	*famous*—or *infamous*—for lying; tendency to falsify is *well-known*
2. *consummate*	great *skill*
3. *incorrigible*	too far gone to be reformed—*impervious to rehabilitation*
4. *inveterate*	lying has become a *deep-rooted habit*
5. *congenital*	lying had *very early beginnings*—as if *from birth over and over*
6. *chronic*	an irresistible *compulsion* to lie—often for no rational reason;

7. *pathological*　　　lying is a *disease*

8. *unconscionable*　　*lack of regret or remorse*

9. *glib*　　　　　　great *smoothness*

10. *egregious*　　　 *viciousness* of the lies

These ten expressive adjectives，needless to say，are not restricted to lying or liars. Note their general meanings：

不用说,这 10 个极具表现力的形容词并不局限于描述撒谎的行为或者撒谎的人。请注意它们笼统的含义：

1. *notorious*　　　　well-known for some bad quality—a *notorious* philanderer

2. *consummate*　　　perfect，highly skilled—*consummate* artistry at the keyboard

3. *incorrigible*　　　beyond reform—an *incorrigible* optimist

4. *inveterate*　　　　long-accustomed，deeply habituated an—*inveterate* smoker（this adjective，like *notorious*，usually has an unfavorable connotation）

5. *congenital*　　　　happening at or during birth—a *congenital* deformity

6. *chronic*　　　　　going on for a long time，or occurring again and again—*chronic* appendicitis

7. *pathological*　　　diseased—a *pathological* condition

8. *unconscionable*　　without pangs of conscience—*unconscionable* cruelty to children

9. *glib*　　　　　　smooth，suspiciously fluent—a *glib* witness

10. *egregious*　　　 outstandingly bad or vicious—an *egregious* error

With the exception of *consummate* and *congenital*，all ten adjectives have strongly derogatory implications and are generally used to describe people，characteristics，or conditions we disapprove of.

这 10 个形容词除 consummate 和 congenital 之外都有强烈的贬义,通常用来形容不为大众接受的人、特征或状况。

USING THE WORDS
单词应用

Can you pronounce the words?
你能读出这些单词吗？

1. *notorious*　　　 nə-TAWR′-ee-əs

2. *consummate*　　 kən-SUM′-ət

3. *incorrigible*　　 in-KAWR′-ə-jə-bəl

4. *inveterate*　　　 in-VET′-ə-rət

5. *congenital*　　　 kən-JEN′-ə-təl

6. *chronic*	KRON′-ik
7. *pathological*	path′-ə-LOJ′-ə-kəl
8. *unconscionable*	un-KON′-shə-nə-bəl
9. *glib*	GLIB
10. *egregious*	ə-GREE′-jəs

Can you work with the words?

你能灵活使用这些词汇了吗？

1. notorious	a. beyond reform
2. consummate	b. continuing over a long period of time; recurring
3. incorrigible	c. diseased
4. inveterate	d. from long-standing habit
5. congenital	e. suspiciously smooth
6. chronic	f. without conscience or scruples
7. pathological	g. outstandingly bad or vicious
8. unconscionable	h. unfavorably known
9. glib	i. from birth
10. egregious	j. finished, perfect, artistic

KEY：1-h，2-j，3-a，4-d，5-i，6-b，7-c，8-f，9-e，10-g

Do you understand the words?

你对这些词汇是否已经透彻地理解？

1. Do people become *notorious* for good acts?	YES	NO
2. Is Beethoven considered a *consummate* musical genius?	YES	NO
3. If a criminal is truly *incorrigible*, is there any point in attempting rehabilitation?	YES	NO
4. Does an *inveterate* smoker smoke only occasionally?	YES	NO
5. Is a *congenital* deformity one that occurs late in life?	YES	NO
6. Is a *chronic* invalid ill much of the time?	YES	NO
7. Is a *pathological* condition normal and healthy?	YES	NO
8. If a person commits an *unconscionable* act of cruelty, is there any regret, remorse, or guilt?	YES	NO
9. Is a *glib* talker awkward and hesitant in	YES	NO

speech?

10. Is an *egregious* error very bad?　　　　　　　　　　YES　　　NO

KEY：1-no，2-yes，3-no，4-no，5-no，6-yes，7-no，8-no，9-no，10-yes

Can you recall the words?
你能够写出这些词汇吗？

1. outstandingly vicious; so bad
   as to be in a class by itself　　　　　　　　1. E _____

2. starting at birth　　　　　　　　　　　　　　2. C _____

3. happening over and over again;
   continuing for a long time　　　　　　　　　3. C _____

4. widely and unfavorably known
   (as for antisocial acts, character
   weaknesses, immoral or unethical behavior, etc.)　　4. N _____

5. beyond correction　　　　　　　　　　　　　5. I _____

6. smooth and persuasive; unusually,
   almost suspiciously, fluent　　　　　　　　　6. G _____

7. long addicted to a habit　　　　　　　　　　7. I _____

8. perfect in the practice of an art;
   extremely skillful　　　　　　　　　　　　　8. C _____

9. unscrupulous; entirely without
   conscience　　　　　　　　　　　　　　　　9. U _____

10. diseased　　　　　　　　　　　　　　　　10. P _____

KEY：1-egregious，2-congenital，3-chronic，4-notorious，5-incorrigible，6-glib，7-inveterate，8-consummate，9-unconscionable，10-pathological

Can you use the words?
你会用这些词汇了吗？

As a result of the tests you are taking, you are becoming more and more familiar with these ten valuable and expressive words. Now, as a further check on your learning, write the word that best fits each blank.

在进行完这些测试后，你对这10个宝贵的极具表现力的单词越来越熟悉了。现在，请你在空格处填上最合适的词，以进一步检验你的学习成果。

1. This person has gambled, day in and day out, for as long as anyone can re-member—gambling has become a deep-rooted habit.

1. An _____ gambler

2. Born with a clubfoot

    2. A _____ deformity

3. Someone known the world over for criminal acts

    3. A _____ criminal

4. An invading army kills, maims, and tortures without mercy, compunction, or regret.

    4. _____ acts of cruelty

5. The suspect answers the detective's questions easily, fluently, almost too smoothly.

    5. _____ responses

6. A person reaches the acme of perfection as an actress or actor.

    6. A _____ performer

7. No one can change someone's absurdly romantic attitude toward life.

    7. An _____ romantic

8. A mistake so bad that it defties description

    8. An _____ blunder

9. Drunk almost all the time, again and again and again—periods of sobriety are few and very, very far between

    9. A _____ alcoholic

10. Doctors find a persistent, dangerous infection in the bladder

    10. A _____ condition

KEY: 1-inveterate, 2-congenital, 3-notorious, 4-unconscionable, 5-glib, 6-consummate, 7-incorrigible, 8-egregious, 9-chronic, 10-pathological

---

(End of Session 14)

SESSION 15
第 15 节

ORINGIN AND RELATED WORDS
词源和相关词汇

1. well-known
闻名

"Widely but unfavorably known" is the common definition for *notorious*. Just as a *notorious* liar is well-known for unreliable statements, so a *notorious* gambler, a *notorious* thief, or a *notorious* killer has achieved a wide reputation for some form of antisocial behavior. The noun is *notoriety* (nō-tə-Rī'-ə-tee).

The derivation is from Latin *notus*, known, from which we also get *noted*. It is an interesting characteristic of some words that a change of syllables can alter the emotional impact. Thus, an admirer of certain business executives will speak of them as "*noted* industrialists"; these same people's enemies will call them "*notorious* exploiters." Similarly, if we admire a man's or a woman's unworldliness, we refer to it by the complimentary term *childlike*; but if we are annoyed by the trait, we describe it, derogatively, as *childish*. Change "*-like*" to "*-ish*" and our emotional tone undergoes a complete reversal.

"臭名昭著"是对 notorious 的定义。a notorious liar 由于不可靠的言语而闻名,而 notorious gambler(赌徒),notorious thief(窃贼)或 notorious killer(杀手)同样由于其反社会行为而广为人知。名词形式是 notoriety。

词源是拉丁语形容词,notus,意为"出名的",noted 也同样源于这个词根。有趣的是,一些词的音节改变之后,其情感含义也发生变化。这样,某些企业高管的崇拜者会将其称为 noted industrialist(知名的企业家);而这些高管的对手则会将他们称为 notorious exploiter(臭名昭著的剥削者)。同样,如果我们欣赏一位男士或女士不谙世事,我们会使用赞美的语言,将其称为 childlike;但是如果我们讨厌这个特点,我们会贬低其为 childish。将-like 改为-ish 的同时,我们的感情色彩变得完全相反。

2. plenty of room at the top
顶端的极大空间

The top of a mountain is called, as you know, the *summit*, a word derived from Latin *summus*, highest, which also gives us the mathematical term *sum*, as in addition. A *consummate* artist has reached the very highest point of perfection; and to *consummate* (KON'-sə-mayt') a marriage, a business deal, or a contract is, etymologically, to bring it to the highest point; that is, to put the final touches to it, to bring it to completion.

山顶最高点被称为 summit,来源于拉丁语 summus,表示"最高的"。数学加法术语 sum(总和)当然也是由此而来。a consummate artist(一位精湛的艺术家)已经达到了艺术的最高峰;从语源学上说,consummate a marriage、a business deal 或 a contract,是将它们引至最高点;换言之,就是对它们进行最后的修正、润色,将其完成。

3. no help
无药可救

Call people *incorrigible* (in-KAWR'-ə-jə-bəl) if they do anything to excess, and if all efforts to correct or reform them are to no avail. Thus，one can be an *incorrigible idealist*，an *incorrigible* criminal，an *incorrigible* optimist，or an *incorrigible* philanderer. The word derives from Latin *corrigo*，to correct or set straight，plus the negative prefix *in-*. (This prefix，depending on the root it precedes，may be negative，may intensify the root，as in *invaluable*，or may mean *in*.)

The noun is *incorrigibility* (in-kawr′-ə-jə-BIL′-ə-tee) or，alternatively，*incorrigibleness*.

如果一个人过分放肆，任何改变他的努力都无济于事，那么我们可以将他称之为 incorrigible。incorrigible idealist 指"无药可救的理想家"；incorrigible criminal 指"屡教不改的罪犯"，incorrigible optimist 指"无可救药的乐观主义者"，incorrigible philanderer 指"积习难改的花心男"。这个单词源于拉丁语 corrigo，意为"改正"或"扶正"，加上否定前缀 in-。(这个前缀，根据其后面的词根，可以表示否定，可以加强原词根的本义，如 invaluable，或表示"在……里")

名词形式是 incorrigibility 或 incorrigibleness。

4. veterans

老手

Inveterate，from Latin *vetus*，old，[1] generally indicates disapproval.

Inveterate gamblers have grown old in the habit，etymologically speaking；*inveterate* drinkers have been imbibing for so long that they，too，have formed old，well-established habits；and *inveterate* liars have been lying for so long，and their habits are by now so deep-rooted，that one can scarcely remember (the word implies) when they ever told the truth.

The noun is *inveteracy* (in-VET′-ər-ə-see) or *inveterateness*.

A *veteran* (VET′-ə-rən)，as of the Armed Forces，grew older serving the country；otherwise a *veteran* is an old hand at the game (and therefore skillful). The word is both a noun and an adjective：a *veteran* at (or in) swimming，tennis，police work，business，negotiations，diplomacy—or a *veteran* actor，teacher，diplomat，political reformer.

inveterate 来源于希腊语词根 vetus(老的)，通常表贬义。

从语源学角度来看，inveterate gamblers(顽固的赌徒)是指赌博已成为他们的"老"习惯；inveterate drinkers(嗜酒成瘾的人)指他们养成了嗜酒成性的"老"习惯；当然，inveterate liar 指"积习已久的骗子"，他们说谎的习惯延续已久，根深蒂固，以至于几乎没有人记得他们什么时候曾经说过实话(inveteran 中的隐含之义)。

名词形式是 inveteracy 或 inveterateness。

部队里的 veteran 指在长年为国服务的过程中变老的人；veteran 也可以指在某个领域中的老手(往往技术熟练)。这个词既可以作为形容词，也可作为名词，例如：a veteran at (or in) swimming，tennis，police work，business，negotiations，diplomacy—or a veteran actor，teacher，diplomat，political reformer 等。

---

1. Latin *senex*，source of *senile* and *senescent*，also，you will recall，means old. In *inveterate*，*in-* means *in*；it is not the negative prefix found，in *incorrigible*.

你应该记得，senile 和 senescent 两词来源于拉丁词根 senex，这个词根也是"老"的意思。inveterate 中的前缀 in-是"在……里面"的意思，与 incorrigible 中的前缀 in-意思不同，后者是表示否定。

5. birth

出生

Greek *genesis*, birth or origin, a root we discovered in discussing *psychogenic* (Chapter 5), is the source of a great many English words.

希腊词根 genesis(意为"出生"或者"起源")在第 5 章中,我们讨论过的单词 psychogenic,就是由此词根演变而来,并且此词根衍生出许多英语词汇。

Genetics (jə-NET′-iks) is the science that treats of the transmission of hereditary characteristics from parents to offspring. The scientist specializing in the field is a *geneticist* (jə-NET′-ə-sist), the adjective is *genetic* (jə-NET′-ik). The particle in the chromosome of the germ cell containing a hereditary characteristic is a *gene* (JEEN).

Genealogy (jeen′-ee-AL′-ə-jee) is the study of family trees or ancestral origins (*logos*, study). The practitioner is a *genealogist* (jeen′-ee-AL′-ə-jist). Can you form the adjective? _____. (And can you pronounce it?)

genetics,"遗传学",是研究父母将遗传基因传递给下一代的科学。研究遗传学的科学家是 geneticist,形容词是 genetic;在生殖细胞的染色体中包含遗传信息的物质就是 gene,"基因"。

genealogy(家谱学)是研究家庭谱系和家族史的学科(后缀 logos 意为"研究"),从业者被称为 genealogist。你能写出它的形容词形式吗?(你会发音吗?)

The *genital* (GEN′-ə-təl), or sexual, organs are involved in the process of conception and birth. The *genesis* (JEN′-ə-sis) of anything—a plan, idea, thought, career, etc.—is its beginning, birth, or origin, and *Genesis*, the first book of the Old Testament, describes the creation, or birth, of the universe.

Congenital is constructed by combining the prefix *con-*, with or together, and the root *genesis*, birth.

genital 意思是"生殖的",与怀孕和出生相关的器官是生殖器官(genital organs)。很多事物的 genesis——如计划、概念、职业生涯等——就是指这些事物的开始,诞生或起源。旧约圣经第一卷为 Genesis(《创世记》),记载宇宙的创造或诞生。

congenital(先天的)是由前缀 con-("和"或"在一起")加词根 genesis(意为"出生")构成。

So a *congenital* defect, deformity, condition, etc. occurs during the nine-month birth process (or period of gestation, to become technical). *Hereditary* (hə-RED′-ə-tair′-ee) characteristics, on the other hand, are acquired at the moment of conception. Thus, eye color, nose shape, hair texture, and other such qualities are *hereditary*; they are determined by the *genes* in the germ cells of the mother and father. But a thalidomide baby resulted from the use of the drug by a pregnant woman, so the deformities were *congenital*.

一个 congenital(先天性的)的缺陷、畸形、状况等,发生在长达 9 个月的生育过程中(或更确切的说是怀孕期间),另一方面,hereditary (hə-RED′-ə-tair′-ee) characteristics(遗传特征)是怀孕的时候被决定的。所以,眼睛的颜色、鼻子的形状、头发质地及其他特性可以用 hereditary 解释,因为这些特性是由受精卵中父母的基因所决定的。但一个"镇静剂宝宝"是孕妇用药所致,因此这种畸形可称为 congenital(先天性的)。

Congenital is used both literally and figuratively. Literally, the word generally refers to some medical deformity or abnormality occurring during gestation. Figuratively, it wildly exaggerates, for effect, the very early existence of some quality:

congenital liar，*congenital* fear of the dark，etc.

congenital 既可以用于本义，也可以用于比喻。从字面意思理解，congenital 指怀孕时造成的畸形等问题。从其比喻义上看，为了增强效果，它可以非常夸张地形容早已存在的一些品质：congenital liar(天生的骗子)，congenital fear of the dark(天生怕黑)，等等。

REVIEW OF ETYMOLOGY
复习词源

PREFIX，ROOT	MEANING	ENGLISH WORD
1. *notus*	known	_____
2. *summus*	highest	_____
3. *corrigo*	to correct，set straight	_____
4. *vetus*	old	_____
5. *senex*	old	_____
6. *genesis*	birth，origin	_____
7. *logos*	science，study	_____
8. *in-*	negative prefix	_____

USING THE WORDS
单词应用

Can you pronounce the words?
你能读出这些单词吗？

1. *notoriety*	nō-tə-Ri′-ə-tee
2. *(to)consumate* (*v.*)	KON′-sə-mayt′
3. *consummacy*	kən-SUM′-ə-see
4. *consummation*	kon′-sə-MAY′-shən
5. *incorrigibility*	in-kawr′-ə-jə-BIL-ə-tee
6. *inveteracy*	in-VET′-ə-tə-see
7. *veteran*	VET′-ə-rən
8. *genetics*	jə-NET′-iks
9. *geneticist*	jə-NET′-ə-sist
10. *genetic*	jə-NET′-ik
11. *gene*	JEEN
12. *genealogy*	jee′-nee-AL′-ə-jee
13. *genealogist*	jee′-nee-AL′-ə-jist
14. *genealogical*	jee′-nee-ə-LOJ′-ə-kəl
15. *genital*	JEN′-ə-təl
16. *genesis*	JEN′-ə-sis
17. *hereditary*	hə-RED′-ə-tair′-ee

Can you work with the words?
你能灵活使用这些词汇了吗？

1. notoriety	a. state of artistic height
2. to consummate (*v.*)	b. state of being long established in a habit
3. consummacy	c. beginning, origin
4. incorrigibility	d. science of heredity
5. inveteracy	e. bring to completion; top off
6. genetics	f. study of ancestry
7. genealogy	g. referring to characteristics passed on to offspring by parents
8. genital	h. referring to reproduction, or to the reproductive or sexual organs
9. genesis	i. ill fame
10. hereditary	j. particle that transmits hereditary characteristics
11. gene	k. state of being beyond reform or correction

KEY: 1-i, 2-e, 3-a, 4-k, 5-b, 6-d, 7-f, 8-h, 9-c, 10-g, 11-j

Do you understand the words?
你对这些词汇是否已经透彻地理解？

1. Does *notoriety* usually come to perpetrators of mass murders?   YES   NO

2. Is the product of a *consummately* skillful counterfeiter likely to be taken as genuine?   YES   NO

3. Is *incorrigibility* in a criminal a sign that rehabilitation is possible?   YES   NO

4. Is a *geneticist* interested in your parents' characteristics?   YES   NO

5. Does *inveteracy* suggest that a habit is new?   YES   NO

6. When you *consummate* a deal, do you back out of it?   YES   NO

7. Is a *veteran* actress long experienced at her art?   YES   NO

8. Do *genes* determine heredity?   YES   NO

9. Is a *genealogist* interested in your family origins?   YES   NO

10. Are the *genital* organs used in reproduction?   YES   NO

11. Is the *genesis* of something the final point?   YES   NO

12. Are *hereditary* characteristics derived   YES   NO
    from parents?

KEY：1-yes，2-yes，3-no，4-yes，5-no，6-no，7-yes，8-yes，9-yes，10-yes，11-no，12-yes

Can you recall the words?
你能够写出这些词汇吗？

1. sexual；reproductive   1. G _____
2. to complete   2. C _____
3. wide and unfavorable reputation   3. N _____
4. particle in the chromosome of   4. G _____
   a cell that transmits a characteristic
   from parent to offspring
5. completion   5. C _____
6. inability to be reformed   6. I _____
7. the science that deals with the   7. G _____
   transmission of characteristics from
   parents to children
8. referring to a quality or characteristic   8. H _____
   that is inherited (*adj.*)
9. beginning or origin   9. G _____
10. student of family roots or origins   10. G _____
11. height of skill or artistry   11. C _____
                                                    or C _____
12. transmitted by heredity   12. G _____
13. quality of a habit that has been   13. I _____
    established over many years   *or* I _____
14. a person long experienced at a   14. V _____
    profession，art，or business
15. pertaining to a study of family   15. G _____
    origins (*adj.*)

KEY：1-genital，2-consummate，3-notoriety，4-gene，5-consummation，6-incorrigibility，7-genetics，8-hereditary，9-genesis，10-genealogist，11-consummacy *or* consummateness，12-genetic，13-inveteracy *or* inveterateness，14-veteran，15-genealogical

(End of Session 15)

SESSION 16
第 16 节

ORIGINS AND RELATED WORDS
词源及相关词汇

1. of time and place
时间与地点

A *chronic* liar lies constantly, again and again and again; a *chronic* invalid is ill time after time, frequently, repeatedly. The derivation of the word is Greek *chronos*, time, The noun form is *chronicity* (krə-NIS′-ə-tee).

chronic liar(积习难改的说谎者)时刻在说谎,没有停歇;chronic invalid 是个"病包儿",总是生病。chronic 是由希腊词 chronos,"时间",演变而来。名词形式是 chronicity。

An *anachronism* (ə-NAK′-rə-niz-əm) is someone or something out of time, out of date, belonging to a different era, either earlier or later. (The prefix *ana-* like *a-*, is negative.) The adjective is *anachronous* (ə-NAK′-rə-nəs) or *anachronistic* (ə-nak′-rə-NIS′-tik).

anachronism 指不合时宜的人或物,他(或它)属于不同于现在的时代,要么比现在早,要么比现在晚。(前缀 ana-,就像 a——一样,是表示否定的前缀)。形容词是 anachronous 或 anachronistic。

Wander along Fifty-ninth Street and Central Park in Manhattan some Sunday. You will see horse-drawn carriages with top-hatted coachmen—a vestige of the 1800s. Surrounded by twentieth-century motorcars and modern skyscrapers, these romantic vehicles of a bygone era are *anachronous*.

某个星期日,你漫步在纽约第 59 街和中央公园,你会看见马车奔驰而过,车上坐着的马车夫戴着高帽——这是 19 世纪的遗迹。被 20 世纪的机动车和摩天大楼所围绕,这些过往时代浪漫的交通工具已经变得不合时宜——anachronous。

Read a novel in which a scene is supposedly taking place in the nineteenth century and see one of the characters turning on a TV set. An *anachronism*!

Your friend talks, thinks, dresses, and acts as if he were living in the time of Shakespeare. Another *anachronism*!

读一本以 19 世纪为背景的小说,却看到书中一个人物打开电视机。这就是算是一个 anachronism(时代错误)!
你的朋友谈话、思想、穿着和行为像是活在莎士比亚时代,也可称为是 anachronism!

Science fiction is deliberately *anachronous*—it deals with phenomena, gadgetry, accomplishments far off (possibly) in the future.

An *anachronism* is out of *time*; something out of *place* is *incongruous* (in-KONG′-groo-əs), a word combining the negative prefix *in-*, the prefix *con-*, with or together, and a Latin verb meaning to *agree* or *correspond*.

Thus, it is *incongruous* to wear a sweater and slacks to a formal wedding; it is *anachronous* to wear the wasp waist, conspicuous bustle, or powdered wig of the eighteenth century. The noun form of *incongruous* is *incongruity* (in-kəng-GROO-ə-tee).

科幻小说会故意设置"时代错误",来呈现未来的现象、机械和有可能取得的成就等。

anachronism 是"不合时宜";不在其恰当位置的东西就显得不协调(incongruous)。incongruous 由表示否定的前缀 in-和表示"和,一起"的前缀 con-加上表示"符合,对应"的拉丁动词组成。

这样,如果婚礼穿毛衣和宽松裤就是 incongruous(不协调);穿 18 世纪的束腰、醒目的裙撑和施粉的假发就是 anachronous(不合时宜)。incongruous 的名词形式是 incongruity。

Chronological (kron-ə-LOJ'-ə-kəl), in correct time order, comes from *chronos*. To tell a story *chronologically* is to relate the events in the time order of their occurrence. *Chronology* (krə-NOL'-ə-jee) is the science of time order and the accurate dating of events (*logos*, *science*)—the expert in this field is a *chronologist* (krə-NOL'-ə-jist)—or a list of events in the time order in which they have occurred or will occur.

chronological,按时间先后顺序排列的,源于 chronos。to tell a story chronologically 就是按照事情的发生先后叙述故事。chronology 是研究时间先后顺序以及事件发生准确日期的科学(logos,科学)——这个领域的专家称为 chronologist——或事件发生先后顺序的列表,其中包括已经发生的和将要发生的。

A *chronometer* (krə-NOM'-ə-tər), combining *chronos* with *metron*, measurement, is a highly accurate timepiece, especially one used on ships. *Chronometry* (krə-NOM'-ə-tree) is the measurement of time——the adjective is *chronometric* (kron'-ə-MET'-rik).

chronometer 由 chronos 和 metron(测量)组成,是一个高度精密的计时器,尤其是应用在船上的。chronometry 是指时间的计量——其形容词是 chronometric。

Add the prefix *syn-*, together, plus the verb suffix *-ize*, to *chronos*, and you have constructed *synchronize* (SIN'-krə-nīz'), etymologically *to time together*, or to move, happen, or cause to happen, at the same time or rate. If you and your friend *synchronize* your watches, you set them at the same time. If you *synchronize* the activity of your arms and legs, as in swimming, you move them at the same time or rate. The adjective is *synchronous* (SIN'-krə-nəs); the noun form of the verb *synchronize* is *synchronization* (sin'-krə-nə-ZAY'-shən).

将 chronos 加上前缀 syn-(一起)和动词后缀-ize,组成单词 synchronize,词源意义为"在时间上连接起来",或者是"在相同的时间或以相同的频率移动,发生或者使……发生"。假如你和你的朋友 synchronize 你们的手表,就是说让你们的手表时间完全一样。当你游泳时,synchronize 你的腿和手臂,就是说你同时或以相同的频率移动它们。形容词是 synchronous;动词 synchronize 的名词形式是 synchronization。

2. disease, suffering, feeling

疾病,苦难,感受

Pathological is *diseased* (a *pathological* condition)—this meaning of the word ignores the root *logos*, science, study.

Pathology (pə-THOL'-ə-jee) *is* the science or study of disease—its nature, cause, cure, etc. However, another meaning of the noun ignores *logos*, and *pathol-*

ogy may be any morbid, diseased, or abnormal physical condition or conditions; in short, simply *disease*, as in "This case involves so many kinds of *pathology* that several different specialists are working on it."

pathological 是指患病的——这个意思与其中的词根 logos(科学,研究),没有关联。

pathology 是研究疾病的本质、病因、治疗方法等的科学。然而,这个名词另外的意思和词根 logo 代表的含义也不太相关,可能是指病态的、生病的、或者不正常的身体症状(可以指一个症状,也可以指多个)。简单的说,就是"disease"的意思,如在句子中"This case involves so many kinds of pathology that several different specialists are working on it.(这个病例涉及许多疾病,几个不同领域的专家正在研究它。)"

A *pathologist* (pə-THOL'-ə-jist) is an expert who examines tissue, often by autopsy or biopsy, to diagnose disease and interpret the abnormalities in such tissue that may be caused by specific diseases.

pathologist 就是检查身体组织的专家,使用尸体解剖或活体器官的方法诊断疾病,对特定疾病引起的组织异常进行分析。

Pathos occurs in some English words with the additional meaning of *feeling*. If you feel or suffer with someone, you are *sympathetic* (sim-pə-THET'-ik)—*sym-* is a respelling before the letter *p* of the Greek prefix *syn-*, with or together. The noun is *sympathy* (SIM'-pə-thee), the verb *sympathize* (SIM'-pə-thīz). Husbands, for example, so the story goes, may have *sympathetic* labor pains when their wives are about to deliver.

在一些英文单词中,pathos 有另外一个意思"感觉"。如果你和某人一同感受或忍受,那么你是 sympathetic——sym-是希腊前缀 syn-在字母 p 前另外一种拼写方式,意为"和……或在一起"。名词形式是 sympathy,动词是 sympathize。例如,妻子要分娩时,据说丈夫也会出现分娩阵痛,这种反应就是 sympathetic。

The prefix *anti-*, you will recall, means *against*. If you experience *antipathy* (an-TIP'-ə-thee) to people or things, you feel *against* them—you feel strong dislike or hostility. The adjective is *antipathetic* (an'-tə-pə-THET'-ik), as in "an *antipathetic* reaction to an authority figure."

But you may have *no* feeling at all—just indifference, lack of any interest, emotion, or response, complete listlessness, especially when some reaction is normal or expected. Then you are *apathetic* (ap-ə-THET'-ik); *a-*, as you know, is a negative prefix. The noun is *apathy* (AP'-ə-thee), as in voter *apathy*, student *apathy*, etc.

你会回想起来,前缀 anti-意为"反对",如果你对某些人或事感到 antipathy,就是说你对他们感到 against(逆反)——即你有强烈的厌恶感和敌意。其形容词是 antipathetic,如短语"an antipathetic reaction to an authority figure(对权势人物的反感)"。

你可能根本没有感觉——只是漠不关心,缺乏兴趣、情绪或反应,完全无动于衷,尤其是在人们期待你做出一些正常反应的时候,那你就是 apathetic;如你所知,a-是一个否定前缀。名词是 apathy,如 voter apathy,student apathy。

On the other hand, you may be so sensitive or perceptive that you not only share the feelings of another, but you also *identify* with those feelings, in fact experience them yourself as if momentarily you were that other person. What you have, then, is *empathy* (EM'-pə-thee); you *empathize* (EM'-pə-thīz'), you are *empathetic* (em-pə-THET′-ik), or, to use an alternate adjective, *empathic* (em-PATH′-ik). *Em-* is a respelling before the letter *p* of the Greek prefix *en-*, in.

另一方面,你可能如此敏感或敏锐,你不仅分担别人的感受,而且认同那种感受,实际上你自己也体验到同样的感受,好像暂时你就是那个人。你的这种感觉就是 empathy;也可以说,你 empathize,你是 empathetic,或用另外一个替代形容词 empathic。在字母 p 前的 em-是希腊前缀 en-的另外一种拼写,意为 in。

Someone is *pathetic* (pə-THET′-ik) who is obviously suffering—such a person may arouse sympathy or pity (or perhaps *antipathy*?) in you. A *pathetic* story is about suffering and, again, is likely to arouse sadness, sorrow, or pity.

当一个人 pathetic 伤感时,显然他是在遭受苦难——这样一个人可能让你感到同情和怜悯(或者让你反感)。一个 pathetic 的故事是跟苦难有关,能激发人们的悲哀、苦痛和怜悯。

Some interesting research was done many years ago by Dr. J. B. Rhine and his associates at Duke University on extrasensory perception; you will find an interesting account of Rhine's work in his book *The Reach of the Mind*. What makes it possible for two people separated by miles of space to communicate with each other without recourse to messenger, telephone, telegraph, or postal service? It can be done, say the believers in *telepathy* (tə-LEP′-ə-thee), also called *mental telepathy*, though they do not yet admit to knowing how. How can one person read the mind of another? Simple—by being *telepathic* (tel-ə-PATH′-ik), but no one can explain the chemistry or biology of it. *Telepathy* is built by combining *pathos*, feeling, with the prefix *tele-*, distance, the same prefix we found in *telephone*, *telegraph*, *telescope*.

Telepathic (tel-ə-PATH′-ik) communication occurs when people can *feel* each other's thoughts from a distance, when they have ESP.

多年前,杜克大学的 J. B. 莱因博士和他的团队对超感官知觉做了一些有趣的研究;他的著作《心灵的延伸》中有许多饶有兴味的论述。两人远隔万里,没有信使、电话、电报或者邮件服务,是什么使他们能够相互交流?相信 telepathy 或者 mental telepathy(心灵感应)的人们认为这的确是可能的,虽然他们承认自己不知道是如何做到的。一个人如何读懂另外一个人的心思? 很简单——就是做个 telepathic(有心灵感应的)的人;但是没有人能够解释其中的化学或者生物原因。telepathy 由 pathos(感觉)和 tele(自远方的)组成。前缀 tele-还见于 telephone(电话),telegraph(电报),和 telescope(望远镜)等词之中。

当人们具备特异功能,能够在远方感受到彼此的想法,就发生了 telepathic communication(心灵感应交流)。

REVIEW OF ETYMOLOGY
复习词源

PREFIX ROOT, SUFFIX	MEANING	ENGLISH WORD
1. *chronos*	time	_____
2. *ana-*, *a-*	negative prefix	_____
3. *con-*	with, together	_____
4. *in-*	negative prefix	_____
5. *logos*	science, study	_____
6. *metron*	measurement	_____

7. *syn-*, *sym-*　　　　with, together　　　　_____

8. *-ize*　　　　　　　verb suffix　　　　　　_____

9. *pathos*　　　　　　disease，suffering，feeling　_____

10. *anti-*　　　　　　against　　　　　　　_____

11. *en-*, *em-*　　　　in　　　　　　　　　_____

12. *tele-*　　　　　　distance　　　　　　_____

USING THE WORDS
单词应用

Can you pronounce the words?（Ⅰ）
你能读出这些单词吗？（Ⅰ）

1. *chronicity*　　　　　　krə-NIS′-ə-tee
2. *anachronism*　　　　　ə-NAK′-rə-niz-əm
3. *anachronous*　　　　　ə-NAK′-rə-nəs
4. *anachronistic*　　　　ə-nak′-rə-NIS′-tik
5. *incongruous*　　　　　in-KONG′-grōō-əs
6. *incongruity*　　　　　in′-kəng-GRŌŌ′-ə-tee
7. *chronological*　　　　kron′-ə-LOJ′-ə-kəl
8. *chronology*　　　　　krə-NOL′-ə-lee
9. *chronologist*　　　　krə-NOL′-ə-jist
10. *chronometer*　　　　krə-NOM′-ə-tər
11. *chronometry*　　　　krə-NOM′-ə-tree
12. *chronometric*　　　　kron′-ə-MET′-rik
13. *synchronize*　　　　SIN′-krə-nīz′
14. *synchronization*　　sin′-krə-nə-ZAY′-shən
15. *synchronous*　　　　SIN′-krə-nəs

Can you pronounce the words?（Ⅱ）
你能读出这些单词吗？（Ⅱ）

1. *pathology*　　　　　pə-THOL′-ə-jee
2. *pathologist*　　　　pə-THOL′-ə-jist
3. *sympathy*　　　　　SIM′-pə-thee
4. *sympathetic*　　　　sim-pə-THET′-ik
5. *sympathize*　　　　SIM′-pə-thīz
6. *antipathy*　　　　　an-TIP′-ə-thee
7. *antipathetic*　　　　an′-tə-pə-THET′-ik
8. *apathy*　　　　　　AP′-ə-thee
9. *apathetic*　　　　　ap-ə-THET′-ik
10. *empathy*　　　　　EM′-pə-thee

11. *empathize*	EM'-pə-thīz'
12. *empathetic*	em-pə-THET'-ik
13. *empathic*	em-PATH'-ik
14. *pathetic*	pə-THET'-ik
15. *telepathy*	tə-LEP'-ə-thee
16. *telepathic*	tel'-ə-PATH'-ik

Can you work with the words? (Ⅰ)

你能灵活使用这些词汇了吗? (Ⅰ)

1. chronicity	a. something, or state of being, out of place
2. anachronism	b. timepiece; device that measures time very accurately
3. incongruity	c. condition of continual or repeated recurrence
4. chronology	d. act of occurring, or of causing to occur, at the same time
5. chronometer	e. calendar of events in order of occurrence
6. chronometry	f. something, or someone, out of time
7. synchronization	g. measurement of time
8. pathology	h. a sharing or understanding of another's feeling
9. sympathy	i. ESP; communication from a distance
10. telepathy	j. disease; study of disease

KEY: 1-c, 2-f, 3-a, 4-e, 5-b, 6-g, 7--d, 8-j, 9-h, 10-i

Can you work with the words? (Ⅱ)

你能灵活使用这些词汇了吗? (Ⅱ)

1. pathologist	a. identification with another's feelings
2. antipathy	b. share another's feelings so strongly as to experience those feelings oneself
3. apathy	c. out of time
4. empathy	d. one who examines tissue to diagnose disease
5. synchronize	e. occurring at the same time or rate
6. empathize	f. relating to extrasensory perception
7. anachronous	g. suffering; arousing sympathy or pity
8. incongruous	h. lack of feeling; non-responsiveness
9. synchronous	i. out of place
10. pathetic	j. happen, or cause to happen, at the same

| | time or rate |
| 11. telepathic | k. hostility; strong dislike |

KEY: 1-d, 2-k, 3-h, 4-a, 5-j, 6-b, 7-c, 8-i, 9-e, 10-g, 11-f

Do you understand the words?
你对这些词汇是否已经透彻地理解?

1. Are these dates in *chronological* order?   YES   NO
   1492, 1941, 1586
2. Is *pathology* the study of healthy tissue?   YES   NO
3. Is *telepathic* communication carried on   YES   NO
   by telephone?
4. Does a *sympathetic* response show an   YES   NO
   understanding of another's feelings?
5. Is one *antipathetic* to things, ideas, or   YES   NO
   people one finds agreeable?
6. Do *apathetic* people react strongly?   YES   NO
7. Does an *empathic* response show   YES   NO
   identification with the feelings of another?
8. Is a swimsuit *incongruous* attire at a   YES   NO
   formal ceremony?
9. Is an *anachronistic* attitude up to date?   YES   NO
10. Are *synchronous* movements out of   YES   NO
    time with one another?

KEY: 1-no, 2-no, 3-no, 4-yes, 5-no, 6-no, 7-yes, 8-yes, 9-no,10-no

Can you recall the words?
你能够写出这些词汇吗?

1. in order of time	1. C _____
2. out of place	2. I _____
3. ,4. out of time (two forms)	3. A _____
	4. A _____
5. something, or state of being, out of place	5. I _____
6. lack of feeling	6. A _____
7. measurer of time	7. C _____

8. study of disease	8. P _____
9. feeling of hostility or dislike	9. A _____
10. to occur, or cause to occur, at the same time or rate	10. S _____
11. evoking sorrow or pity	11. P _____
12. something out of time	12. A _____
13. state of recurring again and again	13. C _____
14. extransensory perception	14. T _____
15. one who examines tissue to diagnose disease	15. P _____
16. identification with the feelings of another	16. E _____
17. happening at the same time or rate (*adj.*)	17. S _____
18. skillful at thought transference without sensory communication	18. T _____
19. calendar of events in time sequence	19. C _____
20. referring to the measurement of time (*adj.*)	20. C _____

KEY: 1-chronological, 2-incongruous, 3, 4-anachronous, anachronistic, 5-incongruity, 6-apathy, 7-chronometer, 8-pathology, 9-antipathy, 10-synchronize, 11-pathetic, 12-anachronism, 13-chronicity, 14-telepathy, 15-pathologist, 16-empathy, 17-synchronous, 18-telepathic, 19-chronology, 20-chronometric

(End of Session 16)

SESSION 17
第 17 节

ORIGINS AND RELATED WORDS
词源及相关词汇

1. knowing
知道

Psychopaths commit antisocial and *unconscionable* acts—they are not troubled by *conscience*, guilt, remorse, etc. over what they have done.

Unconscionable and *conscience* are related in derivation—the first word from Latin *scio*, to know, the second from Latin *sciens*, knowing, and both using the prefix *con*-, with, together.

psychopaths(精神变态者)的行为往往是反社会和没有道德约束的——对于自己的所作所为,他们不会被良心、罪恶感、自责所困扰。

从词语演变上看,unconscionable(没良心的)和 conscience(良心)是有联系的——前者源自拉丁词根 scio,意为"去了解",后者源于拉丁词根 sciens,意为"知道,了解",两者都用到了前缀 con-,"和,在一起"。

Etymologically, then, your *conscience* is your knowledge *with* a moral sense of right and wrong; if you are *unconscionable*, your conscience is not (*un*-) working, or you have no conscience. The noun form is *unconscionableness* or *unconscionability* (un-kon′-shə-nə-BIL′-ə-tee).

那么,从词源角度看,你的 conscience 就是你在道德层面对事物进行对错判断的知识。如果你是 unconscionable(没良心的),那就是你的良心没起作用(un-)、或者说你没有良心。其名词形式是 unconscionableness 或 unconscionability。

Conscious, also from *con*- plus *scio*, is knowledge or awareness of one's emotions or sensations, or of what's happening around one.

Science, from *sciens*, is systematized *knowledge* as opposed, for example, to belief, faith, intuition, or guesswork.

conscious(有意识的)也是来自 con-加 scio,是对个人情绪、感觉或周遭正在发生事件的了解或觉察。

science(科学)来源于 sciens,是系统化的知识,与信念、信仰、直觉或猜测相对。

Add Latin *omnis*, all, to *sciens*, to construct *omniscient* (om-NISH′-ənt), all-knowing, possessed of infinite knowledge. The noun is *omniscience* (om-NISH′-əns).

Add the prefix *pre*-, before, to *sciens*, to construct *prescient* (PREE′-shənt)—knowing about events *before* they occur, i. e., psychic, or possessed of unusual powers of prediction. The noun is *prescience* (PREE′-shəns).

And, finally, add the negative prefix *ne*- to *sciens* to produce *nescient* (NESH′-ənt),—not knowing, or ignorant. Can you, by analogy with the previous two words, write the noun form of *nescient*? _____. (Can you pronounce it?)

把拉丁词根 omnis(意为"全部"),加在 sciens 上,形成了 omniscient,意为"无所不知,拥有无比丰富的知识"。名词是 omniscience。

将 sciens 加上前缀 pre-(前面),构成 prescient——在事件发生前已经提前预知,即能通灵的,或具有非凡的预测能力。名词形式是 prescience。

最后,在 sciens 前加上否定前缀 ne-,就形成了 nescient——不知道的,无知的。通过类比前面这两个单词,你是否能写出 nescient 的名词形式?(你会发音吗?)

2. fool some of the people...

欺骗一些人……

Glib is from an old English root that means *slippery*. *Glib* liars or *glib* talkers are smooth and slippery; they have ready answers, fluent tongues, a persuasive air—but, such is the implication of the word, they fool only the most *nescient*, for their smoothness lacks sincerity and conviction.

The noun is *glibness*.

glib(油腔滑调的)源于一个古老的英语词根,意为"狡猾的"。glib liars 或者 glib talkers 是世故和狡猾的人;他们能应答自如,能说会道,让人觉得很有说服力——但这个词的隐含之义是,他们只能欺骗那些最无知的人,因为他们的世故缺乏真诚和真凭实据。

名词是 glibness。

3. herds and flocks

群

Egregious (remember the pronunciation? ə-GREE′-jəs) is from Latin *grex*, *gregis*, herd or flock. An *egregious* lie, act, crime, mistake, etc. is so exceptionally vicious that it conspicuously stands out (*e-*, a shortened form of the prefix *ex-*, out) from the *herd* or *flock* of other bad things.

The noun is *egregiousness* (ə-GREE′-jəs-nəs).

A person who enjoys companionship, who, etymologically, likes to be with the herd, who reaches out for friends and is happiest when surrounded by people—such a person is *gregarious* (grə- GAIR′-ee-əs).

egregious(记得这个读音吗?)出自拉丁词根 grex,gregis;这两个词根是 herd 或 flock 的意思。[1]

当说一个谎言、行为、罪行、错误等是"egregious"时,就是说它们异常的恶劣,所以比其他的坏事更显突出。

名词是 egregiousness。

一个喜欢和别人"互相做伴"的人,从本意上看就是一个"合群"的人,他喜欢交朋友,并特别享受置身人群的感觉。这样的人是 gregarious。

Extroverts are of course *gregarious*—they prefer human contact, conversation, laughter, interrelationships, to solitude.

The suffix *-ness*, as you know, can be added to an adjective to construct a noun form. Write the noun for *gregarious*:_____.

---

1. flock 用于表示同类的鸟群,或动物群,特别是羊群;在用于表示人群时,指人数众多的人群,例如 Vistors came in flocks to see the new bridge.(参观者成群结队地来观看这座新桥)。herd 表示生有角质蹄子的动物,如牛"群",例如 There we saw herds of cows grazing on the pasture.(我们在那里看到一群群的牛在草地上吃草);herd 在表示人群时,指普通人。——译者注

Add the prefix *con-*, with, together, to *grex*, *gregis*, to get the verb *congregate* (KONG′-grə-gayt′); add the prefix *se-*, apart, to build the verb *segregate* (SEG′-rə-gayt′); add the prefix *ad-*, to, toward (*ad-* changes to *ag-* before a root starting with *g-*), to construct the verb *aggregate* (AG-rə-gayt′).

extroverts(外向性格的人)就是"喜欢交际的"——与独处相比,他们更喜欢和人打交道、交谈、欢笑、交往。

正如你了解的那样,后缀-ness 可以放在形容词的后面而变成名词形式。请写出 gregarious 的名词形式。

把前缀 con-("和""与……在一起")放在 grex, gregis 的前面,而构成动词 congregate;加上前缀 se-(意为"分开")变成动词 segregate;加上前缀 ad-(意为"向、往""对于"[在以 g-开头的词根前,ad-变为 ag-],构成一个动词 aggregate。

Let's see what we have. When people gather *together* in a *herd* or *flock*, they (write the verb)＿＿＿＿＿＿＿＿. The noun is *congregation* (cong′-grə-GAY′-shən), one of the meanings of which is a religious "flock. "

我们回归到前面的例子。当人们聚集在一起变成一个 herd 或 flock 时,他们(写出动词形式)＿＿＿＿＿＿.其名词形式是 congregation,其中一个意思为一个有信仰的群体。

Put people or things apart from the *herd*, and you (write the verb)＿＿＿＿＿＿＿ them. Can you construct the noun by adding the suitable noun suffix? ＿＿＿＿＿＿.

Bring individual items to or toward the *herd* or *flock*, and you (write the verb)＿＿＿＿＿＿＿＿＿＿ them. What is the noun form of this verb? ＿＿＿＿＿＿

把人或事物从 herd(群)里分开,你(写出其动词形式)＿＿＿＿他(它)们,你能加上适当的名词后缀使其变成名词吗?

把个体放入群中,(写出动词形式)＿＿＿＿＿＿他们,这个动词的名词形式是什么?

The verb *aggregate* also means *to come together to or toward the herd*, that is, *to gather into a mass or whole*, or by extension, *to total or amount to*. So *aggregate*, another noun form, pronounced AG′-rə-gət, is a group or mass of individuals considered as a whole, a *herd*, or a *flock*, as in the phrase "people in the *aggregate*. . ."

动词 aggregate 也表示"来到一起"或"向着群走过来",也即"集合成在一大群",或"变成一个整体",或扩展抽象为"总计"或"算在一起"的意思。因此 aggregate 另外一种名词形式读作 AG′-rə-gət,就是一群或很大数量的个体被视作一个整体,"a herd, or a flock",如短语 people in the aggregate...(所有的人)

REVIEW OF ETYMOLOGY
复习词源

PREFIX, ROOT, SUFFIX	MEANING	ENGLISH WORD
1. *grex*, *gregis*	herd, flock	＿＿＿＿＿＿＿
2. *e-*, *ex-*	out	＿＿＿＿＿＿＿
3. *-ness*	noun suffix	＿＿＿＿＿＿＿
4. *con-*	with, together	＿＿＿＿＿＿＿
5. *ad-*, *ag-*	to, toward	＿＿＿＿＿＿＿
6. *un-*	negative prefix	＿＿＿＿＿＿＿

7. *scio*   to know   _____

8. *sciens*   knowing   _____

9. *omnis*   all   _____

10. *pre-*   before   _____

11. *ne-*   negative prefix   _____

12. *se-*   apart   _____

13. *-ion*   noun suffix added to verbs   _____

USING THE WORDS
单词应用

Can you pronounce the words?
你能读出这些单词吗？

1. *unconscionability*   un-kon′-shə-nə-BIL′-ə-tee

2. *omniscient*   om-NISH′-ənt

3. *omniscience*   om-NISH′-əns

4. *prescient*   PREE′-shənt

5. *prescience*   PREE′-shəns

6. *nescient*   NESH′-ənt

7. *nescience*   NESH′-əns

8. *glibness*   GLIB′-nəs

9. *egregiousness*   ə-GREE′-jəs-nəs

10. *gregarious*   grə-GAIR′-ee-əs

11. *gregariousness*   grə-GAIR′-ee-əs-nəs

12. *congregate*   KONG′-grə-gayt′

13. *congregation*   kong′-grə-GAY′-shən

14. *segregate*   SEG′-rə-gayt′

15. *segregation*   seg′-rə-GAY′-shən

16. *aggregate* (*v.*)   AG′-rə-gayt

17. *aggregate* (*n.*)   AG′-rə-gət

18. *aggregation*   ag′-rə-GAY′-shən

Can you work with the words?
你能灵活使用这些词汇了吗？

1. unconscionability   a. ignorance

2. omniscience   b. outstanding badness or viciousness

3. prescience   c. religious group; a massing together

4. nescience   d. total; mass; whole

5. glibness   e. exclusion from the herd; a setting apart

6. egregiousness   f. infinite knowledge

7. gregariousness	g. friendliness; enjoyment of mixing with people
8. congregation	h. lack of conscience
9. segregation	i. suspiciously smooth fluency
10. aggregate (*n.*)	j. foreknowledge

KEY：1-h，2-f，3-j，4-a，5-i，6-b，7-g，8-c，9-e，10-d

Do you understand the words?
你对这些词汇是否已经透彻地理解?

1. Is *unconscionability* one of the signs of the psychopath?	YES	NO
2. Can anyone be truly *omniscient*?	YES	NO
3. Does a *prescient* fear indicate some knowledge of the future?	YES	NO
4. Is *nescience* a result of learning?	YES	NO
5. Does *glibness* make someone sound sincere and trustworthy?	YES	NO
6. Is *egregiousness* an admirable quality?	YES	NO
7. Do *gregarious* people enjoy parties?	YES	NO
8. Do spectators *congregate* at sports events?	YES	NO
9. Do we often *segregate* hardened criminals from the rest of society?	YES	NO
10. Is an *aggregation* of problems a whole mass of problems?	YES	NO

KEY：1-yes，2-no，3-yes，4-no，5-no，6-no，7-yes，8-yes，9-yes，10-yes

Can you recall the words?
你能够写出这些词汇吗?

1. enjoying groups and companionship	1. G	_____
2. ignorant	2. N	_____
3. state of *not* being held back from antisocial behavior by one's conscience	3. U *or* U	_____ _____
4. having knowledge of an event before it occurs (*adj.*)	4. P	_____
5. a religious "flock"	5. C	_____
6. a total, whole, or mass	6. A	_____

	or A _____
7. to separate from the rest	7. S _____
8. suspiciously smooth fluency	8. G _____
9. all-knowing (*adj.*)	9. O _____
10. to come together into a group or mass	10. C _____

KEY：1-gregarious，2-nescient，3-unconscionability *or* unconscionableness，4-prescient，5-congregation，6-aggregate *or* aggregation，7-segregate，8-glibness，9-omniscient，10-congregate

CHAPTER REVIEW
章节复习

A. Do you recognize the words?

你认识这些单词吗？

1. Highly skilled：
   (a) consummate，(b) inveterate，(c) notorious
2. Beyond reform：
   (a) inveterate，(b) incorrigible，(c) glib
3. Dating from birth：
   (a) inveterate，(b) congenital，(c) psychopathic
4. Outstandingly bad：
   (a) egregious，(b) unconscionable，(c) chronic
5. Science of heredity：
   (a) pathology，(b) genetics，(c) orthopedics
6. Out of time：
   (a) incongruous，(b) anachronous，(c) synchronous
7. Study of disease：
   (a) pathology，(b) telepathy，(c) antipathy
8. Fond of company, friends, group activities, etc.：
   (a) apathetic，(b) gregarious，(c) chronological
9. Indifferent：
   (a) antipathetic，(b) pathetic，(c) apathetic
10. Long accustomed in habit：
    (a) incorrigible，(b) notorious，(c) inveterate
11. Study of family ancestry：
    (a) genealogy，(b) genetics，(c) genesis
12. To complete, finish, top off：

(a) synchronize，(b) consummate，(c) empathize

13. Accurate timepiece：

(a) anachronism，(b) chronology，(c) chronometer

14. Identification with the feelings of another：

(a) sympathy，(b) apathy，(c) empathy

15. Thought transference; extrasensory perception：

(a) telepathy，(b) empathy，(c) omniscience

16. Ignorance：

(a) omniscience，(b) prescience，(c) nescience

17. To gather into a group：

(a) congregate，(b) segregate，(c) synchronize

KEY：1-a，2-b，3-b，4-a，5-b，6-b，7-a，8-b，9-c，10-c，11-a，12-b，13-c，14-c，15-a，16-c，17-a

---

B. Can you recognize the roots?

你能认出这些词根吗?

ROOT	MEANING	EXAMPLE
1. *notus*		notorious
2. *summus*		summit
3. *corrigo*		incorrigible
4. *vetus*		veteran
5. *senex*		senile
6. *genesis*		congenital
7. *logos*		genealogy
8. *chronos*		chronic
9. *metron*		chronometer
10. *pathos*		pathology
		pathetic
		empathy
11. *grex*，*gregis*		gregarious
12. *scio*		unconscionable
13. *sciens*		prescience
14. *omnis*		omniscient

KEY：1-known，2-highest，3-to correct，set straight，4-old，5-old，6-birth，7-science，study，8-time，9-measurement，10-disease，suffering，feeling，11-herd，flock，12-to know，13-knowing，14-all

TEASER QUESTIONS FOR THE AMATEUR ETYMOLOGIST
词源小测验

1. "She was one of many *notables* who attended the convention." Recognizing that the italicized word is built on the root *notus*, can you define the noun *notable* in the context of *known*?

_____

_____.

2. *Notify* and *notice* derive from the same root. Can you define these two words, again in the context of *known*? *Notify*: _____. *Notice*: _____. What do you supose the verb suffix -*fy* of *notify* means? (Think also of *simplify*, *clarify*, *liquefy*, etc.)_____.

3. You are familiar with the roots *chronos* and *graphein*. Suppose you came across the word *chronograph* in your reading. Can you make an educated guess as to the meaning? _____

_____.

4. Recognizing the root *genesis* in the verb *generate*, how would you define the word? _____

_____.

How about *regenerate*? _____

_____.

What do you suppose the prefix *re*- means? _____

_____.

5. Recognizing the root *omnis* in *omnipotent* and *omnipresent*, can you define the words?

Omnipotent: _____

Omnipresent: _____

Recalling how we formed a noun from the adjective *omniscient*, write the noun forms of:

Omnipotent: _____

Omnipresent: _____

6. Think of the negative prefix in *anachronism*; think next of the noun *aphrodisiac*. Can you construct a word for *that which reduces* or *eliminates sexual desire*?

_____:

(Answers in Chapter 18)

(答案见第 18 章)

FOUR LASTING BENEFITS
4 个长远利益

You know by now that it is easy to build your vocabulary if you work diligently and intelligently. Diligence is important—to come to the book occasionally is to learn new words and ideas in an aimless fashion, rather than in the continuous way that characterizes the natural, uninterrupted, intellectual growth of a child. (You will recall that children are top experts in increasing their vocabularies.) And an intelligent approach is crucial—new words can be completely understood and permanently remembered only as symbols of vital ideas, never if memorized in long lists of isolated forms.

If you have worked diligently and intelligently, you have done much more than merely learned a few hundred new words. Actually, I needn't tell you what else you've accomplished, since, if you really have accomplished it, you can feel it for yourself; but it may be useful if I verbalize the feelings you may have.

In addition to learning the meanings, pronunciation, back ground, and use of 300-350 valuable words, you have:

1. *Begun to sense a change in your intellectual atmosphere.* (You have begun to do your thinking with many of the words, with many of the ideas behind the words. You have begun to use the words in your speech and writing, and have become alert to their appearance in your reading.)

2. *Begun to develop a new interest in words as expressions of ideas.*

3. *Begun to be aware of the new words you hear and that you see in your reading.*

4. *Begun to gain a new feeling for the relationship between words.* (For you realize that many words are built on roots from other languages and are related to other words which derive from the same roots.)

现在你知道,只要认真、方法得当,你就能够轻松扩大词汇量。恒心很重要——偶尔学习新词或概念只会使学习变得没有目标;而持之以恒的学习才能使你自然地、不中断地学习词汇,就像儿童的智力成长。(你一定还记得,儿童是扩展词汇的专家。)而得当的方法尤为关键——只有将词汇作为表达关键概念的符号,才能完全理解和永久记住新词。如果仅是记忆一长串孤立的单词,你永远达不到这个效果。

如果到现在为止你学习足够勤勉、方法足够得当,你肯定不只是学到了几百个新词。事实上,我无须告知你你还学到了其他的什么东西,因为如果你的确已经学到了这些东西的话,你自己就能够感觉到。但是,如果我将你的感受写成文字,也许会有更好的效果。

除了了解到 300—350 个宝贵单词的意思、发音、背景和用法之外,你还学到了以下 4 点:

1. 你已开始感受到自己知识氛围的变化。(你已经开始用学过的词汇和它们所代表的概念进行思考。你开始在言谈和写作中使用这些词汇。这些词汇出现在文本中时,你对它们更加敏感。)

2. 你开始产生新的兴趣,将词汇看作概念的表现形式。

3. 你开始注意到你听到和读到的新词。

4. 你能够更加深刻地体会词汇之间的关系。(因为你意识到,许多词汇的构建都是基于其他语言的词根,而具有相同词根的词汇之间也有密切的关系。)

Now, suppose we pause to see how successful your learning has been.

In the next chapter, I offer you a comprehensive test on the first part of your work.

现在,我们可以停下来看看你的学习成果。

在下一章中,我会提供一个综合性测验来检验你在第一部分的学习效果。

(End of Session 17)

8

HOW TO CHECK YOUR PROGRESS
如何检验你的进步

(*Comprehensive Test I*)

SESSION 18
第 18 节

If you have worked diligently thus far, you have:

1. Become acquainted, or perhaps reacquainted, with approximately 300-350 expressive words—

2. Learned scores of important Latin and Greek prefixes, roots, and suffixes—

3. Set up valuable habits of self-discipline and self-directed learning—

4. Explored your attitudes toward grammar and current usage, meanwhile erasing any confusion you may once have felt about specific problems of correctness in your use of words—

5. And, finally, taken good, long steps toward your ultimate goal, namely, the development of a better, richer, more expressive—in short, *superior*—vocabulary.

如果你足够勤勉,你一定已经取得了以下成就:

1. 你熟悉了 300—350 个有表现力的词,又或许你重新熟悉了这些词;

2. 你学到了几十个拉丁语和希腊语前缀、词根或者后缀;

3. 你也形成自律的习惯和自学的宝贵方法;

4. 你思考了某些语法和现代用法;同时消除了以前对某些具体的用法是否正确所存的困惑;

5. 最后,你朝着你的最终目标——积累更好、更丰富、更有表现力的词汇,简言之就是超级词汇——迈出了良好的、长远的一步。

Here is your chance both to review and to check your learning. (Bear in mind that without careful and periodic review, a significant amount of learning is lost.)

Methods of scoring your achievement on this test, and the meaning of your results, will be explained at the end of the chapter.

现在,你有机会对你的学习成果进行复习和检验。(记住,如果不能定期进行认真的复习,你学到的大部分知识都会遗忘。)

本次测验的记分方法、测验结果的分析将在本章结尾处说明。

Ⅰ　etymology

ROOT	MEANING	EXAMPLE
1. *ego*		egoism
2. *misein*		misanthrope
3. *gamos*		bigamy
4. *gyne*		gynecology
5. *derma*		dermatology
6. *orthos*		orthodontia
7. *psyche*		psychotic
8. *neuron*		neurology
9. *logos*		biology
10. *bios*		biopsy
11. *opsis, optikos*		autopsy, optical
12. *algos*		neuralgia
13. *agogos*		demagogue
14. *pedis*		pedestrian
15. *paidos* (*ped-*)		pediatrician
16. *demos*		democracy
17. *oculus*		oculist
18. *iatreia*		podiatrist
19. *metron*		optometrist
20. *geras*		geriatrics
21. *soma*		psychosomatic
22. *pathos*		osteopath
23. *odontos*		exodontist
24. *pous, podos*		octopus, podium
25. *cheir* (*chiro-*)		chirography

Ⅱ　more etymology

ROOT	MEANING	EXAMPLE
1. *graphein*		graphology
2. *kallos*		calligrapher
3. *pyge*		callipygian
4. *kakos*		cacophony
5. *senex*		senescent
6. *anthropos*		anthropology
7. *astron*		astronomy
8. *nautes*		astronaut

9. *ge* (*geo-*) _____ geology

10. *zoion* _____ zodiac

11. *lingua* _____ bilingual

12. *philein* _____ Philadelphia

13. *biblion* _____ bibliophile

14. *autos* _____ autonomous

15. *socius* _____ asocial

16. *notus* _____ notorious

17. *summus* _____ consummate

18. *vetus* _____ inveterate

19. *genesis* _____ congenital

20. *chronos* _____ chronic

21. *pathos* _____ empathy

22. *grex*, *gregis* _____ egregious

23. *sciens* _____ prescient

24. *omnis* _____ omniscient

25. *nomos* _____ metronome

Ⅲ　same or opposite

1. egoistic—altruistic   *S   O*

2. misanthropic—philanthropic   *S   O*

3. misogamous—polygamous   *S   O*

4. dexterous—skillful   *S   O*

5. sinister—threatening   *S   O*

6. optical—visual   *S   O*

7. notorious—infamous   *S   O*

8. consummate (*adj.*)—unskilled   *S   O*

9. chronic—acute   *S   O*

10. glib—halting   *S   O*

11. ophthalmologist—oculist   *S   O*

12. geriatric—pediatric   *S   O*

13. endodontist—exodontist   *S   O*

14. calligraphy—cacography   *S   O*

15. astronaut—cosmonaut   *S   O*

16. biopsy—autopsy   *S   O*

17. dichotomous—cut in two   *S   O*

18. congenital—hereditary   *S   O*

19. veteran—"old hand"   *S   O*

20. anachronous—timely   *S*   *O*

IV matching

I

1. dislikes women
2. is pathologically self-interested
3. studies the development of the human race
4. is an expert on insects
5. collects books
6. mounts and stuffs animal skins
7. is an eye doctor
8. is a student of linguistics
9. has "split off" from reality
10. commits antisocial acts without guilt
    or pangs of conscience

II

a. entomologist
b. taxidermist
c. egomaniac
d. bibliophile
e. ophthalmologist
f. psychopath
g. philologist
h. anthropologist
i. psychotic
j. misgynist

V more matching

I

1. delivers babies
2. treats female ailments
3. treats infants
4. treats skin diseases
5. treats skeletal deformities
6. is a heart specialist
7. treats mental or emotional disturbances
8. treats disorders of the nervous system
9. treats minor ailments of the feet
10. treats ailments of the gums

II

a. pediatrician
b. cardiologist
c. psychiatrist
d. podiatrist
e. dermatologist
f. periodontist
g. obstetrician
h. neurologist
i. orthopedist
j. gynecologist

VI recall a word

1. ruthless; without conscience
2. suspiciously fluent or smooth
3. outstandingly bad; vicious
4. out of place
5. study of the family tree; specialty of
   tracing ancestry
6. science of heredity
7. in correct order of time

1. U _____
2. G _____
3. E _____
4. I _____
5. G _____
6. G _____
7. C _____

8. socially awkward   8. G _____
9. record of heart action   9. C _____
10. equally skillful with both the right and   10. A _____
    left hand
11. social scientist who deals with the problems 11. G _____
    of aging
12. extrasensory perception   12. T _____
13. branch of dentistry specializing in the   13. P _____
    care of children's teeth
14. blood-pressure apparatus   14. S _____
15. growing old (*adj.*)   15. S _____
16. palm reader   16. C _____
17. that which arouses sexual desire   17. A _____
18. representation of the whole   18. E _____
19. diseased; pertaining to the study   19. P _____
    of disease (*adj.*)
20. measurement of time   20. C _____
21. hostility; strong dislike; aversion   21. A _____
22. to occur, or cause to occur, at the same   22. S _____
    time or rate
23. ignorant   23. N _____
24. knowledge of an occurrence beforehand   24. P _____
25. enjoying being with the herd; liking   25. G _____
    companionship
26. to identify strongly with the feelings of another 26. E _____
27. instrument to measure atmospheric pressure   27. B _____
28. to separate from the herd   28. S _____
29. possessed of shapely buttocks   29. C _____
30. ugly, illegible handwriting   30. C _____

KEY: A correct answer counts one point. Score your points for each part of the test, then add for a total.

一个正确的答案算 1 分。计算出你每部分测验的分数，然后将各部分所得分数相加。

I

1-I, self, 2-to hate, 3-marriage, 4-woman, 5-skin, 6-straight, correct, 7-mind, soul, spirit, 8-nerve, 9-science, study, 10-life, 11-view, sight, vision, 12-pain, 13-leading, 14-foot, 15-child, 16-people, 17-eye, 18-medical healing, 19-measurement, 20-old age, 21-body, 22-disease, 23-tooth, 24-foot, 25-hand

Your score：＿＿＿＿＿＿＿

Ⅱ

1-to write，2-beauty，3-buttock，4-harsh，ugly，bad，5-old，6-mankind，7-star，8-sailor，9-earth，10-animal，11-tongue，12-to love，13-book，14-self，15-companion，16-known，17-highest，18-old，19-birth（beginning，origin），20-time，21-feeling，22-herd，flock，23-knowing，24-all，25-law，order，arrangement

Your score：＿＿＿＿＿＿＿

Ⅲ

1-O，2-O，3-O，4-S，5-S，6-S，7-S，8-O，9-O，10-O，11-S，12-O，13-O，14-O，15-S，16-O，17-S，18-O，19-S，20-O

Your score：＿＿＿＿＿＿＿

Ⅳ

1-j，2-c，3-h，4-a，5-d，6-b，7-e，8-g，9-i，10-f

Your score：＿＿＿＿＿＿＿

Ⅴ

1-g，2-j，3-a，4-e，5-i，6-b，7-c，8-h，9-d，10-f

Your score：＿＿＿＿＿＿＿

Ⅵ

1-unconscionable，2-glib，3-egregious，4-incongruous，5-genealogy，6-genetics，7-chronological，8-gauche，9-cardiogram，10-ambidextrous，11-gerontologist，12-telepathy，13-pedodontia，14-sphygmomanometer，15-senescent，16-chiromancer，17-aphrodisiac，18-epitome，19-pathological，20-chronometry，21-antipathy，22-synchronize，23-nescient，24-prescience，25-gregarious，26-empathize，27-barometer，28-segregate，29-callipygian，30-cacography

Your score：＿＿＿＿＿＿＿

Your total score：＿＿＿＿＿＿＿

Significance of Your Total Score：

100—120：Masterly work；you are ready to move right along.

80—99：Good work；this review was useful to you.

65—79：Average work；you're getting a good deal out of your study，but perhaps you should review thoroughly after each session.

50—64：Barely acceptable；work harder.

35—49：Poor；further review is suggested before you go on.

0—34：You can do much better if you really try；continue with firmer resolve and more determination.

评价分数：

100—120　你已经熟练掌握所学词汇，再接再厉。

80—99 干得不错;这个复习对你很有用。

65—79 一般;你的学习已让你收获不小,但也许你需要在学完每个章节之后进行全面复习。

50—64 勉强可以接受;继续努力。

35—49 成绩糟糕;全面复习之后再进行下一章的学习。

0—34 如果真正努力,你一定能做得更好;以更坚定、更大的决心继续学习。

PART TWO
GAINING INCREASED MOMENTUM

第二部分
加大马力

9

HOW TO TALK ABOUT ACTIONS
如何描述各种行为

(*Sessions 19—23*)

TEASER PREVIEW
引读

What verb means to：

* *belittle?*

* *be purposely confusing?*

* *tickle someone's fancy?*

* *flatter fulsomely?*

* *prohibit some food or activity?*

* *make unnecessary?*

* *work against?*

* *spread slander?*

* *give implicit forgiveness for a misdeed?*

* *change hostility to friendliness?*

使用哪个动词来表示以下行为：

* 轻视,贬低

* 含糊其词

* 激起想象

* 谄媚

* 禁止某种食物或某项活动

* 消除,排除

* 对……产生不利的影响

* 嚼人舌根;诽谤

* 含蓄地宽恕

* 消除敌意

SESSION 19
第 19 节

Verbs are incalculably useful to you.

Every sentence you think, say, read, or write contains an implied or expressed verb, for it is the verb that carries the action, the movement, the force of your ideas.

As a young child, you used verbs fairly early.

Your first words, of course, were probably *nouns*, as you identified the things or people around you.

Mama, *Dada*, *doll*, *baby*, *bottle*, etc. perhaps were the first standard syllables you uttered, for naming concrete things or real persons is the initial step in the development of language.

Soon there came the ability to express *intangible* ideas, and then you began to use simple verbs—*go*, *stop*, *stay*, *want*, *eat*, *sleep*, etc.

动词对你有不可估量的用处。

你所思考的、说出的、阅读的或者写下的每个句子都包括隐含的或直接的动词,因为只有动词才能传达概念所包含的行动、运动和力量。

在孩童时期,你使用动词相当轻松。

当然,在说出周围的事物和人的名称时,婴儿最初学会的是名词。

一般来说,妈妈、爸爸、娃娃、宝贝、瓶子等是婴儿最早说出的音节,因为在语言能力的发展过程中,说出具体的事物或者真实的人物名称是第一步。

很快,儿童开始具有表达抽象概念的能力,也是在这时,他们开始使用简单的动词——去、停、留、想要、吃、睡等。

As you gained maturity, your verbs expressed ideas of greater and greater complexity; as an adult you can describe the most involved actions in a few simple syllables—if you have a good store of useful verbs at your command.

The richer and more extensive your vocabulary of verbs, the more accurately and expressively you can communicate your understanding of actions, reactions, attitudes, and emotions.

Let's be specific.

儿童不断地成长,他们使用的动词也能够表达越来越复杂的概念;成年人能够使用几个简单音节描述大部分相关行为——当然,前提是他的可用动词储备足够多。

一个人的动词词汇量越丰富、越广泛,就越能够更准确、更生动地表达最细微的动作、反应、态度和情感。

让我们看下面的具体内容。

IDEAS
概念

1. playing it down
   贬低

Ready to go back thirty or more years? Consider some post-World War II American political history:

Harry Truman couldn't win the 1948 election. The pollsters said so, the Republicans heartily agreed, even the Democrats, some in high places, believed it. Mr. Truman himself was perhaps the only voter in the country who was not entirely convinced.

想回到 30 年以前,或者更早的时间吗?这要考虑一下第二次世界大战后美国的政治史:

哈里·杜鲁门不会赢得 1948 选举。民意调查分析者如是说,共和党表示完全赞同,甚至一些身居要职的民主党官员也相信了这个结果。也许,杜鲁门先生是国内唯一不确信此结果的选民。

Came the first Tuesday after the first Monday in November—well, if you were one of those who stayed up most of the night listening to the returns, and then kept your ear to the radio most of the next day, you recall how you reacted to the unique Truman triumph.

11 月第一个星期一过后,第一个星期二到来了——当然,如果你当晚熬夜收听选举结果,第二天的大部分时间也在收听收音机,你一定还记得当时对杜鲁门这次不寻常的胜利是如何反应的。

It was no mean accomplishment, thought many people. Pure accident, said others. If one out of twelve voters in a few key states had changed his ballot, Harry could have gone back to selling ties, one Republican apologist pointed out. It wasn't anything Truman did, said another; it was what Dewey didn't do. No credit to Truman, said a third; it was the farmers—or labor—or the Republicans who hadn't bothered to vote—or the ingenious miscounting of ballots. No credit to Truman, insisted a fourth; it was Wallace's candidacy—it was the Democrats—it was Republican overconfidence—it was sunspots—it was the Communists—it was the civil service workers who didn't want to lose their cushy jobs—it was really Roosevelt who won the election.

许多人想,这根本算不上成功。还有人说,这纯粹是意外。一位共和党辩护人指出,只要几个关键州十二分之一的选民改变投票,哈里可能就会回去卖领带了! 有人说,这与杜鲁门没有一丁点关系;只是杜威表现得不够好而已。有人说,这并不是杜鲁门的功劳;是那些农民——或者工人——或者不愿投票的共和党人的功劳,要不就是有人故意弄错了选票。还有人坚持说,这与杜鲁门无关;是因为华莱士的候选人资格——是因为民主党——是因为共和党的过度自信——是因为太阳黑子——是因为共产党——是因为那些不愿丢掉美差的公务员——真正赢得选举的是罗斯福。

Anyway Harry didn't accomplish a thing—he was just a victim of good fortune. What were the apologists for Dewey's failure doing?

They were *disparaging* Truman's achievement.

无论如何,哈里没有任何成就——他只是运气好罢了。

对于杜威的失败,辩解者又有哪些辩解呢?

他们在贬低(disparaging)杜鲁门的成就。

2. playing it safe

谨慎行事

Willing to look at some more history of the late 1940s?

Of course, Dewey did campaign, in his own way, for the presidency. As the Republican aspirant, he had to take a stand on the controversial Taft-Hartley Act.

Was he for it? He was for that part of it which was *good*. Naturally, he was against any of the provisions which were *bad*. Was he for it? The answer was *yes*— and also *no*. Take whichever answer you wanted most to hear.

What was Dewey doing?

He was *equivocating*.

想看看 20 世纪 40 年代后期更多的历史吗？

当然，杜威以自己的方式投入竞选运动。作为雄心勃勃的共和党人，他不得不对备受争议的"塔夫脱—哈特莱法案"表明立场。

他真的赞成法案吗？他仅赞成其中"好"的部分；当然，他反对法案中任何"不好"的部分。他到底持怎样的立场呢？答案是肯定——也有否定。你只能选择你更倾向的那个答案。

杜威到底在做什么？

他在含糊其词（equivocating）。

3. enjoying the little things

享受生活中的小幸福

Have you ever gone through a book that was so good you kept hugging yourself mentally as you read? Have you ever seen a play or motion picture that was so charming that you felt sheer delight as you watched? Or perhaps you have had a portion of pumpkin-chiffon pie, light and airy and mildly flavored, and with a flaky, delicious crust, that was the last word in gustatory enjoyment?

Now notice the examples I have used. I have not spoken of books that grip you emotionally, of plays and movies that keep you on the edge of your seat in suspense, or of food that satisfies a ravenous hunger. These would offer quite a different, perhaps more lasting and memorable, type of enjoyment. I have detailed, rather, mental or physical stimuli that excite enjoyably but not too sharply—a delightful novel, a charming play, a delicious dessert.

How do such things affect you?

They *titillate* you.

是否有一本书能够让你在阅读的过程中全身心地投入？你是否看过一部非常有趣的戏剧或者电影，在观看的过程中，你的内心感到无穷的喜悦？你是否吃过薄南瓜饼，清淡温和，薄脆美味，觉得是美食至尊？

现在注意我所使用的例子。我说的不是将你的精神紧紧抓住的书籍，不是极具悬念令你坐立不安的戏剧或者电影，也不是能够满足辘辘饥肠的美味甜饼——虽然这些东西会给你带来不同的、更长久、更值得记忆的愉悦。我刚才举的例子说的是那种能带给你愉悦但并不是特别强烈的精神或身体的刺激——一本令人愉快的书，一部引人入胜的剧或者一块可口的甜点。

这些事物如何影响了你？

它们撩起（titillate）你的兴趣。

4. playing it way up

尽情地表演

You know how the teenagers of an earlier generation adored, idolized, and overwhelmed Frank Sinatra, Elvis Presley, the Beatles?

And of course you know how certain people fall all over visiting celebrities—best-selling authors, much publicized artists, or famous entertainers. They show them ingratiating, almost servile attention, worship and flatter them fulsomely. [1]

How do we say it in a single word?

They *adulate* such celebrities.

你知道上一代人年轻的时候是如何仰慕、崇拜、疯狂迷恋弗兰克·辛纳屈、猫王和披头士的吗？

当然，你也知道当一些名人来访时——如畅销书作家、知名艺术家或著名娱乐人——某些人是如何大献殷勤的。他们对这些名人迎合奉承，甚至奴颜媚骨，肉麻地崇拜和吹捧。

我们如何用一个词汇概括这样的行为？

他们对这些名人一味奉承(adulate)。

5. accentuating the negative

过分突出事物负面影响

What does the doctor say to you if you have low blood sugar? "No candy, no pastries, no chocolate marshmallow cookies, no ice cream!", your morale dropping lower and lower as each favorite goody is placed on the forbidden list.

What, in one word, is the doctor doing?

The doctor is *proscribing* harmful items in your diet.

如果你有低血糖，医生会对你说什么？"不能吃糖果，不能吃糕点，不能吃巧克力棉花糖饼干，不能吃冰激凌!"越来越多的食物成为违禁食品，你的情绪也愈加消沉。

如何用一个词来描述医生做的事情？

他在禁止(proscribing)你摄入有害健康的食品。

6. accentuating the affirmative

突出优点

You are warm, friendly, enthusiastic, outgoing, easy to please; you are quick to show appreciation, yet accept, without judgment or criticism, the human weaknesses of others.

You are a fascinating talker, an even better listener.

You believe in, and practice, honest self-disclosure; you feel comfortable with yourself and therefore with everyone else; and you have a passionate interest in experiencing, in living, in relating to people.

Need you have any fears about making friends? Obviously not.

Your characteristics and temperament *obviate* such fears.

---

1. *Fulsome* (FOOL'-səm) does not mean, despite its appearance, *fully* or *completely*, but rather, *offensive because of excessiveness or insincerity*, often in reference to compliments, praise, admiration, or flattery.

fulsome 的意思并不是"全部地"或"彻底地"(虽然它看起来很像)，而是一种"不诚恳"或"过分"带来的冒犯，经常用来指恭维、称赞、羡慕或奉承。

你是温和、友善、热情、外向、容易快乐的。你乐于感恩,能够容忍他人的缺点而不评判、批评别人。

你谈吐迷人,且你更善于聆听。

你相信并实践自我剖析,你很能自我认同,并因而能认同他人;在体验、生活和与他人的交往中你总能找到激情。

你还用在交友方面担忧吗? 当然不用。

你的性格和脾气消除(obviate)了这些疑虑。

7. playing it wrong

玩错

Theodor Reik, in his penetrating book on psychoanalysis *Listening with the Third Ear*, talks about neurotic people who unconsciously wish to fail. In business interviews they say exactly the wrong words, they do exactly the wrong things, they seem intent (as, *unconsciously*, they actually are) on insuring failure in every possible way, though consciously they are doing their best to court success.

What effect does such a neurotic tendency have?

It militates against success.

西奥多·赖克的《第三只耳朵》是一本有关心理分析的、颇有洞察力的著作。在这本书中,他提到一类精神病患者总是无意识地希望失败。在商业会谈中,尽管他们有意识地向成功努力,但是他们总是用错词、做错事,似乎在竭尽全力地专注于确保失败的发生(当然是无意识的状态)。

这样一种精神倾向具有怎样的效果?

它妨碍(militates)成功。

8. playing it dirty

诽谤

"Harry? *He's a closet alcoholic.* Maud? *She's sleeping around*—and her stupid husband doesn't suspect a thing. Bill? *He's embezzling from his own company.* Paul? *He's a child molester.* Sally? You don't know that *she's a notorious husband-beater*?"

What is this character doing?

He's maligning everyone.

"哈里? 他私下里是一个酗酒者。麦迪? 她和男人乱搞,而她愚蠢的丈夫则毫不猜疑。比尔? 他贪污公司里钱。保罗? 他猥亵儿童。莎莉? 你不知道她是臭名远扬的母老虎?"

这种做法的特点是什么?

他诽谤(maligning)每一个人。

9. giving the benefit of any doubt

无罪推断

Do you think it's all right to cheat on your income taxes? At least just a little? It's wrong, of course, but doesn't everybody do it?

How do you feel about marital infidelity? Are you inclined to overlook the occasional philandering of the male partner, since, after all, to invent a cliché, men are essentially polygamous by nature?

If your answers are in the affirmative, how are you reacting to such legal or ethical transgressions?

You *condone* them.

你认为对自己的收入税做手脚对吗？只是一点点手脚？当然这是错误的,但是的确有人这样做,不是吗？
你对婚外情持有怎样的观点？你能够容忍男友偶尔的越轨行为吗？毕竟,借用一句老套话,男人天性就是向往一夫多妻。
如果你对这些问题的回答是肯定的,你对这类违反法律或者道德规范的行为是如何处理的呢？

你宽恕(condone)了这些行为。

10. changing hostility

改变敌意,重归于好

Unwittingly you have done something that has aroused anger and resentment in your best friend. You had no desire to hurt him, yet he makes it obvious that he feels pretty bitter about the whole situation. (Perhaps you failed to invite him to a gathering he wanted to come to; or you neglected to consult him before making a decision on a matter in which he felt he should have some say.) His friendship is valuable to you and you wish to restore yourself in his good graces. What do you do?

You try to *placate* him.

你的无心之举使你最好的朋友很生气、很恼火。你并非有意伤害他,但是他的表现说明他对整件事情非常不满。(可能你没能邀请他参加聚会,而这个聚会对他来说意义非凡;或者你在做决定的时候没有跟他商量,而他认为在这件事上他应该有发言权。)你们的友谊是你宝贵的财富,你希望你们能够重归于好。你会怎样做呢？

你会抚慰(placate)你的朋友。

USING THE WORDS
单词应用

Can you pronounce the words?
你能读出这些单词吗？

1. *disparage*　　dis-PAIR'-əj
2. *equivocate*　　ee-KWIV'-ə-kayt'
3. *titillate*　　TIT'-ə-layt'
4. *adulate*　　AJ'-ə-layt'
5. *proscribe*　　prō-SKRĪB'
6. *obviate*　　OB'-vee-ayt'
7. *militate*　　MIL'-ə-tayt
8. *malign*　　mə-LĪN'
9. *condone*　　kən-DŌN'
10. *placate*　　PLAY'-kayt'

Can you work with the words?
你能灵活使用这些词汇了吗？

1. disparage　　　　a. flatter lavishly
2. equivocate　　　　b. work against
3. titillate　　　　c. prohibit

4. adulate   d. forgive

5. proscribe   e. change hostility to friendliness

6. obviate   f. purposely talk in such a way as to be vague and misleading

7. militate   g. slander

8. malign   h. play down

9. condone   i. make unnecessary

10. placate   j. tickle; stimulate pleasurably

KEY: 1-h, 2-f, 3-j, 4-a, 5-c, 6-i, 7-b, 8-g, 9-d, 10-e

Do you understand the words?
你对这些词汇是否已经透彻地理解？

1. Do you normally *disparage* something you admire?	YES	NO
2. Do you *equivocate* if you think it unwise to take a definite stand?	YES	NO
3. Do pleasant things *titillate* you?	YES	NO
4. Do emotionally mature people need constant *adulation*?	YES	NO
5. Is sugar *proscribed* for diabetics?	YES	NO
6. Does a substantial fortune *obviate* financial fears?	YES	NO
7. Does a worker's inefficiency often *militate* against his keeping his job?	YES	NO
8. Do people enjoy being *maligned*?	YES	NO
9. Do we generally *condone* the faults of those we love?	YES	NO
10. Can you sometimes *placate* a person by apologizing?	YES	NO

KEY: 1-no, 2-yes, 3-yes, 4-no, 5-yes, 6-yes, 7-yes, 8-no, 9-yes, 10-yes

Can you use the words?
你会用这些词汇了吗？

In this exercise you gain the value of actually writing a new word as a meaningful solution to a problem. To think about a word, to say it, to write it, to use it—that is the road to word mastery. Write the verb that best fits each situation.

1. You've been asked to take a stand on a certain issue, but you don't have the courage to be either definitely for or against.

You _____.

2. You spread around an unpleasant story that you know will blacken someone's reputation.

You _____ that person.

3. Your friend is justifiably angry—you asked him to go to a party with you, ignored him all evening, and then finally left with someone else. What must you do if you wish to restore the relationship?

You must try to _____ him.

4. You virtually worship your therapist. You express your admiration in lavish flattery; you praise her in such excessive terms that she appears devoid of all human frailty.

You _____ her.

5. You are crowding 260 on the scales, so your doctor warns against high-calorie meals, rich desserts, second helpings, excessive carbohydrates, etc.

The doctor _____ these foods.

6. Your child Johnnie has smacked the neighbor's kid—entirely without provocation, you are forced to admit. But after all, you think, tomorrow the other kid will, with equal lack of provocation, probably smack Johnnie.

You _____ Johnnie's behavior.

7. When your son, understandably expecting praise, mentions the three B's and two A's he earned in his courses, you respond, callously, "Is that the best you can do? What stopped you from getting *all* A's?"

You _____ his accomplishment.

8. You have run out of cash and plan to go to the bank to make a withdrawal; then unexpectedly you discover a twenty-dollar bill you secreted in your desk drawer months ago.

You find _____ a trip to the bank.

9. You are the soul of honesty, but unfortunately, you have a sneaky, thievish, sinister look—and no one ever trusts you.

Your appearance _____ against you.

10. The centerfold of *Playboy* or *Playgirl* provides a mild and agreeable stimulation.

The centerfold _____ you.

KEY：1-equivocate, 2-malign, 3-placate, 4-adulate, 5-proscribes, 6-condone, 7-disparage, 8-obviates, 9-militates, 10-titillates

---

Can you recall the words?

你能够写出这些词汇吗？

1. change hostility into friendliness	1. P	_____
2. make unnecessary	2. O	_____
3. belittle	3. D	_____
4. overlook or forgive a transgression	4. C	_____
5. tickle; delight; stimulate pleasurably	5. T	_____
6. spread malicious rumors about	6. M	_____
7. purposely use language susceptible of opposite interpretations	7. E	_____
8. act to disadvantage of	8. M	_____
9. forbid	9. P	_____
10. worship; flatter fulsomely	10. A	_____

KEY：1-placate，2-obviate，3-disparage，4-condone，5-titillate，6-malign，7-equivocate，8-militate（against），9-proscribe，10-adulate

(End of Session 19)

SESSION 20
第 20 节

ORINGINS AND RELATED WORDS
词源及相关词汇

1. equality

平等

If you play golf, you know that each course or hole has a certain *par*, the number of strokes allowed according to the results achieved by expert players. Your own accomplishment on the course will be at *par*, above *par*, or below *par*.

Similarly, some days you may feel up to *par*, other days below *par*.

Par is from a Latin word meaning *equal*. You may try, when you play golf, to *equal* the expert score; and some days you may, or may not, feel *equal* to your usual self.

When we speak of *parity* payments to farmers, we refer to payments that show an *equality* to earnings for some agreed-upon year.

So when you *disparage*, you lower someone's *par*, or feeling of *equality*, (*dis-* as you know, may be a negative prefix). The noun is *disparagement* (dis-PAIR'-əj-mənt), the adjective *disparaging* (dis-PAIR'-əj-ing), as in "Why do you always make *disparaging* remarks about me?"

如果你打高尔夫球,你就会知道单一球场或者单一球洞有一定的标准杆数,英语中叫做 par,也就是根据专业选手成绩估计的所需击球次数。你在球场上的表现可以 at par(平标准杆), above bar(高于标准杆)或者 below par(低于标准杆)。

类似的,在某几天里你可能感觉情绪高涨达到 par,在另外几天你低于 par.

par 来源于拉丁语,意为 equal,"平等的"。当你玩高尔夫时,你可以试着去"平"了专家分;在某些日子里你可能感觉自己和你平时状态"一样",或不一样。

当提到向农民支付 parity payments,我们是指按照之前商定好的年收成为他们结款,以示公平。

所以,如果你 disparage(轻视),你就是在降低某人的公平感(dis 如你所了解的那样,是否定前缀)。名词是 disparagement,形容词是 disparaging,例如在 why do you always make disparaging remarks about me(你为何总是用鄙薄的语气谈到我?)中。

Parity (PAIR'-ə-tee) as a noun means *equality*; *disparity* (dis-PAIR'-ə-tee) means a lack of *equality*, or a difference. We may speak, for example, of the *disparity* between someone's promise and performance; or of the *disparity* between the rate of vocabulary growth of a child and of an adult. The adjective *disparate* (DIS'-pə-rət) indicates *essential* or *complete* difference or inequality, as in "Our philosophies are so *disparate* that we can never come to any agreement on action."

The word *compare* and all its forms (*comparable*, *comparative*, etc.) derive from par, equal. Two things are *compared* when they have certain *equal* or similar qualities，(*con-*，*com-*，together，with).

Pair and *peer* are also from *par*. Things (shoes, socks, gloves, etc.) in *pairs* are *equal* or similar; your *peers* are those *equal* to you, as in age, position, rank, or ability. Hence the expression "to be judged by a jury of one's peers."

(British *peers*, however, such is the contradiction of language, were *nobles*.)

名词形式 parity 表示 equality(平等)，反义词 disparity 表示"平等的缺失"或"区别"。例如，我们可以谈论一个人的诺言和行为之间的悬殊：the disparity between someone's promise and performance；或谈论儿童或成年人词汇增长速度的差别：the disparity between the rate of vocabulary growth of a child and of an abult。形容词 disparate，意为"根本的不同"或"完全不同"，如 our philosophies are so disparate that we can never come to any agreement on action(我们的人生哲学截然不同使我们在行为上不可能一致。)

常用词汇 compare 与其派生词 comparable，comparative 等，同样来源于 par。两个被比较的事物之间一定存在同等或者相似的物质。

pair 和 peer 也都由 par 演生而来。成对的东西(鞋、袜子、手套等)是相同或相似的；你的 peers 是和你"相同"的人——在年龄、位置、地位或能力方面。因此有这样的表达法：to be judged by a jury of one's peers. (由与一个人具有相同法律地位的人组成的陪审团来裁决。)

(英国 peers 则是"贵族"的意思。这就是语言中的矛盾现象。)

2. how to say yes and no

如何含糊其辞

Equivocate is built on another Latin word meaning *equal*—*aequus* (the spelling in English is always *equ-*)—plus *vox*, *vocis*, voice.

When you *equivocate* (ə-KWIV'-ə-kayt'), you seem to be saying both *yes* and *no* with *equal voice*. An *equivocal* (ə-KWIV'-ə-kəl) answer, therefore, is by design vague, indefinite, and susceptible of contradictory interpretations, quite the opposite of an *unequivocal* (un'-ə-KWIV'-ə-kəl) response, which says *Yes*! or *No*!, and no kidding. Professional politicians are masters of *equivocation* (ə-kwiv'-ə-KAY'-shən)—they are, on most vital issues, mugwumps; they sit on a fence with their *mugs* on one side and their *wumps* on the other. You will often hear candidates for office say, publicly, that they *unequivocally* promise, if elected, to... ; and then they start *equivocating* for all they are worth, like people who say, "Let me be perfectly *frank* with you"—and then promptly and glibly lie through their teeth.

equivocate 结合了两个词根：一个是表示 equal 的拉丁语词根 aequus(英语中始终拼做 equ-)；另一个是表示声音的词根 vox，vocis。当你 equivocate，你似乎在用"同样的声音"既说"是"又说"否"。所以，equivocal answer 是故意有歧义的回答，这样的回答不确定，容易导致有争议的解释，与 unequivocal answer 恰好相反——后者指或回答"是"，或回答"否"，绝不含糊。职业政客是 equivocation 的高手——在多数关键的问题上，他们是"骑墙派"。他们坐在篱笆上，他们的 mugs(＜俚语＞脸)在一边，而 wumps(臀部)则在另一边。你经常会听见公职候选人这样的表达：unequivocally promises, if elected, to...(如果能够胜选，我明确承诺诺去……)；一旦胜选，他们会开始 equivocate for all they are worth(为一切他该做的事含糊其辞)，就像有些人说 Let me be perfectly frank with you(让我开诚布公地对你说)，之后开始信口开河。

3. statements of various kinds

不同种类的陈述

Do not confuse *equivocal* with *ambiguous* (am'-BIG'-y $\overline{oo}$-əs). An *equivocal* statement is purposely, deliberately (and with malice aforethought) couched in language that will be deceptive; an *ambiguous* statement is *accidentally* couched in such language. *Equivocal* is, in short, purposely *ambiguous*.

You will recall that *ambi-*, which we last met in *ambivert* and *ambidextrous*, is a root meaning *both*; anything *ambiguous* may have *both* one meaning and another meaning. If you say, "That sentence is the height of *ambiguity*," you mean that you find it vague because it admits of both affirmative and negative interpretations, or because it may mean two different things. *Ambiguity* is pronounced am'-bə-GYOO-ə-tee.

Another type of statement or word contains the possibility of two interpretations—one of them suggestive, risqué, or sexy. Such a statement or word is a *double entendre*. This is from the French and translates literally as *double meaning*. Give the word as close a french pronunciation as you can—DOOB'-ləhn-TAHN'-drə. (The *n*'s are nasalized, the *r* somewhat throaty, and the final sylla-ble is barely audible.)

注意不要混淆 equivocal 和 ambiguous。两者虽然都表示"模糊的陈述",但 equivocal statement 是故意的、预谋已久的陈述,用措辞达到欺骗的目的;而 ambiguous statement 是不经意的措辞。简而言之,equivocal 可以理解为 purposely ambiguous(故意的模糊)。

我们在 ambivert 和 ambidextrous 中见过 ambi-,表示 both(两者)。任何 ambiguous 的事物都同时具有两种自相矛盾的含义。所以,如果说 That sentence is the height of ambiguity,你是说句子意思表达模糊,要么对句子的两种解读相互矛盾,要么有两种完全不同的含义。ambiguity 的发音为 am'-bə-G YOO-ə-tee。

另外一个表达同样表示有两种解释的可能性——其中一种是暗示的或者与性有关的。这样的表达或单词是 double entendre(含有猥亵含义的双关语),其来自于法文,可直译为 double meaning(双关语),尽可能按法文发音——DOOB'-ləhn-TAHN'-drə。(n 发鼻音,r 发喉音,最后的音节几乎不发音。)

REVIEW OF ETYMOLOGY
复习词源

PREFIX, ROOT, SUFFIX	MEANING	ENGLISH WORD
1. *par*	equal	_____
2. *-ment*	noun suffix attached to verbs	_____
3. *-ity*	noun suffix attached to adjectives	_____
4. *dis-*	negative prefix	_____
5. *con-*, *com-*	with, together	_____
6. *aequus* (*equ-*)	equal	_____
7. *vox*, *vocis*	voice	_____
8. *-ate*	verb suffix	_____
9. *-ion*	noun suffix attached to verbs ending in *-ate*	_____
10. *-ous*	adjective suffix	_____

11. *ambi-*   both   _____

USING THE WORDS
单词应用

Can you pronounce the words?
你能读出这些单词吗？

1.	*parity*	PAIR′-ə-tee
2.	*disparity*	dis-PAIR′-ə-tee
3.	*disparate*	DIS′-pə-rət
4.	*disparagement*	dis-PAIR′-əj-mənt
5.	*disparaging*	dis-PAIR′-əj-ing
6.	*peer*	PEER
7.	*equivocate*	ə-KWIV′-ə-kayt′
8.	*equivocation*	ə-kwiv′-ə-KAY′-shən
9.	*equivocal*	ə-KWIV′-ə-kəl
10.	*unequivocal*	un′-ə-KWIV′-ə-kəl
11.	*ambiguous*	am-BIG′-yoo-əs
12.	*ambiguity*	am′-bə-GYOO′-ə-tee
13.	*double entendre*	DOOB′-ləhn-TAHN′-drə

Can you work with the words?
你能灵活使用这些词汇了吗？

1. parity	a.	belittlement
2. disparity	b.	act of being deliberately vague or indirectly deceptive; statement that is deceptive or purposely open to contrary interpretations
3. disparagement	c.	quality of being open to misinterpretation; statement with this quality
4. peer	d.	statement or word with two meanings, one of them risque, indelicate, or of possible sexual connotation
5. equivocation	e.	inequality
6. ambiguity	f.	equality
7. double entendre	g.	one's equal

KEY：1-f，2-e，3-a 4-g，5-b，6-c，7-d

Do you understand the words?

你对这些词汇是否已经透彻地理解？

1. Is there a *disparity* in age between a grandfather and his granddaughter?   YES   NO

2. Is an *equivocal* statement clear and direct?   YES   NO

3. Is an *unequivocal* answer vague and misleading?   YES   NO

4. Are politicians often masters of *equivocation*?   YES   NO

5. Are *ambiguous* sentences somewhat confusing?   YES   NO

6. Are people with *disparate* perceptions of life likely to experience reality in the same way?   YES   NO

7. Is a *disparaging* look one of admiration?   YES   NO

8. When people *equivocate*, are they evading the issue?   YES   NO

9. Is the deliberate use of *double entendres* likely to shock puritanical people?   YES   NO

10. Are supervisors and their subordinates *peers*?   YES   NO

KEY：1-yes，2-no，3-no，4-yes，5-yes，6-no，7-no，8-yes，9-yes，10-no

Can your recall the words?

你能够写出这些词汇吗？

1. accidentally vague   1. A _____

2. purposely vague   2. E _____

3. equality   3. P _____

4. word or statement, one meaning of which may be interpreted as risqué   4. D _____

5. lack of equality   5. D _____

6. belittlement   6. D _____

7. clear; direct; capable of only one interpretation   7. U _____

8. essentially or widely unequal or different   8. D _____

9. one's equal in age, rank, etc.   9. P _____

10. to use words in a calculated effort to mislead or to be ambiguous   10. E _____

KEY：1-ambiguous，2-equivocal，3-parity，4-double entendre，5-disparity，6-disparagement，7-unequivocal，8-disparate，9-peer，10-equivocate

(End of Session 20)

SESSION 21
第 21 节

ORIGINS AND RELATED WORDS
词源及相关词汇

1. more on equality
更多关于平等的词

The root *aequus*, spelled *equ-* in English words, is a building block of：

词根 aequus,在英文单词里拼作 equ-,组成了以下单词：

1. *equity* (EK′-wə-tee)—justice, fairness；i. e. , equal treatment. (By extension, stocks in the financial markets are *equities*, and the value of your home or other property over and above the amount of the mortgage you owe is your *equity* in it.) The adjective is *equitable* (EK′-wə-tə-bəl).

1. equity——正义,公平,即平等对待。(可引申为,金融市场上的股票是 equities,你债权之外的房子或其他财产的价值是你的 equity,权益。)其形容词是 equitable。

2. *inequity* (in-EK′-wə-tee)—injustice, unfairness (*equity* plus the negative prefix *in-*). Adjective：*inequitable* (in-EK′-wə-tə-bəl).

2. inequity——不正义、不公平(equity 前面加上前缀 in-)。形容词是 inequitable。

3. *iniquity* (in-IK′-wə-tee)—by one of those delightful surprises and caprices characteristic of language, the change of a single letter (*e* to *i*), extends the meaning of a word far beyond its derivation and original denotation. Injustice and unfairness are sinful and wicked, especially if you naively believe that life is fair. So a "den of *iniquity*" is a place where vice flourishes；an *iniquity* is a sin or vice, or an egregiously immoral act；and *iniquity* is wickedness, sinfulness. Adjective：*iniquitous* (in-IK′-wə-təs).

3. iniquity——仅仅改变一个字母(把 e 换成 i)就可以使一个词的意思和原来的大不相同,这是语言中令人惊奇和变幻莫测的特征之一。不公正和不公平是罪恶的、邪恶的,尤其是你天真地相信生活是公平的。因此 den of iniquity 就是一个道德败坏的地方;iniquity 就是罪孽或恶行,或者极不道德的行为;iniquity 就是邪恶、罪责。形容词是 iniquitous。

4. *equinox* (EE′-kwə-noks′)—etymologically, "equal night," a combination of *aequus* and *nox*, *noctis*, night. The *equinox*, when day and night are of equal length, occurs twice a year：about March 21, and again about September 21 or 22. (The adjective is *equinoctial*—ee′-kwə-NOK′-shəl.) *Nocturnal* (nok-TURN′-əl), derived from *nox*, *noctis*, describes people, animals, or plants that are active or flourish at night rather than during daylight hours. Cats and owls are *nocturnal*, as is the moonflower, whose blossoms open at night；not to mention "night people," whose biorhythms are such that they function better after the sun goes down, and who like to stay up late and sleep well into midmorning. A *nocturne* (NOK′-turn) is

a musical composition of dreamy character (i. e., night music), or a painting of a night scene.

4. equinox(春分,秋分)——从词源上看,就是"平等的夜",由 aequus 和 nox(夜晚)构成。每年有两次昼夜等长:大概是 3 月 21 号,9 月 21 号或 22 号(形容词是 equinoctial)。nocturnal 由 nox(夜晚的)衍变而来,是指在夜间比在白天更为活跃的人或动物或在夜间开花的植物。猫和猫头鹰都是 nocturnal,还有月光花,它在夜里开花;更不用说"夜猫子型的人",他们的生物钟在太阳下山后变得更活跃,并且他们喜欢熬夜,一直睡到快中午的时分。nocturne(夜曲)是指具有梦幻情调的音乐作品(换言之,晚上的音乐)或指描绘夜景的画。

5. *equanimity* (ee′-kwə-NIM′-ə-tee *or* ek′-wə-NIM′-ə-tee)——etymologically *aequus* plus *animus*, mind, hence "equal mind." Maintain your *equanimity*, your evenness of temper, your composure, your coolness or calmness, when everyone around you is getting excited or hysterical, and you will probably be considered an admirable person, though one might wonder what price you pay for such emotional control. (Other words built on *animus*, mind, will be discussed in Chapter 12.)

5. equanimity(平和,镇静)从词源上看,由 aequus 加 animus(精神)构成,意为"平等的精神"。保持你的 equanimity,就是当你周围的人都非常兴奋和情绪激动时,保持你的脾气平顺,平静,冷静等。他们会觉得你是一个值得敬佩的人,虽然也许有人想知道你付出多大努力才能做到如此淡定的。(其他由 animus 构成的单词将在第 12 章讨论。)

6. *Equability* (ee′-kwə-BIL′-ə-tee *or* ek′-wə-BIL′-ə-tee)——a close synonym of *equanimity*. A person of *equable* (EE′-kwə-bəl *or* EK′-wə-bəl) temperament is characteristically calm, serene, unflappable, even-tempered.

6. equability 意思和 equanimity 相近。一个脾气很 equable 的人,是个性平静、安详、镇静、稳重的人。

7. *equilibrium* (ee′-kwə-LIB′-ree-əm)——by derivation *aequus* plus *libra*, balance, weight, pound, hence "equal balance." *Libra* (Lī′-brə) is the seventh sign of the zodiac, represented by a pair of scales. Now you know, in case the question has been bothering you, why the abbreviation for the word *pound* is *lb*. and why the symbol for the British *pound*, the monetary unit, is £. *Equilibrium* is a state of *physical* balance, especially between opposing forces. When you are very drunk you may have difficulty keeping your *equilibrium*——the force of gravity is stronger than your ability to stay upright. An *equilibrist* (ə-KWIL′-ə-brist), as you might guess, is a professional tightrope walker——a performer succesfully defying the law of gravity (when sober) by *balancing* on a thin overhead wire.

7. equilibrium(平衡)由 aequus 加 libra(平衡,重量,英镑,磅)构成,意为"相等的平衡"。Libra 是黄道带的第七宫(天秤座),由一个天平来代表。如果你曾经不明白,现在你就能理解,为什么磅的缩写是 lb。还有,你也可以理解英镑的符号为什么是£。equilibrium 是一种物理的平衡,尤其是指两个相反力量之间的。如果你喝得很醉,那你就很难保持你的 equilibrium,地球重力比你保持站直的力量要强。一个 equilibrist,也许你能猜到,就是一个职业走钢索的人——一个在高空的细索上保持平衡,从而成功地摆脱重力定律(当然是在保持冷静的状态下)的表演者。

The *equator* divides the earth into *equal* halves, and words like *equation*, *equivalent*, *equidistant*, *equiangular*, and *equilateral* (from Latin *latus*, *lateris*, side) are self-explanatory.

赤道(equator)把地球分成两个"相等的"部分,单词 equation,equivalent,equidistant,equiangular 和 equilateral(源于拉丁语 latus,lateris,意为"边")的意思也就不言自明了。

2. not to be confused with horses

不要与"马"混淆

Equestrian (ə-KWES′-tree-ən) is someone on a horse (as *pedestrian* is someone on foot); an *equestrienne* (ə-kwes′-tree-EN′) is a woman on a horse (if you *must* make the distinction); and *equine* (EE′-kwīn) is like a horse, as in appearance or characteristics, or descriptive of horses.

Equestrian is also an adjective referring to horseback riding, as an *equestrian* statue; and *equine* is also a noun, i. e. , a horse,

So the *equ-* in these words, from Latin *equus*, horse, is not to be confused with the *equ-* in the words of the previous section——that *equ-* is from *aequus*, equal. (Remember, also, not to confuse the *ped-* in *pedestrian*, from Latin *pedis*, foot, with the *ped- in pediatrician*, from Greek *paidos*, child.)

equestrian 是指在马上的人(如 pedestrian 是指行人,用脚走路的人);equestrienne 是指一个在马上的女人(如果必须做区分的话);equine 是指"像一匹马",在长相和品格方面,或是与马相关的描述。

equestrian 也可作形容词,指"骑马的",如 an equestrian statue(骑马的雕塑);equine 也可作名词,意为"一匹马"。

所以在这些单词中的 equ-(源于拉丁语 equus,马),不要和之前部分提到的 equ-弄错——那里的 equ-源于 aequus,平等。(此外,还要清楚 pedestrian 的 ped-[源于拉丁语 pedis,脚]不同于 pediatrician 的 ped-[源于希腊语词根 paidos,孩子]);

3. Hear voices?

听声音?

Equivocal, you will recall, combines *aequus* with *vox*. *vocis*, voice; and *vox*, *vocis* combines with *fero*, to bear or carry, to form *vociferous* (vō-SIF′-ər-əs), etymologically "carrying (much) voice," hence loud, noisy, clamorous, as *vociferous* demands (not at all quiet or subtle), or the *vociferous* play of young children ("Please! Try to be quiet so Dad can get his work done?"), though unfortunately TV addiction has abnormally eliminated child noises, at least during the program breaks between commercials. (*Vociferous* will be discussed at greater length in Chapter 10.)

equivocal,你应该能够记起来是由 aequus 和 vox, vocis(声音)组成,由 vox, vocis 和 fero(承担或携带)形成 vociferous,从词源上的意思是"携带很多声音",因此是非常大声、吵闹、喧嚣的意思。vociferous demands 是大声的要求(一点也不安静或含蓄)。vociferous play of young children 指孩子们大声玩闹("劳驾! 能不能安静点,让爸爸做完他的工作?")。不幸的是对电视的痴迷已经以不正常的方式消除了孩子们的噪音,不过即便如此,在电视广告时段孩子们还是会大声玩闹。(关于 vociferous,将要在第 10 章中详细讨论。)

If you are *vocal* (VŌ′-kəl), you express yourself readily and freely by voice; *vocal* sounds are voiced; *vocal* music is sung; and you know what your *vocal* cords are for.

To *vocalize* (VŌ′-kə-līz′) is to give voice to ("*Vocalize* your anger, don't hold it in!"), or to sing the *vocals* (or voice parts) of music. (Can you write the noun form of the verb *vocalize*? _____.) A *vocalist* (VŌ′-kə-list) is a singer. And *Magnavox* (*vox* plus *magnus*, large) is the trade name for a brand of radios and TV sets.

如果说你是"vocal",意即你能流畅地用声音表达自己;人们说的是 vocal sounds(声音),唱的是 vocal music(声乐);你也知道自己的 vocal cords(声带)是做什么的。

vocalize 意为"发出声音"(如 Vocalize your anger, don't hold it in! ——把你的愤怒说出来,别憋着!),或者是唱"声乐"。(你能写出动词 vocalize 的名词形式吗?)vocalist 是歌者。Magnavox(vos 加 magnus,大型的)是一种收音机和电视机的商标。

REVIEW OF ETYMOLOGY
复习词源

PREFIX, ROOT SUFFIX	MEANING	ENGLISH WORD
1. *aequus* (*equ-*)	equal	_____
2. *in-*	negative prefix	_____
3. *nox*, *noctis*	night	_____
4. *animus*	mind	_____
5. *-ity*	noun suffix	_____
6. *libra*	balance, weight, pound	_____
7. *-ist*	person who	_____
8. *latus*, *lateris*	side	_____
9. *equus*	horse	_____
10. *-ine*	like, descriptive of	_____
11. *pedis*	foot	_____
12. *paidos* (*ped-*)	child	_____
13. *vox*, *vocis*	voice	_____
14. *fero*	to bear, carry	_____
15. *magnus*	large	_____

USING THE WORDS
单词应用

Can you pronounce the words? (I)
你能读出这些单词吗?(I)

1. *equity*   EK′-wə-tee
2. *equitable*   EK′-wə-tə-bəl
3. *inequity*   in-EK′-wə-tee
4. *inequitable*   in-EK′-wə-tə-bəl
5. *iniquity*   in-IK′-wə-tee
6. *iniquitous*   in-IK′-wə-təs
7. *equinox*   EE′-kwə-noks′
8. *equinoctial*   ee′-kwə-NOK′-shəl

9. *nocturnal*   nok-TURN′-əl

10. *nocturne*   NOK′-turn

Can you pronounce the words?（Ⅱ）
你能读出这些单词吗?（Ⅱ）

1. *equanimity*   ee′-kwə (*or* ek′-wə) -NIM′-ə-tee

2. *equability*   ee′-kwə (*or* ek′-wə) -BIL′-ə-tee

3. *equable*   EE′-kwə-bəl *or* EK′-wə-bəl

4. *equilibrium*   ee′-kwə-LIB′-ree-əm

5. *equilibrist*   ee-KWIL′-ə-brist

6. *equilateral*   ee-kwə-LAT′-ər-əl

7. *equestrian*   ə-KWES′-tree-ən

8. *equine*   EE′-kwīn

9. *vociferous*   vō-SIF′-ər-əs

10. *vocal*   VŌ′-kəl

11. *vocalize*   VŌ′-kə-līz′

12. *vocalization*   vō′-kə-lə-ZAY′-shən

13. *vocalist*   VŌ′-kə-list

Can you work with the words?（Ⅰ）
你能灵活使用这些词汇了吗?（Ⅰ）

1. equity   a. time when night and day are of equal length

2. inequity   b. balance of mind; composure; calmness under trying circumstances

3. iniquity   c. horseback rider

4. equinox   d. a horse

5. nocturne   e. sinfulness; wickedness; immoral act; sin

6. equanimity   f. unfairness, injustice

7. equilibrium   g. tightrope walker

8. equestrian   h. singer

9. equilibrist   i. fairness, justice

10. equine   j. balance, especially between opposing forces

11. vocalist   k. night music

KEY：1-i，2-f，3-e，4-a，5-k，6-b，7-j，8-c，9-g，10-d，11-h

Can you work with the words? (Ⅱ)

你能灵活使用这些词汇了吗?

1. equitable	a. descriptive of time when night and day are of equal length
2. inequitable	b. give voice to; sing
3. iniquitous	c. having equal sides
4. equinoctial	d. using, or referring to, the voice; freely expressing by voice
5. nocturnal	e. noisy, loud, clamorous
6. equable	f. calm, unruffled, even-tempered
7. equilateral	g. fair, just
8. vociferous	h. referring or pertaining to, or active at, night
9. vocal	i. sinful, wicked, immoral
10. vocalize	j. unfair, unjust

KEY：1-g，2-j，3-i，4-a，5-h，6-f，7-c，8-e，9-d，10-b

Do you understand the words?

你对这些词汇是否已经透彻地理解?

1. Is life always *equitable*?   YES   NO
2. Does the cynic expect more *inequity* than *equity* in life?   YES   NO
3. Do ethical people practice *iniquity*?   YES   NO
4. Does the *equinox* occur once a month?   YES   NO
5. Are *nocturnal* animals active at night?   YES   NO
6. If you generally preserve your *equanimity*, do you often get very excited?   YES   NO
7. Is it easy to maintain your *equilibrium* on icy ground?   YES   NO
8. Is *equability* the mark of a calm, even-tempered person?   YES   NO
9. Does an *equilateral* triangle have equal sides?   YES   NO
10. Is an *equine* a dog?   YES   NO
11. If you demand something *vociferously*, do you make a lot of noise?   YES   NO
12. If you are *vocal*, do you have difficulty   YES   NO

expressing yourself?

13. Is a *vocalist* the same as an instrumentalist?　　　　YES　　NO

KEY：1-no，2-yes，3-no，4-no，5-yes，6-no，7-no，8-yes，9-yes，10-no，11-yes，12-no，13-no

Can you recall the words？（Ⅰ）
你能够写出这些词汇吗？（Ⅰ）

1. to give voice to; to express aloud; to sing

1. V _____

2. tightrope walker

2. E _____

3. active or flourishing at night

3. N _____

4. descriptive or characteristic of, or like, a horse

4. E _____

5. referring to the voice; skillful or fluent in expressing by voice

5. V _____

6. calm and unflappable in temperament

6. E _____

7. wicked, sinful

7. I _____

8. night music

8. N _____

9. fairness, justice

9. E _____

KEY：1-vocalize，2-equilibrist，3-nocturnal，4-equine，5-vocal，6-equable，7-iniquitous，8-nocturne，9-equity

Can you recall the words？（Ⅱ）
你能够写出这些词汇吗？（Ⅱ）

1. loud, noisy, clamorous

1. V _____

2. person on horseback

2. E _____

or E _____

3. calmness or evenness of temper

3. E _____

or E _____

4. unfair, unjust

4. I _____

5. sin; wickedness; grossly immoral behavior

5. I _____

6. time when day and night are of equal length

6. E _____

7. fair, just, evenhanded

7. E _____

8. physical balance; balance between opposing forces

8. E _____

9. having equal sides

9. E _____

10. singer

10. V _____

KEY：1-vociferous, 2-equestrian *or* equestrienne, 3-equanimity *or* equability, 4-inequitable, 5-iniquity, 6-equinox, 7-equitable, 8-equilibrium, 9-equilateral, 10-vocalist

(End of Session 21)

SESSION 22
第 22 节

ORIGINS AND RELATED WORDS
词源及相关词汇

1. how to tickle
如何挠痒痒

Titillate comes from a Latin verb meaning *to tickle*, and may be used both literally and figuratively. That is (literally), you can *titillate* by gentle touches in strategic places; you are then causing an actual (and always very pleasant) physical sensation. Or you can (figuratively) *titillate* people, or their minds, fancies, palates (and this is the more common use of the word), by charm, brilliance, wit, promises, or in any other way your imagination can conceive.

Titillation (tit'-ə-LAY'-shən) has the added meaning of light sexual stimulation. (Note that both noun and verb are spelled with a double *l*, *not* a double *t*.)

titillate(逗引、挑逗)来源于希腊语表示 tickle(挠痒痒)的词根,既可以按字面意思理解,也可以按照引申含义理解。按照字面意思,你可以轻挠身体某个部位,带来实际的(而且总是非常愉快的)身体感觉;按照引申意义,你可以用魅力、聪慧、机智、承诺或其他任何你能想象到的东西逗引人们,或激发他们的头脑,幻想,味觉。

名词形式是 titillation,还有轻度的性挑逗的意味。(注意,其名词和动词都是有两个 l,而不是两个 t。)

2. how to flatter
如何献殷勤

A *compliment* is a pleasant and courteous expression of praise; *flattery* is stronger than a compliment and often considered insincere. *Adulation* (aj'-ə-LAY'-shən) is flattery and worship carried to an excessive, ridiculous degree. There are often public figures (entertainers, musicians, government officials, etc.) who receive widespread *adulation*, but those not in the public eye can also be *adulated*, as a teacher by students, a wife by husband (and vice versa), a doctor by patients, and so on. (The derivation is from a Latin verb meaning to *fawn upon*.)

The adjective *adulatory* (aj'-ə-lə-TAWR'-ee) ends in *-ory*, a suffix we are meeting for the first time in these pages. (Other adjective suffixes: *-al*, *-ic*, *-ical*, *-ous*.)

compliment(恭维),是令人愉快的、彬彬有礼的赞扬方式;flattery(奉承),比恭维强烈,往往不真诚;而 adulation(谄媚),就是 flattery 达到荒谬、怪诞的程度。公众人物(娱乐明星、音乐家、政府官员等)经常能获得大众的"adulation",但一些不是公众人物的人也可能被 adulated,如老师被学生,妻子被丈夫(或反之),医生被病人等。(源于拉丁语中表示"曲意逢迎"的动词。)

其形容词是 adulatory,以-ory 结尾,这也是我们第一次遇到的这个后缀。(其他形容词结尾的后缀有-al,-ic,-ical,-ous。)

3. ways of writing
书写的方式

Proscribe, to forbid, is commonly used for medical, religious, or legal prohibitions.

A doctor *proscribes* a food, drug, or activity that might prove harmful to the patient. The church *proscribes*, or announces a *proscription* (prō-SKRIP′-shən) against, such activities as may harm its parishioners. The law *proscribes* behavior detrimental to the public welfare.

Generally, one might concede, *proscribed* activities are the most pleasant ones—as Alexander Woolcott once remarked, if something is pleasurable, it's sure to be either immoral, illegal, or fattening.

proscribe,"禁止",经常用来指医学、宗教或司法上的禁止。

医生用单子列出可能对病人造成伤害的食物、药品或者行为。教堂 proscribes 或宣布 proscription(禁令)对他们教民有害的行为。法律"proscribes"对公共福利有害的行为。

通常,你可能会同意这种说法,proscribed activities(被禁止的行为)往往是最令人愉快的——正如亚历山大·伍尔科特所说,如果什么事物能够给人带来愉悦,它要么违背道德、违反法律,要么令人发胖。

The derivation is the prefix *pro-*, before, plus *scribo*, *scriptus*, to write. In ancient Roman times, a man's name was written on a public bulletin board if he had committed some crime for which his property or life was to be forfeited; Roman citizens in good standing would thereby know to avoid him. In a similar sense, the doctor writes down those foods or activities that are likely to commit crimes against the patient's health—in that way the patient knows to avoid them.

Scribo, *scriptus* is the building block of scores of common English words: *scribe*, *scribble*, *prescribe*, *describe*, *subscribe*, *script*, *the Scriptures*, *manuscript*, *typescript*, etc. *Describe* uses the prefix *de-*, down—to *describe* is, etymologically, "to write down" about. *Manuscript*, combining *manus*, hand (as in *manual* labor), with *scriptus*, is something handwritten—the word was coined before the invention of the typewriter. *The Scriptures* are holy writings. To *subscribe* (as to a magazine) is to write one's name *under* an order or contract (*sub-*, under, as in *subway*, *subsurface*, etc.); to *subscribe* to a philosophy or a principle is figuratively to write one's name *under* the statement of such philosophy or principle.

To *inscribe* is to write *in* or *into* (a book, for example, or metal or stone). A *postscript* is something written after (Latin *post*, after) the main part is finished.

这个单词是由前缀 pro-(在……之前)加上 scribo, scriptus(写)组成。在古罗马,如果有人犯罪,他的名字会被写在布告板公之于众,没收财产,甚至失去生命;具有良好地位的古罗马公民也会拒绝与其来往。同理,医生会记录可能对病患健康不利的"犯罪行为"———一些食物或活动;这样,病患就能够了解他应该与哪些事物"拒绝来往"。

拉丁语词根 scribo 可以形成几十个常用的英文单词:scribe, scribble, prescribe, describe, subscribe, script, the Scriptures, manuscript, typescript 等。describe 的前缀是 de-(down)———to describe 就是"写下,记下"。manuscript,由 manus,"手"(比如在 manual labor 中)和 scriptus 构成,指"手写"的东西———这个单词出现在打字机出现之前。The Scriptures 就是经文。subscribe,"订阅"(如订阅杂志),就是在订单或合约下面(sub-下面,如 ubway, subsurface 等)写上自己的名字;而"subscribe"某种哲学和原则,就是比喻性地说把名字写在这些哲学和原则的文本下面。

inscribe 是写在或写入(例如书、金属或石头)。Postscript 是指在正文后面的文字。

Note how *-scribe* verbs change to nouns and adjectives:

注意含有-scribe 的动词是如何变成名词或者形容词的:

VERB	NOUN	ADJECTIVE
prescribe	prescription	prescriptive
subscribe	subscription	subscriptive

Can you follow the pattern?
你能根据这个规律写出这些词的名词和形容词吗？

describe	_____	_____
inscribe	_____	_____
proscribe	_____	_____

4. it's obvious
显而易见

You are familiar with the word *via*, by way of, which is from the Latin word for *road*. (The *Via Appia* was one of the famous ways of ancient Roman times.) When something is *obvious*, etymologically it is right there in the middle of the road where no one can fail to see it—hence, easily seen, not hidden, conspicuous. And if you meet an obstacle in the road and dispose of it forthwith, you are doing what *obviate* says. Thus, if you review your work daily in some college subject, frenzied "cramming" at the end of the semester will be *obviated*. A large and steady income *obviates* fears of financial insecurity; leaving for work early will *obviate* worry about being late. *To obviate*, then, is to make unnecessary, to do away with, to prevent by taking effective measures or steps against (an occurrence, a feeling, a requirement, etc.). The noun is *obviation* (ob'-vee-AY'-shən).

你肯定对 via 这个词不陌生，via 来源于拉丁语中表示"道路"的词汇，意为"经由……"。(Via Appia 是古罗马最著名的道路之一。)如果事物是明显的，obvious，从语源学来说是指它位于马路的最中央，任何人都能够看见——所以，obvious 可以解释为"容易看见的、未被隐藏的、显眼的"。如果遇到路障，你毫不犹豫地将其摆脱，你的动作则可以被称为 obviate，去除。这样，在大学学习中，如果每天都能够规律地复习，你在期末考试时就无需疯狂填鸭，可以说你消除了(obviated)临阵磨枪的必要性。保持银行账户余额充足能够消除(obviates)经济危机感；提前空出赶火车的时间能够消除(obviate)迟到的顾虑。简而言之，to obviate 意为采取有效措施使某些事情、感觉或者要求变得没有必要，使其得以消除或预防。名词形式是 obviation。

Surprisingly, *via*, road, is the root in the English word *trivial* (*tri-*, three). Where three roads intersect, you are likely to find busy traffic, lots of people, in short a fairy public place, so you are not going to talk of important or confidential matters, lest you be overheard. You will, instead, talk of *trivial* (TRIV'-ee-əl) things—whatever is unimportant, without great significance; you will confine your conversation to *trivialities* (triv'-ee-AL'-ə-teez) or to *trivia* (also a plural noun, pronounced TRIV'-ee-ə), insignificant trifles.

令人意外的是，via(道路)，是英文单词 trivial(tri-，意为"三个")的词根。在三岔路口，人们可能发现交通拥挤，人多，总而言之是个公共场所，因此不可能谈论重要或秘密的事情，免得被人听到。所以只能谈些 trivial things(琐碎的小事)——即一些不重要的、没什么重大意义的事情；你会把你们的谈话局限在 trivialities(琐事)或者 trivia(琐事，这个词也可作复数名词)方面。

5. war

战争

Militate derives from *militis*, one of the forms of the Latin noun meaning *soldier* or *fighting man*. If something *militates* against you, it fights against you, i. e., works to your disadvantage. Thus, your timidity may *militate* against your keeping your friends. (*Militate* is always followed by the preposition *against* and, like *obviate*, never takes a personal subject—*you* don't *militate* against anyone, but some habit, action, tendency, etc. *militates* against someone or something.)

The adjective *militant* (MIL′-ə-tənt) comes from the same root. A *militant* reformer is one who fights for reforms, a *militant* campaign is one waged aggressively and with determination. The noun is *militancy* (MIL′-ə-tən-see), and *militant* is also a noun for the person—"Sally is a *militant* in the Women's Liberation movement."

Military and *militia* also have their origin in *militis*.

militate(影响,产生作用)源自意为"战士"或"战斗的人"的拉丁名词 militis。说什么事情 militates against 你,就是说它在跟你"作对",也就是对你不利。例如,害羞会对交友不利(your timidity may militate against your keeping your friends)。(militate 总是与 against 搭配使用;此外,与 obviate 相似,人很少充当 militate 的主语——"你"不能 militate against 任何人,而是一些习惯、行为、嗜好等 militates against 某人或某事。)

形容词 militant 也来源于同一个词根。militant reformer(激进的改革者),是指一个人为了坚持自己的改革而斗争;militant campaign(激进的运动),是充满决心的激烈斗争。其名词是 militancy(好斗),militant 也可以作为指代这类人的名词,如 Sally is a militant in the Women liberation movement(莎莉是妇女解放运动的斗士)。

military 和 militia 都源于 militis。

6. first the bad news

先说坏消息

Built on Latin *malus*, bad, evil, to *malign* is to speak evil about, to defame, to slander. *Malign* is also an adjective meaning *bad*, *harmful*, *evil*, *hateful*, as in "the *malign* influence of his unconscious will to fail." Another adjective form is *malignant* (mə-LIG′-nənt), as in "a *malignant* glance," i. e., one showing deep hatred, or "a *malignant* growth," i. e., one that is cancerous (bad).

The noun of *malignant* is *malignancy* (mə-LIG′-nən-see), which, medically, is a cancerous growth, or, generally, the condition, state, or attitude of harmfulness, hatefulness, evil intent, etc. The noun form of the adjective *malign* is *malignity* (mə-LIG′-nə-tee).

由拉丁词根 malus(坏的、邪恶的)组成的单词,malign 意为"中伤,诽谤"。malign 也是形容词,指"坏的,有害的,邪恶的,可恶的",例如 the malign influence of his unconscious will to fail,意为"他想把事情搞砸的潜意识带来的恶劣影响"。另外一个形容词形式是 malignant,例如 a malignant glance,意为"充满恶意的注视";a malignant growth,意为"(肿瘤)恶性的扩散"。

malignant 的名词形式是 malignancy。从医学上讲是癌症的扩散,或一般意义上,指有害的情况、状态、态度,或者不良的意图等。malign 名词形式是 malignity。

Observe how we can construct English words by combining *malus* with other Latin roots.

Add the root *dico*, *dictus*, to say or tell, to form *malediction* (mal′-ə-DIK′-shən), a curse, i. e., an evil saying. Adjective：*maledictory* (mal′-ə-DIK′-tə-ree).

Add the root *volo*, to wish, to will, or to be willing, and we can construct the adjective *malevolent* (mə-LEV′-ə-lent), wishing evil or harm—a *malevolent* glance, attitude, feeling, etc. The noun is *malevolence* (mə-LEV′-ə-ləns).

Add the root *facio*, *factus*, to do or make (also spelled, in English words, *fec-*, *fic-*, *factus*, or, as a verb ending, *-fy*), to form the adjective *maleficent* (mə-LEF′-ə-sənt), doing harm or evil, or causing hurt—*maleficent* acts, deeds, behavior.

Can you figure out, and pronounce, the noun form of *maleficent*? _____ .

看一下如何用 malus 和其他的拉丁词根组成英语单词。

它和词根 dico,dictus(意为"说"或"告诉"),构成 malediction。意为"诅咒",即"恶意的话语"。形容词是 maledictory。

和词根 volo(意为"希望""愿意")构成形容词 malevolent(恶毒的,幸灾乐祸的),充满恶意或伤害的企图——如 malevolent glance ,malevolent attitude,malevolent feeling 等,其名词是 malevolence。

加上词根 facio,factus("做"或"制造",在英语单词中也拼写为 fec-,fic-,factus-或作为动词结尾的-fy),构成形容词 maleficent,意为"伤害、恶意""导致伤害"等——如 maleficent acts, maleficent deeds, maleficent behaviors 等。

你能写出、读出 maleficent 的名词形式吗?

A *malefactor* (MAL′-ə-fak′-tər) is a wrongdoer, an evildoer, a criminal—a *malefactor* commits a *malefaction* (mal′-ə-FAK′- shən), a crime, an evil deed.

French is a "Romance" language, that is, a language based on Roman or Latin (as are, also, Spanish, Portuguese, Italian, and Romanian), and so Latin *malus* became French *mal*, bad, the source of *maladroit* (mal′-ə-DROYT′), clumsy, bungling, awkward, unskillful, etymologically, having a "bad right hand." (See *adroit*, Chapter 3.) The noun is *maladroitness*. Also from French *mal*：*malaise* (mə-LAYZ′), an indefinite feeling of bodily discomfort, as in a mild illness, or as a symptom preceding an illness; etymologically, "bad ease", just as *disease* (dis-ease) is "lack of ease."

Other common words that you are familiar with also spring from Latin *malus*：*malicious*, *malice*, *malady*; and the same *malus* functions as a prefix in words like *maladjusted*, *malcontent*, *malpractice*, *malnutrition*, etc., all with the connotation of *badness*.

malefactor 是一个"做坏事的人""做邪事的人""犯罪者"——malefactor 的行为是 malefaction(犯罪或邪恶的行为)。

法语属于拉丁系语言,它以罗马和拉丁语为基础(西班牙语、葡萄牙语、意大利语、罗马尼亚语都是拉丁系语言)。因此拉丁语 malus 成为法语中的 mal,意为"坏的",并演变出 maladroit,意为"笨拙的""不熟练的",从词源上看,其最初的意思是"坏的右手"(参见第 3 章的 adroit)。名词是 maladroitness,也是来源于法语 mal 的单词还有 malaise,泛指身体上说不出的不舒服感,如小病中的状态,或某种疾病的前兆症状。从词源上看其本义是"坏的舒适"。如 disease 是"缺乏舒适"。

其他一些常见的、由拉丁语 malus 演变而来的单词有:malicious,malice,malady;malus 也可以作为前缀如 maladjusted,malcontent,malpractice,malnutrition 等,都和"坏"相关。

REVIEW OF ETYMOLOGY
复习词源

PREFIX, ROOT, SUFFIX	MEANING	ENGLISH WORD
1. *-ory*	adjective suffix	_____
2. *scribo*, *scriptus*	to write	_____
3. *de-*	down	_____
4. *manus*	hand	_____
5. *sub-*	under	_____
6. *in-*	in, into	_____
7. *post*	after	_____
8. *via*	road	_____
9. *tri-*	three	_____
10. *militis*	soldier	_____
11. *malus*	bad, evil	_____
12. *dico*, *dictus*	to say, tell	_____
13. *volo*	to wish	_____
14. *facio* (*fec-*, *fic-*, *fy*)	to do, make	_____
15. *-ence*, *-ancy*	noun suffix	_____

WORKING WITH THE WORDS
单词应用

Can you pronounce the words?（Ⅰ）
你能读出这些单词吗?（Ⅰ）

1. *titillation*	tit′-ə-LAY′-shən
2. *adulation*	aj′-ə-LAY′-shən
3. *adulatory*	AJ′-ə-lə-tawr′-ee
4. *proscription*	prō-SKRIP′-shən
5. *proscriptive*	prō-SKRIP′-tiv
6. *obviation*	ob′-vee-AY′-shən
7. *trivial*	TRIV′-ee-əl
8. *trivialities*	triv′-ee-AL′-ə-teez
9. *trivia*	TRIV′-ee-ə
10. *militant*	MIL′-ə-tənt
11. *militancy*	MIL′-ə-tən-see
12. *malign* (*adj.*)	mə-LĪN′
13. *malignity*	mə-LIG′-nə-tee

14. *malignant* mə-LIG′-nənt
15. *malignancy* mə-LIG′-nən-see

Can you pronounce the words? (Ⅱ)
你能读出这些单词吗？(Ⅱ)

1. *malediction* mal′-ə-DIK′-shən
2. *maledictory* mal′-ə-DIK′-tə-ree
3. *malevolent* mə-LEV′-ə-lənt
4. *malevolence* mə-LEV′-ə-ləns
5. *maleficent* mə-LEF′-ə-sənt
6. *maleficence* mə-LEF′-ə-səns
7. *malefactor* MAL′-ə-fak′-tər
8. *malefaction* mal′-ə-FAK′-shən
9. *maladroit* mal′-ə-DROYT′
10. *maladroitness* mal′-ə-DROYT′-nəs
11. *malaise* mə-LAYZ′

Can you work with the words? (Ⅰ)
你能灵活使用这些词汇吗？(Ⅰ)

1. titillation
2. adulation
3. proscription
4. militancy
5. malignity

6. malediction
7. maladroitness
8. obviation
9. malevolence
10. malaise

a. prohibition
b. hatefulness；harmfulness
c. clumsiness
d. quality of wishing evil；ill will
e. prevention；fact or act of making unnec-essary or of doing away with
f. worship；excessive flattery
g. vague feeling of bodily discomfort
h. pleasurable stimulation；tickling
i. a curse
j. aggressiveness

KEY：1-h，2-f，3-a，4-j，5-b，6-i，7-c，8-e，9-d，10-g

Can you work with the words? (Ⅱ)
你能灵活使用这些词汇吗？(Ⅱ)

1. adulatory
2. proscriptive
3. militant

a. aggressive；"fighting"
b. of no great consequence
c. bearing ill-will；wishing harm

4. malign	d. of the nature of curses
5. trivial	e. clumsy, awkward
6. maledictory	f. worshipful, adoring
7. malevolent	g. bad, harmful, hurtful
8. maladroit	h. relating or pertaining to prohibitions

KEY: 1-f, 2-h, 3-a, 4-g, 5-b, 6-d, 7-c, 8-e

Do you understand the words?
你对这些词汇是否已经透彻地理解?

1. Does a *malignant* look indicate kindly feelings? YES NO
2. Is a cancer sometimes called a *malignancy*? YES NO
3. Are *trivialties* important? YES NO
4. If your house is cluttered with *trivia*, are these objects of great value? YES NO
5. Do people enjoy having *maledictions* hurled at them? YES NO
6. Is a *maleficent* act likely to cause harm or hurt? YES NO
7. Does *maladroitness* show skill? YES NO
8. Is a *malefactor* a wrongdoer? YES NO
9. Does an *adulatory* attitude show exaggerated admiration? YES NO
10. Is *militancy* the same as passiveness? YES NO

KEY: 1-no, 2-yes, 3-no, 4-no, 5-no, 6-yes, 7-no, 8-yes, 9-yes, 10-no

Can you recall the words? (Ⅰ)
你能够写出这些词汇吗? (Ⅰ)

1. clumsy, awkward 1. M _____
2. bearing ill-will; wishing harm 2. M _____
3. pleasurable stimulation 3. T _____
4. a person aggressively fighting for a cause 4. M _____
5. prohibition against something injurious 5. P _____
6. excessive flattery; exaggerated admiration 6. A _____
7. vague feeling of general physical discomfort 7. M _____

8. a criminal; a wrongdoer   8. M _____

9. a curse   9. M _____

10. a crime; bad or evil act or behavior   10. M _____

KEY: 1-maladroit, 2-malevolent, 3-titillation, 4-militant, 5-proscription, 6-adulation, 7-malaise, 8-malefactor, 9-malediction, 10-malefaction

Can you recall the words? (Ⅱ)

你能够写出这些词汇吗?(Ⅱ)

1. fact or act of making unnecessary or of taking effective steps toward prevention   1. O _____

2. aggressive attitude   2. M _____

3. harmful, hurtful, bad   3. M _____

      or M _____

      or M _____

4. unimportant, insignificant   4. T _____

5. unimportant, insignificant things; trifles   5. T _____

      or T _____

6. cursing; of the nature of, or relating to, curses (*adj.*)   6. M _____

7. worshipful   7. A _____

KEY: 1-obviation, 2-militancy, 3-malign, malignant, *or* maleficent, 4-trivial, 5-trivialities *or* trivia, 6-maledictory, 7-adulatory

(*End of Session 22*)

SESSION 23
第 23 节

ORIGINS AND RELATED WORDS
词源及相关词汇

1. So now what's the good news?

   那么现在什么是好消息?

Malus is *bad*; *bonus* is *good*. The adverb from the Latin adjective *bonus* is *bene*, and *bene* is the root found in words that contrast with the *mal-* terms we studied in the previous session.

So *benign* (bə-NĪN′) and *benignant* (bə-NIG′-nənt) are kindly, good-natured, not harmful, as in *benign* neglect, a *benign* judge, a *benign* tumor (not cancerous), a *benignant* attitude to malefactors and scoundrels. The corresponding nouns are *benignity* (bə-NIG′-nə-tee) and *benignancy* (bə-NIG′-nən-see).

A *malediction* is a curse; a *benediction* (ben′-ə-DIK′-shən) is a blessing, a "saying good." The adjective is *benedictory* (ben′-ə-DIK′-tə-ree).

In contrast to *maleficent* is *beneficent* (bə-NEF′-ə-sənt), doing good. The noun?

_____.

malus 是"坏的";bonus 是"好的"。由拉丁形容词 bonus 衍变而来的副词是 bene,由 bene 组成的单词与我们在前一节里学过的由前缀 mal-组成的单词意思相反。

因此 benign 和 benignant 有"友好的,好脾气的,无害的"意思,如 benign neglect(善意的忽视),a benign judge(充满善意的判决),a benign tumor (良性肿瘤),a benignant attitude to malefactors and scoundrels(对坏人和恶棍的宽容态度),其对应的名词形式是 benignity 和 benignancy。

malediction 是诅咒;而 benediction 是祝福,即"说好话",其形容词是 benedictory。

与 maleficent 相反的是 beneficent,做好事,其名词是什么?

In contrast to *malefactor* is *benefactor* (BEN′-ə-fak′-tər), one who does good things for another, as by giving help, providing financial gifts or aid, or coming to the rescue when someone is in need. If you insist on making sexual distinctions, a woman who so operates is a *benefactress* (BEN′-ə-fak′-trəs). And, of course, the person receiving the *benefaction* (ben-ə-FAK′-shən), the recipient of money, help, etc., is a *beneficiary* (ben′-ə-FISH′-ər-ee *or* ben-ə-FISH′-ee-air-ee). *Benefit* and *beneficial* are other common words built on the combination of *bene* and a form of *facio*, to do or make.

So let others be *malevolent* toward you—confuse them by being *benevolent* (bə-NEV′-ə-lənt) —wish them well. (Turn the other cheek? Why not?) The noun? __

_____.

和 malefactor 相对的是 benefactor,指"有利于他人的人",比如给予他人帮助,在经济方面赠予他人或提供帮助,或救人于困难之中。如果非要在性别方面做一下区分的话,一个这样的女人叫做 a benefactress。当然,获得这些 benefaction 的人,也就是钱财和帮助等的接受者,叫做 beneficiary。benefit 和 beneficial 是另外两个由 bene 和 facio(做,使……

发生)构成的常用单词。

所以，让别人对你恶毒吧(be malevolent foward you)——用我们的善意(being benevolent)让他们感到困惑——为他们祝福。(逆来顺受？为什么不行呢?)benevolent 的名词形式是什么？

The adjective *bonus*, good, is found in English *bonus*, extra payment, theoretically—but not necessarily—for some good act; in *bonbon*, a candy (a "good-good," using the French version of the Latin adjective); and in *bona fide* (BŌ′-nə-FĪD′ or BŌ′-nə-FĪ′-dee), etymologically, "in good faith", hence valid, without pretense, deception, or fraudulent intent—as a *bona fide* offer, a *bona fide* effort to negotiate differences, etc. *Fides* is Latin for *faith* or *trust*, as in *fidelity* (fə-DEL′-ə-tee), faithfulness; *Fido*, a stereotypical name for a dog, one's faithful friend; *infidel* (IN′-fə-dəl), one who does *not* have the right faith or religion (depending on who is using the term), or one who has *no* religion (Latin *in-*, not); and *infidelity* (in′-fə-DEL′-ə-tee), unfaithfulness, especially to the marriage vows.

由形容词词根 bonus(好的)演变而来的单词有：bonus,"额外报酬",理论上是用于奖赏好的行为,但实际不一定；bonbon,"棒棒糖"(法语,由拉丁形容词演变而来,字面意思是一个"好—好"的东西)；bona fide,法语,词源意义为"本着好意",因此这个词的意思是"正当的",没有伪装,没有蒙骗,也没有欺诈意图。拉丁语中的 fides 为 faith(信念)和 trust(信任)的意思,由其演变而来的词有：fidelity,忠诚；Fido,是狗比较典型的名字,意即"人的忠实的朋友"；infidel,指一个人没有正确的信念和信仰(具体要看这个单词用来形容谁),或者一个没有信仰的人(拉丁字母 in-,"没有"的意思)；infidelity,不忠,主要是指对婚姻而言。

2. say, do, and wish
说、做和希望

Benediction and *malediction* derive from *dico, dictus*, to say, tell. *Dictate, dictator, dictation, dictatorial* (dik′-tə-TAWR′-ee-əl)—words that signify telling others what to do ("Do as I say!")—are built on *dico*, as is *predict*, to tell beforehand, i. e., to say that something will occur before it actually does (*pre-*, before, as in *prescient*).

The brand name *Dictaphone* combines *dico* with *phone*, sound; *contradict*, to say against, or to make an opposite statement ("Don't *contradict* me!"; "That *contradicts* what I know!") combines *dico* with *contra-*, against, opposite; and *addiction*, etymologically "a saying to or toward," or the compulsion to say "yes" to a habit, combines *dico* with *ad-*, to, toward.

benediction 和 malediction 源于 dico,dictus(说,告诉)。dictate(命令), dictator(独裁者), dictation(口授,听写,命令), dictatorial(独裁的)——都是具有命令其他人做某事的意味("照我说的做")——这些词都由 dico 演变而来,又如 predict,意思是"事先说出来",即在某事发生之前就提前预测了它的发生并讲出来(pre-,在……前,如 prescient"有预知能力的")。

商标名称 Dictaphone(录音电话),是 dico 加上 phone(意为"声音")。contradict,"表示反对"或"发表相反的意见",如 Don't contradict me!（不要反驳我)；That contradicts what I know(和我了解到的大相径庭)。这个词是 dico 加 contra-(反对,相反)组成的；另外 addiction,从词源看本义为"对着……说",或对某种生活习惯难以抑制地说"yes"的冲动,是 dico 和 ad-(向,往)构成的。

Facio, factus, to do or make (as in *malefactor, benefactor*), has, as noted, variant spellings in English words: *fec-, fic-*, or, as a verb ending, *-fy*.

Thus *factory* is a place where things are *made* (*-ory*, place where); a *fact* is something *done* (i. e. , something that occurs, or exists, or is, therefore, true); *fiction*, something *made* up or invented; *manufacture*, to *make* by hand (*manus*, hand, as in *manuscript*, *manual*), a word coined before the invention of machinery; *artificial*, *made* by human art rather than occurring in nature, as *artificial* flowers, etc. ; and *clarify*, *simplify*, *liquefy*, *magnify* (to *make* clear, simple, liquid, larger) among hundreds of other *-fy* verbs.

facio, factus,"做"或"制造",如 malefactor(犯罪分子),benefactor(捐赠者),我们前面已经提到过,在英文单词里有不同的拼写形式:fec-, fic-,或作为动词结尾的-fy。

因此"factory"就是物品的制造场所(-ory,场所);fact 就是已经做了的事情(即一些已经发生,或存在的事情因此是真实的);fiction,一些制造或发明出来的东西。manufacture,手工制造(manus,"手"如 manuscript, manual),这是一个在机械时代前出现的一个词;artificial,是人的手工制作而不是天然形成,如 artifical flowers(人造花)等;还有诸如 clarify, simplify, liquefy, magnify(使清楚、简单、液化、更大)等数百个以-fy 结尾的动词。

Volo, to wish, to will, to be willing (as in *malevolent*, *benevolent*), occurs in *voluntary*, *involuntary*, *volunteer*, words too familiar to need definition, and each quite obviously expressing *wish* or *willingness*. Less common, and from the same root, is *volition* (vō-LISH′-ən), the act or power of willing or wishing, as in "of her own *volition*", i. e. , *voluntarily*, or "against her *volition*."

volo 表示"希望,愿意,有意愿"(如 malevolent, benevolent),由它构成的词有 voluntary, involuntary,volunteer 等,这些单词因为太常见而不需要再解释了,它们都表达"希望"和"愿意"。不太常见的、同样来自这个词根的是 volition,"愿意"或者"希望"的行为或力量,如 of her own volition(她自己的意愿),即"自愿",或 against her volition(违背她的意愿)。

3. if you please!

只要你愿意!

Placate is built on the root *plac-* which derives from two related Latin verbs meaning, ① *to please*, and ② to *appease*, *soothe*, or *pacify*.

If you succeed in *placating* an angry colleague, you turn that person's hostile attitude into one that is friendly or favorable. The noun is *placation* (play-KAY′-shən), the adjective either *placative* (PLAK′-ə-tiv *or* PLAY′-kə-tiv) or *placatory* (PLAK′-ə-taw-ree *or* PLAY′-kə-taw-ree). A more *placatory* attitude to those you have offended may help you regain their friendship; when husband and wife, or lovers, quarrel, one of them finally makes a *placative* gesture if the war no longer fulfills his or her neurotic needs—one of them eventually will wake up some bright morning in a *placatory* mood.

But then, such is life, the other one may at that point be *implacable* (im-PLAK′-ə-bəl *or* im-PLAY′-kə-bəl)—*im-* is a respelling of *in-*, not, before the letter *p*. One who *can* be soothed, whose hostility *can* be changed to friendliness, is *placable* (PLAK′-ə-bəl *or* PLAY′-kə-bəl).

Implacable has taken on the added meaning of *unyielding* to *entreaty or pity*; hence, *harsh*, *relentless*, as "The governor was *implacable in* his refusal to grant clemency. ”

The noun form of *implacable* is *implacability* (im-plak′-ə-BIL′-ə-tee *or* im-play′-kə-BIL′-ə-tee). Can you write (and pronounce) the noun derived from *placable*? ___

_____.

placate 里有词根 plac-,它由两个相关的拉丁动词演变而来,这两个拉丁动词意思为:① 讨好;② 使其缓和,使其平静。

如果你成功地"placating"一个愤怒的同事,你就是把那个人的敌意,变成"友好"和"赞同"的态度。其名词是 placation,形容词是 placative 或 placatory。对一些你曾经得罪过的人展现更多的 placatory 的态度,有助于重新赢得他的友谊;夫妻、情侣争吵后,如果其中一方发现这种争吵并不能满足其神经质式的需要,而最终做出 placative 的姿态时——他(她)最终就会在明媚的清晨,在 placatory 的心情中醒来。

但是另一方可能仍旧是 implacable(难以和解的),这就是生活——其中的 im-意思是 "不",是前缀 in-在字母 p 前的变化形式。一个人能被安抚,其敌意能化为友善,这就是 placable。

implacable 可引申为对祈求和怜悯无动于衷,也就是残酷的,无情的,如 the governor was implacable in his refusal to grant clemency(州长冷酷地拒绝了给予赦免)。

implacable 的名词形式是 implacability,你能写出(读出)由 placable 演变而成的名词吗?

If you are *placid* (PLAS′-id), you are calm, easygoing, serene, undisturbed—etymologically, you are pleased with things as they are. Waters of a lake or sea, or the emotional atmosphere of a place, can also be *placid*. The noun is *placidity* (plə-SID′-ə-tee).

If you are *complacent* (kəm-PLAY-sənt), you are pleased with yourself (*com-*, from *con-*, with, together); you may, in fact, such is one common connotation of the word, be smug, *too* pleased with your position or narrow accomplishments, too easily self-satisfied, and the hour of reckoning may be closer than you realize. (Humans, as you know, are delighted to be critical of the contentment of others.)

The noun is *complacence* (kəm-PLAY′-səns) or *complacency* (kəm-PLAY′-sən-see).

如果你是 placid,你是平静的,易于相处的,宁静的,泰然自若的——从词源上看其本义为,你是一个安于现状、随遇而安的人。湖水或海水,或者一个地方的气氛也可以是 placid。名词是 placidity。

如果你是 complacent,就是你对自己很满意(com-由 con-演变而来,意为"和""与……在一起");实际上,你可能是一个自鸣得意的人——这是此单词常见的一种隐含意义——你陶醉于自己的地位或小小的成就,太容易自我满足。你不得不清晰的时刻可能比你预想的来得更早。(如你所知,人们都乐于对别人的满足感提出批评。)

名词形式是 complacence 或 complacency。

4. how to give—and forgive
如何给予——如何原谅

To *condone* is to forgive, overlook, pardon, or be uncritical of (an offense, or of an antisocial or illegal act). You yourself might or might not indulge in such behavior or commit such an offense, but you feel no urge to protest, or to demand censure or punishment for someone else who does. You may *condone* cheating on one's income tax, shoplifting from a big, impersonal supermarket, or exceeding the speed limit, though you personally observe the law with scrupulousness. (Not everyone, however, is so charitable or forgiving.) The noun is *condonation* (kon′-dō-NAY′-

shən).

Condone is built on Latin dono, to give, the root found in donor, one who gives; donate, to give; and donation, a gift.

"to condone" 就是宽恕、不介意、原谅或不批评冒犯、反社会、不法行为。你自己可能有也可能没有此类行为,但你并不想去对抗或主张谴责、惩罚有此类行为的人。你可能会对瞒报个人所得税、偷没有人情味的大型超市的商品和驾车超速持宽恕态度,虽然你自己是个遵纪守法的人。(然而不是每个人都如此慷慨宽容。)其名词形式是 condonation。

condone 是由拉丁语 dono(给予)衍生而来;dono 也是 donor(给予者)、donate(给出去)和 donation(礼物)的词根。

REVIEW OF ETYMOLOGY
复习词源

PREFIX, ROOT, SUFFIX	MEANING	ENGLISH WORD
1. bonus, bene	good, well	_____
2. fides	faith	_____
3. dico, dictus	to say, tell	_____
4. pre-	before, beforehand	_____
5. phone	sound	_____
6. contra-	against, opposite	_____
7. ad-	to, toward	_____
8. facio, factus, fec-, fic-, -fy	to make or do	_____
9. -ory	place where	_____
10. manus	hand	_____
11. volo	to wish, to will, to be willing	_____
12. plac-	to please, appease, soothe, pacify	_____
13. -ive	adjective suffix	_____
14. -ory	adjective suffix	_____
15. im- (in-)	not; negative prefix	_____
16. com- (con-)	with, together	_____
17. dono	to give	_____

USING THE WORDS
单词应用

Can you pronounce the words? (I)
你能读出这些单词吗? (I)

1. benign   bə-NĪN′
2. benignity   bə-NIG′-nə-tee

3. *benignant*   bə-NIG'-nənt

4. *benignancy*   bə-NIG'-nən-see

5. *benediction*   ben'-ə-DIK'-shən

6. *benedictory*   ben'-ə-DIK'-tə-ree

7. *beneficent*   bə-NEF'-ə-sənt

8. *beneficence*   bə-NEF'-ə-səns

9. *benefactor*   BEN'-ə-fak'-tər

10. *benefaction*   ben'-ə-FAK'-shən

11. *beneficiary*   ben'-ə-FISH'-ər-ee *or*

               ben'-ə-FISH'-ee-air-ee

12. *benevolent*   bə-NEV'-ə-lənt

13. *benevolence*   bə-NEV'-ə-ləns

14. *bona fide*   BŌ'-nə FĪD' *or* BŌ'-nə FĪ'-dee

15. *fidelity*   fə-DEL'-ə-tee

16. *infidelity*   in'-fə-DEL'-ə-tee

17. *infidel*   IN'-fə-dəl

Can you pronounce the words? (Ⅱ)

你能读出这些单词吗？（Ⅱ）

1. *dictatorial*   dik'-tə-TAWR'-ee-əl

2. *volition*   vō-LISH'-ən

3. *placation*   play-KAY'-shən

4. *placative*   PLAK'-ə-tiv *or* PLAY'-kə-tiv

5. *placatory*   PLAK'-ə-tawr-ee *or*

               PLAY'-kə-tawr-ee

6. *placable*   PLAK'-ə-bəl *or* PLAY'-kə-bəl

7. *implacable*   im-PLAK'-ə-bəl *or*

               im-PLAY'-kə-bəl

8. *placability*   plak'-ə-BIL'-ə-tee *or*

               play'-kə-BIL'-ə-tee

9. *implacability*   im-plak'-ə-BIL'-ə-tee *or*

               im-play'-kə-BIL'-ə-tee

10. *placid*   PLAS'-id

11. *placidity*   plə-SID'-ə-tee

12. *complacent*   kəm-PLAY'-sənt

13. *complacence*   kəm-PLAY'-səns

14. *complacency*   kəm-PLAY'-sən-see

15. *condonation*   kon'-dō-NAY'-shən

Can you work with the words? (Ⅰ)

你能灵活使用这些词汇了吗？（Ⅰ）

1. benign
2. benedictory
3. benevolent
4. bona fide
5. dictatorial
6. placatory
7. implacable
8. placid
9. complacent

a. wishing good things (for another); well disposed

b. domineering; giving orders in a manner permitting no refusal

c. not to be soothed or pacified; unyielding to pity or entreaty

d. tending, or intended, to pacify, to soothe, or to change hostility to friendliness

e. kindly, good-natured; not cancerous

f. calm, unruffled, undisturbed

g. self-satisfied; smug

h. of the nature of, or relating to, blessings

i. in good faith; sincere; valid

KEY: 1-e, 2-h, 3-a, 4-i, 5-b, 6-d, 7-c, 8-f, 9-g

Can you work with the words? (Ⅱ)

你能灵活使用这些词汇了吗？（Ⅱ）

1. benevolence
2. benefaction
3. beneficiary
4. infidelity
5. volition
6. placation
7. fidelity
8. condonation
9. placidity
10. complacency

a. recipient of money, kindness, etc.

b. free will

c. act of overlooking, or of forgiving, an offense or transgression

d. faithfulness

e. self-satisfaction; smugness

f. calmness

g. act of pacifying, or of turning hostility or anger into friendly feelings

h. attitude of wishing good things for another

i. faithlessness

j. good deed; act of charity or kindness

KEY: 1-h, 2-j, 3-a, 4-i, 5-b, 6-g, 7-d, 8-c, 9-f, 10-e

Do you understand the words? (I)
你对这些词汇是否已经透彻地理解？（ I ）

1. Are *benedictions* given in houses of worship?	YES	NO
2. Is it pleasant to be the recipient of a *beneficent* act?	YES	NO
3. Are kind people *benevolent*?	YES	NO
4. Do *placatory* gestures often heal wounds and soothe disgruntled friends?	YES	NO
5. Are some unambitious people *complacent*?	YES	NO
6. Does *benignity* show malice?	YES	NO
7. Is a *benefaction* an act of philanthropy?	YES	NO
8. Is an *implacable* foe of corruption likely to *condone* corrupt acts?	YES	NO
9. Is a *bona fide* offer made insincerely?	YES	NO
10. Does a *benignant* attitude indicate hostility?	YES	NO

KEY：1-yes，2-yes，3-yes，4-yes，5-yes，6-no，7-yes，8-no，9-no，10-no

Do you understand the words? (II)
你对这些词汇是否已经透彻地理解？（ II ）

1. benign—hateful	SAME	OPPOSITE
2. benignant—kindly	SAME	OPPOSITE
3. benediction—malediction	SAME	OPPOSITE
4. benefactor—evildoer	SAME	OPPOSITE
5. beneficiary—giver	SAME	OPPOSITE
6. benevolent—well disposed	SAME	OPPOSITE
7. bona fide—valid	SAME	OPPOSITE
8. fidelity—unfaithfulness	SAME	OPPOSITE
9. infidel—true believer	SAME	OPPOSITE
10. dictatorial—submissive	SAME	OPPOSITE
11. placative—pacifying	SAME	OPPOSITE
12. implacable—unyielding	SAME	OPPOSITE
13. placid—calm	SAME	OPPOSITE
14. complacent—discontented	SAME	OPPOSITE
15. condonation—forgiveness	SAME	OPPOSITE

KEY: 1-O, 2-S, 3-O, 4-O, 5-O, 6-S, 7-S, 8-O, 9-O, 10-O, 11-S, 12-S, 13-S, 14-O, 15-S

Can you recall the words?
你能够写出这些词汇了吗?

1. tending to give orders
2. act of overlooking (an offense, etc.)
3. unyieldingly hostile; beyond soothing; relentless; pitiless
4. intended to soothe or pacify (*adj.*)
5. one's desire, wishes, or unforced will
6. calmness
7. self-satisfaction; smugness
8. non-believer in the "true" religion
9. kindly; well disposed
10. unfaithfulness
11. involving a blessing (*adj.*)
12. doing something good or kind (*adj.*)
13. faithfulness
14. sincere; valid; in good faith
15. one who does something good, kind, or charitable (for another)
16. a kind or charitable deed
17. recipient of kindness, gift, etc.
18. able to be soothed or pacified

1. D ___
2. C ___
3. I ___
4. P ___
or P ___
5. V ___
6. P ___
7. C ___
or C ___
8. I ___
9. B ___
or B ___
or B ___
10. I ___
11. B ___
12. B ___
13. F ___
14. B ___
15. B ___
16. B ___
17. B ___
18. P ___

KEY: 1-dictatorial, 2-condonation, 3-implacable, 4-placatory *or* placative, 5-volition, 6-placidity, 7-complacence *or* complacency, 8-infidel, 9-benign, benignant, *or* benevolent, 10-infidelity, 11-benedictory, 12-beneficent, 13-fidelity, 14-bona fide, 15-benefactor, 16-benefaction, 17-beneficiary, 18-placable

CHAPTER REVIEW

章节复习

A. Do you recognize the words?

你认识这些单词吗？

1. To belittle：

    (a) titillate，(b) disparage，(c) adulate

2. To be purposely confusing：

    (a) equivocate，(b) obviate，(c) proscribe

3. To work to the disadvantage of：

    (a) malign，(b) militate，(c) placate

4. To slander：

    (a) malign，(b) condone，(c) placate

5. Lack of equality：

    (a) parity，(b) disparity，(c) ambiguity

6. Phrase that may have two interpretations, one of them indelicate or off-color：

    (a) equivocation，(b) ambiguity，(c) double entendre

7. Hateful：

    (a) malignant，(b) benignant，(c) malaise

8. Ill will：

    (a) malaise，(b) malevolence，(c) maleficence

9. Kindly：

    (a) benevolent，(b) placid，(c) complacent

10. Inflexibly hostile：

    (a) implacable，(b) placatory，(c) militant

11. Giving orders imperiously：

    (a) benedictory，(b) dictatorial，(c) adulatory

12. Self-satisfaction：

    (a) complacency，(b) placation，(e) placidity

KEY：1-b，2-a，3-b，4-a，5-b，6-c，7-a，8-b，9-a，10-a，11-b，12-a

B. Can you recognize roots?

你能认出这些词根吗？

ROOT	MEANING	EXAMPLE
1. *par*	_____	parity
2. *aeauus (equ-)*	_____	equivocal
3. *vox，vocis*	_____	vocal
4. *nox，noctis*	_____	nocturnal

5. *libra* _____ equilibrist

6. *latus*，*lateris* _____ equilateral

7. *equus* _____ equine

8. *pedis* _____ pedestrian

9. *paidos*（*ped-*） _____ pedagogue

10. *fero* _____ vociferous

11. *magnus* _____ magnify

12. *scribo*，*scriptus* _____ proscribe

13. *manus* _____ manuscript

14. *post* _____ postscript

15. *via* _____ trivial

16. *militis* _____ militate

17. *malus* _____ malefactor

18. *dico*，*dictus* _____ dictatorial

19. *volo* _____ volition

20. *facio*（*fec-*，*fic-*， _____ benefactor

-fy) fiction

simplify

21. *bonus* _____ bona fide

22. *fides* _____ fidelity

23. *phone* _____ Dictaphone

24. *plac-* _____ placate

25. *dono* _____ donation

KEY：1-equal，2-equal，3-voice，4-night，5-balance，6-side，7-horse，8-foot，9-child，10-carry，bear，11-large，12-write，13-hand，14-after，15-road，16-soldier，17-bad，18-say，tell，19-wish，20-do，make，21-good，22-faith，23-sound，24-please，soothe，pacify，25-give

---

TEASER QUESTIONS FOR THE AMATEUR ETYMOLOGIST
词源小测验

1. Keeping in mind the roots *animus* in *equanimity* and *magnus* in *Magnavox* or *magnify*, can you combine these two roots to form a noun meaning, etymologically, *largeness* of *mind*? _____. Can you figure out the adjective form, ending in *-ous*, of the noun you have constucted? _____

2. If *equilateral* means *equal-sided*, can you construct an adjective meaning *two-sided*? _____.

3. *Trans-* is a prefix meaning *across*. Build a verb meaning *to write across* (from

one form or language to another）：_____.
What is the noun derived from this verb? _____.

4. What disease was so named on the erroneous assumption that it was caused by "bad air"? _____.

5. *Facio* may appear in English words as *fec-*. Using the prefix *con-*, together, can you form a noun sometimes used as a synonym for candy, cake, or ice cream (etymologically, "something made together")? _____.

(Answers in Chapter 18)

（答案见第 18 章）

THE THRILL OF RECOGNITION

振奋的识读

You have been adding, over the past twenty-three sessions, hundreds of words to your vocabulary; you have been learning hundreds of prefixes, roots, and suffixes that make it possible for you to figure out the meaning of many unfamiliar words you may come across in your reading.

经过这过去 23 个小节的学习,你已经在自己的词汇库里增加了数百个新单词;也掌握了数百个前缀、词根和后缀,在阅读过程中遇到不熟悉的单词时,你也许能猜出它们的意思。

As time goes on and you notice more and more of the words you have studied whenever you read, or whenever you listen to lectures, the radio, or TV, the thrill of recognition plus the immediate comprehension of complex ideas will provide a dividend of incalculable value.

随着时间的进展,你会在阅读过程中或者在听演讲、听广播、看电视时,遇到越来越多这些学过的单词,认识这些词令人振奋,加之你因而能够立即理解复杂的概念,这些都是无比珍贵的回报。

You will hear these words in conversation, and you will begin to use them yourself, unself-consciously, whenever something you want to say is best expressed by one of the words that exactly verbalizes your thinking. Another priceless dividend!

你会在谈话中听到这些单词,并且还会不自觉地自己加以运用,无论何时,当你想要表达时,这些单词会准确地传递出你的思想,这是另外一个巨大的收获。

So keep on! You are involved in a dividend-paying activity that will eventually make you intellectually rich.

继续努力! 你正在投入一个给你带来回报的活动中,最终会让你智慧丰满。

(End of Session 23)

HOW TO SPEAK NATURALLY
如何自然表达

Consider this statement by Louis Bromfield, a noted author: "If I, as a novelist, wrote dialogue for my characters which was meticulously grammatical, the result would be the creation of a speech which rendered the characters pompous and unreal."

And this one by Jacques Barzun, former literary critic for *Harper's*: "Speech, after all, is in some measure an expression of character, and flexibility in its use is a good way to tell your friends from the robots."

Consider also this puckish remark by the late Clarence Darrow: "Even if you do learn to speak correct English, who are you going to speak it to?"

These are typical reactions of professional people to the old restrictions of formal English grammar. Do the actual teachers of English feel the same way? Again, some typical statements:

"Experts and authorities do not make decisions and rules, by logic or otherwise, about correctness," said E. A, Cross, then Professor of English at the Greeley, Colorado, College of Education. "All they can do is observe the customs of cultivated and educated people and report their findings."

"Grammar is only an analysis after the facts, a post-mortem on usage," said Stephen Leacock in *How To Write*. "Usage comes first and usage must rule."

One way to discover current trends in usage is to poll a cross section of people who use the language professionally, inquiring as to their opinion of the acceptability, in everyday speech, of certain specific and controversial expressions. A questionnaire I prepared recently was answered by eighty-two such people—thirty-one authors, seven book reviewers, thirty-three editors, and eleven professors of English. The results, some of which will be detailed below, may possibly prove startling to you if you have been conditioned to believe, as most of us have, that correct English is rigid, unchangeable, and exclusively dependent on grammatical rules.

思考著名作家路易丝·布鲁姆菲尔德的以下论述:"作为小说家,如果我为人物设计的对话过于墨守陈规,这只会使人物看起来浮夸、虚假。"

《哈珀》的前任文学批评家雅克·巴森说过:"归根结底,语言在某种程度能够体现人物性格,而语言的灵活性是将你的朋友与机器人区分开来的最好途径。"

再来思考下面这句俏皮话,已故的克拉伦斯·丹诺说过:"即使你真的学会了说正确的英语,但是,去哪里找这样的对话对象呢?"

以上是专业人士就正规语法的陈规旧习的典型回答。英语教师是否也有同感? 再来看一些典型论述:

E. A. 克洛斯是科罗拉多州格里利教育学院的教授,他说到:"专家和权威人士并不根据逻辑来判断语法正误;他们能做的只是观察受教育人士的语言习惯并对其作出记录。"

在《如何写作》中,斯蒂芬·李珂克说过:"语法只是对事实发生之后的分析,是对用法的剖析。用法占上风,用法必须统治。"

对当代用法挑错的方法之一是对几个领域的语言专业人士做调研,询问他们对于日常语言中出现的一些具体的、有争议的表达的观点。82 位专家对我最近调查的问卷做出了回复,包括 31 位作家,7 位书评家,33 位编辑和 11 位英语教授。以下是对部分调研结果的详细解释。如果你一直和我们多数人一样,认为正确的英语应该是严格按照英语语法规则的、不可改变的,读过下面的解释,你可能会非常吃惊。

TEST YOURSELF
自我测试

1. Californians boast of the *healthy* climate   RIGHT   WRONG
of their state.
2. Her new novel is not *as* good as her first one.   RIGHT   WRONG
3. We *can't* hardly believe it.   RIGHT   WRONG
4. This is *her*.   RIGHT   WRONG
5. *Who* are you waiting for?   RIGHT   WRONG
6. Please take care of *whomever* is waiting.   RIGHT   WRONG
7. *Whom* would you like to be if you   RIGHT   WRONG
weren't yourself?
8. My wife has been *robbed*.   RIGHT   WRONG
9. Is this *desert* fattening?   RIGHT   WRONG

1. Californians boast of the *healthy* climate of their state.
加州人夸耀加州的健康气候。

RIGHT. There is a distinction, says formal grammar, between *healthy* and *healthful*. A person can be *healthy*—I am still quoting the rule—if he possesses good health. But climate must be *healthful*, since it is *conducive* to health. This distinction is sometimes observed in writing but rarely in everyday speech, as you have probably noticed. Even the dictionaries have stopped splitting hairs—they permit you to say *healthy* no matter which of the two meanings you intend.

"*Healthy* climate" was accepted as current educated usage by twenty-six of the thirty-three editors who answered the questionnaire, six of the seven book reviewers, nine of the eleven professors of English, and twenty of the thirty-one authors. The earlier distinction, in short, is rapidly becoming obsolete.

正确。正规语法认为 healthy 和 healthful 之间有区别。如果拥有健康体魄,可以说一个人 healthy——我仍在引用语法规则。但是修饰气候必须使用 healthful,因为气候是对身体有益的。你一定已经注意到,这个区别仅出现在书面语中,日常交流中并未出现。词典对两者意义的不同已经不做区分——无论你想表达哪种意思,都可以使用 healthy。

回答问卷的 33 位编辑中,26 位接受"healthy climate"的用法。接受这种用法的还有编辑 6 人(共 7 人),英语教授 9 人(共 11 人),作家 20 人(共 31 人)。总之,过去对 healthy 和 healthful 的区分很快就要变得过时。

2. Her new novel is not *as* good as her first one.

    她的新小说没有第一本精彩。

RIGHT. If you have studied formal grammar, you will recall that after a negative verb the "proper" word is *so*, not *as*. Is this rule observed by educated speakers? Hardly ever.

In reference to the sentence under discussion, author Thomas W. Duncan remarked: "I always say—and write—*as*, much to the distress of my publisher's copy-reader. But the fellow is a wretched purist."

The tally on this use of *as* showed seventy-four for, only eight against.

    正确。如果学过正规语法,你一定知道第一个动词之后使用 so 才是"正确"的。受教育人士是否关注过这个语法? 从来没有。

    针对这个句子,作家托马斯·W.邓肯说道:"我在说话和写作时一直使用 as,这着实令我出版商的校对人员苦恼。但是他是个讨厌的语言纯正癖者。"

    接受问卷的 82 人中 74 人支持这种用法,只有 8 人投反对票。

3. We *can't* hardly believe it.

    我几乎无法相信。

WRONG. Of the eighty-two professional people who answered my questionnaire, seventy-six rejected this sentence; it is evident that *can't hardly* is far from acceptable in educated speech. Preferred usage: We *can* hardly believe it.

    错误。接受问卷的 82 位专业人士中,76 人反对此用法;很明显,can't hardly 并不被受教育人士所接受。正确的形式是:We can hardly believe it.

4. This is *her*.

    这是她。

WRONG. This substitution of *her* where the rule requires *she* was rejected by fifty-seven of my eighty-two respondents. Paradoxically enough, although "It's *me*" and "This is *me*" are fully established in educated speech, "This is *her*" still seems to be condemned by the majority of cultivated speakers. Nevertheless, the average person, I imagine, may feel a bit uncomfortable saying "This is *she*"—it sounds almost too sophisticated.

This is more than an academic problem. If the voice at the other end of a telephone conversation makes the opening move with "I'd like to speak to Jane Doe. [your name, for argument's sake]," you are, unfortunately, on the horns of a very real dilemma. "This is *she*" may sound prissy—"This is *her*" may give the impression that you're uneducated. Other choices are equally doubtful. "Talking!" is suspiciously businesslike if the call comes to your home, and "I am Jane Doe!" may make you feel like the opening line of a high school tableau. The need for a decision arises several times in a busy day—and, I am sorry to report, the English language is just deficient enough not to be of much help. I wonder how it would be if you just grunted affably?

    错误。接受问卷的 82 位专业人士中,57 位认为不能用 her 代替语法规则规定的 she。自相矛盾的是,虽然"It's me"和"This is me"是完全被人们所接受的表达方式,但大多数专业人士似乎仍然反对"This is her"的用法。不过我认为,普通人在使用"This is she"时一定会感到别扭——因为这个表达听起来实在复杂。

这不单是一个学术问题。接听电话时,如果电话一端说到"我找 Jane Doe(为了论证的方便,假设你就是 Jane Doe)",你会实在感到左右为难。"This is she"听起来有些刻板——而回答"This is her"会显得你没文化。其他回答同样有问题:对打到你家里的电话,回答"Talking!"听起来过于正式,而回答"I am Jane Doe"又像是高中舞台剧的开场白。繁忙的一天中,人们会多次遇见这样的情景——遗憾的是,英语语言不足以给出最恰当的答复。我在想,如果亲切地咕哝一声是否是最好的办法?

5. *Who* are you waiting for?

　　你在等谁?

RIGHT. *Formal grammar* not only requires *whom* but demands that the word order be changed to: "For whom are you waiting?" (Just try talking with such formality on everyday occasions and see how long you'll keep your friends.)

Who is the normal, popular form as the first word of a sentence, no matter what the grammatical construction; and an opinion by Kyle Crichton, a well-known magazine editor, is typical of the way many educated people feel. Mr. Crichton says: "The most loathsome word (to me at least) in the English language is *whom*. You can always tell a half-educated buffoon by the care he takes in working the word in. When he starts it, I know I am faced with a pompous illiterate who is not going to have me long as company. "

The score for acceptance of the sentence as it stands (with *who*) was sixty-six out of eighty-two. If, like most unpedantic speakers, you prefer *who* to *whom* for informal occasions, or if you feel as strongly about *whom* as Mr. Crichton does, you will be happy to hear that modern trends in English are all on your side.

正确。正规语法不仅要求用 whom 替换 who,还要求将句子结构改变为:"For whom are you waiting?"(你可以尝试在日常生活中使用这样正式的句子结构,看看你能在多长时间内留住你的朋友。)

无论句子的语法结构如何,who 作为句首单词都是正常的、普遍的用法。著名杂志编辑凯尔·克莱顿与许多专业人士的观点相同:"至少对我来说,英语语言中最讨厌的词汇就是 whom。如果一个人非常注意在句子中使用 whom 一词,你就可以知道这是一个半瓶子醋的傻瓜。他只要一张口,我就知道我面对的是一个自负的文盲,我也绝对无法结交这样的朋友。"

接受问卷的 82 人中,66 人接受本句子的用法。如果你与大多数并不迂腐的说话者一样,在非正式场合你更喜欢使用 who,或者你与克莱顿先生对 whom 的用法同样地强烈不满,你会很开心地发现,现代英语用法的趋势和你站在一条战线上。

6. Please take care of *whomever* is waiting.

　　请照顾等待中的每个人。

WRONG. Whomever is awkward and a little silly in this sentence and brings to mind Franklin P. Adams' famous remark on grammar: "'Whom are you?' asked Cyril, for he had been to night school. " It is also contrary to grammatical rule. People who are willing to be sufficiently insufferable to use *whomever* in this construction have been tempted into error by the adjacent word *of*. They believe that since they are following a preposition with an objective pronoun they are speaking impeccable grammar. In actuality, however, *whomever* is not the object of the preposition of but the subject of the verb *is waiting*. Preferable form: Please take care of *whoever* is waiting.

错误。在这个句子中使用 whomever 既奇怪又愚蠢。这使我想起富兰克林·P.亚当关于语法的著名论述:"Cyril 只上过夜校,所以他问:'Whom are you?'"这也是违反语法规则的用法。有些人之所以在这里使用令人难以忍受的 whomever,主要是因为前面的介词 of 诱导他们犯错。人们认为介词之后一定要接宾格形式,这才是毫无瑕疵的语法。但是,实际上,whomever 并不是介词 of 的宾语,而是谓语 is waiting 的主语。正确的形式是:Please take care of whoever is waiting.

7. *Whom* would you like to be if you weren't yourself?

如果能够改变,你想变成谁?

WRONG. Here is another and typical example of the damage which an excessive reverence for *whom* can do to an innocent person's speech. Judged by grammatical rule, *whom* is incorrect in this sentence (the verb *to be* requires *who*); judged by normal speech patterns, it is absurd. This use of *whom* probably comes from an abortive attempt to sound elegant.

错误。这是另一个典型例子,显示无知的人过度尊重 whom 会给他的语言带来多大的破坏。根据语法规则,whom 在本句中的使用是错误的(to be 后需要接 who);而根据正常语言规范,whom 过于荒诞。这里用 whom 可能是出于使语言高雅的动机,只是目的并没有达到。

8. My wife has been *robbed*.

我的妻子被抢。

RIGHT—if something your wife owns was taken by means of thievery. However, if your wife herself was kidnapped, or in some way talked into leaving you, she was *stolen*, not *robbed*. To *rob* is to abscond with the contents of something—to *steal* is to walk off with the thing itself. Needless to say, both forms of activity are highly antisocial and equally illegal.

正确。假如你妻子的财产被人偷窃,这个表达就是正确的。但是,如果你的妻子被诱拐或者被人说服而离开了你,那么应该说 she was stolen,而不是 she was robbed。rob 指带着被劫者的东西逃跑,而 steal 是带着被偷的东西离开。当然,两种都是反社会的行为,同样违反法律。

9. Is this *desert* fattening?

这个甜品会使人发胖吗?

WRONG. The *dessert* that is fattening is spelled with two *s*'s. With one *s*, it's a desert, like the Sahara. Remember the two *s*'s in dessert by thinking how much you'd like *two* portions, if only your waistline permitted.

错误。会使人发胖的是甜品——dessert,两个 s。写成一个 s 便成为沙漠(desert),例如 Sahara Desert(撒哈拉沙漠)。心中谨记你多么想要两份甜品,就能够记住是两个 s——只要你的腰围允许。

10

HOW TO TALK
ABOUT VARIOUS SPEECH HABITS
如何描述多样的语言习惯

(*Sessions 24 — 27*)

TEASER PREVIEW
引读

What adjective describes people who：

* *are disinclined to conversation?*
* *are brief and to the point in their speech?*
* *are blocked or incoherent in their speech?*
* *show by their speech that they are trite and unimaginative?*
* *use more words than necessary?*
* *are forcefully compelling and logical in their speech?*
* *talk rapidly and fluently?*
* *are noisy and clamorous?*
* *are talkative?*

用哪些形容词来描述以下不同类型的人：
* 不爱说话的、沉默寡言的
* 言简意赅的
* 笨口拙舌的、言语不连贯的
* 言谈显示他们陈腐、缺乏想象力
* 啰嗦的、累赘的
* （论据）有说服力的、令人信服的
* 喋喋不休的、口若悬河的
* 吵吵嚷嚷的、叫嚣的
* 爱说话的、嘴碎的

SESSION 24
第 24 节

Perhaps some of your richest and most satisfying experiences have been with people to whom you can just talk，talk，talk. As you speak，previously untapped springs of ideas and emotions begin to flow；you hear yourself saying things you never thought you knew.

What kinds of people might you find yourself in conversation with? In this chapter we start by examining ten types，discovering the adjective that aptly describes each one.

人生最宝贵、最有满足感的经验大多来自交流。交流过程中，之前从未被挖掘的观点和情感开始涌动；你能够听到自己说出意想不到的观点。

你能看出与你交谈的人是什么样的人吗？在本章中我们将检视 10 种类型的人，并找出准确描述各种类型的形容词。

IDEAS
概念

1. saying little
沉默寡言

There are some people who just don't like to talk. It's not that they prefer to listen. Good listeners hold up their end of the conversation delightfully—with appropriate facial expressions；with empathetic smiles，giggles，squeals，and sighs at just the right time；and with encouraging nods or phrases like "Go on!" "Fantastic!" "And then what happened?"

These people like neither to talk nor to listen—they act as if conversation is a bore，even a painful waste of time. Try to engage them，and the best you may expect for your efforts is a vacant stare，a noncommittal grunt，or an impatient silence. Finally，in frustration，you give up，thinking. "Are they self-conscious? Do they hate people? Do they hate *me*?"

The adjective：*taciturn*

有些人就是不喜欢谈话。他们也不是乐于倾听。好的倾听者总是能使谈话保持愉快——整个过程中他们配合恰当的脸部表情，在恰当的时间表现出感同身受的微笑、出声的笑、尖叫和叹息，还会点头鼓励或说"继续讲!""太棒了!""接下来怎么样了?"

这些人不喜欢说或听——对于交谈，他们兴趣索然，或者觉得是浪费时间，令人痛苦。当你试图让他们参与到谈话中时，你得到的只可能是茫然的眼神，不情愿的嘟囔，或缺少耐心的沉默。最后，你可能在沮丧中放弃，并想："他们是害羞吗? 他们厌恶人吗? 他们厌恶我吗?"

形容词 taciturn(沉默寡言的)。

2. saying little—meaning much
言少——意多

There is a well-known anecdote about Calvin Coolidge, who, when he was President，was often called（though probably not to his face）"Silent Cal"：

A young newspaperwoman was sitting next to him at a banquet，so the story goes，and turned to him mischievously.

"Mr. Coolidge，" she said，"I have a bet with my editor that I can get you to say more than two words to me this evening."

"*You lose*，" Coolidge rejoined simply.

The adjective：laconic

有一则关于卡尔文·柯立芝的逸事广为流传,当他还是总统的时候,经常被人称作(虽然可能不能当面)"沉默的卡尔"。

故事是这样的:一次晚宴时,一位年轻的报刊女编辑坐在他身边,转身跟他开玩笑。

"柯立芝先生,"她说,"我和编辑打赌,今天晚上我一定能够让你说出两个字以上。"

柯立芝说道:"你输。"(you lose)。

现在,你又该如何描述柯立芝呢?

形容词 laconic(言简意赅)。

3．when the words won't come

情绪激动,词不达意

Under the pressure of some strong emotion—fear，rage，anger，for example—people may find it difficult，or even impossible，to utter words，to get their feelings unjumbled and untangled enough to form understandable sentences. They undoubtedly have a lot they want to say，but the best they can do is sputter！

The adjective：inarticulate

在很强的情绪压力下,如恐惧、暴怒、愤怒,人们发现要条理清晰地表达自己,并让人能够听懂是非常困难的,甚至不可能。他们无疑有很多话要说,但至多只是嘟囔几声。

形容词 inarticulate(笨口拙舌)。

4．much talk，little sense

言多意少

Miss Bates，a character in *Emma*，a novel by Jane Austen：

"So obliging of you！No，we should not have heard，if it had not been for this particular circumstance，of her being able to come here so soon. My mother is so delighted！For she is to be three months with us at least，Three months，she says so，positively，as I am going to have the pleasure of reading to you. The case is，you see，that the Campbells are going to Ireland. Mrs. Dixon has persuaded her father and mother to come over and see her directly. I was going to say，but，however，different countries，and so she wrote a very urgent letter to her mother，or her father，I declare I do not know which it was，but we shall see presently in Jane's letter..."

The adjective：garrulous

简·奥斯丁所著小说《爱玛》中的人物贝茨小姐这样说:

"你真的是太体贴了! 不,如果不是因为这个特殊情况,我们也不会知道她能够这么早就来。妈妈高兴极了! 因为她至少能和我们待上三个月! 她说过是三个月,一会我会把信读给你听,这真是我的荣幸。你也知道,情况是,坎贝尔一家将要去爱尔兰。迪克逊夫人已经说服她的父亲和母亲直接来这里看她。但是,然而,我要说的是,他们要去不同的国家,所以她给她的父亲或者母亲写了一封紧急信件。我发誓我不知道是哪封信,但是我们现在会从简的信中得知……"

形容词 garrulous(饶舌的,多嘴的)。

5．unoriginal

呆滞、单调

Some people are completely lacking in originality and imagination—and their talk shows it. Everything they say is trite, hackneyed, commonplace, humorless—their speech patterns are full of clichés and stereotypes, their phraseology is without sparkle.

The adjective：banal

有些人实在缺乏原创性和创造力——他们的言语能够说明这一点。他们说的任何话都是陈词滥调,平庸至极,毫无幽默感——他们的语言模式充满了老生常谈,他们的遣词造句毫无智慧火花。

形容词 banal(陈腐的)。

6．Words, words, words！

说不完的话！

They talk and talk and talk—it's not so much the quantity you object to as the repetitiousness. They phrase, rephrase, and re-rephrase their thoughts—using far more words than necessary, overwhelming you with words, drowning you with them; until your only thought is how to escape, or maybe how to die.

The adjective：verbose

他们说呀说,说呀说,总是有说不完的话——令你生厌的不是量的多少,而是不断的重复。他们表达自己的观点,然后改变措辞,再改变措辞——使用太多没有必要的词汇。他不断用词汇压垮你、淹没你,直到你再也无法忍受,唯一的想法就是如何逃离,或者如何自杀！

形容词 verbose(啰嗦的)。

7．words in quick succession

滔滔不绝的谈话

They are rapid, fluent talkers, the words seeming to roll off their tongues with such ease and lack of effort, and sometimes with such copiousness, that you listen with amazement.

The adjective：voluble

他说话又快又流利,他的话能够毫不费力地脱口而出,话多得让你瞠目结舌——你对他的谈话能力惊叹不已。

形容词 voluble(口若悬河的)。

8．words that convince

极具说服力的话

They express their ideas persuasively, forcefully, brilliantly, and in a way that calls for wholehearted assent and agreement from an intelligent listener.

The adjective：cogent

他能够聪慧地、极具影响力地表达思想;他的谈话能够得到有智慧的聆听者全心全意的赞同。

形容词 cogent(有说服力的)。

9．the sound and the fury

喧哗与骚动

Their talk is loud, noisy, clamorous, vehement. What may be lacking in content is compensated for in force and loudness.

The adjective：*vociferous*

他谈话时声音洪亮,吵闹,聒噪,情感强烈——语气和力量足以弥补内容的缺失。

形容词 vociferous(吵吵闹闹的)。

10．quantity

话多

They talk a lot—a *whole* lot. They may be voluble，vociferous，garrulous，verbose，but never inarticulate，taciturn，or laconic. No matter. It's the quantity and continuity that are most conspicuous. "Were you vaccinated with a phonograph needle?" is the question you are tempted to ask as you listen.

The adjective：*loquacious*

他们话多——非常之多。他们可能喋喋不休,吵吵嚷嚷,多嘴,啰嗦,但他们绝对不会辞不达意,沉默寡言或者言简意赅。这些都不重要。重要的是,他们话的数量和连贯性相当显眼。听到他说话,你非常想问这个问题:"你是否接种过贫嘴疫苗?"

形容词 loquacious(爱说话的)。

These ten words revolve around the idea of varying kinds and ways of talking and not talking. Many of the adjectives are close in meaning，but each contains its unique difference.

这 10 个词汇表达各种谈话方式或者沉默的方式。许多形容词虽然意思相近,却都有各自独特的含义。

QUALITY	ADJECTIVE
1. silence，unresponsiveness	taciturn
2. economy，brevity，meaningfulness	laconic
3. awkwardness，sputtering，incoherence	inarticulate
4. rambling chatter	garrulous
5. hackneyed，unoriginal phraseology	banal
6. wordiness，repetitiousness	verbose
7. fluency，rapidity	voluble
8. logic，clarity，persuasiveness	cogent
9. noise，vehemence	vociferous
10. talkativeness	loquacious

USING THE WORDS

单词应用

Can you pronounce the words?

你能读出这些单词吗?

1. taciturn	TAS'-ə-turn
2. laconic	lə-KON'-ik
3. inarticulate	in'-ahr-TIK'-yə-lət
4. garrulous	GAIR'-ə-ləs

5. banal BAY′-nəl
6. verbose vər-BŌS′
7. voluble VOL′-yə-bəl
8. cogent KŌ′-jənt
9. vociferous vō-SIF′-ər-əs
10. loquacious lō-KWAY′-shəs

Can you work with the words?
你能灵活使用这些词汇了吗？

1. taciturn   a. chattering meaninglessly
2. laconic   b. wordy
3. inarticulate   c. trite，hackneyed，unoriginal
4. garrulous   d. fluent and rapid
5. banal   e. noisy，loud
6. verbose   f. sputtering unintelligibly
7. voluble   g. talkative
8. cogent   h. brilliantly compelling, persuasive
9. vociferous   i. unwilling to engage in conversation
10. loquacious   j. using few words packed with meaning

KEY：1-i，2-j，3-f，4-a，5-c，6-b，7-d，8-h，9-e，10-g

Do you understand the words?
你对这些词汇是否已经透彻地理解？

1. Do *taciturn* people usually make others feel comfortable and welcome?   YES   NO
2. Does a *laconic* speaker use more words than necessary?   YES   NO
3. Does rage make some people *inarticulate*?   YES   NO
4. Is it interesting to listen to *garrulous* old men?   YES   NO
5. Do *banal* speakers show a great deal of originality?   YES   NO
6. Is *verbose* a complimentary term?   YES   NO
7. Is if easy to be *voluble* when you don't know the subject you are talking about?   YES   NO
8. Do unintelligent people usually make   YES   NO

cogent statements?

9. Is a *vociferous* demand ordinarily made YES NO
   by a shy, quiet person?

10. Do *loquacious* people spend more time YES NO
    talking than listening?

KEY: 1-no, 2-no, 3-yes, 4-no, 5-no, 6-no, 7-no, 8-no, 9-no, 10-yes

Can you recall the words?
你能够写出这些词汇吗？

Do you know that new nerve patterns are formed by repeated actions? As a very young child, you tied your shoelaces and buttoned your clothing with great concentration—the activity was directed, controlled, purposeful, exciting. As you grew older and more skillful, you tied and buttoned with scarcely a thought of what you were doing. Your fingers flew about their task almost automatically—for the habit had formed a nerve pattern and the action needed little if any conscious attention.

That's simple enough to understand. If you do not remember your own experiences, you can observe the phenomenon of struggling with a skill, mastering it, and finally making it a self-starting habit by watching any young child. Or you can simply take my word for it.

你知道吗？重复的动作能够形成新的神经模式。儿童时期，系鞋带和扣衣服扣子时你非常专注——最初的动作受人指导、控制，动作目的明确，也很有趣。随着年龄增长，你变得越来越有技巧，直到后来你已经意识不到动作的发生。你的手指自动完成动作——因为习惯本身已经形成一套神经模式，动作不再需要任何意识去注意。

这一点很容易理解。如果你忘记了系鞋带的经历，你可以观察小孩子是如何从最初挣扎学习、掌握一个技巧直到最后形成自发的习惯。相信我，没错的！

You need not take my word for the way a mastery of new words is acquired. You can see in yourself, as you work with this book, how adding words to your vocabulary is exactly analogous to a child's mastery of shoelacing. First you struggle with the concepts; then you eventually master them; finally, by frequent work with the new words (now you see the reason for the great number of exercises, the repetitious writing, saying, thinking) you build up new nerve patterns and you begin to use the new words with scarcely any consciousness of what you are doing.

Watch this common but important phenomenon closely as you do the next exercise. Your total absorption of the material so far has given you complete mastery of our ten basic words. Prove that you are beginning to form new nerve patterns in relation to these words by writing the one that fits each brief definition. The more quickly you think of the word that applies, the surer you can be that using these words will soon be as automatic and unself-conscious as putting on your shoes or buttoning/zipping yourself up in the morning.

　　而新词汇是如何获得的呢？这一点你无需信我,你只需要观察自己。通过对本书的学习,你会发现词汇的扩建与儿童掌握系鞋带的动作是类似的。首先,你需要费力理解概念;然后,你终于掌握概念;最后,通过反复练习(现在你一定明白各种练习、反复书写、朗读和思考的意义),你建立起新的神经模式,你可以不费吹灰之力地使用新学到的词汇。

　　做以下练习时,注意观察这个普遍却又非常重要的现象。我坚信,只要专注于学习本章内容,你就一定能够完全掌握 10 个基本词汇。如果能够根据以下的简短定义写出相应词汇,你就已经开始形成新的神经模式。想出词汇的速度越快、准确率越高,自动地、无意识地使用新词就会越快——与系鞋带或早上系衣服扣一样容易!

1. talkative	1. L ＿＿＿＿＿＿
2. noisy, vehement, clamorous	2. V ＿＿＿＿＿＿
3. incoherent; sputtering	3. I ＿＿＿＿＿＿
4. gabbing ceaselessly and with little meaning	4. G ＿＿＿＿＿＿
5. disinclined to conversation	5. T ＿＿＿＿＿＿
6. talking in hackneyed phraseology	6. B ＿＿＿＿＿＿
7. showing a fine economy in the use of words	7. L ＿＿＿＿＿＿
8. forceful and convincing	8. C ＿＿＿＿＿＿
9. talking rapidly and fluently	9. V ＿＿＿＿＿＿
10. using more words than necessary	10. V ＿＿＿＿＿＿

KEY：1-loquacious, 2-vociferous, 3-inarticulate, 4-garrulous, 5-taciturn, 6-banal, 7-laconic, 8-cogent, 9-voluble, 10-verbose

(End of Session 24)

SESSION 25
第 25 节

ORIGINS AND RELATED WORDS
词源及相关词汇

1. about keeping one's mouth shut
有关沉默

If you let your mind play over some of the *taciturn* people you know, you will realize that their abnormal disinclination to conversation makes them seem morose, sullen, and unfriendly. Cal Coolidge's *taciturnity* was world-famous, and no one, I am sure, ever conceived of him as cheerful, overfriendly, or particularly sociable. There are doubtless many possible causes of such verbal rejection of the world: perhaps lack of self-assurance, feelings of inadequacy or hostility, excessive seriousness or introspection, or just plain having nothing to say. Maybe, in Coolidge's case, he was saving up his words—after he did not "choose to run" in 1928, he wrote a daily column for the *New York Herald Tribune* at a rumored price of two dollars a word—and, according to most critics (probably all Democrats), he had seemed wiser when he kept silent. Coolidge hailed from New England, and *taciturnity* (tas-ə-TURN'-ə-tee) in that part of the country, so some people say, is considered a virtue. Who knows, the cause may be geographical and climatic, rather than psychological.

回想你身边不爱说话的朋友,你就会意识到,他们的沉默寡言使他们看起来忧郁、冷漠、没有人情味。卡尔·柯立芝不爱说话的特点是举世闻名的,我确信,没有人会认为他是个欢乐的、过于友善的或者善于交际的人。对于像这样在语言上对外界的抵触,无疑有许多种原因,例如:缺乏自信,感到自卑或者敌意,过度严肃或者过于内向或者就是无话可说。柯立芝可能的确在节省自己的言词——1928 年,在他没有"选择参与竞选"之后,以传闻每个字两美元的稿费为《纽约先驱论坛报》撰写一篇每日专栏——多数评论家认为(可能全部都是民主党),他保持沉默的确更为明智。柯立芝出生于新英格兰,在那里,少言寡语被视为美德。谁知道呢? 很可能是地理和环境因素造成的,并非心理原因。

Taciturn is from a Latin verb *taceo*, to be silent, and is one of those words whose full meaning cannot be expressed by any other combination of syllables. It has many synonyms, among them *silent*, *uncommunicative*, *reticent*, *reserved*, *secretive*, *close-lipped*, and *close-mouthed*; but no other word indicates the *permanent*, *habitual*, and *temperamental* disinclination to talk implied by *taciturn*.

taciturn 来自于拉丁语动词 taceo,意为"变得安静"。有很多词的完整意义是无法用其它的音节组合方式表达出来的,taciturn 就是其中一个。taciturn 的近义词有 silent, uncommunicative, reticent, reserved, secretive, close-lipped 和 close-mouthed;但是,没有任何一个词能够表达 taciturn 所暗含的长久的、沉默寡言的习惯,这个习惯已经成为性格不可分离的一部分。

2. better left unsaid
沉默是金

Tacit (TAS'-it) derives also from *taceo*.

Here is a man dying of cancer. He suspects what his disease is, and everyone else, of course, knows. Yet he never mentions the dread word, and no one who visits him ever breathes a syllable of it in his hearing. It is *tacitly* understood by all concerned that the word will remain forever unspoken.

(Such a situation today, however, may or may not be typical—there appears to be a growing tendency among physicians and family to be open and honest with people who are dying.)

另外一个由 taceo 派生的词语是 tacit,"心照不宣的"。

一个人患有癌症,就要走到生命尽头。他怀疑自己是癌症,当然,其他所有人都知道。但是,他对这个可怕的疾病闭口不谈;前来拜访他的人也从来不泄露只言片语。可以说:It is tacitly understood by all concerned that the word will remain forever unspoken.(所有相关的人都心照不宣,没有人会提癌症这个词。)

(但到了现在,这种情形可能常见,也可能不常见——医生和家人对于垂死的人更加直言以对,这似乎正在成为一种趋势。)

Consider another situation:

An executive is engaging in extracurricular activities with her secretary. Yet during office time they are as formal and distant as any two human beings can well be. Neither of them ever said to the other, "Now, look here, we may be lovers after five o'clock, but between nine and five we must preserve the utmost decorum, okay?" Such speech, such a verbal arrangement, is considered unnecessary—so we may say that the two have a *tacit* agreement (i. e., nothing was ever actually *said*) to maintain a complete employer-employee relationship during office hours.

考虑另外一种情景:

一位高管与她的秘书有婚外情。但是,在办公时间,他们之间的关系跟其他任何两人之间的关系一样正式,一样保持距离。"这样吧,五点之后我们可以是恋人;九点至五点之间我们要尽最大努力维持礼节,好吗?"他们从来不对彼此说出这样的话,因为这样的言语安排是毫无必要的——所以,我们可以说经理和秘书达成了一个 tacit agreement(默契,无需说任何话)——办公时间保持上级和下属关系。

Anything *tacit*, then, is unspoken, unsaid, not verbalized. We speak of a *tacit* agreement, arrangement, acceptance, rejection, assent, refusal, etc. A person is never called *tacit*.

The noun is *tacitness* (TAS′-it-nəs). (Bear in mind that you can transform any adjective into a noun by adding *-ness*, though in many cases there may be a more sophisticated, or more common, noun form.)

所以,任何事物,只要是 tacit,就是未说出口的、不用言语表达的,例如:tacit agreement, tacit arrangement, tacit acceptance, tacit rejection, tacit assent, tacit refusal 等等。注意,不能用 tacit 来描述人。

名词形式是 tacitness。(记住,你可以在任何形容词后面加上-ness 变成名词,虽然很多时候也许已经有其他更复杂,或者更常用的名词形式)。

Changing the *a* of the root *taceo* to *i*, and adding the prefix *re-*, again, and the adjective suffix *-ent*, we can construct the English word *reticent* (RET′-ə-sənt).

Someone is *reticent* who prefers to keep silent, whether out of shyness, embarrassment, or fear of revealing what should not be revealed. (The idea of "againness" in the prefix has been lost in the current meaning of the word.)

We have frequently made nouns out of *-ent* adjectives. Write two possible noun forms of *reticent*：_____，or，less commonly，_____.

把词根 taceo 里的 a 变成 i,然后加上前缀 re-,"再",和形容词后缀-ent,可以构成英文词 reticent。

一个 reticent 的人更愿意保持沉默,可能是因为害羞、尴尬,或者害怕透露一些不该透露的信息。(前缀中"又,再"的意思在这个单词中没有表现出来)。

我们经常能从以-ent 结尾的形容词里面得出其名词形式。写出 reticent 两个可能的名词形式_____;或者不经常使用的_____。

3. Talk，talk，talk！

说个不停！

Loquacious people love to talk. This adjective is not necessarily a put-down，but the implication，when you so characterize such people，is that you wish they would pause for breath once in a while so that *you* can get your licks in. The noun is *loquacity* (lō-KWAS'-ə-tee)，or，of course，*loquaciousness*.

The word derives from Latin *loquor*，to speak，a root found also in：

loquacious 的人喜欢说话。这个形容词未必是贬义,但当你用这个词来描述这类人的时候,你的言下之意是,你希望他们稍微停顿一下,让你能插个话。名词形式是 loquacity,或 loquaciousness。

这个词由拉丁语表示"说话"的词 loquor 衍生而来。由这个词根派生的单词还有：

(1) *soliloquy* (sə-LIL'-ə-kwee)—a speech to oneself (*loquor* plus *solus*，alone)，or，etymologically，a speech when alone.

We often talk to ourselves，but usually silently，the words going through our minds but not actually passing our lips. The term *soliloquy* is commonly applied to utterances made in a play by characters who are speaking their thoughts aloud so the audience won't have to guess. won't have to guess. The *soliloquist* (sə-LIL'-ə-kwist) may be alone；or other members of the cast may be present on stage，but of course they don't hear what's being said，because they're not supposed to know. Eugene O'Neill made novel uses of *soliloquies* in *Mourning Becomes Electra*—the characters made honest disclosures of their feelings and thoughts to the audience，but kept the other players in the dark.

The verb is to *soliloquize* (sə-LIL'-ə-kwīz').

(1) soliloquy 是说给自己听的"独白"(loquor 加上 solus,独自)。或者从词源上看,意为"独处时的自言自语"。

我们经常与自己无声对话,词汇虽然经过大脑,通常却不会从嘴里说出来。术语"独白"常用于戏剧中,剧中角色大声说出他们心中所想,为的只是让听众无需去猜他们想的是什么。"Soliloquist"(独白者)可能是独自一人;或者其他的角色虽在舞台上,但他们听不到这些话,因为他们被假定对此一无所知。尤金·奥尼尔在 *Mourning Becomes Electra* 这出话剧里,对"独白"做了比较新颖的运用——角色们向观众诚实地剖析自己的感情和内心世界,其他的角色则完全不知道。

其动词是 soliloquize。

(2) A *ventriloquist* (ven-TRIL'-ə-kwist) is one who can throw his voice. A listener thinks the sound is coming from some source other than the person speaking. The combining root is Latin *venter*，*ventris*，belly；etymologically，*ventriloquism* (ven-TRIL'-ə-kwiz-əm) is the art of "speaking from the belly." The adjective is *ven-*

triloquistic (ven-tril′-ə-KWIS′-tik). Can you figure out how the verb will end? Write the verb：_____.

(2) ventriloquist 指"口技表演者/腹语术表演者"，听众误认为声音不是出自表演者嘴唇，而是其他地方。这个词源于拉丁语词根 venter，ventris，意为"腹部"；ventriloquism(口技，腹语术)的语源意义是"从腹部发声"的艺术。形容词是 ventriloquistic。你能写出它的动词形式吗？

(3) *Colloquial* (kə-LŌ′-kwee-əl) combines *loquor*, to speak, with the prefix *con-*. (*Con-* is spelled *col-* before a root starting with *l*; *cor-* before a root starting with *r*; *com-* before a root starting with *m*, *p*, or *b*.) When people speak together they are engaging in conversation—and their language is usually more informal and less rigidly grammatical than what you might expect in writing or in public addresses. *Colloquial* patterns are perfectly correct—they are simply informal, and suitable to everyday conversation.

A *colloquialism* (kə-LŌ′-kwee-ə-liz-əm), therefore, is a *conversational-style* expression, like "He hasn't got any" or "Who are you going with?" as contrasted to the formal or literary "He has none" or "With whom are you going?" *Colloquial* English is the English you and I talk on everyday occasions—it is not slangy, vulgar, or illiterate.

(3) colloquial 结合了词根 loquor-("说")和前缀 con-("将……聚在一起")，意为"口语的"。(con-在 l 开头的词根前写作 col-，在以 r 开头的词根前拼作 cor-，在以 m，p 或 b 开头的词根前拼作 com-)。人们在一起的谈话会形成对话——与正式的写作或者公共演讲相比，对话中的语言会变得不那么正式，语法也变得没那么严谨。口语的表达方式是完全正确的，只不过它们是非正式的，适用于日常会话中。

colloquialism(俗话、白话)是一种口语体的表达法。例如，正式用语"He has none"和"With whom are you going?"在白话中就是"He hasn't got any"和"Who are you going with?"colloquial English(会话英语)是指人们在日常会话中使用的英语——既不是俚语、粗俗的语言，也不是文盲的语言。

(4) A *circumlocution* (sur-kəm-lō-KYŌŌ′-shən) is, etymologically, a "talking around" (*circum-*, around). Any way of expressing an idea that is roundabout or indirect is *circumlocutory* (sur′-kəm-LOK′-yə-tawr′-ee)—you are now familiar with the common adjective suffix *-ory*.

(4) 从词源理解，circumlocution 是指"迂回的话语"。以任何方式迂回或者间接的表达都可以被称为 circumlocutory——你现在对形容词后缀-ory 已经很熟悉了。

REVIEW OF ETYMOLOGY
复习词源

PREFIX, ROOT, SUFFIX	MEANING	ENGLISH WORD
1. *taceo*	to be silent	_____
2. *-ity*	noun suffix	_____
3. *-ness*	noun suffix	_____
4. *-ent*	adjective suffix	_____
5. *-ence*, *-ency*	noun suffix	_____

6.	re-	again	_____
7.	loquor	to speak	_____
8.	solus	alone	_____
9.	-ist	one who	_____
10.	-ize	verb suffix	_____
11.	venter, ventris	belly	_____
12.	-ic	adjective suffix	_____
13.	-ous	adjective suffix	_____
14.	con-, col-, com-, cor-	with, together	_____
15.	-al	adjective suffix	_____
16.	-ism	noun suffix	_____

WORKING WITH THE WORDS
单词应用

Can you pronounce the words?
你能读出这些单词吗？

1.	taciturnity	tas-ə-TURN'-ə-tee
2.	tacit	TAS'-it
3.	tacitness	TAS'-ət-nəs
4.	reticent	RET'-ə-sənt
5.	reticence	RET'-ə-səns
6.	reticency	RET'-ə-sən-see
7.	loquaciousness	lō-KWAY'-shəs-nəs
8.	loquacity	lō-KWAS'-ə-tee
9.	soliloquy	sə-LIL'-ə-kwee
10.	solioquist	sə-LIL'-ə-kwist
11.	soliloquize	sə-LIL'-ə-kwīz'
12.	ventriloquist	ven'-TRIL'-ə-kwist
13.	ventriloquism	ven-TRIL'-ə-kwiz-əm
14.	ventriloquistic	ven-tril'-ə-KWIS'-tik
15.	ventriloquize	ven-TRIL'-ə-kwiz'
16.	colloquial	kə-LŌ'-kwee-əl
17.	colloquialism	kə-LŌ'-kwee-ə-liz-əm
18.	circumlocution	sur'-kəm-lō-KYOO'-shən
19.	circumlocutory	sur'-kəm-LOK'-yə-tawr'-ee

Can you work with the words?
你能灵活使用这些词汇了吗？

1. taciturnity		a. unwillingness to talk, or disclose, out of fear, shyness, reserve, etc.
2. tacitness		b. talking, or a speech, "to oneself"
3. reticence		c. art of throwing one's voice
4. loquacity		d. unwillingness to engage in conversation
5. soliloquy		e. informal expression used in everyday conversation
6. ventriloquism		f. state of being understood though not actually expressed
7. colloquialism		g. a talking around; method of talking indirectly or in a roundabout way
8. circumlocution		h. talkativeness

KEY: 1-d, 2-f, 3-a, 4-h, 5-b, 6-c, 7-e, 8-g

Do you understand the words?
你对这些词汇是否已经透彻地理解？

1. A *tacit* understanding is put into words.	TRUE	FALSE
2. Inhibited people are seldom *reticent* about expressing anger.	TRUE	FALSE
3. A *soliloquist* expresses his thoughts aloud.	TRUE	FALSE
4. A *ventriloquistic* performance on stage involves a dummy who appears to be talking.	TRUE	FALSE
5. A *colloquial* style of writing is ungrammatical.	TRUE	FALSE
6. *Circumlocutory* speech is direct and forthright.	TRUE	FALSE
7. *Inarticulate* people are generally given to *loquaciousness*.	TRUE	FALSE
8. A *soliloquy* is a dialogue.	TRUE	FALSE

KEY: 1-F, 2-F, 3-T, 4-T, 5-F, 6-F, 7-F, 8-F

Can you recall the words?

你能够写出这些词汇吗？

1. to speak to oneself	1. S _____
2. to throw one's voice	2. V _____
3. unwillingness to engage in conversation	3. T _____
4. unspoken	4. T _____
5. referring to an indirect, roundabout style of expression (*adj.*)	5. C _____
6. suitable for informal conversation	6. C _____
7. talkativeness	7. L _____ *or* L _____
8. reluctance to express one's feelings or thoughts	8. R _____ *or* R _____
9. a speech to oneself, especially in a play	9. S _____
10. an indirect, roundabout expression	10. C _____

KEY： 1-soliloquize， 2-ventriloquize， 3-taciturnity， 4-tacit， 5-circumlocutory， 6-colloquial， 7-loquaciousness *or* loquacity， 8-reticence *or* reticency， 9-soliloquy， 10-circumlocution

(*End of Session 25*)

SESSION 26
第 26 节

ORIGINS AND RELATED WORDS
词源及相关词汇

1. a Spartan virtue
斯巴达人的美德

In ancient Sparta, originally known as *Laconia*, the citizens were long-suffering, hard-bitten, stoical, and military-minded, and were even more noted for their economy of speech than Vermonters, if that is possible. Legend has it that when Philip of Macedonia was storming the gates of Sparta (or Laconia), he sent a message to the besieged king saying, "If we capture your city we will burn it to the ground." A one-word answer came back: "If." It was now probably Philip's turn to be speechless, though history does not record his reaction.

古代斯巴达原被称为拉科尼亚(Laconia)。斯巴达人虽然长期受苦,却形成了顽强、坚忍的性格,他们时刻准备作战。斯巴达人更以言语的简洁而闻名。相传,当马其顿国王菲利普横扫斯巴达(或拉科尼亚)营地时,他派人送信给被围困的国王:"如果占领此地,我们必将其付之一炬。"国王只用一个词回答他:"If."(如果)。菲利普听到这也许无以应答,历史并未记录他的反应。

It is from the name *Laconia* that we derive our word *laconic*— pithy, concise, economical in the use of words almost to the point of curtness; precisely the opposite of *verbose*.

Like the man who was waiting at a lunch counter for a ham sandwich. When it was ready, the clerk inquired politely, "Will you eat it here, or take it with you?"

"Both," was the *laconic* reply.

laconic 正是由 Laconia 派生而来——简洁、简明,用经济节约的词说话说到点儿上,恰与冗长拖沓相对照。

一个人坐在小吃店等待火腿三明治。三明治做好时,店员礼貌问道:"您在店里吃,还是带走?"

"Both"(都行)是他简洁的回答。

Or like the woman who was watching a lush imbibing dry martinis at a Third Avenue bar in New York City. The drunk downed the contents of each cocktail glass at one gulp, daintily nibbled and swallowed the bowl, then finally turned the glass over and ate the base. The stem he threw into a corner. This amazing gustatory feat went on for half an hour, until a dozen stems were lying shattered in the corner, and the drunk had chewed and swallowed enough bowls and bases to start a glass factory. He suddenly turned to the lady and asked belligerently, "I suppose you think I'm cuckoo, don't you?" "Sure—the stem is the best part," was the *laconic* answer.

纽约第三大道上的酒吧里,一个醉汉正喝着马提尼酒,身旁的一位女士注视着他。醉汉一大口喝完了杯中所有的酒,然后优雅地啃着杯身,慢慢将其全部吞下,最后把杯子倒放,吃掉杯座。他将杯脚扔到墙角。盛宴持续半个小时,直到喝完 12 杯酒。粉碎的 12 个杯脚堆积在墙角;而他吞食下的杯身和杯底足够开设一家玻璃制造厂。醉汉突然转身面向那位女士,挑衅地问道:"我猜你一定认为我傻透了,是不是?"女士回答道:"当然,杯脚最美味了。"——这或许就是一种 laconic answer(简洁的回答)。

(It was doubtless this same gentleman, in his accustomed state of intoxication, who found himself painfully weaving his way along Wilshire Boulevard in Beverly Hills, California—he had somehow gotten on a TWA jetliner instead of the subway—when he realized, almost too late, that he was going to bump into a smartly dressed young woman who had just stepped out of her Mercedes-Benz to go window-shopping along the avenue. He quickly veered left, but by some unexplainable magnetic attraction the woman veered in the same direction, again making collision apparently inevitable. With an adroit maneuver, the drunk swung to the right—the lady, by now thoroughly disoriented, did the same. Finally both jammed on the brakes and came to a dead stop, face to face, and not six inches apart; and as the alcoholic fumes assailed the young lady's nostrils, she sneered at the reeking, swaying man, as much in frustration as in contempt: "Oh! How gauche!" "Fine!" was his happy response. "How goesh with you?" This answer, however, is not *laconic*, merely confused.)

(无疑又是这位先生,在他常态化的醉醺醺中,他发现自己正摇摇晃晃艰难地走在加利福尼亚比弗利山庄维尔雪大道上——他像是坐上了环球航空公司的喷气式飞机而不是地铁——他正撞向一个刚从奔驰车上下来的年轻女人,当他意识到时,已经晚了,年轻女人衣着体面的、正准备逛街买东西。他很快地向左躲,但因为一些无法解释的吸引力,这个女人也正好向同样的方向移,看起来他们又要不可避免地撞在一起了。这个醉汉敏捷地往右躲——这位女士,现在已经彻底丧失方向感了,也往右躲。最终两人都停了下来,脸对着脸,离得不到六英寸;一股酒气直钻女士的鼻子,她鄙夷地看了看这个满身酒气、摇摇晃晃的男人,恼怒而不屑地说:"哎呀,真笨!""很好!"醉汉高兴地回应。"很不错?"这不是一个 laconic,而只是把两个词弄混了。)(gauche 和 goesh 发音相近,gauche 指"笨拙的",而 goesh 则是"不错"或"好的"的意思。——译者注)

We have learned that *-ness*, *-ity*, and *-ism* are suffixes that transform adjectives into nouns——and all three can be used with *laconic*:

... with characteristic *laconicness* (lə-KON'-ək-nəs)
... her usual *laconicity* (lak'-ə-NIS'-ə-tee)
... his habitual *laconism* (LAK'-ə-niz-əm)
... with, for him, unusual *laconicism* (lə-KON'-ə-siz-əm)

A *laconism* is also the expression itself that is pithy and concise, as the famous report from a naval commander in World War II: "Saw sub, sank same."

我们已经学过-ness, -ity,和-ism 是把形容词变成名词的后缀。这三种后缀都适合 laconic(简洁的,简明的):
...特有的 laconicness(简洁)
...她一贯的 laconicity(简洁)
...他惯常的 laconism(简洁)
...用对他来说非同寻常的 laconicism(简洁)
Laconism 这个词还表示一种简洁而准确的表达,如第二次世界大战中一个海军指挥官的著名报告:"看到潜艇,并击沉。"

2. brilliant

毫无破绽

Cogent is a term of admiration. A *cogent* argument is well put, convincing, hardly short of brilliant. *Cogency* (KŌ′-jən-see) shows a keen mind, an ability to think clearly and logically. The word derives from the Latin verb *cogo*, to drive together, compel, force. A *cogent* argument *compels* acceptance because of its logic, its persuasiveness, its appeal to one's sense of reason.

cogent(有说服力的),也是表示赞美的词汇。cogent argument 是"有力的证据",极具说服力,几乎毫无破绽。cogency(中肯、切题),能够显示出缜密的思维和清晰、有逻辑的思考能力。cogent 来自于拉丁语动词 cogo,意为"强迫、迫使"。cogent argument 是"具有说服力的论述",其准确的表意和逻辑性迫使人们接受话语人的观点。

3. back to talk
回到谈话

You will recall that *loquor*, to speak, is the source of *loquacity*, *soliloquy*, *ventriloquism*, *colloquialism*, *circumlocution*. This root is also the base on which *eloquent* (EL′-ə-kwənt), *magniloquent* (mag-NIL′-ə-kwənt), and *grandiloquent* (gran-DIL′-ə-kwənt) are built.

你一定还记得 loquor,它是构成 loquacity, soliloquy, ventriloquism, colloquialism, circumlocution 的词根。这个词根也出现在 eloquent(雄辩的),magniloquent(夸张的)和 grandiloquent(浮夸的)等单词里。

The *eloquent* person speaks *out* (*e-*, from *ex-*, out), is vividly expressive, fluent, forceful, or persuasive in language ("the prosecutor's *eloquent* plea to the jury"). The word is partially synonymous with *cogent*, but *cogent* implies irresistible logical reasoning and intellectual keenness, while *eloquent* suggests artistic expression, strong emotional appeal, the skillful use of language to move and arouse a listener.

一个"eloquent"的人大胆说出自己的想法(e-来自 ex-,出来,外面),其语言表达生动,流利,有感染力或有说服力(如"the prosecutor's eloquent plea to the jury"这位检察官向陪审团提出有说服力的申辩)。这个词和 cogent 部分同义,但 cogent 更强调其非凡的逻辑能力和思维的敏锐,而 eloquent 则强调运用表达的技巧,情感的感染力,熟练的语言能力来打动听众。

Magniloquent (*magnus*, large) and *grandiloquent* (*grandis*, grand) are virtually identical in meaning. *Magniloquence* or *grandiloquence* is the use of high-flown, grandiose, even pompous language; of large and impressive words; of lofty, flowery, or over elegant phraseology. Home is *a place of residence*; wife is *helpmate*, *helpmeet*, or *better half*; women are *the fair sex*; children are *offspring* or *progeny*; a doctor is a *member of the medical fraternity*; people are the *species Homo sapiens*, etc., etc.

magniloquent (magnus, 巨大的)和 grandiloquent (grandis, 宏伟的)实际上是相同的意思。magniloquence 或 grandiloquence 是用夸张的、浮夸的、华而不实的语言,是用复杂的、令人印象深刻的词汇,用华丽、虚华或过度优雅的表达方式。如 Home is a place of residence; wife is helpmate, helpmeet, or better half; women are the fair sex; children are offspring or progeny; a doctor is a member of the medical fraternity; people are the species Homo sapiens, 等等。

Loquacious, *verbose*, *voluble*, and *garrulous* people are all talkative; but each type, you will recall, has a special quality.

If you are *loquacious*, you talk a lot because you *like* to talk and doubtless have a lot to say.

If you are *verbose*, you smother your ideas with excess words, with such an overabundance of words that your listener either drops into a state of helpless confusion or falls asleep.

If you are *voluble*, you speak rapidly, fluently, glibly, without hesitation, stutter, or stammer; you are vocal, verbal, and highly articulate.

If you are *garrulous*, you talk constantly, and usually aimlessly and meaninglessly, about trifles. We often hear the word used in "a *garrulous* old man" or "a *garrulous* old woman," since in very advanced age the mind may wander and lose the ability to discriminate between the important and the unimportant, between the interesting and the dull.

loquacious，verbose，voluble 和 garrulous 的人都是 talkative(喜欢说话的)，但每种都有自己的特质。

如果你是 loquacious，你之所以说很多话就是因为你喜欢说并且无疑有好多事要说。

如果你是 verbose，你过多的言语模糊了你本想要表达的东西，从而让听你讲话的人如坠云雾里或者昏昏欲睡。

如果你是 voluble，那你说的很快、很流利、很熟练，没有犹豫、停顿和结巴。你善于口头表达，并且能言善辩。

如果你是 garrulous，你能滔滔不绝，并且常常是无重点、无目的地说些琐事。我们经常说用在"a garrulous old man"和"a garrulous old woman"里，因为人在年岁很大的时候，思维就容易信马由缰，并且失去了分辨事情的重要与否、有趣与否的能力。

Verbose is from Latin *verbum*, word—the *verbose* person is wordy.

Voluble comes from Latin *volvo*, *volutus*, to roll—words effortlessly roll off the *voluble* speaker's tongue.

And *garrulous* derives from Latin *garrio*, to chatter—a *garrulous* talker chatters away like a monkey.

The suffix *-ness* can be added to all these adjectives to form nouns. Alternate noun forms end in *-ity*:

verbose 源于拉丁语的 verbum，"词句"—— verbose 的人就是唠叨的人。

voluble 源于拉丁语 volvo, volutus，"转动"——话语不停歇地在 voluble 说话者的舌头上转动。

garrulous 由拉丁语 garrio 演变而来，"喋喋不休的说"——"garrulous"的说话者就像猴子一样喋喋不休。

后缀-ness 能加到所有这些形容词的后面而变成名词，也可在后面加上-ity 变为名词：

verbosity	(vər-BOS'-ə-tee)
volubility	(vol'-yə-BIL'-ə-tee)
garrulity	(gə-ROOL'-ə-tee)

4. at large

与"大"相关

We discovered *magnus*, large, big, great, in Chapter 9, in discussing *Magnavox* (etymologically, "big voice"), and find it again in *magniloquent* (etymologically, "talking big"). The root occurs in a number of other words:

在第 9 章我们讨论 Magnavox(词源上看其意思是"大声")时发现了词根 magnus(巨大，大，伟大)，在 magniloquent (本义 "说大话")中也出现过这个词根。这个词根也出现在以下单词中：

(1) *Magnanimous* (mag-NAN'-ə-məs)—big-hearted, generous, forgiving (etymologically, "great-minded"). (*Magnus* plus *animus*, mind.) We'll discuss this word in depth in Chapter 12.

(1) magnanimous——心怀宽广的，慷慨的，宽容的(语源学意义是"心灵伟大的")。(Magnus 加 animus——心灵。)我们会在第 12 节深入讨论这个单词。

(2) *Magnate* (MAG′-nayt)—a person of great power or influence, a big wheel, as a business *magnate*.

(2) magnate——是指一个具有很大权力和影响力的人，领导者，如一个 business magnate(商业领袖)。

(3) *Magnify*—to make larger, or make seem larger (magnus plus -*fy* from *facio*, to make), as in "*magnify* your problems."

(3) magnify——使变大(magnus 加上后缀-fy；这个后缀源于 facio，制造，使……)，或使看起来变大，如在"magnify your problems"(放大了你的问题)。

(4) *Magnificent*—*magnus* plus *fic-*, from *facio*.

(4) magnificent(宏伟的)——Magnus 加 fic-(来自 facio)。

(5) *Magnitude*—*magnus* plus the common noun suffix -*tude*, as in *fortitude*, *multitude*, *gratitude*, etc.

(5) magnitude(宏大)——magnus 加上常见的名词后缀-tude，如在 fortitude, multitude, gratitude 等中。

(6) *Magnum* (as of champagne or wine)—a large bottle, generally two fifths of a gallon.

(6) magnum (与香槟或酒有关)—— 一个大瓶子，一般有 2/5 加仑那么大。

(7) *Magnum opus* (MAG′-nəm Ō′-pes)—etymologically, a "big work"; actually, the greatest work, or masterpiece, of an artist, writer, or composer. *Opus* is the Latin word for *work*; the plural of *opus* is used in the English word *opera*, etymologically, "a number of works," actually a musical drama containing overture, singing, and other forms of music, i. e., many musical works. The verb form *opero*, to work, occurs in *operate*, *co-operate*, *operator*, etc.

(7) magnum opus——从词源上看是"大作品"的意思；实际上是指一个艺术家、作家或一个作曲者的最伟大、最杰出的作品。opus 是拉丁语，意为"作品"，它的复数是英语中的单词 opera，词源的本义为"很多作品"，事实上，opera 指一个音乐剧包括序曲、歌唱和其他音乐形式，即许多"音乐作品"。动词形式是 opero"工作"，出现在单词 operate, co-operate, operator 等词中。

5. Words, words, words!

单词、单词、单词!

Latin *verbum* is *word*. A *verb* is the important word in a sentence; *verbatim* (vər-BAY′-tim) is word-for-word (a *verbatim* report).

Verbal (VUR′-bəl), ending in the adjective suffix -*al*, may refer either to a *verb*, or to words in general (a *verbal* fight); or it may mean, loosely, *oral* or *spoken*, rather than written (*verbal* agreement or contract); or, describing people ("she is quite *verbal*"), it may refer to a ready ability to put feelings or thoughts into words.

Working from *verbal*, can you add a common verb suffix to form a word meaning to *put into words*? _____.

Verbiage (VUR′-bee-əj) has two meanings: an excess of words ("Such *verbiage*!"); or a style or manner of using words (medical *verbiage*, military *verbiage*).

拉丁语 verbum 是 word 的意思。verb(动词)在句子中很重要;verbatim 是 word-for-word(一字一字的,逐字的)如 a verbatim report(一字不差的报告)。

verbal 以形容词后缀-al 结尾,可以用来指动词,也可以指其他性质的词,如 a verbal fight(言语上的争执);通常宽泛地指口头的而非书面的,如 verbal agreement or contract(口头约定或合约);或用来描述人,如 she is quite verbal(她是个很擅长表达的人),可能是指具有用语言来准确表达思想和感情的能力。

你是否能在 verbal 上加一个常见的动词后缀变成"put into words"(行诸于语言)?

verbiage 有两个意思:冗长的、废话连篇的语言,如"Such verbiage!"(这么多废话);或是指一种使用语言的风格和形式(即"术语"),如 medical verbiage(医学用语), military verbiage(军事术语)。

6. Roll on, and on!

滚啊滚!

Volvo, *volutus*, to roll, the source of *voluble*, is the root on which many important English words are based.

滚啊滚!

Volvo, volutus 都是"滚动"的意思,voluble(爱说话的,喋喋不休的)就是源于这两个词根,很多英语单词也是由此衍变而来。

Revolve (rə-VOLV′)—roll again (and again), or keep turning round. Wheels *revolve*, the earth *revolves* around the sun, the cylinder of a revolver *revolves*. (The prefix is *re-*, back or again.)

The noun is *revolution* (rev-ə-LŌŌ′-shən), which can be one such complete rolling, or, by logical extension, a radical change of any sort (TV was responsible for a *revolution* in the entertainment industry), especially political (the American, or French, *Revolution*). The adjective *revolutionary* (rev′-ə-LŌŌ′-shən-air′-ee) introduces us to a new adjective suffix, *-ary*, as in *contrary*, *disciplinary*, *stationary*, *imaginary*, etc. (But *-ary* is sometimes also a noun suffix, as in *dictionary*, *commentary*, etc.)

revolve——不停地滚动或转动,轮子转动,地球围绕着太阳转动,旋转装置的圆筒在转动。(前缀 re-,是来回往返的意思)。

其名词形式是 revolution,指大幅度的转动,或在逻辑上引申为某种事物的巨变,如 TV was responsible for a revolution in the entertainment industry(电视改变了娱乐业的面貌),尤其指政治方面的(如美国革命或法国革命)。其形容词是 revolutionary,让我们了解到一种新的形容词后缀-ary,如 contrary, disciplinary, stationary, imaginary 等(但-ary 有时也可是名词后缀,如 dictionary, commentary 等)。

Add different prefixes to *volvo* to construct two more English words:

(1) *involve*—etymologically, "roll in" ("I didn't want to get *involved*!"). Noun: *involvement*.

(2) *evolve* (ə-VOLV′)—etymologieally, "roll out" (*e-*, out); hence to unfold, or gradually develop ("The final plan *evolved* from some informal discussions"; "The political party *evolved* from a group of interested citizens who met frequently to protest government actions").

By analogy with the forms derived from *revolve*, can you construct the noun and adjective of *evolve*? Noun:＿＿＿＿＿＿＿＿. Adjective:＿＿＿＿＿＿＿＿
＿＿＿＿＿.

volvo 加上不同的前缀形成另外两个英文词:

(1) involve——从词源看,其意为"滚进",如"I didn't want to get involved!"(我不想卷进来)名词形式是 involvement。

(2) evolve——从词源上看本义是"滚出"(e-,出来,外面);因此,有"展开,或者逐渐发展"的意思,如 The final plan evolved from some informal discussions(最终的计划在非正式的讨论中逐渐形成);The political party evolved from a group of interested citizens who met frequently to protest government actions(政治党派就由经常聚会反对政府的公民群体演变而来)。

REVIEW OF ETYMOLOGY
复习词源

PREFIX, ROOT, SUFFIX	MEANING	ENGLISH WORD
1. *Laconia*	Sparta	_____
2. *-ness*	noun suffix	_____
3. *-ism*	noun suffix	_____
4. *-ity*	noun suffix	_____
5. *e- (ex-)*	out	_____
6. *-ent*	adjective suffix	_____
7. *-ence*	noun suffix	_____
8. *magnus*	big	_____
9. *grandis*	grand	_____
10. *verbum*	word	_____
11. *volvo, volutus*	to roll	_____
12. *garrio*	to chatter	_____
13. *animus*	mind	_____
14. *-fy*	to make	_____
15. *-tude*	noun suffix	_____
16. *opus*	work	_____
17. *opero*	to work	_____
18. *-al*	adjective suffix	_____
19. *-ize*	verb suffix	_____
20. *re-*	again, back	_____
21. *-ary*	adjective suffix	_____
22. *in-*	in	_____

USING THE WORDS
单词应用

Can you pronounce the words? (1)
你能读出这些单词吗?(Ⅰ)

1. *laconicity*   lak′-ə-NIS′-ə-tee
2. *laconism*   LAK′-ə-niz-əm

3. *laconicism*   lə-KON′-ə-siz-əm

4. *eloquent*   EL′-ə-kwənt

5. *eloquence*   EL′-ə-kwəns

6. *magniloquent*   mag-NIL′-ə-kwənt

7. *magniloquence*   mag-NIL′-ə-kwəns

8. *grandiloquent*   gran-DIL′-ə-kwənt

9. *grandiloquence*   gran-DIL′-ə-kwəns

10. *verbosity*   vər-BOS′-ə-tee

11. *volubility*   vol′-yə-BIL′-ə-tee

12. *garrulity*   gə-ROO′-lə-tee

13. *cogency*   KŌ′-jən-see

Can you pronounce the words? （Ⅱ）
你能读出这些单词吗？（Ⅱ）

1. *magnanimous*   mag-NAN′-ə-məs

2. *magnate*   MAG′-nayt

3. *magnum opus*   MAG′-nəm Ō′-pəs

4. *verbatim*   vər-BAY′-tim

5. *verbal*   VUR′-bəl

6. *verbalize*   VUR′-bə-līz′

7. *verbiage*   VUR′-bee-əj

8. *revolve*   rə-VOLV′

9. *revolution*   rev′-ə-LOO′-shən

10. *revolutionary*   rev′-ə-LOO′shə-nair′-ee

11. *evolve*   ə-VOLV′

12. *evolution*   ev′-ə-LOO′-shən

13. *evolutionary*   ev′-ə-LOO′-shə-nair′-ee

Can you work with the words? （Ⅰ）
你能灵活使用这些词汇了吗？（Ⅰ）

1. laconicity   a. floweriness, pompousness, or elegance in speech

2. eloquence   b. incessant chatter with little meaning

3. magniloquence   c. big wheel; important or influential person

4. verbosity   d. great artistic work; masterpiece

5. volubility   e. a gradual unfolding or development; "a rolling out"

6. garrulity   f. "a rolling round"; radical change; political upheaval

7. magnum opus	g. great economy in speech
8. magnate	h. fluency, ease, and/or rapidity of speech
9. revolution	i. great, artistic, or emotional expressiveness
10. evolution	j. wordiness
11. cogency	k. persuasiveness through logic; keen-mindedness in reasoning

KEY: 1-g, 2-i, 3-a, 4-j, 5-h, 6-b, 7-d, 8-c, 9-f, 10-e, 11-k

Can you work with the words? (Ⅱ)
你能灵活使用这些词汇了吗？(Ⅱ)

1. laconism	a. word for word
2. verbiage	b. to put into words
3. verbalize	c. causing, or resulting from, radical change; new and totally different
4. verbal	d. resulting or developing gradually from (something)
5. verbatim	e. expressive; emotionally moving
6. revolutionary	f. pithiness or economy of expression; word or phrase packed with meaning
7. evolutionary	g. big-hearted; generous, forgiving
8. grandiloquent	h. referring or pertaining to, or involving, words; oral, rather than written
9. eloquent	i. using flossy, flowery, elegant, or impressive phraseology
10. magnanimous	j. wordiness; style or manner of using words; type of words

KEY: 1-f, 2-j, 3-b, 4-h, 5-a, 6-c, 7-d, 8-i, 9-e, 10-g

Do you understand the words?
你对这些词汇是否已经透彻地理解？

1. Is *laconicism* characteristic of a verbose speaker?	YES	NO
2. Does a *magniloquent* speaker use short, simple words?	YES	NO
3. Does a frog *evolve* from a tadpole?	YES	NO

4. Is an *eloquent* speaker interesting to listen to?　　　　YES　　NO

5. Do verbose people use a lot of *verbiage*?　　　　YES　　NO

6. Is *volubility* characteristic of an inarticulate person?　　　　YES　　NO

7. Does *verbosity* show a careful and economical use of words?　　　　YES　　NO

8. Is a *verbal* person usually inarticulate?　　　　YES　　NO

9. Is a *magnum opus* one of the lesser works of a writer, artist, or composer?　　　　YES　　NO

10. Is a *magnanimous* person selfish and petty-minded?　　　　YES　　NO

KEY: 1-no, 2-no, 3-yes, 4-yes, 5-yes, 6-no, 7-no, 8-no, 9-no, 10-no

Can you recall the words?

你能够写出这些词汇吗?

1. gradually unfolding, resulting, or developing (*adj.*)　　1. E _____

2. causing, or resulting from, radical change (*adj.*)　　2. R _____

3. quality of conciseness and economy in the use of words　　3. L _____
　　or L _____
　　or L _____
　　or L _____

4. expressiveness in the use of words　　4. E _____

5. turn round and round　　5. R _____

6. important person, as in the commercial world　　6. M _____

7. unselfish; generous; noble in motive; big-hearted; forgiving　　7. M _____

8. using words easily; vocal; articulate; referring to, or involving, words; oral, rather than written　　8. V _____

9. style of word usage; type of words; overabundance of words　　9. V _____

10. wordiness; quality of using excess words　　10. V _____

11. elegance in word usage   11. M _____
                                                   or G _____

12. quality of chattering on and on   12. G _____
    about trivia, or with little meaning

13. fluency and ease in speech   13. V _____

14. word for word   14. V _____

15. masterpiece; great artistic work   15. M _____ O _____

16. persuasiveness and forcefulness   16. C _____
    in speech or writing through
    closely reasoned logic

KEY: 1-evolutionary, 2-revolutionary, 3-laconism, laconicism, laconicity, *or* laconicness, 4-eloquence, 5-revolve, 6-magnate, 7-magnanimous, 8-verbal, 9-verbiage, 10-verbosity, 11-magniloquence *or* grandiloquence, 12-garrulity, 13-volubility, 14-verbatim, 15-magnum opus, 16-cogency

(End of Session 26)

SESSION 27
第 27 节

ORIGINS AND RELATED WORDS
词源及相关词汇

1. front and back—and uncles
前面和后面——和叔叔们

The *ventriloquist* appears to talk from the belly (*venter*, *ventris* plus *loquor*) rather than through the lips (or such was the strange perception of the person who first used the word).

Venter, *ventris*, belly, is the root on which *ventral* (VEN'-trəl) and *ventricle* are built.

ventriloquist (口技表演者)看起来是从肚子(venter, ventris 加 loquor)发音而非通过嘴唇(或这就是第一个用这个单词的人的奇怪的理解)。

venter, ventris, "肚子,腹部",也是组成 ventral(腹部)和 ventricle(心室、脑室)的词根。

The *ventral* side of an animal, for example, is the front or anterior side—the belly side.

例如,一个动物的 ventral 一侧,就是腹部的前面或前侧。

A *ventricle* (VEN'-trə-kəl) is a hollow organ or cavity, or, logically enough, belly, as one of the two chambers of the heart, or one of the four chambers of the brain. The *ventricles* of the heart are the lower chambers, and receive blood from the *auricles*, or upper chambers. The *auricle* (AW'-rə-kəl), so named because it is somewhat ear-shaped (Latin *auris*, ear), receives blood from the veins; the *auricles* send the blood into the *ventricles*, which in turn pump the blood into the arteries. (It's all very complicated, but fortunately it works.)

ventricle 是指具有空腔的器官或腔、洞等,或者从逻辑上顺理成章地指"腹部",如两个心室其中的一个,或者是四个脑室其中的一个。心脏的"ventricles"就是下面的那个心室,它接受心耳或上面的心室过来的血液。auricle(心耳)之所以叫这个名字,就是因为它的形状很像是耳朵(拉丁语中的 auris 就是"耳朵"的意思),它接受从静脉流过来的血液;心耳把血液输入到下心室中,然后下心室把血液压入动脉(这个过程很复杂,不过幸好它们能顺利进行)。

The adjective form of *ventricle* is *ventricular* (ven-TRIK'-yə-lər), which may refer to a *ventricle*, or may mean *having a belly like bulge*.

Now that you see how *ventricular* is formed from *ventricle*, can you figure out the adjective of *auricle*? _____ .
How about the adjective of *vehicle*? _____ .
Of *circle*? _____ .

ventricle 的形容词是 ventricular,它可以指 ventricle,也可指一个突出的肚子。

现在你已经了解到 ventricle 是怎样演变成 ventricular 的,那你能猜出 auricle 的形容词是什么吗? 那 vehicle 的形容词又是什么呢? circle 的呢?

No doubt you wrote *auricular* (aw-RIK′-yə-lər)，*vehicular*，and *circular*，and have discovered that nouns ending in *-cle* from adjectives ending in *-cular*.

So you can now be the first person on your block to figure out the adjective derived from：

无疑你能写出 auricular, vehicular 和 circular,并且可以发现这些名词都是以-cle 结尾,是由以-cular 结尾的形容词形式发展而来。

因此你可以成为你所在街区第一个能写出以下名词的形容词形式的人：

clavicle：_____

cuticle：_____

vesicle：_____

testicle：_____

uncle：_____

The answers of course are *clavicular*，*cuticular*，*vesicular*，*testicular*—and for *uncle* you have every right to shout "No fair!" (But where is it written that life is fair?)

The Latin word for *uncle* (actually，uncle on the mother's side) is *avunculus*，from which we get *avuncular* (ə-VUNG′-kyə-lər)，referring to an uncle.

答案当然是 clavicular, cuticular, vesicular, testicular,对于 uncle 你会喊道"不公平!"(但哪里又写明生活就是公平的呢?)

uncle(实际上是指母亲一方的亲属)在拉丁语中为 avunculus,由此而演变出 avuncular,指"uncle"。

Now what about an uncle? Well，traditional or stereotypical uncles are generally kindly，permissive，indulgent，protective—and often give helpful advice. So anyone who exhibits one or more of such traits to another (usually younger) person is *avuncular* or acts in an *avuncular* capacity.

那 uncle 到底意味着什么呢？这个嘛,无论是传统印象还是常规的观念,uncles 通常是亲切的、宽容的、从容的、保护性的——经常给出有用的建议。因此凡是对他人显示出其中一种或几种品格的人就是 avuncular,"像叔叔似的""如长辈般的",或者"做出叔叔般的行为"。

So，at long last，to get back to *ventral*. If there's a front or belly side，anatomically，there must be a reverse—a back side. This is the *dorsal* (DAWR′-səl) side，from Latin *dorsum*，the root on which the verb *endorse* (en-DAWRS′) is built.

所以,说了这么多,我们再回到 ventral。如果有前侧或肚皮,那么从解剖学上来说就一定会有相反的一面——后侧。这就是 dorsal side,由拉丁语 dorsum 衍变而来,动词 endorse 也是源于这个词根。

If you *endorse* a check，you sign it on the back side; if you *endorse* a plan，an idea，etc.，you *back* it，you express your approval or support. The noun is *endorsement* (en-DAWRS′-mənt).

签支票时,你签在它的 back side(后面);如果你同意一项计划,一个想法等,你 back(back 既是"后面",又有"支持"的意思)它,以表达你的赞同和支持。其名词形式是 endorsement。

2．the noise and the fury

喧哗与骚乱

Vociferous derives from Latin *vox*，*vocis*，voice (a root you met in Chapter 9)， *plus fero*, to bear or carry. A *vociferous* rejoinder carries a lot of voice—i. e. , it is vehement，loud，noisy，clamorous，shouting. The noun is *vociferousness* (vō-SIF′-ə-rəs-nəs)；the verb is to *vociferate* (vō-SIF′-rayt′). Can you form the noun derived from the verb? ＿＿＿＿＿＿＿＿＿．

vociferous 也来自于拉丁语 vox, vocis,"声音"(这个词根你在第 9 章的时候遇到过)；加上词根 fero("承担")。a vociferous rejoinder,"喧闹的辩驳",发出许多声音——声音激昂、响亮、吵闹、聒噪、喊叫。名词形式是 vociferousness；动词是 vociferate。你能写出其从动词演变出来的名词形式吗？

3. to sleep or not to sleep—that is the question

睡或不睡——那是个问题

The root *fero* is found also in *somniferous* (som-NIF′-ə-rəs)，carrying，bearing，or bringing sleep. So a somniferous lecture is so dull and boring that it is sleep-inducing.

Fero is combined with *somnus*，sleep，in *somniferous*. (The suffix *-ous* indicates what part of speech? ＿＿＿＿＿＿＿＿＿＿＿＿＿．)

Tack on the negative prefix *in-* to *somnus* to construct *insomnia* (in-SOM′-nee-ə)，the abnormal inability to fall asleep when sleep is required or desired. The unfortunate victim of this disability is an *insomniac* (in-SOM′-nee-ak)，the adjective is *insomnious* (in-SOM′-nee-əs). (So *-ous*，in case you could not answer the question in the preceding paragraph，is an *adjective* suffix.)

somniferous 中也包含词根 fero("承担")，意为"催眠的"。所以，a somniferous lecture "催眠的讲座",枯燥乏味的程度足以勾起睡眠。

在 somniferous 里,fero 和 somnus(意为"睡眠")组合在一起(后缀-ous 表示什么词性?)。

把否定前缀 in-加在 somnus 上,组成 insomnia(失眠),指睡眠障碍。有这种睡眠障碍的人叫做 insomniac(失眠症患者),形容词是 insomnious(患有失眠症的)。(万一你不能回答出上一段中的问题,告诉你吧,-ous 是形容词后缀。)

Add a different adjective suffix to *somnus* to derive *somnolent* (SOM′-nə-lənt)，sleepy，drowsy. Can you construct the noun form of *somnolent*? ＿＿＿＿＿＿＿＿＿＿ *or* ＿＿＿＿＿＿＿＿＿＿．

Combine *somnus* with *ambulo*，to walk，and you have *somnambulism* (som-NAM′-byə-liz-əm)，walking in one's sleep. With your increasing skill in using etymology to form words，write the term for the person who is a sleepwalker. ＿＿＿＿＿＿＿＿＿. Now add to the word you wrote a two-letter adjective suffix we have learned，to form the adjective：＿＿＿＿＿＿＿＿＿＿．

在 somnus 上加一个不同的形容词后缀就变成了 somnolent,"困的""昏昏欲睡的"。你能写出 somnolent 的名词形式吗？

把 somnus 和 ambulo("走")放在一起,形成一个新的词 somnambulism(梦游病),"在睡梦中走"。根据你掌握的、利用词源推测词语形式的技能,写出意指"梦游症状患者"的词＿＿＿＿。在这个词上加上你已经学过的两个字母的形容词后缀,形成其形容词形式＿＿＿＿。

4. a walkaway

走开

An *ambulatory* (AM′-byə-lə-taw′-ree) patient，as in a hospital or convalescent home, is finally well enough to get out of bed and walk around. A *perambulator* (pə-RAM′-byə-lay′-tər), a word used more in England than in the United States, and often shortened to *pram*, is a baby carriage, a vehicle for walking an infant through the streets (*per-*, through). To *perambulate* (pə-RAM′-byə-layt′) is, etymologically, "to walk through"; hence, to stroll around. Can you write the noun form of this verb? _____.

一个"ambulatory"病人，就是在医院或者疗养院里，已经恢复得足够好，能离开床到处走走的人。perambulator，在英格兰比美国应用的更广泛，并且经常简写为 pram，是种婴儿车(per-是"经过"的意思)。perambulate 从词源上看有"走过"的意思，因此这个词的意思是"闲逛""溜达"。你能写出这个动词的名词形式吗？

To *amble* (AM′-bəl) is to walk aimlessly; an *ambulance* is so called because originally it was composed of two stretcher-bearers who *walked* off the battlefield with a wounded soldier; and a *preamble* (PREE′-am-bəl) is, by etymology, something that "walks before" (*pre-*, before, beforehand), hence an introduction or introductory statement, as the *preamble* to the U. S. Constitution ("We the people..."), a *preamble* to the speech, etc; or any event that is introductory or preliminary to another, as in "An increase in inflationary factors in the economy is often a *preamble* to a drop in the stock market."

amble 就是"毫无目的地走"；一个 ambulance(救护车)之所以是这种拼法，因为它最初是指两个抬担架的人，抬着受伤的士兵从战场"走开"；preamble 从词源上看其本意为，一些"走在前面的"事物，(pre-，在……前面)，因此，它指介绍或介绍性陈述，如 preamble to the U. S. Constitution("We the people...")"美国宪法的序言"，a preamble to the speech"一个演讲正式开始前的介绍"等；或是某些 "介绍"或"预兆"之类的事件，如"An increase in inflationary factors in the economy is often a preamble to a drop in the stock market."（通货膨胀因素的增加，是证券市场下跌的前兆。）

5. back to sleep

回去睡觉

Somnus is one Latin word for sleep——*sopor* is another. A *soporific* (sop′-ə-RIF′-ik) lecture, speaker, style of delivery, etc. will put the audience to sleep (*fic-* from *facio*, to make), and a *soporific* is a sleeping pill.

somnus 是一个拉丁语里相当于"sleep"的单词——和另外一个拉丁语 sopor 同义。"a soporific"演讲、说话者或说话的方式等，会令人昏昏欲睡(fic- 来自 facio，意为"制造")。soporific 是安眠药片。

6. noun suffixes

名词后缀

You know that *-ness* can be added to any adjective to construct the noun form. Write the noun derived from *inarticulate*: _____. *Inarticulate* is a combination of the negative prefix *in-* and Latin *articulus*, a joint. The *inarticulate* person has trouble joining words together coherently. If you are quite *articulate* (ahr-TIK′-yə-lət), on the other hand, you join your words together easily, you are verbal, vocal, possibly even voluble. The verb to *articulate* (ahr-TIK′-yə-layt′) is to join (words), i. e., to express your vocal sounds——as in "Please *articulate* more clearly." Can you write the noun derived from the verb *articulate*? _____.

-ness 能加在形容词后面而变成名词,写出 inarticulate 的名词形式＿＿＿＿＿＿＿。inarticulate 是由否定前缀 in-和拉丁语 articulus(连接点)构成。一个"inarticulate"的人,就是在"把词语条理分明地连在一起时有困难"。相反地,如果你很"articulate",就是说你把词语连接在一起很轻松,你口头表达不错,甚至比较流畅,或者口若悬河。动词 articulate 就是把(词语)连在一起表达出来——如"Please articulate more clearly."(请再说清楚点),你能写出 articulate 的名词形式吗?

Another, and very common, noun suffix attached to adjectives is, as you have discovered, -ity. So the noun form of *banal* is either *banalness*, or, more commonly, *banality* (bə-NAL′-ə-tee).

Bear in mind, then, that -*ness* and -*ity* are common noun suffixes attached to adjectives, and -*ion* (or -*ation*) is a noun suffix frequenty affixed to verbs (to *articulate—articulation*; to *vocalize—vocalization*; to *perambulate—perambulation*).

正如你已经发现的,另外一个常见的放在形容词后面而变成名词的后缀是-ity。因此 banal 的名词形式是 banalness,或是更为普遍的 banality。

请记住,-ness 和-ity 是常见的形容词变名词的后缀,-ion(或-ation)是动词变名词后缀。(如 to articulate—articulation; to vocalize—vocalization; to perambulate—perambulation。)

REVIEW OF ETYMOLOGY
复习词源

PREFIX, ROOT, SUFFIX	MEANING	ENGLISH WORD
1. *venter, ventris*	belly	_____
2. *loquor*	to speak	_____
3. *auris*	ear	_____
4. *avunculus*	uncle	_____
5. *dorsum*	back	_____
6. *vox, vocis*	voice	_____
7. *fero*	to carry, bear	_____
8. *somnus*	sleep	_____
9. -*ous*	adjective suffix	_____
10. *in-*	negative suffix	_____
11. *ambulo*	to walk	_____
12. -*ory*	adjective suffix	_____
13. *per-*	through	_____
14. *pre-*	before, beforehand	_____
15. *sopor*	sleep	_____
16. *fic-* (*facio*)	to make or do	_____
17. -*ness*	noun suffix	_____
18. -*ity*	noun suffix	_____
19. -*ion* (-*ation*)	noun suffix attached to verbs	_____
20. -*ent*	adjective suffix	_____

21. *-ence*，*-ency*　　　　　　noun suffix　　　　_____

USING THE WORDS
单词应用

Can you pronounce the words?（Ⅰ）
你能读出这些单词吗?（Ⅰ）

1. *ventral*　　　　　　　　　　VEN′-trəl
2. *ventricle*　　　　　　　　　VEN′-trə-kəl
3. *auricle*　　　　　　　　　　AWR′-ə-kəl
4. *ventricular*　　　　　　　　ven-TRIK′-yə-lər
5. *auricular*　　　　　　　　　aw-RIK′-yə-lər
6. *avuncular*　　　　　　　　　ə-VUNG′-kyə-lər
7. *dorsal*　　　　　　　　　　DAWR′-səl
8. *endorse*　　　　　　　　　　en-DAWRS′
9. *endorsement*　　　　　　　en-DAWRS′-mənt
10. *vociferousness*　　　　　　vō-SIF′-ə-rəs-nəs
11. *vociferate*　　　　　　　　vō-SIF′-ə-rayt′
12. *vociferation*　　　　　　　vō-sif′-ə-RAY′-shən

Can you pronounce the words?（Ⅱ）
你能读出这些单词吗?（Ⅱ）

1. *somniferous*　　　　　　　som-NIF′-ər-əs
2. *insomnia*　　　　　　　　　in-SOM′-nee-ə
3. *insomniac*　　　　　　　　in-SOM′-nee-ak′
4. *insomnious*　　　　　　　　in-SOM′-nee-əs
5. *somnolent*　　　　　　　　SOM′-nə-lənt
6. *somnolence*　　　　　　　　SOM′-nə-ləns
7. *somnolency*　　　　　　　　SOM′-nə-lən-see
8. *somnambulism*　　　　　　som-NAM′-byə-liz-əm
9. *somnambulist*　　　　　　som-NAM′-byə-list
10. *somnambulistic*　　　　　som-nam′-byə-LIST′-ik

Can you pronounce the words?（Ⅲ）
你能读出这些单词吗?（Ⅲ）

1. *ambulatory*　　　　　　　AM′-byə-lə-tawr′-ee
2. *perambulator*　　　　　　pə-RAM′-byə-lay′-tər
3. *perambulate*　　　　　　　pə-RAM′-byə-layt′
4. *perambulation*　　　　　　pə-ram′-byə-LAY′-shən

5. *amble*   AM'-bəl
6. *preamble*   PREE'-am-bəl
7. *soporific*   sop-ə-RIF'-ik
8. *inarticulateness*   in'-ahr-TIK'-yə-lət-nəs
9. *articulate*   ahr-TIK'-yə-lət
10. *banality*   bə-NAL'-ə-tee

Can you work with the words? (Ⅰ)
你能灵活使用这些词汇了吗?(Ⅰ)

1. ventral	a. unable to fall asleep
2. dorsal	b. pertaining to sleepwalking
3. somniferous	c. drowsy
4. insomnious	d. able to walk, after being bedridden
5. somnolent	e. verbal, vocal
6. somnambulistic	f. like an uncle; kindly; protective
7. ambulatory	g. pertaining to one of the chambers of the heart
8. articulate	h. referring to the front or belly side
9. ventricular, auricular	i. sleep-inducing
10. avuncular	j. referring to the back side

KEY:1-h, 2-j, 3-i, 4-a, 5-c, 6-b, 7-d, 8-e, 9-g, 10-f

Can you work with the words? (Ⅱ)
你能灵活使用这些词汇了吗?(Ⅱ)

1. ventricle, auricle	a. inability to fall asleep
2. endorsement	b. sleepwalking
3. vociferousness	c. introduction; preliminary or introductory occurrence
4. insomnia	d. incoherence; sputtering; inability to get words out
5. somnolence	e. chamber of the heart
6. somnambulism	f. sleeping pill
7. perambulator	g. support; approval
8. preamble	h. lack of originality; lack of imagination
9. soporific	i. drowsiness
10. inarticulateness	j. baby buggy; stroller
11. banality	k. loudness; clamorousness

KEY: 1-e, 2-g, 3-k, 4-a, 5-i, 6-b, 7-j, 8-c, 9-f, 10-d, 11-h

Can you work with the words? (Ⅲ)

你能灵活使用这些词汇了吗？（Ⅲ）

1. endorse	a. one who cannot fall asleep
2. vociferate	b. sleepwalker
3. insomniac	c. walk aimlessly
4. somnolency	d. stroll through; walk around
5. somnambulist	e. to sign on the back; support; approve of
6. perambulate	f. drowsiness
7. amble	g. say loudly and with great vehemence
8. soporific	h. causing sleep
9. insomnious	i. wakeful; unable to fall asleep

KEY: 1-e, 2-g, 3-a, 4-f, 5-b, 6-d, 7-c, 8-h, 9-i

Do you understand the words?

你对这些词汇是否已经透彻地理解？

1. Does an *insomniac* often need a *soporific*?	YES	NO
2. Does a *somnambulist* always stay in bed when asleep?	YES	NO
3. Are *ambulatory* patients bedridden?	YES	NO
4. Does a *preamble* come after another event?	YES	NO
5. Are *articulate* people verbal?	YES	NO
6. Does *banality* show creativeness?	YES	NO
7. Does an *avuncular* attitude indicate affection and protectiveness?	YES	NO
8. Is *vociferation* habitual with quiet, shy people?	YES	NO
9. Is a *somnolent* person wide awake?	YES	NO
10. Is a *somniferous* speaker stimulating and exciting?	YES	NO

KEY: 1-yes, 2-no, 3-no, 4-no, 5-yes, 6-no, 7-yes, 8-no, 9-no, 10-no

Can you recall the words?

你能够写出这些词汇吗？

1. lack of imagination or originality in speech, actions, or style of life; hackneyed or trite phraseology	1. B _____
2. sleep-inducing	2. S _____
	or S _____
3. unable to fall asleep (*adj.*)	3. I _____
4. verbal, vocal, speaking fluently	4. A _____
5. acting like an uncle	5. A _____
6. referring to the front; anterior	6. V _____
7. referring to the back; posterior	7. D _____
8. approve of; support; sign on the back of	8. E _____
9. shout vehemently	9. V _____
10. one who cannot fall asleep	10. I _____
11. drowsy; sleepy	11. S _____
12. sleepwalker	12. S _____
13. now able to walk, though previously bedridden	13. A _____
14. walk aimlessly	14. A _____
15. introduction; introductory event	15. P _____
16. incoherence	16. I _____

KEY: 1-banality, 2-somniferous *or* soporific, 3-insomnious, 4-articulate, 5-avuncular, 6-ventral, 7-dorsal, 8-endorse, 9-vociferate, 10-insomniac, 11-somnolent, 12-somnambulist, 13-ambulatory, 14-amble, 15-preamble, 16-inarticulateness

CHAPTER REVIEW

章节复习

A. Do you recognize the words?

你认识这些单词吗？

1. Disinclined to conversation:
   (a) loquacious, (b) laconic, (c) taciturn
2. Trite:
   (a) inarticulate, (b) banal, (c) verbose
3. Rapid and fluent:
   (a) voluble, (b) verbose, (c) garrulous
4. Forceful and compelling:

(a) vociferous, (b) cogent, (c) laconic

5. Unspoken:

(a) verbatim, (b) eloquent, (c) tacit

6. Using elegant and impressive words:

(a) verbose, (b) grandiloquent, (c) colloquial

7. Back:

(a) dorsal, (b) ventral, (c) somniferous

8. Sleep-inducing:

(a) soporific, (b) somnolent, (c) ventral

9. Inability to fall asleep:

(a) somnambulism, (b) ambulatory, (c) insomnia

10. Talkativeness:

(a) reticence, (b) ventriloquism, (c) loquacity

11. Expressing indirectly or in a roundabout way:

(a) circumlocutory, (b) colloquial, (c) laconic

12. Elegance in expression:

(a) magniloquence, (b) grandiloquence, (c) verbiage

13. Wordiness:

(a) laconism, (b) cogency, (c) verbosity

14. Big-hearted, generous, unselfish:

(a) grandiloquent, (b) magnanimous, (c) garrulous

15. Causing radical changes:

(a) evolutionary, (b) revolutionary, (c) ventricular

16. To shout vehemently:

(a) endorse, (b) perambulate, (c) vociferate

17. Like an uncle:

(a) ventricular, (b) auricular, (c) avuncular

18. Drowsy:

(a) somniferous, (b) somnolent, (c) soporific

19. Sleepwalking:

(a) insomnia, (b) somnolency, (c) somnambulism

20. Introduction:

(a) preamble, (b) perambulator, (c) evolution

KEY: 1-c, 2-b, 3-a, 4-b, 5-c, 6-b, 7-a, 8-a, 9-c, 10-c, 11-a, 12-a *and* b, 13-c, 14-b, 15-b, 16-c, 17-c, 18-b, 19-c, 20-a

---

B. Can you recognize the roots?

你能认出这些词根吗?

ROOT	MEANING	EXAMPLE
1. *taceo*	_____	taciturn
2. *loquor*	_____	loquacity
3. *solus*	_____	soliloquize
4. *venter*, *ventris*	_____	ventral
5. *magnus*	_____	magniloquent
6. *grandis*	_____	grandiloquent
7. *verbum*	_____	verbatim
8. *volvo*, *volutus*	_____	revolution
9. *garrio*	_____	garrulous
10. *animus*	_____	magnanimous
11. *opus*	_____	magnum opus
12. *opero*	_____	operator
13. *auris*	_____	auricle
14. *avunculus*	_____	avuncular
15. *dorsum*	_____	dorsal
16. *vox*, *vocis*	_____	vociferate
17. *fero*	_____	somniferous
18. *ambulo*	_____	preamble
19. *sopor*	_____	soporific
20. *somnus*	_____	somnolency

KEY: 1-to be silent, 2-to speak, 3-alone, 4-belly, 5-big, large, great, 6-grand, 7-word, 8-to roll, 9-to chatter, 10-mind, 11-work, 12-to work, 13-ear, 14-uncle, 15-back, 16-voice, 17-to carry or bear, 18-to walk, 19-sleep, 20-sleep

TEASER QUESTIONS FOR THE AMATEUR ETYMOLOGIST
词源小测验

1. The present participle (or -*ing* form) of the Latin verb *opero*, to work, is *operans*, working. The form *operandi* means *of working*. Can you figure out the literal meaning of the phrase *modus operandi*, sometimes used to signify the characteristic methods or procedures used by certain criminals? _____.

2. *Circum-*, we have learned, is a prefix meaning *around*, as in *circumlocution*, *circumference*, *circumcision*, *circumnavigation*, etc. Thinking of the root *scribo*, *scriptus*, to write, can you figure out the word meaning *writing*, *or written material*, *around* (the edge of something)? _____.

3. You know the roots *somnus* and *loquor*. Can you combine these two roots to form an adjective meaning *talking in one's sleep*? _____. Can you write the noun form of this adjective? _____.

4. We have discovered *auris*, ear, as in *auricle*. Can you figure out the specialty of the physician called an *aurist*? _____.

5. *Verbal*, from *verbum*, refers to words; *oral*, from *os*, *oris*, the mouth, refers to spoken words or sounds. Can you analyze *aural* and decide on its meaning? _____.

6. A *somnambulist* walks in his sleep. What does a *noctambulist* do? _____.

7. *Soporific*, combining *sopor*, sleep, with *fic-* (from *facio*), to make, means *inducing or causing sleep*. Use *somnus*, another root for sleep, to construct a word that has the same form and meaning as *soporific*: _____.

8. *Perambulate* is *to walk through*. Use another Latin prefix to construct a verb meaning *to walk around*. _____.

(*Answers in Chapter 18*)
(答案见第18章)

BECOMING ALERT TO NEW IDEAS
增强对新思想、观念的敏感

Some chapters back I suggested that since words are symbols of ideas, one of the most effective means of building your vocabulary is to read books that deal with new ideas. Along that line, I further suggested that the fields of psychology, psychiatry, and psychoanalysis would be good starting points, and I mentioned a number of exciting books to work with.

Needless to say, you will not wish to neglect other fields, and so I want to recommend, at this point, highly readable books in additional subjects. All these books will increase your familiarity with the world of ideas—all of them, therefore, will help you build a superior vocabulary.

在之前的章节里,我已经讲过一个观点,因为词语是思想和观念的表达,所以最有效的学习词汇的方法,就是读一些介绍新观念和思想的书。继续发挥一下我的这个观念,我觉得心理学、精神病学、精神分析学是个好的起点,我会提到这些领域内值得一读的书。

毋庸置疑,你也不希望忽视其他领域,基于这点,我也会介绍其他领域内可读性很强的书。所有的这些书,将会让你熟悉不同的知识领域——这都有助于你积累超级词汇量。

SEMANTICS(语义学方面):

Language in Thought and Action, by S. I. Hayakawa

People in Quandaries, by Wendell Johnson

EDUCATION AND LEARNING(教与学方面)：

How to Survive in Your Native Land，by James Herndon
Education and the Endangered Individual，by Brian V. Hill
How Children Fail and What Do I Do on Monday? by John Holt
Teaching Human Beings，by Jeffrey Schrank
Education and Ecstasy，by George B. Leonard
Human Teaching for Human Learning，by George Isaac Brown

SEX，LOVE，MARRIAGE(性，爱，婚姻方面)：

Couple Therapy，by Gerald Walker Smith and Alice I. Phillips
Your Fear of Love，by Marshall Bryant Hodge
Sexual Suicide，by George F. Gilder
Intimacy，by Gina Allen and Clement G. Martin，M. D.
How to Live with Another Person，by David Viscott，M. D.
Pairing，by George R. Bach and Ronald M. Deutsch
The Intimate Enemy，by George R. Bach and Peter Wyden
The Rape of the A. P. E. by Allan Sherman（Humor）
The Hite Report，by Shere Hire
Sex in Human Loving，by Eric Berne，M. D.

WOMEN，FEMINISM，ETC.（女人，女性主义等方面）：

Rebirth of Feminism，by Judith Hole and Ellen Levine
The Way of All Women，by M. Esther Harding
Knowing Woman，by Irene Claremont de Castillejo
Sexist Justice，by Karen De Crow
Our Bodies，Our Selves，by The Boston Women's Health Book Collective

CHILDREN，CHILD-RAISING，ETC.（儿童，儿童教养等方面）：

Between Parent and Child and Between Parent and Teenager，by Dr. Haim Ginott
Children Who Hate，by Fritz Redl and David Wineman
Parent Effectiveness Training，by Dr. Thomas Gordon
How to Parent，by Dr. Fitzhugh Dodson
Escape from Childhood，by John Holt
One Little Boy，by Dorothy W. Baruch

HEALTH(健康方面)：

Save Your Life Diet Book，by David Reuben，M. D.
Folk Medicine，by D. C. Jarvis，M. D.
Get Well Naturally，by Linda Clark
Let's Eat Right to Keep Fit，by Adelle Davis

PHILOSOPHY(哲学):

The Way of Zen and *What Does It Matter*? by Alan W. Watts

Love's Body, by Norman O. Brovm

BUSINESS, ECONOMICS, FINANCE(商业,经济,金融):

The Affluent Society, by John Kenneth Galbraith

Parkinson's Law, by C. Northcote Parkinson

The Peter Principle, by Laurence J. Peter

Up the Organization, by Robert Townsend

SOCIOLOGY(社会学):

Passages, by Gail Sheehy

Future Shock, by Alvin Toffler

Hard Times, by Studs Terkel

Roots, by Alex Haley

DEATH AND DYING(死亡和濒死):

Life After Life, by Raymond A. Moody, Jr., M. D.

On Death and Dying, by Elizabeth Kubler Ross

All but one or two of these stimulating and informative books are available in inexpensive paperback editions—most of them can be found in any large public library. Any one of them will provide an evening of entertainment and excitement far more rewarding than watching TV, will possibly open for you new areas of knowledge and-understanding, and will undoubtedly contain so many of the words you have learned in this book that you will again and again experience the delicious shock of recognition that I spoke of in an earlier chapter.

除了一两本书之外,以上这些信息量丰富、给人以启迪的书大都是价钱不贵的平装本———一般都能在大一点的公共图书馆找到。每本书都能给你带来远大于电视的乐趣,或为你开启一个崭新的知识领域,当然在阅读这些书的过程中,也必然会遇到本书之前章节里介绍的一些词汇,你会一次次地体验我在前面的章节中提到的认出这些词带来的美妙的震撼感。

Additionally, you may encounter words you have never seen before that are built on roots you are familiar with-and you will then realize how simple it is to figure out the probable meaning of even the most esoteric term once you have become an expert in roots, prefixes, and suffixes.

另外,你还会遇到一些你从未见过的、以你熟悉的词根构建而成的单词———你会意识到猜出它们大概的意思是件非常简单的事,一旦你成为词根、前缀、后缀方面的专家,你甚至能轻易猜出那些深奥术语的意思。

(End of Session 27)

Brief Intermission Six
简短插叙六

DO YOU ALWAYS USE THE PROPER WORD
你总是能够恰当地使用词语吗

The fact is that grammar is getting more liberal every day. Common usage has put a stamp of approval on many expressions which your grandmother would not have dared utter in her most intimate conversation——not if she believed she was in the habit of using good English. It is me; have you got a cold?; it's a nice day; can I have another piece of cake?; she is a most aggravating child; will everybody please remove their hats—all these today represent perfectly correct grammar for everyday conversation. Modern grammar research reports that these expressions have become universal in educated speech.

语法越来越自由,这是事实。当代用法为一些表达方式打上赞同的印记,而即使在最亲密的对话当中,这些表达方式也是你的祖父、祖母不敢使用的——如果他们自认为习惯了使用正确的英语,他们就不会用这些表达法。It is me; have you got a cold?; it's a nice day; can I have another piece of cake?; she is a most aggravating child; will everybody please remove their hats——今天,所有这些表达都完全符合正确的语法规则。当代对语法的研究也表明,这些表达也在规范的语言中普遍使用。

However, such a liberal policy does not mean that all bars are down. Only a person whose speech borders on the illiterate would make such statements as: can you learn me to swim?; he don't live here no more; we ain't working so good; me and my husband are glad to see you. There are still certain minimum essentials of good English that the cultivated speaker carefully observes.

然而,这样的一个"自由政策"并不意味所有限制的解除。只有欠缺正当教育的人才会使用以下的表达:Can you learn me to swim?; he don't live here no more; we ain't working so good; me and my husband are glad to see you。正确的英语表达仍然包括一些最基本的语法规则,而这些规则正是受教育人士极度重视的。

Is your grammar as good as the next person's? Here's a quick test by which you can measure your ability.

Check the preferable choice in each sentence, then compare your results with the key at the end. Allowing 4 percent for each correct answer, consider 92—100 excellent, 76—88 good, 68—72 average.

你的语法跟别人一样好吗? 完成以下快速测验,衡量你的语言能力。

从每句话给出的选项中选出最恰当的表达,然后将你的答案与题后的答案做比较。每个正确选项4分。如果你能够达到92—100分,你的语法非常好;76—88分,好;68—72分,普通水平。

1. What (a-effect, b-affect) does Farrah Fawcett-Majors have on you?
2. What's the sense (a-in, b-of) looking for a needle in a haystack?

3. She won't (a-leave, b-let) us meet her new boy friend.

4. What (a-kind of, b-kind of a) dress do you want?

5. Her (a-principle, b-principal) objection to neurotics is that they are difficult to live with.

6. The murderer was (a-hanged, b-hung) two hours before the governor's pardon arrived.

7. Many men feel great affection for their (a-mother-in-laws, b-mothers-in-law).

8. For a light cake, use two (a-spoonfuls, b-spoonsful) of baking powder.

9. Everyone likes you but (a-she, b-her).

10. Sally sent a gift for (a-him and me, b-he and I).

11. The criteria you are using (a-is, b-are) not valid.

12. The cost of new houses (a-is, b-are) finally stabilizing.

13. Irene as well as her husband (a-has, b-have) come to see you.

14. (a-Is, b-Are) either of your sisters working?

15. As soon as the editor or her secretary (a-comes, b-come) in, let me know.

16. One or two of her features (a-is, b-are) very attractive.

17. Can you visit Mary and (a-I, b-me) tonight?

18. He is totally (a-uninterested, b-disinterested) in your personal affairs.

19. She (a-laid, b-lay) on the beach while her son splashed at the water's edge.

20. (a-Who, b-Whom) would you rather be if you weren't yourself?

21. You should not (a-have, b-of) spoken so harshly.

22. She is one of those women who (a-believes, b-believe) that husbands should share in doing housework and taking care of the children.

23. Was it you who (a-was, b-were) here yesterday?

24. What we need in this country (a-is, b-are) honest politicians.

25. I'm smarter than Gladys, but she's richer than (a-I, b-me).

KEY: 1-a, 2-a, 3-b, 4-a, 5-b, 6-a, 7-b, 8-a, 9-b, 10-a, 11-b, 12-a, 13-a, 14-a, 15-a, 16-b, 17-b, 18-a, 19-b, 20-a, 21-a, 22-b, 23-b, 24-a, 25-a

11

HOW TO INSULT YOUR ENEMIES
如何侮辱敌人

（Sessions 28 — 31）

TEASER PREVIEW
引读

What do you call a person who：

* *insists on complete and blind obedience?*

* *toadies to the rich or influential?*

* *dabbles in the fine arts?*

* *is a loud-mouthed，quarrelsome woman?*

* *has a one-track mind?*

* *sneers at other people's cherished traditions?*

* *does not believe in God?*

* *has imaginary ailments?*

你如何称呼以下不同类型的人：

* 要求别人完全地、盲目地服从

* 善于谄媚富人或者有影响力的人

* 对艺术浅尝辄止

* 胡吹乱侃的、动辄争吵的女人

* 脑子一根筋

* 对别人敬奉的传统冷嘲热讽

* 不信上帝

* 幻想自己有病

SESSION 28
第 28 节

There are few of us who do not need warm and nourishing relationships to lead a fulfilled life.

Psychology makes clear that loving and being loved are important elements in e-motional health, but also points out the necessity for expressing, rather than re-pressing, our hostilities. (You know how good you feel once you blow off steam? And how much closer you can become attached to someone once you directly and honestly vent your anger, resentment, or irritation instead of bottling it up and seeth-ing in fury?)

It is a mark of your own emotional maturity if you can accept hostility as well as dish it out. So let us pretend, in order to encourage you to become personally in-volved in the introductory ten words of this chapter, that each paragraph in the next few pages accurately describes you. What label exactly fits your personality?

几乎没有人不需要温暖健康的人际关系来实现一个圆满的人生。

心理学研究发现，爱与被爱对人的心理健康非常重要，也发现表达出敌意比压抑更有利于心理健康。（你知道发顿脾气后感觉会多好吗？当你直接和诚实地表达出你的愤怒、怨恨和生气，而不是把它们压抑、隐藏起来后，你知道你和别人的关系会拉近很多吗？）

接受敌意，并把它展示出来，是你心理成熟的标志。为了增加你对本章要介绍的 10 个单词的参与感，可以假定下面几页每段都准确描述了你，那适合你的性格标签是什么？

IDEAS
概念

1. slave driver

奴隶监工

You make everyone toe the mark—right down to the last centimeter. You exact blind, unquestioning obedience; demand the strictest conformity to rules, however arbitrary or tyrannical; and will not tolerate the slightest deviation from your or-ders. You are, in short, the very epitome of the army drill sergeant.

You are a *martinet*.

你要求每个人都听从你，精确度达到毫米。你要求别人对命令从不质疑、盲目服从；要求无论规则多么荒谬、专横，别人都最严格地遵守规则；你绝不容许执行你的命令时有丝毫偏差。简而言之，你就是典型的军事训练长官。

他是严格执行纪律的人（martinet）。

2. bootlicker

拍马屁

You toady to rich or influential people, catering to their vanity, flattering their ego. You are the personification of the traditional ward heeler, you out-yes the Hol-lywood yes men. And on top of all these unpleasant characteristics, you're a complete hypocrite. All your servile attentions and unceasing adulation spring from your own selfish desires to get ahead, not out of any sincere admiration. You cultivate people of power or property so that you can curry favor at the opportune moment.

You are a sycophant.

你谄媚富人和有影响力的人士,迎合他们的虚荣心,奉承他们的自负心理。你是依附政客之人的化身,比好莱坞应声虫更为唯唯诺诺。在所有这些令人作呕的特征之上,你还是十足的伪君子。你所有卑躬屈膝的行为和谄媚都并非出于真诚的崇拜,目的只有一个:攀高枝。你结交有钱有势之人,以便于关键时刻及时谋取福利。

你是谄媚者(sycophant)。

3. dabbler

浅尝辄止者

Often, though not necessarily, a person of independent income, you engage superficially in the pursuit of one of the fine arts—painting, writing, sculpturing, composing, etc. You do this largely for your own amusement and not to achieve any professional competence; nor are you at all interested in monetary rewards. Your artistic efforts are simply a means of passing time pleasantly.

You are a dilettante.

你涉猎某种艺术形式——绘画、写作、雕刻、作曲等等。虽然并不一定全是如此,但通常来说,你有这些艺术之外的收入。你的目的仅限于娱乐,不以达到任何专业成就为目标,也不追求任何金钱回报。对于你来说,这仅仅是打发时间的乐事。

你是个浅涉文艺的人(dilettante)。

4. battle-ax

战斧

You are a loud-mouthed, shrewish, turbulent woman; you're quarrelsome and aggressive, possessing none of those gentle and tender qualities stereotypically associated with femininity. You're strong-minded, unyielding, sharp-tongued, and dangerous. You can curse like a stevedore and yell like a fishwife—and often do.

You are a virago.

你是一个高谈阔论的女人,你泼辣、蛮横、动辄争吵、争强好胜,完全不具备传统观念中女性应有的温柔、细腻等品质。你固执、倔强、刻薄、危险。你会向码头工人一样骂街,像卖鱼妇一样大声叫嚷。

你是个泼妇(virago)。

5. superpatriot

超级爱国者

Anything you own or belong to is better—simply because you own it or belong to it, although you will be quick to find more justifiable explanations. Your religion, whatever it may be, is far superior to any other; your political party is the only honest one; your neighborhood puts all others in the city in the shade; members of your own sex are more intelligent, more worthy, more emotionally secure, and in every way far better than people of the opposite sex; your car is faster, more fun to drive, and gets better gas mileage than any other, no matter in what price range; and of course your country and its customs leave nothing to be desired, and inhabitants of other nations are in comparison barely civilized. In short，you are exaggeratedly，aggressively，absurdly，and excessively devoted to your own affliafions—and you make no bones about advertising such prejudice.

You are a chauvinist.

你认为你所拥有的东西或所在环境都是最好的——原因就在于这是你所拥有的东西、是你所在的环境，虽然你会很快给出更多看似合理的解释。无论你有怎样的信仰，你的信仰都优于别人的信仰；你所在的党派是最诚实的党派；你所在的社区使得城市中其他社区暗淡无光；与自己相同性别的人远比异性的人更聪明、更有价值、情绪更稳定；你的轿车不管是什么价位，都比别的车更快，更好开，更省油；当然，你的祖国及其习俗完美无缺，相比而言，别的国家的居民都是野蛮人。简而言之，你喜欢你对自己所属的一切忠诚到了夸张、好斗、荒谬和过分的地步——而你毫不掩饰地显示你的这种偏见。

你是个沙文主义者(chauvinist)。

6. fanatic
狂热者

You have a one-track mind—and when you're riding a particular hobby, you ride it hard. You have such an excessive, all-inclusive zeal for one thing (and it may be your business, your profession, your husband or wife, your children, your stomach, your money, or whatever) that your obsession is almost absurd. You talk, eat, sleep that one thing—to the point where you bore everyone to distraction.

You are a monomaniac.

你是一个独行其是的人——一旦培养某种爱好，你的热忱就会过度。你对某种事物会表现出夸张的、全身心投入的热情(这种事物可能是事业、专业、丈夫或妻子、孩子、胃、钱或者任何其他事物)，几乎达到疯狂的程度。无论是说话还是吃饭，你只谈这一件事，甚至睡觉心里也只想着这一件事——这使得每个人都因觉得非常乏味而走神。

你是一个偏执狂(monomaniac)。

7. attacker
攻击者

You are violently against established beliefs, revered traditions, cherished customs—such, you say, stand in the way of reform and progress and are always based on superstition and irrationality. Religion, family, marriage, ethics—you weren't there when these were started and you're not going to conform simply because most unthinking people do.

You are an iconoclast.

你强烈反对已有的信仰、受尊敬的传统和被珍惜的习俗——你认为，这些都建立在迷信和非理性基础之上，都会阻拦改革和发展。信仰、家庭、婚姻和道德开始存在时，你尚未出生，你也不打算去遵从这些东西，因为这是从不思考的人才会遵从的。

你是个攻击传统观念的人(iconoclast)。

8. skeptic
怀疑论者

There is no God—that's your position and you're not going to budge from it.

You are an atheist.

上帝并不存在——这就是你的观点，决不动摇。

你是个无神论者(atheist)。

9. self-indulger

自我放纵

You are, as a male, lascivious, libidinous, lustful, lewd, wanton, immoral—but more important, you promiscuously attempt to satisfy (and are often successful in so doing) your sexual desires with any woman within your arm's reach.

You are a lecher.

你淫荡,性欲强烈,好色,放肆,不道德——最重要的是,你不加选择地与你身边的任何女人滥交,试图满足(而且经常成功)你的性欲。

你是个色鬼(lecher)。

10. worrier

杞人忧天

You are always sick, though no doctor can find an organic cause for your ailments. You know you have ulcers, though medical tests show a healthy stomach. You have heart palpitations, but a cardiogram fails to show any abnormality. Your headaches are caused (you're sure of it) by a rapidly growing brain tumor—yet X rays show nothing wrong. These maladies are not imaginary, however; to you they are most real, non-existent as they may be in fact. And as you travel from doctor to doctor futilely seeking confirmation of your imminent death, you become more and more convinced that you're too weak to go on much longer. Organically, of course, there's nothing the matter with you. Perhaps tensions, insecurities, or a need for attention is taking the form of simulated bodily ills.

You are a hypochondriac.

你总像个病秧子,但是医生却无法找出疾病的器质性原因。你觉得自己有胃溃疡,虽然医疗检查显示你的胃非常健康。你觉得心悸,但是心电图显示你的心脏完全正常。你认为脑袋里一颗脑瘤的快速生长是你头疼的原因(你非常确定)——但是X光查不出任何问题。但是,不要认为这些病是假想的;对于你来说,虽然病患的确不存在,但这些病再真实不过。你拜访不同的医生,为即将来临的死亡寻找佐证却徒劳无功,于是,你越来越确定,你的身体过于虚弱,无法继续维持。当然,从生理上来说,你的身体完全健康。或许,是紧张的精神、不安感和获得关注的需求使你感觉身体的某个部分患病。

你是个疑病症患者(hypochondriac)。

USING THE WORDS
单词应用

Can you pronounce the words?
你能读出这些单词吗?

1.	martinet	mahr-tə-NET′
2.	sycophant	SIK′-ə-fənt
3.	dilettante	dil′-ə-TAN′-tee
4.	virago	və-RAY′-gō
5.	chauvinist	SHŌ′-və-nist

6. monomaniac   mon′-ə-MAY′-nee-ak
7. iconoclast   ī-KON′-ə-klast′
8. atheist   AY′-thee-ist
9. lecher   LECH′-ər
10. hypochondriac   hī′-pə-KON′-dree-ak

Can you work with the words?
你能灵活使用这些词汇了吗?

WORDS	KEY IDEAS
1. martinet	a. superficiality
2. sycophant	b. patriotism
3. dilettante	c. godlessness
4. virago	d. single-mindedness
5. chauvinist	e. antitradition
6. monomaniac	f. sex
7. iconoclast	g. illness
8. atheist	h. discipline
9. lecher	i. turbulence
10. hypochondriac	j. flattery

KEY: 1-h, 2-j, 3-a, 4-i, 5-b, 6-d, 7-e, 8-c, 9-f, 10-g

Do you understand the words?
你对这些词汇是否已经透彻地理解?

1. Does a *martinet* condone carelessness and neglect of duty?　　　　YES　NO
2. Is a *sycophant* a sincere person?　　　　YES　NO
3. Is a *dilettante* a hard worker?　　　　YES　NO
4. Is a *virago* sweet and gentle?　　　　YES　NO
5. Is a *chauvinist* modest and self-effacing?　　　　YES　NO
6. Does a *monomaniac* have a one-track mind?　　　　YES　NO
7. Does an *iconoclast* scoff at tradition?　　　　YES　NO
8. Does an *atheist* believe in God?　　　　YES　NO
9. Is a *lecher* misogynous?　　　　YES　NO
10. Does a *hypochondriac* have a lively imagination?　　　　YES　NO

KEY：1-no，2-no，3-no，4-no，5-no，6-yes，7-yes，8-no，9-no，10-yes

Can you recall the words?
你能够写出这些词汇吗？

1. a person whose emotional disorder is reflected in non-organic or imaginary bodily ailments	1. H	_____
2. a strict disciplinarian	2. M	_____
3. a lewd and sexually aggressive male	3. L	_____
4. a toady to people of wealth or power	4. S	_____
5. a disbeliever in God	5. A	_____
6. a dabbler in the arts	6. D	_____
7. a shrewish, loud-mouthed female	7. V	_____
8. a scoffer at tradition	8. I	_____
9. person with a one-track mind	9. M	_____
10. a blatant superpatriot	10. C	_____

KEY：1-hypochondriac，2-martinet，3-lecher，4-sycophant，5-atheist，6-dilettante，7-virago，8-iconoclast，9-monomaniac，10-chauvinist

Can you use the words?
你会使用这些词汇了吗？

1. She scoffs at beliefs you have always held dear.　1. _____
2. You know he's hale and hearty—but he constantly complains of his illness.　2. _____
3. She insists her political affliations are superior to yours.　3. _____
4. She insists on her subordinates toeing the mark.　4. _____
5. He makes sexual advances to everyone else's wife—and is too often successful.　5. _____
6. He cultivates Mends that can do him good—financially.　6. _____
7. She dabbles with water colors.　7. _____
8. She insists there is no Deity.　8. _____
9. She's a shrew, a harridan, a scold, and a nag.　9. _____

10. His only interest in life is his fish
    collection—and he is fanatically, almost
    psychotically, devoted to it.

10. _____

KEY: 1-iconoclast, 2-hypochondriac, 3-chauvinist, 4-martinet, 5-lecher, 6-sycophant, 7-dilettante, 8-atheist, 9-virago, 10-monomaniac

(End of Session 28)

SESSION 29
第 29 节

ORIGINS AND RELATED WORDS
词源及相关词汇

1. the French drillmaster
法国教官

Jean Martinet was the Inspector General of Infantry during the reign of King Louis XIV—and a stricter, more fanatic drillmaster France had never seen. It was from this time that the French Army's reputation for discipline dated, and it is from the name of this Frenchman that we derive our English word *martinet*. The word is always used in a derogatory sense and generally shows resentment and anger on the part of the user. The secretary who calls his boss a *martinet*, the wife who applies the epithet to her husband, the worker who thus refers to the foreman—these speakers all show their contempt for the excessive, inhuman discipline to which they are asked to submit.

Since *martinet* comes from a man's name (in the Brief Intermission which follows we shall discover that a number of picturesque English words are similarly derived), there are no related forms built on the same root. There is an adjective *martinetish* (mahr-tə-NET'-ish) and another noun form, *martinetism*, but these are used only rarely.

让·马蒂内(Jean Martinet)是法国国王路易十四在位期间的步兵总检察长——是法国历史上最严格、最狂热的教官。也正是从他开始,法国军队以纪律严格著称,正是马蒂内的名字 Martinet 派生出了 martinet 这个词语。这个词的用法基本为贬义,通常能够表露使用者的厌恶和气愤。无论是将她的老板称为 martinet 的秘书,还是用 martinet 形容丈夫的妻子,还是将其领班称为 martinet 的工人——这些人都对他们必须服从的人表现出的过度的、非人性的原则表示蔑视。

因为 martinet 这个词来源于人名(本章后的简短插叙中,我们会发现许多生动的英语词汇都是以这个方式派生的),所以它并没有派生出基于相同词根的词形。人们很少使用另外两个形式:形容词形式 martinetish(严格的)和名词形式 martinetism(严格的训练)。

2. a Greek "fig-shower"
古希腊"无花果告发者"

Sycophant comes to us from the Greeks. According to *Shipley's Dictionary of Word Origins*:

When a fellow wants to get a good mark, he may polish up an apple and place it on teacher's desk; his classmates call such a lad an apple-shiner. Less complimentary localities use the term bootlicker. The Greeks had a name for it: *fig-shower*. Sycophant is from Gr. *sykon*, fig, [and] *phanein*, to show. This was the fellow that informed the officers in charge when (1) the figs in the sacred groves were being taken, or (2) when the Smyrna fig-dealers were dodging the tariff.

sycophant,"谄媚者",来自于希腊语。根据《希普利词源词典》：

"学生如果想得高分，他就会削好一个苹果，把它放到老师的桌子上；同学们会把他称为削苹果的家伙——apple-shiner。一些地区使用另外一个不太光彩的词语，舔靴子的人——bootlicker。古希腊人则将这样的人称为 fig-shower。sycophant 来自于希腊语 sykon,"无花果",和 phanein,"给……看"。这是一个通知主管官员的家伙，他要么告知(1)有人正在偷取神圣之林中的无花果；要么告知(2)有无花果商人正在逃税。"

Thus, a *sycophant* may appear to be a sort of "stool pigeon," since the latter curries the favor of police officials by "peaching" on his fellow criminals. *Sycophants* may use this means of ingratiating themselves with influential citizens of the community; or they may use flattery, servile attentions, or any other form of insinuating themselves into someone's good graces. A sycophant practices *sycophancy* (SIK′-ə-fən-see), and has a *sycophantic* (sik-ə-FAN′-tik) attitude. All three forms of the word are highly uncomplimentary—use them with care.

因此,从某种程度上说,a sycophant 看起来有"密探"的意思,因为后者通过揭发同伴的罪行来讨好警官。谄媚者会使用手段讨好身边有影响的人士；或者阿谀奉承,或者卑躬屈膝,使用各种暗示的方法讨人欢心。sycophant 的行为被称为 sycophancy,"谄媚";持有的态度是 sycophantic,"阿谀奉承的"。三个形式都是绝对的贬义词——注意要小心使用。

Material may be so delicate or fine in texture that anything behind it will show through. The Greek prefix *dia-* means *through*; and *phanein*, as you now know, means *to show*—hence such material is called *diaphanous* (dī-AF′-ə-nəs). Do not use the adjective in reference to all material that is transparent (for example, you would not call glass *diaphanous*, even though you can see right through it), but only material that is silky, gauzy, filmy, and, in addition, transparent or practically transparent. The word is often applied to female garments—nightgowns, negligees, etc.

一些纺织品的材质十分纤细、精致,透过它们能够看到后面的任何物体。希腊语前缀 dia-表示 through(透过);phanein 表示 to show(展示),正如我们刚讨论过的一样——这样的东西都是 diaphanous,"(织物等)透明的"。注意不要用这个形容词修饰任何透明的材质(例如,尽管玻璃是透明的,你也不能用这个词来修饰),只有透明的或者近乎透明的丝质的、薄纱的、薄膜的材料才能用这个词来修饰。diaphanous 经常修饰女性服装——睡袍、晨衣等。

3. just for one's own amusement

仅为个人娱乐

Dilettante is from the Italian verb *dilettare*, to delight. The *dilettante* paints, writes, composes, plays a musical instrument, or engages in scientific experiments purely for amusement—not to make money, become famous, or satisfy a deep creative urge (the latter, I presume, being the justifications for the time that professional artists, writers, composers, musicians, poets, and scientists spend at their chosen work). A *dilettantish* (dil-ə-TAN′-tish) attitude is superficial, unprofessional; *dilettantism* (dil-ə-TAN′-tiz-əm) is superficial, part-time dabbling in the type of activity that usually engages the full time and energy of the professional artist or scientist.

dilettante(浅涉艺术的人)来自于意大利语动词 dilettare,意为"使……感到高兴"。dilettante 可能绘画、写作、作曲、玩乐器或者参加科学实验,但目的仅为娱乐或者消遣——而不是为了赚钱、搏出名或者满足一种深刻的创作欲望(这种创作欲望在我看来是评判专业艺术家、作家、作曲家、音乐家、诗人或科学家的常规标准)。一种 dilettantish 态度是肤浅的、非专业的;dilettantism,"浅涉文艺",是指涉猎本该是艺术家或科学家付出所有时间和精力参与的艺术活动。

Do not confuse the *dilettante*, who has a certain amount of native talent or ability, with the *tyro* (TĪ′-rō), who is the inexperienced beginner in some art, but who may be full of ambition, drive, and energy. To call a person a *tyro* is to imply that he is just starting in some artistic, scientific, or professional field—he's not much good yet because he has not had time to develop his skill, if any. The *dilettante* usually has some skill but isn't doing much with it. On the other hand, anyone who has developed consummate skill in an artistic field, generally allied to music, is called a *virtuoso* (vur′-chōō-Ō′-sō)—like Heifetz or Menuhin on the violin, Horowitz or Rubinstein on the piano. Pluralize *virtuoso* in the normal way—*virtuosos*; or if you wish to sound more sophisticated, give it the continental form—*virtuosi* (vur′-chōō-Ō′-see). Similarly, the plural of *dilettante* is either *dilettantes* or *dilettanti* (dil-ə-TAN′-tee).

The *i* ending for a plural is the Italian form and is common in musical circles. For example, *libretto*, the story (or book) of an opera, may be pluralized to *libretti*; *concerto*, a form of musical composition, is pluralized *concerti*. However, the Anglicized *librettos* and *concertos* are perfectly correct also. *Libretto* is pronounced lə-BRET′-ō; *libretti* is lə-BRET′-ee; *concerto* is kən-CHUR′-tō; and *concerti* is kən-CHUR′-tee. Suit your plural form, I would suggest, to the sophistication of your audience.

注意不要将 dilettante 与 tyro 相混淆。dilettante 具有一定程度的天赋或能力；而 tyro 是指对某种艺术形式毫无经验的生手,但是他可能充满热情、动力和能量。将一个人称为 tyro 会暗示出这个人仅仅刚刚开始进入某种艺术、科学或者专业领域——因为没有足够的时间去发展他的技巧(如果具有技巧),所以他做得还不够好。而 dilettante 通常具有一定的技巧,只是不太会运用技巧。另一方面,任何在某种艺术领域,尤其是音乐领域达到精湛技巧的人都被称为 virtuoso,"艺术大师"——例如小提琴家海菲兹或者梅纽因、钢琴家霍洛维茨或鲁宾森。virtuoso 的复数形式是规则变法——virtuosos;如果你希望自己听起来更高贵,可以使用欧洲大陆的复数变法——virtuosi。同样,dilettante 的复数形式是 dilettantes 或者 dilettanti。

复数形式以 i 结尾是意大利语复数的变法,在音乐领域比较常见。例如,libretto,"(歌剧等的)剧本",复数形式为 libretti;concerto,"协奏曲",复数形式为 concerti. 但是根据英语的复数变法,librettos 和 concertos 也是完全正确的形式。libretto 的发音是 lə-BRET′-o;libretti 的发音是 lə-BRET′-ee;concerto 的发音是 kən-CHUR′-tə;concerti 的发音是 kən-CHUR′-tee. 我的建议是根据对话对象选择恰当的复数形式。

4. "masculine" women

"女汉子"

Virago comes, oddly enough, from the Latin word for man, *vir*. Perhaps the derivation is not so odd after all; a *virago*, far from being stereotypically feminine (i. e. , timid, delicate, low-spoken, etc.), is stereotypically masculine in personality: coarse, aggressive, loud-mouthed. *Termagant* (TUR′-mə-gənt) and *harridan* (HAIR′-ə-dən) are words with essentially the same uncomplimentary meaning as *virago*. To call a brawling woman a *virago*, a *termagant*, and a *harridan* is admittedly repetitious, but is successful in relieving one's feelings.

奇怪的是,virago,"泼妇",来源于拉丁语中的 vir,意为"男人"。也许这个派生并非特别奇怪;泼妇与传统的女性形象大相径庭(例如羞怯、细腻、低声细语等),而在个性上与男性形象更为相近——粗野,好斗,高声大气。另外两个与

virago具有同样贬义词义的同义词是 termagant 和 harridan。用 virago、termagant 和 harridan 三个词一起修饰一个喧嚷的女人虽然有些重复,但是十分有助于发泄情绪。

5. the old man

老男人

Nicolas Chauvin, soldier of the French Empire, so vociferously and unceasingly aired his veneration of Napoleon Bonaparte that he became the laughingstock of all Europe. Thereafter, an exaggerated and blatant patriot was known as a *chauvinist*— and still is today. *Chauvinism* (SHŌ'-və-niz-əm), by natural extension, applies to blatant veneration of, or boastfulness about, any other affiliation besides one's country.

To be *patriotic* is to be normally proud of, and devoted to, one's country—to be *chauvinistic* (shō'-və-NIS'-tik) is to exaggerate such pride and devotion to an obnoxious degree.

We might digress here to investigate an etymological side road down which the word *patriotic* beckons. *Patriotic* is built on the Latin word *pater*, *patris*, father— one's country is, in a sense, one's fatherland.

尼古拉斯·沙文是法兰西帝国的一位战士,他不停地吵嚷着宣扬对拿破仑·波拿马的敬仰之情,以至于他的名字成为了整个欧洲的笑柄。此后,任何夸大的、露骨的爱国主义者都被称为 chauvinist,"沙文主义者、本国至上主义者",一直到现在。chauvinism(沙文主义)自然引申出的含义,是指某人除了对国家以外,对他所附属的任何组织也表现出露骨的尊崇并大肆吹嘘。

patriotic,爱国的,是指对自己国家正常的自豪感和奉献——而 chauvinistic,沙文主义的,是将这种自豪感和奉献发挥至令人讨厌的、病态的程度。

这里我们或许需要偏离主题来研究 patriotic 的词源。patriotic 来源于拉丁语词语 pater,patris(父亲)——祖国在一定意义上来说就是 fatherland。

Let us see what other interesting words are built on this same root.

(1) *patrimony* (PAT'-rə-mō-nee)—an inheritance from one's father. The *-mony* comes from the same root that gives us *money*, namely *Juno Moneta*, the Roman goddess who guarded the temples of finance. The adjective is *patrimonial* (pat'-rə-MŌ'-nee-əl).

(2) *patronymic* (pat'-rə-NIM'-ik)—a name formed on the father's name, like *Johnson* (son of John), *Martinson*, *Aaronson*, etc. The word combines pater, patris with Greek onyma, name. Onyma plus tho Greek prefix syn-, with or together, forms synonym (SIN'-ə-nim), a word of the same name (or meaning), etymologically "a together name." Onyma plus the prefix anti against, forms antonym (AN'-tə-nim), a word of opposite meaning, etymologically "an against name." Onyma plus Greek homos, the same, forms homonym (HOM'-ə-nim), a word that sounds like another but has a different meaning and spelling, like bare bear, way-weigh, to-too-two, etc., etymologically "a same name." A homonym is more accurately called a homophone (HOM'-ə-fən'), a combination of homos, the same, and phone, sound. The adjective form of synonym is synonymous (sə-NON'-ə-məs). Can you write,

and pronounce，the adjective derived from：

antonym? _____

homonym? _____

homophone? _____

（3）*paternity*（pə-TUR′-nə-tee）—fatherhood，as to question someone's *paternity*，to file a *paternity* suit in order to collect child support from the assumed，accused，or self-acknowledged father. The adjective is *paternal*（pə-TUR′-nəl），fatherly. *Paternalism*（pə-TUR′-nə-liz-əm）is the philosophy or system of governing a country；or of managing a business or institution，so that the citizens，employees，or staff are treated in a manner suggesting a father children relationship. （Such a system sounds，and often is，benign and protective，but plays havoc with the initiative，independence，and creativity of those in subordinate roles. ）The adjective is *paternalistic*（pə-turn′-ə-LIS′-tik）.

（4）*patriarch*（PAY′-tree-ark′）—a venerable，fatherlike old man；an old man in a ruling，fatherlike position. Here *pater*，*patris* is combined with the Greek root *archein*，to rule. The adjective is *patriarchal*（pay′-tree-AHR′-kəl），the system is a *patriarchy*（PAY′-tree-ahr′-kee）.

（5）*patricide*（PAT′-rə-sīd′）—the killing of one's father. *Pater*，*patris* combines with *-cide*，a suffix derived from the Latin verb *caedo*，to kill. The adjective is *patricidal*（pat-rə-SĪ′-dəl）.

现在,我们来看基于相同词根的其他有趣词汇。

（1）patrimony——"遗产",从父亲继承的财物。-mony 与 money(钱)来自相同词根,Juno Moneta——朱诺·莫尼塔,守护财政圣殿的罗马女神。形容词是 patrimonial。

（2）patronymic——"取自父名的",例如,Johnson(John 的儿子)、Martinson(Martin 的儿子)、Aaronson(Aaron 的儿子)等。这个单词是由 pater, patris 加上希腊语 onyma(意为"名字")构成。onyma 加上希腊前缀 syn-(意为"和"或"在一起"),构成 synonym,意即"同名或同义",从词源上看其意思为"一个共同的名字"。Onyma 加上前缀 anti-(意为"相反的")形成 antonym,意为"反义词",从词源上看,意为"一个相反的名字"。Onyma 加上希腊语中的 homos,形成 homonym 意即"同音词"——发音相似,但意思和拼写则都不一样,如 bare—bear, way——weigh, to——too——two 等,从词源上意为"一个相同的名字"。一个"homonym"更准确的叫法是"homophone",由 homos(意为"相同的"),和 phone(意为"声音")构成。Synonym 的形容词形式是 synonymous。你能写出、读出下列单词的形容词形式吗?

antonym? _____

homonym? _____

homophone? _____

（3）paternity——"父亲的身份、父权"。比如质疑某人的父亲身份,发起一场 paternity 诉讼以从父亲那里获得孩子的赡养费——此人可能被认为是孩子的父亲,也可能是别人指称他是父亲,还可能他自己声称是父亲。paternalism(家长制)是一种管理国家、管理企业或机构的哲学或系统,其对待公民、雇员或者职员的方式有点像父子关系。(这种系统听起来是良性的、保护性的,而且事实也常常如此,但是它对处于从属地位的角色的主动性、独立性和创造性有很大的破坏作用。)其形容词形式是 paternalistic。

（4）patriarch——"家长、元老",令人尊重的、像父亲一样的老者;占统治地位的、占有父亲一样地位的老者。这个词由 pater,patris 加上希腊词根 archein(统治)组成,其形容词形式是 patriarchal,这种系统称为 patriarchy(父权制)。

（5）patricide——"弑父",杀害父亲。这个词由 pater,patris 加后缀-cide(由拉丁动词 caedo,"杀害",派生而来)。形容词是 patricidal。

This list does not exhaust the number of words built on *pater*, father, but is sufficient to give you an idea of how closely related many English words are. In your reading you will come across other words containing the letters *pater* or *patr*—you will be able to figure them out once you realize that the base is the word *father*. You might, if you feel ambitious, puzzle out the relationship to the "father idea" in the following words, checking with a dictionary to see how good your linguistic intuition is:

虽然无法详尽以 pater(父亲)为词根的所有词汇,但是以上举例足以说明英语词汇间的紧密联系。当你阅读其他包括 pater 或者 patr 的词汇时——只要意识到是 father 的词根,你就能够明白词汇的含义。如果你现在踌躇满志,你可以猜测以下词汇与"父亲"的关系,然后查阅词典,检验你的语言直觉是否足够灵敏。

1. patrician
2. patron
3. patronize
4. patronizing (*adj.*)
5. paterfamilias
6. padre

6. the old lady

老女人

Pater, *patris* is *father*. *Mater*, *matris* is *mother*.

For example:

(1) *matriarch* (MAY'-tree-ahrk')—the mother-ruler; the "mother person" that controls a large household, tribe, or country. This word, like *patriarch*, is built on the root *archein*, to rule. During the reign of Queen Elizabeth or Queen Victoria, England was a *matriarchy* (MAY'-tree-ahr'-kee). Can you figure out the adjective form? _____.

(2) *maternity* (mə-TUR'-nə-tee)—motherhood

(3) *maternal* (mə-TURN'-əl)—motherly

(4) *matron* (MAY'-trən)—an older woman, one sufficiently mature to be a mother. The adjective *matronly* (MAY'-trən-lee) conjures up for many people a picture of a woman no longer in the glow of youth and possibly with a bit of added weight in the wrong places, so this word should be used with caution; it may be hazardous to your health if the lady you are so describing is of a tempestous nature, or is a *virago*.

(5) *alma mater* (AL'-mə MAY'-tər *or* AHL'-mə MAH'-tər)—etymologically, "soul mother"; actually, the school or college from which one has graduated, and which in a sense is one's intellectual mother.

(6) *matrimony* (MAT'-rə-mō'-nee)—marriage. Though this word is similar to

patrimony in spelling, it does not refer to *money*, as *patrimony* does; unless, that is, you are cynical enough to believe that people marry for money. As the language was growing, marriage and children went hand in hand—it is therefore not surprising that the word for *marriage* should be built on the Latin root for *mother*. Of course, times have changed, but the sexist nature of the English language has not. The noun suffix *-mony* indicates state, condition, or result, as in *sanctimony*, *parsimony*, etc. The adjective is *matrimonial* (mat'-rə-MŌ'-nee-əl).

(7) *matricide* (MAT'-rə-sīd')—the killing of one's mother. The adjective? ＿＿＿
＿＿＿＿＿＿＿＿＿＿＿＿＿.

　　"父亲"的词根是 pater,patris。"母亲"的词根是 matris。

　　例如：

　　(1) matriarch——"女家长"；是控制一个大家族、部落或者国家的"母亲式人物"。这个词与 patriarch 同样基于词根 archein,"统治"。无论是伊丽莎白女王或是维多利亚女王在位期间,英国都被称为 matriarchy,"母权制"。你能写出它的形容词形式吗？

　　(2) maternity——"母性,为母之道"。

　　(3) maternal——"母亲的,母系的"。

　　(4) matron——一个有些年龄、足可以当妈妈的女人。形容词 matronly 让人们联想到一个韶华不再,并可能有些发胖的女人,因此要谨慎使用这个词；如果你用这个词来描述一个脾气火爆的女人或是一个泼妇,那可能会对你的健康有害。

　　(5) alma mater——"母校",逐字翻译应该是"灵魂母亲"。一个人学习过的学校或者大学在某种意义上是"智慧母亲"。

　　(6) matrimony——"婚姻生活"。虽然这个词与 patrimony 的拼写相似,但是它与钱无关；除非是愤世嫉俗的你坚决认为女性只会为金钱而结婚。婚姻会为家庭带来孩子,语言是这样发展的——因此,marriage(婚姻)也是基于拉丁语表示 mother 的词根。当然,时代在变,现代人即使结婚也不一定会生育。名词后缀-mony 表"状态""状况"或"结果",如 sanctimony,parsimony 等,形容词是 matrimonial。

　　(7) matricide——"弑母"。形容词形式是什么？

7. murder most foul...

各种谋杀

Murder unfortunately is an integral part of human life, so there is a word for almost every kind of killing you can think of. Let's look at some of them.

(1) *suicide* (SOO'-ə-sīd')—killing oneself (intentionally); *-cide* plus *sui*, of oneself. This is both the act and the person who has been completely successful in performing the act (*partially* doesn't count); also, in colloquial usage, *suicide* is a verb. The adjective? ＿＿＿＿＿＿＿.

(2) *fratricide* (FRAT'-rə-sīd')—the killing of one's brother; *-cide* plus *frater*, *fratris*, brother. The adjective? ＿＿＿＿＿＿＿.

(3) *sororicide* (sə-RAWR'-ə-sīd')—the killing of one's sister; *-cide* plus *soror*, sister. The adjective? ＿＿＿＿＿＿＿.

(4) *homicide* (HOM'-ə-sīd')—the killing of a human being; *-cide* plus *homo*,

person. In law, *homicide* is the general term for any slaying. If intent and premeditation can be proved, the act is murder and punishable as such. If no such intent is present, the act is called *manslaughter* and receives a lighter punishment. Thus, if your mate/lover/spouse makes your life unbearable and you slip some arsenic into his/her coffee one bright morning, you are committing murder—that is, if he/she succumbs. On the other hand, if you run your victim down—quite accidentally—with your car, bicycle, or wheelchair, with no intent to kill, you will be accused of *manslaughter*—that is, if death results and if you can prove you didn't really mean it. It's all rather delicate, however, and you might do best to put thoughts of justifiable *homicide* out of your mind. The adjective? _____.

(5) *regicide* (REJ′-ə-sīd′)—the killing of one's king, president, or other governing official. Booth committed *regicide* when he assassinated Abraham Lincoln. Adjective? _____.

Derivation: Latin *rex*, *regis*, king, plus *-cide*.

很不幸,谋杀总与人类生活相伴,你能想到的各种谋杀都有词与之对应。

(1) suicide——自杀(故意为之);-cide 加上 sui("自己"),这个词既指这种行为,也指成功实行这种行为的人(部分成功不算),在口语中 suicide 也可作为动词,其形容词是什么?

(2) fratricide——杀害同胞兄弟;-cide 加上 frater,fratris(兄弟)。形容词是什么?

(3) sororicide——杀亲姐妹;-cide 加上 soror(姐妹)。形容词是什么?

(4) homicide——杀人(行为或罪);-cide 加上 homo(人)。按照法律,homicide 是杀戮的统称。如果能够确定杀人的动机和预谋,就能够确定是否为"谋杀"——murder,并以此定罪。如果没有明显的杀人动机,就是过失杀人——manslaughter,惩罚也相对轻。这样,如果你的伴侣/情人/配偶使你的生活无法忍受,你决定在一个明媚的清晨在她的咖啡中放上一块砒霜,你就是在谋杀——如果他或她死亡。但是,如果你用轿车、自行车或者轮椅十分偶然地将其撞倒,你并没有杀她的动机,你所犯的就是过失杀人罪——也就是说,如果她死亡,而你能够证明你并非有意。然而,这两个罪行之间的区别十分微妙,所以,即使你使用暴力的理由再合理,你也最好不要有这样的想法。形容词是什么?

(5) regicide——"弑君(者)",杀害国王、总统或者统治官员。当布斯刺杀林肯总统时,他实施的这种行为就是 regicide。其形容词是什么?演变:拉丁语 rex,regis(意为"国王""总统")加上-cide。

(6) *uxoricide* (uk-SAWR′-ə-sīd′)—the killing of one's wife. Adjective? _____ _____. Derivation: Latin *uxor*, wife, plus *-cide*.

(7) *mariticide* (mə-RIT′-ə-sīd′)—the killing of one's husband. Adjective? ____ _____. Derivation: Latin *maritus*, husband, plus *-cide*.

(8) *infanticide* (in-FAN′-tə-sīd′)—the killing of a newborn child. Adjective? ____ _____. Derivation: Latin *infans*, *infantis*, baby, plus *-cide*.

(9) *genocide* (JEN′-ə-sīd′)—the killing of a whole race or nation. This is a comparatively new word, coined in 1944 by a UN official named Raphael Lemkin, to refer to the mass murder of the Jews, Poles, etc. ordered by Hitler. Adjective? ____ _____. Derivation: Greek *genos*, race, kind, plus *-cide*.

(10) *parricide* (PAIR′-ə-sīd′)—the killing of either or both parents. Adjective?

_____

Lizzie Borden was accused of, and tried for, *parricide* in the 1890s, but was not convicted. A bit of doggerel that was popular at the time, and, so I have been told, little girls jumped rope to，went somewhat as follows：

> Lizzie Borden took an ax
> And gave her mother forty whacks—
> And when she saw what she had done，
> She gave her father forty-one.

(6) uxoricide——"杀妻(者)"。其形容词是什么？演变：拉丁语 uxor(妻子)加上-cide。

(7) mariticide——"杀夫(者)"。其形容词是什么？演变：拉丁语 maritus(丈夫)加上-cide。

(8) infanticide——"杀婴(者)"，杀害新生儿。其形容词是什么？演变：拉丁语 maritus(丈夫)加上-cide。

(9) genocide——"种族灭绝"，将一整个民族或者国家的人全部杀害。这个词相对新，是 1944 年由一个名为拉法尔·莱姆金的联合国官员制造出来的，用来指希特勒及其党羽谋杀犹太人和波兰人的罪行。其形容词是什么？演变：希腊语 genes(种族，类别)加-cide.

(10) parricide——杀自己父母中的一个或两个。其形容词是什么？

利兹·波登在 19 世纪 90 年代曾被指控谋杀自己的父母，但没有被定罪。那时流行一首打油诗，小女孩跳绳时会经常念，好像是这样的：

> 利兹·波登拿着把斧子，
> 猛砍他母亲四十下，
> 当她看到她做的这些，
> 她砍了她父亲四十一下。

REVIEW OF ETYMOLOGY
复习词源

PREFIX，ROOT，SUFFIX	MEANING	ENGLISH WORD
1. *sykon*	fig	_____
2. *phanein*	to show	_____
3. *dia-*	through	_____
4. *vir*	man（male）	_____
5. *pater*，*patris*	father	_____
6. *syn-*	with，together	_____
7. *onyma*	name	_____
8. *anti*	against	_____
9. *homos*	the same	_____
10. *phone*	sound	_____
11. *-ity*	noun suffix	_____
12. *-ism*	noun suffix	_____
13. *-al*	adjective suffix	_____
14. *-ic*	adjective suffix	_____
15. *archein*	to rule	_____
16. *-cide*	killing	_____
17. *mater*，*matris*	mother	_____
18. *alma*	soul	_____

19.	*-mony*	noun suffix	_____
20.	*sui*	of oneself	_____
21.	*frater*，*fratris*	brother	_____
22.	*soror*	sister	_____
23.	*homo*	person，human	_____
24.	*rex*，*regis*	king	_____
25.	*uxor*	wife	_____
26.	*maritus*	husband	_____
27.	*infans*，*infantis*	baby	_____
28.	*genos*	race，kind	_____

USING THE WORDS
单词应用

Can you pronounce the words?（Ⅰ）
你能读出这些单词吗?（Ⅰ）

1.	*martinetish*	mahr-tə-NET′-ish
2.	*sycophancy*	SIK′-ə-fən-see
3.	*sycophantic*	sik′-ə-FAN′-tik
4.	*diaphanous*	dī-AF′-ə-nəs
5.	*dilettanti*	dil′-ə-TAN′-tee
6.	*dilettantism*	dil-ə-TAN′-tiz-əm
7.	*dilettantish*	dil-ə-TAN′-tish
8.	*tyro*	TĪ′-rō
9.	*virtuoso*	vur′-choo-Ō′-sō
10.	*virtuosi*	vur′-choo-Ō′-see
11.	*termagant*	TUR′-mə-gənt
12.	*harridan*	HAIR′-ə-dən

Can you pronounce the words?（Ⅱ）
你能读出这些单词吗?（Ⅱ）

1.	*chauvinism*	SHŌ′-və-niz-əm
2.	*chauvinistic*	shō-və-NIS′-tik
3.	*patrimony*	PAT′-rə-mō-nee
4.	*patronymic*	pat′-rə-NIM′-ik
5.	*synonym*	SIN′-ə-nim
6.	*synonymous*	sə-NON′-ə-məs
7.	*antonym*	AN′-tə-nim
8.	*antonymous*	an-TON′-ə-məs

9. *homonym*   HOM′-ə-nim

10. *homonymous*   hə-MON′-ə-məs

11. *homophone*   HOM′-ə-fōn

12. *homophonous*   hə-MOF′-ə-nəs

Can you pronounce the words？（Ⅲ）

你能读出这些单词吗？（Ⅲ）

1. *paternity*   pə-TUR′-nə-tee

2. *paternal*   pə-TUR′-nəl

3. *paternalism*   pə-TUR′-nə-liz-əm

4. *paternalistic*   pə-turn′-ə-LIS′-tik

5. *patriarch*   PAY′-tree-ahrk′

6. *patriarchal*   pay′-tree-AHR′-kəl

7. *patriarchy*   PAY′-tree-ahr′-kee

8. *patricide*   PAT′-rə-sīd′

9. *patricidal*   pat′-rə-SĪ′-dəl

Can you pronounce the words？（Ⅳ）

你能读出这些单词吗？（Ⅳ）

1. *matriarch*   MAY′-tree-ahrk′

2. *matriarchy*   MAY′-tree-ahr′-kee

3. *matriarchal*   may′-tree-AHR′-kəl

4. *maternity*   mə-TUR′-nə-tee

5. *maternal*   mə-TURN′-əl

6. *matron*   MAY′-trən

7. *matronly*   MAY′-trən-lee

8. *alma mater*   AL′-mə MAY′-tər
           or AHL′-mə MAH′-tər

9. *matrimony*   MAT′-rə-mō-nee

10. *matrimonial*   mat-rə-MŌ′-nee-əl

11. *matricide*   MAT′-rə-sīd′

12. *matricidal*   mat-rə-SĪ′-dəl

Can you pronounce the words？（Ⅴ）

你能读出这些单词吗？（Ⅴ）

1. *suicide*   SŌO-ə-sīd′

2. *suicidal*   sōo-ə-SĪ′-dəl

3. *fratricide*   FRAT′-rə-sīd′

4. *fratricidal*   frat-rə-SĪ′-dəl

5. *sororicide*   sə-RAWR′-ə-sīd′

6. *sororicidal*   sə-rawr′-ə-SĪ′-dəl

7. *homicide*   HOM′-ə-sīd′

8. *homicidal*   hom′-ə-SĪ′-dəl

9. *regicide*   REJ′-ə-sīd′

10. *regicidal*   rej′-ə-SĪ′-dəl

Can you pronounce the words?（Ⅵ）

你能读出这些单词吗?（Ⅵ）

1. *uxoricide*   uk-SAWR′-ə-sīd′

2. *uxoricidal*   uk-sawr′-ə-SĪ′-dəl

3. *mariticide*   mə-RIT′-ə-sīd′

4. *mariticidal*   mə-rit′-ə-SĪ′-dəl

5. *infanticide*   in-FAN′-tə-sīd′

6. *infanticidal*   in-fan′-tə-SĪ′-dəl

7. *genocide*   JEN′-ə-sīd′

8. *genocidal*   jen′-ə-SĪ′-dəl

9. *parricide*   PAIR′-ə-sīd′

10. *parricidal*   pair′-ə-SĪ′-dəl

Can you work with the words?（Ⅰ）

你能灵活使用这些词汇了吗?（Ⅰ）

1. sycophancy   a. murder of one's father

2. dilettantism   b. excessive patriotism

3. chauvinism   c. murder of one's ruler

4. patrimony   d. inheritance from one's father

5. patricide   e. murder of one's sister

6. matricide   f. murder of one's brother

7. fratricide   g. murder of a person

8. sororicide   h. toadying

9. homicide   i. murder of one's mother

10. regicide   j. dabbling

KEY：1-h，2-j，3-b，4-d，5-a，6-i，7-f，8-e，9-g，10-c

Can you work with the words?（Ⅱ）
你能灵活使用这些词汇了吗？（Ⅱ）

1. uxoricide	a. marriage
2. infanticide	b. killing of one's child
3. genocide	c. fatherhood
4. matrimony	d. mother-ruler
5. matriarch	e. killing of one's wife
6. maternity	f. older woman
7. matron	g. one's school or college
8. alma mater	h. motherhood
9. paternity	i. old man in governing position
10. patriarch	j. killing of whole groups of people

KEY：1-e，2-b，3-j，4-a，5-d，6-h，7-f，8-g，9-c，10-i

Can you work with the words?（Ⅲ）
你能灵活使用这些词汇了吗？（Ⅲ）

1. parricide	a. catering to people of power or position
2. patronymic	b. name from father
3. chauvinistic	c. dabblers
4. sycophantic	d. an accomplished musician
5. diaphanous	e. filmy, gauzy
6. dilettanti	f. blatantly overpatriotic
7. tyro	g. loud-mouthed woman
8. virtuoso	h. a beginner
9. termagant	i. killing of either or both parents

KEY：1-i，2-b，3-f，4-a，5-e，6-c，7-h，8-d，9-g

Can you work with the words?（Ⅳ）
你能灵活使用这些词汇了吗？（Ⅳ）

1. synonyms	a. system in which those in power have a father-child relafionship with subordinates
2. antonyms	b. like a strict disciplinarian
3. homonyms	c. self-killing

4. paternalism   d. fatherly

5. suicide   e. referring to or like, those who "play at" an art

6. mariticide   f. words that sound alike but are spelled differently and have unrelated meanings

7. martinetish   g. words of similar meaning

8. dilettantish   h. referring to, or like, an older woman

9. paternal   i. husband-killing

10. matronly   j. words of opposite meaning

KEY：1-g, 2-j, 3-f, 4-a, 5-c, 6-i, 7-b, 8-e, 9-d, 10-h

Can you work with the words? (Ⅴ)
你能灵活使用这些词汇了吗?

1. harridan   a. motherly

2. homophones   b. similar in meaning

3. maternal   c. referring to a system in which older men are in power

4. matrimonial   d. the same in sound but not in spelling or meaning

5. synonymous   e. likely to kill; referring to the killing of a person

6. antonymous   f. referring to a system in which older women are in power

7. homonymous   g. virago

8. patriarchal   h. opposite in meaning

9. matriarchal   i. referring to marriage

10. homicidal   j. words that sound the same

KEY：1-g, 2-j, 3-a, 4-i, 5-b, 6-h, 7-d, 8-c, 9-f, 10-e

Do you understand the words?
你对这些词汇是否已经透彻地理解?

1. Does a *sycophantic* attitude show sincere admiration?   YES   NO

2. Is a *diaphanous* gown revealing?   YES   NO

3. Does *dilettantism* show firmness and   YES   NO
   tenacity?

4. Is a *tyro* particularly skillful?   YES   NO

5. Is a violin *virtuoso* an accomplished   YES   NO
   musician?

6. Is a *termagant* a pleasant person?   YES   NO

7. Does *chauvinism* show modesty?   YES   NO

8. Does a substantial *patrimony* obviate   YES   NO
   financial insecurity?

9. If you know a person's *patronymic* can   YES   NO
   you deduce his father's name?

10. Is a *patriarch* a male?   YES   NO

11. Does a *matriarch* have a good deal of power?   YES   NO

12. Does *fratricide* mean murder of   YES   NO
    one's sister?

13. Did the assassin of Abraham Lincoln   YES   NO
    commit *regicide*?

14. Do dictators and tyrants sometimes   YES   NO
    commit *genocide*?

15. Are an *uxoricidal* husband and his   YES   NO
    mariticidal wife likely to have a peaceful
    and affectionate marriage?

KEY：1-no, 2-yes, 3-no, 4-no, 5-yes, 6-no, 7-no, 8-yes, 9-yes, 10-yes, 11-yes, 12-no, 13-yes, 14-yes, 15-no

---

Can you recall the words? (Ⅰ)
你能够写出这些词汇吗？(Ⅰ)

1. father-killing (*noun*)   1. P _____

2. wife-killing (*noun*)   2. U _____

3. mature woman   3. M _____

4. toadying to people of influence   4. S _____
   (*adj.*)

5. skilled musician   5. V _____

6. exaggerated patriotism   6. C _____

7. turbulent female (three   7. T _____
   words)   *or* H _____

                                    or V _____

8. name derived from father's name   8. P _____

9. powerful father figure in a ruling position   9. P _____

10. powerful mother figure in a ruling position   10. M _____

11. motherly   11. M _____

12. motherhood   12. M _____

13. marriage   13. M _____

14. one's school or college   14. A _____

15. attitude of catering to wealth or prestige (*noun*)   15. S _____

16. killing of a race or nation   16. G _____

17. dabbling in the fine arts (*noun*)   17. D _____

18. a beginner in a field   18. T _____

19. plural of *virtuoso* (Italian form)   19. V _____

20. having an attitude of excessive patriotism (*adj.*)   20. C _____

21. inheritance from father   21. P _____

22. sheer, transparent   22. D _____

23. mother-killing (*noun*)   23. M _____

24. brother-killing (*noun*)   24. F _____

25. sister-killing (*noun*)   25. S _____

26. killing of a human being   26. H _____

27. killing of one's ruler   27. R _____

28. killing of a baby   28. I _____

29. killing of one's husband   29. M _____

30. killing of either parent or of both parents   30. P _____

KEY：1-patricide，2-uxoricide，3-matron，4-sycophantic，5-virtuoso，6-chauvinism，7-termagant，harridan，virago，8-patronymic，9-patriarch，10-matriarch，11-maternal，12-maternity，13-matrimony，14-alma mater，15-sycophancy，16-genocide，17-dilettantism，18-tyro，19-virtuosi，20-chauvinistic，21-patrimony，22-diaphanous，23-matricide，24-fratricide，25-sororicide，26-homicide，27-regicide，28-infanticide，29-mariticide，30-parricide

Can you recall the words? (Ⅱ)

你能够写出这些词汇吗?（Ⅱ）

1. words of similar meaning	1. S _____ s
2. words of opposite meaning	2. A _____ s
3. words of the same sound	3. H _____ s
	or H _____ s
4. fatherly	4. P _____
5. protective and fatherly toward one's subordinates (*adj.*)	5. P _____
6. older woman	6. M _____
7. self-destructive	7. S _____
8. meaning the same (*adj.*)	8. S _____
9. having opposite meanings (*adj.*)	9. A _____
10. sounding the same but spelled differently (*adj.*)	10. H _____
	or H _____

KEY：1-synonym，2-antonym，3-homonym *or* homophone，4-paternal，5-paternalistic，6-matron，7-suicidal，8-synonymous，9-antonymous，10-homonymous *or* homophonous

(*End of Session 29*)

SESSION 30
第 30 节

ORIGINS AND RELATED WORDS
词源及相关词汇

1. brothers and sisters, wives and husbands
兄弟姐妹,妻子丈夫

Frater, brother; *soror*, sister; *uxor*, wife; and *maritus*, husband—these roots are the source of a number of additional English words:

Frater,"兄弟"; soror,"姐妹"; uxor,"妻子"; maritus,"丈夫"——英语中很多单词来自这些词根。

(1) to *fraternize* (FRAT'-ər-nīz')—etymologically, to have a brotherly relationship (with). This verb may be used to indicate social intercourse between people, irrespective of sex, as in, "Members of the faculty often *fraternized* after school hours."

Additionally, and perhaps more commonly, there may be the implication of having a social relationship with one's subordinates in an organization, or even with one's so-called inferiors, as in, "The president of the college was reluctant to *fraternize* with faculty members, preferring to keep all her contacts with them on an exclusively professional basis"; or as in, "The artist enjoyed *fraternizing* with thieves, drug addicts, prostitutes, and pimps, partly out of social perversity, partly to find interesting faces to put in his paintings."

The verb also gained a new meaning during and after World War II, when soldiers of occupying armies had sexual relations with the women of conquered countries, as in, "Military personnel were strictly forbidden to *fraternize* with the enemy." (How euphemistic can you get?)

Can you write the noun form of *fraternize*? _____.

(1) to fraternize——从词源角度看,意为"建立兄弟关系",这个动词也可以描述人们之间的社会关系,和性别无关,如"Members of the faculty often fraternized after school hours."(很多教职员在课后经常厮混在一起)。

另外,这个单词更为普遍的用法可能是表示在一个组织中的从属关系,以及和下属部门的关系,如"The president of the college was reluctant to fraternize with faculty members, preferring to keep all her contacts with them on an exclusively professional basis"(大学校长不太愿意和教职工的关系过于亲密,她更愿意和员工的关系限于工作层面);或者如"The artist enjoyed fraternizing with thieves, drug addicts, prostitutes, and pimps, partly out of social perversity, partly to find interesting faces to put in his paintings."(这位画家愿意和盗贼、吸毒者、妓女、皮条客等打成一片,部分原因是出于其执拗的性情,部分原因是希望捕捉到他们生动的表情和面貌,画在自己的作品中)。

这个动词在第二次世界大战中和战后有了新的涵义,可用来指占领的军队和被占领国家的妇女发生性关系,如"Military personnel were strictly forbidden to fraternize with the enemy."(部队人员严禁与敌人发生亲密关系。)(你看懂这种委婉说法了吗?)

你能写出 fraternize 名词形式吗?

(2) *fraternal* (frə-TUR'-nəl)—brotherly. The word also designates *non-*

identical（twins）.

（3）*fraternity*（frə-TUR'-nə-tee）——a men's organization in a high school or college, often labeled with Greek letters（the Gamma Delta Epsilon *Fraternity*）; or any group of people of similar interests or profession（the medical *fraternity*, the financial *fraternity*）.

（4）*sorority*（sə-RAWR'-ə-tee）—a women's organization in high school or college, again usually Greek-lettered; or any women's social club.

（5）*uxorious*（uk-SAWR'-ee-əs）—an adjective describing a man who excessively, even absurdly, caters to, dotes on, worships, and submits to the most outlandish or outrageous demands of, his wife. This word is *not* synonymous with *henpecked*, as the henpecked husband is dominated by his wife, perhaps because of his own fear or weakness, while the *uxorious* husband is dominated only by his neurosis, and quite likely the wife finds his *uxoriousness*（uk-SAWR'-ee-əs-nəs）comical or a pain in the neck.（There can, indeed, be too much of a good thing!）

（6）*uxorial*—pertaining to, characteristic of, or befitting, a wife, as *uxorial* duties, privileges, attitudes, etc.

（7）*marital*（MAIR'-ə-təl）—etymologically, pertaining or referring to, or characteristic of, a husband; but the meaning has changed to include the marriage relationship of both husband *and* wife（don't ever let anyone tell you that our language is not sexist!）, as *marital* duties, obligations, privileges, arguments, etc. Hence *extramarital* is literally *outside the marriage*, as in *extramarital* affairs（hanky-panky with someone other than one's spouse）. And *premarital*（Latin prefix *pre-*, before）describes events that occur before a planned marriage, as *premarital* sex, a *premarital* agreement as to the division of property, etc.

（2）fraternal——兄弟的。这个词也用来指不完全一样的（双胞胎）。

（3）fraternity——在高中或大学的男生组织，经常用希腊字母写出来（the Gamma Delta Epsilon Fraternity）；或具有类似兴趣或专业的群体（如 the medical fraternity, the financial fraternity）。

（4）sorority——在高中或大学的女生组织，也经常用希腊字母拼写，也可指任何女生的社会团体。

（5）uxorious——是一个形容词，用来描述过度地甚至荒唐地顺从、溺爱、崇拜或无条件服从妻子任何要求的男人。这个词和 henpecked 并不是同义词，一个"henpecked husband"只是因为害怕自己的妻子，或者软弱而被妻子主导，而一个"uxorious husband"是被他的神经机能病所主导，妻子很可能觉得丈夫这种"uxoriousness"很滑稽可笑或者很讨厌（的确，有些事情过犹不及）。

（6）uxorial——和妻子相关的，妻子的。如妻子的责任、权益、态度等。

（7）marital——从词源上看，marital 意为"丈夫的"；但这个单词逐渐演变可指婚姻关系（不要相信任何人宣称的、我们的语言不是性别主义的！），如婚姻义务，责任，益处，争论等。因此，extramarital 字面上的意思就是"婚姻之外的"，如 extramarital affairs（婚外情）。premarital（拉丁语中的前缀 pre-，在……之前），指发生在"计划的婚姻"之前的事，如 premarital sex（婚前性行为），a premarital agreement as to the division of property（婚前财产协议）等。

2. of cabbages and kings（without the cabbage）

白菜和国王的（没有"cabbage"）

Rex, *regis* is Latin for *king*. *Tyrannosaurus rex* was the king（i. e., the largest）of the dinosaurs（etymologically, "king of the tyrant lizards"）. Dogs are often named *Rex* to fool them into thinking they are kings rather than slaves. And *regal* (REE′-gəl) is royal, or fit for a king, hence magnificent, stately, imperious, splendid, etc., as in *regal* bearing or manner, a *regal* mansion, a *regal* reception, etc. The noun is *regality* (rə-GAL′-ə-tee).

Regalia (rə-GAYL′-yə), a plural noun, designated the emblems or insignia or dress of a king, and now refers to any impressively formal clothes; or, more commonly, to the decorations, insignia, or uniform of a rank, position, office, social club, etc. "The Shriners were dressed in full *regalia*", "The five-star general appeared in full *regalia*", etc.

rex, regis 在拉丁语中意为"国王",tyrannosaurus rex 是"恐龙的国王"(意即"最大的"),源于"king of the tyrant lizards"(邪恶的蜥蜴之王)。狗崽被起名为 Rex,就是为了让它觉得它是国王而非奴隶。regal,意为"皇家的",或"为国王的",意味着高贵,庄严,专横,华美等,如 regal bearing or manner,a regal mansion,a regal reception。名词形式是 regality。

复数形式是 regalia (rə-GAYL′-yə),指国王的标志、徽章或者衣服。现在指令人印象深刻的正式服装。更普遍的用法是指装饰物,徽章,或者有阶位高低的、官员,社会俱乐部的制服等。"The Shriners were dressed in full regalia"(圣地兄弟会的会员们一身盛装),"The five-star general appeared in full regalia"(五星级上将一身戎装)等。

3. "madness" of all sorts

各种"疯狂"

The *monomaniac* develops an abnormal obsession in respect to one particular thing (Greek *monos*, one), but is otherwise normal. The obsession itself, or the obsessiveness, is *monomania* (mon′-ə-MAY′-nee-ə), the adjective is *monomaniacal* (mon′-ə-mə-NĪ′-ə-kəl). *Monomaniacal*, like the adjective forms of various other manias, is tricky to pronounce—practice carefully to make sure you can say it correctly without stuttering.

monomaniac 是指变态地着迷于某种事物的人,但在其他方面却是个正常的人。迷恋的状态就是 monomania,其形容词是 monomaniacal。像 manias 所演化的其他的形容词一样,monomaniacal 不太容易发音——认真练习,以使你能正确流畅地读出来。

Psychology recognizes other abnormal states, all designating obsessions, and built on Greek *mania*, madness.

(1) *dipsomania* (dip′-sə-MAY′-nee-ə)—morbid compulsion to keep on absorbing alcoholic beverages (Greek *dipsa*, thirst). The *dipsomaniac* has been defined as the person for whom one drink is too many, a thousand not enough. Recent investigations suggest that *dipsomania*, or alcoholism, may not necessarily be caused by anxieties or frustrations, but possibly by a metabolic or physiological disorder.

Adjective: *dipsomaniacal* (dip′-sə-mə-NĪ′-ə-kəl).

心理学还研究另外一些与迷恋有关的非正常状态,这些词也都基于希腊语词根 mania,"疯狂"。

(1) dipsomania——"嗜酒症",对含酒精饮料有着病态的强烈欲望(希腊语 dipsa 是"饥渴"的意思)。dipsomaniac 被定义为嗜酒徒,对他们来说,一杯就会醉,但一千杯也不嫌多。最近的研究表明,嗜酒症不一定由焦虑或者挫败感引发,而可能由新陈代谢或者生理紊乱引发。

形容词形式:dipsomaniacal。

(2) *kleptomania* (klep′-tə-MAY′-nee-ə)—morbid compulsion to steal, not from

any economic motive, but simply because the urge to take another's possessions is irresistible. The *kleptomaniac* (Greek *klepte*, thief) may be wealthy, and yet be an obsessive shoplifter. The *kleptomaniac*, for reasons that psychologists are still arguing about, is more often a female than a male, and may pinch her best friend's valueless trinket, or a cheap ashtray or salt shaker from a restaurant, not because she wants, let alone needs, the article, but because she apparently can't help herself; she gets carried away. (When she arrives home, she may toss it in a drawer with other loot, and never look at it again.)

Can you write (and *correctly* pronounce) the adjective? _____.

（2）kleptomania——"窃盗癖"，对偷盗有着病态的强烈欲望。这种欲望不具有任何经济动机，仅仅是因为无法压抑想要盗窃的欲望。kleptomaniac（希腊语 klepte，"贼"）可能很富有，但是痴迷于扒窃，其心理动机仍然没有定论，并且常常女性比男性多，她可能会盗窃最好朋友不值钱的小饰品，或便宜的托盘，或饭馆里盛盐的小瓶子，不是因为她想要，更不是需要，仅仅是因为她无法控制自己。她会带走。（到家后，她也许会把偷来的东西塞进抽屉里，和其他偷来的东西放在一起，然后再也不会看它一眼。）

你能写出（并正确读出）它的形容词形式吗？

（3）*pyromania* (pī'-rə-MAY'-nee-ə)——morbid compulsion to set fires. *Pyromania* should not be confused with *incendiarism* (in-SEN'-dee-ə-riz-əm), which is the malicious and deliberate burning of another's property, and is *not* a compulsive need to see the flames and enjoy the thrill of the heat and the smoke. Some *pyromaniacs* join volunteer fire companies, often heroically putting out the very blazes they themselves have set. An *incendiary* (in-SEN'-dee-air-ee) is antisocial, and usually sets fires for revenge. Either of these two dangerous characters is called, colloquially, a "firebug."

In law, setting fire to another's, or to one's own, property for the purpose of economic gain (such as the collection of the proceeds of an insurance policy) is called *arson* (AHR'-sən) and is a felony. The *pyromaniac* sets fire for the thrill; the *incendiary* for revenge; the *arsonist* (AHR'-sə-nist) for money.

Pyromania is built on Greek *pyros*, fire; *incendiarism* on Latin *incendo*, *incensus*, to set fire; *arson* on Latin *ardo*, *arsus*, to burn.

Can you write, and pronounce, the adjective form of *pyromaniac*? _____.

（3）pyromania——"纵火癖"，对纵火有着病态的强烈欲望。注意不要混淆 pyromania 和 incendiarism，后者虽然也是纵火，却是恶意烧毁他人财物，并不受病态精神状态的驱使。一些 pyromaniacs 会自愿加入救火队，经常英勇地扑灭他们自己放的火。而 incendiary 的行为则是反社会的，经常为了报复而纵火。有这两种危险性格特质的人，都可以用一个比较直白的词"firebug"来指代。

法律上，放火烧毁他人或者自己的财产以谋取经济利益的行为被称为 arson，"纵火罪"，属于重罪，例如想从某种保险政策谋利。这样的罪犯被称为 arsonist，"纵火犯"。简而言之，pyromaniac 纵火是要陶醉其中；incendiary 为报仇；arsonist 为钱财。

pyromania 是由希腊语 pyros（意为"火"）演变而来；incendiarism 是由拉丁语 incendo, incensus，（意为"放火"）演变而来；arson 是由拉丁语 ardo, arsus，（意为"点燃"）演变而来。

你能写出并读出 pyromaniac 的形容词形式吗？

（4）*megalomania* (meg'-ə-lə-MAY'-nee-ə)——morbid delusions of grandeur, power, importance, godliness, etc. Jokes accusing the heads of governments of *megalomania* are common. Here's an old chestnut from the forties:

Churchill, Roosevelt, and Stalin were talking about their dreams.

Churchill: I dreamed last night that God had made me *Prime Minister* of the whole world.

Roosevelt: I dreamed that God had made me *President* of the whole world.

Stalin: How could you gentlemen have such dreams? *I* didn't dream of offering you those positions!

(4) megalomania——"自大狂",对自己的伟大、重要性和神圣性等有病态的妄想。谴责患有自大狂的政府首脑的笑话为数不少,这里有一个来自 20 世纪 40 年代的、广为流传的段子:

丘吉尔、罗斯福和斯大林在谈论他们的梦想。

丘吉尔:昨晚我梦见上帝使我成为了整个世界的首相。

罗斯福:我梦见上帝使我成为整个世界的总统。

斯大林:你们怎么能做这样的梦? 我并没有梦见自己给你们提供这样的职位!

Hitler, Napoleon, and Alexander the Great have been called *megalomaniacs*—all three certainly had delusions about their invincibility.

Can you write (and pronounce correctly) the adjective derived from *megalomaniac*? _____.

Megalomania is built on Greek *megas*, great, big, large, plus *mania*.

Can you think of the word for what someone speaks through to make the *sound* (phone) of his voice *greater*? _____.

希特勒、拿破仑、亚历山大大帝都曾经被称为 megalomaniacs——三个人都有"自己是不可战胜"的妄想。

根据 megalomaniac,你能写出(或者正确读出)其形容词形式吗?

megalomania 是由希腊语 megas(意为"大的,巨大的")加上 mania 构成。

你能想起某个单词吗——一些人通过说这个单词以他的声音听起来"更棒"?

(5) *nymphomania* (nim'-fə-MAY'-nee-ə)—morbid, incessant, uncontrollable, and intense desire, on the part of a female, for sexual intercourse (from Greek *nymphe*, bride, plus *mania*).

The person? _____.

The adjective? _____.

(5) nymphomania——指女性病态的、无止境的、强烈的性交欲望(由希腊语 nymphe,意为"新娘",加上 mania 构成)。

具有这种精神特征的人叫什么?

其形容词是什么?

(6) *satyromania* (sə-teer'-ə-MAY'-nee-ə)—the same morbid, incessant, etc. desire on the part of a male (from Greek *satyros*, satyr, plus *mania*).

The person? _____.

The adjective? _____.

A *satyr* (SAY'-tər) was a mythological Greek god, notorious for lechery. He had horns, pointed ears, and the legs of a goat; the rest of him was in human form. *Satyromania* is also called *satyriasis* (sat'-ə-RĪ'-ə-sis).

(6) satyromania——指男性病态的、无止境的、强烈的性交欲望（由希腊语 satyros，意为"性欲极强的男人"，加上 mania 构成）。

具有这种精神特征的人叫什么？

其形容词是什么？

satyr 是希腊神话中的神，以其好色而臭名昭著。他有角、尖耳和山羊腿；身体的其他部分则是人形。satyromania 也可称为 satyriasis。

4. and now phobias

各种恐惧症

So much for *maniacs*. There is another side to the coin. Just as personality disorders can cause morbid *attraction* toward certain things or acts (stealing, fire, power, sex, etc.), so also other emotional ills can cause violent or morbid *repulsions* to certain conditions, things, or situations. There are people who have irrational and deep-seated dread of cats, dogs, fire, the number thirteen, snakes, thunder or lightning, various colors, and so on almost without end. Such morbid dread or fear is called, in the language of psychology, a *phobia*, and we might pause to investigate the three most common ones. These are:

各种病态的狂热讲完了，现在看看与其相反的一面。人格错乱能够导致人对某种事物或者行为的病态痴迷（对偷窃、纵火、权力、性等等），其他情绪问题也同样能够使人对某些情况、事物或者境遇产生暴力或者病态的反感。有些人对猫、狗、火、数字 13、蛇、雷电、彩色等等不计其数的事物有着荒谬的、根深蒂固的恐惧。从精神病学角度，这样的恐惧被称为 phobia。我们现在需要停下来研究三个最常见的词汇，它们是：

(1) *claustrophobia* (klaw'-strə-FŌ'-bee-ə)—morbid dread of being physically hemmed in, of enclosed spaces, of crowds, etc. From Latin *claustrum*, enclosed place, plus Greek *phobia*, morbid fear. The person: *claustrophobe* (KLAW'-strə-fōb'). Adjective: *claustrophobic* (klaw'-strə-FŌ'-bik).

(1) claustrophobia——"闭室恐怖症"，对身处封闭的空间、人群感到恐惧。由拉丁语 claustrum（意为"封闭的地方"）加上希腊语 phobia（意为"病态的恐惧"）构成。指代人时为：claustrophobe。形容词为：claustrophobic。

(2) *agoraphobia* (ag'-ə-rə-FŌ'-bee-ə)—morbid dread of open space, the reverse of *claustrophobia*. People suffering from *agoraphobia* prefer to stay shut in their homes as much as possible, and become panic-stricken in such places as open fields, large public buildings, airport terminals, etc. From Greek *agora*, market place, plus *phobia*.

The person? _____.

The adjective? _____.

(2) agoraphobia——"旷野恐怖症"，与 claustrophobia 相反。患有 agoraphobia 的人会尽量把自己关在家里，在空旷的田野、机场航站楼等大型公共建筑等地会惊慌失措。由希腊语 agora（意为"市场"）加 phobia 构成。

具有这种精神特征的人叫什么？

其形容词是什么？

(3) *acrophobia* (ak'-rə-FŌ'-bee-ə)—morbid dread of high places. The victims of this fear will not climb ladders or trees, or stand on tops of furniture. They refuse to go onto the roof of a building or look out the window of one of the higher floors. From Greek *akros*, highest, plus *phobia*.

The person? _____.

The adjective? _____.

（3）acrophobia——"恐高症"。恐高症患者无法爬梯子或者爬树，无法站在家具顶端。他们拒绝登上建筑屋顶或者从较高楼层向外望。由希腊语 akros(意为"最高的")加 phobia 构成。

具有这种精神特征的人叫什么？

其形容词是什么？

REVIEW OF ETYMOLOGY
复习词源

PREFIX, ROOT, SUFFIX	MEANING	ENGLISH WORD
1. *frater*, *fratris*	brother	_____
2. *soror*	sister	_____
3. *uxor*	wife	_____
4. *maritus*	husband	_____
5. *rex*, *regis*	king	_____
6. *mania*	madness	_____
7. *monos*	one	_____
8. *-ac*	noun suffix, "one who"	_____
9. *-al*	adjective suffix	_____
10. *dipsa*	thirst	_____
11. *klepte*	thief	_____
12. *pyros*	fire	_____
13. *incendo*, *incensus*	to set fire	_____
14. *ardo*, *arsus*	to burn	_____
15. *mega*	great, large, big	_____
16. *phone*	sound	_____
17. *satyros*	satyr	_____
18. *nymphe*	bride	_____
19. *claustrum*	enclosed place	_____
20. *agora*	market place	_____
21. *akros*	highest	_____
22. *-ic*	adjective suffix	_____
23. *phobia*	morbid dread	_____
24. *pre-*	before	_____
25. *extra-*	outside	_____

USING THE WORDS
单词应用

Can you pronounce the words? (Ⅰ)
你能读出这些单词吗? (Ⅰ)

1. *fraternize*	FRAT′-ər-nīz′
2. *fraternization*	frat′-ər-nə-ZAY′-shən
3. *fraternal*	frə-TUR′-nəl
4. *fraternity*	frə-TUR′-nə-tee
5. *sorority*	sə-RAWR′-ə-tee
6. *uxorious*	uk-SAWR′-ee-əs
7. *uxorial*	uk-SAWR′-ee-əl
8. *marital*	MAIR′-ə-təl
9. *extramarital*	ek′-strə-MAIR′-ə-təl
10. *premarital*	pree-MAIR′-ə-təl
11. *regal*	REE′-gəl
12. *regality*	rə-GAL′-ə-tee
13. *regalia*	rə-GAYL′-yə

Can you work with the words? (Ⅰ)
你能灵活使用这些词汇了吗? (Ⅰ)

1. fraternize	a. pertaining to, characteristic of, or befitting, a wife
2. fraternal	b. outside the marriage
3. sorority	c. kingly, royal; splendid, stately, magnificent, etc.
4. uxorious	d. referring to marriage
5. uxorial	e. before marriage
6. marital	f. socialize
7. extramarital	g. excessively indulgent to, or doting on, one's wife
8. premarital	h. brotherly
9. regal	i. badges, insignia, dress, etc. of rank or office
10. regalia	j. sisterhood

KEY: 1-f, 2-h, 3-j, 4-g, 5-a, 6-d, 7-b, 8-e, 9-c, 10-i

Can you pronounce the words?（Ⅱ）

你能读出这些单词吗？（Ⅱ）

1.	*monomania*	mon′-ə-MAY′-nee-ə
2.	*monomaniac*	mon′-ə-MAY′-nee-ak
3.	*monomaniacal*	mon′-ə-mə-NĪ′-ə-kəl
4.	*dipsomania*	dip′-sə-MAY′-nee-ə
5.	*dipsomaniac*	dip′-sə-MAY′-nee-ak
6.	*dipsomaniacal*	dip′-sə-mə-NĪ′-ə-kəl
7.	*kleptomania*	klep′-tə-MAY′-nee-ə
8.	*kleptomaniac*	klep′-tə-MAY′-nee-ak
9.	*kleptomaniacal*	klep′-tə-mə-NĪ′-ə-kəl
10.	*pyromania*	pī′-rə-MAY′-nee-ə
11.	*pyromaniac*	pī′-rə-MAY′-nee-ak
12.	*pyromaniacal*	pī′-rə-mə-NĪ′-ə-kəl

Can you work with the words?（Ⅱ）

你能灵活使用这些词汇了吗？（Ⅱ）

1. monomania	a.	obsession for alcohol
2. dipsomania	b.	obsession for setting fires
3. kleptomania	c.	obsession in one area
4. pyromania	d.	obsession for thievery

KEY：1-c，2-a，3-d，4-b

Can you pronounce the words?（Ⅲ）

你能读出这些单词吗？（Ⅲ）

1.	*incendiarism*	in-SEN′-dee-ə-riz-əm
2.	*incendiary*	in-SEN′-dee-air-ee
3.	*arson*	AHR′-sən
4.	*arsonist*	AHR′-sə-nist
5.	*megalomania*	meg′-ə-lə-MAY′-nee-ə
6.	*megalomaniac*	meg′-ə-lə-MAY′-nee-ak
7.	*megalomaniacal*	meg′-ə-lə-mə-NĪ′-ə-kəl
8.	*nymphomania*	nim′-fə-MAY′-nee-ə
9.	*nymphomaniac*	nim′-fə-MAY′-nee-ak
10.	*nymphomaniacal*	nim′-fə-mə-NĪ′-ə-kəl
11.	*satyromania*	sə-teer′-ə-MAY′-nee-ə

12. *satyromaniacal*   sə-teer'-ə-mə-NĪ'-ə-kəl

13. *satyriasis*   sat'-ə-RĪ'-ə-sis

Can you work with the words? (Ⅲ)
你能灵活使用这些词汇了吗？（Ⅲ）

1. incendiarism
2. arson
3. megalomania
4. nymphomania
5. satyromania
6. claustrophobia
7. agoraphobia

8. acrophobia

a. delusions of grandeur
b. compulsive sexual needs on the part of a male
c. morbid dread of open spaces
d. morbid dread of enclosed places
e. malicious setting of fires, as for revenge, etc.
f. morbid dread of heights
g. compulsive sexual needs on the part of a female

h. felony of setting fire for economic gain

KEY：1-e，2-h，3-a，4-g，5-b，6-d，7-c，8-f

Can you pronounce the words? (Ⅳ)
你能读出这些单词吗？（Ⅳ）

1. *claustrophobia*   klaw'-strə-FŌ'-bee-ə
2. *claustrophobe*   KLAW'-strə-fōb'
3. *claustrophobic*   klaw'-strə-FŌ'-bik
4. *agoraphobia*   ag'-ə-rə-FŌ'-bee-ə
5. *agoraphobe*   AG'-ə-rə-fōb'
6. *agoraphobic*   ag'-ə-rə-FŌ'-bik
7. *acrophobia*   ak'-rə-FŌ'-bee-ə
8. *acrophobe*   AK'-rə-fōb'
9. *acrophobic*   ak'-rə-FŌ'-bik

Can you work with the words? (Ⅳ)
你能灵活使用这些词汇了吗？（Ⅳ）

1. incendiary
2. arsonist
3. megalomaniac
4. nymphomaniac
5. satyriasis
6. claustrophobe
7. agoraphobe

a. one who has delusions of greatness or power
b. male compulsion for sexual intercourse
c. one who fears shut-in or crowded places
d. one who sets fires out of malice
e. one who fears heights
f. one who fears large or open spaces
g. one who sets fires for economic and illegal profit

8. acrophobe   h. woman with compulsive, incessant sexual desire

KEY: 1-d, 2-g, 3-a, 4-h, 5-b, 6-c, 7-f, 8-e

Do you understand the words?
你对这些词汇是否已经透彻地理解?

1. Is a *sorority* a men's organization?   YES   NO
2. Is an *uxorious* husband likely to be
   psychologically dependent on his wife?   YES   NO
3. Are *extramarital* affairs adulterous?   YES   NO
4. Do VIPs often receive *regal* treatment?   YES   NO
5. Is an admiral of the fleet in *regalia*
   informally dressed?   YES   NO
6. Do *monomaniacal* people have varied
   interests?   YES   NO
7. Can a *dipsomaniac* safely indulge in
   social drinking?   YES   NO
8. Do people of *pyromaniacal* tendencies
   fear fire?   YES   NO
9. Is *incendiarism* an uncontrollable
   impulse?   YES   NO
10. Does an *arsonist* expect a reward for
    his actions?   YES   NO
11. Is it necessary to seduce a
    nymphomaniac?   YES   NO
12. Do *megalomaniacs* have low opinions
    of themselves?   YES   NO
13. Is a *satyromaniac* lecherous?   YES   NO
14. Are *satyriasis* and *asceticism*
    compatible conditions?   YES   NO
15. Does a *claustrophobe* enjoy cramped
    quarters?   YES   NO
16. Would an *agoraphobe* be comfortable
    in a small cell-like room?   YES   NO
17. Does an *acrophobe* enjoy
    mountain-climbing?   YES   NO

KEY：1-no，2-yes，3-yes，4-yes，5-no，6-no，7-no，8-no，9-no，10-yes，11-no，12-no，13-yes，14-no，15-no，16-yes，17-no

Can you recall the words?
你能够写出这些词汇吗？

1. to socialize	1. F _____
2. excessively indulgent to, and doting on, one's wife	2. U _____
3. full dress, with ribbons, insignia, badges of office, etc.	3. R _____
4. obsessed in one area or with one overriding interest (*adj.*)	4. M _____
5. having a compulsion to set fires (*adj.*)	5. P _____
6. having a psychological compulsion to steal (*adj.*)	6. K _____
7. person who sets fires for revenge	7. I _____
8. felony of putting the torch to property for economic profit	8. A _____
9. obsessive need for sexual gratification by a male	9. S _____ *or* S _____
10. morbidly dreading enclosed or cramped places (*adj.*)	10. C _____
11. morbidly dreading heights (*adj.*)	11. A _____
12. morbidly dreading wide-open spaces (*adj.*)	12. A _____
13. having delusions of grandeur or power (*adj.*)	13. M _____
14. referring to a female who obsessively needs sexual gratification (*adj.*)	14. N _____
15. alcoholism	15. D _____
16. stealing for thrills or out of psychological compulsion (*adj.*)	16. K _____
17. brotherly	17. F _____
18. characteristic of, or befitting, a wife	18. U _____

19. referring to, characteristic of, or involved in, the matrimonial relationship
19. M _____

20. kingly; royal; splendid; etc.
20. R _____

21. outside the marriage (*adj.*)
21. E _____

22. before marriage (*adj.*)
22. P _____

KEY: 1-fraternize, 2-uxorious, 3-regalia, 4-monomaniacal, 5-pyromaniacal, 6-kleptomaniacal, 7-incendiary, 8-arson, 9-satyromania *or* satyriasis, 10-claustrophobic, 11-acrophobic, 12-agoraphobic, 13-megalomaniacal, 14-nymphomaniacal, 15-dipsomania, 16-kleptomaniacal, 17-fraternal, 18-uxorial, 19-marital, 20-regal, 21-extramarital, 22-premarital

(End of Session 30)

SESSION 31
第 31 节

ORIGINS AND RELATED WORDS
词源及相关词汇

1. no reverence
漠视一切

The *iconoclast* sneers at convention and tradition, attempts to expose our cherished beliefs, our revered traditions, or our stereotypical thinking as shams and myths. H. L. Mencken was the great *iconoclast* of the 1920s; Tom Wolfe (*The Kandy-Kolored Tangerine-Flake Streamline Baby*), of the 1960s.

Adolescence is that confused and rebellious time of life in which *iconoclasm* (i-KON′-ə-klaz′-əm) is quite normal—indeed the adolescent who is not *iconoclastic* (i-kon′-ə-KLAST′-ik) to some degree might be considered either immature or maladjusted. The words are from *eikon*, a religious image, plus *klaein*, to break. *Iconoclasm* is not of course restricted to religion.

iconoclast 是鄙视规矩和传统的人,他常常试图揭示出我们一直习以为常的信念、我们尊敬的传统、或我们常规的思想,不过是种假象。H. L. 麦肯和汤姆·沃尔夫(其作品 *The Kandy-Kolored Tangerine-Flake Streamline Baby*)分别是20 世纪 20 年代和 60 年代的 iconoclast。

adolescence(青春期)是一个充满迷茫和反叛的年龄段,在这段时间内表现出"iconoclasm"是非常正常的——事实上一个不鄙视规矩和传统的青春期孩子可能被认为是不成熟和某种失调的表现。这个单词源自 eikon,意为"一个宗教形象",加上 klaein(意为"打破")构成。当然,iconoslasm 并不限于指宗教方面。

2. Is there a God?
上帝真的存在吗?

Atheist combines the Greek negative prefix a- with *theos*, God. Do not confuse *atheism* (AY′-thee-iz-əm) with *agnosticism* (ag- NOS′-tə-siz-əm), the philosophy that claims that God is unknowable, that he may or may not exist, and that human beings can never come to a final conclusion about Him. The *agnostic* (ag-NOS′-tik) does not deny the existence of a deity, as does the *atheist*, but simply holds that no proof can be adduced one way or the other.

atheist 由希腊语否定前缀 a-和 theos 组成,a 表示"不、没有",theos 表示"神灵"。注意不要混淆 atheism(无神论)和agnosticism(不可知论),后者的哲学认为上帝是否存在是不可知的,上帝可能存在,也可能不存在,但是人类永远也无法得出确定的结论。agnostic(不可知论者)并不否认神灵的存在,这点与 atheist(无神论者)相反;agnostic 只是认为人类无法给出任何证据表明上帝存在或不存在。

3. how to know
怎样了解

Agnostic (which is also an adjective) is built on the Greek root *gnostos*, known, and the negative prefix *a-*. An *agnostic* claims that all but material phenomena is unknown, and, indeed, unknowable.

A *diagnosis* (di-əg-NŌ′-sis), constructed on the allied Greek root *gnosis*, knowledge, plus *dia-*, through, is a knowing through examination or testing. A *prognosis* (prog-NŌ′-sis), on the other hand, is etymologically a knowing beforehand, hence a prediction, generally, but not solely, as to the course of a disease. (The Greek prefix *pro-*, before, plus *gnosis*.)

Thus, you may say to a doctor, "What's the *diagnosis*, Doc?"

"Diabetes."

Then you say, "And what's the *prognosis*?"

"If you take insulin and watch your diet, you'll soon be as good as new."

The doctor's *prognosis*, then, is a forecast of the development or trend of a disease. The doctor knows beforehand, from previous similar cases, what to expect.

agnostic(也可作形容词)由希腊词根 gnostos(已知的)和否定前缀 a-组成。一个 agnostic(不可知论者)宣称,所有非有形的事物都是未知的,也是不可知的。

diagnosis 由希腊词根 gnosis(知识)加上 dia-(通过)组成,指通过检查和测试去了解。而与之相对,prognosis,从词源上看是"事先知道"的意思,指对疾病发展的一般性而非唯一性的预测(希腊语前缀 pro-,在……之前,加上 gnosis)。

所以,如果你问医生:"医生,我的诊断结果如何?"

"糖尿病。"

然后你又问:"我的病情预断是什么?"

"如果你能够注射胰岛素而且注意饮食,你就会恢复健康。"

所以,prognosis 是对疾病发展或者趋势的预测。依照之前的相似病例,医生知道病情的发展。

The verb form of *diagnosis* is diagnose (dī′-əg-NŌS′); the verb form of *prognosis* is *prognosticate* (prog-NOS′-tə-kayt′). To use the verb *prognosticate* correctly, be sure that your meaning involves the forecasting of developments from a consideration of symptoms or conditions—whether the problem is physical, mental, political, economic, psychological, or what have you.

In school, you doubtless recall taking *diagnostic* (dī′-əg-NOS′- tik) tests; these measured not what you were supposed to have learned during the semester, but your general knowledge in a field, so that your teachers would know what remedial steps to take, just as doctors rely on their *diagnosis* to decide what drugs or treatments to prescribe.

In a reading center, various *diagnostic* machines and tests are used—these tell the clinician what is wrong with a student's reading and what measures will probably increase such a student's reading efficiency.

The medical specialist in *diagnosis* is a *diagnostician* (dī′-əg-nos-TISH′-ən).

The noun form of the verb *prognosticate* is *prognostication* (prog-nos′-tə-KAY′-shən).

diagnosis 的动词形式是 diagnose;prognosis 的动词形式是 prognosticate。注意 prognosticate 的用法,确保你要表达的意思包含了考虑症状或某种状况之后对其发展的预测——无论这个问题是身体上的,精神上的,政治上的,经济上的,心理上或其他方面的。

你一定记得上学时经历的 diagnostic tests——诊断性测试;这些测试的目的并不在于对整个学期的学习内容进行

评估,而是测试你对某一领域的常识,这样你的老师才能够知道采取怎样的辅导,与医生根据诊断确定开哪些处方药或者进行怎样的治疗是一个道理。

在阅读中心,人们使用各种各样的诊断仪器和测试,以找出学生阅读问题,确定应该采取哪些手段来提高学生的阅读效率。

从事医疗诊断的专家称为 diagnostician,动词 prognosticate 的名词形式是 prognostication。

4. getting back to God

继续讲上帝

Theos, God, is also found in:

(1) *Monotheism* (MON′-ə-thee-iz-əm)—belief in *one* God. (*Monos*, one, plus *theos*, God.)

Using *atheism*, *atheist*, and *atheistic* as a model, write the word for the person who believes in one God: _____.

The adjective? _____.

(2) *Polytheism* (POL′-ee-thee-iz-əm)—belief in *many* gods, as in ancient Greece or Rome. (*Polys*, many, plus *theos*.)

The person with such a belief? _____

The adjective? _____.

(3) *Pantheism* (PAN′-thee-iz-əm)—belief that God is not in man's image, but is a combination of all forces of the universe. (*Pan*, all, plus *theos*.) The person?

_____

The adjective? _____.

(4) *Theology* (thee-OL′-ə-jee)—the study of God and religion. (*Theos* plus *logos*, science or study.)

The student is a *theologian* (thee′-ə-LŌ′-jən), the adjective is *theological* (thee′-ə-LOJ′-ə-kəl).

Theos(神,上帝)还见于以下词汇中:

(1) monotheism——只信仰"一个"上帝。(monos,"一个",加上 theos——"上帝")。

仿照 atheism, atheist 和 atheistic,写出这种只信仰一个上帝的人叫什么? 其形容词是什么?

(2) polytheism——信仰很多个神,如古希腊和古罗马。(polys,"很多",加上 theos。)

有这种信仰的人叫做什么? 其形容词是什么?

(3) pantheism——相信上帝非人形,而是宇宙所有力量的组合。(Pan,"所有",加上 theos。)

有这种信仰的人叫什么? 其形容词是什么?

(4) theology——研究上帝和信仰。(theos 加上 logos——"科学""研究"。)

这门学科的学生是 theologian,形容词是 theological。

5. of sex and the tongue

性和舌头的

A *lecher* practices lechery (LECH′-ər-ee). The derivation is Old French *lechier*, to lick. The adjective *lecherous* (LECH′-ə-rəs) has many close or not-so-close synonyms, most of them also, and significantly, starting with the letter *l*, a sound formed with the tongue, supposedly the seat of sensation.

(1) *libidinous* (lə-BID′-ə-nəs)—from *libido*, pleasure.

(2) *lascivious* (lə-SIV′-ee-əs)—from *lascivia*, wantonness.

(3) lubricious (lōo-BRISH′-əs)—from *lubricus*, slippery, the same root found in *lubricate*. The noun is *lubricity* (lōo-BRIS′-ə-tee).

(4) licentious (lī-SEN′-shəs) —from *licere*, to be permitted, the root from which we get *license*, etymologically, "permission," and *illicit*, etymologically, "not permitted."

(5) *lewd*—the previous four words derive from Latin, but this one is from Anglo-Saxon *lewed*, vile.

(6) *lustful*—from an Anglo-Saxon word meaning *pleasure*, *desire*. Noun：*lust*. *Libidinous*, *lascivious*, *lubricious*, *licentious*, *lewd*, *lecherous*, **lustful** are seven adjectives that indicate sexual desire and/or activity. The implication of all seven words is more or less derogatory.

Each adjective becomes a noun with the addition of the noun suffix *-ness*；*lubricity* and *lust* are alternate noun forms of two of the adjectives.

lecher,好色之徒,是 lechery(淫荡)的热衷者。lecher 来自于法语动词 lechier,意为"舔"。形容词形式是 lecherous,意为"好色的"。lecherous 有许多同义词,重要的是,这些同义词中大部分都以 l 开头,原因可能是 l 的发音由舌头这个感觉器官形成。

(1) libidinous——来源于 libido,"寻欢作乐"。

(2) lascivious——来源于 lascivia,"淫乱"。

(3) lubricious——来源于 lubricus,"狡猾"。lubricate 也有同样的词根。名词是 lubricity。

(4) licentious——来源于 licere,"被允许",也是 license(许可证)的词根,从词源上看,意为"同意",而 illicit 则为"不允许"。

(5) lewd——以上四个词语都来源于拉丁语,但是 lewd 来源于盎格鲁-撒克逊语 lewed,"粗鄙"。

(6) lustful——同样来源于盎格鲁-撒克逊语,表示"寻欢作乐、欲望"。名词为：lust。

libidinous,lascivious,lubricious,licentious,lewd,lecherous,lustful 是 7 个表达性欲望或性活动的形容词,这 7 个单词或多或少都有贬义。

每个形容词后面加上后缀-ness 就变成名词,lubricity 和 lust 是其中两个形容词另外的名词形式。

6. of sex and the itch

性和痒的

Prurient (PROO′-ee-ənt), from Latin *prurio*, to itch, to long for, describes someone who is filled with great sexual curiosity, desire, longing, etc. Can you form the noun? _____.

Pruritis (prōor-Ī′-tis), from the same root, is a medical condition in which the skin is very itchy, but without a rash or eruptions. (Scratch enough, of course, as you will be irresistibly tempted to do, and something like a rash will soon appear.) The adjective is *pruritic* (prōor-IT′-ik).

prurient 源于拉丁语 prurio,意为"痒""渴望",用来描述对性充满好奇、欲望和渴求等的人。你能写出其名词形式吗?

pruritis 源于同一词根,指一种皮肤瘙痒的病症,但没有皮疹和痘痘出现。(当然,如果控制不住而用手老挠的话,就会有类似皮疹的东西出现。)形容词是 pruritic。

7. under and over

下面和上面

Hypochondria (hī-pə-KON′-dree-ə) is built on two Greek roots：*hypos*，under，and *chondros*，the cartilage of the breastbone. This may sound farfetched until you realize that under the breastbone is the abdomen；the ancient Greeks believed that morbid anxiety about one's health arose in the abdomen—and no one is more morbidly, unceasingly, and unhappily anxious about health than the *hypochondriac*.

Hypochondriac is also an adjective—an alternate and more commonly used adjective form is *hypochondriacal* (hī′-pə-kən-DRĪ′-ə-kəl).

Hypos，under，is a useful root to know. The *hypodermic* needle penetrates *under* the skin；a *hypothyroid* person has an *underworking* thyroid gland；*hypotension* is abnormally low blood pressure.

On the other hand，*hyper* is the Greek root meaning *over*. The *hypercritical* person is excessively fault-finding；*hyperthyroidism* is an overworking of the thyroid gland；*hypertension* is high blood pressure；and you can easily figure out the meanings of *hyperacidity*，*hyperactive*，*hypersensitive*，etc.

The adjective forms of *hypotension* and *hypertension* are *hypotensive* and *hypertensive*.

hypochondria，"疑病症"，建立在两个希腊语词根基础上；hypos——在……之下；chondros——胸骨的软骨。这看起来有些牵强，但是，当你意识到胸骨以下是腹部时，意义就会变得明了；古希腊人认为对于个人健康病态的忧虑来自于腹部——没有人比 hypochondriac(疑病症患者)对健康担忧的程度更变态、更持续、更忧伤。

hypochondriac 也是一个形容词——而更为常用的形容词形式是 hypochondriacal.

hypos 表示"在……之下"，是个有用的词根。hypodermic，"皮下注射"；hypothyroid 是"甲状腺功能减退者"；hypotension 是"低血压"。

相反，希腊语词根 hyper 是指"在……之上"。hypercritical person 是过度吹毛求疵的人；hyperthyroidism 是甲状腺机能亢进；hypertension 是血压过高；你也一定能够轻松理解以下词语：hyperacidity, hyperactive, hypersensitive, hyperconscious 等。

hypotension 和 hypertension 的形容词是 hypotensive 和 hypertensive。

REVIEW OF ETYMOLOGY

复习词源

PREFIX，ROOT，SUFFIX	MEANING	ENGLISH WORD
1. *eikon*	religious image	_____
2. *klaein*	to break	_____
3. *a-*	negative prefix	_____
4. *theos*	God	_____
5. *gnostos*	known	_____
6. *-ism*	noun suffix	_____
7. *-ic*	adjective suffix	_____
8. *gnosis*	knowledge	_____

9. *dia-*   through   _____

10. *pro-*   before   _____

11. *-ate*   verb suffix   _____

12. *-ion*   noun suffix for   _____
                    verbs ending in *-ate*   _____

13. *-ician*   one who; expert   _____

14. *monos*   one   _____

15. *polys*   many   _____

16. *pan*   all   _____

17. *logos-*   science, study   _____

18. *-al*   adjective suffix _____

19. *prurio*   to itch, to long for   _____

20. *hypos*   under   _____

21. *hyper*   over   _____

22. *-ive*   adjective suffix _____

USING THE WORDS
单词应用

Can you pronounce the words? (Ⅰ)
你能读出这些单词吗？(Ⅰ)

1. *iconoclasm*   ī-KON′-ə-klaz-əm

2. *iconoclastic*   ī-kon′-ə-KLAS′-tik

3. *atheism*   AY′-thee-iz-əm

4. *atheistic*   ay′-thee-IS′-tik

5. *agnostic*   ag-NOS′-tik

6. *agnosticism*   ag-NOS′-tə-siz-əm

7. *diagnosis*   dī′-əg-NŌ′-sis

8. *diagnose*   DĪ′-əg-nōs′

9. *diagnostic*   di′-əg-NOS′-tik

10. *diagnostician*   dī′-əg-nos-TISH′-ən

11. *prognosis*   prog-NŌ′-sis

12. *prognostic*   prog-NOS′-tik

13. *prognosticate*   prog-NOS′-tə-kayt′

14. *prognostication* prog-nos′-tə-KAY′-shən

Can you pronounce the words?（Ⅱ）

你能读出这些单词吗？（Ⅱ）

1.	*monotheism*	MON'-ə-thee-iz-əm
2.	*monotheist*	MON'-ə-thee'-ist
3.	*monotheistic*	mon'-ə-thee-IS'-tik
4.	*polytheism*	POL'-ee-thee-iz-əm
5.	*polytheist*	POL'-ee-thee'-ist
6.	*polytheistic*	pol'-ee-thee-IS'-tik
7.	*pantheism*	PAN'-thee-iz-əm
8.	*pantheist*	PAN'-thee-ist
9.	*pantheistic*	pan'-thee-IS'-tik
10.	*theology*	thee-OL'-ə-jee
11.	*theologian*	thee'-ə-LŌ'-jən
12.	*theological*	thee'-ə-LOJ'-ə-kəl

Can you pronounce the words?（Ⅲ）

你能读出这些单词吗？（Ⅲ）

1.	*lechery*	LECH'-ər-ee
2.	*lecherous*	LECH'-ər-əs
3.	*libidinous*	lə-BID'-ə-nəs
4.	*lascivious*	lə-SIV'-ee-əs
5.	*lubricious*	loo-BRISH'-əs
6.	*lubricity*	loo-BRIS'-ə-tee
7.	*licentious*	lī-SEN'-shəs
8.	*lewd*	LOOD
9.	*lustful*	LUST'-fəl
10.	*lust*	LUST

Can you pronounce the words?（Ⅳ）

你能读出这些单词吗？（Ⅳ）

1.	*prurient*	PROOR'-ee-ənt
2.	*prurience*	PROOR'-ee-əns
3.	*pruritis*	proor-Ī'-tis
4.	*pruritic*	proor-IT'-ik
5.	*hypochondria*	hī'-pə-KON'-dree-ə
6.	*hypochondriacal*	hī'-pə-kən-DRĪ'-ə-kəl
7.	*hypotension*	hī'-pō-TEN'-shən
8.	*hypertension*	hī'-pər-TEN'-shən

9. *hypotensive*   hī'-pō-TEN'-siv

10. *hypertensive*   hī'-pər-TEN'-siv

This has been a long chapter，and we have discussed，more or less in detail，over one hundred words. Just to keep everything straight in your mind now，see how successfully you can work out the following matching exercises，which will concern any of the words discussed in this chapter.

Can you work with the words? (Ⅰ)
你能灵活使用这些词汇了吗？（Ⅰ）

1. martinet	a. lack of seriousness in an art or profession
2. sycophancy	b. harridan，shrew
3. dilettantism	c. excessive patriotism
4. tyro	d. name from father
5. virtuoso	e. venerable and influential old man
6. termagant	f. beginner
7. chauvinism	g. brilliant performer
8. patrimony	h. bootlicking
9. patronymic	i. inheritance from father
10. patriarch	j. strict disciplinarian

KEY：1-j，2-h，3-a，4-f，5-g，6--b，7-c，8-i，9-d，10-e

Can you work with the words? (Ⅱ)
你能灵活使用这些词汇了吗？（Ⅱ）

1. patricide	a. mother-killing
2. alma mater	b. tending to fixate obsessively on one thing
3. matricide	c. wife-killing
4. fratricide	d. father-killing
5. uxoricide	e. tending to set fires
6. uxorious	f. alcoholic
7. monomaniacal	g. wife-doting
8. pyromaniacal	h. school or college from which one has graduated
9. megalomaniacal	i. tending to delusions of grandeur
10. dipsomaniacal	j. brother-killing

KEY：1-d，2-h，3-a，4-j，5-c，6-g，7-b，8-e，9-i，10-f

Can you work with the words? (Ⅲ)

你能灵活使用这些词汇了吗？(Ⅲ)

1. kleptomania	a. disbelief in God
2. libidinous	b. belief in many gods
3. atheism	c. lewd
4. agnosticism	d. belief that God is nature
5. polytheism	e. morbid anxiety about health
6. monotheism	f. belief in one God
7. theology	g. study of religion
8. pantheism	h. obsessive thievery
9. satyriasis	i. abnormal male sexual needs
10. hypochondria	j. skepticism about God

KEY：1-h，2-c，3-a，4-j，5-b，6-f，7-g，8-d，9-i，10-e

Can you work with the words? (Ⅳ)

你能灵活使用这些词汇了吗？(Ⅳ)

1. hypotension	a. high blood pressure
2. lascivious	b. malicious fire-setting
3. hypertension	c. abnormally low blood pressure
4. agnostic	d. fire-setting for illegal gain
5. incendiarism	e. to forecast (probable developments)
6. arson	f. a determination through examination or testing of the nature, type, causes, etc. of a condition
7. iconoclasm	g. one who claims that ultimate reality is unknowable
8. prognosticate	h. sexually immoral
9. diagnosis	i. a foretelling of probable developments
10. prognosis	j. a scoffing at tradition

KEY：1-c，2-h，3-a，4-g，5-b，6-d，7-j，8-e，9-f，10-i

Can you work wlth the words?（Ⅴ）
你能灵活使用这些词汇了吗？（Ⅴ）

1. prurience	a. abnormal need for sexual intercourse by a male
2. satyromania	b. fear of enclosed places
3. agoraphobia	c. student of religion
4. claustrophobia	d. sexual longing or curiosity
5. acrophobia	e. fear of heights
6. theologian	f. fear of open spaces
7. lubricious	g. having, or referring to, abnormally low blood pressure
8. hypochondriacal	h. itching
9. hypotensive	i. having, or referring to, high blood pressure
10. hypertensive	j. sexually immoral; lewd
11. pruritis	k. beset by anxieties about one's health

KEY：1-d，2-a，3-f，4-b，5-e，6-c，7-j，8-k，9-g，10-i，11-h

Can you recall the words?（Ⅰ）
你能够写出这些词汇吗？（Ⅰ）

Ⅰ. manias and phobias

1. single fixed obsession	1. M _____
2. irresistible compulsion to set fires	2. P _____
3. unceasing desire, on the part of a woman, for sexual intercourse	3. N _____
4. obsessive desire to steal	4. K _____
5. delusions of grandeur	5. M _____
6. alcoholism	6. D _____
7. compulsion for sexual intercourse by a male	7. S _____ or S _____
8. dread of heights	8. A _____
9. dread of open spaces	9. A _____
10. dread of cramped quarters	10. C _____

KEY：1-monomania, 2-pyromania, 3-nymphomania, 4-kleptomania, 5-megalomania, 6-dipsomania, 7-satyromania *or* satyriasis, 8-acrophobia, 9-agoraphobia,

10-claustrophobia

Can you recall the words？（Ⅱ）

你能够写出这些词汇吗？（Ⅱ）

II. sex

Write seven adjectives；all starting with L，more or less meaning "sexually immoral，desirous，etc."；write the adjective starting with P meaning "sexually curious or longing".

1. L _____   5. L _____
2. L _____   6. L _____
3. L _____   7. L _____
4. L _____   8. P _____

KEY：（1-7 *in any order*）1-lecherous，2-libidinous，3-lascivious，4-lubricious，5-licentious，6-lewd，7-lustful，8-prurient

Can you recall the words？（Ⅲ）

你能够写出这些词汇吗？（Ⅲ）

Ⅲ. God

1. study of religion   1. T _____
2. belie that God is the sum total   2. P _____
   of natural forces
3. belief that there is no God   3. A _____
4. belief that God's existence is   4. A _____
   unknowable
5. belief in one God   5. M _____
6. belief in many gods   6. P _____

KEY：1-theology，2-pantheism，3-atheism，4-agnosticism，5-monotheism，6-polytheism

Can you recall the words？（Ⅳ）

你能够写出这些词汇吗？（Ⅳ）

1. morbid anxiety about one's   1. H _____
   health

2. high blood pressure   2. H _____

3. malicious fire-setting   3. I _____

4. the felony of setting fire for economic gain   4. A _____

5. sneering contempt for convention or tradition   5. I _____

6. a forecast of development (of a disease, etc.)   6. P _____

7. designed to discover causes or conditions (*adj.*)   7. D _____

8. abnormally low blood pressure   8. H _____

9. to forecast (probable future developments) by examining present conditions   9. P _____

10. to determine the nature of a disease, condition, or state by examination   10. D _____

11. the act of forecasting (probable future developments) by examining present conditions   11. P _____

12. doctor who is an expert at recognizing the nature of a disease or condition   12. D _____

13. possessed of, or referring to, high blood pressure   13. H _____

14. possessed of, or referring to, abnormally low blood pressure   14. H _____

15. one who studies religion   15. T _____

KEY: 1-hypochondria, 2-hypertension, 3-incendiarism, 4-arson, 5-iconoclasm, 6-prognosis, 7-diagnostic, 8-hypotension, 9-prognosticate, 10-diagnose, 11-prognostication, 12-diagnostician, 13-hypertensive, 14-hypotensive, 15-theologian

---

CHAPTER REVIEW
章节复习

A. Do you recognize the words?

你认识这些单词吗?

1. Disciplinarian:

(a) martinet, (b) virago, (c) dilettante

2. Bootlicker:

(a) chauvinist, (b) sycophant, (c) lecher

3. Scoffer at tradition:

(a) monomaniac, (b) hypochondriac, (c) iconoclast

4. Disbeliever in God:

(a) agnostic, (b) atheist, (c) chauvinist

5. Accomplished musician:

(a) tyro, (b) dilettante, (c) virtuoso

6. Sheer, flimsy:

(a) diaphanous, (b) uxorious, (c) paternal

7. Abusive woman:

(a) termagant, (b) virtuoso, (c) matriarch

8. Murder of one's wife:

(a) genocide, (b) uxoricide, (c) sororicide

9. Old man in ruling position:

(a) matriarch, (b) patricide, (c) patriarch

10. Morbid compulsion to steal:

(a) dipsomania, (b) nymphomania, (c) kleptomania

11. Delusions of grandeur:

(a) megalomania, (b) egomania, (c) pyromania

12. Lewd, lustful:

(a) prurient, (b) agnostic, (c) hypochondriac

13. Belief in many gods:

(a) polytheism, (b) monotheism, (c) agnosticism

14. Setting fire for economic gain:

(a) pyromania, (b) incendiarism, (c) arson

15. Morbid fear of heights:

(a) agoraphobia, (b) acrophobia, (c) claustrophobia

16. High blood pressure:

(a) hypotension, (b) hypertension, (c) hypochondria

17. Abnormal need for sexual intercourse by a male:

(a) lechery, (b) lubricity, (c) satyriasis

KEY: 1-a, 2-b, 3-c, 4-b, 5-c, 6-a, 7-a, 8-b, 9-c, 10-c, 11-a, 12-a, 13-a, 14-c, 15-b, 16-b, 17-c

---

B. Can you recognize the roots?

你能认出这些词根吗?

ROOT	MEANING	EXAMPLE
1. *sykon*	_____	sycophant
2. *phanein*	_____	diaphanous
3. *vir*	_____	virago
4. *pater*, *patris*	_____	paternal
5. *onyma*	_____	synonym
6. *homos*	_____	homonym
7. *phone*	_____	homophone
8. *archein*	_____	matriarchy
9. *mater*, *matris*	_____	maternity
10. *alma*	_____	alma mater
11. *sui*	_____	suicide
12. *caedo* (*-cide*)	_____	parricide
13. *frater*, *fratris*	_____	fraternity
14. *soror*	_____	sorority
15. *homo*	_____	homicide
16. *rex*, *regis*	_____	regal
17. *uxor*	_____	uxorious
18. *maritus*	_____	mariticide
19. *infans*, *infantis*	_____	infanticide
20. *genos*	_____	genocide
21. *mania*	_____	egomania
22. *monos*	_____	monomania
23. *dipsa*	_____	dipsomania
24. *klepte*	_____	kleptomania
25. *pyros*	_____	pyromania
26. *incendo*, *incensus*	_____	incendiarism
27. *ardo*, *arsus*	_____	arson
28. *mega*	_____	megalomaniac
29. *satyros*	_____	satyriasis
30. *nymphe*	_____	nymphomaniac
31. *claustrum*	_____	claustrophobia
32. *agora*	_____	agoraphobia
33. *akros*	_____	acrophobia
34. *phobia*	_____	zoophobia
35. *eikon*	_____	iconoclastic
36. *klaein*	_____	iconoclasm

37. *theos*	_____	monotheism
38. *gnostos*	_____	agnostic
39. *gnosis*	_____	prognosis
40. *polys*	_____	polytheism
41. *pan*	_____	pantheism
42. *logos*	_____	theology
43. *prurio*	_____	pruritis
44. *hypos*	_____	hypotension
45. *hyper*	_____	hypertension

KEY：1-fig，2-to show，3-man（male），4-father，5-name，6-the same，7-sound，8-to rule，9-mother，10-soul，11-of oneself，12-to kill，killing，13-brother，14-sister，15-person，16-king，17-wife，18-husband，19-baby，20-race，kind，21-madness，22-one，23-thirst，24-thief，25-fire，26-to set fire，27-to burn，28-great，large，29-satyr，30-bride，31-enclosed place，32-market place，33-highest，34-morbid dread，35-religious image，36-to break，37-God，38-known，39-knowledge，40-many，41-all，42-science，study，43-to itch，44-under，45-over

TEASER QUESTIONS FOR THE AMATEUR ETYMOLOGIST
词源小测验

1. If a *patronymic* is a name derived from the name of one's father, can you figure out the word for a name derived from one's *mother's* name? _____.

2. *Incendo*, *incensus*, to set on fire, is the origin of the adjective *incendiary*, the noun *incense*, and the verb to *incense*.

(a) What is an *incendiary* statement or speech? _____.

(b) Why do people use *incense*, and why is it called *incense*? _____.

(c) If someone *incenses* you, or if you feel *incensed*, how does the meaning of the verb derive from the root? _____.

3. *Ardo*, *arsus* to burn, is the source of *ardent* and *ardor*. Explain these two words in terms of the root.

(a) ardent: _____.

(b) ardor: _____.

4. What is used to make sound greater (use the roots for *great* and *sound*)? _____.

5. A *metropolis*, by etymology, is the mother city (Greek *meter*, mother, plus *polis*, city, state). Construct a word for a great city (think of *megalomania*, delusions of greatness): _____.

6. *Polis*, city, state, is the origin of the word for the uniformed group guarding

the city or state. The English word? _____. Can you think of the word from the same root for the art of governing the city or state? ____ _____.

7. What is a *bibliokleptomaniac*? _____ _____.

Coin a word for one who has an irresistible compulsion to steal *women*: _____ _____. To steal *children* (uso the Greek, not the Latin, root for *child*): ____ _____. To steal *males* (use the Greek root): _____. To steal *people* (use the Greek root): _____.

8. What word can you coin for someone who has an obsession to reach the highest places? _____. To be in the market place, or in wide-open spaces? _____. To be in confined places? _____.

9. Coin a word for one who has a morbid dread of thieves: _____ ; of fire:_____ ; of women: _____ ; of males: _____ ; of people: _____.

10. Guess at the meaning, thinking of the roots you have learned, of *gnosiology*: _____ _____.

11. Wolfgang Amadeus Theophilus Gottlieb Mozart was a famous eighteenth-century Austrian composer. You can recognize the roots in *Theophilus*. How are his other two middle names similar to *Theophilus*? _____ _____.

12. Thinking of the root *phanein*, define *cellophane*: _____ _____.

13. Recognizing the root *hypos*, can you define *hypoglycemia*? _____ _____.

Construct a word that is the opposite of *hypoglycemia*: _____.

14. *Pan*, all, occurs in *Pantheon*, *pandemonium*, and *panorama*. Can you figure out the meanings?

(a) Pantheon: _____ _____.

(b) pandemonium: _____ _____.

(c) panorama: _____ _____.

15. Recognizing the roots in *monarchy*, define the word: _____ _____.

(*Answers in Chapter 18*)

(答案见第 18 章)

MAGAZINES THAT WILL HELP YOU

有助于学习的期刊

When a pregnant woman takes calcium pills, she must make sure also that her diet is rich in vitamin D, since this vitamin makes the absorption of the calcium possible. In building your vocabulary by learning great quantities of new words, you too must take a certain vitamin, metaphorically speaking, to help you absorb, understand, and remember these words. This vitamin is reading—for it is in books and magazines that you will find the words that we have been discussing in these pages. To learn new words without seeing them applied in the context of your reading is to do only half the job and to run the risk of gradually forgetting the additions to your vocabulary. To combine your vocabulary-building with increased reading is to make assurance doubly sure.

You are now so alert to the words and roots we have discussed that you will find that most of your reading will be full of the new words you have learned—and every time you do see one of the words used in context in a book or magazine, you will understand it more fully and will be taking long steps toward using it yourself.

Among magazines, I would like particularly to recommend the following, which will act both to keep you mentally alert and to set the new words you are learning:

1. *Harper's Magazine*
2. *Atlantic Monthly*
3. *The New Yorker*
4. *Time*
5. *Newsweek*
6. *Esquire*
7. *Psychology Today*
8. *Saturday Review*
9. *Ms.*
10. *Mother Jones*

孕妇食用钙片之前，一定要确定她的饮食富含维生素 D，因为维生素 D 才能保证钙的吸收。而当你通过学习大量新词扩建词汇时，你同样需要一种"维生素"来帮助你吸收、理解以及记忆这些新词。这种维生素就是阅读——因为只有在书籍和期刊中你才会找到我们一直在讨论的这些词汇。在学习新词的过程中，如果你无法看见它们在阅读语境中的具体应用，你的工作只完成了一半，忘记新词的风险也很大。将词汇扩建与增长的阅读量相结合才是双保险。

现在，你对我们讨论过的词汇和词根一定非常敏感，以至于你会发现你的阅读材料中充满了这些词汇——每一次在书籍或者期刊的具体语境中看到这些词汇，你都会更加全面地理解它们，也距离自己使用这些词汇越来越近。

众多期刊中，我尤其推荐以下几本，它们既能够保持头脑的机智，也能够使你接触学习过的新词：

11. *Signs*
12. *National Geographic*
13. *Smithsonian*
14. *Human Nature*
15. *Scientific American*
16. *Natural History*

These periodicals are aimed at the alert, verbally sophisticated, educated reader; you will see in them, without fail, most of the words you have been studying in this book—not to mention hosts of other valuable words you will want to add to your vocabulary, many of which you will be able to figure out once you recognize their etymological structure.

这些期刊的目标读者是那些头脑机智、词汇丰富、受过教育的读者;你在这些期刊中一定会发现我们学习过的大多数词汇——不用说,还有大量你希望增加到你的词汇库的宝贵词汇,其中很多单词只要你认识它们的词源结构就可以推断出含义。

(End of Session 31)

Brief Intermission Seven
简短插叙七

SOME INTERESTING DERIVATIONS
一些有趣的词源

PEOPLE WHO MADE OUR LANGUAGE
铸造我们语言的那些人

Bloomers

灯笼裤

Mrs. Elizabeth Smith Miller invented them in 1849, and showed a working model to a famous women's fights advocate, *Amelia J. Bloomer*. Amelia was fascinated by the idea of garments that were both modest (they then reached right down to the ankles) and convenient — and promptly sponsored them...

伊丽莎白·史密斯·米勒夫人在 1849 年发明了灯笼裤,并将样式展示给当时著名的女权倡导者艾米丽·J. 布鲁姆(Amelia J. Bloomer)。艾米丽非常喜欢这个既适度又舒适的裤子(当时的长度直到脚踝),并立即给予赞助……

Boycott

抵制

Charles C. Boycott was an English land agent whose difficult duty it was to collect high rents from Irish farmers. In protest, the farmers ostracized him, not even allowing him to make purchases in town or hire workers to harvest his crops.

查尔斯·C. 博伊科特(Charles C. Boycott)曾是英国一位土地代理人,他的职责是从爱尔兰农夫收取高额租金。这份工作并不容易。农夫们为了表示抵抗,处处排挤博伊科特,甚至不允许他在城镇购买物品或雇佣工人收获庄稼。

Marcel

烫发

Marcel was an ingenious Parisian hairdresser who felt he could improve on the button curls popular in 1875. He did, and made a fortune.

马歇尔(Marcel)是巴黎一位极具天赋的发型师,他认为自己能够改良 1875 年流行的按钮卷。他做到了,并从中赚到一大笔钱。

Silhouette

轮廓

Finance Minister of France just before the Revolution, *Etienne de Silhouette* advocated the *simple* life, so that excess money could go into the treasury instead of into luxurious living. And the profile is the *simplest* form of portraiture, if you get the connection.

艾蒂安·德·西路爱特(Etienne de Silhouette)是法国大革命爆发之前的财务部长，他倡导生活从简，这样剩余货币就会流入国库，而不是花费在奢华的生活上。而如果你能够联想得到，肖像画的最简形式就是画轮廓。

Derrick
井架

A seventeenth-century English hangman, *Derrick* by name, hoisted to their death some of the most notorious criminals of the day.

德瑞克(Derrick)是17世纪时的一位绞刑吏，是将当时最臭名昭著的罪犯处以绞刑的人。

Sadist
施虐狂者

Because *Marquis de Sade*, an eighteenth-century Frenchman, found his greatest delight in torturing friends and mistresses, the term *sadist* was derived from his name. His works shocked his nation and the world by the alarming frankness with which he described his morbid and bloodthirsty cruelty.

萨德侯爵是18世纪法国人，折磨朋友和情妇是他最大的乐趣，sadist 也正是从他的名字得来。他的回忆录震惊了整个国家和世界，回忆录中，他以惊人坦率的文笔记录了他病态的、血腥的残忍。

Galvanism
电疗法

Luigi Galvani, the Italian physiologist, found by accident that an electrically charged scalpel could send a frog's corpse into muscular convulsions. Experimenting further, he eventually discovered the principles of chemically produced electricity. His name is responsible not only for the technical expressions *galvanism*, *galvanized iron*, and *galvanometer*, but also for that highly graphic phrase, "*galvanized into action.*"

路易吉·伽伐尼(Luigi Galvani)是意大利的生理学家，他偶然发现充电的手术刀可以使死了的青蛙肌肉抽搐。通过进一步实验，他最终发现化学发电的原理。他的名字不仅衍生出几个技术术语，例如 galvanism(电疗法)、galvanized iron (镀锌铁)和 galvanometer(电流表)，还衍生出一个非常生动的短语：galvanized into action，意为"激励"。

Guppies
虹鳉

In 1868, *R. J. Lechmere Guppy*, president of the Scientific Association of Trinidad, sent some specimens of a tiny tropical fish to the British Museum. Ever since, fish of this species have been called *guppies*.

1868年，特立尼达岛科学学会主席 R. J. 雷克米尔·格皮(R. J. Lechmere Guppy)将一种体型非常小的热带鱼标本送到了大英博物馆。从那时起，这种鱼就被命名为 guppies，虹鳉。

Nicotine
尼古丁

Four hundred years ago, *Jean Nicot*, a French ambassador, bought some tobacco seeds from a Flemish trader. Nicot's successful efforts to popularize the plant in

Europe brought him linguistic immortality.

　　400 多年前,法国大使让·尼科从弗莱芒商人手中购买了一些烟草种子。尼科成功地将这种植物普及欧洲大陆的同时,也使他的名字在语言史上永垂不朽。

PLACES THAT MADE OUR LANGUAGE
铸造我们语言的那些地点

Bayonne, France
巴约纳,法国

Where first was manufactured the daggerlike weapon that fits over the muzzle end of a rifle—the *bayonet*.

在巴约纳,一种外形酷似匕首的武器被最早制造出来,这种武器适合安置在步枪的枪口处——the bayonet,"刺刀"。

Cantalupo, Italy
坎特卢波,意大利

The first place in Europe to grow those luscious melons we now call *cantaloupes*.

坎特卢波是欧洲最早种植那些甘美多汁瓜类的地方,我们现在将这些瓜称为——cantaloupes,"哈密瓜"。

Calicut, India
卡利卡特,印度

The city from which we first imported a kind of cotton cloth now known as *calico*.

我们最早从卡利卡特进口了一种棉布,这种棉布现在被称为——calico,"白棉布"。

Tuxedo Park, New York
塔克西多帕克,纽约

In the country club of this exclusive and wealthy community, the short (no tails) dinner coat for men, or *tuxedo*, was popularized.

在这个高档的富裕社区的乡村俱乐部里,一种男士短晚装非常流行——tuxedo,"无尾晚礼服"

Egypt
埃及

It was once supposed that the colorful, fortunetelling wanderers, or *Gypsies*, hailed from this ancient land.

曾有人认为,有趣的、能够预知未来的吉普赛人(Gypsies)就来自于埃及这片古老的土地。

Damascus, Syria
大马士革,叙利亚

Where an elaborately patterned silk, *damask*, was first made.

一种样式精巧的丝绸最早在大马士革被制作——damask,"绸缎"。

Tzu-t'ing, China
泉州,中国

Once a great seaport in Fukien Province. Marco Polo called it *Zaitun*, and in time a silk fabric made there was called *satin*.

泉州曾经是福建省一个重要的海港。马可·波罗称其为 Zaitun,那时,一种丝织品被称为 satin,"缎子"。

Frankfurt，Germany

法兰克福,德国

Where the burghers once greatly enjoyed their smoked beef and pork sausages, which we now ask for in delicatessen stores and supermarkets by the name of *frankfurters*, *franks*, or *hot dogs*.

法兰克福中产阶级曾经非常享受的熏牛肉和猪肉香肠,我们现在也能够在熟食店买到——frankfurters,franks,hot dogs,"熏肠"。

12

HOW TO FLATTER YOUR FRIENDS
如何奉承朋友

(Sessions 32 — 37)

TEASER PREVIEW
引读

What adjective aptly describes people who are:

* *friendly and easy to get along with?*
* *tireless?*
* *simple, frank, aboveboard?*
* *keen-minded?*
* *generous, noble, and forgiving?*
* *able to do many things skillfully?*
* *unflinching in the face of pain or disaster?*
* *brave, fearless?*
* *charming and witty?*
* *smooth, polished, cultured?*

哪些词能够巧妙地描述以下几类人：
* 友善、容易相处
* 孜孜不倦
* 简单、直率、光明正大
* 思维敏捷
* 慷慨、高尚、仁慈
* 能够熟练地做很多事情
* 在痛苦和灾难面前无所畏惧
* 勇敢、无畏
* 迷人、诙谐
* 温和、优雅、有教养

SESSION 32
第 32 节

Words are the symbols of emotions, as well as ideas. You can show your feeling by the tone you use ("You're silly" can be an insult, an accusation, or an endearment, depending on how you say it) or by the words you choose (you can label a quality either "childish" or "childlike," depending on whether you admire it or condemn it—it's the same quality, no matter what you call it).

In Chapter 11 we discussed ten basic words that you might use to show your disapproval. In this chapter we discuss ten adjectives that indicate wholehearted approval.

Consider the interesting types of people described in the following paragraphs, then note how accurately the adjective applies to each type.

词汇是情绪和概念的象征符号。你可以通过声调表现情感("你真傻"既可能是侮辱,也可能是指责或嗔爱,这取决于你的声调),也可以通过措辞达到同样的效果(你可以将一个人的特点描述为"幼稚"或"单纯",这取决于你要表达的是褒义或是贬义——无论使用怎样的声调,特点是同样的)。

我们在第 11 章中讨论了 10 个基本词汇,你可以使用这些词汇来表示反对。本章我们将讨论另外十个词汇,这些词汇表示完全赞成。

思考一下下文描述的有意思的几类人,然后注意一下这些形容词是如何准确形容不同类型的人的。

IDEAS
概念

1. put the kettle on, Polly

波利,烧水

They are friendly, happy, extroverted, and gregarious—the sort of people who will invite you out for a drink, who like to transact business around the lunch table, who put the coffee to perking as soon as company drops in. They're sociable, genial, cordial, affable—and they like parties and all the eating and drinking that goes with them.

The adjective is: *convivial*

他们友好、快乐、外向、爱交际。这类人会叫你出去喝上一杯,喜欢在午餐时谈工作,只要有朋友在,他会马上去煮咖啡。他擅长交际、和蔼、友好、平易近人——他喜欢聚会,喜欢和大家一起吃吃喝喝。

形容词是 convivial。

2. you can't tire them

不会感到疲倦

Arnold Bennett once pointed out that we all have the same amount of time—twenty-four hours a day. Strictly speaking, that's as inconclusive an observation as Bennett ever made. It's not time that counts, but energy—and of that wonderful quality we all have very different amounts, from the persons who wake up tired, no matter how much sleep they've had, to lucky, well-adjusted mortals who hardly ever need to sleep.

Energy comes from a healthy body, of course; it also comes from a psychological balance, a lack of conflicts and insecurities.

Some people apparently have boundless, illimitable energy— they're on the go from morning to night, and often far into the night, working hard, playing hard, never tiring, never "pooped" or "bushed"—and getting twice as much done as any three other human beings.

The adjective is: indefatigable

阿诺德·伯奈特曾经指出,所有人都拥有相同的时间———一天 24 小时。严格说来,这是伯奈特得出的无法令人信服的结论之一。 时间并不重要,重要的是精力——每个人所拥有的这个特质都不尽相同:有些人无论睡了多久,起床时仍然感觉疲倦;而有些人却非常幸运,自身调节能力强,几乎不需要睡眠。

当然,精力源于健康的身体;也源于平衡的内心,没有纷争、没有不安感的内心。

有些人明显具有无边无际的精力——他能够从早到晚甚至一直到深夜不停地努力工作、尽情玩耍,从不疲倦,不会"筋疲力尽"或是"疲惫不堪"——他做成的事情甚至是三个平常人相加的两倍。

形容词是 indefatigable。

3. no tricks, no secrets
不要手段、不藏秘密

They are pleasingly frank, utterly lacking in pretense or artificiality, in fact quite unable to hide their feelings or thoughts—and so honest and aboveboard that they can scarcely conceive of trickery, chicanery, or dissimulation in anyone. There is, then, about them the simple naturalness and unsophistication of a child.

The adjective is: ingenuous

他们的坦诚惹人喜欢,他毫不矫饰或做作。实际上,他根本不会隐藏情感或想法——他的诚实和率直使他根本想象不到别人的诡计、欺诈或虚伪。在他的身上,我们能看到孩子一样的自然和质朴。

形容词是 ingenuous。

4. sharp as a razor
像剃刀一样锋利

They have minds like steel traps; , their insight into problems that would confuse or mystify people of less keenness or discernment is just short of amazing.

The adjective is: perspicacious

他的思维好像捕兽夹;对于使洞察力或识别能力稍差的人困惑不解的问题,他的鉴别能力会使你惊讶不已。

形容词是 perspicacious。

5. no placating necessary
无需安抚

They are most generous about forgiving a slight, an insult, an injury. Never do they harbor resentment, store up petty grudges, or waste energy or thought on means of revenge or retaliation. How could they? They're much too big-hearted.

The adjective is: magnanimous

他会非常慷慨地原谅轻蔑、侮辱和伤害。他不会怀恨在心,隐藏怨恨,或将精力和思想浪费在思考报仇或反击的手段上。他是如何做到的? 他的内心非常强大。

形容词是 magnanimous。

6．one-person orchestras
一个人的管弦乐队

The range of their aptitudes is truly formidable. If they are writers, they have professional facility in poetry, fiction, biography, criticism, essays—you just mention it and they've done it, and very competently. If they are musicians, they can play the oboe, the bassoon, the French horn, the bass viol, the piano, the celesta, the xylophone, even the clavichord if you can dig one up. If they are artists, they use oils, water colors, *gouache*, charcoal, pen and ink—they can do anything! Or maybe the range of their abilities cuts across all fields, as in the case of Michelangelo, who was an expert sculptor, painter, poet, architect, and inventor. In case you're thinking "Jack of all trades . . ." you're wrong—they're masters of all trades.

The adjective is: *versatile*

他的天赋之多令人惊叹。如果他是作家,他在诗歌、小说、传记、评论和散文等方面都十分精通——你可能只能谈及,而他却能够做到,而且做得很好。如果他是音乐家,他会精通双簧管、巴松管、圆号、低音提琴、钢琴、钢片琴、木琴,如果你能够为他挖掘出击弦古钢琴,他同样能够演奏。如果他是艺术家,他对油画、水彩、水粉画、木炭画、钢笔画和墨水画都精通——他什么都能做! 他的才华也可能会跨越领域的界限,例如米开朗基罗,他既是专业雕刻家,又是画家、诗人、建筑家、发明家。如果你认为他是"万事皆通一无所长",你错了——他个个精通。

形容词是 versatile。

7．no grumbling
从不抱怨

They bear their troubles bravely, never ask for sympathy, never yield to sorrow, never wince at pain. It sounds almost superhuman, but it's true.

The adjective is: *stoical*

他勇敢忍受困苦,从不乞求同情,从不向悲伤低头,从不畏缩痛苦。听起来他像超人,但这的确是事实。

形容词是 stoical。

8．no fear
无所畏惧

There is not, as the hackneyed phrase has it, a cowardly bone in their bodies. They are strangers to fear, they're audacious, dauntless, contemptuous of danger and hardship.

The adjective is: *intrepid*

他的身上没有懦弱的骨头,尽管这是陈词滥调。对于恐惧,他是陌生人;他大胆,无畏,蔑视危险和困苦。

形容词是 intrepid。

9．no dullness
从不沉闷

They are witty, clever, delightful; and naturally, also, they are brilliant and entertaining conversationalists.

The adjective is: *scintillating*

他诙谐幽默、聪明、开心,他是才华横溢的令人开心的健谈者。

形容词是 scintillating。

10. city slickers

时髦的城市人

They are cultivated, poised, tactful, socially so experienced, sophisticated, and courteous that they're at home in any group, at ease under all circumstances of social intercourse. You cannot help admiring (perhaps envying) their smoothness and self-assurance, their tact and congeniality.

The adjective is: *urbane*

他举止文雅、沉着冷静、圆滑老练,他在社交场合富有经验,彬彬有礼,所以,他能够适应任何群体,能够适应任何社交场合。你忍不住会羡慕(可能嫉妒)他的圆滑、自信、爽快、机智和亲和力。

形容词是 urbane。

USING THE WORDS
单词应用

Can you pronounce the words?
你能读出这些单词吗?

1.	*convivial*	kən-VIV′-ee-əl
2.	*indefatigable*	in′-də-FAT′-ə-gə-bəl
3.	*ingenuous*	in-JEN′-yoo-əs
4.	*perspicacious*	pur′-spə-KAY′-shəs
5.	*magnanimous*	məg-NAN′-ə-məs
6.	*versatile*	VUR′-sə-təl
7.	*stoical*	STŌ′-ə-kəl
8.	*intrepid*	in-TREP′-id
9.	*scintillating*	SIN′-tə-layt-ing
10.	*urbane*	ur-BAYN′

Can you work with the words?
你能灵活使用这些词汇了吗?

1.	convivial	a.	frank
2.	indefatigable	b.	unflinching
3.	ingenuous	c.	noble
4.	perspicacious	d.	capable in many directions
5.	magnanimous	e.	tireless
6.	versatile	f.	fearless
7.	stoical	g.	keen-minded

8. intrepid	h. witty
9. scintillating	i. friendly
10. urbane	j. polished, sophisticated

KEY: 1-i, 2-e, 3-a, 4-g, 5-c, 6-d, 7-b, 8-f, 9-h, 10-j

Do you understand the words? (Ⅰ)
你对这些词汇是否已经透彻地理解?(Ⅰ)

1. *Convivial* people are unfriendly.		TRUE	FALSE
2. Anyone who is *indefatigable* tires easily.		TRUE	FALSE
3. An *ingenuous* person is artful and untrustworthy.		TRUE	FALSE
4. A *perspicacious* person is hard to fool.		TRUE	FALSE
5. A *magnanimous* person is easily insulted.		TRUE	FALSE
6. A *versatile* person does many things well.		TRUE	FALSE
7. A *stoical* person always complains of his hard lot.		TRUE	FALSE
8. An *intrepid* explorer is not easily frightened.		TRUE	FALSE
9. A *scintillating* speaker is interesting to listen to.		TRUE	FALSE
10. Someone who is *urbane* is always making enemies.		TRUE	FALSE

KEY: 1-F, 2-F, 3-F, 4-T, 5-F, 6-T, 7-F, 8-T, 9-T, 10-F

Do you understand the words? (Ⅱ)
你对这些词汇是否已经透彻地理解?(Ⅱ)

1. convivial—hostile	SAME	OPPOSITE
2. indefatigable—enervated	SAME	OPPOSITE
3. ingenuous—worldly	SAME	OPPOSITE
4. perspicacious—obtuse	SAME	OPPOSITE
5. magnanimous—petty	SAME	OPPOSITE
6. versatile—well-rounded	SAME	OPPOSITE
7. stoical—unemotional	SAME	OPPOSITE

8. intrepid—timid	SAME	OPPOSITE
9. scintillating—banal	SAME	OPPOSITE
10. urbane—erude	SAME	OPPOSITE

KEY: 1-O，2-O，3-O，4-O，5-O，6-S，7-S，8-O，9-O，10-O

Can you recall the words?

你能够写出这些词汇吗？

1. witty	1. S _____
2. noble，forgiving	2. M _____
3. capable in many fields	3. V _____
4. keen-minded	4. P _____
5. uncomplaining	5. S _____
6. friendly	6. C _____
7. poised；polished	7. U _____
8. courageous	8. I _____
9. tireless	9. I _____
10. simple and honest；frank	10. I _____

KEY：1-scintillating，2-magnanimous，3-versatile，4-perspicacious，5-stoical，6-convivial，7-urbane，8-intrepid，9-indefatigable，10-ingenuous

(End of Session 32)

SESSION 33
第 33 节

ORIGINS AND RELATED WORDS
词源及相关词汇

1. eat, drink, and be merry
吃、喝、开心

The Latin verb *vivo*, to live, and the noun *vita*, life, are the source of a number of important English words.

Convivo is the Latin verb to *live together*; from this, in Latin, was formed the noun *convivium* (don't get impatient; we'll be back to English directly), which meant a *feast* or *banquet*; and from *convivium* we get our English word *convivial*, an adjective that describes the kind of person who likes to attend feasts and banquets, enjoying (and supplying) the jovial good fellowship characteristic of such gatherings.

Using the suffix *-ity*, can you write the noun form of the adjective *convivial*? ___
_____. (Can you pronounce it?)

拉丁语动词 vivo(意为"生活")及其相应的名词 vita(意为"生活")派生出许多重要的英语词汇。

convivo 是拉丁语动词,表示"在一起生活";在拉丁语中,它的名词形式是 convivium(不要失去耐心,我们很快就会回到英语),表示"盛宴或者宴会";我们从 convivium 得到英语形容词 convivial,用来形容喜欢参加盛宴或者宴会的那一类人,因为他们喜欢(并提供)快活的交际,这也正是聚会的最大特点。

用后缀 ity,你能写出形容词 convivial 的名词形式吗?(你能读出来吗?)

2. living it up
快乐生活

Among many others, the following English words derive from Latin *vivo*, to live:

(1) *vivacious* (vī-VAY′-shəs)—full of the joy of living; animated; peppy—a *vivacious* personality. Noun: *vivacity* (vī-VAS′-ə-tee). You can, as you know, also add *-ness* to any adjective to form a noun. Write the alternate noun form of *vivacious*: _____.

(2) *vivid*—possessing the freshness of life; strong; sharp—a *vivid* imagination; a *vivid* color. Add *-ness* to form the noun: _____.

(3) *revive* (rə-VIV′)—bring back to life. In the 1960s, men's fashions of the twenties were *revived*. Noun: *revival* (rə-VĪ′-vəl).

(4) *vivisection* (viv′-ə-SEK′-shən)—operating on a live animal. *Sect-* is from a Latin verb meaning *to cut*. *Vivisection* is the process of experimenting on live animals to discover causes and cures of disease. *Antivivisectionists* object to the procedure, though many

of our most important medical discoveries were made through *vivisection*.

以下英语词汇来自拉丁语词汇，vivo，表示生活：

（1）vivacious——充满快乐感的；活泼的；精神充沛的——a vivacious personality（活泼的性情）。名词形式：vivacity。正如你所了解的，你可以在任何形容词尾添加-ness 来形成名词。写出 vivacious 的另外一个名词形式：

（2）vivid——具有鲜活的特点；强烈的；鲜明的——a vivid imagination；a vivid color。添加-ness 形成名词：_____。

（3）revive——复活、复兴。20 世纪 20 年代的男性时尚在 60 年代得到复兴。名词形式 revival。

（4）vivisection（viv′-ə-SEK′-shən）——动物活体解剖。sect-是拉丁语词根，表示"切割"。vivisection 是科学家解剖活着的动物的过程，目的是为了找出疾病的原因和治疗方法。antivivisectionists 是反对活体解剖者，但是，我们大多数重要的医学发现都是通过活体解剖得到的。

（5）*Viviparous*（vī-VIP′-ər-əs）—producing live babies. Human beings and most other mammals are *viviparous*. *Viviparous* is contrasted to *oviparous*（ō-VIP′-ər-əs）, producing young from eggs. Most fish, fowl, and other lower forms of life are *oviparous*.

The combining root in both these adjectives is Latin *pareo*, to give birth (*parent* comes from the same root). In *oviparous*, the first two syllables derive from Latin *ovum*, egg.

Ovum, egg, is the source of *oval* and *ovoid*, egg-shaped; *ovulate*（O′-vyə-layt′）, to release an egg from the *ovary*: *ovum*（Ō-vəm）, the female germ cell which, when fertilized by a sperm, develops into an embryo, then into a *fetus*（FEE′-təs）, and finally, in about 280 days in the case of humans, is born as an infant.

The adjective form of *ovary* is *ovarian*（ō-VAIR′-ee-ən）; of *fetus*, *fetal*（FEE′-təl）. Can you write the noun form of the verb *ovulate*? _____.

Love, you may or may not be surprised to hear, also comes from *ovum*.

No, not the kind of love you're thinking of. Latin *ovum* became *oeuf* in French, or with "the" preceding the noun (*the* egg), *l'oeuf*, pronounced something like LOOF. *Zero* (picture it for a moment) is shaped like an egg (0), so if your score in tennis is *fifteen*, and your opponent's is *zero*, you shout triumphantly, "Fifteen love! Let's go!"

（5）viviparous——胎生的。人类和其他大多数哺乳动物都需要这种方式。与 oviparous 相对，后者表示"卵生的"，是大多数鱼类、家禽类和其他低等生物的繁殖方式。

组成这两个形容词的词根是拉丁语 pareo，表示"使……出生"（parent 也来自于同一词根）。oviparous 的前两个音节派生自拉丁语 ovum，表示"卵"。

ovum，卵，是以下词汇的来源：oval 和 ovoid，表示"卵形的"；ovulate，表示"从卵巢释放卵子"；ovum 是女性生殖细胞，与精子结合后受精，发展成为胚胎，然后成为胎儿（fetus），经历 280 天孕育后（对人类来说）出生，成为婴儿。

ovary 的形容词形式是 ovarian；fetus 的形容词形式是 fetal。你能够写出动词 ovulate 的名词形式吗？

你或许曾经听说，love（爱）也来自于 ovum。

并不是你想到的那种爱。拉丁语 ovum 在法语中变成 oeuf，名词前加上定冠词后变成 l'oeuf（这个蛋），发音与 LOOF 颇为相似。零（想象）的形状与蛋十分相似（0），所以，如果你在打网球时得到 15 分，你的对手得到零分，你会胜利地叫喊"15 比 0！加油！"

3. more obout life

更多关于生活的词汇

Latin *vita*, life, is the origin of：

(1) *vital*(VĪ′-təl)—essential to life; of crucial importance—a *vital* matter; also full of life, strength, vigor, etc. Add the suffix *-ity* to form the noun: _____ _____. Add a verb suffix to construct the verb: _____ _____ (meaning: *to give life to*). Finally, write the noun derived from the verb you have constructed: _____.

(2) *Revitalize*(ree-VĪ′-tə-līz′) is constructed from the prefix *re-*, again, back, the root *vita*, and the verb suffix. Meaning? _____. Can you write the noun formed from this verb? _____.

(3) The prefix *de-* has a number of meanings, one of which is essentially negative, as in *defrost*, *decompose*, *declassify*, etc. Using this prefix, can you write a verb meaning *to rob of life*, *to take life from*? _____. Now write the noun form of this verb: _____.

(4) *Vitamin*—one of the many nutritional elements on which life is dependent. Good eyesight requires vitamin A (found, for example, in carrots); strong bones need vitamin D (found in sunlight and cod-liver oil); etc.

Vitalize, *revitalize*, and *devitalize* are used figuratively for example, a program or plan is *vitalized*, *revitalized*, or *devitalized*, according to how it's handled.

拉丁语名词 vita,"生命/生活",也出现在以下词汇中:

(1) vital——对生命必不可少,至关重要的——a vital matter,一件至关重要的事,也指充满生命、力量和活力等。加上后缀-ity 形成名词_____。加上动词后缀形成动词_____(意为"赋予生命")。最后写出从动词衍生出来的名词_____。

(2) revitalize——是由前缀 re-("再一次""又"),加上词根 vita 和动词后缀,它是什么意思呢? _____。你能写出由这个动词衍变而来的名词形式吗? _____。

(3) 前缀 de-有不同的意思,其中最常见的意思之一就是表否定,如在 defrost,decompose,declassify 等。加上一个动词前缀,你能写出一个表示"剥夺生命"的动词吗? _____。你能写出这个动词的名词形式吗? _____。

(4) vitamin——维生素,生命赖以生存的元素之一。良好的视力需要维生素 A(例如,胡萝卜中含有维生素 A);坚固的骨骼需要维生素 D(光照和鱼油中含有维生素 D)等;

vitalize, revitalize 和 devitalize 都有其引申用法——例如,根据处理项目或计划的方法,a program or plan is vitalized, revitalize or devitalized,"项目或者计划被启动、重新启动或否定"。

4. French life

法式生活

Sometimes, instead of getting our English words directly from Latin, we work through one of the Latin-derived or Romance languages. (As you will recall, the Romance languages—French, Spanish, Italian, Portuguese, and Romanian—are so called because they were originally dialects of the old Roman tongue. English, by the way, is not a Romance language, but a Teutonic one. Our tongue is a development of a German dialect imposed on the natives of Britain by the Angles, Saxons, and Jutes of early English history. Though we have taken over into English more than 50 percent of the Latin vocabulary and almost 30 percent of the classical Greek vocabulary as roots and prefixes, our basic language is nevertheless German.)

The French, using the same Latin root *vivo*, to live, formed two expressive phrases much used in English. French pronunciation is, of course, tricky, and if you are not at least superficially acquainted with that language, your pronunciation may sound a bit awkward to the sophisticated ear—but try it anyway. These phrases are:

有时候,英语单词并非直接来自于拉丁语,而来自于一种拉丁语派生的或者属于拉丁语系的语言。(拉丁语系包括法语、西班牙语、意大利语、葡萄牙语和罗马尼亚语——它们最初都是古罗马人的语言的方言。顺便说一下,英语并不属于拉丁语系,而是日耳曼语。英语是一种德语方言的发展,是由英国历史早期的盎格鲁人、撒克逊人和朱特人给当地英国人语言带来的影响。尽管我们从拉丁语获得了 50% 的词汇,从希腊语获得了 30% 的词汇,我们的基本语言基本上还是德语语系的。)

运用同样的拉丁语词根 vivo(生活),法语构成了两个表现力丰富的短语,这两个短语在英语中也被广泛使用。当然,法语发音比较困难,如果你对法语一无所知,对于老练的耳朵来说,你的发音听起来可能会有点别扭——但是你还是要去试一试。这些词组是:

(1) *joie de vivre*—pronounced something like zhwahd′-VEEV′ (*zh* is identical in sound to the *s* of *pleasure*).

Literally *joy of living*, this phrase describes an immense delight in being alive, an effervescent keenness for all the daily activities that human beings indulge in. People who possess *joie de vivre* are never moody, depressed, bored, or apathetic—on the contrary, they are full of sparkle, eager to engage in all group activities, and, most important, always seem to be having a good time, no matter what they are doing. *Joie de vivre* is precisely the opposite of *ennui* (this is also a word of French origin, but is easy to pronounce: AHN′-wee), which is a feeling of boredom, discontent, or weariness resulting sometimes from having a jaded, oversophisticated appetite, sometimes from just finding all of life tedious and unappetizing, and sometimes implying in addition physical lassitude and general inactivity. Young children and simple people rarely experience *ennui*—to them life is always exciting, always new.

(1) joie de vivre——发音与 zhwahd′-VEEV′ 比较相近(zh 与 pleasure 中 s 的发音相同)。

字面意思表示"活着的快乐",这个短语描述了活着的极大幸福,对于人们的日常活动表现出强烈的热情。拥有 joie de vivre 的人从不会喜怒无常、失落、厌烦或者冷淡——相反,他们充满活力和参加所有团体活动的渴望。最重要的是,不论做什么,他们总会非常尽兴。joie de vivre 的反义词是 ennui(这个词虽然也是法语词源,但是发音相对容易 AHN′-wee),表示厌烦感、不满足感和疲倦感,这样的感觉有时源自腻烦的、过度复杂的饮食,有时源自对枯燥无味的生活的厌倦,有时源自身体的疲劳和缺乏运动。青少年和单纯的人很少经历 ennui——对于他们来说,生活总是多姿多彩,每一天都是新的。

(2) *bon vivant*, pronounced something like BŌNG′-vee-VAHNG′—the -NG a muted nasal sound similar to the *-ng* in *sing*.

A *bon vivant* is a person who lives luxuriously, especially in respect to rich food, good liquor, expensive theater parties, operas, and other accouterments of upper-class life. *Bon vivant* means, literally, a *good liver*; actually, a *high liver*, one who lives a luxurious life. When you think of a *bon vivant* (usually, language being sexist, a male), you get the picture of someone attired in top hat, "soup and fish" or tuxedo, raising his cane to call a taxi while a beautiful, evening-gowned and sophisticated-looking woman, sparkling in diamonds and furs, waits at his side. They're going to a champagne and partridge supper at an outrageously expensive restaurant, etc.—fill in your own details of the high life.

The *bon vivant* is of course a *convivial* person—and also likely to be a *gourmet* (gŏor-MAY′), another word from French.

（2）bon vivant——发音与 BŌNG′-vee-VAHNG′相似——-NG 是个特殊的弱鼻音，与 sing 中的-ng 发音类似。

a bon vivant 是指过着奢侈的生活的人，尤其喜欢食物、美酒、昂贵的剧院派对、歌剧以及其他上流社会的活动。bon vivant 的字面意思是 a good liver，生活得好的人；事实上是个 high liver，锦衣玉食者。联想 bon vivant 时，你的脑海中浮现出一个穿着整齐的人，他戴着高帽，穿着晚礼服，抬起手杖叫车，身边站着一位穿了美丽晚礼服的女士，她看起来优雅得体，身上的钻石和裘皮熠熠生光。他们要去豪华餐馆享用香槟酒和山鹑晚宴，等等——其他上流社会的细节由你自己填充。

bon vivant 当然会是 convivial(好交际的)人——也是美食主义者(gourmand)，这是法语的另一个单词。

5. food and how to enjoy it

食物和享受食物的方法

The *gourmand* （GŎOR′-mənd） enjoys food with a sensual pleasure. To *gourmands* the high spots of the day are the times for breakfast, lunch, dinner, and midnight supper; in short, they like to eat, but the eating must be good. The verb form, *gormandize* （GAWR′-mən-dīz′）, however, has suffered a degeneration in meaning—it signifies to *stuff oneself like a pig*.

A *gourmand* is significantly different from a *gourmet*, who has also a keen interest in food and liquor, but is much more fastidious, is more of a connoisseur, has a most discerning palate for delicate tastes, flavors, and differences; goes in for rare delicacies (like humming birds' tongues and other such absurdities); and approaches the whole business from a scientific, as well as a sensual, viewpoint. *Gourmet* is always a complimentary term, *gourmand* somewhat less so.

gourmand,美食主义者,视食物为一种感官享受。对于他来说,一天里最重要的时光就是早餐、午餐、晚餐和午夜夜宵。简而言之,他喜欢吃,但是必须吃得好。但是,动词形式 gormandize 在词义上有所贬低——它表示像猪一样狼吞虎咽。

gourmet 的词义与 gourmand 有很大不同。gourmet 指"美食家",对食物和酒也具有浓厚的兴趣,但是他更讲究,更像鉴赏家,对微妙的味道、香味和它们的不同口味更加挑剔;他喜欢罕见的佳肴(例如蜂鸟的舌头和其他类似离谱的事物);对于整个美食业的态度,他以科学的态度对待,而非感官视角。gourmet 总是被视为褒义词来使用,gourmand 相比稍差。

The person who eats voraciously, with no discernment whatever, but merely for the purpose of stuffing himself ("I know I haven't had enough to eat till I feel sick"), is called a *glutton* (GLUT′-ən)—obviously a highly derogatory term. The verb *gluttonize* is stronger than *gormandize*; the adjective *gluttonous* （GLUT′-ə-nəs） is about the strongest epithet you can apply to someone whose voracious eating habits you find repulsive. Someone who has a voracious, insatiable appetite for money, sex, punishment, etc. is also called a *glutton*.

仅仅是为了填饱肚子(他会说"我会一直吃,直到恶心为止")而一点也不会品位味道的贪吃鬼被称为 glutton——饕餮之徒,极度贬义词。动词 gluttonize 比 gormandize 的贬义意味更为强烈,"暴食";形容词 gluttonous,"暴食的",是非常强烈的贬义词语,你可以用它来指你认为非常厌恶的具有暴食习惯的人。gluttonous 有时也用来形容对金钱、性欲和惩罚等有着贪婪的、无法满足欲望的人,也可以称他是一个"glutton"。

REVIEW OF ETYMOLOGY
复习词源

PREFIX, ROOT, SUFFIX	MEANING	ENGLISH WORDS
1. *vivo*	to live	_____
2. *-ous*	adjective suffix	_____
3. *re-*	again, back	_____
4. *sectus*	cut	_____
5. *anti-*	against	_____
6. *ovum*	egg	_____
7. *pareo*	to give birth, produce	_____
8. *vita*	life	_____
9. *-ize*	verb suffix	_____
10. *-ation*	noun suffix	_____
	added to verbs	_____
	ending in *-ize*	_____
11. *de-*	negative prefix	_____
12. *bon*	good	_____
13. *-ate*	verb suffix	_____

USING THE WORDS
单词应用

Can you pronounce the words?（Ⅰ）
你能读出这些单词吗？（Ⅰ）

1. *conviviality*	kən-viv′-ee-AL′-ə -tee
2. *vivacious*	vī-VAY′-shəs
3. *vivacity*	vī-VAS′-ə-tee
4. *vivid*	VIV′-id
5. *vividness*	VIV′-id-nəs
6. *revive*	rə-VĪV′
7. *revival*	rə-VĪV′-əl
8. *vivisection*	viv′-ə-SEK′-shən
9. *antivivisectionist*	an′-tee (or tī)-viv′-ə-SEK′-shən-ist
10. *viviparous*	vī-VIP′-ər-əs
11. *oviparous*	ō-VIP′-ər-əs
12. *oval*	Ō′-vəl.
13. *ovoid*	Ō′-voyd′

14. *ovary*   Ō′-və-ree

15. *ovarian*   ō-VAIR′-ee-ən

16. *ovulate*   Ō-vyə-layt′

17. *ovulation*   ō-vyə-LAY′-shən

Can you pronounce the words? (Ⅱ)

你能读出这些单词吗？(Ⅱ)

1. *vital*   VĪ′-təl

2. *vitality*   vī-TAL′-ə-tee

3. *vitalize*   VĪ′-tə -līz′

4. *vitalization*   vī′-tə -lə-ZAY′-shən

5. *revitalize*   ree-VĪ′-tə-līz′

6. *revitalization*   ree-vī′-tə-lə-ZAY′-shən

7. *devitalize*   dee-VĪ′-tə-līz′

8. *devitalization*   dee-vī′-tə-lə-ZAY′-shən

9. *joie de vivre*   zhwahd′-VEEV′

10. *ennui*   AHN′-wee

11. *bon vivant*   BŌNG′ vee-VAHNG′

12. *gourmand*   GŎOR′-mənd

13. *gourmet*   gŏor-MAY′

14. *gormandize*   GAWR′-mən-dīz′

15. *glutton*   GLUT′-ən

16. *gluttonous*   GLUT-ə-nəs

17. *gluttonize*   GLUT′-ə-nīz′

18. *vitamin*   VĪ′-tə-min

Can you work with the words? (Ⅰ)

你能灵活使用这些词汇了吗？(Ⅰ)

1. oval, ovoid   a. peppy

2. revitalize   b. bearing live young

3. gluttonous   c. strong, sharp

4. vivacious   d. piggish; greedy

5. vivid   e. egg-shaped

6. viviparous   f. bearing young in eggs

7. oviparous   g. give new life to

KEY：1-e, 2-g, 3-d, 4-a, 5-c, 6-b, 7-f

Can you work with the words? (II)
你能灵活使用这些词汇了吗？(II)

1. conviviality	a. release of the egg
2. vivisection	b. a "high liver"
3. antivivisectionist	c. experimentation on live animals
4. ovulation	d. one who is a connoisseur of good food
5. vitality	e. effervescence; joy of living
6. *joie de vivre*	f. one who enjoys food
7. ennui	g. one who eats greedily; one who is greedy (as for punishment, etc.)
8. *bon vivant*	h. boredom
9. gourmand	i. congeniality
10. gourmet	j. strength, vigor
11. glutton	k. one who is against experimen-tation on live animals

KEY：1-i, 2-c, 3-k, 4-a, 5-j, 6-e, 7-h, 8-b, 9-f, 10-d, 11-g

Can you work with the words? (III)
你能灵活使用这些词汇了吗？(III)

1. revive	a. rob of life or strength
2. vital	b. nutritional element necessary for life
3. vitalize	c. important, crucial
4. devitalize	d. stuff oneself like a pig
5. gluttonize	e. breathe life into
6. vitamin	f. bring back to life

KEY：1-f, 2-c, 3-e, 4-a, 5-d, 6-b

Do you understand the words? (I)
你对这些词汇是否已经透彻地理解？(I)

1. conviviality—asceticism	SAME	OPPOSITE
2. vivacious—apathetic	SAME	OPPOSITE
3. vivid—dull	SAME	OPPOSITE
4. revive—kill	SAME	OPPOSITE
5. revitalize—rejuvenate	SAME	OPPOSITE

6. ennui—boredom   SAME   OPPOSITE
7. *bon vivant*—"man about town"   SAME   OPPOSITE
8. gormandize—starve   SAME   OPPOSITE
9. glutton—ascetic   SAME   OPPOSITE
10. *joie de vivre*—boredom   SAME   OPPOSITE

KEY：1-O，2-O，3-O，4-O，5-S，6-S，7-S，8-O，9-O，10-O

Do you understand the words? (Ⅱ)
你对这些词汇是否已经透彻地理解？（Ⅱ）

1. vivacity—liveliness   SAME   OPPOSITE
2. revival—renewal   SAME   OPPOSITE
3. vivisection—experimentation on corpses   SAME   OPPOSITE
4. ovulation—egg-releasing   SAME   OPPOSITE
5. devitalize—reinvigorate   SAME   OPPOSITE
6. vitality—fatigue   SAME   OPPOSITE
7. gluttonous—greedy   SAME   OPPOSITE
8. gourmand—ascetic   SAME   OPPOSITE
9. ovoid—egg-shaped   SAME   OPPOSITE

KEY：1-S，2-S，3-O，4-S，5-O，6-O，7-S，8-O，9-S

Do you understand the words? (Ⅲ)
你对这些词汇是否已经透彻地理解？（Ⅲ）

1. Humans are *viviparous*.   TRUE   FALSE
2. Cows are *oviparous*.   TRUE   FALSE
3. *Ovulation* takes places in females only when they are married.   TRUE   FALSE
4. An *antivivisectionist* believes in experimenting on live animals.   TRUE   FALSE
5. *Vitamins* are essential to good health.   TRUE   FALSE
6. A *bon vivant* lives like a hermit.   TRUE   FALSE
7. A *gourmet* stuffs himself with food.   TRUE   FALSE
8. It is normal for young children to be overwhelmed with *ennui*.   TRUE   FALSE
9. People who are keenly alive possess *joie de vivre*.   TRUE   FALSE

KEY：1-T，2-F，3-F，4-F，5-T，6-F，7-F，8-F，9-T

Can you recall the words?

你能够写出这些词汇吗?

1. bearing young by eggs (*adj.*)	1. O _____
2. bearing live young (*adj.*)	2. V _____
3. good-fellowship	3. C _____
4. operating on live animals	4. V _____
5. one who is opposed to such an activity	5. A _____
6. the process of releasing an egg from the ovary	6. O _____
7. to remove life or vigor from	7. D _____
8. joy of living	8. J _____
9. one who eats like a pig	9. G _____
10. a "high liver"	10. B _____
11. one who is a connoisseur of good food	11. G _____
12. one who gets a sensual enjoyment from good food	12. G _____
13. to stuff oneself like a pig; to eat greedily	13. G _____ *or* G _____
14. boredom; discontent; tedium	14. E _____
15. liveliness, pep	15. V _____ *or* V _____ *or* V _____
16. egg-shaped	16. O _____ *or* O _____
17. to bring renewed life or vigor to	17. R _____ *or* R _____
18. referring to the ovary (*adj.*)	18. O _____
19. essential to life; crucial; of utmost importance	19. V _____

KEY: 1-oviparous, 2-viviparous, 3-conviviality, 4-vivisection, 5-antivivisectionist, 6-ovulation, 7-devitalize, 8-*joie de vivre*, 9-glutton, 10-*bon vivant*, 11-gourmet, 12-gourand, 13-gluttonize *or* gormandize, 14-ennui, 15-vivacity, vivaciousness, *or* vitality, 16-oval *or* ovoid, 17-revitalize *or* revive, 18-ovarian, 19-vital

(*End of Session 33*)

SESSION 34
第 34 节

ORIGINS AND RELATED WORDS
词源及相关词汇

1. no fatigue
不疲劳

Indefatigable is a derived form of *fatigue——in-* is a negative prefix，the suffix -*able* means *able to be*；hence，literally，*indefatigable* means *unable to be fatigued*. The noun is *indefatigability* (in′-də-fat′-ə-gə-BIL′-ə-tee).

indefatigable 由 fatigue 演变而来——in-是否定前缀,后缀-able 表示"能够……"——这样,从字面理解,indefatigable 表示"不能疲倦的"。名词形式是 indefatigability。

2. How simple can one be?
怎么会有如此坦率之人?

Ingenuous is a complimentary term，though its synonyms *naïve*，*gullible*，and *credulous* are faintly derogatory.

To call people *ingenuous* implies that they are frank，open，artless——in other words，not likely to try to put anything over on you，nor apt to hide feelings or thoughts that more sophisticated persons would consider it wise，tactful，or expedient to conceal.

Ingenuous should not be confused with *ingenious* (in-JEEN′-yəs)——note the slight difference in spelling——which on the contrary means *shrewd*，*clever*，*inventive*.

The noun form of *ingenuous* is *ingenuousness*；of *ingenious*，*ingenuity* (in′-jə-N OO′-ə-tee) or ingeniousness.

To call people *naive* (nah-EEV′) is to imply that they have not learned the ways of the world，and are therefore idealistic and trusting beyond the point of safety；such idealism and trust have probably come from ignorance or inexperience. The noun is *naivete* (nah-eev-TAY′).

Credulous (KREJ′-ə-ləs) implies a willingness to believe almost anything，no matter how fantastic. *Credulity* (krə-JOO′-lə-tee)，like *naivete*，usually results，again，from ignorance or inexperience，or perhaps from an inability to believe that human beings are capable of lying.

Gullible (GUL′-ə-bəl) means *easily tricked*，*easily fooled*，*easily imposed on*. It is a stronger word than *credulous* and is more derogatory. *Gullibility* (gul′-ə-BIL′-ə-tee) results more from stupidity than from ignorance or inexperience.

These four synonyms, *ingenuous*, *naive*, *credulous*, and *gullible*, are fairly close, but they contain areas of distinction worth remembering. Let's review them:

(1) *ingenuous*——frank, not given to concealment

(2) *naive*——inexperienced, unsophisticated, trusting

(3) *credulous*——willing to believe; not suspicious or skeptical

(4) *gullible*——easily tricked

ingenuous 是褒义词,但是它的同义词 naive、gullible 和 credulous 都略有贬义。

称一个人为 ingenuous 暗示出他很坦诚、直接、单纯——换句话说,他不会欺骗任何人,也不会刻意隐藏任何感觉或者想法,虽然一些更世故的人认为这不是聪明、机智的权宜之计。

注意不要混淆 ingenuous 和 ingenious(同时注意读音的不同)。相反,ingenious 表示"精明的、聪明的、别出心裁的"。ingenuous 的名词形式是 ingenuousness。ingenious 的名词形式是 ingenuity 或 ingeniousness。

称一个人为 naive(天真的)会暗示出他因为不懂得世道,因此过于理想主义容易轻信,超出了基本的安全范围;这样的态度来自于无知和经历的匮乏。名词形式为 naivete。

credulous(轻信的)则暗示出对于任何事物都报以信任的态度,无论事物有多么不切实际。与 naivete 相似,轻信的态度也是由于无知和经历的匮乏造成的,或者没有能力去认识到人类会撒谎。

gullible 表示"容易上当受骗的",比 credulous 表意强烈,词义上也更加贬义。gullibility 更多是由于愚蠢,而不是无知或经历的匮乏。

ingenuous、naive、credulous 和 gullible 这 4 个近义词词义非常接近,但也具有值得谨记的区别。我们稍作复习:

(1) ingenuous——直率的、毫无隐藏的;

(2) naive——无经验的、不世故的、容易轻信的;

(3) credulous——轻信的、不会猜测或怀疑的;

(4) gullible——容易上当受骗的。

3. belief and disbelief

　　信与不信

Credulous comes from Latin *credo*, to believe, the same root found in *credit* (if people *believe* in your honesty, they will extend *credit* to you; they will *credit* what you say). *-Ous* is an adjective suffix that usually signifies *full of*. So, strictly, *credulous* means *full of believingness*.

Do not confuse *credulous* with *credible* (KRED'-ə-bəl). In the latter word we see combined the root *credo*, believe, with *-ible*, a suffix meaning *can be*. Something *credible* can be believed.

Let's chart some differences:

Credulous listeners—those who fully believe what they hear

A *credible* story—one that can be believed

An *incredulous* (in-KREJ'-ə-ləs) attitude—an attitude of skepticism, of non-belief

An *incredible* (in-KRED'-ə-bəl) story—one that cannot be believed

Incredible characters—persons who are so unique that you can scarcely believe they exist.

Nouns are formed as follows:

credulous—credulity (krə-JOO'-lə-tee)

incredulous—incredulity (in-krə-JOO′-lə-tee)

credible—credibility (kred′-ə-BIL′-ə-tee)

incredible—incredibility (in-kred′-ə-BIL′-ə-tee)

credulous 来自于拉丁语 credo(相信),与 credit(信用)的词根相同(如果人们相信你的诚实,他们就会给你信誉,也会相信你说的话)。-ous 是形容词后缀,通常表示"充满……的"。所以,严格意义上,credulous 表示"充满信任的"。

注意不要混淆 credulous 和 credible。credible 结合了词根 credo(相信)和表示"能够……的"后缀-ible。用 credible 形容的事物是"能够被相信的",是"可信的"。

以下罗列出几个词汇词义的区别:

a credulous listener——对听见的事物完全信任的人;

a credible story——可信的故事;

an incredulous attitude——怀疑的态度;

an incredible story——难以置信的故事;

incredible characters——十分独一无二的人物,你无法相信他们的真实存在。

名词形式分别为:

credulous—credulity

incredulous—incredulity

credible—credibility

incredible—incredibility

To check your understanding of these distinctions，try the next test.

完成以下测试,检验自己对词汇意义的区别是否完全理解。

Can you use these words correctly？

你能正确使用这些单词吗?

Use *credulous*，*credible*，or corresponding negative or noun forms in the following sentences：

1. She listened _____ly to her husband's confession of his frequent infidelity，for she had always considered him a paragon of moral uprightness.

2. He told his audience an _____ and fantastic story of his narrow escapes.

3. He'll believe you—he's very _____.

4. Make your characters more _____ if you want your readers to believe in them.

5. We listened dumb-struck，full of _____，to the shocking details of corruption and vice.

6. He has the most _____ good luck.

7. The _____ of it！How can such things happen？

8. Naive people accept with complete _____ whatever anyone tells them.

9. "Do you believe me？" "Sure—your story is _____

_____ enough. ”

10. I'm not objecting to the total _____ of your story, but only to your thinking that I'm _____ enough to believe it!

KEY：1-incredulously，2-incredible，3-credulous，4-credible，5-incredulity，6-incredible，7-incredibility，8-credulity，9-credible，10-incredibility，credulous

4. what people believe in
人们所相信的

Credo，to believe，is the origin of four other useful English words.

(1) _Credo_（KREE′-do）—personal belief，code of ethics；the principles by which people guide their actions.

(2) _Creed_—a close synonym of _credo_；in addition，a religious belief，such as Catholicism，Judaism，Protestantism，Hinduism，etc.

(3) _Credence_（KREE′-dəns）—belief，as in，"I place no _credence_ in his stories. " or "Why should I give any _credence_ to what you say?"

(4) _Credentials_（krə-DEN′-shəls）—a document or documents proving a person's right to a title or privilege (i. e. ，a right to be believed)，as in，"The new ambassador presented his _credentials_ to the State Department. "

credo(相信)是另外 4 个有用的英语词汇的词根。

(1) credo——信条,个人信仰,道德准则,一些人依照其行为的原则。

(2) creed——与 credo 意义十分接近的近义词;此外还表示一种宗教信仰,例如天主教、犹太教、新教、印度教等。

(3) credence——信任、相信,例如"I place no credence in his stories. "(我不相信他编造的故事),或者"Why should I give any credence to what you say?"(我为什么要相信你的话?)

(4) credentials——凭证,能够证明一个人得到某种头衔或者优先权的文件(也就是一种使人相信你的权利),例如: "The new ambassador presented his credentials to the State Department. "(新大使向国务院递交了国书。)

5. heads and tails
有头有尾

We can hardly close our book on the words suggested by _ingenuous_ without looking at the other side of the coin. If _ingenuous_ means _frank，open_，then _disingenuous_（dis-in-JEN′-yoo-əs）should mean _not frank or open_. But _disingenuous_ people are far more than simply _not ingenuous_. They are crafty，cunning，dishonest，artful，insincere，untrustworthy—and they are all of these while making a pretense of being simple，frank，and aboveboard. You are thinking of a wolf in sheep's clothing? It's a good analogy.

Similarly，a remark may be _disingenuous_，as may also a statement，an attitude，a confession，etc.

Add -ness to form the noun derived from _disingenuous_： _____.

如果不提及与 ingenuous 相反的另外一个词汇,我们很难为本部分的讨论收尾。如果 ingenuous 表示"直率的、坦诚的",那么它的反义词 disingenuous 应该表示"不直率的"。但是一个用 disingenuous 修饰的人远比"不直率"的人复杂得多。他们狡猾、奸诈、不诚实、虚伪、不真诚、不值得信任——他们具备以上一切特点,同时还装出一副简单、坦诚、率直的模样。你一定想到了披着羊皮的狼,是吗? 真是个不错的类比。

disingenuous 可以用来修饰言语、陈述、态度、供述等。

在 disingenuous 后加上-ness 构成名容词:

REVIEW OF ETYMOLOGY
复习词源

PREFIX, ROOT, SUFFIX	MEANING	ENGLISH WORD
1. *in-*	negative prefix	_____
2. *-ness*	noun suffix	_____
3. *credo*	to believe	_____
4. *-ous*	adjective suffix	_____
5. *-ible*	can be; able to be	_____
6. *-ity*	noun suffix	_____
7. *-ence*	noun suffix	_____
8. *dis-*	negative prefix	_____

USING THE WORDS
单词应用

Can you pronounce the words?
你能读出这些单词吗?

1. *indefatigability*   in'-də-fat'-ə-gə-BIL'-ə-tee
2. *ingenuousness*   in-JEN'-yoo-əs-ness
3. *ingenious*   in-JEEN'-yəs
4. *ingenuity*   in'-jə-NOO'-ə-tee
5. *naive*   nah-EEV'
6. *naivete*   nah-eev-TAY'
7. *credulous*   KREJ'-ə-ləs
8. *incredulous*   in-KREJ'-ə-ləs
9. *gullible*   GUL'-ə-bəl
10. *gullibility*   gul'-ə-BIL'-ə-tee
11. *credible*   KRED'-ə-bəl
12. *incredible*   in-KRED'-ə-bəl
13. *credulity*   krə-JOO'-lə-tee
14. *incredulity*   in'-krə-JOO'-lə-tee
15. *credibility*   kred'-ə-BIL'-ə-tee
16. *incredibility*   in-kred'-ə-BIL'-ə-tee

17. *credo*   KREE'-dō
18. *creed*   KREED
19. *credence*   KREE'-dəns
20. *credentials*   krə-DEN'-shəlz
21. *disingenuous*   dis'-in-JEN'-yōo-əs
22. *disingenuousness* dis'-in-JEN'-yōo-əs-nəs

Can you work with the words? (Ⅰ)
你能灵活使用这些词汇了吗？(Ⅰ)

WORDS	DEFINITIONS
1. indefatigability	a. cunning
2. ingenuousness	b. skepticism
3. disingenuousness	c. personal code of ethics
4. naivete	d. frankness
5. credibility	e. belief, trust
6. incredulity	f. tirelessness
7. credence	g. believability
8. credo	h. inexperience; unworldliness

KEY：1-f，2-d，3-a，4-h，5-g，6-b，7-e，8-c

Can you work with the words? (Ⅱ)
你能灵活使用这些词汇了吗？(Ⅱ)

1. ingenious	a. easily tricked
2. credulous	b. religious belief
3. gullible	c. inexperienced; unworldly
4. incredible	d. document proving privileges, identity, etc.
5. creed	e. unbelievable
6. credentials	f. shrewdness; cleverness
7. ingenuity	g. clever; inventive; shrewd
8. naïve	h. willing to believe

KEY：1-g，2-h，3-a，4-e，5-b，6-d，7-f，8-c

Do you understand the words?

你对这些词汇是否已经透彻地理解？

1. Is *indefatigability* a sign of physical and emotional health?   YES   NO
2. Is *ingenuousness* a normal quality of young childhood?   YES   NO
3. Is *ingenuity* a characteristic of inventors?   YES   NO
4. Are some adolescents *naïve*?   YES   NO
5. Are unintelligent people often *gullible*?   YES   NO
6. Is *incredulity* the mark of the agnostic?   YES   NO
7. Does an *incredible* story invite belief?   YES   NO
8. Do people generally live by a *credo*?   YES   NO
9. Does our Constitution guarantee certain rights to Americans irrespective of their *creed*?   YES   NO
10. Are *ingenious* people sometimes *disingenuous*?   YES   NO
11. Do we generally give *credence* to *incredible* statements?   YES   NO

KEY：1-yes，2-yes，3-yes，4-yes，5-yes，6-yes，7-no，8-yes，9-yes，10-yes，11-no

Can you recall the words?

你能够写出这些词汇吗？

1. inexperience; unsophistication   1. N _____
2. believing (*adj.*)   2. C _____
3. religious belief   3. C _____
4. believable   4. C _____
5. great reservoir of energy   5. I _____
6. frankness   6. I _____
7. crafty; dishonest   7. D _____
8. inventive; clever   8. I _____
9. easily tricked   9. G _____
10. skeptical   10. I _____
11. unbelievable   11. I _____
12. personal code   12. C _____

KEY：1-naive，2-credulous，3-creed，4-credible，5-indefatigability，6-ingenuousness，7-disingenuous，8-ingenious，9-gullible，10-incredulous，11-incredible，12-credo

(End of Session 34)

SESSION 35
第 35 节

ORIGINS AND RELATED WORDS
词源及相关词汇

1. how to look
如何看

The Latin root *specto*, to look, is the source of a host of common English words: *spectacle*, *spectator*, *inspect*, *retrospect* (a looking back), *prospect* (a looking a-head), etc. In a variant spelling, *spic-*, the root is found in *conspicuous* (easily seen or looked at), *perspicacious*, and *perspicuous*.

A *perspicacious* (pur'-spə-KAY'-shəs) person is keen-minded, mentally sharp, astute. *Per-* is a prefix meaning *through*; so the word etymologically means *looking through* (matters, etc.) keenly, intelligently. The noun: *perspicacity* (pur'-spə-KAS'-ə-tee). Write an alternate noun ending in -ness:_____.

Perspicacity is a synonym of *acumen* (ə-KYOO'-mən), mental keenness, sharpness, quickness; keen insight. The root is Latin *acuo*, to sharpen.

拉丁语动词 specto 表示"看",并衍生出许多常见的英语词汇:spectacle(眼镜)、spectator(观众)、inspect(检查)、retrospect(回顾)、prospect(前景)等等。其变体 spic-也出现在许多词语中,例如:conspicuous(显眼的)、perspicacious(有洞察力的)和 perspicuous(明了的)。

如果用 perspicacious 形容一个人,这个人则是头脑敏锐的、思维敏捷的、聪慧的。per-是一个前缀,意为"穿过";因此这个单词从词源上看,意为"敏锐地、聪明地看透"。名词形式是 perspicacity. 请写出另外一个以-ness 结尾的名词形式_____。

perspicacity 的同义词是 acumen,意为"头脑敏锐,敏捷""敏锐的洞察力"。词根是拉丁语 acuo,意为"使锋利"。

2. sharpness
锋利

From *acuo*, to sharpen, come such words as *acute*, sharp, sudden, as *acute pain*, an *acute* attack of appendicitis, *acute* reasoning, etc; and *acupuncture* (AK'-yoo-punk'-chər), the insertion of a (sharp) needle into the body for medical purposes. The noun form of *acute*, referring to the mind or thinking, is *acuteness* or *acuity* (ə-KYOO-ə-tee); in other contexts, *acuteness* only.

Acupuncture combines *acuo*, to sharpen, with *punctus*, point. When you *punctuate* a sentence, you put various *points* (periods, commas, etc.) where needed; when lightning *punctuates* the storm, or when the silence is *punctuated* by the wailing of police sirens, again *points*, etymologically speaking, interrupt the atmosphere, the quiet, etc.

acuo 表示"使……锋利",它派生出 acute 和 acupuncture。acute 表示"锋利的、突然的",例如 acute pain(剧痛)、acute attack of apprendicitis(突发阑尾炎)和 acute reasoning(敏锐的推理)等;acupuncture 表示出于医学目的的将(锋利的)针头

插入身体。acute 的名词形式在表示思维或思考的敏锐程度时是 acuteness 或 acuity；在其他语境下仅有 acuteness 形式。

　　acupuncture 结合了 acuo，"使……变锋利"和 punctus，"点"。当你 punctuate 一个句子，你是在为句子添加各种标点符号（句号、逗号等）；当"闪电不时打断（punctuate）暴风雨"，或"安静被警笛的鸣叫声不时打断（punctuate）"，从词源角度讲，"点"再次将气氛、宁静等打扰。

If you are *punctual*, you're right on the point of time（noun：*punctuality*）; if you're *punctilious*（punk-TIL′-ee-əs）, you are exact, scrupulous, very careful to observe the proper *points* of behavior, procedure, etc.（noun：*punctiliousness*）. And to *puncture* something, of course, is to make a hole in it with a sharp *point*—as to *puncture* someone's tire, or figuratively, illusions, fantasies, or ego. *Pungent*（PUN′-jənt）comes from another form of the root *punctus*（*pungo*, to pierce sharply）, so a *pungent* smell or taste is sharp, spicy, pricking the nose or taste buds, so to speak; and a *pungent* wit sharply pierces one's sense of humor. Can you write the noun forms of this adjective? _____ or _____.

　　如果你 punctual，你会谨守时刻（名词形式：punctuality）；如果你 punctilious，你是一个严谨、一丝不苟的人，你十分认真地遵守有关行为、程序的合适的要点（名词形式：punctiliousness）。当然，如果将某种事物 puncture，你是在用一个锋利的点在上面钻洞，例如刺穿轮胎；或比喻用法，将假想、幻想或自尊心戳穿。pungent 来自词根 punctus 的另外一个形式（pungo，猛刺），所以，如果气味或味道由 pungent 修饰，那么它们十分强烈、辛辣，可以说能够刺伤鼻子或味蕾；而 pungent wit 是一针见血的机智，能够准确击中人们的幽默感。你能够写出这个形容词的名词形式吗？

3. some more looking

　　更多的"看"

Perspicacious should not be confused with *perspicuous*（pər-SPIK′-yo͞o-əs）. Here is the important distinction：

Perspicacious means *smart, sharp, able to look through and understand quickly*. This adjective applies to persons, their reasoning, minds, etc.

Perspicuous is the obverse side of the coin—it means *easily understood from one look*, and applies to writing, style, books, and like things that have to be understood. Hence it is a synonym of *clear, simple, lucid*. If you write with *perspicuous* style, your language is clear, easy to understand. If you are perspicacious, you understand quickly, easily.

The noun form of *perspicuous* is *perspicuity*（pur′-spə-KYo͞o-ə-tee）, or, of course, *perspicuousness*.

　　注意不要混淆 perspicacious 和与其形式十分相近的 perspicuous。两个词汇的主要区别在于：

　　perspicacious 的含义是："聪慧的、能够看透并快速理解的"，用来修饰人、推理、思维等等。

　　perspicuous 则是硬币的反面——用来指"明白易懂的"，可以用来修饰写作、文体、书籍及其他需要理解的事物。这样，它与 clear、simple、lucid 是近义词。如果你的写作风格是 perspicuous，你的语言则非常明晰、简单易懂。如果你 perspicacious，你理解得更快速、更容易。

　　perspicuous 的名词形式是 perspicuity，当然，也可以是 perspicuousness。

A *spectacle* is something to *look at*; *spectacles*（eyeglasses）are the means by which you get a comfortable and accurate look at the world. Anything *spectacular* is, etymologically, worth *looking* at.

A *spectator* is one who *looks* at what's happening.

To *inspect* is to *look into* something.

Retrospect (RET′-rə-spekt′) is a backward *look*—generally the word is preceded by the preposition *in*, for instance,"His life in *retrospect* seemed dreary and dull," or "Most experiences seem more enjoyable in *retrospect* than in actuality" (*retro-*, backward).

Prospect (PROS′-pekt′) is a forward *look*; *prospective* (prə-SPEK′-tiv) is the adjective. What's the *prospect* for inflation, for world peace, for the domestic energy supply? Your *prospective* mother-in-law is the one you can look forward to if you marry a certain person; similarly, your *prospective* bride, groom, child, job, vacation, etc. is the person, thing, or activity in the future that you look forward to. (The prefix is *pro-*, forward, ahead, before.)

a spectacle 是用来看的工具;spectacles 指"眼镜",佩戴眼镜你能够更舒适、更准确地观察世界。任何事物如果用 spectacular 修饰,从词源理解,这种事物值得观看。

a spectator 是观众,是观察事件的人物。

to inspect 是检查,是"to look into something"。

retrospect 是回顾,一种向后的看——通常与介词 in 连用,例如:"His life in retrospect seemed dreary and dull."(他过去的生活似乎枯燥乏味。)或者 "Most experiences seem more enjoyable in retrospect than in actuality."(大多数经历回顾起来要比当时有趣得多。)(retro-表示向后的。)

prospect 是前景,是一种向前的看;形容词形式是 prospective。通货膨胀、世界和平和国内能源供应会有怎样的 prospect 呢? prospective mother-in-law(未来的岳母或婆婆)则是那个只要结婚就要遇见的人;同样,你可能会有 prospective bride, groom, child, job, vacation 等等,他们是你期望在将来得到的人、事物或活动。(前缀是 pro-,表示向前的、在……前面的、在……之前的。)

If you enjoy looking at yourself, figuratively speaking, then you like to examine your mental processes and emotional reactions, in the intense way characteristic of the *introvert* (see Chapter 3). Your mind's eye turns inward, and you spend a good deal of time analyzing yourself, your character, your personality, your actions. Hence, since you look *inward*, you are *introspective* (in′-trə-SPEK′-tiv)—the prefix is *intro-*, inside, within. If you *introspect* (in′-trə-SPEKT′), you look inward and examine your inner reactions. Too much introspection (in′-trə-SPEK′-shən) or *introspectiveness* may lead to unhappiness or to depressing thoughts or feelings of anxiety—few people have the courage to see themselves as they really are.

There are times when you have to look *around* most carefully; you must then be *circumspect* (SUR′-kəm-spekt′)—watchful, cautious, alert (*circum-*, around).

The noun is *circumspection* (sur′-kem-SPEK-shən) or *circumspectness*.

If something looks good or sensible, but actually is not, we call it *specious* (SPEE′-shəs). A *specious* argument sounds plausible, but in reality is based on an error, a fallacy, or an untruth. The noun is *speciousness*.

如果说你是一个"喜欢看自己的人",从修辞角度可以理解为你喜欢审视自己的思维过程和情感反应,与性格内向型的人(introvert,见第3章)具有相似的鲜明特点。你的思维是内敛的,你花费许多时间分析自己、自己的性格、人品和行为。这样,因为你"向内部看",所以你是 introspective,"内省的"——前缀是 intro-,表示"里面的、内部的"。如果你 introspect,你会"向内部看",审视内部的反应。过多的内省通常会导致痛苦、消沉的情绪或焦虑情感——极少数人拥有面对真实自我的勇气。

有时你需要仔细地"观察周围";你必须是 circumspect——小心的、谨慎的、警觉的(circum-表示"周围")。名词形式是 circumspection 或 circumspectness。

如果事物看起来好或者合理,但事实并非如此,我们将其称为 specious,(似是而非的)。a specious argument 听起来似乎合理,事实上却建立在错误、谬论或者谎言的基础之上。名词形式是 speciousness。

REVIEW OF ETYMOLOGY
复习词源

PREFIX, ROOT, SUFFIX	MEANING	EXAMPLE
1. *specto*	to look	_____
2. *per-*	through	_____
3. *acuo*	to sharpen	_____
4. *punctus*	point	_____
5. *-ate*	verb suffix	_____
6. *-al*	adjective suffix	_____
7. *pungo*	to pierce sharply	_____
8. *-ent*	adjective suffix	_____
9. *-ence*, *-ency*	noun suffixes	_____
10. *-ness*	noun suffix	_____
11. *-ity*	noun suffix	_____
12. *retro-*	backward	_____
13. *pro-*	forward, ahead, before	_____
14. *intro-*	inside, within	_____
15. *-ion*	noun suffix	_____
16. *-ive*	adjective suffix	_____
17. *circum-*	around	_____

USING THE WORDS
单词应用

Can you pronounce the words? (Ⅰ)
你能读出这些单词吗?(Ⅰ)

1. *perspicacious*	pur-spə-KAY′-shəs
2. *perspicacity*	pur′-spə-KAS′-ə-tee
3. *acumen*	ə-KYOO′-mən
4. *acute*	ə-KYOOT′
5. *acuity*	ə-KYOO′-ə-tee
6. *acupuncture*	AK′-yoo-punk′-chər
7. *punctuate*	PUNK′-choo-ayt′
8. *punctilious*	punk-TIL′-ee-əs

9. *puncture*   PUNK'-chər
10. *pungent*   PUN'-jənt
11. *pungence*   PUN'-iəns
12. *pungency*   PUN'-jən-see

Can you pronounce the words？（Ⅱ）
你能读出这些单词吗？（Ⅱ）

1. *perspicuous*   pər-SPIK'-yoo-əs
2. *perspicuity*   pur'-spə-KYOO'-ə-tee
3. *retrospect*   RET'-rə-spekt'
4. *prospect*   PROS'-pekt'
5. *prospective*   prə-SPEK'-tiv
6. *introspective*   in'-trə-SPEK'-tiv
7. *introspect*   in'-trə-SPEKT'
8. *introspection*   in'-trə-SPEK'-shən
9. *circumspect*   SUR'-kəm-spekt'
10. *circumspection*   sur'-kəm-SPEK'-shən
11. *specious*   SPEE'-shəs

Can you work with the words？（Ⅰ）
你能灵活使用这些词汇了吗？（Ⅰ）

1. perspicacious   a. extremely careful, exact, or proper in procedure
2. acumen   b. clear; easy to understand
3. acupuncture   c. a forward look
4. punctilious   d. looking inside, or examining or analyzing, oneself
5. pungent   e. keen-minded
6. perspicuous   f. sharp; spicy; piercing
7. retrospect   g. careful, watchful, wary, cautious; "looking around"
8. prospect   h. sharpness of mind or thinking
9. introspective   i. a backward look
10. circumspect   j. medical insertion of needles

KEY：1-e, 2-h, 3-j, 4-a, 5-f, 6-b, 7-i, 8-c, 9-d, 10-g

Can you work with the words?（Ⅱ）

你能灵活使用这些词汇了吗？（Ⅱ）

1. acute	a.	pierce; make a hole in; (noun) a small hole
2. acuity	b.	clarity; lucidity; ability to be understood quickly and easily
3. punctuate	c.	sounding plausible, or looking right, but actually false or untrue
4. puncture	d.	in the future; describing that which, or one who, can be looked forward to
5. pungence, pungency	e.	care; watchfulness; caution
6. perspicuity	f.	sharp; sudden; keen-minded
7. prospective	g.	tending to examine and to think about one's motives, feelings, etc.
8. introspective	h.	interrupt sharply or suddenly
9. circumspection	i.	sharpness or spiciness of taste, smell, wit, etc.
10. specious	j.	keeness of mind, thinking, or intellect

KEY：1-f，2-j，3-h，4-a，5-i，6-b，7-d，8-g，9-e，10-c

Do you understand the words?

你对这些词汇是否已经透彻地理解？

1. perspicacious—dull-witted	SAME	OPPOSITE
2. acumen—stupidity	SAME	OPPOSITE
3. acute—sharp	SAME	OPPOSITE
4. acuity—perspicacity	SAME	OPPOSITE
5. punctilious—casual	SAME	OPPOSITE
6. pungent—flat, dull	SAME	OPPOSITE
7. perspicuous—clear	SAME	OPPOSITE
8. retrospect—backward look	SAME	OPPOSITE
9. prospect—expectation	SAME	OPPOSITE
10. introspective—extroverted	SAME	OPPOSITE
11. prospective—in the past	SAME	OPPOSITE
12. circumspect—careless	SAME	OPPOSITE
13. specious—true	SAME	OPPOSITE

KEY: 1-O, 2-O, 3-S, 4-S, 5-O, 6-O, 7-S, 8-S, 9-S, 10-O, 11-O, 12-O, 13-O

Can you recall the words? (Ⅰ)
你能够写出这些词汇吗? (Ⅰ)

1. plausible, but false or incorrect	1. S _____
2. spiciness, sharpness; piercing quality	2. P _____ or P _____
3. clear; easily understood	3. P _____
4. sharpness of mind or of intelligence	4. A _____ or A _____ or A _____
5. care and caution; wariness	5. C _____ or C _____
6. piercing of the skin with needles for medical purposes	6. A _____
7. tending to examine one's motives, etc.; loooking inward (*adj.*)	7. I _____
8. exact in the observance of proper procedure	8. P _____
9. to pierce and make a small hole in	9. P _____
10. a backward look or view	10. R _____

KEY: 1-specious, 2-pungence *or* pungency, 3-perspicuous, 4-acumen *or* acuteness *or* acuity, 5-circumspection *or* circumspectness, 6-acupuncture, 7-introspective, 8-punctilious, 9-puncture, 10-retrospect

Can you recall the words? (Ⅱ)
你能够写出这些词汇吗? (Ⅱ)

1. keenness of mind	1. P _____ or P _____
2. sharp; sudden; keen-minded	2. A _____
3. to interrupt suddenly	3. P _____
4. spicy; piercing in taste, smell, wit, etc.	4. P _____
5. clarity; clearness of style or language	5. P _____ or P _____
6. keen-minded; perceptive	6. P _____

7. a look forward   7. P _____

8. act or process of looking inward   8. I _____

9. carefully looking around; cautious;   9. C _____
   wary

10. anticipated; "to be"; looked   10. P _____
    forward to (*adj.*)

KEY: 1-perspicacity *or* perspicaciousness, 2-acute, 3-punctuate, 4-pungent, 5-perspicuity *or* perspicuousness, 6-perspicacious, 7-prospect, 8-introspection, 9-circumspect, 10-prospective

---

(*End of Session 35*)

SESSION 36
第 36 节

ORIGINS AND RELATED WORDS
词源及相关词汇

1. the great and the small
伟大和渺小

You are familiar with Latin *animus*, mind. *Animus* and a related root, *anima*, life principle, soul, spirit (in a sense, these meanings are all very similar), are the source of such words as *animal*, *animate* and *inanimate*, *animated*, and *animation*; knowing the meaning of the roots, you have a better understanding of any word built on them.

Magnanimous contains, in addition to *animus*, mind, the root *magnus*, large, great, which you recall from *magniloquent*. *Magnanimous* people have such great, noble minds or souls that they are beyond seeking petty revenge.

The noun is *magnanimity* (mag′-nə-NIM′-ə-tee).

On the other hand, people who have tiny, tiny minds or souls are *pusillanimous* (py oo′-sə-LAN′-ə-mes)—Latin *pusillus*, tiny. Hence, they are contemptibly petty and mean. The noun is *pusillanimity* (py oo′-sə-lə-NIM′-ə-tee).

你应该熟悉拉丁语 animus(意识)。animus 和相关词根 anima-(灵魂、精神、生命之气息),是许多词的词根,例如 animal(动物)、animate(使……有生气)和 inanimate(无生命的)、animated(活泼的)和 animation(动画片);了解了词根的含义,对于包括这个词根的任何词汇就会有更好的理解。

magnanimous 除了包括词根 animus,还包括词根 magnus,表示"大的",你能够回忆起 magniloquent 也包括同样的词根。a magnanimous person 具有非常慷慨的、大度的心灵,绝对不会有想要报复的狭隘念头。

名词形式是 magnanimity。

相反,具有狭隘之心的人被称为 pusillanimous——这个词使用了拉丁语 pusillus,表示"非常小的"。这样,他就是非常狭隘、吝啬之人,被人们所鄙视。名词形式是 pusillanimity。

Other words built on *animus*, mind:

(1) *unanimous* (y oo-NAN′-ə-məs)—of one *mind*. If the Supreme Court hands down a *unanimous* opinion, all the judges are of *one* mind (Latin *unus*, one). The noun is *unanimity* (y oo′-nə NIM′-ə-tee).

(2) *equanimity* (ee′kwə-NIM′-ə-tee or ek′-wə-NIM′-ə-tee)—etymologically, "e-qual (or balanced) mind." Hence, evenness or calmness of mind; composure. If you preserve your *equanimity* under trying circumstances, you keep your temper, you do not get confused, you remain calm (Latin *aequus*, equal).

(3) *animus* (AN′-ə-məs)—hostility, ill will, malevolence. Etymologically, *animus* is simply *mind*, but has degenerated, as words often do, to mean *unfriendly mind*. The word is most often used in a pattern like, "I bear you no *animus*, even

though you have tried to destroy me. " (Such a statement shows real *magnanimity*!)

(4) *animosity* (an'-ə-MOS'-ə-tee)—ill will, hostility. An exact synonym of *animus*, and a more common word. It is used in patterns like, "You feel a good deal of *animosity*, don't you?" "There is real *animosity* between Bill and Ernie." "If you bear me no *animosity*, why do you treat me so badly?"

其他由 animus(意识)构成的单词：

(1) unanimous——一致同意的。如果最高法院宣布一个 unanimous opinion,所有的法官都具有相同的意见(拉丁语词 unus,表示"一个")。名词形式是 unanimity。

(2) equanimity——镇静;字面理解,平静的或者平衡的心境;思维的平整或冷静。如果在难堪的境遇维持 equanimity,你克制脾气,不感到困惑,保持冷静。

(3) animus——敌意、恶意、居心不良。在词源学意义上,animus 指简单的头脑,但是与许多其他词汇相似,其词义发生了变化,现在用来表示"不友好的心境"。这个词常有以下用法："I bear you no animus, even though you have tried to destroy me."(即使你试图摧毁我,我对你仍然没有恶意。)(这句话显示了真正的宽宏大量!)

(4) animosity——恶意、敌意。是 animus 的同义词,而且更为常见,常见用法是："You feel a good deal of animosity, don't you?"(你感受到许多敌意,不是吗?)"There is real animosity between Bill and Ernie,"(比尔和恩尼之间充满敌意)"If you bear me no animosity, why do you treat me so badly?"(如果你对我没有敌意,你为什么对我如此糟糕?)

2. turning

转弯

Versatile comes from *verto*, *versus*, to turn—*versatile* people can turn their hand to many things successfully. The noun is *versatility* (vur'-sə-TIL'-ə-tee).

versatile 源于 verto,versus,意为"转"——"versatile people"就是有多种技能的人。其名词形式是 versatility。

3. Zeno and the front porch

芝诺和门廊

Centuries ago, in ancient Greece, the philosopher Zeno lectured on a topic that still piques the human mind, to wit: "How to Live a Happy Life. " Zeno would stand on a porch (the Greek word for which is *stoa*) and hold forth somewhat as follows: people should free themselves from intense emotion, be unmoved by both joy and sorrow, and submit without complaint to unavoidable necessity.

Today, psychologists suggest pretty much the exact opposite—let your emotions flow freely, express your love or animosity, don't bottle up your feelings. But in the fourth century B. C. , when Zeno was expounding his credo, his philosophy of control of the passions fell on receptive ears. His followers were called *Stoics*, after the *stoa*, or porch, from which the master lectured.

If we call people *stoical*, we mean that they bear their pain or sorrow without complaint, they meet adversity with unflinching fortitude. This sounds very noble, you will admit—actually, according to modern psychological belief, it is healthier not to be so *stoical*. *Stoicism* (STŌ'-ə-siz-əm) may be an admirable virtue (mainly because we do not then have to listen to the *stoic's* troubles), but it can be overdone.

很多世纪之前的古希腊,哲学家芝诺针对"如何快乐生活"的主题进行演讲,直到今天,他的观点仍然能够激发人们的兴趣。芝诺站在门廊上(古希腊语中的门廊是 stoa),说出下面这些话:人应该从强烈的情感之中解放自己,不为快乐和悲伤所动,甘心顺从不可避免的必然。

现在的哲学家宣扬的恰好相反——自由地表达情感、爱或者敌意,不要封锁你的情绪。但是,芝诺阐释自己的信条是在公元前4世纪,他所表达的控制欲望的哲学被人们广为接纳。他的追随者被称为 Stoics,斯多葛(廊下)学派,由芝诺演讲时所在的门廊(stoa)派生。

如果将一个人称为 stoical,我们认为他是一个能够忍受疼痛或者痛苦却毫不抱怨的人,即使遇到不幸,他也会无所畏惧地坚毅面对。你必须承认,这需要相当的雅量——当然,根据当代心理学观点,不如此 stoical 才更有利于健康。stoicism 可能是一种值得赞扬的美德(主要是因为我们不必分担斯多葛学派追随者的苦难),但这样做有可能过头。

4. fear and trembling

恐惧与颤抖

Intrepid is from Latin *trepido*, to tremble. *Intrepid* people exhibit courage and fearlessness (and not a single tremble!) when confronted by dangers from which you and I would run like the cowards we are. (You recognize the negative prefix *in-*.)

The noun: *intrepidity* (in'-trə-PID'-ə-tee), or, of course, *intrepidness*.

Trepido is the source also of *trepidation* (trep'-ə-DAY'-shən)—great fear, trembling, or alarm.

intrepid 来自于拉丁语 trepido(表示"颤抖")。Intrepid(无畏)的人在面临危险时会表现出勇气和无畏(一点也不颤抖!),而你我面对这些危险会像懦夫一样逃之夭夭(你认识表示否定的前缀 in-)。

名词形式是 intrepidity 或者 intrepidness。

trepido 也出现在 trepidation 中——极大的恐惧、颤抖、惊恐。

5. quick flash

快速的闪光

Scintilla, in Latin, is a quick, bright spark; in English the word *scintilla* (sin-TIL'-ə) may also mean a *spark*, but more commonly refers to a very small particle (which, in a sense, a spark is), as in, "There was not a *scintilla* of evidence against him."

In the verb *scintillate* (SIN'-tə-layt'), the idea of the spark remains; someone who *scintillates* sparkles with charm and wit, flashes brightly with humor. The noun is *scintillation* (sin'-tə LAY'-shən).

拉丁语 scintilla 表示"快速的、明亮的闪光";在英语中,这个词也有闪光的含义,但是更多用来表示非常小的颗粒(某种意义上讲,闪光的确是个小颗粒),例如,"There was not a scintilla of evidence against him."(对他不利的一丁点证据都没有。)

在动词 scintillate 中,闪光的概念仍然保留;一个 scintillates 的人会闪烁魅力和智慧的光芒,也会明亮地闪耀出幽默感。名词形式是 scintillation。

6. city and country

城市和乡村

People who live in the big city go to theaters, attend the opera, visit museums and picture galleries, browse in bookstores, and shop at Robinson's, Bloomingdale's, Marshall Field, or other large department stores.

These activities fill them with culture and sophistication.

Also, they crowd into jammed subway trains or buses, squeeze into packed elevators, cross the street in competition with highpowered motorcars, patiently stand in line outside of movie houses, and then wait again in the lobby for seats to be vacated.

Also, they have the privilege of spending two hours a day going to and coming from work.

As a result, city-dwellers are refined, polished, courteous—or so the etymology of *urbane* (from Latin *urbs*, city) tells us. (And you must be absurdly credulous, if not downright gullible, to believe it.) The noun is *urbanity* (ur-BAN'-ə-tee).

大城市居民会去剧院、看歌剧、参观博物馆和画廊、逛书店、逛梅西百货、马歇尔或者其他大型商店。
这些活动填补着他们的文化和修养。

同时，他们也聚集在拥堵的铁路和公交上，挤进满满的电梯里，与大马力的电车争相过路，在电影院门外耐心排队等待，在大厅里等空座等上几个小时。他们还有上下班两个小时的消遣。因此，城市居民是高雅的，优雅的，文质彬彬的——或如 urbane(源自拉丁语 urbs,意为"城市")描述的那一样。（如果你真相信如此,那你一定轻信得可笑,即使算不上赤裸裸的易上当。）名词形式为 urbanity。

So *urbane* people are gracious, affable, cultivated, suave, tactful—add any similar adjectives you can think of.

Urban (UR'-bən) as an adjective simply refers to cities—*urban* affairs, *urban* areas, *urban* populations, *urban* life, *urban* development, etc.

Consider some prefixes: *sub-*, near; *inter-*, between; *intra-*, inside, within; *ex-*, out,

Add each prefix to the root *urbs*, using the adjective suffix *-an*:

 sub ＿＿＿＿＿＿＿: near the city

 (*Sub-* has a number of meanings: *under*, *near*, *close to*, etc.)

 inter ＿＿＿＿＿＿＿: between cities

 intra ＿＿＿＿＿＿＿: within a city

 ex ＿＿＿＿＿＿＿: out of the city

The *suburbs* are residential sections, or small communities, close to a large city; Larchmont is a *suburb* of New York City, Whittier a *suburb* of Los Angeles.

Suburbia (sə-BUR'-bee-ə) may designate *suburbs* as a group; *suburban* residents, or *suburbanites* (sə-BUR'-bə-nīts'), as a group; or the typical manners, modes of living, customs, etc. of suburban residents.

An *interurban* bus travels *between* cities, an *intraurban* bus *within* a single city.

An *exurb* (EKS'-urb) lies well beyond, way outside, a large city, and generally refers to a region inhabited by well-to-do families. *Exurb* has derived forms corresponding to those of *suburb*. Can you construct them?

 Plural noun: ＿＿＿＿＿＿＿＿＿＿＿＿＿

 Adjective: ＿＿＿＿＿＿＿＿＿＿＿＿＿

 Resident: ＿＿＿＿＿＿＿＿＿＿＿＿＿

 As a group; manners, customs, etc.: ＿＿＿＿＿＿＿＿＿＿＿

Urbs is the city; Latin *rus*, *ruris* is the country, i. e. , farmland, fields, etc. So *rural* (ROOR'-əl) refers to country or farm regions, agriculture, etc.—a wealthy *rural* area.

Rustic (RUS′-tik) as an adjective may describe furniture or dwellings made of roughhewn wood，or furnishings suitable to a farmhouse；or，when applied to a person，is an antonym of *urbane*—unsophisticated，boorish，lacking in social graces，uncultured. Noun：*rusticity* (rus-TIS′-ə-tee). *Rustic* is also a noun designating a person with such characteristics，as in，"He was considered a *rustic* by his classmates，all of whom came from cultured and wealthy backgrounds."

urbane 的人是和蔼的、友善的、有修养的、文雅的、圆通的——可用你能想到的任何类似的形容词修饰。

urban 做形容词的时候，只指"城市"——如"城市事务""城市面积""城市人口""城市发展"等。

结合一些前缀：sub-（近的）；inter-（在……之间）；intra-（在里面）；ex-（外面）。

在词根 urbs 前面加上这些前缀，然后再加上形容词后缀-an：

sub ＿＿＿＿＿＿＿＿＿：接近城市

（sub 有很多意思：如 under，near，close to，等）

inter ＿＿＿＿＿＿＿＿：在城市之间。

intra ＿＿＿＿＿＿＿＿：在城市里。

ex ＿＿＿＿＿＿＿＿＿：在城市外。

suburbs（郊区）靠近大城市的居住区或小的社区；如拉赤蒙是纽约的 suburb；惠蒂尔是洛杉矶的 suburb。

suburbia 可以把 suburbs 作为一个群体来指代；suburban residents 或 suburbanites 即作为一个群体的郊区居民，或者用来指代郊区居民特有的生活方式、风俗习惯等。

"interurban bus"往返于城市之间，"intraurban bus"则是在一个城市内。

exurb 是指离大都市较远、富裕家庭的聚居地。exurb 有很多和 suburban 类似的变形，你能写出来吗？

复数形式是什么：

形容词形式是什么：

居民怎表示：

作为一个群体，行为方式、生活习惯等：

urbs 是城市，拉丁语中的 rus，ruris 是指"乡村"，即田地、田野等。因此 rural 是指乡村、农场，或农业等——如"a wealthy rural area"（一个富裕的农村地区）。

rustic 作为形容词时可以指简陋的木头家具或住所，或农家式的装修样式。当指人时，是 urbane 的反义词——单纯的、粗鲁的、缺乏社交礼仪的、没文化的。名词形式是 rusticity。rustic 也可作为一个名词来指有这些特质的人，如："He was considered a rustic by his classmates，all of them come from cultured and wealthy background"（他被有教养和有富裕家庭背景的同学们视为乡巴佬）。

Urbane and *rustic*，when applied to people，are emotionally charged words. *Urbane* is complimentary，*rustic* derogatory. [1]

To *rusticate* (RUS′-tə-kayt′) is to spend time in the country，away from the turmoil and tensions of big-city life. Can you construct the noun？ ＿＿＿＿＿＿＿＿＿．

urbane 和 rustic 用来形容人时，会带有强烈的感情色彩。urbane 是高度赞扬，rustic 是极度贬义。

to rusticate 指"去乡下"，远离城市生活的喧嚣和紧张。你能写出它的名词吗？

---

1. Incidentally，a word used with a derogatory connotation (*bitch*，*piggish*，*glutton*，*idiot*，etc.) is called a *pejorative* (pe-JAWR′-ə-tiv). *Pejorative* is also an adjective，as in，"She spoke in *pejorative* terms about her exhusband." The derivation is Latin *pejor*，worse.

顺便提一句，带有贬义的单词称为 pejorative（贬义词）。贬义词也是形容词，例如："She spoke in pejorative terms about her ex-husband."这源自拉丁语 pejor（糟糕的）。

REVIEW OF ETYMOLOGY
复习词源

PREFIX, ROOT, 　　SUFFIX	MEANING	ENGLISH WORD
1. *animus*	mind	_____
2. *anima*	soul, spirit, life principle	_____
3. *magnus*	large, great	_____
4. *pusillus*	tiny	_____
5. *unus*	one	_____
6. *aequus* (*equ-*)	equal	_____
7. *verto*, *versus*	to turn	_____
8. *stoa*	porch	_____
9. *in-*	negative prefix	_____
10. *trepido*	to tremble	_____
11. *scintilla*	a spark	_____
12. *urbs*	city	_____
13. *sub-*	near, close to, under	_____
14. *inter-*	between	_____
15. *intra-*	within, inside	_____
16. *ex-*	out	_____
17. *rus*, *ruris*	country, farmlands	_____
18. *-ate*	verb suffix	_____
19. *-ion*	noun suffix aded to -ate verbs	_____

USING THE WORDS
单词应用

Can you pronounce the words? （Ⅰ）
你能读出这些单词吗？（Ⅰ）

1. *magnanimity*　　　mag′-nə-NIM′-ə-tee
2. *pusillanimous*　　pyo͞o′-sə-LAN′-ə-məs
3. *pusillanimity*　　pyo͞o′-sə-lə-NIM′-ə-tee
4. *unanimous*　　　yo͞o-NAN′-ə-məs
5. *unanimity*　　　yo͞o-nə-NIM′-ə-tee
6. *equanimity*　　　eek′ (*or* ek′)-wə-NIM′-ə-tee
7. *animus*　　　　　AN′-ə-məs
8. *animosity*　　　an′-oə-MOS′-ə-tee
9. *versatility*　　　vur′-sə-TIL′-ə-tee

10. *stoic*　　　　　　　STŌ′-ik
11. *stoicism*　　　　　 STŌ′-ə-siz-əm

Can you pronounce the words?（Ⅱ）
你能读出这些单词吗？（Ⅱ）

1. *intrepidity*　　　　in′-trə-PID′-ə-tee
2. *trepidation*　　　　trep′-ə-DAY′-shən
3. *scintilla*　　　　　sin-TIL′-ə
4. *scintillate*　　　　SIN′-tə-layt′
5. *scintillation*　　　sin′-tə-LAY′-shən
6. *urbanity*　　　　　ur-BAN′-ə-tee
7. *suburbia*　　　　　sə-BUR′-bee-ə
8. *interurban*　　　　in′-tər-UR′-bən
9. *intraurban*　　　　in′-trə-UR′-bən
10. *exurbs*　　　　　EKS′-urbz
11. *exurban*　　　　　eks-UR′-bən
12. *exurbanite*　　　　eks-UR′-bən-īt′
13. *exurbia*　　　　　eks-UR′-bee-ə

Can you pronounce the words?（Ⅲ）
你能读出这些单词吗？（Ⅲ）

1. *rural*　　　　　　ROOR′-əl
2. *rustic*　　　　　　RUS′-tik
3. *rusticity*　　　　rus-TIS′-ə-tee
4. *rusticate*　　　　RUS′-tə-kayt′
5. *rustication*　　　rus′-tə-KAY′-shən
6. *pejorative*　　　pə-JAWR′-ə-tiv

Can you work with the words?（Ⅰ）
你能灵活使用这些词汇了吗？（Ⅰ）

1. magnanimity　　　a. calmness, composure
2. pusillanimity　　　b. ability either to do many different things well, or to function successfully in many areas
3. unanimity　　　　c. fearlessness; great courage
4. equanimity　　　 d. unemotionality; bearing of pain, etc. without complaint
5. animosity　　　　e. big-heartedness; generosity; quality of forgiving easily
6. versatility　　　 f. a sparkling with wit or cleverness

7. stoicism	g. fear and trembling; alarm
8. intrepidity	h. complete agreement, all being of one mind
9. trepidation	i. petty-mindedness
10. scintillation	j. anger, hostility, resentment, hatred

KEY: 1-e, 2-i, 3-h, 4-a, 5-j, 6-b, 7-d, 8-c, 9-g, 10-f

Can you work with the words? (Ⅱ)
你能灵活使用这些词汇了吗？(Ⅱ)

1. urbanity	a. referring to the countryside
2. suburbia	b. word with negative or derogatory connotation; describing such a word or words
3. exurbia	c. to spend time in the country
4. animus	d. residential areas near big cities; customs, etc. of the inhabitants of such areas
5. interurban	e. residential areas far from big cities; customs, etc. of the inhabitants of such areas
6. intraurban	f. between cities
7. rural	g. roughhewn, farmlike; unsophisticated, uncultured
8. rustic	h. sophistication, courtesy, polish, etc.
9. rusticate	i. anger, hatred, hostility
10. pejorative	j. within one city

KEY: 1-h, 2-d, 3-e, 4-i, 5-f, 6-j, 7-a, 8-g, 9-c, 10-b

(End of Session 36)

SESSION 37
第 37 节

READY FOR A STRONG REVIEW?
准备好强化复习了吗?

Drill, drill, drill! This is the important secret of learning words thoroughly.

Review, review, review! This is the secret of remembering, assimilating, digesting, and keeping as permanent acquisitions all the new words you have learned.

So pitch in with enthusiasm to the rest of this chapter, made up of a series of valuable tests on all the chapter words. Ready?

Can you work with the words? (I)
你能灵活使用这些词汇了吗? (I)

1. retrospect	a. complete agreement
2. acumen	b. pettiness
3. magnanimity	c. malevolence
4. pusillanimity	d. backward look
5. unanimity	e. calmness
6. equanimity	f. ability in many fields
7. animosity	g. mental keenness
8. versatility	h. generosity

KEY:1-d, 2-g, 3-h, 4-b, 5-a, 6-e, 7-c, 8-f

Can you work with the words? (II)
你能灵活使用这些词汇了吗? (II)

1. stoicism	a. fearlessness
2. intrepidity	b. sparkle
3. trepidation	c. inward look
4. scintillation	d. uncomplaining attitude to pain or trouble
5. urbanity	e. falsity
6. introspection	f. polish, cultivation
7. circumspection	g. care, cautiousness
8. speciousness	h. fear

KEY:1-d, 2-a, 3-h, 4-b, 5-f, 6-c, 7-g, 8-e

Can you work with the words? (Ⅲ)
你能灵活使用这些词汇了吗？（Ⅲ）

1. exurbs		a. of one mind
2. pusillanimous		b. ill will
3. unanimous		c. pertaining to the city
4. animus		d. petty
5. rustic		e. self-analytical
6. urban		f. regions far from the city
7. introspective		g. cautious
8. circumspect		h. false, though plausible
9. specious		i. countrified

KEY: 1-f, 2-d, 3-a, 4-b, 5-i, 6-c, 7-e, 8-g, 9-h

Can you work with the words? (Ⅳ)
你能灵活使用这些词汇了吗？（Ⅳ）

1. perspicacity	a. clearness
2. perspicuity	b. to be witty
3. stoic	c. spend time in the country
4. scintilla	d. one who controls his emotions
5. scintillate	e. to look inward
6. rural	f. a very small amount
7. rusticate	g. keen intelligence
8. introspect	h. clear, understandable
9. perspicuous	i. keen-minded
10. perspicacious	j. pertaining to the country

KEY: 1-g, 2-a, 3-d, 4-f, 5-b, 6-j, 7-c, 8-e, 9-h, 10-i

Do you understand the words? (Ⅰ)
你对这些词汇是否已经透彻地理解？（Ⅰ）

1. Does life often seem pleasanter in *retrospect*?	YES	NO
2. Are people of *acuity* gullible?	YES	NO
3. Is *perspicacity* a common characteristic?	YES	NO
4. Is a person of *acumen* likely to be naive?	YES	NO
5. Is a *perspicuous* style of writing easy to read?	YES	NO

6. Should all writers aim at *perspicuity*?   YES   NO

7. Is *magnanimity* a characteristic of small-minded   YES   NO
   people?

8. Does a person of *pusillanimous* mind often think   YES   NO
   of petty revenge?

9. Is a *unanimous* opinion one in which all concur?   YES   NO

KEY：1-yes，2-no，3-no，4-no，5-yes，6-yes，7-no，8-yes，9-yes

Do you understand the words? (Ⅱ)
你对这些词汇是否已经透彻地理解？(Ⅱ)

1. Is it easy to preserve one's *equanimity* under trying   YES   NO
   circumstances?

2. Do we bear *animus* toward our enemies?   YES   NO

3. Do we usually feel great *animosity* toward our friends?   YES   NO

4. Do we admire *versatility*?   YES   NO

5. Does a *stoic* usually complain?   YES   NO

6. Is *stoicism* a mark of an uninhibited personality?   YES   NO

7. Do cowards show *intrepidity* in the face of danger?   YES   NO

8. Do cowards often feel a certain amount of *trepidation*?   YES   NO

9. Is a *scintilla* of evidence a great amount?   YES   NO

10. Do dull people *scintillate*?   YES   NO

11. Is *urbanity* a characteristic of boorish people?   YES   NO

KEY：1-no，2-yes，3-no，4-yes，5-no，6-no，7-no，8-yes，9-no，10-no，11-no

Do you understand the words? (Ⅲ)
你对这些词汇是否已经透彻地理解？(Ⅲ)

1. Is New York City a *rural* community?   YES   NO

2. Is a village an *urban* community?   YES   NO

3. Do you *rusticate* in the city?   YES   NO

4. Are extroverts very *introspective*?   YES   NO

5. Does an introvert spend a good deal of time in   YES   NO
   introspection?

6. In dangerous circumstances, is it wise to be   YES   NO
   circumspect?

7. Do *specious* arguments often sound convincing?   YES   NO

KEY:1-no，2-no，3-no，4-no，5-yes，6-yes，7-yes

Do you understand the words? (Ⅳ)
你对这些词汇是否已经透彻地理解？(Ⅳ)

1. retrospect—prospect	SAME	OPPOSITE
2. acute—perspicacious	SAME	OPPOSITE
3. acumen—stupidity	SAME	OPPOSITE
4. perspicuous—confused	SAME	OPPOSITE
5. magnanimous—noble	SAME	OPPOSITE
6. pusillanimous—petty	SAME	OPPOSITE
7. unanimous—divided	SAME	OPPOSITE
8. equanimity—nervousness	SAME	OPPOSITE
9. animosity—hostility	SAME	OPPOSITE
10. animus—friendliness	SAME	OPPOSITE
11. versatility—monomania	SAME	OPPOSITE
12. stoicism—cowardice	SAME	OPPOSITE
13. intrepidity—fear	SAME	OPPOSITE
14. trepidation—courage	SAME	OPPOSITE
15. scintilla—slight amount	SAME	OPPOSITE
16. urbanity—refinement	SAME	OPPOSITE
17. rustic—crude	SAME	OPPOSITE
18. rural—urban	SAME	OPPOSITE
19. introspective—serf-analytic	SAME	OPPOSITE
20. circumspect—careless	SAME	OPPOSITE
21. specious—true	SAME	OPPOSITE

KEY:1-O，2-S，3-O，4-O，5-S，6-S，7-O，8-O，9-S，10-O，11-O，12-O，13-O，14-O，15-S，16-S，17-S，18-O，19-S，20-O，21-O

Can you recall the words? (Ⅰ)
你能够写出这些单词吗？(Ⅰ)

1. ability in many fields	1. V	_____
2. pertaining to the city (*adj.*)	2. U	_____
3. to spend time in the country	3. R	_____
4. merest spark; small mount	4. S	_____
5. courage	5. I	_____

KEY:1-versatility，2-urban，3-rusticate，4-scintilla，5-intrepidity

Can you recall the words? (Ⅱ)
你能够写出这些单词吗？(Ⅱ)

1. unflinching fortitude   1. S _____
2. countrified；unpolished   2. R _____
3. pertaining to the countryside   3. R _____
   (*adj.*)
4. a looking back to the past   4. R _____
5. nobleness of mind or spirit   5. M _____

KEY:1-stoicism，2-rustic，3-rural，4-retrospect，5-magnanimity

Can you recall the words? (Ⅲ)
你能够写出这些词汇吗？(Ⅲ)

1. keen-mindedness   1. A _____
2. clear，lucid   2. P _____
3. petty，mean   3. P _____
4. all of one mind or opinion   4. U _____
5. ill will   5. A _____
        or A _____

KEY:1-acuity，2-perspicuous，3-pusillanimous，4-unanimous，5-animus *or* animosity

Can you recall the words? (Ⅳ)
你能够写出这些词汇吗？(Ⅳ)

1-4. keenness of mind   1. P _____
        or P _____
        2. A _____
        3. A _____
        4. A _____
5. clearness of style or language   5. P _____
6. one who keeps his emotions，   6. S _____
   during times of trouble, hidden

7. sophistication, courtesy,
   refinement

7. U _____

KEY: 1-perspicacity *or* perspicaciousness, 2-acumen, 3-acuity, 4-acuteness (2-4 in any order), 5-perspicuity, 6-stoic, 7-urbanity

Can you recall the words? (V)
你能够写出这些词汇吗? (V)

1. pettiness of character
2. noun form of *unanimous*
3. mental calmness, balance
4. fear and trembling
5. to sparkle with wit and humor

1. P _____
2. U _____
3. E _____
4. T _____
5. S _____

KEY: 1-pusillanimity, 2-unanimity, 3-equanimity, 4-trepidation, 5-scintillate

Can you recall the words? (VI)
你能够写出这些词汇吗? (VI)

1. a looking inward; an examining
   of one's mental processes
   or emotional reactions
2. cautious
3. seemingly true, actually false
4. to think of one's mental processes
5. care, watchfulness

1. I _____
2. C _____
3. S _____
4. I _____
5. C _____

KEY: 1-introspective, 2-circumspect, 3-specious, 4-introspect, 5-circumspection

THREE FURTHER TESTS
三个补充测试

I. matching

WORD	MEANING
1. convivial	a. frank
2. indefatigable	b. noble, forgiving
3. ingenuous	c. unflinching; unemotional

4. perspicacious   d. courteous; polished; suave
5. magnanimous   e. companionable, gregarious
6. versatile   f. witty
7. stoical   g. capable in many directions
8. intrepid   h. brave
9. scintillating   i. keen-minded
10. urbane   j. tireless

KEY: 1-e, 2-j, 3-a, 4-i, 5-b, 6-g, 7-c, 8-h, 9-f, 10-d

Ⅱ. same or opposite?

1. vivacious—sluggish   SAME   OPPOSITE
2. vital—crucial   SAME   OPPOSITE
3. ennui—boredom   SAME   OPPOSITE
4. *bon vivant*—gourmand   SAME   OPPOSITE
5. gourmet—ascetic   SAME   OPPOSITE
6. ingenuous—crafty   SAME   OPPOSITE
7. *naive*—sophisticated   SAME   OPPOSITE
8. credulous—skeptical   SAME   OPPOSITE
9. disingenuous—insincere   SAME   OPPOSITE
10. credo—belief   SAME   OPPOSITE

KEY: 1-O, 2-S, 3-S, 4-S, 5-O, 6-O, 7-O, 8-O, 9-S, 10-S

Ⅲ. changing parts of speech

Change these adjectives to nouns *not* ending in *-ness*.

1. indefatigable   1. _____
2. perspicacious   2. _____
3. stoical   3. _____
4. urbane   4. _____
5. naive   5. _____
6. incredulous   6. _____
7. incredible   7. _____
8. perspicuous   8. _____
9. magnanimous   9. _____
10. pusillanimous   10. _____

KEY：1-indefatigability，2-perspicacity，3-stoicism，4-urbanity，5-naivete，6-incredulity，7-incredibility，8-perspicuity，9-magnanimity，10-pusillanimity

CHAPTER REVIEW
章节复习

A. Do you recognize the words?
你认识这些单词吗？
1. Tireless：
   (a) convivial，(b) indefatigable，(c) versatile
2. Frank，unsophisticated：
   (a) ingenuous，(b) ingenious，(c) intrepid
3. Unflinching，uncomplaining：
   (a) perspicacious，(b) urbane，(c) stoical
4. Noble，forgiving，generous：
   (a) pusillanimous，(b) unanimous，(c) magnanimous
5. Between cities：
   (a) interurban，(b) intraurban，(c) exurban
6. Giving birth to live young：
   (a) oviparous，(b) ovulation，(c) viviparous
7. Tedium，boredom：
   (a) ennui，(b) *joie de vivre*，(c) vitality
8. Connoisseur of choice food：
   (a) gourmet，(b) gourmand，(c) glutton
9. Inexperienced in the ways of the world：
   (a) credulous，(b) naive，(c) credible
10. Easily tricked：
    (a) gullible，(b) incredulous，(c) ingenious
11. Backward look：
    (a) prospect，(b) retrospect，(c) introspection
12. Clearness：
    (a) perspicacity，(b) perspicuity，(c) intrepidity
13. Resentment：
    (a) animosity，(b) stoicism，(c) urbanity
14. Countrified：
    (a) rustic，(b) specious，(c) circumspect

B. Can you recognize roots?

你能认出这些词根吗?

ROOT	EXAMPLE	MEANING
1. *vivo*	_____	vivacious
2. *sectus*	_____	vivisection
3. *pareo*	_____	viviparous
4. *ovum*	_____	oviparous
5. *vita*	_____	vital
6. *bon*	_____	*bon vivant*
7. *credo*	_____	credible
8. *specto*	_____	spectator
9. *acuo*	_____	acupuncture
10. *punctus*	_____	punctuate
11. *pungo*	_____	pungent
12. *animus*	_____	animosity
13. *pusillus*	_____	pusillanimous
14. *magnus*	_____	magnanimous
15. *unus*	_____	unanimous
16. *aequus（equ-）*	_____	equanimity
17. *verto, versus*	_____	versatile
18. *stoa*	_____	stoical
19. *trepido*	_____	trepidation
20. *scintilla*	_____	scintillate
21. *urbs*	_____	urban
22. *rus, ruris*	_____	rural, rustic

KEY: 1-to live, 2-cut, 3-to give birth, produce, 4-egg, 5-life, 6-good, 7-to believe, 8-to look, 9-to sharpen, 10-point, 11-to pierce sharply, 12-mind, 13-tiny, 14-big, great, large, 15-one, 16-equal, 17-to turn, 18-porch, 19-to tremble, 20-spark, 21-city, 22-country, countryside

TEASER QUESTIONS FOR THE AMATEUR ETYMOLOGIST
词源小测验

1. Recalling the root *vivo*, to live, can you think of the verb that means to *live on*? Can you write the noun form? _____

2. How would you explain a *vivarium*? _____

3. Recalling the meanings of Latin *vita*, what would you understand if someone asked you for your *vita* before you appeared for an interview for a professional position? _____

4. *Unus* is Latin for *one*. Can you use this root to construct words meaning：

(a) animal with *one* horn：_____

(b) of one form：_____

(c) to make *one*：_____

(d) *one*ness：_____

(e) *one*-wheeled vehicle：_____

5. *Annus* is Latin for *year*；*verto*, *versus*, as you know, means to *turn*. Can you, then, explain the word *anniversary* in terms of its roots? _____.

6. How about *universe* and *university* in terms of their roots (*unus*, one；*verto*, *versus*, to turn)?

(a) universe：_____

(b) university：_____

7. Use *inter-*, between, to form words of the following meanings：

(a) *between* states (*adj.*)：_____

(b) *between* nations (*adj.*)：_____

(c) in the middle *between* elementary and advanced (*adj.*)：_____

(d) to break in (*between* people conversing)：_____

(e) *between persons* (*adj.*)：_____

8. Use *intra-*, within, to form words with the following meanings (all *adjectives*)：

(a) *within* one state：_____

(b) within one nation：_____

(c) within one's own person or mind：_____

(d) within the muscles：_____

(*Answers in Chapter* 18)
(答案见第 18 章)

WORDS INFLUENCE YOUR THINKING
词汇影响你的思想

By now, you have thoroughly explored hundreds upon hundreds of valuable words and scores upon scores of important Greek and Latin roots.

As you went along you stopped at frequent intervals to say aloud, think about, work with, and recall the words you were adding to your vocabulary.

By now, therefore, the words you have been learning are probably old friends of yours; they have started to influence your thinking, have perhaps begun to appear in your conversation, and have certainly become conspicuous in your reading. In short, they have been effective in making changes in your intellectual climate.

Let us pause now for another checkup of the success of your study. In the next chapter, you will find a second Comprehensive Test. Take the test cold if you feel that all the material is at your fingertips; or spend a little time reviewing Chapters 9, 10, 11, and 12 if you believe such review is necessary.

(End of Session 37)

到现在为止,你已经彻底地探究了数百个有价值的单词以及几十个重要的希腊和拉丁词根。

在此过程中,你每隔一段时间停下来,大声地念出、思考、使用和回忆你正在加进自己词汇库的单词。

因此,你一直在学习的单词可能成为了你的老朋友;它们已开始影响你的思维,或许已开始在你的谈话中出现,并肯定在你的阅读中变得显眼。简言而之,它们已经有效地改变了你的智力氛围。

让我们暂停一下,来做另外一次测试,检验你学习的效果。在下一章里,你将进行第二个综合测试。如果你感觉对所有的内容都了如指掌,就直接做测试;如果你相信有必要复习的话,花点时间复习第9章、第10章、第11章和第12章。

13

HOW TO CHECK YOUR PROGRESS
如何检验你的进步

(*Comprehensive Test II*)

SESSION 38
第 38 节

Ⅰ. etymology

ROOT	MEANING	EXAMPLE
1. *scribo*, *scriptus*		proscribe
2. *aequus*（*equ-*）		equivocal
3. *malus*		malign
4. *dico*, *dictus*		malediction
5. *volo*		malevolent
6. *facio*		malefactor
7. *bonus*, *bene*		benevolent
8. *fides*		infidelity
9. *dono*		condone
10. *nox*, *noctis*		equinox
11. *equus*		equestrian
12. *libra*		equilibrium
13. *taceo*		taciturn
14. *loquor*		loquacious
15. *solus*		soliloquy
16. *venter*, *ventris*		ventral
17. *magnus*		magniloquence
18. *verbum*		verbatim
19. *volvo*, *volutus*		voluble
20. *animus*		pusillanimous
21. *dorsum*		endorse

22. *vox, vocis* _____ vocal

23. *fero* _____ vociferous

24. *ambulo* _____ somnambulist

25. *somnus* _____ somnolent

Ⅱ. more etymology

ROOT	MEANING	EXAMPLE
1. *phanein*	_____	sycophant
2. *vir*	_____	virago
3. *pater, patris*	_____	patricide
4. *onyma*	_____	synonym
5. *homos*	_____	homonym
6. *phone*	_____	homophone
7. *archein*	_____	matriarch
8. *mater, matris*	_____	matron
9. *caedo (-cide)*	_____	suicide
10. *homo*	_____	homicide
11. *uxor*	_____	uxorious
12. *maritus*	_____	mariticide
13. *pyros*	_____	pyromania
14. *theos*	_____	atheist
15. *vivo*	_____	viviparous
16. *credo*	_____	credulous
17. *pungo*	_____	pungency
18. *unus*	_____	unanimous
19. *trepido*	_____	intrepid
20. *scintilla*	_____	scintillate
21. *urbs*	_____	urbanity
22. *rus, ruris*	_____	rural, rustic
23. *gnosis*	_____	prognosis
24. *pan*	_____	pantheism
25. *omnis*	_____	omniscient

Ⅲ. same or opposite

1. disparage—praise   S   O

2. proscribe—prohibit   S   O

3. placate—irritate   S   O

4. taciturn—talkative   S   O

5. cogent—brilliant   S   O

6. atheistic—religious   S   O
7. convivial—unfriendly   S   O
8. ingenuous—naive   S   O
9. perspicacious—keen-minded   S   O
10. intrepid—fearful   S   O
11. malign—praise   S   O
12. inarticulate—verbal   S   O
13. verbose—laconic   S   O
14. tyro—virtuoso   S   O
15. megalomania—modesty   S   O
16. satyriasis—nymphomania   S   O
17. claustrophobia—agoraphobia   S   O
18. indefatigability—tirelessness   S   O
19. credulous—skeptical   S   O
20. animosity—hostility   S   O

IV. matching

1. is lewd and lustful   a. chauvinist
2. caters to the rich   b. sycophant
3. is an accomplished musician   c. dilettante
4. sneers at traditions   d. iconoclast
5. is the mother-ruler or a family tribe，or nation   e. lecher
6. has an irresistable urge to steal   f. tyro
7. is excessively patriotic   g. virtuoso
8. is a loud-mouthed woman   h. termagant
9. is a beginner   i. matriarch
10. is a dabbler   j. kleptomaniac

V. more matching

1. does not know whether or not God exists   a. dipsomaniac
2. is a criminal   b. pyromaniac
3. is a connoisseur of good food   c. agnostic
4. sets fires for revenge   d. hypochondriac
5. meets adversity or pain without flinching   e. gourmet
6. walks in his sleep   f. stoic
7. is obsessively addicted to drink   g. malefactor
8. has imaginary ailments   h. somnambulist
9. compulsively sets fires   i. nymphomaniac

10. is a woman who is sexually insatiable   j. incendiary

VI. recall a word

1. to make unnecessary   1. O _____
2. to flatter fulsomely   2. A _____
3. to spread slander about   3. M _____
4. economical in speech   4. L _____
5. trite and hackneyed   5. B _____
6. word for word   6. V _____
7. killing of masses of people   7. G _____
8. inheritance from one's father   8. P _____
9. belief in many gods   9. P _____
10. a person aggressively fighting for a cause   10. M _____
11. sincere; valid; in good faith   11. B _____
    F _____
12. babbling ceaselessly about trivia (*adj.*)   12. G _____
13. to speak to oneself, as in a play   13. S _____
14. masterpiece   14. M _____
    O _____
15. unselfish; not revengeful   15. M _____
16. able to walk after being bedridden   16. A _____
17. inability to fall asleep   17. I _____
18. morbid fear of heights   18. A _____
19. the killing of one's brother   19. F _____
20. opposite in meaning (*adj.*)   20. A _____
21. "joy of life"   21. J _____ D _____
    V _____
22. to rob of life or vigor   22. D _____
23. inexperience, unsophistication   23. N _____
24. scrupulously careful in the observance of proper procedure   24. P _____
25. clear, understandable (of style or language)   25. P _____
26. wary, cautious, watchful   26. C _____
27. a backward look   27. R _____
28. all of one mind (*adj.*)   28. U _____
29. uncomplaining in face of pain, misfortune, or emotional difficulties (*adj.*)   29. S _____

30. between cities (*adj.*) 30. I _____

KEY: A correct answer counts one point. Score your points for each part of the test, then add for a total.

I

1-to write, 2-equal, 3-bad, evil, 4-to say or tell, 5-to wish, 6-to do or make, 7-good, well, 8-faith, 9-to give, 10-night, 11-horse, 12-balance, pound, 13-to be silent, 14-to speak, 15-alone, 16-belly, 17-big, large, great, 18-word, 19-to roll, 20-mind, 21-back, 22-voice, 23-to bear or carry, 24-to walk, 25-sleep

Your score: _____

II

1-to show, 2-man, male, 3-father, 4-name, 5-the same, 6-sound, 7-to rule, 8-mother, 9-to kill, killing, 10-person, 11-wife, 12-husband, 13-fire, 14-God, 15-to live, 16-to believe, 17-to pierce sharply, 18-one, 19-to tremble, 20-spark, 21-city, 22-country (countryside), 23-knowledge, 24-all, 25-all

Your score: _____

III

1-O, 2-S, 3-O, 4-O, 5-S, 6-O, 7-O, 8-S, 9-S, 10-O, 11-O, 12-O, 13-O, 14-O, 15-O, 16-O, 17-O, 18-S, 19-O, 20-S

Your score: _____

IV

1-e, 2-b, 3-g, 4-d, 5-i, 6-j, 7-a, 8-h, 9-f, 10-c

Your score: _____

V

1-c, 2-g, 3-e, 4-j, 5-f, 6-h, 7-a, 8-d, 9-b, 10-i

Your score: _____

VI

1-obviate, 2-adulate, 3-malign, 4-laconic, 5-banal, 6-verbatim, 7-genocide, 8-patrimony, 9-polytheism, 10-militant, 11-bona fide, 12-garrulous, 13-soliloquize, 14-magnum opus, 15-magnanimous, 16-ambulatory, 17-insomnia, 18-acrophobia, 19-fratricide, 20-antonymous, 21-*joie* de *vivre*, 22-devitalize, 23-naivete, 24-punctilious, 25-perspicuous, 26-circumspect, 27-retrospect, 28-unanimous, 29-stoical, 30-interurban

Your score: _____
Your total score: _____

Significance of Your Total Score:

100—120: Masterly work; you are ready to move right along.

80—99: Good work; this review was useful to you.

65—79: Average work; you're getting a good deal out of your study, but perhaps you should review thoroughly after each session.

50—64: Barely acceptable; work harder.

35—49: Poor; further review is suggested before you go on.

0—34: You can do much better if you really try.

You might turn back for a moment to Chapter 8, in which you recorded your score on the first Comprehensive Test. Did you do better this time? Let's make a record of both scores at this point for the sake of comparison and to give you a mark to shoot at in the Comprehensive Test you will take in Chapter 17.

你总分的意义:

100—120:出色的工作;你已经准备就绪,可以继续前进了。

80—99:不错的工作;这个复习对你有用。

65—79:一般;你的学习有了不少收获,但也许你应该在每一节后彻底复习。

50—64:勉强可接受;再努力。

35—49:很差;在你继续之前,建议你再做复习。

0—34:如果你真的努力,你可以做得更好。

在第8章里,你已经记下了综合测验Ⅰ的成绩,建议你回到那一章看一看。你这次测验进步了吗?现在把这两次分数都记录下来,以资比较,同时也为你在第17章的综合测验Ⅲ确立一个目标。

SCORES

Test I (Chapter 8): _____ out of 120

Test II (Chapter 13): _____ out of 120

PART THREE
FINISHING WITH A FEELING OF COMPLETE SUCCESS

第三部分
以圆满成功的感觉收尾

14

HOW TO TALK ABOUT COMMON PHENOMENA AND OCCURRENCES

如何描述普遍现象和事件

(*Sessions 39 — 41*)

TEASER PREVIEW

引读

What word aptly describes：

* *dire poverty?*
* *emotion experienced without direct participation?*
* *something which lasts a very short time?*
* *an inoffensive word for an unpleasant idea?*
* *light and easy banter?*
* *someone who is cowlike in his stolidity?*
* *homesickness?*
* *harsh sound?*
* *a meat-eating animal?*
* *something kept secret?*

哪些词汇能够恰当描述以下情景：
* 赤贫
* 间接感受到的情绪
* 短暂的、瞬息的事物
* 委婉语
* 打趣、玩笑
* 迟钝如牛的人
* 乡愁、怀旧
* 刺耳嘈杂的声音
* 食肉动物
* 秘密

SESSION 39
第 39 节

This world, Robert Louis Stevenson once claimed—with, I think, questionable logic—is so full of a number of things that we should all be as happy as kings.

I doubt very strongly that happiness comes from the outside, or that kings are necessarily happy. But I will go this far (and no further) with Stevenson: the world is certainly full of a number of things. For instance, poverty and misery, hospitals and insane asylums, slums and racial restrictions, cut-down forests and once fertile lands becoming progressively more arid, war and death and taxes and bumbling diplomats. I know that Stevenson had a different sort of thing in mind, for romantic poets tend to view the world through rose-tinted spectacles, but it is often necessary to counter one extreme with another—and I simply wish to set the record straight.

In this chapter we are going to discuss a number of things to be found in the world and in the minds of its inhabitants—poverty and wealth; secondhand emotions; the relativity of time; praise of various sorts; small talk and how to indulge in it; animals; longings for the past; sounds; eating habits; and many kinds and conditions of secrecy.

As you see, when you start exploring ideas, as we constantly do in these chapters, you never know what will turn up.

罗伯特·路易斯·史蒂文森[1]曾经宣称,这个世界包罗万象,我们应该像帝王一样快乐。我对他的逻辑有所疑问。

我非常质疑快乐来自外界的观点,也不认为所有帝王都快乐。我只赞同史蒂文森的前半句话(仅此而已):这个世界的确包罗万象。例如:贫穷和苦难,医院和精神病院,贫民窟和种族歧视,森林被破坏,曾经富饶的土地愈加贫瘠,战争、死亡、税收,还有装模作样的外交官。我知道史蒂文森有着另外一套思维方式,作为一个浪漫的诗人,他透过玫瑰色的眼镜观察世界。但是,我认为提出问题的对立面十分有必要。我只是希望澄清是非。

本章,我们将讨论一些在世界中发现和人类头脑中的一些事物——贫穷和富裕;间接的情绪;时间的相对性;各种各样的赞扬;闲谈和如何享受闲谈;动物;对过去的眷顾;声音;饮食习惯;以及秘密的许多种类和情况。

与之前章节的学习方法相同,开始探讨概念时,你会发现你学到了过去从未想过的观点。

IDEAS
概念

1. for want of the green stuff
需要绿色的生活

There are those people who are forced (often through no fault of their own) to pursue an existence not only devoid of such luxuries as radios, television sets, sunken bathtubs, electric orange-juice squeezers, automobiles, Jacuzzis, private swimming pools, etc., but lacking also in many of the pure necessities of living—sufficient food, heated homes, hot water, vermin- and rodent-free surroundings, decent

---

1. 罗伯特·路易斯·史蒂文森,英国浪漫主义代表作家之一。代表作品有《沃尔特·斯科特爵士》《金银岛》等。——译者注

clothing，etc.

Such people live：

in penury

有一些人被迫(通常不是他们自己的错)过着潦倒的生活,不仅无法享受我们习以为常的奢侈品,如:收音机、电视机、浴缸、电动榨橘汁机、汽车、按摩浴缸、私人游泳池等,连最基本的生活必需品也十分匮乏——足够的食物、有暖气的房子、热水、干净的居住环境和得体的衣服等。

这些人濒临赤贫的境地(penury)。

2．at least watch it

至少能够看到

All normal people want and need love and at least a modicum of excitement in their lives—so say the psychologists. If no one loves them，and if they can find no one on whom to lavish their own love，they may often satisfy their emotional longings and needs by getting their feelings secondhand—through reading love stories，attending motion pictures，watching soap operas，etc.

These are：

vicarious feelings

所有正常的人都向往和需要爱,至少需要在生命中有一点点令人激动的东西——这是心理学家的观点。如果没有人爱她们,如果她们找不到人去挥霍自己的爱,她们通常会通过二手的情感来满足内心对情感的渴望和需求——阅读爱情小说、看动画片和电视肥皂剧等。

这些是间接体验到的情感(vicarious)。

3．time is fleeting

时光飞逝

During the late winter and early spring of 1948—1949，great numbers of people went practically berserk joining and forming "pyramid clubs." If you have not heard of this amazing phenomenon，I won't attempt to describe it in any of its multifarious ramifications，but the main point was that you paid two dollars，treated some people to coffee and doughnuts，and shortly thereafter (if you were gullible enough to fall for this get-rich-quick scheme) supposedly received a return of some fantastic amount like＄2,064 for your investment.

For a short time，pyramid clubs were a rage—soon they had vanished from the American scene.

Anything that lasts for but a short time and leaves no trace is：

ephemeral

1948 年深冬到 1949 年初春,许多人发疯似的参加并组成了"金字塔俱乐部"。如果你从未听说过这个惊人事件,我并不打算描述任何其带来的多种影响,但要点是,如果你花费两美元为一些人购买咖啡和甜甜圈,很快(如果你足够轻信,来参加这个一夜成为富翁的计划)你的投资将获得 2064 美元的回报。

"金字塔俱乐部"风靡一时——但很快便从美国历史舞台上消失。

任何流行一时并在之后不留任何痕迹的事物都可以被称为"短暂的"(ephemeral)。

4. how not to call a spade. . .

如何遮遮掩掩

Words are only *symbols of* things—they are not the things themselves. (This, by the way, is one of the basic tenets of semantics.) But many people identify the word and the thing so closely that they fear to use certain words that symbolize things that are unpleasant to them.

I know that this is confusing, so let me illustrate.

Words having to do with death, sex, certain portions of the anatomy, excretion, etc. are avoided by certain people.

These people prefer circumlocutions—words that "talk around" an idea or that mean or imply something but don't come right out and say so directly.

For example：

词汇只是事物的象征符号——词汇本身并不是事物。(顺便提及,这一点是语义学的基本原则。)但是,许多人认为词汇与事物之间具有非常紧密的关系,他们不敢使用对于他们来说象征不快事物的词汇,唯恐这些词汇会带来这些不快之事。

我知道这的确令人困惑,所以请允许我进一步说明。

有几种人会拒绝使用与死亡、性、身体的某些部位、排泄等相关的词汇。

这些人喜欢委婉曲折的表达方法——虽然间接却能表达同样概念的词汇。

例如：

WORD	CIRCUMLOCUTION
die	expire; depart this life; pass away; leave this vale of tears
sexual intercourse	(intimate) relations; "playing house"; "shacking up"
prostitute	lady of the evening; *fille de joie*; painted woman; lady of easy virtue; *fille de nuit*; streetwalker; hooker
house of prostitution	house of ill-fame; bawdyhouse; house of ill-repute; bagnio; brothel; bordello; "house"; "massage parlor"
buttocks, behind	derrière; rear end; butt; tail
breasts	bosom; bust; curves
toilet	powder room; little girl's room; facilities; washroom; lavatory; head

The left-hand column is the direct, non-pussyfooting word. The right-hand column is made up of:

euphemisms

左栏中是直接的、不委婉的表达方法,右栏中由 euphemisms(委婉语)构成。

5. small talk

俏皮话

"Whenever I'm in the dumps, I get a new suit."

"Oh, so that's where you get them!"

"Lend me a dime—I want to phone one of my friends."

"Here's a quarter—call them all."

"The doctor says I have snoo in my blood!"

"Snoo? What's snoo?"

"Not a darn! What's new with you?"

"What are twins?"

"Okay, what are twins?"

"Womb mates!"

"I took a twip yesterday."

"A twip?"

"Yes, I took a twip on a twain!"

These are examples of:

badinage

"被抛弃的时候，我总会为自己买一件新套装。"

"哦，所以你总是从垃圾场捡套装！"

（dump 即表示被抛弃，又表示垃圾场。）

"借我一毛钱硬币——我要给一个朋友打电话。"

"这是 25 分钱——你可以打给你所有的朋友。"

"医生说我血液里'snoo'（油脂）太多！"

"snoo? 什么是 snoo?"[1]

"没什么！你最近怎么样?"

"什么是双胞胎?"

"好的,什么是双胞胎?"

"子宫里的伙伴。"

"昨天我用了一个 twip"

"一个 twip?"

"对,在 twain 上!"[2]

以上是打趣的具体例子（badinage）。

6. everything but give milk

只是不产奶

You've seen a cow contentedly munching its cud. Nothing seems capable of disturbing this animal—and the animal seems to want nothing more out of life than to lead a simple, vegetable existence.

Some people are like a cow—calm, patient, placid, phlegmatic, vegetable-like. They are:

---

1. snoo 有很多意思,可指"油脂",也可以是"what is new"的简写形式。——译者注

2. twip 和 twine 都是计算机相关术语,这几句是把 twip 仿照成 trip 的诙谐说法。——译者注

bovine[1]

你一定看见过奶牛满意地反刍。似乎没有任何事能够打扰这种动物——除了简单地以草为生，它们无欲无求。

有些人很像奶牛——冷静、耐心、平和、冷静、呆板。

他们呆头呆脑（bovine）。

7. good old days

过去的美好时光

Do you sometimes experience a keen, almost physical, longing for associations or places of the past?

When you pass the neighborhood in which you were born and where you spent your early years, do you have a sharp, strange reaction, almost akin to mild nausea?

When you are away from home and friends and family, do pleasant remembrances crowd in on your mind to the point where your present loneliness becomes almost unbearable, and you actually feel a little sick?

This common feeling is called:

nostalgia

有时，你是否会对过去的关系或地方经历一种强烈的、几乎是生理上的渴望？

经过你出生和早期成长的地方，你是否会经历一种近似于轻度头晕的强烈的奇怪反应？

当你远离故土、朋友和家人，你的脑海中是否会充满愉快的回忆，以至于此时的孤独变得无法忍受，就好像生病了一样？

这种普遍的感觉被称为乡愁（nostalgia）。

8. sounds that grate

刺耳的声音

Some sounds are so harsh, grating, and discordant that they offend the ear. They lack all sweetness, harmony, pleasantness. Traffic noises of a big city, electronic rock music, chalk squeaking on a blackboard...

Such blaring, ear-splitting, or spine-tingling sounds are called:

cacophonous

一些声音非常粗糙、刺耳、不和谐，听起来不舒服。这些声音缺少甜美、和谐和令人舒适的感觉。大城市的交通噪音，电子摇滚乐，黑板上粉笔的响声等。

这些高声、刺耳或令人后背发麻的声音是嘈杂的（cacophonous）。

9. eating habits

饮食习惯

Lions, tigers, wolves, and some other mammals subsist entirely on flesh. No spinach, salad greens, whole-wheat cereals, sugar, or spices—just good, red meat.

These mammals are:

carnivorous

---

1. Remember Ogden Nash's delightful definition?

      The cow is of the bovine ilk,

      One end moo, the other end milk.

记得奥格登·纳什的令人发笑的定义吗？奶牛属牛类，一端哞哞叫，一端出牛奶。

狮子、老虎、狼和其他动物是完全的肉食动物。不吃菠菜、绿色蔬菜沙拉、全麦谷物、糖或辣椒——只吃新鲜的红肉。他们是食肉的(carnivorous)。

10. private and public

私下的和公开的

There are certain things most of us do in private, like taking a bath. Some people like to engage in other activities in complete privacy—eating, reading, watching TV, sleeping, for example.

The point is that, while these activities may be conducted in privacy, there is never any reason for keeping them secret.

But there are other activities that are kept not only private, but well-shrouded in secrecy and concealed from public knowledge. These activities are unethical, illegal, or unsafe—like having an affair with someone whose spouse is your best friend, betraying military secrets to the enemy, trading in narcotics, bribing public officials, etc.

Arrangements, activities, or meetings that fall under this category are called:

clandestine

有些事自然而然要私下去做,例如洗澡。一些人也喜欢完全在私下里做其他一些事——例如吃饭、阅读、看电视和睡觉。

问题是,虽然这些活动可以私密进行,但是没有任何理由值得保密。

还有一些活动不仅需要私下进行,而且需要完全保密,要掩人耳目。这些活动通常被视为不道德的、非法的、违法的或者危险的——例如与你最好的朋友的配偶有染、向敌军泄露军事秘密、贩卖毒品和向政府官员行贿等。

这一类安排、活动或者会面被称为暗中的(clandestine)。

USING THE WORDS

单词应用

Can you pronounce the words?

你能读出这些单词吗?

1.	*penury*	PEN′-yə-ree
2.	*vicarious*	vī-KAIR′-ee-əs
3.	*ephemeral*	ə-FEM′-ə-rəl
4.	*euphemism*	YOO′-fə-miz-əm
5.	*badinage*	BAD′-ə-nəj
6.	*bovine*	BŌ-vīn′
7.	*nostalgia*	nə-STAL′-jə
8.	*cacophony*	kə-KOF′-ə-nee
9.	*carnivorous*	kahr-NIV′-ər-əs
10.	*clandestine*	klan-DES′-tin

Can you work with the words?

你能灵活使用这些词汇了吗?

1. penury		a. impermanent
2. vicarious		b. banter
3. ephemeral		c. homesickness
4. euphemism		d. meat-eating
5. badinage		e. circumlocution
6. bovine		f. harsh noise
7. nostalgia		g. poverty
8. cacophony		h. secret
9. carnivorous		i. placid; stolid; cowlike
10. clandestine		j. secondhand

KEY:1-g, 2-j, 3-a, 4-e, 5-b, 6-i, 7-c, 8-f, 9-d, 10-h

Do you understand the words? (I)

你对这些词汇是否已经透彻地理解? (I)

1. Do wealthy people normally live in *penury*?　　　　　YES　　NO
2. Is a *vicarious* thrill one that comes from direct participation?　　　　　YES　　NO
3. Do *ephemeral* things last a very short time?　　　　　YES　　NO
4. Is a *euphemism* the substitution of an inoffensive term for another of the same meaning that may sound offensive, vulgar, or indelicate?　　　　　YES　　NO
5. Does *badinage* show lighthearted frivolity?　　　　　YES　　NO
6. Are *bovine* people high-strung and nervous?　　　　　YES　　NO
7. Does one get a feeling of *nostalgia* for past occurrences and relationships?　　　　　YES　　NO
8. Is *cacophony* pleasant and musical?　　　　　YES　　NO
9. Do *carnivorous* animals eat meat?　　　　　YES　　NO
10. Is a *clandestine* meeting conducted in secrecy?　　　　　YES　　NO

KEY:1-no, 2-no, 3-yes, 4-yes, 5-yes, 6-no, 7-yes, 8-no, 9-yes, 10-yes

Do you understand the words?（Ⅱ）

你对这些词汇是否已经透彻地理解？（Ⅱ）

1. penury—affluence	SAME	OPPOSITE
2. vicarious—actual	SAME	OPPOSITE
3. ephemeral—eternal	SAME	OPPOSITE
4. euphemism—less offensive word	SAME	OPPOSITE
5. badinage—light，teasing talk	SAME	OPPOSITE
6. bovine—high-strung	SAME	OPPOSITE
7. nostalgia—longing for the past	SAME	OPPOSITE
8. cacophony—euphony	SAME	OPPOSITE
9. carnivorous—herbivorous	SAME	OPPOSITE
10. clandestine—hidden	SAME	OPPOSITE

KEY：1-O，2-O，3-O，4-S，5-S，6-O，7-S，8-O，9-O，10-S

（The new words used in this test will be discussed in later sections of this chapter.）

Can you recall the words?

你能够写出这些词汇吗？

1. harsh sound	1. C _____
2. having a short life	2. E _____
3. dire poverty	3. P _____
4. substitution of an indirect or pleasant word or phrase for a possibly offensive one of the same meaning	4. E _____
5. experienced as a spectator, rather than as a participant	5. V _____
6. acute feeling of homesickness	6. N _____
7. light，half-teasing banter	7. B _____
8. subsisting solely on meat	8. C _____
9. cowlike；stolid	9. B _____
10. secret；concealed	10. C _____

KEY：1-cacophony, 2-ephemeral, 3-penury, 4-euphemism，5-vicarious, 6-nostalgia, 7-badinage, 8-carnivorous, 9-bovine, 10-clandestine

(End of Session 39)

SESSION 40
第 40 节

ORIGINS AND RELATED WORDS
词源及相关词汇

1. money, and what it will buy
钱和钱能买到的东西

The modern world operates largely by means of a price structure—wealth and poverty are therefore words that indicate the possession, on the one hand, or the lack, on the other, of money. *Penury*, from Latin *penuria*, need, neediness, is dire, abject poverty, complete lack of financial resources. It is one of the two strongest English words there are to denote absence of money. The adjective form, *penurious* (pə-NYOOr′-ee-əs *or* pə-NOOR′-ee-əs), strangely enough, *may* mean *poverty-stricken*, but more commonly signifies *stingy*, *close-fisted*, *niggardly*; so sparing in the use of money as to give the appearance of *penury*.

当今世界从很大程度上通过价值结构运作——因此，一方面，与财富有关的词汇能表示拥有金钱；另一方面，与贫穷相关的词汇显示金钱的匮乏。penury 来自拉丁语 penuria，表示"需求"；penury 是极端的、境况凄惨的贫穷，是资金的完全匮乏，是两个表示金钱匮乏的表意最强烈的词语之一。奇怪的是，形容词形式 penurious 可能用来表示贫穷，但更多用来指过分节俭的、小气的、吝啬的，而不指经济上的窘迫；因为在金钱方面过于节俭，所以给人一种贫困的感觉。

Penurious is a synonym of *parsimonious* (pahr′-sə-MŌ′-nee-əs), but is much stronger in implication. A *parsimonious* person is stingy; a *penurious* person is twice as stingy. *Penury*, then, is poverty; *penuriousness* is stinginess, excessive frugality. The noun form of *parsimonious* is *parsimony* (PAHR′-sə-mō′-nee).

A somewhat milder word than *penury* for poverty (if you can imagine a mild degree of poverty) is *indigence* (IN′-də-jəns). *Indigent* (IN′-də-jənt) people are not absolutely penniless—they are simply living in reduced circumstances, forgoing many creature comforts, forced to undergo the type of hardships that may accompany a lack of sufficient funds.

penurious 与 parsimonious 是同义词，但在表意上更为强烈。a parsimonious person 很小气；而 a penurious person 是他吝啬程度的两倍。所以，penury 指赤贫；penuriousness 指吝啬、过度节俭。parsimonious 的名词形式是 parsimony。

表示贫困但程度不及 penury 严重的词汇（如果你能够想象出贫困的适中程度）是 indigence。indigent person 不是完全的身无分文——他只是生活拮据，不得不放弃物质享受，可能由于缺少足够的资金而忍受艰难。

On the other hand, a close synonym of *penury*, and one of equal strength, is *destitution* (des′-tə-TOO′-shən). *Destitute* (DES′-tə-toot) people do not even have the means for mere subsistence—as such, they are perhaps on the verge of starvation. *Penury and destitution* are not merely straitened circumstances—they are downright desperate circumstances.

另外,penury 有一个表意同样强烈的近义词 destitution。destitute person 连最起码的生活都无法维持——因此,他在饥饿的边缘挣扎;penury 和 destitution 不仅仅生活在窘迫的环境中——他们本身就是彻头彻尾的窘迫。

To turn now to the brighter side of the picture, the possession of money, especially in increasing amounts, is expressed by *affluence* (AF′-lo͞o-əns). *Affluent* (AF′-lo͞o-ənt) people, people of *affluence*, or those living in *affluent* circumstances, are more than comfortable; in addition, there is the implication that their wealth is increasing. People who live in *affluence* probably own large and costly homes, run big, new cars, belong to expensive golf or country clubs, etc.

现在我们来看较光明的一面。富有,尤其是日益增长的财富,被称为 affluence。an affluent person,a man of affluence 或 one living in affluent circumstances 会生活得特别舒适;此外还暗示出他的财富在日益增长,而生活富足的人很可能拥有自己宽敞昂贵的房子,驾驶宽敞的崭新轿车,是昂贵的高尔夫俱乐部的会员。

A much stronger term is *opulence* (OP′-yə-ləns), which not only implies much greater wealth than *affluence*, but in addition suggests lavish expenditures and ostentatiously luxurious surroundings. People of *opulence* own estates; drive only outrageously expensive and specially equipped cars (Rolls-Royces, Mercedes-Benzes, Porsches, etc.); have a corps of servants, including a major-domo; belong to golf and yacht and country clubs, etc., etc. Embroider the fantasy as much as you wish to. *Opulent* (OP′-yə-lənt) may describe people, surroundings, styles of life, or the like.

Affluent is a combination of the prefix *ad-*, to, toward (changing to *af-* before a root beginning with *f*), plus the Latin verb *fluo*, to flow—*affluence* is that delightful condition in which money keeps flowing to us, and no one ever turns off the spigot. Other words from the same root, *fluo*, to flow, are *fluid*, *influence*, *confluence* (a "flowing together"), *fluent* (the words flow smoothly), etc.

Opulent is from Latin *opulentus*, wealthy. No other English words derive from this root.

另一个表意更为强力的词语是 opulence(阔绰、富丽堂皇),不仅表示比 affluence 更多的财富,还暗示出挥霍的花销和故意炫耀的奢侈生活。people of opulence 拥有庄园;只驾驶超级昂贵和专门装备的汽车(罗尔斯-罗伊斯、奔驰、保时捷等);由大批的仆人来服侍,并雇佣一个大总管来管理;是高尔夫、游艇和乡村俱乐部的会员。尽可能极尽想象。opulent 可以用来描述人、环境、生活方式等。

affluent 由前缀 ad-(朝,朝着;在以 f 开始的词根前为 af-),加拉丁动词后缀 fluo(流)组成——affluent 就是金钱源源朝我们流来的令人愉悦状态,没有人去关龙头。由同一词根 fluo(流)派生的词有 fluid, influence, confluence(流到一起),fluent(话语顺畅地流)等。

opulent 源于拉丁语中的 opulentus,意为"富裕的",没有别的英语单词由这个词根派生。

2. doing and feeling

体验与感受

If you watch a furious athletic event, and *you* get tired, though the athletes expend all the energy—that's *vicarious* fatigue.

If your friend goes on a bender, and as you watch him absorb one drink after another, *you* begin to feel giddy and stimulated, that's *vicarious* intoxication.

If you watch a mother in a motion picture or dramatic play suffer horribly at the death of her child, and *you* go through the same agony, that's *vicarious* torment.

观看激烈的体育赛事，即使耗费体能的是运动员，你也会感到疲倦——这种疲倦可以被称为 vicarious fatigue(间接体验的疲劳)。

如果你的朋友不停喝酒，你看着他喝了一杯又一杯，你也开始感到头昏、兴奋，这种酒醉可以被称为 vicarious intoxication(间接体验的酒醉)。

在电影或者戏剧中看到母亲因丧子而痛苦，你会感到经历了同样的痛苦，这样的折磨可以被称为 vicarious(间接体验的)。

You can experience an emotion, then, in two ways: firsthand, through actual participation; or *vicariously*, by becoming empathetically involved in another person's feelings.

Some people, for example, lead essentially dull and colorless lives. Through their children, through reading or attending the theater, however, they can experience all the emotions felt by others whose lives move along at a swift, exciting pace. These people live at second hand; they live *vicariously*.

所以，你能够通过两种方式经历情感：通过直接参与所经历的一手情感；通过感受另一个人的感受而经历的二手情感，这样的情感就是间接获得的——vicarious。

例如，有些人过着枯燥、无趣的生活。但是，通过自己的孩子、通过阅读或者观赏戏剧，他们能够经历到以轻松、令人兴奋的节奏生活的人们的所有情感。这些人过着二手的生活；可以说"they live vicariously"，他们过着间接感受的生活。

3. time is relative

时间是相对的

Elephants and turtles live almost forever; human beings in the United States have a life expectancy in general of sixty-eight to seventy-six years (though the gradual conquest of disease is constantly lengthening our span)[1]; dogs live from seven to ten years; and some insects exist for only a few hours or days.

One such short-lived creature is the dayfly, which in Greek was called *ephemera*. Hence anything so short-lived, so unenduring that it scarcely seems to outlast the day, may be called *ephemeral*.

大象和乌龟似乎永远不会死；美国人的预期寿命大约 68—76 年(虽然不断战胜疾病使得人类寿命不断延长)；狗能活 7—10 年；一些昆虫只能存活几个小时或数天。

蜉蝣就是如此短命的生物，古希腊人称之为 ephemera。所以，任何如此短命的、甚至活不过一天的事物都被称为 ephemeral。

A synonym of *ephemeral* is *evanescent* (ev-ə-NES'-ənt), fleeting, staying for a remarkably short time, vanishing. Something intangible, like a feeling, may be called *evanescent*; it's here, and before you can quite comprehend it, it's gone—vanished.

The noun is *evanescence* (ev'-ə-NES'-əns); the verb is to evanesce (ev-ə-NES').

---

1. Latest figures, 1978, for the United States: males, 68.5 years; females, 76.4 years.

美国 1978 年最新数据：男性平均寿命为 68.5 岁；女性平均寿命为 76.4 岁。

ephemeral 的近义词是 evanescent，表示"短暂的、停留时间非常短的、迅速消失的"。像感觉这类无形的事物可以用 evanescent 来修饰，它在这里，但在你还没完全体验到之前，它就消失了—vanished。

名词形式是 evanescence，动词形式是 evanesce。

Evanescent is built on the prefix *e-*（*ex-*），out，the root *vanesco*，to vanish，and the adjective suffix *-ent*.

The suffix *-esce* often，but not always，means *begin to*. *-Escent* may mean *becoming* or *beginning to*. Thus：

Adolescent—beginning to grow up；
　　　　　　　 beginning to become an adult

evanesce—begin to vanish

convalesce—begin to get well after illness

putrescent—beginning to rot；
　　　　　　　　 beginning to become putrid

obsolescent—becoming obsolete

evanescent 是由前缀 e-(ex，外面的)，词根 vanesco(消失)和形容词后缀-ent 三部分构成的。

后缀-esce 通常(但不总是)意为"开始"，-escent 可能意为"变成"或"开始"。因此：

词根-esce 通常表示"正在开始……"。这样：

adolescent(青春期的)——开始长大；开始成为成人

evanesce(消散)——开始消失

convalesce(康复)——病后开始恢复

putrescent(将要腐烂的)——开始腐烂、腐臭

obsolescent(即将过时的)——开始过时

4. an exploration of various good things

探索各种美好的事物

A *euphemism* is a word or expression that has been substituted for another that is likely to offend—it is built on the Greek prefix *eu-*，good，the root *pheme*，voice，and the noun suffix *-ism*. （Etymologically，"something said in a good voice！"）Adjective：*euphemistic*（y oo′-fə′-MIS′-tik）.

Other English words constructed from the prefix *eu-*：

euphemism 是替换可能冒犯言辞的一个词汇或一种表达——它由希腊语 eu-(好的)和 pheme(声音)，加上名词后缀-ism 组成。(从语源学角度看，"用好声音说出的东西！")形容词形式是 euphemistic。

由前缀 eu-组成的其他英文单词有：

（1）*euphony*（YOO′-fə-nee）—good sound；pleasant lilt or rhythm（*phone*，sound）

Adjective：*euphonic*（y oo-FON′-ik）*or* euphonious（y oo-FŌ′- nee-əs）

（2）*eulogy*（YOO′-lə-jee）—etymologically，"good speech"；a formal speech of praise，usually delivered as a funeral oration. *Logos* in this term means *word or speech*，as it did in *philology*（Chapter 6）. *Logos* more commonly means *science or study*，but has the alternate meaning in *eulogy*，*philology*，*monologue*，*dialogue*， *epilogue* (words upon the other words, or "after-words"), and *prologue* (words before the main part, "before-words," or introduction).

Adjective：*eulogistic* (yōō-lə-JIS′-tik)；verb：*eulogize* (YŌŌ-lə-jiz′)；person who delivers a *eulogy*：*eulogist* (YŌŌ-lə-jist)

(3) *euphoria* (yōō-FAWR′-ee-ə)—good feeling, a sense of mental buoyancy and physical well-being.

Adjective：*euphoric* (yōō-FAWR′-ik)

(4) *euthanasia* (yōō′-thə-NAY′-zhə)—etymologically, "good death"; method of painless death inflicted on people suffering from incurable diseases—not legal at the present time, but advocated by many people. The word derives from *eu-* plus Greek *thanatos*, death.

(1) euphony——悦耳的声音、愉悦的调子或节奏(phone,声音)。

形容词形式：euphonic 或 euphonious

(2) eulogy——从词源上看,其本义为"好的演讲";通常是在葬礼上,对死者充满溢美之词的正式演讲。logos 在这个单词中意为"词语"或"演讲",和其在 philology(在第 6 章中)中的一样。logos 更常见的意思是"科学"或"研究",但其在 eulogy,philology,monologue, dialogue, epilogue(其他语句上面的或"之后"的话),还有 prologue(在主要部分之前的话,"前面的话",或介绍)中是第一个意思。

形容词是 eulogistic;动词是 eulogize,发表 eulogy 的人是：eulogist

(3) euphoria——幸福感;精神欢快感、身体舒适感。

形容词形式：euphoric

(4) euthanasia——安乐死,从词源学讲,"好的死法";对患有不治之症的病人采取的一种无痛死亡方法——安乐死现在在美国不合法,但是许多医生倡导。它由 eu-加希腊语 thanatos(死亡)组成。

5. exploration of modes of expression
探索各种表达方法

Badinage is a half-teasing, non-malicious, frivolous banter, intended to amuse rather than wound. *Badinage* has a close synonym, *persiflage* (PUR′-sə-flahzh′), which is a little more derisive, a trifle more indicative of contempt or mockery—but still totally unmalicious.

In line with *badinage* and *persiflage*, there are four other forms of expression you should be familiar with：*cliché*(klee-SHAY′), *bromide* (BRŌ′-mīd′), *platitude* (PLAT′-ə-tōōd), and *anodyne* (AN′-ə-dīn′).

A *cliché* is a pattern of words which was once new and fresh, but which now is so old, worn, and threadbare that only banal, unimaginative speakers and writers ever use it. Examples are：*fast and furious*；*unsung heroes*；*by leaps and bounds*；*conspicuous by its absence*；*green with envy*；*etc.* The most devastating criticism you can make of a piece of writing is to say, "It is full of *cliché*"; the most pointed insult to a person's way of talking is, "You speak in *clichés*."

badinage 是一种半开玩笑的、非恶意的、无聊的玩笑,仅供娱乐,而非伤害。与 badinage 词义非常相近的词是 persiflage,相比之下,persiflage 略带嘲笑之意,多了一丝轻蔑和嘲讽的意味——但也是完全没有恶意的。

除了 badinage 和 persiflage,你还应该熟悉另外四种表达形式：cliché、bromide、platitude 和 anodyne。

cliché 是指曾经耳目一新而在现在是古老、陈旧、乏味的表达,只有陈腐和毫无想象力的演讲者和作家才会使用这样的表达。例如：fast and furious(飞快地)；unsung heros(幕后英雄)；by leaps and bounds(突飞猛进地)；conspicuous by its absence(因缺席而变得显眼)；green with envy(心中充满妒忌)等等。一篇文章能够得到的最致命的评论就是："It is full of cliche."("文章充满陈词滥调。")；而对于一个人说法方式最直接的侮辱就是："He speaks in cliches."("他满嘴陈词滥调。")

A *bromide* is any trite, dull, and probably fallacious remark that shows little evidence of original thinking, and that therefore convinces a listener of the total absence of perspicacity on the part of the speaker.

For instance, some cautious, dull-minded individual might warn you not to take a chance in these words："Remember it's better to be safe than sorry!"

Your sneering response might be："Oh, that old *bromide*!"

bromide 是指老生常谈的、枯燥的、很大程度上靠不住的言语，未经过具有一丁点新意的思考，因此它会使听者确信说话者毫无洞察力。

例如，一些谨慎、呆板的人会警告你不要冒险使用这类老套的话语："记住，事后追悔不如事前稳妥。"

你会鄙视地答道："天呐，又是这套老话！"

A *platitude* is similar to a *cliché* or *bromide*, in that it is a dull, trite, hackneyed, unimaginative pattern of words—but, to add insult to injury (*cliché*), the speaker uses it with an air of novelty—as if he just made it up, and isn't he the brilliant fellow!

An *anodyne*, in the medical sense, is a drug that allays pain without curing an illness, like aspirin or morphine. Figuratively, an *anodyne* is a statement made to allay someone's fears or anxieties, not believed by the speaker, but intended to be believed by the listener. "Prosperity is just around the corner" was a popular *anodyne* of the 1930s.

platitude 与 cliché 和 bromide 意义相近，因为它也指陈旧的、腐朽的、呆板的、缺乏想象力的表达——但雪上加霜的是(cliché)，说话者却装出一副言辞新颖的模样——就好像他刚刚编造出这个表达，难道他不是聪明的家伙吗！

anodyne 的本义是指一种能够减轻疼痛却无法治愈疾病的药物，例如阿司匹林或者吗啡。anodyne 的引申含义表示减缓听话者恐惧或焦虑的陈述，说话者不以为然，但其目的是为了说服听话者。20 世纪 30 年代一句著名的 anodyne 就是："Prosperity is just around the corner."(繁荣指日可待)

A *bromide* is also a drug, formerly used as a sedative. Sedatives dull the senses—the statement labeled a *bromide* comes from a speaker of dull wit and has a sedative effect on the listener. The adjective is *bromidic* (brō-MID'-ik), as in "his *bromidic* way of expressing himself."

Platitude derives from Greek *platys*, broad or flat, plus the noun suffix *-tude*. Words like *plateau* (flat land), *plate* and *platter* (flat dishes), and *platypus* (flat foot) all derive from the same root as *platitude*, a flat statement, i. e., one that falls flat, despite the speaker's high hopes for it. The adjective is *platitudinous* (plat'-ə-TŌO-də-nəs), as in, "What a *platitudinous* remark."

Anodyne is a combination of the negative prefix *an-* with Greek *odyne*, pain. *Anodynes*, as drugs, lessen pain; as statements, they are intended to reduce or eliminate emotional pain or anxiety.

　　bromide 也是一种药,以前用作镇静剂。镇静剂会使感觉变得迟钝——一个缺乏智慧的令人昏昏欲睡的演讲者的演讲,就像是 bromide。其形容词是 bromidic,就如"his bromidic way of express himself"(他总是陈词滥调)。

　　platitude 源于希腊语 platys(宽阔的或平的),加上名词后缀—tude,如 plateau(平地),plate,platter(平的盘子),plat-ypus(平足)都和 platitude(一个平淡的讲话,即虽然演讲者虽然有很高的期望,但其演讲还是流于平淡)一样,来源于同样的词根。形容词是 platitudinous,如"what a platitudinous remark"(一个多么陈腐的评论)。

　　anodyne 是由否定前缀 an-和希腊语 odyne(疼痛)构成,anodyne 是一种减少疼痛的药物。可指代消除精神痛苦和焦虑的谈话。

REVIEW OF ETYMOLOGY
复习词源

PREFIX, ROOT, SUFFIX	MEANING	ENGLISH WORD
1. *penuria*	need, neediness	_____
2. *ad-* (*af,*)	to, toward	_____
3. *fluo*	to flow	_____
4. *opulentus*	wealthy	_____
5. *ephemera*	dayfly	_____
6. *e-*, *ex*	out	_____
7. *vanesco*	to vanish	_____
8. *-esce*	begin to	_____
9. *-ent*	adjective suffix	_____
10. *-ence*	noun suffix	_____
11. *eu-*	good	_____
12. *pheme*	voice	_____
13. *-ism*	noun suffix	_____
14. *phone*	sound	_____
15. *-ic*	adjective suffix	_____
16. *-ous*	adjective suffix	_____
17. *logos*	word, speech	_____
18. *-ize*	verb suffix	_____
19. *thanatos*	death	_____
20. *platys*	broad or flat	_____
21. *an-*	negative prefix	_____
22. *odyne*	pain	_____

USING THE WORDS
单词应用

Can you pronounce the words? （Ⅰ）
你能读出这些单词吗?（Ⅰ）

1. *penurious*　　　　　pə-NYŎO′-ee-əs or
2. *penuriousness*　　　pə-NYŎOR′-ee-əs-nəs or
　　　　　　　　　　　　pə-NŎOR′-ee-əs-nəs

3. *parsimonious*   pahr′-sə-MŌ′-nee-əs

4. *parsimony*   PAHR′-sə-mō′-nee

5. *indigence*   IN′-də-jəns

6. *indigent*   IN′-də-jənt

7. *destitution*   des′-tə-TŌO′-shən

8. *destitute*   DES′-tə-tŏot

9. *affluence*   AF′-lŏo-o-əns

10. *affluent*   AF′-lŏo-ənt

11. *opulence*   OP′-yə-ləns

12. *opulent*   OP′-yə-lənt

Can you pronounce the words?（Ⅱ）

你能读出这些单词吗？（Ⅱ）

1. *evanescent*   ev′-ə-NES′-ənt

2. *evanescence*   ev′-ə-NES′-əns

3. *evanesce*   ev′-ə-NES′

4. *euphemistic*   yŏo-fə-MIS′-tik

5. *euphony*   YOO′-fə-nee

6. *euphonic*   yŏo′-FON′-ik

7. *euphonious*   yŏo-FO′-nee-əs

8. *eulogy*   YOO′-lə-jee

9. *eulogistic*   yŏo′-lə-JIS′-tik

10. *eulogize*   YŌO′-lə-jiz′

Can you pronounce the words?（Ⅲ）

你能读出这些单词吗？（Ⅲ）

1. *euphoria*   yŏo-FAWR′-ee-ə

2. *euphoric*   yŏo-FAWR′-ik

3. *euthanasia*   yŏo-thə-NAY′-zha

4. *persiflage*   PUR′-sə-flahzh′

5. *cliché*   klee-SHAY′

6. *bromide*   BRŌ′-mid′

7. *bromidic*   brō-MID′-ik

8. *platitude*   PLAT′-v-tŏod

9. *platitudinous*   plat′-ə-TOO′-də-nəs

10. *anodyne*   AN′-ə-dīn′

Can you work with the words? (Ⅰ)

你能灵活使用这些词汇了吗？（Ⅰ）

1. penurious	a. poor; of limited means
2. indigent	b. inoffensive
3. affluent	c. flat, trite
4. evanescent	d. feeling tiptop
5. euphemistic	e. wealthy
6. euphonious	f. pleasant in sound
7. euphoric	g. stingy; tight-fisted
8. platitudinous	h. fleeting

KEY: 1-g, 2-a, 3-e, 4-h, 5-b, 6-f, 7-d, 8-c

Can you work with the words? (Ⅱ)

你能灵活使用这些词汇了吗？（Ⅱ）

1. parsimony	a. lavish luxury
2. destitution	b. painless death
3. opulence	c. pleasant sound
4. evanescence	d. trite remark
5. euphony	e. impermanence
6. euphoria	f. feeling of well-being
7. euthanasia	g. stinginess
8. platitude	h. poverty

KEY: 1-g, 2-h, 3-a, 4-e, 5-c, 6-f, 7-b, 8-d

Can you work wlth the words? (Ⅲ)

你能灵活使用这些词汇了吗？

1. anodyne	a. light, teasing banter
2. bromide	b. tightfistedness
3. persiflage	c. statement intended to allay anxiety
4. eulogy	d. poverty, want
5. penuriousness	e. high, formal praise
6. indigence	f. wealth
7. affluence	g. trite statement

KEY: 1-c, 2-g, 3-a, 4-e, 5-b, 6-d, 7-f

Can you work with the words?（Ⅳ）
你能灵活使用这些词汇了吗？（Ⅳ）

1. parsimonious
2. destitute
3. opulent
4. vicarious
5. euphonic
6. eulogistic
7. evanesce
8. eulogize
9. bromidic
10. cliché

a. begin to vanish
b. stingy, frugal
c. highly praising
d. hackneyed phrase
e. ostentatiously wealthy
f. stilted in expression
g. pleasant-sounding
h. in want
i. secondhand
j. praise

KEY：1-b，2-h，3-e，4-i，5-g，6-c，7-a，8-j，9-f，10-d

Do you understand the words?（Ⅰ）
你对这些词汇是否已经透彻地理解？（Ⅰ）

1. Do *penurious* people satisfy their extravagant desires?　　　　　YES　NO
2. Is *penuriousness* the characteristic of a miser?　　　　　YES　NO
3. If you are *parsimonious* with praise, do you lavish it on others?　　　　　YES　NO
4. Are people with extremely low incomes forced to live a life of *parsimony*?　　　　　YES　NO
5. Is *indigence* a sign of wealth?　　　　　YES　NO
6. Are *indigent* people often aided by state welfare?　　　　　YES　NO
7. If you live in a state of *destitution*, do you have all the money you need?　　　　　YES　NO
8. Is a completely *destitute* person likely to have to live in want?　　　　　YES　NO
9. Does a person of *affluence* generally have petty money worries?　　　　　YES　NO
10. Are *opulent* surroundings indicative of great wealth?　　　　　YES　NO

KEY：1-no，2-yes，3-no，4-yes，5-no，6-yes，7-no，8-yes，9-no，10-yes

Do you understand the words? (Ⅱ)

你对这些词汇是否已经透彻地理解? (Ⅱ)

1. Can you engage in *vicarious* exploits by reading spy novels?   YES   NO

2. Does an *evanescent* feeling remain for a considerable time?   YES   NO

3. Do parents generally indulge in *euphemisms* in front of young children?   YES   NO

4. Is poetry generally *euphonious*?   YES   NO

5. Does a sincere *eulogy* indicate one's feeling of admiration?   YES   NO

6. Is *euphoria* a feeling of malaise?   YES   NO

7. Is *euthanasia* practiced on animals?   YES   NO

8. Is *persiflage* an indication of seriousness?   YES   NO

9. Does a liberal use of *cliches* show original thinking?   YES   NO

10. Is an *anodyne* intended to relieve fears?   YES   NO

KEY: 1-yes, 2-no, 3-yes, 4-yes, 5-yes, 6-no, 7-yes, 8-no, 9-no, 10-yes

Do you understand the words? (Ⅲ)

你对这些词汇是否已经透彻地理解? (Ⅲ)

1. Is a *platitude* flat and dull?   YES   NO

2. If a person uses *bromides*, is he likely to be an interesting conversationalist?   YES   NO

3. If you indulge in *persiflage*, are you being facetious?   YES   NO

4. Are the works of Beethoven considered *euphonious*?   YES   NO

5. Can parents receive a *vicarious* thrill from their children's triumphs?   YES   NO

KEY: 1-yes, 2-no, 3-yes, 4-yes, 5-yes

Can you recall the words?

你能够写出这些词汇吗?

1. a statement, usually untrue, meant to alleviate fear   1. A _____

2. light banter   2. P _____

3. a hackneyed phrase   3. C _____

4. fleeting—lasting a very short time (*adj.*)   4. E _____

5. laudatory—delivered in tones of formal praise (*adj.*)   5. E _____

6. process of painlessly putting to death a victim of an incurable disease
  6. E _____

7. stingy (*adj.*)
  7. P _____
  or P _____

8. in want (*adj.*)
  8. D _____

9. wealth
  9. A _____

10. immense wealth
  10. O _____

11. adverb describing the manner of responding empathetically to another's acts
  11. V _____

12. stinginess (*noun*)
  12. P _____
  or P _____

13-14. poverty
  13. I _____
  14. D _____

15. impermanence
  15. E _____

16. pleasing sound
  16. E _____

17. substituting inoffensive words (*adj.*)
  17. E _____

18. sense of well-being
  18. E _____

19. trite remark
  19. B _____

20. banal remark
  20. P _____

21. begin to vanish (*v.*)
  21. E _____

22. poverty-stricken (*adj.*)
  22. I _____

23-24. wealthy (two *adjs.*)
  23. A _____
  24. O _____

25. feeling tiptop (*adj.*)
  25. E _____

26. pleasant in sound (*adj.*)
  26. E _____
  or E _____

27. formal praise
  27. E _____

28. trite (*adj.*)
  28. B _____

29. flat, dull (*adj.*)
  29. P _____

30. to praise
  30. E _____

KEY: 1-anodyne, 2-persiflage, 3-cliche, 4-evanescent, 5-eulogistic, 6-euthanasia, 7-parsimonious *or* penurious, 8-destitute, 9-affluence, 10-opulence, 11-vicariously, 12-parsimony *or* penuriousness, 13-indigence, 14-destitution, 15-evanescence, 16-euphony, 17-euphemistic, 18-euphoria, 19-bromide, 20-platitude, 21-evanesce, 22-indigent, 23-affluent, 24-opulent, 25-euphoric, 26-euphonic *or* euphonious, 27-eulogy, 28-bromidic, 29-platitudinous, 30-eulogize

(End of Session 40)

SESSION 41
第 41 节

ORIGINS AND RELATED WORDS
词源及相关词汇

1. people are the craziest animals
人类是最疯狂的动物

Bovine, placid like a cow, stolid, patient, unexcitable, is built on the Latin word for *ox* or *cow*, *bovis*, plus the suffix *-ine*, like, similar to, or characteristic of. To call someone *bovine* is of course far from complimentary, for this adjective is considerably stronger than *phlegmatic*, and imaplies a certain mild contempt on the part of the speaker. A *bovine* person is somewhat like a vegetable: eats and grows and lives, but apparently is lacking in any strong feelings.

Humans are sometimes compared to animals, as in the following adjectives:

bovine 指像牛一样宁静、迟钝、耐心、无动于衷,是拉丁语词汇表示公牛或者奶牛的 bovis 和词尾-ine(类似,具有……特征)的结合。称某人为 bovine 绝非称赞,因为普遍认为这个形容词的表意比 phlegmatic(迟钝的)更为强烈。使用这个词能够表现出说话者的不屑。a bovine person 在某种程度上与蔬菜相似:只顾吃、生长、生存,但是明显缺少强烈的情感。

人类有时被比作其他动物,以下形容词就是这方面的表现:

(1) *leonine* (LEE′- ə -nīn′)—like a lion in appearance or temperament.

(2) *canine* (KAY′-nīn)—like a dog. As a noun, the word refers to the species to which dogs belong. Our *canine* teeth are similar to those of a dog.

(3) *feline* (FEE′-līn′)—catlike. We may speak of *feline* grace; or (insultingly) of *feline* temperament when we mean that a person is "catty."

(4) *porcine* (PAWR′-sīn′)—piglike.

(5) *vulpine* (VUL′-pīn′)—foxlike in appearance or temperamemt. When applied to people, this adjective usually indicates the shrewdness of a fox.

(6) *ursine* (UR′-sīn′)—bearlike.

(7) *lupine* (LŌO′-pīn)—wolflike.

(8) *equine* (EE′-kwīn′) — horselike; "horsy".

(9) *piscine* (PIS′-īn′)—fishlike.

(1) leonine——外貌或者性情好像狮子般的。

(2) canine——似狗的。作为名词使用时,表示犬科。canine teeth 是指类似犬牙的尖牙。

(3) feline——似猫的。我们可以说某人具有 feline grace,像猫一样的优雅;或者说某人具有 feline temperament(阴险的秉性),是侮辱性的表达。

(4) porcine——像猪一样的。

(5) vulpine——外貌或者性情好像狐狸的。用来修饰人时,通常用来表示像狐狸一样的狡猾。

(6) ursine——像熊的。

(7) lupine ——像狼的。

(8) equine ——像马的。

(9) piscine ——像鱼的。

All these adjectives come from the corresponding Latin words for the animals; and, of course, each adjective also describes, or refers to, the specific animal as well as to the person likened to the animal.

所有的这些形容词均来自相应的拉丁语指此类动物的单词;当然,这类形容词除了描述、指代动物外,也可以用来形容被比作这种动物的人。

1. *leo*   lion
2. *canis*   dog
3. *felis*   cat
4. *porcus*   pig
5. *vulpus*   fox
6. *ursus*   bear
7. *lupus*   wolf
8. *equus*   horse
9. *piscis*   fish

The word for meat from a pig—*pork*—derives, obviously, from *porcus*. *Ursa Major* and *Ursa Minor*, the *Great Bear* and the *Little Bear*, the two conspicuous groups of stars in the northern sky (conspicuous, of course, only on a clear night), are so labeled because in formation they resemble the outlines of bears. The feminine name *Ursula* is, by etymology, "a little bear," which, perhaps, is a strange name to burden a child with. The skin disease *lupus* was so named because it eats into the flesh, as a wolf might.

表示猪肉的单词"pork",很明显来源于 porcus。Ursa Major 和 Ursa Minor,也就是大熊和小熊星座,北方天空中比较明显的两个星系(当然,只有在晴朗的夜晚才会那么显眼),之所以这样命名是因为它们连在一起的形状比较像熊。女性的名字 Ursula,从词源看是"小熊"的意思,这也许是会让孩子感到困扰的奇怪名字。皮肤病 lupus(狼疮)之所以这样命名,是因为它会像狼一样吞噬鲜肉。

2. you can't go home again

你无法再次回家

Nostalgia, built on two Greek roots, *nostos*, a return, and *algos*, pain (as in *neuralgia*, *cardialgia*, etc.), is a feeling you can't ever understand until you've experienced it—and you have probably experienced it whenever some external stimulus has crowded your mind with scenes from an earlier day.

You know how life often seems much pleasanter in retrospect? Your conscious memory tends to store up the pleasant experiences of the past (the trauma and unpleasant experiences may get buried in the unconscious), and when you are lonely or unhappy you may begin to relive these pleasant occurrences. It is then that you feel the emotional pain and longing that we call *nostalgia*.

The adjective is *nostalgic*, as in "motion pictures that are *nostalgic* of the fifties," or as in, "He feels *nostalgic* whenever he passes 138th Street and sees the house in which he grew up. "

nostalgia 是两个希腊语词根的组合:nostos,"回家";algos,"痛苦"(例如 neuralgia,神经痛;cardialgia 胃痛等)。没有经历过乡愁的人无法真正理解乡愁的含义——只要外界的刺激使你的头脑充满了过去日子的场景,你就会体会到乡愁。

你知道,回忆中的生活总是更快乐吗?你有意识的思维倾向于储备过去的快乐经历(创伤和不愉快的经历可能储存在无意识中),当你感到孤独或者悲伤时,你可能会开始释放这些愉快的经历。也正是在这时,你感受到了感情上的痛苦和渴望,我们将这种情感称为 nostalgia。

形容词形式是 nostalgic,例如:"motion pictures that are nostalgic of the fifties"(50 年代的怀旧影片)或"He feels nostalgic whenever he passes 138th Street and sees the house in which he grew up. "(每次经过第 138 街,看到自己成长的地方,他总会感到怀旧。)

3. soundings

各种声音

Cacophony is itself a harsh-sounding word—and is the only one that exactly describes the unmusical, grating, ear-offending noises you are likely to hear in man-made surroundings:the New York subway trains thundering through their tunnels (they are also, these days in the late 1970s, eye-offending, for which we might coin the term *cacopsis*, noun, and *cacoptic*, adjective), the traffic bedlam of rush hours in a big city, a steel mill, an automobile factory, a blast furnace, etc. Adjective:*cacophonous* (kə-KOF′-ə- nəs).

These words are built on the Greek roots *kakos*, bad, harsh, or ugly, and *phone*, sound.

Phone, sound, is found also in:

(1) *telephone*—etymologically, "sound from afar"

(2) *euphony*—pleasant sound

(3) *phonograph*—etymologically, "writer of sound"

(4) *saxophone*—a musical instrument (hence *sound*) invented by Adolphe Sax

(5) *xylophone*—a musical instrument; etymologically, "sounds through wood" (Greek *xylon*, wood)

(6) *phonetics* (fə-NET′-iks)—the science of the sounds of language; the adjective is *phonetic* (fə-NET′-ik), the expert a *phonetician* (fō′-nə-TISH′-ən)

(7) *phonics*—the science of sound; also the method of teaching reading by drilling the sounds of letters and syllables

caocophony 本身的发音就很刺耳——也是唯一一个能够准确描述你可能在人为环境中听到的不悦耳、甚至刺耳的词汇:纽约地铁轰鸣着穿过隧道(在 20 世纪 70 年代后期,它们看起来也让人不舒服,我们可以因此造出两个词:cacopsis,不悦目,这是名词形式,形容词形式是 cacoptic),大城市里上班高峰期的拥堵喧闹、钢铁厂、汽车厂、鼓风炉的喧嚣声,等等。其形容词是 cacophonous。

cacophony 结合了两个希腊语词根:kakos(坏的,刺耳的,丑陋的)和 phone(声音)。

表示声音的 phone 也出现在以下词汇中:

(1) telephone——电话,从远方传来的声音;

(2) euphony——悦耳的声音;

(3) phonograph——留声机,语源意义是"声音记录器";

(4) saxophone——萨克斯风,一种由阿道夫·萨克斯发明的乐器(所以有 phone);

(5) xylophone——木琴,语源意义是"穿过木头的声音"(希腊语 xylon,木头);

(6) phonetics——语音学。形容词是 phonetic，phonetician 表示"语音专家"；

(7) phonics—声音科学；也是一种通过练习字母和音节发音来教阅读的方法。

4. the flesh and all
食肉类和其他所有类别

Carnivorous combines *carnis*, flesh, and *voro*, to devour. A *carnivorous* animal, or *carnivore* (KAHR′-nə-vawr′), is one whose main diet is meat.

Voro, to devour, is the origin of other words referring to eating habits：

(1) *herbivorous* (hur-BIV′-ər-əs)—subsisting on grains, grasses, and other vegetation, as cows, deer, horses, etc. The animal is a *herbivore* (HUR′-bə-vawr′). Derivation：Latin *herba*, herb, plus *voro*, to devour

carnivorous 结合了 carnis，"肉"，和 voro，"狼吞虎咽地吃、吞食"。carnivorous animal 是食肉动物，也可以称之为 carnivore，"食肉动物"，主要以肉为生。

voro，"吞食"，为我们提供了另外三个表示饮食习惯的词汇：

(1) herbivorous——以谷物、草和其他植物为生，例如：奶牛、鹿、马和其他素食类。这种动物是 herbivore。衍变：拉丁语 herba，草，加 voro，吞没。

(2) *omnivorous* (om-NIV′-ər-əs)—eating everything：meat, grains, grasses, fish, insects, and anything else digestible. The only species so indiscriminate in their diet are humans and rats, plus, of course, some cats and dogs that live with people (in contrast to *felines* and *canines*—lions, tigers, bobcats, wolves, etc.—that are not domesticated). *Omnivorous* (combining Latin *omnis*, all, with *voro*, plus the adjective suffix *-ous*) refers not only to food. An *omnivorous* reader reads everything in great quantities (that is, devours *all* kinds of reading matter).

(2) omnivorous——杂食的，吃肉、谷物、草、鱼、昆虫和其他任何易消化的食物。当然，饮食习惯上如此不加选择的物种就是人类和老鼠，当然还加上一些家养的猫和狗（而猫科动物和犬科动物如狮子、老虎、山猫和狼等，都非家养）。omnivorous 是在 voro，"吞食"的前面添加了拉丁语词汇 omnis，表示"全部"，再加上形容词后缀-ous。这个词的用法并不仅限于食物。an omnivorous reader 是博览群书的读者（他大量"吞食"各种各样的阅读材料）。

(3) *voracious* (vaw-RAY′-shəs)—*devouring*; hence, greedy or gluttonous; may refer either to food or to any other habits. One may be a *voracious* eater, *voracious* reader, *voracious* in one's pursuit of money, pleasure, etc. Think of the two noun forms of *loquacious*. Can you write two nouns derived from *voracious*?

① _____ ② _____.

(3) voracious——字面理解是"狼吞虎咽"，表示"贪婪的、贪吃的"，既可以针对食物，也可以指其他习惯。具体用法有：a voracious eater，"贪吃的食客"；voracious reader，"如饥似渴的读者"；voracious in one's pursuit of money, pleasure，"对金钱或者快感贪婪的"。思考一下 loquacious 两个名词形式。你能写出两个由 voracious 衍变而来的两个名词吗？

5. "allness"
全部

Latin *omnis*, all, is the origin of：

(1) *omnipotent* (om-NIP′-ə-tənt)—all-powerful, an adjective usually applied to God；also, to any ruler whose governing powers are unlimited, which allows for some exaggeration, as King Canute the Great proved to his sycophantic courtiers

when he ordered the tide to come so far up the beach and no further. He got soaking wet! (*Omnis* plus Latin *potens*, *potentis*, powerful, as in *potentate*, a powerful ruler; *impotent* (IM'-pə-tənt), powerless; *potent*, powerful; and *potential*, possessing power or ability not yet exercised). Can you write the noun form of *omnipotent*? ___

_____

(2) *omniscient* (om-NISH'-ənt)—all-knowing; hence, infinitely wise. (*Omnis* plus *sciens*, knowing.) We have discussed this adjective in a previous chapter, so you will have no problem writing the noun:_____.

拉丁语中的 omnis(全部)是以下单词的词根：

(1) omnipotent——全能的，通常用来形容上帝或者任何掌握无限统治权力的统治者；当然带有些夸张的描述，如卡努特大帝用命令潮汐的涨停来向阿谀谄媚者显示自己的力量，但他浑身透湿！(这个词由 omnis 加上拉丁语 potens，potentis，"强有力的"组成；后者派生出来的词如 potentate，强有力的统治者；impotent，无力的；potent，强有力的；potential，具有尚未发挥的能力。)你能写出 omnipotent 的名词形式吗？

(2) omniscient——无所不知的；博闻广识的(omnis 加上 sciens，"知道"。)；我们在之前的章节里曾经讨论过这个形容词，因此，你应该能够写出其名词形式。

(3) *omnipresent* (om'-nə-PREZ'-ənt)—present in all places at once. Fear was *omnipresent* in Europe during 1939 just before World War II. A synonym of *omnipresent* is *ubiquitous* (yōō-BIK'-wə-təs), from Latin *ubique*, everywhere. The *ubiquitous* ice cream vendor seems to be *everywhere* at the same time, tinkling those little bells, once spring arrives. The *ubiquitous* little red wagon rides around *everywhere* in airports to refuel departing planes. "*Ubiquitous* laughter greeted the press secretary's remark," i. e., laughter was heard *everywhere* in the room. The noun forms are *ubiquity* (yōō-BIK'-wə-tee) or _____. (Can you think of the alternate form?)

(3) omnipresent——无所不在的。1939 年的欧洲，在第二次世界大战前恐惧无所不在(omnipresent)。omnipresent 的同义词 ubiquitous 源自拉丁语 ubique，"到处"。春天一到，似乎无处不在的冰淇淋小贩看起来同时出现在每个地方，摇着小铃铛。The ubiquitous little red wagon rides around in airports to refuel departing planes. (机场上随处可见的红色小车来回穿梭着给飞机加油。)Ubiquitous laughter greeted the press secretary's remark(新闻秘书的评论引起了哄堂的笑声)，也就是说笑声在房间里每处都能听到。其名词形式是 ubiquity 或 _____。(你能想出另一种形式吗?)

(4) *omnibus* (OM'-nə-bəs)—etymologically, "for all, including all." In the shortened form *bus* we have a public vehicle for *all* who can pay; in a John Galsworthy *omnibus* we have a book containing *all* of Galsworthy's works; in an *omnibus* legislative bill we have a bill containing *all* the miscellaneous provisions and appropriations left out of other bills.

(4) omnibus——语源意义是"所有的，包括全部的"。词汇包含的 bus 是所有人都能支付的起的交通方式；John Galsworthy omnibus 是约翰·高尔斯华绥选集，里面包括所有高尔斯绥的作品；omnibus legislative bill 是综合法案，其中包括所有其他法案缺少的杂项规定和拨款。

6. more flesh

更多的肉

Note how *carnis*, flesh, is the building block of:

(1) *carnelian* (kahr-NEEL′-yən)—a reddish color, the color of red *flesh*.

(2) *carnival* (KAHR′-nə-vəl)—originally the season of merrymaking just before Lent, when people took a last fling before saying "*Carne vale*!" "Oh *flesh*, fare-well!" (Latin *vale*, farewell, goodbye). Today a *carnival* is a kind of outdoor enter-tainment with games, rides, side shows, and, of course, lots of food—also any exu-berant or riotous merrymaking or festivities.

(3) *carnal* (KAHR′-nəl)—most often found in phrases like "*carnal* pleasures" or "*carnal* appetites," and signifying pleasures or appetites of the *flesh* rather than of the spirit—hence, sensual, lecherous, lascivious, lubricious, etc. The noun is *car-nality* (kahr-NAL′-ə-tee).

词根 carnis,"肉",也出现在以下词汇中:

(1) carnelian——一种红颜色,红肉的颜色;

(2) carnival——原指四旬斋之前的狂欢节,人们会在说"哦肉,再见了(Carne Vale)"之前进行最后的放纵。现在用来指一种室外娱乐,有各种游戏、骑马和穿插表演;当然,还有许多食物——或者任何兴高采烈的、欢腾的狂欢或节日;

(3) carnal——经常出现在 carnal pleasure 或者 carnal appetite 等表达中,表示肉体上的、非精神上的愉悦或者欲望——所以表示肉欲的、性的、好色的等等;名词形式 carnality 表示放纵性欲、淫荡。

(4) *carnage* (KAHR′-nəj)—great destruction of life (that is, of human *flesh*), as in war or mass murders.

(5) *reincarnation* (ree′-in-kahr-NAY′-shən)—a rebirth or reappearance. Believ-ers in *reincarnation* maintain that one's soul persists after it has fled the *flesh*, and eventually reappears in the body of a newborn infant or animal, or in another form. Some of us, according to this interesting philosophy, were once Napoleon, Alexan-der the Great, Cleopatra, etc. The verb is to *reincarnate* (ree-in-KAHR′-nayt), to bring (a soul) back in another bodily form.

(6) *incarnate* (in-KAHR′-nət)—in the *flesh*. If we use this adjective to call someone "the devil *incarnate*," we mean that here is the devil in the *flesh*. Or we may say that someone is evil *incarnate*, that is, the personification of evil, evil in-vested with human or bodily form. The verb to *incarnate* (in-KAHR′-nayt) is to embody, give bodily form to, or make real.

(4) carnage——(战争中的)大屠杀(对人们的肉体的残杀);

(5) reincarnation——重生或者重现。reincarnation 的信仰者坚决认为,精神会在人死后离开肉体,最后以另一种形态重新出现在新生儿或动物的身体里。根据这种有意思的哲学,我们当中的一些人曾经是拿破仑、亚历山大大帝、克莉奥佩特拉等;动词是 reincarnate,意为"把灵魂带回到另一个身体上"。

(6) incarnate——化身的、(神灵)现身的。如果我们将某个人称为 devil incarnate,我们是指他是魔鬼的化身。我们也可以说某个人是 evil incarnate,那么他是恶魔的化身,是恶魔以人形或人体的存在。动词是 incarnate,意为"体现,给予肉体形态,或者使……成真"。

7. dark secrets

暗中的秘密

Clandestine comes from Latin *clam*, secretly, and implies secrecy or concealment in the working out of a plan that is dangerous or illegal. *Clandestine* is a close syno-nym of *surreptitious* (sur′-əp-TISH′-əs), which means *stealthy*, *sneaky*, *furtive*, generally because of fear of detection.

The two words cannot always, however, be used interchangeably. We may speak of either *clandestine* or *surreptitious* meetings or arrangements; but usually only of *clandestine* plans and only of *surreptitious* movements or actions. Can you write the noun form of *surreptitious*? _____.

clandestine 由 clam("秘密地")派生,表示在制订危险的或者违法的计划时的秘密或隐藏。与其意义十分相近的是 surreptitious,表示"鬼鬼祟祟的、偷偷摸摸的、贼头贼脑的",通常因为害怕被发现。

但是,这两个词并不是在所有情况下都可以互换。clandestine 和 surreptitious 都可以用来修饰 meetings 或 arrangements;但只能用 clandestine 修饰 plans;只能用 surreptitious 修饰 movements 或 actions。你能写出 surreptious 的名词形式吗?

REVIEW OF ETYMOLOGY
复习词源

PREFIX, ROOT, SUFFIX	MEANING	ENGLISH WORD
1. *-ine*	like, similar to, characteristic of	_____
2. *leo*	lion	_____
3. *felis*	cat	_____
4. *porcus*	pig	_____
5. *canis*	dog	_____
6. *vulpus*	fox	_____
7. *ursus*	bear	_____
8. *lupus*	wolf	_____
9. *equus*	horse	_____
10. *piscis*	fish	_____
11. *nostos*	a return	_____
12. *algos*	pain	_____
13. *-ic*	adjective suffix	_____
14. *kakos*	bad, harsh, ugly	_____
15. *phone*	sound	_____
16. *xylon*	wood	_____
17. *carnis*	flesh	_____
18. *voro*	to devour	_____
19. *herba*	herb	_____
20. *omnis*	all	_____
21. *-ous*	adjective suffix	_____
22. *potens, potentis*	powerful	_____
23. *sciens*	knowing	_____
24. *ubique*	everywhere	_____

25. *-ity*   noun suffix   _____
26. *vale*   farewell   _____
27. *-al*   adjective suffix   _____
28. *re-*   again，back   _____
29. *-ate*   verb suffix   _____
30. *in-*   in   _____
31. *clam*   secretly   _____
32. *-ent*   adjective suffix   _____
33. *-ence*   noun suffix   _____

USING THE WORDS
单词应用

Can you pronounce the words?（Ⅰ）
你能读出这些单词吗?（Ⅰ）

1. *leonine*   LEE′-ə-nīn′
2. *canine*   KAY′-nīn′
3. *feline*   FEE′-līn′
4. *porcine*   PAWR′-sīn′
5. *vulpine*   VUL′-pīn′
6. *ursine*   UR′-sīn′
7. *lupine*   LŌO′-pīn′
8. *equine*   EE′-kwīn′
9. *piscine*   PIS′-īn′
10. *nostalgic*   nos-TAL′-jik

Can you pronounce the words?（Ⅱ）
你能读出这些单词吗?（Ⅱ）

1. *cacophonous*   kə-KOF′-ə-nəs
2. *phonetics*   fə-NET′-iks
3. *phonetic*   fə-NET′-ik
4. *phonetician*   fō-nə-TISH′-ən
5. *carnivore*   KAHR′-nə-vawr′
6. *herbivore*   HUR′-bə-vawr′
7. *herbivorous*   hur-BIV′-ər-əs
8. *omnivorous*   om-NIV′-ər-əs
9. *voracious*   vaw-RAY′-shəs
10. *voracity*   vaw-RAS′-ə-tee
11. *omnipotent*   om-NIP′-ə-tənt

12. *impotent*   IM′-pə-tənt

13. *impotence*   IM′-pə-təns

14. *omnipotence*   om-NIP′-ə-təns

Can you pronounce the words?（Ⅲ）
你能读出这些单词吗？（Ⅲ）

1. *omniscient*   om-NISH′-ənt

2. *omniscience*   om-NISH′-əns

3. *omnipresent*   om′-nə-PREZ′-ənt

4. *omnipresence*   om′-nə-PREZ′-əns

5. *ubiquitous*   yōō-BIK′-wə-təs

6. *ubiquity*   yōō-BIK′-wə-tee

7. *ubiquitousness*   yōō-BIK′-wə-təs-nəs

8. *omnibus*   OM′-nə-bəs

Can you pronounce the words?（Ⅳ）
你能读出这些单词吗？（Ⅳ）

1. *carnelian*   kahr-NEEL′-yən

2. *carnal*   KAHR′-nəl

3. *carnality*   kahr-NAL′-ə-tee

4. *carnage*   KAHR′-nəj

5. *reincarnation*   ree′-in-kahr-NAY′-shən

6. *reincarnate* (*v.*)   ree′-in-KAHR′-nayt

7. *incarnate* (*adj.*)   in-KAHR′-nət

8. *incarnate* (*v.*)   in-KAHR′-nayt

9. *surreptitious*   sur′-əp-TISH′-əs

10. *surreptitiousness*   sur′-əp-TISH′-əs-nəs

Can you work with the words?（Ⅰ）
你能灵活使用这些词汇了吗？（Ⅰ）

1. leonine   a. doglike

2. canine   b. greedy, devouring

3. feline   c. foxlike

4. porcine   d. all-powerful

5. vulpine   e. stealthy, clandestine

6. ursine   f. lionlike

7. voracious   g. all-knowing

8. omnipotent   h. bearlike

9. omniscient   i. catlike

10. surreptitious   j. piglike

KEY：1-f，2-a，3-i，4-j，5-c，6-h，7-b，8-d，9-g，10-e

Can you work with the words? (Ⅱ)
你能灵活使用这些词汇了吗？(Ⅱ)

1. nostalgic		a. harsh-sounding
2. cacophonous		b. eating everything
3. herbivorous		c. lewd, lecherous, lubricious
4. omnivorous		d. found everywhere
5. ubiquitous		e. homesick
6. carnal		f. grass-eating
7. incarnate		g. in the flesh

KEY：1-e，2-a，3-f，4-b，5-d，6-c，7-g

Can you work with the words? (Ⅲ)
你能灵活使用这些词汇了吗？(Ⅲ)

1. phonetics		a. universality
2. carnivore		b. a color
3. voracity		c. infinite power
4. omnipotence		d. furtiveness; stealth; sneakiness
5. omniscience		e. lechery, lasciviousness, lubricity
6. omnipresence		f. infinite wisdom
7. omnibus		g. science of speech sounds
8. carnelian		h. slaughter
9. carnality		i. a collection of all things
10. carnage		j. greediness
11. surreptitiousness		k. meat-eater
12. reincarnation		l. a return to life in a new body or form

KEY：1-g，2-k，3-j，4-c，5-f，6-a，7-i，8-b，9-e，10-h，11-d，12-l

Can you work with the words? (Ⅳ)
你能灵活使用这些词汇了吗？(Ⅳ)

1. lupine		a. fishlike
2. equine		b. powerless
3. piscine		c. wolflike

4. phonetician	d. bring back into a new body or form
5. impotent	e. occurrence, or existence, everywhere
6. ubiquity	f. horselike
7. reincarnate (*v.*)	g. expert in speech sounds
8. incarnate (*v.*)	h. embody; make real; put into bodily form

KEY: 1-c, 2-f, 3-a, 4-g, 5-b, 6-e, 7-d, 8-h

Do you understand the words? (Ⅰ)
你对这些词汇是否已经透彻地理解？（Ⅰ）

1. A person of *leonine* appearance looks like a tiger.	TRUE	FALSE
2. *Canine* habits refers to the habits of dogs.	TRUE	FALSE
3. *Feline* grace means catlike grace.	TRUE	FALSE
4. *Porcine* appearance means wolflike appearance.	TRUE	FALSE
5. *Vulpine* craftiness means foxlike craftiness.	TRUE	FALSE
6. *Ursine* means bearlike.	TRUE	FALSE
7. *Nostalgic* feelings refer to a longing for past experiences.	TRUE	FALSE
8. *Cacophonous* music is pleasant and sweet.	TRUE	FALSE
9. An elephant is a *carnivore*.	TRUE	FALSE
10. Deer are *herbivorous*.	TRUE	FALSE

KEY: 1-F, 2-T, 3-T, 4-F, 5-T, 6-T, 7-T, 8-F, 9-F, 10-T

Do you understand the words? (Ⅱ)
你对这些词汇是否已经透彻地理解？（Ⅱ）

1. An *omnivorous* reader does very little reading.	TRUE	FALSE
2. A *voracious* eater is gluttonous.	TRUE	FALSE
3. True *omnipotence* is unattainable by human beings.	TRUE	FALSE
4. No one is *omniscient*.	TRUE	FALSE

5.	Fear of economic ruin was practically *omnipresent* in the early nineteen-thirties	TRUE	FALSE
6.	When an airplane lands for refueling, the *ubiquitous* little red gasoline wagon comes rolling up.	TRUE	FALSE
7.	An author's *omnibus* contains all his published writings.	TRUE	FALSE
8.	*Carnelian* is a deep blue color.	TRUE	FALSE
9.	*Carnality* is much respected in a puritanical society.	TRUE	FALSE
10.	There is considerable *carnage* in war.	TRUE	FALSE
11.	A *surreptitious* glance is meant to be conspicuous.	TRUE	FALSE
12.	A person who is evil *incarnate* is a vicious character.	TRUE	FALSE

KEY：1-F，2-T，3-T，4-T，5-T，6-T，7-T，8-F，9-F，10-T，11-F，12-T

Can you recall the words?
你能够写出这些词汇吗？

I. adverbs

1-2. secretly (two forms)	1. C _____
	2. S _____
3. in a harsh and noisy manner	3. C _____
4. in a homesick manner	4. N _____
5. in a greedy, devouring manner	5. V _____

KEY：1-clandestinely，2-surreptitiously，3-cacophonously，4-nostalgically，5-voraciously

II. nouns

1. greediness	1. V _____
2. unlimited power	2. O _____
3. infinite knowledge	3. O _____
4. a gathering of all things	4. O _____
5. lechery; indulgence in fleshly pleasures	5. C _____
6. slaughter	6. C _____

7. stealthiness; secretiveness　　　　　7. S _____

8. harsh sound　　　　　　　　　　　8. C _____

9. science of speech sounds　　　　　　9. P _____

10. a return to life in new form　　　　10. R _____

KEY：1-voracity，2-omnipotence，3-omniscience，4-omnibus，5-carnality，6-carnage，7-surreptitiousness，8-cacophony，9-phonetics，10-reincarnation

---

III. adjectives

1. lionlike　　　　　　　　　　　　　1. L _____

2. doglike　　　　　　　　　　　　　2. C _____

3. catlike　　　　　　　　　　　　　3. F _____

4. cowlike　　　　　　　　　　　　　4. B _____

5. foxlike　　　　　　　　　　　　　5. V _____

6. bearlike　　　　　　　　　　　　　6. U _____

7. homesick　　　　　　　　　　　　7. N _____

8. grating in sound　　　　　　　　　8. C _____

9. meat-eating　　　　　　　　　　　9. C _____

10. grass-eating　　　　　　　　　　10. H _____

11. all-eating; indiscriminate　　　　　11. O _____

12. devouring; greedy　　　　　　　　12. V _____

13. in the flesh　　　　　　　　　　　13. I _____

KEY：1-leonine，2-canine，3-feline，4-bovine，5-vulpine，6-ursine，7-nostalgic，8-cacophonous，9-carnivorous，10-herbivorous，11-omnivorous，12-voracious，13-incarnate

---

IV. more adjectives

1. all-powerful　　　　　　　　　　　1. O _____

2. all-knowing　　　　　　　　　　　2. O _____

3. present or existing everywhere　　　3. O _____

4. found everywhere　　　　　　　　4. U _____

5. lewd, lascivious, lecherous　　　　　5. C _____

6. secret　　　　　　　　　　　　　6. C _____

KEY：1-omnipotent，2-omniscient，3-omnipresent，4-ubiquitous，5-carnal，6-clandestine

---

V. final mop-up

1. wolflike   1. L _____
2. horselike   2. E _____
3. fishlike   3. P _____
4. referring to speech sounds   4. P _____
5. expert in speech sounds   5. P _____
6. powerless   6. I _____
7-8. existence everywhere   7. U _____
                                                    or U _____
                                                     8. O _____

9. to bring back into another pleasures   9. R _____
10. to embody, make real, or put into bodily form   10. I _____

KEY: 1-lupine, 2-equine, 3-piscine, 4-phonetic, 5-phonetician, 6-impotent, 7-ubiquity *or* ubiquitousness, 8-omnipresence, 9-reincarnate, 10-incarnate

CHAPTER REVIEW
章节复习

A. Do you recognize the words?
你认识这些单词吗?

1. Utter want:
   (a) affluence, (b) opulence, (c) penury
2. Experienced secondhand:
   (a) ephemeral, (b) vicarious, (c) evanescent
3. Inoffensive circumlocution:
   (a) badinage, (b) persiflage, (c) euphemism
4. Homesick:
   (a) nostalgic, (b) bromide, (c) clandestine
5. Meat-eating:
   (a) herbivorous, (b) voracious, (c) carnivorous
6. Stingy:
   (a) indigent, (b) parsimonious, (c) opulent
7. Extreme financial need:
   (a) destitution, (b) affluence, (c) parsimony
8. Great and increasing wealth:
   (a) penuriousness, (b) affluence, (c) omnipresence
9. Remaining for a short time:

　　（a）euphemistic，（b）evanescent，（c）eulogistic

10. Sweet-sounding：

　　（a）euphonious，（b）cacophonous，（c）euphoric

11. Praise glowingly：

　　（a）evanesce，（b）eulogize，（c）reincarnate

12. Sense of physical well-being：

　　（a）euthanasia，（b）euphoria，（c）persiflage

13. Hackneyed expression：

　　（a）anodyne，（b）badinage，（c）cliche

14. catlike：

　　（a）leonine，（b）feline，（c）canine

15. Bearlike：

　　（a）vulpine，（b）ursine，（c）porcine

16. All-knowing：

　　（a）omnipotent，（b）omniscient，（c）omnipresent

17. Found everywhere：

　　（a）ubiquitous，（b）omnivorous，（c）omnibus

18. Destruction：

　　（a）carnage，（b）carnality，（c）reincarnation

19. Stealthy：

　　（a）voracious，（b）surreptitious，（c）incarnate

KEY：1-c，2-b，3-c，4-a，5-c，6-b，7-a，8-b，9-b，10-a，11-b，12-b，13-c，14-b，15-b，16-b，17-a，18-a，19-b

---

B. Can you recognize roots?

你能认出这些词根吗？

ROOT	MEANING	EXAMPLE
1. *penuria*	_____	penury
2. *fluo*	_____	affluent
3. *opulentus*	_____	opulent
4. *ephemera*	_____	ephemeral
5. *vanesco*	_____	evanescent
6. *pheme*	_____	euphemism
7. *phone*	_____	phonetics
8. *logos*	_____	eulogy
9. *thanatos*	_____	euthanasia
10. *platys*	_____	platitude, platypus
11. *odyne*	_____	anodyne

12. *leo*	_____	leonine
13. *felis*	_____	feline
14. *porcus*	_____	porcine
15. *canis*	_____	canine
16. *vulpus*	_____	vulpine
17. *lupus*	_____	lupine
18. *equus*	_____	equine
19. *piscis*	_____	piscine
20. *nostos*	_____	nostalgia
21. *algos*	_____	nostalgic
22. *kakos*	_____	cacophonous
23. *xylon*	_____	xylophone
24. *carnis*	_____	carnivorous
25. *voro*	_____	omnivorous
26. *herba*	_____	herbivorous
27. *omnis*	_____	omnipotent
28. *potens, potentis*	_____	impotent
29. *sciens*	_____	omniscience
30. *ubique*	_____	ubiquitous
31. *vale*!	_____	carnival
32. *clam*	_____	clandestine

KEY：1-want, neediness, 2-to flow, 3-wealthy, 4-dayfly, 5-to vanish, 6-voice, 7-sound；8-word, speech, 9-death, 10-flat, broad, 11-pain, 12-lion, 13-cat, 14-pig, 15-dog, 16-fox, 17-wolf；18-horse, 19-fish, 20-a return, 21-pain, 22-bad, harsh, ugly, 23-wood, 24-flesh, 25-to devour, 26-herb, 27-all, 28-powerful, 29-knowing, 30-everywhere, 31-farewell！, 32-secretly

TEASER QUESTIONS FOR THE AMATEUR ETYMOLOGIST
词源小测验

1. American poet William Cullen Bryant wrote a poem in 1811 called *Thanatopsis*. You are familiar with both roots in the word. Can you figure out the meaning?

_____.

2. If you wanted to coin a word for the study or science of death and dying, what would you come up with? _____.

3. *Pheme*, as you know from *euphemism*, means *voice*. This root derives from a Greek verb *phanai*, to speak, which, as it traveled through Latin, Old French, and

Middle English, finally took on the spelling *phet-*, *phec-*, or *phes-*. And you recall that the Greek prefix *pro-* means *beforehand* or *ahead* (as in *prognosis*, *prologue*, etc.). Can you now combine elements to form a word meaning:

(a) to say beforehand; to foretell (art occurrence before it actually happens)?

_____.

(b) the foretelling of such an occurrence? _____.

(c) the person who foretells? _____.

4. Can you combine a *Latin* prefix and root to form words of the same meaning?

(a) to foretell: _____.

(b) the act of foretelling: _____.

5. An eminent psychoanalyst, Richard Karpe of Connecticut, has coined the term *nostopathy* (nos-TOP'-ə-thee) for an emotional disorder he diagnosed among a number of his patients who were returning veterans of World War II and of the Korean and Vietnam wars. You know both roots in the word. Can you figure out the meaning?

_____

_____

_____.

6. Coin a word that means:

(a) the killing of foxes: _____.

(b) the killing of wolves: _____.

(c) the killing of lions, tigers, and other cats: _____.

(d) the killing of bears: _____.

7. Figure out an adjective that means:

(a) fish-eating: _____.

(b) insect-eating: _____.

8. Have you ever wondered whether the Canary Islands were named after the Latin root *canis*, dog? They were. Large, wild dogs inhabited the area. Pretty songbirds also abounded there. What were these birds called? _____.

9. A new verb was coined some years ago, based on the Latin root *potens*, *potentis*, meaning (of a drug) *to make more effective or powerful; to augment the effect of another drug*. Can you figure out what this verb would be? _____

_____.

(Answers in Chapter 18)
（答案见第 18 章）

GETTING USED TO NEW WORDS
对新词习以为常

Reference has been made, in previous chapters, to the intimate relationship between reading and vocabulary building. Good books and the better magazines will not only acquaint you with a host of new ideas (and, therefore, new words, since every word is the verbalization of an idea), but also will help you gain a more complete and a richer understanding of the hundreds of words you are learning through your work in this book. If you have been doing a sufficient amount of stimulating reading—and that means, at minimum, several magazines a week and at least three books of non-fiction a month—you have been meeting, constantly, over and over again, the new words you have been learning in these pages. Every such encounter is like seeing an old friend in a new place. You know how much better you understand your friends when you have a chance to see them react to new situations; similarly, you will gain a much deeper understanding of the friends you have been making among words as you see them in different contexts and in different places.

My recommendations in the past have been of non-fiction titles, but novels too are a rich source of additions to your vocabulary—provided you stay alert to the new words you will inevitably meet in reading novels.

The natural temptation, when you encounter a brand-new word in a novel, is to ignore it—the lines of the plot are perfectly clear even if many of the author's words are not.

I want to counsel strongly that you resist the temptation to ignore the unfamiliar words you may meet in your novel reading: resist it with every ounce of your energy, for only by such resistance can you keep building your vocabulary as you read.

What should you do? Don't rush to a dictionary, don't bother underlining the word, don't keep long lists of words that you will eventually look up *en masse*—these activities are likely to become painful and you will not continue them for any great length of time.

Instead, do something quite simple—and very effective.

在之前的章节中,我们已经提及阅读与构建词汇之间的紧密关系。优质的书籍和杂志不仅可以使你接触新概念(由此学习新的词汇,因为词汇是概念的语言实现),也能够帮助你更全面、更丰富地理解从本书中学到的几百个词汇。如果你的阅读量足够充足,能够不断刺激学到的新词——这就意味着:每周至少阅读几本杂志,每个月至少完成三本非小说类书籍——你一定会反复不断地遇到从本书中学到的新词。与新词的每次会面好比在一个新的地点遇见老朋友。有机会观察老朋友对新环境的反应,你知道自己是如何加深对朋友的理解;同样,只有在不同的语境和不同的文体中阅读到这些词汇,你才能够对这些词汇老朋友有更深刻的理解。

虽然之前我所推荐的书籍都属于非小说类文体,但是小说同样是扩充词汇的另一丰富资源——如果你能够保持对新词的敏感度,你一定会在阅读小说时注意到这些新词。

在小说中遇见崭新的词汇时,最自然的反应是忽略它们的存在——即使对作者所使用的很多词汇的词义并不清楚,你仍然能够明白故事的情节。

我想强烈建议大家,在阅读小说时,一定要抵挡忽略生词的诱惑;用你的每分力量抵挡,因为只有通过抵挡你才能够在阅读的过程中扩建词汇。

你应该怎样做? 不要急于查词典,不需要用下画线标记那么麻烦,也不需要罗列出所有生词以备最后一同复习——这样的做法都会使你痛苦,你很可能无法长时间坚持。

相反,采取非常简单——却又非常奏效的方法。

When you meet a new word, underline it with a *mental* pencil. That is, pause for a second and attempt to figure out its meaning from its use in the sentence or from its etymological root or prefix, if it contains one you have studied. Make a mental note of it, say it aloud once or twice—and then go on reading.

That's all there is to it. What you are doing, of course, is developing the same type of mind-set toward the new word that you have developed toward the words you have studied in this book. And the results, of course, will be the same—you will begin to notice the word occurring again and again in other reading you do, and finally, having seen it in a number of varying contexts, you will begin to get enough of its connotation and flavor to come to a fairly accurate understanding of its meaning. In this way you will be developing alertness not only to the words you have studied in this book, but to all expressive and meaningful words. And your vocabulary will keep growing.

But of course that will happen only if you keep reading.

I do not wish to recommend any particular novels or novelists, since the type of fiction one enjoys is a very personal matter. You doubtless know the kind of story you like—mystery, science fiction, spy, adventure, historical, political, romantic, Western, biographical, one or all of the above. Or you may be entranced by novels of ideas, of sexual prowess, of fantasy, of life in different segments of society from your own. No matter. Find the kind of novel or novelist *you* enjoy by browsing in the public library or among the thousands of titles in bookstores that have a rich assortment of paperbacks as well as hardbacks.

And then read! And keep on the alert for new words! You will find them by the hundreds and thousands. Bear in mind: *people with rich vocabularies have been reading omnivorously, voraciously, since childhood*—including the ingredients listed in small print on bread wrappers and cereal boxes.

(End of Session 41)

遇见新词时,用一只"脑子里的铅笔"做出下划线标记。也就是说,你要停下片刻,尝试从新词在句子中的用法判断其含义;如果词中包含你所学习的词根或前缀,你可以由词根或前缀判断词义。在脑海中记忆新词,大声朗读一次或两次——然后继续阅读。

这就是扩建词汇的秘诀。当然,你所做的与你在本书中学习词汇的方法相同,是对新词发展出相同的思维定式。当然,结果也是相同的——你会开始在阅读材料中反复注意到这些词汇;最终,因为熟知它们所出现的许多不同语境,对它们的含义和特点也越来越熟悉,逐渐完全地、准确地理解它们的含义。运用这种方法,你不仅会对本书中学到的词汇越来越敏感,对所有表意和词义丰富的词汇也能十分警觉。你的词汇会不断扩展。

当然,一切的前提是你要不断地阅读。

我不准备给你推荐任何小说或小说作者,因为对不同虚构作品的喜好是非常个人化的,你自己最清楚自己喜欢什么样的故事类型——推理、科幻、间谍、冒险、历史、政治、言情、西部、自传,其中一种或者全部。或者你可能被有关理念、性技巧、幻想或者与你不同的社会阶层生活经历的小说所吸引。不管哪类都如此。你可以在公共图书馆、或在书店里数以千计的精装书、平装书中发现你喜欢的小说或小说作者。

然后就开始读吧!并且注意遇到的新单词!你将会学到数以百计或千计的新单词。要记住:词汇丰富的人都是从小就随处贪婪阅读的人——包括印在面包包装纸上和谷物盒子上面的营养成分表。

HOW TO SPELL A WORD
如何拼写单词

The spelling of English words is archaic, it's confusing, it's needlessly complicated, and, if you have a sense of humor, it's downright comical. In fact, any insulting epithet you might wish to level against our weird methods of putting letters together to form words would probably be justified—but it's our spelling, and we're stuck with it.

How completely stuck we are is illustrated by a somewhat ludicrous event that goes back to 1906, and that cost philanthropist Andrew Carnegie $75,000.

Working under a five-year grant of funds from Carnegie, and headed by the esteemed scholar Brander Matthews, the Simplified Spelling Board published in that year a number of recommendations for bringing some small semblance of order out of the great chaos of English spelling. Their suggestions affected a mere three hundred words out of the half million then in the language. Here are a few examples, to give you a general idea:

词汇拼写历史古老、令人混淆,不仅复杂得没有必要,还荒谬得使人发笑(如果你有足够的幽默感)。其实,使用任何侮辱性的词语来修饰我们这种将字母拼凑在一起形成词汇的方法都可能有道理——但是我们就是这么拼写的,而且我们还一直使用这些拼法。

无法摆脱的程度能够由一个需要追溯到 1906 年的荒谬事件说明,这个事件花费了慈善家安德鲁·卡耐基 75,000 美元。

卡耐基提供 5 年资金保证,在著名学者布兰德·马修斯的带领下,简化拼写委员会在 1906 年出版了许多建议,为非常混乱的英语拼写带来表象的秩序。他们的建议仅仅影响了当时英语 50 万词汇中的 300 个。以下几个例子能够使你大体了解:

SPELLING THEN CURRENT	SIMPLIFIED SPELLING
mediaeval	*medieval*
doubt	*dout*
debtor	*dettor*
head	*hed*
though	*tho*
through	*thru*
laugh	*laf*
tough	*tuf*
knife	*nife*

theatre	*theater*
centre	*center*
phantom	*fantom*

These revisions seemed eminently sensible to no less a personage than the then President of the United States, Theodore Roosevelt. So delighted was he with the new garb in which these three hundred words could be clothed that he immediately ordered that all government documents be printed in simplified spelling. And the result? Such a howl went up from the good citizens of the republic, from the nation's editors and schoolteachers and businessmen, that the issue was finally debated in the halls of Congress. Almost to a man, senators and representatives stood opposed to the plan. Teddy Roosevelt, as you have doubtless heard, was a stubborn fellow— but when Congress threatened to hold up the White House stationery appropriation unless the President backed down, Teddy rescinded the order. Roosevelt ran for re-election some time later, and lost. That his attitude toward spelling contributed to his defeat is of course highly doubtful— nevertheless an opposition New York newspaper, the day the returns were in, maliciously commented on the outgoing incumbent in a one-word simplified-spelling editorial: "THRU!"

这些修改甚至连当时的美国总统都觉得非常合乎情理。他对于这 300 个穿着新装的词汇非常满意,以至于他立即命令所有政府文件用简体拼写印刷。结果呢?公众中意识清醒的公民、全国的编辑、教师和商人对此反响非常强烈,事件的最终结果是在国会大厅里开始讨论。参议院和众议院几乎所有人都反对这个计划。你肯定听说过,泰迪·罗斯福是个固执的家伙——但是当国会威胁道,除非总统撤销命令,否则他们将阻止对白宫的文具拨款时,泰迪才废除命令。一段时间之后,罗斯福参与连任竞选,最后以失败告终。是否是他对拼写的态度造成了连任的失败仍然很不确定——但是,投票结果出来的那一天,纽约一家反对派报纸的报道在社论部分对即将卸任的现任总统进行了恶意评论,他们只使用一个简体拼写的词汇:"THRU!"(结束)

Roosevelt was not the first President to be justifiably outraged by our ridiculous orthography. Over a hundred years ago, when Andrew Jackson was twitted on his poor spelling, he is supposed to have made this characteristic reply, "Well, sir, it is a damned poor mind that cannot think of more than one way to spell a word?" And according to one apocryphal version, it was Jackson's odd spelling that gave birth to the expression "okay." Jackson thought, so goes the story, that "all correct" was spelled "orl korrect," and he used O. K. as the abbreviation for these words when he approved state papers.

罗斯福并不是第一个被我们荒谬的拼字法激怒的总统。大约 100 年前,当安德鲁·杰克逊由于自己糟糕的拼写被嘲笑时,他应该用自己别具一格的回答方式回答:"好吧,先生,人类该死的大脑如此愚笨,竟然无法想出词汇的多种拼写方式?"一个杜撰的版本甚至制造出正是杰克逊的奇怪拼写造就了"okay"这个表达方式。其中还继续写道,杰克逊认为 "all correct" 可以拼写为"orl korrect",所以,当他批阅政府文件时,使用 O. K. 作为简写。

---

1. 按照简体拼写,thru 原型是 through,表示"结束",讽刺即将卸任的罗斯福对简体拼写的赞同态度。——译者注

Many years ago, the British playwright George Bernard Shaw offered a dramatic proposal for reducing England's taxes. Just eliminate unnecessary letters from our unwieldy spelling, he said, and you'll save enough money in paper and printing to cut everyone's tax rate in half. Maybe it would work, but it's never been put to the test—and the way things look now, it never will be. Current practice more and more holds spelling exactly where it is, bad though it may be. It is a scientific law of language that if enough people make a "mistake," the "mistake" becomes acceptable usage. That law applies to pronunciation, to grammar, to word meanings, but not to spelling. Maybe it's because of our misbegotten faith in, and worship of, the printed word—maybe it's because written language tends to be static, while spoken language constantly changes. Whatever the cause, spelling today successfully resists every logical effort at reform. "English spelling," said Thorstein Veblen, "satisfies all the requirements of the canons of reputability under the law of conspicuous waste. It is archaic, cumbrous, and ineffective." Perfectly true. Not withstanding, it's here to stay.

多年前,英国剧作家萧伯纳为减少英国的税收提供了一个戏剧性的建议。他认为,仅仅从我们笨拙的拼写中减少不必要的字母,你就能够在报纸和印刷品上省下足够多的资金,将每个人的税率减半。也许他的方法有效,但是从未有人真正试验过——从现在的情况来看,这种方案永远不会有效。目前的情况是拼写越来越忠实原本的模样,尽管原本的模样非常糟糕。语言的一个科学法则是:如果足够多人犯下一个"错误",这个"错误"就变得能够被接受。这个法则适用于发音、语法、词义,但唯独不适用于拼写。也许是因为人们对印刷词汇固执的信仰和崇拜——也可能因为书写语言更稳定,而语言表达时刻在变。无论什么原因,今天的拼写成功抵制了每一次合理的改革努力。托斯丹·韦伯伦写道:"如果明显的浪费也值得尊重的话,英语拼写完全符合要求。英语拼写陈旧过时、累赘低效。"他的话完全正确。但是无论如何,英语拼写不会发生任何变化。

Your most erudite friend doubtless misspells the name of the Hawaiian guitar. I asked half a dozen members of the English department of a large college to spell the word—without exception they responded with *ukelele*. Yet the only accepted form is *ukulele*.

Judging from my experience with my classes at Rio Hondo College, half the population of the country must think the word is spelled *alright*. Seventy-five percent of the members of my classes can't spell *embarrassing* or *coolly*. People will go on misspelling these four words, but the authorized spellings will remain impervious to change.

你最有学问的朋友也可能将夏威夷四弦琴的英语拼写拼错。我曾经让一所大学英语系的 6 个教职工拼写这个词——他们的回答都是 ukelele,无一例外。但是,唯一被承认的正确拼写是 ukulele。

根据我在深河学院的教学经验判断,全国肯定有一半人认为 alright 是正确的拼写方法。但是唯一正确的形式是 all right。我班上 75％的学生无法正确拼写 embarrassing 或 coolly。将来一定还有人会将这 4 个词汇拼错,但是权威拼写方法不会受到任何影响。

Well, you know the one about Mohammed and the mountain. Though it's true that we have modernized spelling to a microscopic extent in the last eighty years (*traveler*, *center*, *theater*, *medieval*, *labor*, and *honor*, for example, have pretty much replaced *traveller*, *centre*, *theatre*, *mediaeval*, *labour*, and *honour*), still the resistance to change has not observably weakened. If spelling won't change, as it probably won't, those of us who consider ourselves poor spellers will have to. We'll just have to get up and go to the mountain.

你可能听过默罕默德和山的典故。虽然在过去的 80 年英语拼写发生了非常微小的现代化变化(例如,traveler, center, theater, medieval, labor 和 honor 基本已经完全替代了 traveller, centre, theatre, mediaeval, labour 和 honour), 但是,变革的阻力从未被显著削弱。如果拼写不变,认为自己拼写糟糕的人们也将不得不接受这个事实,因为拼写极有可能不会发生任何变化。我们只能站起身来开始爬山。

Is it hard to become a good speller? I have demonstrated over and over again in my classes that anyone of normal intelligence and average educational background can become a good speller in very little time.

What makes the task so easy?

做个完美的拼写者真的这么困难吗?我曾经反复向我的学生展示,任何具有正常智商、具有普通教育背景的人都能在很短的时间内变成完美的拼写者。

什么能够使这项任务变得如此简单?

First—investigations have proved that 95 percent of the spelling errors that educated people make occur in just one hundred words. Not only do we all misspell the same words—but we misspell them in about the same way.

Second—correct spelling relies exclusively on memory, and the most effective way to train memory is by means of association or, to use the technical term, mnemonics.

首先——已有调查表明,受教育人士所犯的拼写错误中的 95％集中体现为 100 个词汇。我们不仅将同样的词汇错误拼写——就连错误的拼写方式也一样。

第二——正确的拼写唯独依靠记忆,而训练记忆最有效的方式是通过联想,或使用记忆法(心理学术语)。

If you fancy yourself an imperfect or even a terrible speller, the chances are very great that you've developed a complex solely because you misspell some or all of the hundred words with which this Intermission deals. When you have conquered this single list, and I shall immediately proceed to demonstrate how easy it is, by means of mnemonics, to do so, 95 percent of your spelling difficulties will in all likelihood vanish.

Let us start with twenty-five words from the list. In the first column you will find the correct spelling of each, and in the second column the simple mnemonic that will forevermore fix that correct spelling in your memory.

如果你认为自己的拼写不完美,甚至非常糟糕,那么极有可能已经形成了一种情结,而原因只是你拼错了本篇介绍的几百个单词中的部分或全部单词。当你完成以下列表,我将马上向你证明,通过记忆法做到正确拼写有多么简单,你95％的拼写困难大多会消失。

我们从 25 个词汇开始。左栏给出每个词汇的正确拼写方法;右栏提供的简单记忆法会使你永远记住正确的拼写。

CORRECT SPELLING	MNEMONIC
1. all right	Two words, no matter what it means. Keep in mind that it's the opposite of *all wrong*.
2. coolly	Of course you can spell *cool*—simply add the ad-

verbial ending -ly.

3. supersede — This is the only word in the language ending in -sede (the only one, mind you—there isn't a single other one so spelled).

4. succeed — The only three words in the entire

5. proceed — language ending in -ceed. When you

6. exceed — think of the three words in the order given here, the initial letters form the beginning of SPEED.

7. cede, precede, recede, etc. — All other words with a similar-sounding final syllable end in -cede.

8. procedure — One of the double e's of proceed moves to the end in the noun form, procedure.

9. stationery — This is the word that means paper, and notice the -er in paper.

10. stationary — In this spelling, the word means standing, and notice the -a in stand.

11. recommend — Commend, which we all spell correctly, plus the prefix re-.

12. separate

13. comparative — Look for a rat in both words.

14. ecstasy — to sy (sigh) with ecstasy

15. analyze — The only two non-technical words in

16. paralyze — the whole language ending in -yze.

17. repetition — First four letters identical with those in the allied form repeat.

18. irritable — Think of allied forms irritate and

19. inimitable — imitate.

20. absence — Think of the allied form absent, and you will not be tempted to misspell it abscence.

21. superintendent — The superintendent in an apartment house collects the rent—thus you avoid superintendant.

22. conscience — Science plus prefix con-.

23. anoint — Think of an ointment, hence no double n.

24. ridiculous — Think of the allied form ridicule, which we usually spell correctly, thus avoiding rediculous.

25. despair — Again, think of another form—desperate—and so avoid dispair.

正确拼写	记忆法
1. all right	无论具体表示什么含义,总是两个词语。记住,它与 all wrong 相反。

2. coolly	当然你会拼写 cool——只是简单添加副词词尾-ly。
3. supersede	这是英语中唯一一以-sede 结尾的词汇（唯一的一个，注意——没有任何其他词汇以-sede 结尾。）
4-6. succeed，proceed，exceed	这三个是英语中以-ceed 结尾的所有词汇。当你按照先后顺序回想这三个词汇，你会发现三个词汇的首字母构成了 SPEED 的前三个字母。
7. cede，precede，recede 等等	所有其他具有相似发音的最后音节都以-cede 结尾。
8. procedure	想象 proceed 中的两个 ee 的其中一个在名词形式中挪动了词尾。
9. stationery	这个词义与纸相关，联想 paper 中的 er。
10. stationary	这个词义与站立相关，联想 stand 中的 a。
11. recommend	只是在我们能够正确拼写的 commend 之前加上 re-。
12. separate、13. comparative	两个词中都包含大老鼠"rat"。
14. ecstasy	无法控制的叹息 sy(sigh)。
15. analyze、16. paralyze	英语中仅有的两个以-yze 结尾的非技术性词汇。
17. repetition	只有前四个字母与动词原形 repeat 相同。
18. irritable、19. inimitable	联想两个词的动词原形 irritate 和 imitate。
20. absence	联想形容词形式 absent，你就不会将其错误拼写为 abscence。
21. superintendent	公寓管理人 superintendent(管理人)会收取 rent(房租)——这样你就不会将其错误拼写为 superintendant。
22. conscience	science 加上前缀-con。
23. anoint	联想 ointment(软膏)，这样就不会错误拼写为双写 n。
24. ridiculous	联想我们能够正确拼写的动词原形 ridicule，这样就能够避免错误拼写为 rediculous。
25. despair	再一次联想另外一个形式——desperate——避免错误拼写为 dispair。

Whether or not you have much faith in your spelling ability, you will need very little time to conquer the preceding twenty-five demons. Spend a few minutes, now, on each of those words in the list that you're doubtful of, and then test your success by means of the exercise below. Perhaps to your astonishment, you will find it easy to make a high score.

无论你对自己的拼写能力有多大的信心，战胜以上 25 个词汇都仅需要很短时间。对于以上列表中有疑虑的词汇，你要多拿出几分钟消化；然后通过以下练习测验学习效果。也许结果会出乎预料，你会发现得到满意的分数竟然如此简单。

A test of your learning

检验学习效果

Instructions：After studying the preceding list of words，fill in the missing letters correctly.

要求：完全消化以上列表中的词汇之后，填写下面省去的字母。

1. a _____ right
2. coo _____ y
3. super _____
4. suc _____
5. pro _____
6. ex _____
7. pre _____
8. proc _____ dure
9. station _____ ry（paper）
13. re _____ o _____ end
14. ecsta _____ y
15. anal _____ e
16. paral _____ e
17. rep _____ tition
18. irrit _____ ble
19. inimit _____ ble
20. ab _____ ence
21. superintend _____ nt

10. station _____ ry (still)

11. sep _____ rate

12. compar _____ tive

22. con _____ nce

23. a _____ oint

24. r _____ diculous

25. d _____ spair

Mere repetitious drill is of no value in learning to spell a word correctly. You've probably heard the one about the youngster who was kept after school because he was in the habit of using the ungrammatical expression "I have went." Miss X was going to cure her pupil, even if it required drastic measures. So she ordered him to write "I have gone" one thousand times. "Just leave your work on my desk before you go home," she said, "and I'll find it when I come in tomorrow morning." Well, there were twenty pages of neat script on her desk next morning, one thousand lines of "I have gone's," and on the last sheet was a note from the child. "Dear Teacher," it read, "I have done the work and I have went home." If this didn't actually happen, it logically could have, for in any drill, if the mind is not actively engaged, no learning will result. If you drive a car, or sew, or do any familiar and repetitious manual work, you know how your hands can carry on an accustomed task while your mind is far away. And if you hope to learn to spell by filling pages with a word, stop wasting your time. All you'll get for your trouble is writer's cramp.

只是机械地重复对正确拼写词汇是没有价值的。你可能听说过这样一个故事:一个小孩因为习惯使用不符合语法规则的表达方式"I have went"而被老师留在学校。即使需要严厉的措施,X 老师也要纠正学生的错误。于是,她命令学生将"I have gone"写上 1000 遍。她说:"回家之前把作业放在我的桌子上,明天一早我会检查。"第二天早上,她的桌上放着 20 页笔迹工整的作业,上面写了 1000 行"I have gone"。最后一页是学生写给老师的便条:"Dear Teacher, I have done the work and I have went home."即使这个故事是虚构的,在逻辑上也确实有可能发生。如果没有大脑的积极参与,任何操练都不能带来学习效果。如果是开车、缝纫或者任何其他相似的反复手工工作,你知道,即使心不在焉,你也能够完成这样的熟练工作。但是,如果你希望通过写满纸张就为了记住一个词汇的拼写,还是不要浪费你的时间了。最后得到的只能是手抽筋。

The only way to learn to spell those words that now plague you is to devise a mnemonic for each one.

If you are never quite sure whether it's *indispensible* or *indispensable*, you can spell it out one hundred, one thousand, or one million times—and the next time you have occasion to write it in a sentence, you'll still wonder whether to end it with *-ible* or *-able*. But if you say to yourself *just once* that *able* people are generally *indispensable*, that thought will come to you whenever you need to spell the word; in a few seconds you've conquered another spelling demon. By engineering your own mnemonic through a study of the architecture of a troublesome word, you will become so quickly and completely involved with the correct spelling of that word that it will be impossible for you ever to be stumped again.

正确拼写使你痛苦的那些词汇的唯一方法是为每个词汇发明一个记忆法。

如果你总是无法确定 indispensible 和 indispensable 哪个才是正确的拼写,你可以写上 100 遍、1000 遍,甚至 100 万遍——但是,下一次有机会在句子中使用这个词汇时,你仍然不确定结尾到底是-ible 还是-able。但是,只要你告诉自己,有能力的人（able men）是必不可少的（indispensable），这样，下一次无论什么时候需要拼写这个词汇，你都能想到这个联想；短短几秒钟，你又战胜了另外一个拼写恶魔。通过研究令人头痛的词汇的结构，设计出自己的记忆法，你就能够快速、完全地参与到词汇的正确拼写中，你也绝对不会再被它们难倒。

Let us start at once. Below you will find another twenty-five words from the list of one hundred demons, each offered to you in both the correct form and in the popular misspelling. Go through the test quickly, checking off what you consider a proper choice in each case. In that way you will discover which of the twenty-five you would be likely to get caught on. Then devise a personal mnemonic for each word you flunked, writing your ingenious result out in the margin of the page. And don't be alarmed if some of your mnemonics turn out kind of silly—the sillier they are the more likely you are to recall them in an emergency. One of my pupils, who could not remember how many *l*'s to put into *tranquillity* (or is it *tranquility*?), shifted his mind into high gear and came up with this: "In the old days life was more *tranquil* than today, and people wrote with *quills* instead of fountain pens. Hence—*tranquil-lity*!" Another pupil, a girl who always chewed her nails over *irresistible* before she could decide whether to end it with *-ible* or *-able*, suddenly realized that a certain brand of *lipstick* was called *irresistible*, the point being of course that the only vowel in *lipstick* is *i*—hence, *-ible*! Silly, aren't they? But they work. Go ahead to the test now; and see how clever—or silly—you can be.

让我们马上开始这样的联想方法。下面的练习中，你会发现 100 个难拼写的词中的另外 25 个，练习给出了正确的形式和最常见的错误拼写。快速完成测验，选出每组中的正确形式。这样，你会发现这 25 个词汇中的哪些词是你容易拼写错误的词汇。然后为你拼写错误的每个词汇设计一个记忆法，在页面空白处写下你别具一格的设计。不要担心自己的设计有多么荒唐——设计越是荒唐，在紧急时刻越是容易想起。我的一个学生曾经无法记忆 tranquillity（或是 tranquility?）中到底有几个 l，他快速转动脑筋，想到这个方法："人类过去的生活比现在安静（tranquil）许多，人们当时用羽毛笔（quills）写字，而不使用钢笔。这样——tranquillity!"另外一个女学生总是无法分辨 irresistible 和 irresistable 哪个才是正确的拼写，直到她突然意识到一种口红（lipstick）的品牌就是 irresistible，原因当然是 lipstick 的唯一一个原音字母就是 i——这样就是-ible! 想法很荒唐，不是吗？但是的确非常奏效。完成以下测试；看一看你到底能有多么聪明——或是多么荒唐！

SPELLING TEST
拼写测验

1. a. supprise   b. surprise
2. a. inoculate   b. innoculate
3. a. definitely   b. definately
4. a. priviledge   b. privilege
5. a. incidently   b. incidentally
6. a. predictible   b. predictable
7. a. dissipate   b. disippate
8. a. descriminate   b. discriminate
9. a. description   b. discription
10. a. baloon   b. balloon

11. a. occurence	b. occurrence
12. a. truely	b. truly
13. a. arguement	b. argument
14. a. assistant	b. asisstant
15. a. grammer	b. grammar
16. a. parallel	b. paralell
17. a. drunkeness	b. drunkenness
18. a. suddeness	b. suddenness
19. a. embarassment	b. embarrassment
20. a. weird	b. wierd
21. a. pronounciation	b. pronunciation
22. a. noticeable	b. noticable
23. a. developement	b. development
24. a. vicious	b. viscious
25. a. insistent	b. insistant

KEY：1-b，2-a，3-a，4-b，5-b，6-b，7-a，8-b，9-a，10-b，11-b，12-b，13-b，14-a，15-b，16-a，17-b，18-b，19-b，20-a，21-b，22-a，23-b，24-a，25-a

By now you're well on the way toward developing a definite superiority complex about your spelling—which isn't a half-bad thing, for I've learned, working with my students, that many people think they're awful spellers, and have completely lost faith in their ability, solely because they get befuddled over no more than two dozen or so common words that they use over and over again and always misspell. Every other word they spell perfectly, but they still think they're prize boobs in spelling until their self-confidence is restored. So if you're beginning to gain more assurance, you're on the right track. The conquest of the one hundred common words most frequently misspelled is not going to assure you that you will always come out top man in a spelling bee, but it's certain to clean up your writing and bolster your ego.

现在,你已经开始确立起对自己拼写技能的良好感觉——这可是件不错的事,因为通过教学我发现,许多人仅仅因为二十几个反复使用却经常拼写错误的词汇就认为自己的拼写非常糟糕,甚至对自己的拼写能力完全失去信心。虽然他们能够正确拼写其他词汇,但却始终认为自己是蠢材,直到重新树立自信心。所以,如果你开始相信自己,你就已经步入正轨。战胜经常拼写错的100个常用词汇虽然不能保证你得到拼写竞赛的金奖,但确实能够使你的写作更加清晰、提高自我满足感。

So far you have worked with fifty of the one hundred spelling demons. Here, now, is the remainder of the list. Test yourself, or have someone who can keep a secret test you, and discover which ones are your Waterloo. Study each one you miss as if it were a problem in engineering. Observe how it's put together and devise whatever association pattern will fix the correct form in your mind.

Happy spelling!

至此,你已经见过了 100 个拼写恶魔中的 50 个。以下是其余的词汇。自己测验自己,或者让一个能够为你保密的人测验自己,找到哪些才是你在滑铁卢战役中的对手。研究每个错误,把它当成工程中遇到的问题。研究词汇的构成,在头脑中思考任何有助于正确拼写的联想。

祝拼写愉快!

SPELLING DEMONS
拼写恶魔

These fifty words complete the list of one hundred words that most frequently stump the inexpert spellers:

1. embarrassing		26. panicky
2. judgment		27. seize
3. indispensable		28. leisure
4. disappear		29. receive
5. disappoint		30. achieve
6. corroborate		31. holiday
7. sacrilegious		32. existence
8. tranquillity		33. pursue
9. exhilaration		34. pastime
10. newsstand		35. possesses
11. license		36. professor
12. irresistible		37. category
13. persistent		38. rhythmical
14. dilemma		39. vacuum
15. perseverance		40. benefited
16. until (but till)		41. committee
17. tyrannize		42. grievous
18. vacillate		43. conscious
19. oscillate		44. plebeian
20. accommodate		45. tariff
21. dilettante		46. sheriff
22. changeable		47. connoisseur
23. accessible		48. necessary
24. forty		49. sergeant
25. desirable		50. misspelling

15

HOW TO TALK ABOUT WHAT GOES ON
如何描述正在发生的事情

(*Sessions 42 — 44*)

TEASER PREVIEW
引读

What verb, ending in -*ate*, means:

* *to exhaust?*
* *to scold severely?*
* *to deny oneself?*
* *to repeat the main points?*
* *to be a victim of mental or intellectual stagnation?*
* *to pretend?*
* *to hint?*
* *to make (something) easier to bear?*
* *to show sympathy?*
* *to waver indecisively?*

哪个以-ate 结尾的动词具有以下含义：
* 使……衰弱、失去活力
* 严厉批评、斥责
* 自我否定
* 重复要点
* 心灵与智力停滞不前
* 假装、冒充
* 暗示、提示
* 减轻、缓和
* 怜悯、同情
* 犹豫不定

SESSION 42
第 42 节

WORDS are symbols of ideas—and we have been learning, discussing, and working with words as they revolve around certain basic concepts.

Starting with an idea (personality types, doctors, occupations, science, lying, actions, speech, insults, compliments, etc.), we have explored the meanings and uses of ten basic words; then, working from each word, we have wandered off toward any ideas and additional words that a basic word might suggest, or toward any *other* words built on the same Latin or Greek roots.

By this natural and logical method, you have been able to make meaningful and lasting contact with fifty to a hundred or more words in each chapter. And you have discovered, I think, that while five *isolated* words may be difficult to learn in one day, fifty to a hundred or more *related* words are easy to learn in a few sessions.

In this session we learn words that tell what's going on, what's happening, what people do to each other or to themselves, or what others do to *them*.

词汇是概念的象征符号——我们一直学习、讨论和练习的词汇都紧紧围绕一些基本概念。

从概念出发(个性种类、医生、职业、科学、谎言、行为、话语、侮辱、赞扬等等),我们分别探讨 10 个基本词汇的含义和用法;然后我们以每个词汇为基础,探讨了与之相关的概念和更多的词汇或与其有相同拉丁词根、希腊词根的词汇。

通过这种自然的、逻辑清晰的方法,我们在每一章都能够接触到 50 至 100 个词汇,不仅能够理解词汇的丰富含义,也能够达到长久记忆。我认为,你可能已发现,花费一天时间记忆 5 个孤立词汇非常困难,而在几个小节中记忆 50 至 100 个相关词汇反而容易。

在这部分中我们要学习一些描述"正在发生什么"的单词,人们对彼此或者对他们自己做些什么,或者别人如何对待他们。

IDEAS
概念

1. complete exhaustion
筋疲力尽

You have stayed up all night. And what were you doing? Playing poker, a very pleasant way of whiling away time? No. Engaging in some creative activity, like writing a short story, planning a political campaign, discussing fascinating questions with friends? No.

The examples I have offered are exciting or stimulating—as psychologists have discovered, it is not work or effort that causes fatigue, but boredom, frustration, or a similar feeling.

You have stayed up all night with a very sick husband, wife, child, or dear friend. And despite all your ministrations, the patient is sinking. You can see how this long vigil contains all the elements of frustration that contribute to mental, physical, and nervous fatigue.

And so you are bushed—but completely bushed. Your exhaustion is mental, it is physiological, it is emotional.

What verb expresses the effect of the night's frustrations on you?

to enervate

你熬了一整夜。你做了些什么？是打扑克吗，一种令人开心的消遣？不是。或是参加具有创造性的活动吗，例如写短篇故事，筹划政治竞选，与朋友讨论引人入胜的问题？也不是。

以上我所提到的例子都会让人兴奋、感到刺激——心理学家发现，使人感到疲惫的并不是工作或辛苦，而是厌倦、挫败感和其他相似的感觉。

你熬了一整夜陪在重病的丈夫、妻子、孩子或者挚友的身边。即使你关心备至，病人仍然每况愈下。你能够体会到这种漫长的守夜包含了挫败感的各种要素，这一切使你精神、身体、神经倍感疲惫。

你感到疲倦——筋疲力尽。你的疲惫既是精神上的、生理上的，也是情感上的。

哪个以-ate 结尾的动词能够描述通宵的挫败感对你造成的影响？

使……衰弱(to enervate)

2. tongue-lashing

大声斥责

You suddenly see the flashing red light as you glance in your rear-view mirror. It's the middle of the night, yet the police flasher is clear as day—and then you hear the low growl of the siren. So you pull over, knowing you were speeding along at 70 on the 55-mile-an-hour-limit freeway—after all, there was not another car in sight on the deserted stretch of road you were traveling.

The cop is pleasant, courteous, smiling; merely asks for your driver's license and registration; even says "Please."

Feeling guilty and stupid, you become irritated. So what do you do?

You lash out at the officer with all the verbal vituperation welling up in you from your self-anger. You scold him harshly for not spending his time looking for violent criminals instead of harassing innocent motorists; you call into question his honesty, his ambition, his fairness, even his ancestry. To no avail, of course you stare at the traffic morosely as the police cruiser pulls away.

What verb describes how you reacted?

to castigate

你忽然从后视镜里看到了闪烁的红灯，已经是午夜时分，但警用闪光灯却如白天一般清晰——然后你听到警车喇叭的低吼声，因此你靠边停车，并且忽然意识到在这条限速是 55 英里的高速公路上，你的时速却达到了 70 英里——然而，在你正在旅行着的这条偏远的公路上，目之所及，再也看不到另外一辆车。

警察态度友好，满脸笑容；只让你拿出驾照，并做了登记，甚至说"请"。

你感到内疚而愚蠢，进而恼羞成怒。这时你会做什么呢？

你突然忍不住对这个警官脱口大骂，表达你内心的愤怒。你狠狠地责骂他不去花时间对付暴力犯罪却来纠缠一个无辜的司机。你质疑他的诚实，他的企图，他的公平，甚至他的祖宗。但完全没用，你只能愁眉苦脸地眼睁睁地看着巡逻警车开走。

用什么动词来描述你的反应？

严厉批评(to castigate)

3. altruistic

利他的

Phyllis is selfless and self-sacrificing. Her husband's needs and desires come first—even when they conflict with her own. Clothes for her two daughters are her main concern—even if she has to wear a seven-year-old coat and outmoded dresses so that Paula and Evelyn can look smart and trim. At the dinner table, she heaps everyone's plate—while she herself often goes without. Phyllis will deny herself, will scrimp and save—all to the end that she may offer her husband and children the luxuries that her low self-esteem does not permit her to give herself.

What verb expresses what Phyllis does?

to self-abnegate

菲利斯无私,勇于自我牺牲。她丈夫的欲望是最为重要的,即使与她自己的欲望相悖。两个女儿的着装是她的首要考虑——即使她不得不穿着 7 年前买的大衣和过时的裙子,她也要宝拉和伊芙琳看起来靓丽、整洁。在餐桌上,她会装满其他每个人的盘子——而自己通常什么都不需要。她会牺牲自己,精打细算,省吃俭用———一切的目的就是给丈夫和孩子提供他们已经习惯了的奢侈生活,而她自己卑微的自尊不允许她享用这种奢侈。

哪个以-ate 结尾的动词能够最恰当地描述菲利斯所为?

自我牺牲(to self-abnegate)

4. repetition

重复

You have delivered a long, complicated lecture to your class, and now, to make sure that they will remember the important points, you restate the key ideas, the main thoughts. You offer, in short, a kind of brief summary, step by step, omitting all extraneous details.

What verb best describes what you do?

to recapitulate

在给你的班级上了一堂长篇大论、内容复杂的课之后,为了使大家记住重要内容,你重新陈述关键概念、主要观点。简而言之,你提供一种分步骤的简要概括,省去所有不必要的细节。

哪个以-ate 结尾的动词能够最准确地描述你的行为?

总结、扼要重述(to recapitulate)

5. no joie de vivre

缺少生活的乐趣

Perhaps you wake up some gloomy Monday morning (why is it that Monday is always the worst day of the week?) and begin to think of the waste of the last five years. Intellectually, there has been no progress—you've read scarcely half a dozen books, haven't made one new, exciting friend, haven't had a startling or unusual thought. Economically, things are no better—same old debts to meet, same old hundred dollars in the bank, same old job, same old routine of the eight-to-five workdays, the tuna fish or chicken salad sandwich for lunch, the same dreary ride home. What a life! No change, nothing but routine, sameness, monotony—and for what? (By now you'd better get up—this type of thinking never leads anywhere, as you've long since learned.)

What verb describes how you think you live?

to vegetate

一个令人抑郁的星期一早晨(为什么星期一总是一周中最糟糕的一天?)你醒来后开始思考被浪费了的过去 5 年。你在智力上没有任何进步——你甚至没有读完 6 本书,没有结交下一个令人开心的新朋友,没有任何不同寻常的想法。经济上也没有任何好转——面对同样的旧债,银行里还是过去的几百美元存款,仍然做着过去的工作,朝八晚五,午餐还是金枪鱼和鸡肉沙拉,下班乘车回家之路仍那么乏味。多么无趣的生活! 没有任何变化,只有不变的日程、单调、乏味——为什么会这样? (现在你最好赶快起床——这样的思维不会使你有任何的进步,正如我们之前所说到的一样。)

哪个以-ate 结尾的动词能够描述你过去五年的生活?

过着单调、呆板的生活(to vegetate)

6. pretense
假装

Your neighbor, Mrs. Brown, pops in without invitation to tell you of her latest troubles with (a) her therapist, (b) her hairdresser, (c) her husband, (d) her children, and/or (e) her gynecologist.

Since Florence Brown is dull to the point of ennui, and anyway you have a desk piled high with work you were planning to light into, you find it difficult to concentrate on what she is saying. However, you do not wish to offend her by sending her packing, or even by appearing to be uninterested, so you pretend rapt attention, nodding wisely at what you hope are the right places.

What verb describes this feigning of interest?

to simulate

邻居布朗夫人不请自来到了你家,告诉你她最近与(a)治疗师、(b)美发师、(c)丈夫、(d)孩子和(e)妇科医生等人之间的不愉快。

因为弗洛伦斯·布朗是个非常无聊的人,而你桌上又堆满了需要处理的工作材料,你发现自己很难集中精力去听她的谈话内容。但是,你既无法把她送走,又不能表现出对她的话不感兴趣,因为你不想冒犯她。所以,你假装全神贯注,明智地点头,希望点头的时机恰到好处。

哪个以-ate 结尾的动词能够准确描述这种伪装的兴趣?

假装、冒充(to simulate)

7. slight hint, no more
细小的暗示

You are an author and are discussing with your editor the possible avenues of publicity and advertising for your new book. At one point in the conversation the editor makes several statements which might—or might not—be construed to mean that the company is, going to promote the book heavily. For example, "If we put some real money behind this, we might sell a few copies," or "I wonder if it would be a good idea to get you on a few talk shows..." No unequivocal commitments, no clear-cut promises, only the slight and oblique mention of possibilities.

What verb expresses what the editor is doing?

to intimate

假如你是作家,正在与出版商讨论新书可行的宣传和广告方法。对话的某一时刻,出版商的表态可能意味着出版公司打算大力推销你的书,也可能没有这个意思。比如他说:"如果我们在这本书上切实花点钱,也许能多卖出几本。"或者:"我不知道让你参加几场脱口秀会不会是个好主意……"这些话里没有明确的承诺,只是轻描淡写地提到了各种可能性。

哪个以-ate 结尾的动词能够最恰当地表达出版商所做的事?

to intimate：暗示

8. helpful

有帮助的

Aspirin doesn't cure any diseases. Yet this popular and inexpensive drug is universally used to lighten and relieve various unpleasant symptoms of disease: aches and pains, fever, inflammations, etc.

What verb expresses the action of aspirin?

to alleviate

阿司匹林不能治愈任何疾病。但这种大众的便宜药普遍用来减轻、缓和各种各样的不舒服症状,例如疼痛、发烧、炎症等。

哪个以-ate结尾的动词能够表示阿司匹林的作用?

减轻、缓和(to alleviate)

9. when the bell tolls

当丧钟鸣起

John Donne's lines (made famous by Ernest Hemingway):

No man is an Island, *intire of itselfe*; *every man is a peece of the* Continent, *a part of the* maine; *if a* Clod *bee washed away by the* Sea, Europe *is the lesse*, *as well as if a* Promontorie *were*, *as well as if a* Manner *of thy* friends *or of* thine owne *were*; *any mans* death *diminishes* me, *because I am involved* in Mankinde; *And therefore never send to know for whom the* bell *tolls*; *It tolls for thee.*

They are truer than you may think; any person who views another's pain with complete detachment or indifference is shutting off important feelings.

When people have suffered a bereavement (as through death); when they have been wounded by life or by friends; then is the time they most need to feel that they are not alone, that you share their misery with them even if you cannot directly alleviate their sorrow. Your sympathy and compassion are, of course, alleviation enough.

What verb signifies this vicarious sharing of sorrow with someone who directly suffers?

to commiserate

以下是约翰·多恩的诗行(因为欧内斯特·海明威的引用而出名)

没有谁是一座孤岛,在大海里独踞;每个人都是一块小小的泥土,是整个陆地的一部分;如果有一块泥土被海水冲刷,欧洲就会失去一角,这如同一座山岬,也如同你或是你朋友的一片庄园;无论谁死了,我都有一部分在消逝,因为我总是人类的一部分;因此,不要问丧钟为谁而鸣,丧钟为你而鸣。

这些诗行比你的想象更加真实;任何面对其他人的困苦完全无动于衷的人都是封闭了一些重要的情感。

经历丧亲之痛时,被生活或朋友伤害时,他最大的需要是感到自己并不孤单,即使你无法直接减轻他的悲哀,但总能够分享他的不幸。当然,你的同情就足以减轻痛苦了。

哪个以-ate结尾的动词能够表达出这种间接地分享一个直接遭受痛苦的人的情感?

怜悯、同情(to commiserate〔with〕)

10. when two men propose

当两个男人同时向你求婚

Should you marry John or George? (You're strongly and equally attracted to both.) John is handsome, virile, tender; George is stable, reliable, dependable, always there when you need him. George loves you deeply; John is more exciting. You decide on John, naturally.

But wait—marrying John would mean giving up George, and with George you always know where you stand; he's like the Rock of Gibraltar (and sometimes almost as dull). So you change your mind—it's George, on more mature reflection.

But how happy can you be with a husband who is not exciting? Maybe John would be best after all....

The pendulum swings back and forth—you cannot make up your mind and stick to it. (You fail to realize that your indecision proves that you don't want to marry either one, or perhaps don't want to give either one up, or possibly don't even want to get married.) First it's John, then it's George, then back to John, then George again. *Which is it, which is it*?

What verb describes your pendulum-like indecision?

to vacillate

你会嫁给约翰还是乔治?(你被两个人同样强烈地吸引。)约翰帅气、强健、温柔;乔治沉稳,值得依赖、依靠,当你需要他的时候,他总会陪伴在你的左右。乔治对你情深意浓;约翰使你更加心动。当然,你选择了约翰。

但是,等等! 嫁给约翰意味着放弃乔治,和乔治在一起时,你总是知道自己的位置;他好似直布罗陀巨石(虽然有时几乎与巨石一样无趣)。所以你改变了主意——通过更成熟的考虑,你决定嫁给乔治。

但是嫁给一个不会使人兴奋的丈夫会开心吗? 也许约翰才是最好的选择……

钟摆摇摆不定——你无法下定决心并不再改变。(你没有意识到,你的犹豫不决证明你不想嫁给两者中的任何一个,或你不想放弃两者中的任何一个,或你甚至不想结婚。)最初你想要嫁给约翰,然后变成乔治,然后又变回约翰,然后再次变回乔治。你想要嫁给谁? 谁?

哪个以 -ate 结尾的动词能够最准确地描述你的犹豫不决?

犹豫、踌躇(to vacillate)

USING THE WORDS

单词应用

Can you pronounce the words?

你能读出这些单词吗?

1. *enervate*	EN′-ər-vayt′
2. *castigate*	KAS′-tə-gayt′
3. *self-abnegate*	self-AB′-nə-gayt′
4. *recapitulate*	ree′-kə-PICH′-ə-layt′
5. *vegetate*	VEJ′-ə-tayt′
6. *simulate*	SIM′-yə-layt′
7. *intimate*	IN′-tə-mayt′
8. *alleviate*	ə-LEE′-vee-ayt′

9. *commiserate*   kə-MIZ′-ə-rayt

10. *vacillate*   VAS′-ə-layt

Can you work with the words?
你能灵活使用这些词汇了吗?

1. enervate	a. deny oneself
2. castigate	b. stagnate
3. self-abnegate	c. suggest; hint
4. recapitulate	d. sympathize
5. vegetate	e. waver
6. simulate	f. exhaust
7. intimate	g. lessen; lighten
8. alleviate	h. summarize
9. commiserate	i. pretend
10. vacillate	j. censure; scold; slash at verbally

KEY: 1-f, 2-j, 3-a, 4-h, 5-b, 6-i, 7-c, 8-g, 9-d, 10-e

Do you understand the words? (Ⅰ)
你对这些词汇是否已经透彻地理解? (Ⅰ)

1. Should you feel *enervated* after a good night's sleep?   YES   NO

2. Do motorists who have been caught speeding sometimes start *castigating* the traffic officer?   YES   NO

3. Do people who are completely *self-abnegating* say "No!" to their needs and desires?   YES   NO

4. When you *recapitulate*, do you cover new material?   YES   NO

5. Do people possessed of *joie de vivre* usually feel that they are *vegetating*?   YES   NO

6. When you *simulate* alertness, do you purposely act somnolent?   YES   NO

7. When you *intimate*, do you make a direct statement?   YES   NO

8. Does aspirin often have an *alleviating* effect on pain?   YES   NO

9. Do we naturally *commiserate* with people who have suffered a bereavement?   YES   NO

10. Do decisive people often *vacillate*?　　　　　　　　YES　　NO

KEY：1-no，2-yes，3-yes，4-no，5-no，6-no，7-no，8-yes，9-yes，10-no

Do you understand the words? (Ⅱ)
你对这些词汇是否已经透彻地理解？(Ⅱ)

1. enervated—exhilarated	SAME	OPPOSITE
2. castigate—praise	SAME	OPPOSITE
3. self-abnegate—deny oneself	SAME	OPPOSITE
4. recapitulate—summarize	SAME	OPPOSITE
5. vegetate—stagnate	SAME	OPPOSITE
6. simulate—pretend	SAME	OPPOSITE
7. intimate—hint	SAME	OPPOSITE
8. alleviate—make worse	SAME	OPPOSITE
9. commiserate—sympathize	SAME	OPPOSITE
10. vacillate—decide	SAME	OPPOSITE

KEY：1-O，2-O，3-S，4-S，5-S，6-S，7-S，8-O，9-S，10-O

Can you recall the words?
你能够写出这些词汇吗？

1. pretend	1. S＿＿＿＿＿＿
2. scold	2. C＿＿＿＿＿＿
3. sacrifice one's desires	3. S＿＿＿＿＿＿
4. waver	4. V＿＿＿＿＿＿
5. exhaust	5. E＿＿＿＿＿＿
6. sympathize	6. C＿＿＿＿＿＿
7. summarize	7. R＿＿＿＿＿＿
8. lighten	8. A＿＿＿＿＿＿
9. hint	9. I＿＿＿＿＿＿
10. stagnate	10. V＿＿＿＿＿＿

KEY：1-simulate，2-castigate，3-self-abnegate，4-vacillate，5-enervate，6-commiserate，7-recapitulate，8-alleviate，9-intimate，10-vegetate

(End of Session 42)

SESSION 43
第 43 节

ORIGINS AND RELATED WORDS
词源及相关词汇

1. more than fatigue

筋疲力尽

When you are *enervated*, you feel as if your nerves have been ripped out—or so the etymology of the word indicates.

当你是"enervated"的时候,你会感觉就像你的神经已经被扯了出来——从词源上看,这大概就是这个词的本义。

Enervate is derived from *e-* (*ex-*), out, and Latin *nervus*, nerve. *Enervation* (en'-ər-VAY'-shən) is not just fatigue, but complete devitalization—physical, emotional, mental—as if every ounce of the life force has been sapped out, as if the last particle of energy has been drained away.

enervate 是 e-(ex-),(外面的)和拉丁语 nervus(神经)衍变而来。enervation 不仅是劳累,而是彻底的失去活力——身体上的,情绪上的,精神上的——如同每一点生命力都被吸了出来,所有的能量都被耗尽。

Despite its similar appearance to the word *energy*, *enervation* is almost a direct antonym. *Energy* is derived from the Greek prefix *en-*, in, plus the root *ergon*, work; *erg* is the term used in physics for a unit of work or energy. *Synergism* (SIN'-ər-jiz-əm)—the prefix *syn-*, together or with, plus *ergon*—is the process by which two or more substances or drugs, by working together, produce a greater effect in combination than the sum total of their individual effects.

尽管这个词和 energy 看上去相似,但 enervation 的意思却几乎和 energy 完全相反。energy 是由希腊语前缀 en-("在里面")加上词根 ergon(功)衍变而来;erg 在物理学上是"功"或"能量"的计量单位。synergism——前缀 syn-(一起,共同),加上 ergon——是两种或以上药物共同作用,比两种药物各自的作用加起来产生的效果更大。

Alcohol, for example, is a depressant. So are barbiturates and other soporifics. Alcohol and barbiturates work *synergistically* (sin'-ər-JIS'-tik'-lee)—the effect of each is increased by the other if the two are taken together.

比如酒精是一种镇静剂。巴比妥酸盐和其他的安眠药也是。酒精和巴比妥酸盐 work synergistically(共同作用)——效果就会比单独一种要大。

So if you're drinking, don't take a sleeping pill—or if you *must* take a pill for your insomnia, don't drink—the combination, if not lethal, will do more to you than you may want done!

Synergy (SIN'-ər-jee), by the way, is an alternate form of *synergism*.

如果你正在饮酒,就别吃安眠药——或者如果你因为失眠而必须吃安眠药,那就不要饮酒——它们的共同作用,如果不是致命的,也会比你想要的大。

顺便说一下,synergy 是 synergism 的另一种拼法。

2. verbal punishment

大声斥责

Castigate is derived from a Latin verb meaning *to punish*; in present-day usage, the verb generally refers to verbal punishment, usually harsh and severe. It is somewhat synonymous with *scold*, *criticize*, *rebuke*, *censure*, *reprimand*, or *berate*, but much stronger than any of these—*rail at*, *rant at*, *slash at*, *lash out at*, or *tongue lash* is a much closer synonym. When candidates for office *castigate* their opponents, they do not mince words.

Can you construct the noun form of *castigate*? _____.

castigate 源于一个拉丁语动词,意为"惩罚";现在的用法是指言语上的惩罚,经常是严厉而苛刻的。在某种程度上,它和 scold, criticize, rebuke, censure, reprimand, 或 berate 意思差不多,但比这些单词表达的程度都要强——意思上和 rail at, rant at, slash at, lash out at, 或 tongue lash 更为接近。当官员候选人"castigate"他们的对手时,他们是不会用比较委婉温和的词句的。

你能写出 castigate 的名词形式吗?

3. saying "No!" to oneself

对自己说"不"

Abnegate is derived from Latin *ab-*, away (as in *absent*), plus *nego*, to deny—*self-abnegation* (ab'-nə-GAY'-shən), then, is self-denial. *Nego* itself is a contraction of Latin *neg-*, not, no, and *aio*, I say; to be *self-abnegating* is to say "No!" to what you want, as if some inner censor were at work whispering, "No, you can't have that, you can't do that, you don't deserve that, you're not good enough for that..."

abnegate 是由拉丁语中的 ab-(离开,如 absent)加上 nego(否认)——因此,self-abnegation 就是自我否认。nego 是拉丁单词 neg-(不)的缩写加 aio 的缩写(我说);self-abnegating 就是对自己的需求说"不",如同一个内在的监督者在低声说:"不,你不能要,你不能那么做,你没资格拥有那些,你还不配……"

To *negate* (nə-GAYT') is to deny the truth or existence of, as in "The atheist *negates* God"; or, by extension, to destroy by working against, as in, "His indulgence in expensive hobbies *negates* all his wife's attempts to keep the family solvent." Can you write the noun form of the verb *negate*? _____.

Negative and *negativity* obviously spring from the same source as *negate*.

to negate 就是否认事实和某些事物的存在,如 The atheist negates God(无神论者不承认有上帝);或者是通过采取阻碍行动来进行"破坏",如 His indulgence in expensive hobbies negates all his wife's attempts to keep the family solvent(他奢侈的爱好使他妻子还清债务的努力毁于一旦)。你能写出 negate 的名词形式吗? _____。

negative 和 negativity 很明显和 negate 有着相同的来源。

4. heads and headings

头和标题

Latin *caput*, *capitis* means *head*. The *captain* is the *head* of any group; the *capital* is the "*head* city" of a state or nation; and to *decapitate* (dee-KAP'-ə-tayt') is to chop off someone's *head*, a popular activity during the French Revolution after the guillotine was invented. Write the noun form of *decapitate*: _____.

拉丁语 caput，capitis(头部)。captain 是任何一个组织的"头"；capital 是一个州或国家的"领头城市"；decapitate 是砍头，这种行刑方式在铡刀被发明后的法国大革命时期盛极一时。写出 decapitate 的名词形式 _____。

Latin *capitulum* is a little head，or，by extension，the heading，or title，of a chapter. So when you *recapitulate*，you go through the chapter headings again (*re-*)，etymologically speaking，or you summarize or review the main points.

Remembering how the noun and adjective forms are derived from *adulate* (Chapter 9)，can you write the required forms of *recapitulate*?

拉丁语 capitulum 意为"一个小头"，或引申为一个章节的标题或题目。因此，当 recapitulate 时，意即再次继续阅读章节的标题，或从词源上看其意思是，归纳或复习文章主旨、要点。

请回想一下 adulate 的名词和形容词形式是如何从 adulate(第 9 章)派生而来的。你能写出 recapitulate 的以下形式吗？

NOUN(名词)：_____

ADJECTIVE(形容词)：_____

When you *capitulate* （kə-PICH′-ə-layt′），etymologically you arrange in headings，or，as the meaning of the verb naturally evolved，you arrange conditions of surrender，as when an army *capitulates* to the enemy forces under prearranged conditions；or，by further natural extension，you stop resisting and give up，as in，"He realized there was no longer any point in resisting her advances，so he reluctantly *capitulated*." Can you write the noun form of *capitulate*? _____。

当你 capitulate 时，从词源上看，其意思为"做出纲领性的安排"，或如这个动词的引申义，是布置投降计划，就是一个部队在提前议定好的条件下，向对方部队投降；或进一步延伸为"停止抵制"和"放弃"，如 He realized there was no longer any point in resisting her advances，so he reluctantly capitulated.（他意识到试图阻止她的进攻已毫无意义，因此他只能不情愿地放弃了。）你能写出 capitulate 的名词形式吗？

5. mere vegetables

纯蔬菜

Vegetable is from Latin *vegeto*，to live and grow，which is what vegetables do—but that's *all* they do，so to *vegetate*，is，by implication，to do no more than stay alive，stuck in a rut，leading an inactive，unstimulating，emotionally and intellectually stagnant existence. *Vegetation* （vej′-ə-TAY′-shən） is any dull，passive，stagnant existence；also any plant life，as the thick *vegetation* of a jungle.

vegetable 源于拉丁语 vegeto(活着或生长)——这也是蔬菜的状态，也是它们唯一的状态，因此，to vegetate 意即只是活着，其他的什么都不做，因循守旧，过着一种懒散，没有激情，情感上和智力上迟钝的生活。vegetation 就是一种迟钝、消极、停滞的存在；它也指任何植物生命，如丛林中厚厚的植被。

REVIEW OF ETYMOLOGY

复习词源

PREFIX，ROOT，SUFFIX	MEANING	ENGLISH WORD
1. *e-* （*ex-*）	out	_____
2. *nervus*	nerve	_____

3. *en-*   in   _____

4. *ergon*   work   _____

5. *syn-*   with，together   _____

6. *-ic*   adjective suffix   _____

7. *-ion*   noun suffix   _____

8. *ab-*   away   _____

9. *nego*   to deny   _____

10. *caput，capitis*   head   _____

11. *de-*   negative prefix   _____

12. *capitulum*   little head，
chapter heading   _____

13. *re-*   again   _____

14. *-ory*   adjective suffix   _____

15. *vegeto*   to live and grow   _____

USING THE WORDS
单词应用

Can you pronounce the words?
你能读出这些单词吗？

1. *enervation*   en′-ər-VAY′-shən

2. *synergism*   SIN′-ər-jiz-əm

3. *synergy*   SIN′-ər-jee

4. *synergistic*   sin′-ər-JIS′-tik

5. *castigation*   kas′-tə-GAY′-shən

6. *self-abnegation*   self-ab′-nə-GAY′-shən

7. *negate*   nə-GAYT′

8. *negation*   nə-GAY′-shən

9. *decapitate*   dee-KAP′-ə-tayt′

10. *decapitation*   dee-kap′-ə-TAY′-shən

11. *recapitulation*   ree-kə-pich′-ə-LAY′-shən

12. *recapitulatory*   ree-kə-PICH′-ə-lə-tawr′-ee

13. *capitulate*   kə-PICH′-ə-layt′

14. *capitulation*   kə-pich′-ə-LAY′-shən

Can you work with the words?
你能灵活使用这些词汇了吗？

1. enervation   a. tongue-lashing

2. synergism，synergy   b. denial；destruction

3. castigation   c. a lopping off of one's head

4. self-abnegation	d. summary; review of main points
5. negation	e. self-denial
6. decapitation	f. utter exhaustion; mental, emotional, and physical drain
7. recapitulation	g. a working together for greater effect
8. capitulation	h. surrender

KEY: 1-f, 2-g, 3-a, 4-e, 5-b, 6-c, 7-d, 8-h

Do you understand the words?

你对这些词汇是否已经透彻地理解？

1. enervating—refreshing	SAME	OPPOSITE
2. synergistic—neutralizing	SAME	OPPOSITE
3. castigation—scolding	SAME	OPPOSITE
4. self-abnegation—egoism	SAME	OPPOSITE
5. negate—accept	SAME	OPPOSITE
6. decapitate—behead	SAME	OPPOSITE
7. recapitulatory—summarizing	SAME	OPPOSITE
8. capitulate—resist	SAME	OPPOSITE

KEY: 1-O, 2-O, 3-S, 4-O, 5-O, 6-S, 7-S, 8-O

Can you recall the words?

你能够写出这些词汇吗？

1. to give in	1. C	_____
2. working together for greater effect (*adj.*)	2. S	_____
3. total fatigue	3. E	_____
4. for the purpose of summarizing or review (*adj.*)	4. R	_____
5. self-denial	5. S _____ A _____	
6. deny; render ineffective; nullify	6. N	_____
7. process by which two or more substances produce a greater effect than the sum of the individual effects	7. S *or* S	_____
8. to cut off the head of	8. D	_____
9. strong censure	9. C	_____

10. to surrender   10. C _____

KEY：1-capitulate，2-synergistic，3-enervation，4-recapitulatory，5-self-abnega-tion，6-negate，7-synergism *or* synergy，8-decapitate，9-castigation，10-capitulate

(End of Session 43)

SESSION 44
第 44 节

ORIGINS AND RELATED WORDS
词源及相关词汇

1. not the real McCoy
不是真货

Simulate is from Latin *simulo*, to copy; and *simulo* itself derives from the Latin adjective *similis*, like or similar.

Simulation (sim′-yə-LAY′-shən), then, is copying the real thing, pretending to be the genuine article by taking on a similar appearance. The *simulation* of joy is quite a feat when you really feel depressed.

simulate 来源于拉丁语 simulo(复制),simulo 自身又由拉丁形容词 similis(相像的,类似的)派生而来。

因此,simulation 就是复制真的事物,展示出类似的外表达到以假乱真。当你真正难过的时候,强颜欢笑绝非易事。

Genuine pearls grow inside oysters; *simulated* pearls are synthetic, but look like the ones from oysters. (Rub a pearl against your teeth to tell the difference—the natural pearl feels gritty.)So the frequent advertisement of an inexpensive necklace made of "genuine *simulated* pearls" can fool you if you don't know the word—you're being offered a genuine fake.

真正的珍珠从牡蛎里生出;模拟的珍珠是人工合成的,但看起来与牡蛎里长出来的一样。(拿一颗珍珠在你牙齿上摩擦,就能看出两者的区别——自然的珍珠感觉有沙砾。)如果你不知道 simulated 这个词的意思,那么经常播放的由"真正的模拟珍珠"制成的廉价项链广告就会愚弄你——你实际得到的是真正的假货。

Dissimulation (də-sim′-yə-LAY′-shən) is something else! When you *dissimulate* (də-SIM′-yə-layt′), you hide your true feelings by making a pretense of opposite feelings. (Then again, maybe it's not something completely else!)

Sycophants are great *dissimulators*—they may feel contempt, but show admiration; they may feel negative, but express absolutely positive agreement.

dissimulation 则有完全不同的意思。当你 dissimulate 的时候,你隐藏自己真正的感觉,而假装出与其相反的感觉。(话说回来,也许其意义并非完全不同。)

马屁精是出色的 dissimulators——他们可能心存不屑,但对你表现出崇拜;他们可能内心反对,但表现出的却是绝对热情的附和。

A close synonym of *dissimulate* is *dissemble* (də-SEM′-bəl), which also is to hide true feelings by pretending the opposite; or, additionally, to conceal facts, or one's true intentions, by deception; or, still further additionally, to pretend ignorance of facts you'd rather not admit, when, indeed, you're fully aware of them.

The noun is *dissemblance* (də-SEM′-bləns).

In *dissimulate* and *dissemble*, the negative prefix *dis-* acts largely to make both words pejorative.

dissimulate 的一个非常接近的同义词是 dissemble,也是表示装出相反的感觉来隐藏真正的感觉;另外的意思是用欺骗来隐瞒事实或者真实意图;更深的意思是,对你不愿承认的事实假装毫不知情,而实际上你心知肚明。

名词形式是 dissemblance。

在 dissimulate 和 dissemble 中的否定前缀 dis-主要作用是赋予这两个词以贬义。

2. hints and helps

暗示和帮助

The verb *intimate* is from Latin *intimus*, innermost, the same root from which the adjective *intimate* (IN′-tə-mət) and its noun *intimacy* (IN′-tə-mə-see) are derived; but the relationship is only in etymology, not in meaning. An *intimation* (in′-tə-MAY′-shən) contains a significance buried deep in the innermost core, only a hint showing. As you grow older, you begin to have *intimations* that you are mortal; when someone aims a .45 at you, or when a truck comes roaring down at you as you drive absent-mindedly against a red light through an intersection, you are suddenly *very sure* that you are mortal.

动词 intimate 来源于拉丁词 intimus(最里面的),形容词 intimate 及其名词形式 intimacy 也由这个词根派生,但是它们之间的关系只限于语源方面,意义上并没有联系。intimation 包含了深藏于最核心部分的意义,但在外表上只轻微地做出暗示。当你慢慢变老的时候,你开始得到提示,你终有一天会死去;而当某人拿着一支 0.45 口径的枪对着你,或者你漫不经心地开车闯过十字路口的红灯,这时一辆卡车冲你呼啸而来时,你突然非常肯定地意识到你终有一死。

Alleviate is a combination of Latin *levis*, light (not heavy), the prefix *ad-*, to, and the verb suffix. (*Ad-* changes to *al-* before a root starting with *l-*.)

If something *alleviates* your pain, it makes your pain lighter for you; if I *alleviate* your sadness, I make it lighter to bear; and if you need some *alleviation* (ə-lee′-vee-AY′-shən) of your problems, you need them made lighter and less burdensome. To *alleviate* is to relieve only temporarily, not to cure or do away with. (*Relieve* is also from *levis*, plus *re-*, again—to make light or easy again.) The adjective form of *alleviate* is *alleviative* (ə-LEE′-vee-ay′-tiv)—aspirin is an *alleviative* drug.

alleviate 由拉丁语 levis(轻的)加前缀 ad-(向)和动词后缀组成。(ad-在以 l-开头的词根前拼写为 al-。)

如果什么东西 alleviates 你的疼痛,它使你的疼痛变得更轻;如果我 alleviate 你的悲伤,我让它变得更轻,可以承受;如果你的问题需要一些 alleviation,你希望它们变得更轻,没那么沉重。alleviate 只是暂时减轻,而不是彻底根治或者消除。(relieve 也来源于 levis,加上前缀 re-[又]——使……再变轻或容易)。alleviate 的形容词是 alleviative——阿司匹林就是一种 alleviative 的药。

Anything light will rise—so from the prefix *e-* (*ex-*), out, plus *levis*, we can construct the verb *elevate*, etymologically, to raise out, or, actually, raise up, as to *elevate* one's spirits, raise them up, make them lighter; or *elevate* someone to a higher position, which is what an *elevator* does.

Have you ever seen a performance of magic in which a person or an object apparently rises in the air as if floating? That's *levitation* (lev′-ə-TAY′-shən)—rising through no visible means. (I've watched it a dozen times and never *could* figure it out!) The verb, to so rise, is *levitate* (LEV′-ə-tayt′).

轻的东西会上升——所以，前缀 e-(ex-)，"出来"，加上 levis，我们可以组成动词 elevate。从词源学来讲，"升出去"或"升上去"，如 elevate 一个人的精神，就是将它们"提升上去"，让它们变轻；或 elevate 一个人到更高的位置，就像电梯的功能一样。

你是否见过这样的魔术表演，一个人或物体看起来在空中上升，像飘浮起来一样？那就是 levitation——不通过可见的方法上升。(我看过十几次这样的表演，始终搞不明白是怎么做的！)表示以这种方式上升的动词是 levitate。

And how about *levity* (LEV'-ə-tee)? That's lightness too, but of a different sort—lightness in the sense of frivolity, flippancy, joking, or lack of seriousness, especially when solemnity, dignity, or formality is required or more appropriate, as in "tones of *levity*," or as in, "Levity is out of place at a funeral, in a house of worship, at the swearing-in ceremonies of a President or Supreme Court Justice," or as in, "Okay, enough *levity*—now let's get down to business!"

levity 是什么意思？它也表示"轻"，但是所指不同——是"轻浮""轻率""调侃"，或缺乏严肃，尤其是在要求庄重、庄严和正式的时候，或者庄重、庄严和正式更合适的时候——这个词用于"轻浮的语气"，或"在葬礼上、在礼拜堂、在总统或最高法院法官就职仪式上轻浮不合时宜"，或者"好吧，玩笑开够了——现在让我们谈正事吧！"

3. sharing someone's misery
分担不幸

Latin *miser*, wretched, the prefix *con-* (which, as you know, becomes *com-* before a root beginning with *m-*), together or with, and the verb suffix *-ate* are the building blocks from which *commiserate* is constructed. "I *commiserate* with you," then, means, "I am wretched together with you—I share your misery." The noun form? _____.

Miser, *miserly*, *miserable*, *misery* all come from the same root.

拉丁词根 miser 表示"悲惨的"，加上前缀 con-(表示"一起""与"的意思，如你所知，在以 m-开头的词根前拼写改为 com-)，再加动词后缀-ate，就构成了动词 commiserate(同情)。所以，I commiserate with you 的意思就是，"我跟你一起悲伤——我分担你的悲惨。"名词形式是什么？

miser，miserly，miserable，misery 全部来自同一个词根。

4. swing and sway
摇摆

Vacillate—note the single *c*, double *l*—derives from Latin *vacillo*, to swing back and forth. The noun form? _____.

People who swing back and forth in indecision, who are irresolute, who can, unfortunately, see both, or even three or four, sides of every question, and so have difficulty making up their minds, are *vacillatory* (VAS'-ə-lə-tawr'-ee). They are also, usually, *ambivalent* (am-BIV'-ə-lənt)—they have conflicting and simultaneous emotions about the same person or thing; or they want to go but they also want to stay; or they love something, but they hate it too. The noun is *ambivalence* (am-BIV'-ə-ləns)—from *ambi* both. (Remember *ambivert* and *ambidextrous* from Chapter 3?)

vacillate——注意是一个 c，两个 l——由拉丁词根 vacillo 派生，意为"前后摆动"。名词形式是什么？

人们在犹豫不决的时候会前后摇摆，在不坚定的时候会摇摆，在能够同时看到每个问题的两面甚至三四面的时候会摇摆，难以决断，所有这些人都可用 vacillatory 来形容。他们通常也 ambivalent——即对于同一个人或事同时有着相互冲突的情绪,或去留不定,或既爱又恨。名词形式是 ambivalence,来源于 ambi(都)。(记得第 3 章中学过的 ambivert 和 ambidextrous 吗?)

Ambivalence has best been defined (perhaps by Henny Youngman—if he didn't say it first, he should have) as watching your mother-in-law drive over a cliff in your new Cadillac.

To *vacillate* is to swing mentally or emotionally. To sway back and forth physically is *oscillate*—again note the double *l*—(OS'-ə-layt'), from Latin *oscillum*, a swing. A pendulum *oscillates*, the arm of a metronome *oscillates*, and people who've had much too much to drink *oscillate* when they try to walk. The noun? _____.

ambivalence 的最佳定义(也许是由喜剧演员亨尼·扬曼诠释出来的——哪怕他没有第一个说出来,他也本来应该说出)就是看着你的丈母娘开着你的凯迪拉克冲过悬崖。

vacillate 是精神上或情绪上的摇摆。形体上的前后摆动是 oscillate——再注意词中两个 l——来源于拉丁词根 oscillum,秋千。钟摆、节拍器的臂、醉酒者走路时都会摇摆(oscillate)。名词形式是什么?

REVIEW OF ETYMOLOGY
复习词源

PREFIX, ROOT, SUFFIX	MEANING	ENGLISH WORD
1. *simulo*	to copy	_____
2. *similis*	like, similar	_____
3. *dis-*	pejorative prefix	_____
4. *ad-* (*al-*)	to, toward	_____
5. *levis*	light	_____
6. *-ate*	verb suffix	_____
7. *-ion*	noun suffix	_____
8. *e-* (*ex-*)	out	_____
9. *intimus*	innermost	_____
10. *miser*	wretched	_____
11. *vacillo*	to swing back and forth	_____
12. *ambi-*	both	_____
13. *oscillum*	a swing	_____

USING THE WORDS
单词应用

Can you pronounce the words?
你能读出这些单词吗?

1. *simulation*　　　　　sim'-yə-LAY'-shən
2. *dissimulate*　　　　 də-SIM'-yə-layt'

3. *dissimulation*　　　　də-sim′-yə-LAY′-shən

4. *dissemble*　　　　　　də-SEM′-bəl

5. *dissemblance*　　　　　də-SEM′-bləns

6. *intimation*　　　　　　in′-tə-MAY′-shən

7. *alleviation*　　　　　　ə-lee′-vee-AY′-shən

8. *alleviative*　　　　　　ə-LEE′-vee-ay′-tiv

9. *levitate*　　　　　　　LEV′-ə-tayt′

10. *levitation*　　　　　　lev′-ə-TAY′-shən

11. *levity*　　　　　　　LEV′-ə-tee

12. *commiseration*　　　　kə-miz′-ə-RAY′-shən

13. *vacillation*　　　　　　vas′-ə-LAY′-shən

14. *vacillatory*　　　　　　VAS′-ə-lə-tawr′-ee

15. *ambivalent*　　　　　am-BIV′-ə-lənt

16. *ambivalence*　　　　　am-BIV′-ə-ləns

17. *oscillate*　　　　　　　OS′-ə-layt′

18. *oscillation*　　　　　　os′-ə-LAY′-shən

Can you work with the words?（Ⅰ）
你能灵活使用这些词汇了吗?（Ⅰ）

1. simulation　　　　　　a. hint

2. dissemble　　　　　　b. flippancy or joking when seriousness is required

3. intimation　　　　　　c. a sharing of grief

4. alleviation　　　　　　d. physical swaying; swinging action，as of a pendulum

5. levitate　　　　　　　e. a swinging back and forth in indecision

6. levity　　　　　　　　f. pretense

7. commiseration　　　　g. conflicted and contrary feelings

8. vacillation　　　　　　h. rise in the air（as by magic or illusion）

9. ambivalence　　　　　i. pretend

10. oscillation　　　　　　j. a lightening; a making less severe

KEY：1-f，2-i，3-a，4-j，5-h，6-b，7-c，8-e，9-g，10-d

Can you work with the words?（Ⅱ）
你能灵活使用这些词汇了吗?（Ⅱ）

1. dissimulate　　　　　　a. pretense of ignorance

2. dissemblance　　　　　b. a rising and floating in air

3. alleviative　　　　　　c. having simultaneous and contrary feelings

4. levitation   d. tending to swing back and forth in indecision

5. vacillatory   e. to swing back and forth like a pendulum

6. ambivalent   f. to hide real feelings by pretending opposite feelings

7. oscillate   g. tending to ease (pain, burdens, suffering, etc.)

KEY: 1-f, 2-a, 3-g, 4-b, 5-d, 6-c, 7-e

Do you understand the words?
你对这些词汇是否已经透彻地理解?

1. simulated—genuine   SAME   OPPOSITE
2. dissimulate—pretend   SAME   OPPOSITE
3. dissemble—be truthful   SAME   OPPOSITE
4. intimation—hint   SAME   OPPOSITE
5. alleviation—reduction   SAME   OPPOSITE
6. levitate—sink   SAME   OPPOSITE
7. levity—flippancy   SAME   OPPOSITE
8. vacillation—decisiveness   SAME   OPPOSITE
9. ambivalent—confused   SAME   OPPOSITE
10. oscillate—sway   SAME   OPPOSITE

KEY: 1-O, 2-S, 3-O, 4-S, 5-S, 6-O, 7-S, 8-O, 9-S, 10-S

Can you recall the words?
你能够写出这些词汇吗?

1. to swing back and forth — 1. O _____
2. feeling both ways at the same time (*adj.*) — 2. A _____
3. to conceal real feelings — 3. D _____ *or* D _____
4. pretense — 4. S _____
5. to pretend ignorance though knowing the facts — 5. D _____
6. joking; frivolity; flippancy — 6. L _____

7. indecisive

    7. V _____

    or V _____

8. to rise in the air, as by illusion

    8. L _____

9. tending to ease (pain, etc.)

    9. A _____

  (*adj.*)

    or A _____

10. a sharing of another's grief (*n.*)

    10. C _____

KEY: 1-oscillate, 2-ambivalent, 3-dissimulate *or* dissemble, 4-simulation, 5-dissemble, 6-levity, 7-vacillatory *or* vacillating, 8-levitate, 9-alleviative *or* alleviating, 10-commiseration

CHAPTER REVIEW
章节复习

A. Do you recognize the words?

你认识这些单词吗?

1. Complete exhaustion:

  (a) synergism, (b) enervation, (c) negation

2. Co-operation in producing effects:

  (a) synergy, (b) castigation, (c) capitulation

3. Lop off the head of:

  (a) castigate, (b) capitulate, (c) decapitate

4. deny; render ineffective:

  (a) castigate, (b) negate, (c) recapitulate

5. stagnate:

  (a) intimate, (b) simulate, (c) vegetate

6. concealment of true feelings:

  (a) simulation, (b) dissimulation, (c) dissemblance

7. sympathy:

  (a) levity, (b) ambivalence, (c) commiseration

8. indecisiveness:

  (a) vacillation, (b) oscillation, (c) dissimulation

9. aware of contrary feelings:

  (a) alleviative, (b) dissimulating, (c) ambivalent

KEY: 1-b, 2-a, 3-c, 4-b, 5-c, 6-b *and* c, 7-c, 8-a, 9-c

B. Can you recognize roots?

你能认出这些词根吗？

ROOT	MEANING	EXAMPLE
1. *nervus*	_____	enervate
2. *ergon*	_____	energy
3. *nego*	_____	self-abnegation
4. *caput, capitis*	_____	decapitate
5. *capitulum*	_____	recapitulate
6. *vegeto*	_____	vegetate
7. *simulo*	_____	dissimulate
8. *similis*	_____	similarity
9. *levis*	_____	levity
10. *intimus*	_____	intimation
11. *miser*	_____	commiserate
12. *vacillo*	_____	vacillate
13. *ambi-*	_____	ambivalent
14. *oscillum*	_____	oscillate

KEY：1-nerve, 2-work, 3-deny, 4-head, 5-little head, chapter heading, 6-live and grow, 7-to copy, 8-like, similar, 9-light, 10-innermost, 11-wretched, 12-swing back and forth, 13-both, 14-a swing

TEASER QUESTIONS FOR THE AMATEUR ETYMOLOGIST

词源小测验

We have previously met the Greek prefix *syn-*, together or with, in *synonym* ("names together") and *sympathy* ("feeling with"), and again in this chapter in *synergism* ("working together").

Syn- is a most useful prefix to know. Like Latin *con-*, (together or with) and *ad-* (to, toward), the final letter changes depending on the first letter of the root to which it is attached. *Syn-* becomes *sym-* before *b*, *m*, and *p*.

Can you construct some words using *syn-*, or *sym-*?

1. Etymologically, Jews are "led together" in a house of worship (*agogos*, leading). Can you construct the word for this temple or place of worship? _____

2. There is a process by which dissimilar organisms live together (*bios*, life) in close association, each in some way helping, and getting help from, the other (like the shark and the pilot fish). What word, ending in *-sis*, designates such a process? _____

What would the adjective form be? _____.

3. Using Greek *phone*, sound, write the word that etymologically refers to a musical composition in which the sounds of all instruments are in harmony together. _____. Using the suffix *-ic*, write the adjective form of this word: _____.

4. Combine *sym-* with *metron*, measurement, to construct a word designating similarity of shape on both sides (i. e., "measurement together"): _____. Write the adjective form of this word: _____.

5. *Syn-* plus *dromos*, a running, are the building blocks of a medical word designating a group of symptoms that occur (i, e., run) together in certain diseases. Can you figure out the word? _____.

6. The same *dromos*, a running, combines with Greek *hippos*, horse, to form a word referring to a place in ancient Greece in which horse and chariot races were run. The word? _____.

7. *Hippos*, horse, plus Greek *potamos*, river, combine to form a word designating one of the three pachyderms we discussed in an earlier chapter. The word?

_____.

(Answers in Chapter 18.)

（答案见第18章）

PICKING YOUR FRIENDS' BRAINS
听取朋友的见解

You can build your vocabulary, I have said, by increasing your familiarity with new ideas and by becoming alert to the new words you meet in your reading of magazines and books.

There is still another productive method, one that will be particularly applicable in view of all the new words you are learning from your study of these pages.

That method is *picking your friends' brains*.

Intelligent people are interested in words because words are symbols of ideas, and the person with an alert mind is always interested in ideas.

You may be amazed, if you have never tried it, to find that you can stir up an animated discussion by asking, in a social group that you attend, "What does ____ _____ mean?" (Use any word that particularly fascinates you.) Someone in the group is likely to know, and almost everyone will be willing to make a guess. From that point on, others in the group will ask

我已经反复强调，通过对新概念的熟悉和保持阅读杂志和书籍时的遇见新词的敏感度，你就能够不断扩充词汇。

但是，另外一个方法也能够使你快速、大量扩展词汇，而对于我们在本书中所学的所有词汇尤其适用。

直截了当地说，这个方法就是"听取朋友的见解"。

每个充满智慧的人都对词汇颇感兴趣，这很大程度上因为词汇是概念的象征；机警的头脑总是对概念感兴趣。

如果过去从未尝试，这个方法的效果会使你非常惊讶：在你所参加的社团中提出这样的问题："_____是什么意思?"（使用任何你感兴趣的词汇），你能够激发起活跃的讨论。社团中的某个人很可能了解这个词的含义，而且，几乎每个人都愿意参与词义的猜测。从这个问题出发，

questions about their own favorite words (most people do have favorites), or about words that they themselves have in some manner recently learned. As the discussion continues along these lines, you will be introduced to new words yourself, and if your friends have fairly good vocabularies you may strike a rich vein of pay dirt and come away with a large number of words to add to your vocabulary.

This method of picking your friends' brains is particularly fruitful because you will be learning not from a page of print (as in this book or as in your other reading) but from real live persons—the same sources that children use to increase their vocabularies at such prodigious rates. No learning is quite as effective as the learning that comes from other people—no information in print can ever be as vivid as information that comes from another human being. And so the words you pick up from your friends will have an amazingly strong appeal, will make a lasting impression on your mind.

Needless to say, your own rich vocabulary, now that you have come this far in the book, will make it possible for you to contribute to your friends' vocabulary as much as, if not more than, you take away—but since giving to others is one of the greatest sources of a feeling of self-worth, you can hardly complain about this extra dividend.

(End of Session 44)

社团中的其他人也会提出关于他们感兴趣的词汇的问题(大多数人还是能够说出自己感兴趣的词汇),或者是有关他们最近所学新词的问题。随着话题的继续,你自己了解到许多新词;如果你的朋友词汇量丰富,你也可能会挖到宝藏,从而进一步为自己的词汇库增添许多新词汇。

这个"听取朋友见解"的方法尤其有效,因为你的学习并不来源于一页印刷纸(例如本书或其他阅读材料),而是从真实的、活着的人口中得到——儿童能够以惊人的速度增加词汇量也正是使用了同样的方法。没有任何学习方法能够比从别人口中得到更为有效——以印刷形式出现的任何信息都无法达到从人类身上得到的信息那样生动逼真。所以,你从朋友口中学到的词汇会惊人地引人入胜,会给你留下长久的印象。

既然你已经学习到本书的这个部分,你的词汇量已经相当丰富,可能你给予朋友的新词汇并不比你从朋友那里得到的少,也许还要更多——但是因为给予是得到真正快乐的最有效渠道之一,你绝对不会抱怨这个额外的红利。

简短插叙九

TAKE THIS SPELLING TEST
拼写测验

Even in the most painstakingly edited of magazines, a silly little misspelling of a perfectly common word will occasionally appear. How the error eluded the collective and watchful eyes of the editor, the associate editor, the assistant editor, the type-setter, and the proofreader, no one will ever know—for practically every reader of the magazine spots it at once and writes an indignant letter, beginning: "Didn't you ever go to school...?"

即使经过了最缜密的编辑,杂志上的常见词语拼写仍然可能出现低级的小错误。没有人知道这样的错误如何逃脱编辑、副主编、助理主编、排字工作人员和校对人员共同的警觉监视——而事实是,几乎杂志的每个读者都能够马上看出错误,并愤愤不平地给出版社写信,信的开头是:"你难道没读过书吗……?"

Even if you went to school, you're going to have plenty of trouble spotting the one misspelled word in each group below. And not one of these words will be a de-mon like *sphygmomanometer* (a device for measuring blood pressure) or *piccalilli* (a highly seasoned relish), which no one would ever dare spell without first checking with a dictionary. On the contrary, every word will be of the common or garden variety that you might use every day in your social or business correspondence.

即使你读过书,将以下每组测验中的一个有拼写错误的词汇挑选出来也不是容易的事。这些词汇不是像 sphygmo-manometer(血压仪)或 piccalilli(辣泡菜)一样的魔鬼词汇,不查阅词典,任何正常人都不敢轻易拼写。相反,每个词都是日常社交和工作中使用的常用词。

Nevertheless, you're letting yourself in for ten minutes of real trouble, for you will be working with fifty particularly difficult spelling words. So put on your think-ing cap before you begin.

A half-dozen high school teachers who took this test were able to make an aver-age score of only five proper choices. Can you do better? Six or seven fight is *very good*, eight or nine right is *excellent*, and 100 percent success marks you as an abso-lute expert in English spelling.

但是,接下来的 10 分钟将是真正困难的 10 分钟,因为你要面对的是 50 个十分难拼写的词汇。所以在开始前要做好思想准备。

参与这个测验的 6 个高中老师的平均分数为 5 分。你能做得更好吗? 6 至 7 分是良好,8 至 9 分是优秀,如果全部答对,你绝对是英语拼写的权威专家。

Check the only misspelled word in each group.

要求:选出每组拼写有错误的词汇。

A：1-surprise，2-disappear，3-innoculate，4-description，5-recommend

B：1-privilege，2-separate，3-incidentally，4-dissipate，5-occurence

C：1-analyze，2-argument，3-assistant，4-comparative，5-truly

D：1-grammar，2-drunkeness，4-parallel，4-sacrilegious，5-conscience

E：1-precede，2-exceed，3-accede，4-procede，5-concede

F：1-pronunciation，2-noticable，3-desirable，4-holiday，5-anoint

G：1-wierd，2-seize，3-achieve，4-receive，5-leisure

H：1-superintendent，2-persistent，3-resistant，4-insistent，5-perseverence

I：1-accessible，2-permissible，3-inimitable，4-irresistable，5-irritable

J：1-pursue，2-pastime，3-kidnapped，4-rhythmical，5-exhillarate

KEY：A-3（inoculate），B-5（occurrence），C-1（analize），D-2（drunkenness），E-4（proceed），F-2（noticeable），G-1（weird），H-5（perseverance），I-4（irresistible），J-5（exhilarate）

16

HOW TO TALK ABOUT
A VARIETY OF PERSONAL CHARACTERISTICS
如何描述各种个性特征

(*Sessions 45 — 46*)

TEASER PREVIEW
引读

What word, ending in -*ous*, describes someone who is:

* *fawning, servilely attentive, transparently self-ingratiating?*
* *nagging, dissatisfied, complaining?*
* *snobbish, haughtily contemptuous, arrogant?*
* *noisily troublesome, unmanageable?*
* *habitually short of cash?*
* *attentive and courteous to women?*
* *harmless?*
* *fond of liquor?*
* *pale, gaunt, haggard?*
* *melancholy, sorrowful?*

哪个以-ous结尾的词汇能够恰当地描绘以下人物：

* 奉承的、卑躬屈膝的
* 爱抱怨的、爱发牢骚的
* 高傲的、目空一切的
* 吵闹的、难以管束的
* 总是没钱的、一贫如洗的
* 彬彬有礼的、殷勤的
* 无害的
* 嗜酒的
* 面色苍白的、面容枯槁的
* 悲伤的、悲哀的

SESSION 45
第 45 节

There are thousands of English words that end in the letters *-ous*—a Latin suffix meaning *full of*.

The central theme about which the words in this chapter revolve is the idea of "fullness"—and as you will shortly see, you can be full of compliance and servility; full of complaints; full of snobbery; full of noise; full of no money; full of horsemanship; full of harmlessness; full of liquor; full of deathly pallor; and full of sorrows.

For each of these ideas English has a word—and the person with a rich vocabularly knows the exact word to describe what someone is full of.

英语中有成千上万个词汇以-ous 结尾——这是一个表示"充满……的"拉丁后缀。

本章所讲词汇的核心就是这个"充满"的概念——你很快就会发现,你可能充满谄媚和奉承;充满牢骚;充满傲慢;充满噪音;充满了贫穷;充满骑士风度;充满无害性;充满酒精;充满死人一样的苍白;充满悲伤。

对于以上每个概念,英语中都有一个词汇与其对应——而词汇量丰富的人了解描述每种情况的准确词汇。

IDEAS
概念

1. compliance
服从

The Latin root *sequor* means to *follow*—and those who follow rather than lead are usually in a menial, subordinate, or inferior position. People who engage in certain fields of endeavor—waiters, clerks, and servants, for example—are forced, often contrary to their natural temperaments, to act excessively courteous, pleasant, obliging, even subservient and humble. They must follow the lead of their customers or employers, bending their own wills according to the desires of those they serve. They are, etymologically, *full of following after*, or—

obsequious

拉丁语词根 sequor 表示"跟随"——跟随而不去领导别人的人通常处于卑贱的、附属的或下级的地位。从事某些行业的人——例如:服务员、文员和仆人——不得不违逆自己的本性而表现出过度的礼貌、友好、热情,甚至屈从或者卑贱。他们必须"跟随"顾客或者雇主的领导,根据他们所服务的人的欲望改变自己的意愿。从词源上讲,他们"充满了跟随他人的心理",或者称他们为——obsequious。

RELATED WORDS:
相关词汇:

（1）*obsequies*—In a funeral cortege, the mourners *follow* after the corpse. Hence, *obsequies* are the burial ceremonies, the funeral rites.

（2）*subsequent*—A *subsequent* letter, paragraph, time, etc. is one that *follows* another.

（3）*sequel*—A *sequel* may be a literary work, such as a novel, that *follows* another, continuing the same subject, dealing with the same people or village, etc. or it may be an occurrence that grows out of or *follows* another, as in, "Just wait until you hear the *sequel* to the story!"

（4）*sequence*—In order, one item *following* another, as in, "The *sequence* of events of the next few days left him breathless."

(1) obsequies——在送葬列队中,送葬者会"跟随"尸体。这样,obsequies 指"葬礼,埋葬仪式"。

(2) subsequent——a subsequent letter, paragraph, time 等等是指"跟随"另外一个字母、段落、时间的事物。

(3) sequel——A sequel 可能是一部文学作品(例如小说)的"续集",是延续同样主题、"跟随"之前一部的另一部作品,主题是同样的人或村庄等等;也可能指出一个事件衍生出或"跟随"之前的事件出现的"结局",例如:"Just wait until you hear the sequel to the story!"(敬请等待故事的续集!)

(4) sequence——"顺序",一个事物接着另一个事物,例如:"The sequence of events of the next few days left him breathless."("接下来几天内发生的一系列事情使他喘不过气来。")

Any other word containing the root *sequ-* is likely to have some relationship to the idea of *following*.

任何其他包含"sequ-"词根的词汇都很可能与"跟随"的概念相关。

2. complaints

抱怨

The Latin root *queror* means *to complain*—and anyone full of complaints, constantly nagging, harping, fretful, petulant, whining, never satisfied, may accordingly be called—

querulous

拉丁语词根 queror 表示"抱怨"——这样的人心中满是抱怨,他们不停找茬、喋喋不休、狂躁不安、容易发怒、爱唠叨,从不感到满足。他们可以被称为——querulous。

3. snobbery

高傲

The Latin root *cilium* means *eyelid*; *super* means *above*; and above the eyelid, as anyone can plainly see, is the eyebrow. Now there are certain obnoxious people who go around raising their eyebrows in contempt, disdain, and sneering arrogance at ordinary mortals like you and me, Such contemptuous, sneering, overbearingly conceited people are called—

supercilious

拉丁语词根 cilium 表示"眼皮";super 表示"在……之上";每个人都知道,眼皮上面是眉毛。现在,总是有一些令人生厌的人,他们喜欢抬起眉毛,鄙视地、轻蔑的、傲慢地看着周围你我一样正常的人类。这样轻蔑的、傲慢的、极度自大的人被称为——supercilious。

4. noise

噪音

The Latin root *strepo* means *to make a noise*. Anyone who is unruly, boisterous, resistant to authority, unmanageable—and in a noisy, troublesome manner—is

obstreperous

拉丁语词根 strepo 表示"制造噪音"——任何任性的、喧闹的、不守规矩的、难以管理并且以吵闹、制造麻烦的方式表现出来 obstreperous。

5. moneyless

身无分文

The Latin root *pecus* means *cattle*—and at one time in human history a person's wealth was measured not by stocks and bonds but by stocks of domestic animals, which was a lot more logical, since you get milk and leather and meat from cattle—true wealth—and all you get from the stock market is a headache.

Someone who had lots of *pecus*, then, was rich—someone without *pecus* was indigent, destitute, "broke." And so today we call someone who is habitually without funds, who seems generally to be full of a complete lack of money—

impecunious

拉丁语词根 pecus 表示"牛"——在人类历史上某个时期,人的财富由饲养动物的多少来衡量,而不是股票和债券。这样的衡量方法似乎更符合逻辑,因为我们从牛身上可以得到牛奶、皮革和肉——真正的财富——我们从股票市场得到的只有头疼。

所以,任何拥有许多牛(pecus)的人都很富有——没有牛的人则贫穷、贫困、"一贫如洗"。今天,我们将那些经常没钱、生活中充满了没钱的状况的人称为——impecunious。

This word is not a synonym of *indigent*, *destitute*, or *poverty-stricken*; it does not necessarily imply living in reduced circumstances or want, but quite simply being short of cash—habitually.

注意这个词并不是 indigent、destitute 或 poverty-stricken 的同义词;它并没有暗示出生活在窘迫的环境下或贫困当中,只是缺钱——并习以为常。

RELATED WORD:
相关词汇:

pecuniary—pertaining to money, as in, a *pecuniary* consideration, *pecuniary* affairs, etc.

pecuniary——"金钱上的、与钱相关的",例如:a pecuniary consideration(出于金钱的考虑),pecuniary affairs(金钱事务),等等。

6. horses

马匹

The French word *cheval* means *horse*; and in medieval times only gentlemen and knights rode on horses—common people walked. Traditionally (but not, I understand, actually) knights were courteous to women, attentive to female desires, and self-sacrificing when their own interests came in conflict with those of the fair sex. Hence, we call a modern man who has a knightly attitude to women—

chivalrous

法语词根 cheval 表示"马";在中世纪,只有绅士和骑士骑马——普通百姓步行。根据传统(虽然我知道事实并非如此),骑士对女性彬彬有礼,关注女性的意愿,当自己的意愿与异性相冲突时,他们会自我牺牲。这样,我们将对女士具有骑士风度的现代男性称为——chivalrous。

RELATED WORDS:

相关词汇:

(*Cheval*, horse, comes from Latin *caballus*, an inferior horse. *Callabus* is found in English words in the spelling *caval-*.)

(cheval,"马",来自于拉丁词 caballus,是一种劣种马。caballus 在英语中拼写为 caval-。)

(1) *cavalcade*—A procession of persons on horseback, as in a parade.

(1) cavalcade——骑马队伍,例如游行时的队伍。

(2) *cavalier*—As a noun, a *cavalier* was once a mounted soldier. As an adjective, *cavalier* describes actions and attitudes that are haughty, unmindful of others' feelings, too offhand, such attributes often being associated with people in power (the military being one of the powers-that-be). Thus, "He answered in a *cavalier* manner" would signify that he was arrogant in his answer, as if the questioner were taking a little too much privilege with him. Or, "After the *cavalier* treatment I received, I never wished to return," signifying that I was pretty much made to feel unimportant and inferior. Or, "After her *cavalier* refusal, I'll never invite her to another party," signifying that the refusal was, perhaps, curt, offhand, without any attempt at apology or courtesy.

(2) cavalier——名词形式曾用来指骑兵。形容词形式用来形容自大的、对他人情感不屑一顾的、不礼貌的行为或态度,这样的品行常与有权势的人联系在一起(军人也是掌权者之一)。这样,"He answered in a cavalier manner."是指他的回答十分傲慢,就好像问话人沾了他太多的光一样。"After the cavalier treatment I received, I never wished to return,"表示出我受够了这种渺小的、低人一等的感觉。"After her cavalier refusal, I'll never invite her to another party,"表明了她的拒绝唐突无理、不假思索,没有一点道歉或礼貌的意思。

(3) *cavalry*—The mounted, or "horsed" part of an army.

(3) cavalry——骑兵部队。

(4) *chivalry*—Noun form of *chivalrous*. Can you write the alternate noun form ending in *-ness*? _____.

(4) chivalry—chivalrous 的名词形式,你能写出以-ness 结尾的另外一个名词形式吗? _____。

(5) *chivalric*—Less commonly used adjective form, identical in meaning to *chivalrous*.

(5) chivalric——是一种不太常用的形容词形式,意思和 chivalrous 一样。

Another Latin root for *horse*, as you know, is *equus*, found in words we have already discussed:

(1) *equestrian*—A horseman.

(2) *equestrienne*—A horsewoman.

(3) *equine*—Horselike.

另外一个表示马的拉丁词是 equus,包含这个词的英语词有:

(1) equestrian——骑手、骑马者、马戏演员;

(2) equestrienne——女骑手;

(3) equine——像马的。

7. no harm done

无害

The latin root *noceo* means to *injure*; someone who need cause you no fear, so harmless is that person, so unable to interfere, so unlikely to get you into trouble, is called—

innocuous

拉丁语词根 noceo 表示"伤害";有些人无需使你恐惧,他们不会给你带来伤害,不会打扰你,不会使你陷入困境,这些人被称为——innocuous。

RELATED WORDS:
相关词汇:

(1) *innocent*—Not guilty of crime or injury.

(2) *noxious*—Harmful, poisonous; unwholesome.

(1) innocent——无罪的、清白的;

(2) noxious——有害的、有毒的;令人厌恶的。

8. alcoholic

酒鬼

The Latin root *bibo* means to *drink*; and one who is generally found with one foot up on the brass rail, who likes to tipple beyond the point of sobriety—who, in short, has an overfondness for drinks with a pronounced alcoholic content, is called, usually humorously—

bibulous

拉丁语词根 bibo 表示"喝";有些人总是被发现一只腿翘起,搭在黄铜围栏上;他们总是喝酒喝到不清醒的地步——简而言之,他们过度喜爱富含酒精成分的饮料,这类人通常被幽默地称为——bibulous。

RELATED WORDS:
相关词汇:

(1) *imbibe*—To drink in, soak up, absorb. If we use this verb without specifying what is drunk, as in, "He likes to *imbibe*," the implication, of course, is always liquor; but *imbibe* may also be used in patterns like "*imbibe* learning" or "In early infancy she *imbibed* a respect for her parents."

(1) imbibe——喝、吸干、吸收。如果使用这个动词时不对饮料做特殊说明,例如"He likes to imbibe,"显然这里是指酒精饮品;但是,imbibe 也有其他用法,例如:"imbibe learning"(吸取知识)或"in early infancy she imbibed a respect for her parents."(幼年时她就学会了要尊重父母。)

(2) *bib*—Upper part of an apron, or an apronlike napkin tied around a child's neck. In either case, the *bib* prevents what is drunk (or eaten) from spilling over, or dribbling down, on the wearer's clothing.

(2) bib——围裙的上半部,或是一个系在孩子脖子上的、围裙似的餐巾。这两个用途都是避免喝(或吃)的东西溅在或滴在穿着者的衣服上。

9. like death itself

像死人一样的

The Latin root *cado* means *to fall*—one's final fall is of course always in death, and so someone who looks like a corpse (figuratively speaking), who is pale, gaunt, thin, haggard, eyes deep-sunk, limbs wasted, in other words the extreme opposite of the picture of glowing health, is called—

cadaverous

拉丁语词根 cado 表示"倒下"——当然，人们最后的"倒下"就是死亡；所以，如果一个人看起来好像尸体一般（打个比方），他会面色苍白、憔悴、骨瘦如柴、面容枯槁、眼球深陷、四肢无力。换句话说，他与容光焕发恰好是完全相反的状态，这样的状态被称为——cadaverous。

RELATED WORDS:

相关词汇:

(1) *cadaver*—A corpse, literally, especially one used for surgical dissection.

(1) cadaver——从字面上看，表示"死尸"，尤其是用于外科解剖的尸体。

(2) *decadent*—Etymologically, "*falling down*" (*de-* is a prefix one meaning of which is *down*, as in *descend*, climb down; *decline*, turn down; etc.). If something is in a *decadent* state, it is deteriorating, becoming corrupt or demoralized. *Decadence* is a state of decay. Generally *decadent* and *decadence* are used figuratively—they refer not to actual physical decay (as of a dead body), but to moral or spiritual decay.

(2) decadent——从词源理解，表示"落下"（de 是表示"向下"的前缀，例如 descend 表示"爬下来"；decline 表示"拒绝"；等等）。如果某种事物处于 decadent 状态，它就是在腐化，变得越来越堕落、颓废。decadence 表示 decay 的状态。decadent 和 decadence 通常都用作比喻含义——它们并不指实际身体上的腐烂（例如死尸），而是道德或精神上的腐朽。

10. pain and misery

痛苦与悲哀

The Latin root *doleo* means *to suffer* or *grieve*—one who is mournful and sad, whose melancholy comes from physical pain or mental distress, who seems to be suffering or grieving, is called—

dolorous

拉丁语词根 doleo 表示"遭受痛苦"——一个哀痛的、悲伤的人，遭受身体痛苦或精神苦恼的人被称为——dolorous。

RELATED WORDS:

相关词汇:

(1) *dolor*—A poetic synonym of *grief*.

(1) dolor——是 grief（悲哀）的同义词，更具有诗意。

(2) *doleful*—A word referring somewhat humorously to exaggerated dismalness, sadness, or dreariness.

(2) doleful——用来形容夸张的惨烈、悲哀或沮丧，具有某种程度的幽默口吻。

(3) *condole*—Etymologically, to suffer or grieve with (Latin *con-*, with, togeth-

er). *Condole* is a somewhat less commonly used synonym of *commiserate*, a verb we discussed in Chapter 15. The noun *condolence* is much more frequently heard than the verb, as in, "Let me offer you my *condolences*," usually said to someone mourning the death of a friend or relative. You have heard of *condolence* cards, and no doubt have sent your share of them. When you *condole* with somebody who has sustained a loss, usually by death, you are saying, in effect, "I am suffering or grieving with you."

　　(3) condole——从词源上看,意为"一起受苦"或"一起悲伤"(拉丁语中 con-,意为"和""一起")。condole 是 commiserate 一个较少使用的同义词(我们在第 15 章讨论过的一个动词)。condolence 比其他动词常见,如 Let me offer you my condolences(向你表示哀悼)经常表示对别人亲友的死表示哀悼。你一定听说过慰问卡,并且无疑已用过。当你"condole"那些遭受某种损失(通常是与死亡相关)的人时,事实上,你就是在说:"我对你的痛苦和悲哀感同身受!"

REVIEW OF ETYMOLOGY
复习词源

PREFIX, ROOT, SUFFIX	MEANING	ENGLISH WORD
1. *sequor*	to follow	
2. *queror*	to complain	
3. *cilium*	eyelid	
4. *super*	above	
5. *strepo*	to make a noise	
6. *pecus*	cattle	
7. *-ary*	adjective suffix	
8. *im-* (*in-*)	negative prefix	
9. *cheval*	horse	
10. *callabus* (*caval-*)	inferior horse	
11. *-ous*	adjective suffix	
12. *-ic*	adjective suffix	
13. *equus*	horse	
14. *-ine*	like, similar to, characteristic of	
15. *bibo*	to drink	
16. *im-* (*in-*)	in	
17. *cado*	to fall	
18. *de-*	down	
19. *-ent*	adjective suffix	
20. *-ence*	noun suffix	
21. *con-*	with, together	

USING THE WORDS
单词应用

A. THE BASIC WORDS
　　基础单词

Can you pronounce the words?
你能读出这些单词吗?

1.	*obsequious*	ob-SEEK′-wee-əs
2.	*querulous*	KWAIR′-ə-ləs
3.	*supercilious*	soo′-pər-SIL′-ee-əs
4.	*obstreperous*	əb-STREP′-ər-əs
5.	*impecunious*	im′-pə-KYOO′-nee-əs
6.	*chivalrous*	SHIV′-əl-rəs
7.	*innocuous*	ə-NOK′-yoo-əs
8.	*bibulous*	BIB′-yə-ləs
9.	*cadaverous*	kə-DAV′-ər-əs
10.	*dolorous*	DOL′-ər-əs *or* DŌ′-lər-əs

Can you work with the words? (Ⅰ)
你能灵活使用这些词汇了吗? (Ⅰ)

1.	obsequious	a.	snobbish
2.	querulous	b.	harmless
3.	supercilious	c.	gaunt
4.	obstreperous	d.	short of funds
5.	impecunious	e.	fawning; excessively, ingratiatingly, polite
6.	chivalrous	f.	sorrowful
7.	innocuous	g.	addicted to drink
8.	bibulous	h.	courteous to women
9.	cadaverous	i.	complaining
10.	dolorous	j.	unmanageable

KEY: 1-e, 2-i, 3-a, 4-j, 5-d, 6-h, 7-b, 8-g, 9-c, 10-f

Can you work with the words? (Ⅱ)
你能灵活使用这些词汇了吗? (Ⅱ)

Match each word in the first column with one from the second column that is *opposite* in meaning.

1. obsequious	a. content; uncomplaining; satisfied
2. querulous	b. affluent
3. supercilious	c. healthy
4. obstreperous	d. rude
5. impecunious	e. sober
6. chivalrous	f. dangerous
7. innocuous	g. humble
8. bibulous	h. misogynous
9. cadaverous	i. happy; cheerful
10. dolorous	j. quiet

KEY: 1-d, 2-a, 3-g, 4-j, 5-b, 6-h, 7-f, 8-e, 9-c, 10-i

Do you understand the words?

你对这些词汇是否已经透彻地理解?

1. Do *obsequious* people, usually command our respect?	YES	NO
2. Are *querulous* people satisfied?	YES	NO
3. Are *supercilious* people usually popular?	YES	NO
4. Is a person of affluence *impecunious*?	YES	NO
5. Do some women like *chivalrous* men?	YES	NO
6. Are *innocuous* people dangerous?	YES	NO
7. Is a *bibulous* character a teetotaler?	YES	NO
8. Is a *cadaverous*-looking individual the picture of health?	YES	NO
9. Is a *dolorous* attitude characteristic of jovial people?	YES	NO
10. Is an *obstreperous* child difficult to manage?	YES	NO

KEY: 1-no, 2-no, 3-no, 4-no, 5-yes, 6-no, 7-no, 8-no, 9-no, 10-yes

Can you recall the words?

你能够写出这些词汇吗?

1. sorrowful	1. D _____
2. servilely attentive; overly polite	2. O _____
3. haggard; gaunt; pale	3. C _____

4. complaining; whining

5. addicted to alcohol; likely to drink past the point of sobriety

6. arrogant; haughty

7. harmless

8. noisily unmanageable

9. attentive and courteous to women

10. short of money; without funds

4. Q _____

5. B _____

6. S _____

7. I _____

8. O _____

9. C _____

10. I _____

KEY: 1-dolorous, 2-obsequious, 3-cadaverous, 4-querulous, 5-bibulous, 6-supercilious, 7-innocuous, 8-obstreperous, 9-chivalrous, 10-impecunious

(End of Session 45)

SESSION 46
第 46 节

B. RELATED WORDS
相关词汇

Can you pronounce the words? (I)
你能读出这些单词吗? (I)

1.	*obsequies*	OB′-sə-kweez
2.	*subsequent*	SUB′-sə-kwənt
3.	*sequel*	SEE′-kwəl
4.	*sequence*	SEE′-kwəns
5.	*pecuniary*	pə-KYŌŌ′-nee-air′-ee
6.	*noxious*	NOK′-shəs
7.	*imbibe*	im-BĪB′
8.	*dolor*	DŌ′-lər
9.	*doleful*	DŌL′-fəl
10.	*cavalcade*	KAV′-əl-kayd′
11.	*cavalier* (*adj.*)	kav-ə-LEER′

Can you pronounce the words? (II)
你能读出这些单词吗? (II)

1.	*cavalry*	KAV′-əl-ree
2.	*chivalry*	SHIV′-əl-ree
3.	*chivalric*	shə-VAL′-rik
4.	*condole*	kən-DŌL′
5.	*condolence*	kən-DŌ′-ləns
6.	*equestrian*	ə-KWES′-tree-ən
7.	*equestrienne*	ə-KWES′-tree-en′
8.	*equine*	EE′-kwīn′
9.	*cadaver*	kə-DAV′-ər *or* kə-DAY′-vər
10.	*decadent*	DEK′-ə-dənt *or* də-KAY′-dənt
11.	*decadence*	DEK′-ə-dəns *or* də-KAY′-dəns

Can you work with the words?
你能灵活使用这些词汇了吗?

1.	obsequies	a. proper order
2.	subsequent	b. drink; absorb; take in

3. sequel	c. harmful, poisonous
4. sequence	d. pain, sorrow (*poetic*)
5. pecuniary	e. coming later or afterward
6. noxious	f. procession of mounted riders
7. imbibe	g. offhand, haughty
8. dolor	h. a following event or literary work
9. doleful	i. horsewoman
10. cavalcade	j. pertaining to money
11. cavalier (*adj.*)	k. mounted military division; soldiers on horseback
12. cavalry	l. funeral rites
13. equestrian	m. exaggeratedly sorrowful
14. equestrienne	n. horselike
15. equine	o. horseman
16. cadaver	p. spiritual decline
17. decadent	q. morally decaying
18. decadence	r. corpse
19. chivalry	s. expression of sympathy
20. condolence	t. gallant courtesy to women

KEY：1-l，2-e，3-h，4-a，5-j，6-c，7-b，8-d，9-m，10-f，11-g，12-k，13-o，14-i，15-n，16-r，17-q，18-p，19-t，20-s

Do you understand the words? (Ⅰ)

你对这些词汇是否已经透彻地理解？(Ⅰ)

1. Are speeches usually made during *obsequies*?　　　　　　　　　YES　　NO

2. Did Margaret Mitchell write a *sequel* to *Gone with the Wind*?　　　　YES　　NO

3. Are these numbers in *sequence*：5，6，7，8，9，10，11?　　　　　YES　　NO

4. Do banks often handle the *pecuniary* details of an estate?　　　　　YES　　NO

5. Is arsenic a *noxious* chemical?　　　　YES　　NO

6. Do children sometimes *imbibe* wisdom from their parents?　　　　　YES　　NO

7. If a song is sung in tones of *dolor*，is it a happy song?　　　　　　YES　　NO

8. Is a *doleful* countenance a happy one?	YES	NO
9. Does a *cavalcade* contain horses?	YES	NO
10. Does a *cavalier* attitude show a spirit of humility?	YES	NO

KEY：1-yes，2-no，3-yes，4-yes，5-yes，6-yes，7-no，8-no，9-yes，10-no

Do you understand the words? (II)
你对这些词汇是否已经透彻地理解? (II)

1. Is a *cavalry* officer usually a good horseman?	YES	NO
2. Would an *equestrian* statue of General Grant show him with or on a horse?	YES	NO
3. Is an *equestrienne* a man?	YES	NO
4. Do humans possess many *equine* characteristics?	YES	NO
5. Is a *cadaver* alive?	YES	NO
6. Is an iconoclast likely to consider religion a *decadent* institution?	YES	NO
7. Is *decadence* a desirable quality?	YES	NO
8. Is *chivalry* dead?	YES	NO
9. Is it appropriate to *condole* with someone who has suffered a loss through death?	YES	NO
10. Are *condolences* appropriate at a wedding ceremony?	YES	NO

KEY：1-yes，2-yes，3-no，4-no，5-no，6-yes，7-no，8-yes，*or* no, depending on your point of view，9-yes，10-no (unless you're misogamous)

Do you understand the words? (III)
你对这些词汇是否已经透彻地理解? (III)

1. obsequies—rites	SAME	OPPOSITE
2. subsequent—preceding	SAME	OPPOSITE
3. pecuniary—financial	SAME	OPPOSITE
4. sequence—order	SAME	OPPOSITE
5. noxious—harmful	SAME	OPPOSITE

6. imbibe—drink	SAME	OPPOSITE
7. dolor—delight	SAME	OPPOSITE
8. doleful—merry	SAME	OPPOSITE
9. cavalier—courteous	SAME	OPPOSITE
10. cadaver—corpse	SAME	OPPOSITE
11. decadent—resurgent	SAME	OPPOSITE
12. chivalry—gallantry to women	SAME	OPPOSITE
13. condolences—congratulations	SAME	OPPOSITE

KEY：1-S，2-O，3-S，4-S，5-S，6-S，7-O，8-O，9-O，10-S，11-O，12-S，13-O

Can you recall the words?

你能够写出这些词汇吗?

1. harmful	1. N _____
2. a literary work or an event that follows another	2. S _____
3. drink in	3. I _____
4. poetic word for sorrow	4. D _____
5. burial ceremonies	5. O _____
6. horseman	6. E _____
7. horsewoman	7. E _____
8. horselike	8. E _____
9. following (*adj.*)	9. S _____
10. relating to money (*adj.*)	10. P _____
11. exaggeratedly sad	11. D _____
12. proper order	12. S _____
13. parade of mounted riders	13. C _____
14. offhand; unmindful of another's feelings	14. C _____
15. mounted soldiers	15. C _____
16. a corpse	16. C _____
17. morally deteriorating (*adj.*)	17. D _____
18. spiritual decay	18. D _____
19. expression of sympathy	19. C _____
20. gallantry to women	20. C _____

KEY：1-noxious，2-sequel，3-imbibe，4-dolor，5-obsequies，6-equestrian，7-equestrienne，8-equine，9-subsequent，10-pecuniary，11-doleful，12-sequence，

13-cavalcade，14-cavalier，15-cavalry，16-cadaver，17-decadent，18-decadence，19-condolence，20-chivalry *or* chivalrousness

CHAPTER REVIEW
章节复习

A. Do you recognize the words?

你认识这些单词吗？

1. Excessively polite and fawning：
   (a) querulous，(b) obsequious，(c) supercilious
2. Noisily troublesome：
   (a) querulous，(b) impecunious，(c) obstreperous
3. Courteous and attentive to women：
   (a) querulous，(b) chivalrous，(c) supercilious
4. Complaining，nagging：
   (a) querulous，(b) supercilious，(c) innocuous
5. Haughtily disdainful：
   (a) supercilious，(b) bibulous，(c) dolorous
6. Gaunt，corpselike：
   (a) noxious，(b) cadaverous，(c) doleful
7. Highhanded：
   (a) supercilious，(b) cavalier，(c) decadent
8. Moral decay：
   (a) decadence，(b) obsequies，(c) sequence
9. Expression of sympathy：
   (a) bibulousness，(b) dolefulness，(c) condolence
10. Courtesy to women：
    (a) dolor，(b) chivalry，(c) decadence

KEY：1-b，2-c，3-b，4-a，5-a，6-b，7-b，8-a，9-c，10-b

B. Can you recognize roots?

你能认出这些词根吗？

ROOT	MEANING	EXAMPLE
1. *sequor*		subsequent
2. *queror*		querulous
3. *cilium*		supercilious
4. *super*		supervision
5. *strepo*		obstreperous

6. *pecus*	_____	pecuniary
7. *cheval*	_____	chivalry
8. *caballus* (*caval-*)	_____	cavalier
9. *equus*	_____	equine
10. *cado*	_____	decadence

KEY: 1-to follow, 2-to complain, 3-eyelid, 4-above, 5-to make a noise, 6-cattle, 7-horse, 8-(inferior) horse, 9-horse, 10-to fall

TEASER QUESTIONS FOR THE AMATEUR ETYMOLOGIST
词源小测验

1. In logic, a conclusion not based on the evidence is called a *non sequitur*; by extension, the term is applied to any statement that appears to have no connection or relevance to what was said before. Knowing the root *sequor*, how would you define this term etymologically? _____

_____.

2. *Sequor*, like many other Latin verbs, has another form somewhat differently spelled. (Remember *verto*, *versus* and *loquor*, *locutus*?) The other form of *sequor* is *secutus*. Can you define the following words in terms of the root?

(a) second: _____

(b) consecutive: _____

(c) persecute: _____

(d) prosecute: _____

3. Latin *super*, above or over, is used as a prefix in hundreds of English words. Can you figure out the word starting with *super-* that fits each etymological definition?

(a) above others (in quality, position, etc.) _____

_____

(b) above the surface; not in depth (*adj.*) _____

_____

(c) (flowing) above what is necessary; more than needed (*adj.*) _____

(d) above (or beyond) the natural (*adj.*) _____

_____

(e) to oversee; be in charge of (*v.*) _____

4. *Cado*, to fall, is found in the following English words (sometimes the root is spelled *-cid*). Can you define each word in terms of its etymological parts?

(a) cadence: _____

    (b) occidental: _____

    (c) deciduous: _____

    (d) incident: _____

    (e) accident: _____

    (f) coincidence: _____

    5. The negative prefix *in-* plus *doleo*, to suffer, forms an adjective that *etymologically* means *not suffering* (*pain*), but *actually* means *idle; lazy; disliking effort or work*. Can you figure out the English word? _____.
Can you write the noun form? _____.

    6. What does the feminine name Dolores mean etymologically? _____.

(End of Session 46)

Brief Intermission Ten
简短插叙十

ANOTHER CHECK ON YOUR SPELLING
另一个拼写测验

In each line you will find four words—one of them purposely, subtly, and perhaps unexpectedly misspelled. It's up to you to check the single error. If you can come out on top at least fifteen times out of twenty, you're probably a better speller than you realize.

每道题给出了四个词汇——其中有一个是有目的地、刻意拼写错误的词汇,也可能是意外的错误。由你来找出这个唯一的错误。如果 20 道题能够答对 15 道以上,你的拼写可能要比自己想象中厉害得多。

1. (a) alright, (b) coolly, (c) supersede, (d) disappear
2. (a) inoculate, (b) definately, (c) irresistible, (d) recommend
3. (a) incidentally, (b) dissipate, (c) seperate, (d) balloon
4. (a) argument, (b) ecstasy, (c) occurrance, (d) analyze
5. (a) sacrilegious, (b) weird, (c) pronunciation, (d) repitition
6. (a) drunkeness, (b) embarrassment, (c) weird, (d) irritable
7. (a) noticeable, (b) superintendant, (c) absence, (d) development
8. (a) vicious, (b) conscience, (c) panicy, (d) amount
9. (a) accessible, (b) pursue, (c) exhilarate, (d) insistant
10. (a) naivete, (b) necessary, (c) catagory, (d) professor
11. (a) rhythmical, (b) sergeant, (c) vaccuum, (d) assassin
12. (a) benefitted, (b) allotted, (c) corroborate, (d) despair
13. (a) diphtheria, (b) grandeur, (c) rediculous, (d) license
14. (a) tranquillity, (b) symmetry, (c) occassionally, (d) privilege
15. (a) tarriff, (b) tyranny, (c) battalion, (d) archipelago
16. (a) bicycle, (b) geneology, (c) liquefy, (d) bettor
17. (a) defense, (b) batchelor, (c) stupefy, (d) parallel
18. (a) whisky, (b) likable, (c) bookkeeper, (d) accomodate
19. (a) comparitive, (b) mayonnaise, (c) indispensable, (d) dexterous
20. (a) dictionary, (b) cantaloupe, (c) existance, (d) ukulele

KEY：1-a（all right），2-b（definitely），3-c（separate），4-c（occurrence），5-d（repetition），6-a（drunkenness），7-b（superintendent），8-c（panicky），9-d（insistent），10-c（category），11-c（vacuum），12-a（benefited），13-c（ridiculous），14-c（occasionally），15-a（tariff），16-b（genealogy），17-b（bachelor），18-d（accommodate），19-a（comparative），20-c（existence）

17

HOW TO CHECK YOUR PROGRESS
如何检验你的进步

(Comprehensive Test III)

SESSION 47
第 47 节

I. etymology

ROOT	MEANING	EXAMPLE
1. *fluo*		affluent
2. *pheme*		euphemism
3. *platys*		platitude
4. *felis*		feline
5. *piscis*		piscine
6. *nostos*		nostalgia
7. *kakos*		cacophony
8. *carnis*		carnivorous
9. *voro*		voracious
10. *omnis*		omnivorous
11. *potens, potentis*		impotent
12. *ubique*		ubiquity
13. *lupus*		lupine
14. *doleo*		dolorous
15. *porcus*		porcine
16. *thanatos*		euthanasia
17. *canis*		canine
18. *vulpus*		vulpine
19. *algos*		nostalgic
20. *odyne*		anodyne
21. *logos*		eulogy

22. *sciens，scientis* _____ omniscient
23. *ursus* _____ ursine
24. *phone* _____ euphonious
25. *penuria* _____ penury

Ⅱ. more etymology

ROOT，PREFIX   EXAMPLE

1. *nervus* _____ enervate
2. *ergon* _____ energy
3. *nego* _____ negation
4. *caput，capitis* _____ decapitate
5. *capitulum* _____ recapitulate
6. *vegeto* _____ vegetate
7. *simulo* _____ simulate
8. *similis* _____ similarity
9. *levis* _____ alleviate
10. *intimus* _____ intimate (*v.*)
11. *miser* _____ commiserate
12. *vacillo* _____ vacillate
13. *ambi-* _____ ambivalent
14. *oscillum* _____ oscillate
15. *sequor，secutus* _____ obsequious
16. *queror* _____ querulous
17. *cilium* _____ supercilious
18. *super-* _____ superior
19. *strepo* _____ obstreperous
20. *pecus* _____ impecunious
21. *equus* _____ equine
22. *caballus（caval-）* _____ cavalier
23. *loquor，locutus* _____ circumlocution
24. *cado* _____ decadence
25. *vanesco* _____ evanescent

Ⅲ. same or opposite

1. penury—affluence   S   O
2. vicarious—secondhand   S   O
3. ephemeral—evanescent   S   O
4. badinage—persiflage   S   O

5.	cacophony—euphony	S	O
6.	clandestine—surreptitious	S	O
7.	parsimonious—extravagant	S	O
8.	indigent—opulent	S	O
9.	destitute—impecunious	S	O
10.	euphemistic—indirect	S	O
11.	cliché—bromide	S	O
12.	platitudinous—original	S	O
13.	voracious—gluttonous	S	O
14.	omniscient—ignorant	S	O
15.	omnipresent—ubiquitous	S	O
16.	carnal—libidinous	S	O
17.	carnage—slaughter	S	O
18.	enervated—exhilarated	S	O
19.	castigate—condone	S	O
20.	simulate—pretend	S	O

IV. matching

WORDS	DEFINITIONS
1. alleviating	a. excessively polite or servile
2. cavalier (*adj.*)	b. gaunt，corpselike
3. vacillating	c. noisy
4. obsequious	d. poisonous
5. querulous	e. highhanded
6. obstreperous	f. sad
7. innocuous	g. nagging；complaining
8. cadaverous	h. harmless
9. dolorous	i. soothing
10. noxious	j. constantly changing one's mind

V. more matching

1. condolence	a. a rising into the air
2. decadent	b. harsh sound
3. levity	c. powerlessness
4. levitation	d. a return to life in a new form
5. surreptitious	e. devouring all；eating everything
6. cacophony	f. expression of sympathy
7. reincarnation	g. cowlike；phlegmatic；stolid

8. omnivorous   h. morally deteriorating
9. impotence   i. joking
10. bovine   j. stealthy，secret

VI. recall a word

1. lionlike   1. L _____
2. doglike   2. C _____
3. catlike   3. F _____
4. piglike   4. P _____
5. foxlike   5. V _____
6. bearlike   6. U _____
7. horselike   7. E _____
8. all-powerful   8. O _____
9. in the flesh   9. I _____
10. to stagnate   10. V _____
11. secret   11. C _____
12. meat-eating (*adj.*)   12. C _____
13. lasting a very short time   13. E _____
14. stingy; tight-fisted   14. P _____
                                   or P _____
15. feeling contradictory ways at 15. A _____
    the same time (*adj.*)
16. speech of praise   16. E _____
17. a feeling of well-being, both 17. E _____
    physical and emotional
18. statement intended to allay   18. A _____
    pain or anxiety
19. mercy death   19. E _____
20. science of speech sounds   20. P _____
21. all-powerful   21. O _____
22. to give in; to stop resisting 22. C _____
23. a working together for greater 23. S _____
    effect   *or* S _____
24. to behead   24. D _____
25. relating to, pertaining to, or 25. P _____
    involving money (*adj.*)
26. harmless   26. I _____
27. tending to drink a lot (*adj.*) 27. B _____

28. to express sympathy; to share
　　suffering, pain, or grief (with)
29. snobbish; contemptuous;
　　haughty; arrogant
30. mounted soldiers

28. C ＿＿＿＿＿＿＿＿＿＿＿
　or C ＿＿＿＿＿＿＿＿＿＿＿
29. S ＿＿＿＿＿＿＿＿＿＿＿

30. C ＿＿＿＿＿＿＿＿＿＿＿

KEY: A correct answer counts one point. Score your points for each part of the test, then add for a total.

I

1-to flow, 2-voice, 3-flat, broad, 4-cat, 5-fish, 6-a return, 7-harsh, bad, ugly; 8-flesh, 9-to devour, 10-all, 11-powerful, 12-everywhere, 13-wolf, 14-to suffer, grieve, 15-pig, 16-death, 17-dog, 18-fox, 19-pain, 20-pain, 21-word, speech, 22-knowing, 23-bear, 24-sound, 25-want, neediness

Your score: ＿＿＿＿＿＿＿

II

1-nerve, 2-work, 3-to deny, 4-head, 5-little head, chapter heading, 6-to live and grow, 7-to copy, 8-like, similar, 9-light, 10-innermost, 11-wretched, 12-to swing back and forth, 13-both, 14-a swing, 15-to follow, 16-to complain, 17-eyelid, 18-above, 19-to make a noise, 20-cattle, 21-horse, 22-(inferior) horse, 23-to speak, 24-to fall, 25-to vanish

Your score: ＿＿＿＿＿＿＿

III

1-O, 2-S, 3-S, 4-S, 5-O, 6-S, 7-O, 8-O, 9-S, 10-S, 11-S, 12-O, 13-S, 14-O, 15-S, 16-S, 17-S, 18-O, 19-O, 20-S

Your score: ＿＿＿＿＿＿＿

IV

1-i, 2-e, 3-j, 4-a, 5-g, 6-c, 7-h, 8-b, 9-f, 10-d

Your score: ＿＿＿＿＿＿＿

V

1-f, 2-h, 3-i, 4-a, 5-j, 6-b, 7-d, 8-e, 9-c, 10-g

Your score: ＿＿＿＿＿＿＿

VI

1-leonine, 2-canine, 3-feline, 4-porcine, 5-vulpine, 6-ursine, 7-equine, 8-omnipotent, 9-incarnate, 10-vegetate, 11-clandestine, 12-carnivorous, 13-ephemeral, 14-penurious *or* parsimonious, 15-ambivalent, 16-eulogy, 17-euphoria, 18-anodyne, 19-euthanasia, 20-phonetics, 21-omnipotent, 22-capitulate, 23-synergism *or* syner-

gy，24-decapitate，25-pecuniary，26-innocuous，27-bibulous，28-condole *or* commis-
erate，29-supercilious，30-cavalry

Your score：＿＿＿＿＿＿＿＿

Your total score：＿＿＿＿＿＿＿＿

Significance of Your Total Score：

100—120：Masterly

80—99：Good

65—79：Average

50—64：Barely acceptable

35—49：Poor

0—34：Terrible！

Record your score in the appropriate space below as well as your scores from Chapters 8 and 13. You will then have a comparison chart of all three achievement tests.

你的总分的意义：

100—120：出色

80—99：不错

65—79：一般

50—64：勉强可接受

35—49：很差

0—34：很糟糕

在下面的空格中同时填上你在第 8 章和第 13 章的测试成绩。你会看到三个测试成绩的对比情况。

SCORES

TEST I (Chapter 8)：＿＿＿＿＿＿＿＿＿＿＿＿＿ out of 120.

TEST II (Chapter 13)：＿＿＿＿＿＿＿＿＿＿＿ out of 120.

TEST III (Chapter 17)：＿＿＿＿＿＿＿＿＿＿ out of 120.

(End of Session 47)

18

HOW TO CHECK YOUR STANDING AS
AN AMATEUR ETYMOLOGIST
如何检验你对词源掌握的程度

(*Answers to Teaser Questions in*
Chapters 3-7, 9-12, and 14-16)

CHAPTER 3:

1. *Anthropocentric* (an'-thrə-pə-SEN'-trik), an adjective built on *anthropos*, mankind; Greek *kentron*, center, and the adjective suffux *-ic*, describes thinking, assumptions, reasoning, etc. that see mankind as the central fact, or ultimate aim, of the universe. The noun forms are either *anthropocentrism* (an'-thrə-pə-SEN'-triz-əm) or *anthropocentricity* (an'-thrə-pō'-sən-TRIS'-ə-tee).

2. *Andromania* (an'-drə-MAY'-nee-ə), a combination of *andros*, man (male), plus *mania*, madness, signifies an obsession with males. Person: *andromaniac*, one who is mad about men; adjective: *andromaniacal* (an'-drə-mə-NĪ'-ə-kəl).

3. *Gynandrous* (jī-NAN'-drəs), combining *gyne*, woman, with *andros*, man (male), describes:

a. plants in which the male and female organs are united in the same column; *or*

b. people who physically have both male and female sexual organs, often one or both in rudimentary form; *or*

c. (*a more recent meaning*) people who exhibit, or are willing to own up to, the male *and* female *emotional* characteristics that everyone possesses.

The word may have the roots in reverse, becoming *androgynous* (an-DROJ'-ə-nəs), with all three meanings identical to those of *gynandrous*.

Hermaphroditic (hur-maf'-rə-DIT'-ik), a combination of *Hermes*, the Greek god who served as messenger or herald (in Roman mythology, this god was known as *Mercury*, and is conventionally pictured with wings on his heels), and *Aphrodite*, the Greek goddess of love and beauty (in Roman mythology, *Venus*), has either of the first two meanings of *gynandrous*.

The noun form of *gynandrous* is *gynandry* (ji-NAN′-dree); of *androgynous*, *androgyny* (an-DROJ′-ə-nee); of *hermaphroditic*, *hermaphroditism* (hur-MAF′-rə-di′-tiz-əm).

The individual plant is an *andrognye* (AN′-drə-jin); plant or person, a *hermaphrodite* (hur-MAF′-rə-dīt′).

4. *Monomania* (mon-ə-MAY′-nee-ə), combining *monos*, one, and *mania*, madness, is an obsession with one thing, or obsessiveness in one area. Person: *monomaniac*; adjective: *monomaniacal* (mon′-ə-mə-NĪ′-ə-kəl).

5. A *misandrist* (mis-AN′-drist), combining *misein*, to hate, with *andros*, man (male), hates men. Noun: *misandry* (mis-AN′-dree). Adjective: *misandrous* (mis-AN′-drəs).

Check your learning

ROOT	MEANING	EXAMPLE
1. *anthropos*	_____	anthropocentric
2. *kentron*	_____	anthropocentrism
3. *andros*	_____	andromania
4. *mania*	_____	andromaniac
5. *gyne*	_____	gynandrous
6. *Hermes*	_____	hermaphrodite
7. *Aphrodite*	_____	hermaphroditic
8. *monos*	_____	monomania
9. *misein*	_____	misandry

KEY: 1-mankind, 2-center, 3-man (male), 4-madness, 5-woman, 6-Hermes, the messenger of the gods, 7-Aphrodite, goddess of love and beauty, 8-one, 9-to hate

CHAPTER 4:

1. *Pedodontia* (pee-də-DON′-shə) is the specialty of child dentistry—*paidos*, child, plus *odontos*, tooth. Specialist: *pedodontist*. Adjective: *pedodontic*.

2. *Cardialgia* (kahr′-dee-AL′-jə), heart pain—*kardia*, heart, plus *algos*, pain.

3. *Odontalgia* (ō′-don-TAL′-jə), toothache.

4. *Nostalgia* (nos-TAL′-jə). Adjective: *nostalgic*.

Check your learning

PREFIX, ROOT	MEANING	EXAMPLE
1. *padios* (*ped-*)	_____	pedodontia

2. *kardia*	_____	cardialgia
3. *algos*	_____	odontalgia
4. *odontos*	_____	pedodontist
5. *nostos*	_____	nostalgia

KEY：1-child，2-heart，3-pain，4-tooth，5-a return

CHAPTER 5：

1. Eighty to eighty-nine years old. From Latin *octoginta*, eighty. People of other ages are as follows：

(a) 50—59：*quinquagenartan* (kwin′-kwə-jə-NAIR′-ee-ən)

(b) 60—69：*sexagenarian* (seks′-ə-jə-NAIR′-ee-ən)

(c) 70—79：*septuagenarian* (sep′-chōo-ə-jə-NAIR′-ee-ən)

(d) 90—99：*nonagenarian* (non′-ə-jə-NAIR′-ee-ən)

(e) 100 and over：*centenarian* (sen′-te-NAIR′-ee-ən)

2. *Cacophony* (kə-KOF′-ə-nee). Adjective：*cacophonous* (kə-KOF′-ə-nəs).

3. *Cacopygian* (kak′-ə-PIJ′-ee-ən).

4. *Telescope* (*tele-* plus *skopein*, to view) or *telebinoculars*；*telephone*；*television*.

Check your learning

PREFIX，ROOT	MEANING	EXAMPLE
1. *octoginta*	_____	octogenarian
2. *quinquaginta*	_____	quinquagenarian
3. *sexaginta*	_____	sexagenarian
4. *septuaginta*	_____	septuagenarian
5. *nonaginta*	_____	nonagenarian
6. *centum*	_____	centenarian
7. *kakos*	_____	cacophony
8. *phone*	_____	cacophonous
9. *pyge*	_____	cacopygian
10. *tele-*	_____	television
11. *skopein*	_____	telescope

KEY：1-eighty, 2-fifty, 3-sixty, 4-seventy, 5-ninety, 6-one hundred, 7-ugly, harsh, bad, 8-sound, 9-buttock, 10-distance, from afar, 11-to view

CHAPTER 6:

1. *Sophomore*; from *sophos* plus *moros*, foolish, the word etymologically designates one who is half wise and half foolish. The adjective *sophomoric* (sof-ə-MAWR′-ik) describes people, attitudes, statements, writings, etc. that are highly opinionated, self-assured, and coming off as if wise, but which in reality are immature, inexperienced, foolish, etc.

2. *Sophisticated* (sə-FIS′-tə-kay′-təd). The verb is *sophisticate*, the noun *sophistication*. One who is worldly-wise is a *sophisticate* (sə-FIS′-tə-kət).

Sophisticated has in recent years taken on the added meaning of *highly developed*, *mature*, or *complicated*; *appealing to a mature intellect*; or *aware and knowledgeable*. Examples: *sophisticated* machinery, electronic equipment; a *sophisticated* approach; a *sophisticated* audience, group, staff, faculty, etc.

3. One who is obsessed with books, especially with collecting books.

4. (a) speaking one language, (b) speaking two languages, (c) speaking three languages.

Multilingual (*multus*, many, plus *lingua*)—speaking many languages.

A *linguist* is one who is fluent in many languages, or else an expert in *linguistics* (or both).

Multus, as indicated, means *many*, as in *multitude*, *multiply*, *multiple*, *multicolored*, *multifarious*, *multilateral*, etc., etc.

5. (a) France, (b) Russia, (c) Spain, (d) Germany, (e) Japan, (f) China.

6. (a) *androphile*, (b) *gynephile* (or *philogynist*), (c) *pedophile*, (d) *zoophile*, (e) *botanophile*.

But *pedophilia* (pee′-də-FIL′-ee-ə) is another story. A *pedophiliac* sexually molests young children—such love little kids can do without!

Check your learning

PREFIX,ROOT	MEANING	EXAMPLE
1. *sophos*	_____	sophomore
2. *moros*	_____	sophomoric
3. *biblion*	_____	bibliomaniac
4. *mania*	_____	bibliomania
5. *lingua*	_____	linguist
6. *monos*	_____	monolingual
7. *bi-*	_____	bilingual
8. *tri-*	_____	trilingual
9. *multus*	_____	multilingual

10. *Franco-*	_____	Francophile
11. *Russo-*	_____	Russophile
12. *Hispano-*	_____	Hispanophile
13. *Germano-*	_____	Germanophile
14. *Nippono-*	_____	Nipponophile
15. *Sino-*	_____	Sinophile
16. *andros*	_____	androphile
17. *gyne*	_____	gynephile
18. *philein*	_____	philogynist
19. *paidos* (*ped-*)	_____	pedophile
20. *zoion*	_____	zoophile
21. *botane*	_____	botanophile

KEY: 1-wise, 2-foolish, 3-book, 4-madness, 5-tongue, 6-one, 7-two, 8-three, 9-many, 10-France, 11-Russia, 12-Spain, 13-Germany, 14-Japan, 15-China, 16-man (male), 17-woman, 18-to love, 19-child, 20-animal, 21-plant

CHAPTER 7:

1. A *notable* is someone well-*known*.

2. To *notify* is, etymologically, to make *known*—*notus* + *-fy*, a derivation of *facio*, to make.

Notice, as a noun, is what makes something *known*; to *notice*, as a verb, is to observe (something or someone) so that it, he, or she becomes *known* to the observer.

-Fy, as a verb suffix, means *to make*. So *simplify* is to make simple, *clarify*, to make clear; *liquefy*, to make liquid; *putrefy*, to make (or become) rotten or putrid; *stupefy*, to make stupid, or dumb, with astonishment (note the *-e* preceding the suffix in *liquefy*, *putrefy*, *stupefy*); *fortify*, to make strong; *rectify*, to make right or correct; etc., etc.

3. *Chronograph* (KRON'-ə-graf') is an instrument that measures and records short intervals of time.

4. To *generate* is to give birth to, figuratively, or to create or produce, as a turbine *generates* power, a person's presence *generates* fear, etc. The noun is *generation*, which, in another context, also designates the people born and living about the same time (the older, previous, or next *generation*, the Depression *generation*, etc.), or a period, conventionally set at about thirty years, between such groups of people.

To *regenerate* is to give birth to again, or to be born again. Some creatures can *regenerate new limbs or parts off these are lost or cut off—or the limbs or parts regenerate.*

Re- means, of course, *again*; or, in some words, as *recede*, *regress*, etc., *back.*

5. *Omnipotent* (om-NIP′-ə-tənt)—all-powerful; *omnis* plus *potens*, *potentis*, powerful.

Omnipresent (om′-nə-PREZ′-ənt)—present all over, or everywhere.

Nouns: *omnipotence*, *omnipresence.*

6. *Anaphrodisiac* (ən-af′-rə-DIZ′-ee-ak′)—both a noun and an adjective. Saltpeter is supposedly an *anaphrodisiac*; so, some people say, is a cold shower, which is highly doubtful. The best temporary *anaphrodisiac* is probably sexual intercourse. Some women who were teen-agers when Elvis Presley was at the height of his popularity have told me that the young man's gyrating hips were *aphrodisiacal*—I will take their word for it, as Elvis has never turned me on. On the other hand, if you want to talk about Diane Keaton or Raquel Welch … or especially Marilyn Monroe…

Check your learning

PREFIX,ROOT	MEANING	EXAMPLE
1. *notus*	_____	notify
2. *chronos*	_____	chronograph
3. *graphein*	_____	chronographic
4. *genesis*	_____	generate
5. *re-*	_____	regenerate
6. *omnis*	_____	omnipotent
7. *potens, potentis*	_____	omnipotence
8. *an-*	_____	anaphrodisiac

KEY: 1-known, 2-time, 3-to write, 4-birth, 5-again, 6-all, 7-powerful, 8-not (negative)

CHAPTER 9:

1. *Magnanimity* (mag′-nə-NIM′-ə-tee). Adjective: *magnunimous* (mag-NAN′-ə-məs).

2. *Bilateral* (bī-LAT′-ər-əl), as in a *bilateral* decision, i. e., one made by the two sides or two people involved. On the other hand, a *unilateral* (yoo-nə-LAT′-ər-əl) decision is made by *one* person, without consultation with others.

3. *Transcribe*. Noun: *transcription*. A stenographer *transcribes* shorthand notes into English words, or a musical *transcriber* arranges or adapts a musical composition for an instrument, group, etc. other than the one for which the work was originally written.

4. *Malaria* was once thought to have been caused by the "bad air" of swamps; actually, it was (and is) transmitted to humans by infected anopheles mosquitoes breeding and living in swamps and other places where there is stagnant water.

5. *Confection*. The word is hardly used much today with this meaning, except perhaps by members of an older generation who remember *confectioner's* shops and *confectionery* stores. Now such places are called *ice cream stores* (or *ice cream parlors*) and are run, at least on the west coast, by Baskin-Robbins or Farrell's; or they are called *candy shops*; or, when I was growing up, *candy stores*, where the kids all hung out, and candies could be bought for a penny apiece, with Hershey bars selling for a nickel (that's why they are called "the good old days").

Check your learning

PREFIX,ROOT	MEANING	EXAMPLE
1. *magnus*		magnanimous
2. *animus*		magnanimity
3. *bi-*		bilateral
4. *unus*		unilateral
5. *latus, lateris*		unilateral
6. *trans-*		transcribe
7. *scribo, scriptus*		transcription
8. *malus*		malaria
9. *con-*		confection
10. *facio (fec-)*		confectionery

KEY: 1-big, large, great, 2-mind, 3-two, 4-one, 5-side, 6-across, 7-to write, 8-bad, evil, 9-together, 10-to make

CHAPTER 10:

1. *Modus operandi*. Method (or mode) of working (or operating). Pronounced MŌ'-dəs op'-ə-RAN'-dī, the word is not, of course, restricted to the special methods used by a criminal, but may refer to the method or style of operating characteristic of any other professional. *Modus vivendi* (MŌ'dəs və-VEN'-dī), etymologically "method of living," is the style of life characteristic of a person or group.

2. *Circumscription*. To *circumscribe* also means, figuratively, to write (a line) *around* (*one's freedom of action*), so that one is restricted, limited, hemmed in, as in, "a life *circumscribed* by poverty, by parental injunctions, or by an overactive conscience, etc.," or "actions *circumscribed* by legal restraints." The noun *circumscription* has the figurative meaning also.

3. *Somniloquent* (səm-NIL'-ə-kwənt). Noun: *somniloquence* (səm-NIL'-ə-kwəns) or *somniloquy* (səm-NIL'-ə-kwee), the latter noun also designating the words spoken by the sleeper. One who habitually talks while asleep is a *somniloquist* (səm-NIL'-ə-kwist).

4. An *aurist* is an ear specialist, more commonly called an *otologist* (ō-TOL'-ə-jist), from Greek *otos*, ear. Noun: *otology*, Adjective: *otological* (ō-tə-LOJ'-ə-kəl).

It is difficult at this point to resist telling a well-known story about medical specialists. In fact it's impossible to resist, so here it is:

A dentist, doing his first extraction on a patient, was understandably nervous. When he got the molar out, his hand shook, he lost his grip on the instrument, and the tooth dropped down into the patient's throat.

"Sorry," said the doctor. "You're outside my specialty now. You should see a laryngologist! [lair'-ing-GOL'-ə-jist—a larynx or throat specialist]."

By the time the unfortunate victim got to the laryngologist, the tooth had worked its way much further down.

The laryngologist examined the man.

"Sorry," said the doctor, "You're outside my specialty now. You should see a gastrologist! [gas-TROL'-ə-jist—a stomach specialist]."

The gastrologist X-rayed the patient. "Sorry," said the doctor, "the tooth has traveled into your lower intestines. You should see an enterologist! [en'-tə-ROL'-ə-jist—an intestinal specialist]."

The enterologist took some X rays. "Sorry, the tooth isn't there. It must have gone down farther. You should see a proctologist! [prok-TOL'-ə-jist—a specialist in diseases of the rectum; from Greek *proktos*, anus]."

Our patient is now on the proctologist's examining table, in the proper elbow-knee position. The doctor has inserted a proctoscope and is looking through it.

"Good heavens, man! You've got a tooth up there! You should see a dentist!"

5. *Aural* (AWR-əl) refers to the ears or to the sense or phenomenon of hearing. *Monaural* reproduction, as of music over a radio or by a phonograph record, for example, has only one source of sound, and technically should be called *monophonic* (mon'-ə-FON'-ik)—*monos*, one, plus *phone*, sound. *Binaural* may mean *having two ears or involving the use of both ears*, or, recently, *descriptive of sound from two sources*, giving a *stereophonic* (steer'-ee-ə-FON'-ik) effect—*stereos*, deep, sol-

id，plus *phone*.

6. A *noctambulist*（nok-TAM'-byə-list）walks at night—*nox*，*noctis*，night，plus *ambulo*，to walk. Noun：*noctambulism*（nok- TAM'-byə-liz-əm）.

7. *Somnific*（som-NIF'-ik）：*a somnific* lecture，movie，effect，etc.

8. *Circumambulate*（sur'-kəm-AM'-byə-layt'）. To *circumnavigate* is to sail around—*circum*，around，plus *navis*，ship.

Check your learning

PREFIX，ROOT	MEANING	EXAMPLE
1. *modus*		*modus operandi*
2. *operandi*		*modus operandi*
3. *vivo*		*modus vivendi*
4. *circum-*		circumscribe
5. *scribo，scriptus*		circumscription
6. *somnus*		somniloquent
7. *loquor*		somniloquence
8. *aurus*		aurist
9. *otos*		otology
10. *proktos*		proctologist
11. *stereos*		stereophonic
12. *phone*		stereophonic
13. *monos*		monaural
14. *bi-*		binaural
15. *nox，noctis*		noctambulist
16. *ambulo*		noctambulism
17. *facio（fic-）*		somnific

KEY：1-mode，method，2-of working，3-to live，4-around，5-to write，6-sleep；7-to speak，to talk，8-ear，9-ear，10-anus，11-deep，solid，12-sound，13-one，14-two，15-night，16-to walk，17-to make

CHAPTER 11：

1. *Matronymic*（mat'-rə-NIM'-ik）. Or，if you prefer to use the Greek root for mother（*meter*，*metr-*），*metronymic*. The Greek word *metra*，uterus，derives from *meter*，naturally enough，so *metritis* is inflammation of the uterus；*metralgia* is uterine pain；*endometriosis*（en'-dō-mee'-tree-Ō'-sis）is any abnormal condition of the uterine lining—*endo*，inside；*metra*，uterus；*-osis*，abnormal condition.

2. (a) An *incendiary* statement, remark, speech, etc. figuratively enflames an audience, sets them afire, gets them excited, galvanizes them into action, etc.

(b) *Incense* (IN′-sens) is a substance that sends off a pleasant odor when burned—often, but not necessarily, to mask unpleasant or telltale smells, as of marijuana smoke, etc.

(c) To *incense* (in-SENS′) is to anger greatly, i. e., to "burn up." "I'm all burned up" is etymologically an accurate translation of "I'm *incensed*."

3. (a) *Ardent* (AHR′-dənt)—burning with zeal, ambition, love, etc., as an *ardent* suitor, worker, etc.

(b) *Ardor* (AHR′-dər)—the noun form of *ardent*—burning passion, zeal, enthusiasm, etc. Alternate noun: *ardency* (AHR′-dən-see).

4. *Megaphone.*

5. *Megalopolis* (meg′-ə-LOP′-ə-lis).

6. *Police. Politics.*

7. *Bibliokleptomaniac* (bib′-lee-ō-klep′-tə-MAY′-nee-ak): one who has an obsession for stealing books. Not too many years ago, an author titled his book, *Steal This Book*! perhaps hoping to appeal to *bibliokleptomaniacs*; if the appeal was successful enough, his royalty statements must have been minuscule indeed!

Gynekleptomaniac.

Pedokleptomaniac.

Androkleptomaniac.

Demokleptomaniac.

If you prefer to use shorter words, *compulsive kidnapper* or *obsessive abductor* will do as well for these words.

8. *Acromaniac.*

Agoramaniac.

Claustromaniac.

9. *Kleptophobe*; *pyrophobe*; *gynephobe*; *androphobe*; *demophobe*.

Triskaidekaphobia (tris′-kī-dek′-ə-FŌ′-bee-ə) is the morbid dread of the number 13, from Greek *triskai*, three, *deka*, ten, and *phobia*.

10. *Gnosiology* (nō′-see-OL′-ə-jee), the science or study of knowledge.

11. *Amadeus* is love (Latin *amor*) God (Latin *deus*). *Theophilus* is love (Greek *philos*) God (Greek *theos*). Gottlieb is love (German *Lieb*) God (German *Gott*).

Perhaps this explains why he started composing at the age of four and wrote forty-one symphonies.

12. *Cellophane*—cellulose made to be transparent, i. e., to *show* what's wrapped in it.

13. *Hypoglycemia* (hī-pō-glī-SEE′-mee-ə)—low blood sugar, a common ailment today, though I believe the AMA has called it a "non-disease" (Greek *hypos*, under;

glykys, sweet; *haima*, blood).

Haima, blood, is found in many English words, the root spelled either *hem-* or *-em*. Here are a few, with their etymological interpretations:

(a) *Hemorrhage*—excessive blood flow.

(b) *Anemia*—"no blood"—actually a pathological reduction of red blood corpuscles.

(c) *Hemotology*—science of blood (and its diseases).

(d) *Hemophilia*—"love of blood"—actually a hereditary condition, occurring in males, in which the blood clots too slowly.

(e) *Hemoglobin*—"blood gobules"—actually the red coloring matter of the red blood corpuscles.

Hyperglycemia is the opposite of *hypoglycemia*.

14. (a) *Pantheon* (PAN′-thee-on′)—a temple built in Rome in 27 B. C. for "all the gods."

(b) *Pandemonium* (pan′-də-MŌ′-nee-əm)—a word supposedly coined by poet John Milton in *Paradise Lost* to signify the dwelling place of all the demons; now any wild and noisy disorder.

(c) *Panorama* (pan′-ə-RAM′-ə *or* pan′-ə-RAH′-mə)—a view (or a picture of such a view) all around—*pan*, all, plus *horama*, view. The adjective: *panoramic* (pan′-ə-RAM′-ik).

15. *Monarchy*—rule by one person.

Check your learning

PREFIX, ROOT	MEANING	EXAMPLE
1. *mater*, *matris*	_____	matronymic
2. *onyma*	_____	metronymic
3. *meter*	_____	metronymic
4. *metra*	_____	metritis
5. *endo-*	_____	endometriosis
6. *incendo*, *incensus*	_____	incendiary
7. *ardo*	_____	ardent
8. *megalo-*	_____	megalopolis
9. *polis*	_____	police
10. *demos*	_____	demokleptomaniac
11. *akros*	_____	acromaniac
12. *agora*	_____	agoramaniac
13. *claustrum*	_____	claustromaniac
14. *triskai*	_____	triskaidekaphobia
15. *deka*	_____	triskaidekaphobia

16. *gnosis*	_____	gnosiology
17. *amor*	_____	Amadeus
18. *deus*	_____	deity
19. *theos*	_____	Theophilus
20. *philos*	_____	hemophilia
21. *phanein*	_____	cellophane
22. *hypos*	_____	hypoglycemia
23. *glykys*	_____	hypoglycemia
24. *haima*	_____	hemorrhage
25. *an-*	_____	anemia
26. *hyper-*	_____	hyperglycemia
27. *pan*	_____	Pantheon
28. *horama*	_____	panorama
29. *archein*	_____	monarch
30. *monos*	_____	monarchy

KEY：1-mother，2-name，3-mother，4-uterus，5-inside，6-to set on fire，7-to burn，8-big, large, great，9-city，10-people，11-highest，12-market place，13-enclosed place，14-three，15-ten，16-knowledge，17-love，18-God，19-God，20-love，21-to show，22-under，23-sweet，24-blood，25-not, negative，26-over，27-all，28-view，29-to rule，30-one

CHAPTER 12：

1. *Survive*. Noun：*survival*.

2. *Vivarium* (vī-VAIR′ee-əm)—enclosed area in which plants and (small) animals live in conditions resembling their natural habitat. The suffix *-ium* usually signifies *place where*—*solarium*, a place for the sun to enter, or where one can sunbathe；*aquarium*, a place for water (Latin *aqua*, water), or fish tank；*podium*, a place for the feet (Greek *podos*, foot), or speaker's platform；*auditorium*, a place for hearing (or listening to) concerts, plays, etc. (Latin *audio*, to hear).

3. *Vita* (VĪ′-tə), etymologically, *life*, is one's professional or career resume：

4. (a) *Unicorn* (Latin *cornu*, horn).

(b) *Uniform*.

(c) *Unify* (*-fy*, from *facio*, to make).

(d) *Unity*.

(e) *Unicycle* (Greek *kyklos*, circle, wheel).

5. *Anniversary*—a year has turned.

6. (a) *Universe*—everything turning as one.

(b) *University*—highest institute of education—universal subjects taught，learned，etc.，i.e.，the curriculum covers the universe，is in no way restricted，etc.

7. (a) *Interstate*.

(b) *International*.

(c) *Intermediate*.

(d) *Interrupt* (*Latin rumpo*，*ruptus*，to break).

(e) *Interpersonal*.

8. (a) *Intrastate*.

(b) *Intranational*.

(c) *Intrapersonal* or *intrapsychic*.

(d) *Intramuscular*.

Check your learning

PREFIX，ROOT	MEANING	EXAMPLE
1. *vive*		survive
2. *podos*		podium
3. *vita*		*vita*
4. *cornu*		unicorn
5. *kyklos*		unicycle
6. *annus*		anniversary
7. *verto，versus*		universe
8. *unus*		university
9. *inter-*		interstate
10. *intra-*		intrapsychic

KEY：1-to live，2-foot，3-life，4-horn，5-circle，wheel，6-year，7-to turn，8-one，9-between，10-within

CHAPTER 14：

1. "View of Death. "

2. *Thanatology*.

3. (a) *Prophesy* (PROF'-ə-sī').

(b) *Prophecy* (PROF'-ə-see).

(c) *Prophet* (PROF'-ət).

4. (a) *Predict*.

(b) *Prediction*.

5. *Nostopathy*—"disease" (tensions, insecurities, conflicts) on returning home after leaving the service. Some veterans could not face the freedom and responsibilities of being on their own. The Army, Navy, or Air Force had fed and clothed them and made decisions for them; now they had to read just to civilian life.

6. (a) *Vulpicide*.

(b) *Lupicide*.

(c) *Felicide*.

(d) *Ursicide*.

7. (a) *Piscivorous* (pə-SIV′-ər-əs).

(b) *Insectivorous* (in′-sek-TIV′-ər-əs).

8. *Canaries*, what else?

9. *Potentiate* (pə-TEN′-shee-ayt′).

Check your learning

PREFIX, ROOT	MEANING	EXAMPLE
1. *thanatos*		thanatology
2. *logos*		thanatology
3. *opsis*		*Thanatopsis*
4. *pheme*		prophecy
5. *pro-*		prophet
6. *pre-*		predict
7. *dico, dictus*		predict
8. *nostos*		nostopathy
9. *pathos*		nostopathy
10. *vulpus*		vulpicide
11. *lupus*		lupicide
12. *felis*		felicide
13. *ursus*		ursicide
14. *piscis*		piscivorous
15. *voro*		insectivorous
16. *caedo (-cide)*		insecticide
17. *canis*		canary
18. *potens, potentis*		potentiate

KEY: 1-death, 2-science, study, 3-view, 4-voice, 5-beforehand, 6-before, 7-to say or tell, 8-a return, 9-disease, 10-fox, 11-wolf, 12-cat, 13-bear, 14-fish, 15-devour, 16-to kill (killing), 17-dog, 18-powerful

CHAPTER 15：

1. *Synagogue*.

2. *Symbiosis* (sim'-bī-Ō'-sis). Adjective：*symbiotic* (sim'-bī-OT'-ik).
People (for example lovers，spouses，parent and child，etc.) also may live in a *symbiotic* relationship，each depending on the other for important services，emotional needs，etc.；each also providing these for the other.

3. *Symphony*；*symphonic*.

4. *Symmetry* (SIM'-ə-tree)；*symmetrical* (sə-MET'-rə-kəl) or *symmetric* (sə-MET'-rik).

5. *Syndrome* (SIN'-drōm).

6. *Hippodrome* (HIP'-ə-drōm')；the word today is often used as the name of a movie theater or other place of entertainment.

7. *Hippopotamus*.

Check your learning

PREFIX，ROOT	MEANING	EXAMPLE
1. *syn-*	_____	synagogue
2. *agogos*	_____	synagogue
3. *bios*	_____	symbiosis
4. *phone*	_____	symphonic
5. *metron*	_____	symmetry
6. *dromos*	_____	syndrome
7. *hippos*	_____	hippodrome
8. *potamos*	_____	hippopotamus

KEY：1-with，together，2-leader，leading，3-life，4-sound，5-measurement，6-a running，7-horse，8-river

CHAPTER 16：

1. *Non sequitur* (non SEK'-wə-tər)—"it does not follow."

2. (a) *Second*—following after the first.

(b) *Consecutive*—following in proper order.

(c) *Persecute*—to follow (i. e. ，pursue) through and through；hence to annoy，harass continually for no good reason.

(d) *Prosecute*—to follow before；hence to pursue (something) diligently or vigorously in order to complete it successfully (*prosecute* a campaign); or to start, or engage in, legal proceedings against, especially in an official capacity.

3. (a) *Superior*.

(b) *Superficial*.

(c) *Superfluous* (sə-PUR'-floo-əs). Noun: superfluity (soo'-pər-FLOO'-ə-tee).

(d) *Supernatural*.

(e) *Supervise*.

4. (a) *Cadence* (KAY'-dəns)—fall and rise of the voice in speaking; hence inflection, rhythm beat, etc. of sound or music. Adjective: *cadent* (KAY'-dənt).

(b) *Occidental* (ok'-sə-DEN'-təl)—etymologically, falling. Hence relating to western countries, since the sun falls in the west; also, a native of such a country. Noun: *Occident* (OK'-sə-dənt). The sun rises in the east, so Latin *orior*, to rise, is the origin of the *Orient*, *oriental*, etc., and also of the verb *orient* (AW'-ree-ent'). To *orient* is to adjust to a place or situation; etymologically, to turn, or face, east. Noun: *orientation*. "I'm finally oriented" does not mean that I'm easternized or facing east, but that I have become familiar with, and comfortable in, a place, job, situation, etc. So to *disorient* (dis-AW'-ree-ent') is to remove (someone's) *orientation*, or to confuse or bewilder, especially in reference to locality, direction, etc. Noun: *disorientation*.

(c) *Deciduous* (də-SIJ'-oo-əs)—falling down (Latin prefix *de-*). This adjective refers to trees whose leaves fall (down) every autumn.

(d) *Incident*—that which falls upon, befalls, or happens.

(e) *Accident*—that which falls to (*ac-* is a respelling of *ad-*, to, toward) someone or something (by chance).

(f) *Coincidence*—*co-* is a respelling of *con-*, together. A *coincidence* occurs when two things befall, or happen, together, or at the same time, and by chance.

5. *Indolent* (IN'-də-lənt). Noun: *indolence* (IN'-də-ləns).

6. *Dolores*—from Spanish *Maria de los Dolores*, Mary of the Sorrows; hence, I guess, someone who is generally sorrowful, though the few Doloreses I have known do not live up to their etymology.

Check your learning

PREFIX, ROOT	MEANING	EXAMPLE
1. *sequor*,	_____	non sequitur,
secutus		second
2. *per-*	_____	persecute
3. *pro-*	_____	prosecute
4. *super-*	_____	superior
5. *fluo*	_____	superfluous

6. *cado* ＿＿＿＿＿＿＿＿＿ cadence

7. *orior* ＿＿＿＿＿＿＿＿＿ Orient

8. *dis-* ＿＿＿＿＿＿＿＿＿ disorient

9. *ad-* (*ac-*) ＿＿＿＿＿＿＿＿＿ accident

10. *doleo* ＿＿＿＿＿＿＿＿＿ indolent

11. *in-* ＿＿＿＿＿＿＿＿＿ indolence

KEY： 1-to follow，2-through，3-beforehand，4-above，5-to flow，6-to fall，7-to rise，8-negative prefix，9-to, toward，10-to suffer, to grieve，11-negative prefix

19

HOW TO KEEP BUILDING YOUR VOCABULARY
如何不断扩建词汇

At commencement exercises, whether in elementary school, high school, or college, at least one of the speakers will inevitably point out to the graduates that this is not the end—not by a long shot. It is only the beginning; that's why it is called "commencement," etc., etc.

在毕业典礼活动上，无论是小学、高中、还是大学，至少其中一位演讲者，会直截了当地告诉毕业生们，今天并不是最后一天——至少长远看来并不是。今天只是一个开始；所以，毕业当天也被称为"commencement"诸如此类的话。

Of course the speaker is right—no educative process is ever the end; it is always the beginning of more education, more learning, more living.

当然，演讲者是正确的——任何教育过程都没有尽头；一个阶段的教育、学习或生活只能是更多阶段的开始。

And that is the case here. What has happened to you as a result of your reaction to the material and suggestions in this book is only the beginning of your development. To stop increasing your vocabulary is to stop your intellectual growth. You will wish, I am sure, to continue growing intellectually as long as you remain alive. And with the momentum that your weeks of hard work have provided, continuing will not be at all difficult.

这同样符合我们的词汇学习。你对本书材料和建议的习得只是词汇扩展的开始。停止扩展词汇就相当于停止智慧的增长。我敢说，只要你活着，你就希望增长智慧。通过这几周以来刻苦的努力，你已经获得了极大的动力，继续扩建词汇也绝不是难事。

Let me offer, as a summary of all I have said throughout the book, a recapitulation of the steps you must take so that your vocabulary will keep growing and growing.

再次，我要给大家提供五个步骤，作为我在本书中所强调的所有建议的总结，这样，你就可以不断增长词汇（同样增长智慧）。

STEP ONE. *You must become actively receptive to new words.*

Words won't come chasing after you—you must train yourself to be on a constant lookout, in your reading and listening, for any words that other people know and you don't.

第一步：你必须积极地乐于接受新词汇。

词汇不会主动追逐你——你必须训练自己时刻保持警觉，在阅读或者听力中获取别人知道而你不知道的词汇。

STEP TWO. *You must read more.*

As an adult, you will find most of the sources of your supply of new words in books and magazines. Is your reading today largely restricted to a quick perusal of the daily newspaper? Then you will have to change your habits. If your aim is to have a superior vocabulary, you will have to make the time to read at least one book and several magazines *every week*. Not just this week and next week—but every week for the rest of your life. I have never met a single person who possessed a rich vocabulary who was not also an omnivorous reader.

第二步:你必须不断扩大阅读量。

作为成年人,你的新词汇主要来源是书籍和杂志。你今天的阅读是否仅限于浏览当日日报? 如果是,你必须改变自己的习惯。如果你的目标是积累超级词汇量,你一周至少抽出时间阅读完一本书或者几本杂志。不仅是这周或下周——而是余下生命的每一周。在我见过的词汇量丰富的所有人当中,没有一个人不是博览群书的。

STEP THREE. *You must learn to add to your own vocabulary the new words you meet in your reading.*

When you see an unfamiliar word in a book or magazine, do not skip over it impatiently. Instead, pause for a moment and say it over to yourself—get used to its sound and appearance. Then puzzle out its possible meaning in the context of the sentence. Whether you come to the right conclusion or not, whether indeed you are able to come to any intelligent conclusion at all, is of no importance. What is important is that you are, by this process, becoming superconscious of the word. As a result, you will suddenly notice that this very word pops up unexpectedly again and again in all your reading—for you now have a mind-set for it. And of course after you've seen it a few times, you will know fairly accurately not only what it means but the many ways in which it can be used.

第三步:你必须使自己在阅读中遇到的新词成为自己词汇的一部分。

在书籍或者杂志中看到不熟悉的词汇时,不要没有耐心地将其忽略,而是停下来读出这个词汇——熟悉它的发音和拼写。然后根据句中语境分析它的可能含义。你的结论正确与否,你的总结是否合理,这些都不重要。重要的是,通过这个过程,你对于这个新词的意识越来越强烈。结果是,你会发现,这个词出乎意料地反复出现在你的阅读中——因为你对它已经确立起一种思维模式。当然,见过这个词几次之后,你不仅十分准确地掌握了它的含义,对它的几种用法也会了如指掌。

STEP FOUR. *You must open your mind to new ideas.*

Every word you know is the translation of an idea.

Think for a few minutes of the areas of human knowledge that may possibly be unknown to you—psychology, semantics, science, art, music, or whatever. Then attack one of these areas methodically—by reading books in the field. In every field, from the simplest to the most abstruse, there are several books written for the average, untrained lay reader that will give you both a good grasp of the subject and at the same time add immeasurably to your vocabulary. College students have large vocabularies because they are required to expose themselves constantly to new areas of learning. You must do the same.

第四步:你必须打开思维,接受新概念。

你知道的每个词汇都是对概念的解释。

想一想,有哪些人类知识领域是你所不了解的——心理学、语义学、科学、艺术、音乐或其他领域。然后通过阅读书籍有条不紊地钻研一个领域。每个领域的书籍难度各不相同,从最简单的到最晦涩的,但总有几本书是写给大众的、非专业的普通读者。这样的书不仅能够使你对本领域的大致情况有所了解,同时也会极大地增加你的词汇量。大学生时期词汇量较大的原因就是他们必须不断接受新领域的学习。你也必须这样做。

STEP FIVE. *You must set a goal.*

If you do *nothing* about your vocabulary, you will learn, at most, twenty-five to fifty new words in the next twelve months. *By conscious effort you can learn several thousand.* Set yourself a goal of finding several new words *every day*. This may sound ambitious—but you will discover as soon as you start actively looking for new words in your reading, and actively doing reading of a more challenging type, that new words are all around you—that is, if you're ready for them. And understand this: vocabulary building *snowballs*. The results of each new day's search will be greater and greater—once you provide the necessary initial push, once you gain momentum, once you *become addicted* to looking for, finding, and taking possession of new words.

And this is one addiction well worth cultivating!

第五步:你必须设定明确的目标。

如果你不做任何努力,在接下来的 12 个月中,你最多只能学到 25 到 50 个新词。但是,通过有意识的努力,你能够学到成千上万个词汇。为自己定下目标,每天去发现并吸收几个新词。这个任务听起来可能过于艰巨——但是你很快就会发现,只要你开始积极地在阅读中寻找新词,主动地做更有挑战的阅读,新词就会经常围绕着你——前提是你必须做好准备。并且理解这点:学习词汇就像是滚雪球,每天学习的成果会越来越明显——只要你为自己提供必要的原始动力,只要你获得了惯性,只要你养成了嗜好,去搜寻、发现,并掌握这些新词,而这是最值得培养的嗜好!